The Aircraft-Spotter's
Film and Television
Companion

The Aircraft-Spotter's Film and Television Companion

SIMON D. BECK

Foreword by James H. Farmer

McFarland & Company, Inc., Publishers
Jefferson, North Carolina

ISBN (print) 978-1-4766-6349-4
ISBN (ebook) 978-1-4766-2293-4

LIBRARY OF CONGRESS CATALOGUING DATA ARE AVAILABLE

British Library cataloguing data are available

Front cover image: TBM-3 from *Close Encounters of the
Third Kind*, 1977 (courtesy Matt Gunsch)

Printed in the United States of America

*McFarland & Company, Inc., Publishers
Box 611, Jefferson, North Carolina 28640
www.mcfarlandpub.com*

For Yee Miin, Maegan and Ellie

Contents

Abbreviations

AAF—(U.S.) Army Air Field

AFB—(U.S.) Air Force Base

AFR—(U.S.) Air Force Reserve

ANG—(U.S.) Air National Guard

BAPC—British Aviation Preservation Council (founded 1967)

CAC—Commonwealth Aircraft Corp., Melbourne, Australia

CAF—Canadian Armed Forces

CASA—Contrucciones Aeronauticas SA, Madrid, Spain

CCF—Canadian Car & Foundry Co., Ontario, Canada

CGI—Computer Generated Image (visual effect)

EAA—(U.S.) Experimental Aircraft Association

MASDC—Military Aircraft Storage and Disposition Center

MCAS—(U.S.) Marine Corps. Air Station

msn—Manufacturer's Serial Number

NACA—National Advisory Committee for Aeronautics

NAF—(U.S.) Naval Air Field

NAS—(U.S.) Naval Air Station

NASA—National Aeronautics and Space Administration

RAAF—Royal Australian Air Force

RAF—(UK) Royal Air Force

RC—Remote Control (radio controlled flying models)

RCAF—Royal Canadian Air Force

reg.—(Civil) Registration

RFC—(UK) Royal Flying Corps.

RMAF—Royal Malaysian Air Force

RN—(UK) Royal Navy

RNZAF—Royal New Zealand Air Force

RTAF—Royal Thai Air Force

SAC—(U.S.) Strategic Air Command

SAM—Surface to Air Missile

SAR—Search And Rescue

s/n—Serial Number

TVM—Television Movie

TVMS—Television Mini-Series

TVS—Television Series

UK—United Kingdom

USAAC—United States Army Air Corps

USAAF—United States Army Air Force

USAF—United States Air Force

USAFR—United States Air Force Reserve

USCG—United States Coast Guard

USMC—United States Marine Corps

USN—United States Navy

Preface

For a number of years I've been interested in developing a book devoted to aviation films and the histories of the aircraft featured in them, in particular a book recording their serial numbers and registrations. On many occasions while watching a favorite movie I'd considered how useful it would be to have a single, concise reference book which listed aircraft identities and airfield locations for each of the major aviation films and cult favorites among the aviation community.

Over the course of the last eight years, right up to the point of publishing, I have personally viewed around 250 of the 350 titles featured for this book. Many of the unseen titles were simply not available on DVD or VHS, or sadly no longer available in any format, the original negatives or prints having long since been lost or decayed. Readers will note much of the information in the following pages is presented in a "notebook" format designed both for space-saving and convenience of reference while reviewing a specific title.

Although there is a growing abundance of excellent aviation film material available in various books and magazines and on the Internet, it does tend to require some lengthy, in-depth searching to find what you're looking for. Furthermore, many of the excellent books published in the past on the subject of film aviation have mostly focused on one specific area, usually stunt flying or films from one specific period in history. Information on aircraft identities in movies across the whole genre is scattered, inaccurate and troublesome to locate and authenticate.

So, I considered, why not bring it all together— aircraft types, serial numbers, registrations, locations and brief histories? This book is the result.

Foreword by James H. Farmer

Numbers. Numbers and nonsensical combinations of letters may seem mundane, cold, even impersonal things.

Yet for serious aviation buffs, and aviation *film* buffs, such multi-digit and letter combinations, military aircraft serial numbers and national civil aircraft registrations, can open an entirely new world, a decidedly personal view into the aircraft appearing in your favorite international screen productions. These numbers offer a window into the real aircraft behind the fiction or historical dramatization. Specifically, what type was it? From which military unit was it loaned out to the producers? Or from which civilian corporation or individual aircraft owner did the featured airplane come? The answers are all in the numbers and letters.

More than a quarter century ago my own curiosity had led me to begin seeking out such identities for my own volume on early aviation films, *Celluloid Wings*. But I had only scratched the surface—the idea worthy of little more than a brief appendix. Back in 1984 I'd simply identified the early shark-tailed Flying Fortress known as the *Mary Ann*—as it appeared in the classic 1943 Howard Hawks film *Air Force*—as an unknown B-17C. No actual serial number was then available. Yet fast-forward a quarter century and speculation runs hot and fast between aviation historians that the bomber, which was the heart and soul of that aviation classic, was actually a B-17B variant upgraded to "C" standards. Is there now a serial number attached to this speculation? You bet! And with it comes into focus the actual life and history of this early Boeing bomber which avoided a one-way trip into the Pacific during the early months of World War II to instead become a Hollywood star!

And now a serial number has been found for even the long unappreciated B-17G acquired for the studio-based sequences in one of the most honored aviation films of all time, *Twelve O'Clock High* (1949). That simple serial number opens a wonder-filled window onto that disassembled and dissected aircraft's entire history through its military aircraft record cards—from the day it left the Douglas Long Beach assembly line till that day in April of 1949 when it was resurrected from a USAF surplus facility in Texas for its final trip back to Southern California and the Fox Studios.

And what of the actual identity of the Halifax bomber lost below the fresh skin of the fictional *Reindeer* airliner as featured in the 1951 British classic *No Highway in the Sky*? Did you even know there was a Halifax used in that film? Well, look no further for this and a thousand other answers, which await within this truly exciting and concise volume.

Yes, strange combinations of numbers and letters can be everything to an aviation film historian and no historian has taken to the task as intensely or as determinedly as has Simon D. Beck. Where my book only began to look into this fascinating subject, Mr. Beck's heroic eight-year efforts, which have coalesced into this remarkable work, provide answers I'd only dreamed of finding back in 1984. "It struck me back in 2006," shared Mr. Beck, "that no one had ever done a book on film aircraft identities. I began by watching 1941's *Dive Bomber* thinking this project would only take a year. I must admit the Internet has a fair range of access to aircraft identities, but by no means everything. My research has led me to contacts in the United States, the United Kingdom, Australia and Canada, many, many people. It has taken me to the FAA, CAA, military aircraft record cards, museums and a multitude of civilian aviation companies all over the world."

The scope of Simon D. Beck's book is un-matched and unimagined even a decade earlier. His book is a remarkably important addition to the library of any aviation film buff truly worth his salt!

James H. Farmer is a leading aviation film historian, having written some 300 aviation film-related articles for aircraft magazines both in the U.S. and overseas. He has also written four books including Celluloid Wings, *a work covering aviation film history. A former associate editor for* The American Historical Society Journal, *he was a high school art and history teacher for forty years and is now retired in Glendora, California.*

Introduction

What is an aviation film? You could say it's a specialist genre that fits neatly into any of the broader, classic genres such as war, adventure, thriller, action, romance and in some cases science fiction. As described on its own, however, an aviation film can best be summed up as any feature film whose central characters, key events or story center on the subject of aircraft or aviation in either a military or civilian setting.

Over the years most aviation films have been of the military or war genre, often with actors playing heroic pilots on Hollywood backlots while film editors expertly cut in around them actual combat newsreel footage or filmed material from an aerial second unit. Alternatively, the civilian aviation film has become, almost from day one, synonymous with the disaster film genre, the starring airplane almost always coming to grief at some point during the story. There are, of course, thousands of films that feature aircraft at some point, often as traveling links between scenes; but unless aircraft are an integral part of a film's story or narrative, such a movie cannot truly be called an *aviation film*.

In essence, this book is an aircraft identification reference aimed at anyone keen to find out the history of a particular aircraft or location as seen in one of the many Hollywood aviation films made over the years. Although no book can list all such feature films ever made, I feel there's a fair representation in this publication of most of the mainstream and likely "favorites" of the aviation film genre. Gathering the various military serial numbers, civil registrations and histories of these "film star aircraft" has been a challenging quest. Older films, it was found, had less research material available, so identifying aircraft was a more

challenging and often unsuccessful task. During the early, fledgling development of the motion picture industry, and of aviation around the same time, aircraft types were easy to recognize in films, but their registration identities were not. Three of the industry's biggest films of the time, *Wings* (1927), *Hell's Angels* (1930), and *The Dawn Patrol* (1930), for example, featured a multitude of biplanes, most of them impossible to identify by registration or military serial number.

Later, in the 1930s, some regulation was introduced into a growing airline industry, and registration markings on aircraft became bold and clear. Aircraft numbers could easily be read and so their histories noted. Such was the case with many an airframe in *Without Orders* (1936), *Test Pilot* (1938), and *Men with Wings* (1938), to name but a few. Military aircraft serial numbers during the 1930s underwent a similar makeover, with both army and naval aircraft often giving themselves away with that telltale set of numbers on the tail. *Dive Bomber* (1941) is a prime example, with many naval numbers visible on the N3N Canary fighters lined up at NAS San Diego in California.

During World War II, aviation films, on occasion, would alter numbers and registrations for security reasons. One famous example is the B-17 *Mary Ann* from the Warner Bros. film *Air Force* (1943), which in reality was serial number "8584" but was cleverly doctored to "05564" for the film. Bogus serial numbers and registrations have become an annoying practice in the aviation film world, with numbers often being changed for the purposes of the storyline; but thankfully, the registration and serial numbers we see in most motion pictures are usually the real ones. Occasionally aircraft markings are removed altogether, saving a logistical continuity nightmare for the director in the cutting room. One of the best examples of this practice was the Japanese replicas built for the 1970 epic *Tora! Tora! Tora!* The brilliantly converted Zeros, Kates and Vals were all initially given historically accurate tail numbers, but these were unceremoniously removed once filming began in Hawaii!

Of course, not all aircraft histories are obtained through watching a copy of the film. Many of the aircraft featured in this book were discovered through other sources such as photographs, aircraft records, and the pilots and technicians who flew them in the film industry. Just such a few of these long-lost identities are the C-82 Packets from *The Flight of the Phoenix* (1965), the mysterious Flight 19 Avengers in *Close Encounters of the Third Kind* (1977), the menacing Hughes 500 and fleeing Stearman from *Capricorn One* (1978), and several of the aircraft featured in the James Bond films.

So, pull up a chair, turn on a favorite "flyer movie" and have a copy of this book on hand next to the remote control, a ready reference to the many aircraft that have flown on the big screen.

Section One—Feature Films

All entries for this section are feature-length motion pictures, listed in an alphabetical order with numerical titles listed alphabetically according to their letter-based spelling. International or alternative titles for each entry are listed under the original title. These alternative titles are also listed separately throughout the book to assist a reader who may not know a film by its original title but only by its alternative or international one.

Each title features the technical aspects of the production: country of origin, film studio and/or distributor, year of initial release, black and white or color, and the running time. The film's director and principal cast members are then listed, followed by a brief story synopsis, critique, and description of the aviation content. Some titles have a table detailing the aircraft that make appearances, listed by original type, manufacturer's serial number, military or civilian serial number, and film markings, to aid the viewer with on-screen identification. After this is a detailed write-up about the aircraft and relevant material relating to the aeronautical aspects of the production. Some entries will also have relevant anecdotes or brief descriptions of other unique information related to that production. Lastly, there's a description of relevant filming locations and, where possible, a list of GPS coordinates, which are useful in searching for locations with Google Earth or other similar programs.

Where actual aircraft were hired for a production, the type is listed in **bold** lettering in the text. Listed aircraft that appear in the form of stock footage, models, CGI effects or footage from previous motion pictures or documentaries are not presented in bold type.

Some film entries have a "Factual Background" included, outlining details of the historical significance, actual events, or a biographical description of individuals the particular film is based on.

To help readers identify the "pure" aviation films from those of broader genres, the tag "(Non–Aviation Themed Title)" has been added next to each such particular entry. These are titles that aren't aviation films as such but contain a sizeable aeronautical content at some point in the story. The C-47 Dakotas in *A Bridge Too Far* (1977) or the P-40 fighters provided for *1941* (1979) are two excellent examples.

Information that could not be confirmed by the time of publication is listed under the heading "UNCONFIRMED DATA." It is information that is speculative on the author's part; though based on the best available data, it should not be regarded as confirmed fact.

The length of individual film entries is basically directly proportional to the number of aircraft used in that particular film. So titles such as *Battle of Britain* (1969) and *Tora! Tora! Tora!* (1970), with a large aircraft content, receive a longer, more detailed analysis than entries with only a few aircraft.

Above and Beyond

USA / Metro-Goldwyn-Mayer / 1952 / B&W / 122 minutes

Directors: Melvin Frank and Norman Panama

Cast: Robert Taylor, Eleanor Parker, James Whitmore, Larry Keating, Larry Gates, Marilyn Erskine, Robert Burton, Hayden Rorke

Synopsis / Aviation Content: Accurate, intriguing story of the development and use of the first atomic bomb, in particular the impact it has on the life of Col. Paul Tibbets, the pilot

The *Above and Beyond* (1952) Boeing B-29 (s/n 42-65401) fuselage was also used for *The Wild Blue Yonder* (1951) and the TV movie *Enola Gay* (1980). Photograph: Taigh Ramey, www.twinbeech.com.

chosen to lead the first atomic mission over Japan. Well-cast film doesn't dwell on melodrama or lose its way, retaining a tight and tense atmosphere throughout. The screen story was penned by Eighth Air Force veteran and aviation writer Beirne Lay, Jr. of *Twelve O'Clock High* (1949) fame; Lay also co-wrote the screenplay. Many sharp views of the B-29 make this one of the must-see pictures for Superfortress fans and a definite all-round must-see aviation film.

Filmed at Davis-Monthan AFB, Arizona, with USAF SAC **Boeing B-29 Superfortress** bombers from the 43rd and 303rd Bomb Groups. Other featured aircraft were the **Boeing B-17 Flying Fortress**, including stock footage from World War II, and two **Douglas C-47B Skytrain** transports (s/n 43-16269 / msn 20735; and s/n 43-49198 / msn 15014/26459). Background aircraft were several **Douglas C-54 Skymaster** transports, a **Beechcraft C-45 Expeditor** and a **Curtiss C-46 Commando**. A B-29-35-MO fuselage (s/n 42-65401) was also used for studio filming of aircraft interiors. The camera-plane was Mantz Air Services B-25H (reg. N1203), owned and flown for the film by Hollywood pilot Paul Mantz. Actor Robert Taylor was a World War II U.S.

Navy flight instructor and a postwar recreational pilot, flying a Beechcraft Twin.

FACTUAL BACKGROUND: THE ATOMIC BOMBERS

Type: Boeing B-29-45-MO Superfortress
Serial number: 44-86292
Notes: Aircraft named *Enola Gay*, dropped the 15-kiloton *Little Boy* bomb on Hiroshima, August 6, 1945.
Type: Boeing B-29-35-MO Superfortress
Serial number: 44-27297
Notes: Aircraft named *Bockscar* (also *Bock's Car*), dropped the 21-kiloton *Fat Man* bomb on Nagasaki, August 9, 1945.

The Ace   see   *The Great Santini*

The Ace   see   *Hell in the Heavens*

Ace Eli and Rodger of the Skies

USA / 20th Century–Fox / 1973 / Color / 92 minutes
Director: John Erman
Cast: Cliff Robertson, Pamela Franklin, Eric Shea, Bernadette Peters, Rosemary Murphy

Synopsis / Aviation Content: A largely forgotten film about a down-and-out 1920s pilot who goes on a barnstorming tour with his only son after the boy's mother is killed. The only aircraft was renowned Hollywood pilot Frank Tallman's **Standard J-1** (reg. N62505 / msn T4595) and an unidentified **DeHavilland DH-82 Tiger Moth** doubling as a Standard J-1, which was crashed through a fake barn by Tallman at the top of the film. Made in Kansas with the story written by a then unknown Steven Spielberg!

Ace of Aces

USA / RKO Radio Pictures / 1933 / B&W / 76 minutes
Director: J. Walter Ruben
Cast: Richard Dix, Elizabeth Allan, Ralph Bellamy, Theodore Newton, Nella Walker, Anderson Lawler
Synopsis / Aviation Content: Interesting story of a young pacifist, played by Dix, who reluctantly enters World War I as a fighter pilot and subsequently develops a thirst for blood and killing. Co-written by John Monk Saunders, based on his short story "Birds of Prey." Aircraft include the **Curtiss JN-1 Jenny**; **Lincoln-Garland LF-1**; several **Nieuport 28** fighters and **Waco Model 7** biplanes. Filmed in California.

Aces High

UK / EMI Films / 1976 / Color / 109 minutes
Director: Jack Gold
Cast: Malcolm McDowell, Christopher Plummer, Simon Ward, Peter Firth, David Wood, John Gielgud, Trevor Howard, Richard Johnson, Ray Milland
Synopsis / Aviation Content: Burnt-out squadron leader McDowell and his pilots receive a bright and enthusiastic new pilot to their ranks who quickly learns the horrors of war. All the usual World War I film trappings, such as long drinking bouts, but a top cast and solid aerial sequences throughout with some excellent stunt work. Highlights include a cunning aerial ploy by McDowell to fool his German pursuers. Based on the 1930s play *Journey's End* by R.C. Sherriff and the memoir *Sagittarius Rising* by Cecil Lewis. Produced by S. Benjamin Fisz of *Battle of Britain* (1969) fame.

Type	msn	Civil Reg.	Film Markings
Avro 504K	BAPC.177	G-AACA	G1381
Avro 504K	BAPC.178	—	E373
Bucker Bu. 133C Jungmeister	38	G-AYSJ	E622
DeHavilland DH.82A Tiger Moth	83653	G-AOBX	—
Fokker E.III Eindecker	PPS/FOK/6	G-AVJO	—
Sopwith Pup	BAPC.179	—	A7317
Stampe SV.4B	64	G-AZSA	E954
Stampe SV.4C	120	G-AZGC	—
Stampe SV.4C	163	G-AXYW	—
Stampe SV.4C	360	G-AWXZ	E639, E943
Stampe SV.4C	376	G-AZGE	E940
Valton Lentokonetehdas VL Viima II	unknown	G-BAAY	C-1501

All aircraft were either supplied or operated by Personal Plane Services Ltd., based at the filming location on Booker Airfield (Wycombe Air Park), High Wycombe, Buckinghamshire, England in 1975. Technical advisors were Air Commodore Allen Wheeler and Group Captain Dennis David. Pilots were Tony Bianchi (owner of Personal Plane Services Ltd.), James Gilbert, Iain Weston and Neil Williams.

The Avro 504K was an original British fighter that first flew in 1913. Production continued up to 1932, with over 8,300 produced, making it the most produced World War I–era aircraft to be built. Two non-flying replicas were built and used in the film (BAPC.177, BAPC.178), one with a working engine for taxiing shots.

The Bucker Bu. 133, G-AYSJ, and DeHavilland Tiger Moth, G-AOBX, doubled as German fighter types, G-AYSI had the white wings with red trim and is seen prominently in the final scene. G-AOBX is seen throughout is various dogfights. The Fokker E.III *Eindecker* (Monoplane) was a replica built in 1965 based on the 1915 German fighter, 249 of which were produced. It flew, of course, as the German monoplane in the film. The VL Viima II, G-BAAY, was a rare Finnish-built primary trainer, only twenty-five of which were built in 1935 and 1936. This one (ex–Finnish

Air Force s/n VI-3 / civil reg. OH-VIG), was imported into England in 1972 and flew extensively in the film as the all-red German biplane.

The five Belgian-designed Stampe SV.4 biplanes were conversions doubling as the **Royal Aircraft Factory S.E.5a** fighter. Only three flew in the film, and the remaining two were used for background set dressing. A non-flying Sopwith Pup (BAPC.179) replica was also apparently used for background.

Some use was made of models and special effects for explosions and various angles of no-man's land. Brief snippets of footage from *The Blue Max* (1966) and *Von Richthofen and Brown* (1971) were used featuring the **Fokker Dr.I**, **Fokker D.VII** and other **S.E.5a** replicas.

Aces: Iron Eagle III

USA-UK / New Line Cinema / 1992 / Color / 98 minutes

Director: John Glen

Cast: Louis Gossett Jr., Rachel McLish, Paul Freeman, Christopher Cazenove, Horst Buchholz, Sonny Chiba

Synopsis / Aviation Content: Third *Iron Eagle* film sees veteran World War II fighter pilots combine their talents to mount a private war against a drug dealer in Peru. Although the story is thin on credibility, there is a surprisingly large and varied amount of excellent Warbird action throughout, let down mainly by unconvincing studio-based cockpit mock-ups. Arguably the best of the *Iron Eagle* films for aerial action and flying scenes. Followed by *Iron Eagle IV* (1995).

The Japanese Zero, marked as 3-183, is an original *Tora! Tora! Tora!* (1970) conversion from a Canadian built Harvard Mk. 4, provided here by the Mid-Atlantic Air Museum. The P-38J and Spitfire were provided by the Palm Springs Air Museum. The P-51A "Messerstang," as it was known, doubled for the Messerschmitt Bf. 109 and came from Planes of Fame at Chino, California.

The C-123 Provider, marked in a random USAF livery, was a C-123K (jet-pods), conversion owned and operated by Thunderbird Aviation, Inc. The fictional Messerschmitt 263 seen at the end of the movie is the Scaled Composites Model 151 prototype demonstrator, also known as the Rutan ARES mudfighter after its designer Burt Rutan. Conceived in the 1980s as a low-cost tactical support (ARES: Agile Responsive Effective Support) aircraft for the U.S. Army, it first flew on February 19, 1990, with no other examples built. The mudfighter subsequently flew in support of aviation research experiments.

The four jet fighters sent to intercept the "Aces" squadron are Yugoslavian-built **SOKO G-2A** Galeb aircraft, *Galeb* is Croatian for sea gull. A two-seat, single-engined advanced trainer and ground-attack aircraft, the Galeb was produced in Yugoslavia from 1964 to 1985 with a total of 248 examples built. Of these, 132 served with the Yugoslav Air Force, with the rest sold overseas. The small fighter has become a popular Warbird flyer with at least a dozen sold to U.S.-based owners.

Background aircraft include a **Bell Model 205** and **Model 206 Jet Ranger**, several **Boeing-Stearman** biplanes, a **Cessna 425 Corsair** (N55CH), a **General Dynamics F-16**, three **McDonnell Douglas F-15** fighters, a **North American T-28 Trojan**, **Ryan PT-22 Recruit** (marked as 217) and several biplane aerobatic types. Partly filmed in Avra Valley northwest of Tucson, Arizona.

Type	msn	military s/n	civil reg.
Aces Aircraft			
CCF Harvard Mk. 4	CCF4-16	(RCAF) 20225	N15796
Lockheed P-38J-20-LO Lightning	422-4318	44-23314	N38BP
North American P-51A-10-NA Mustang	99-22354	43-6251	N4235Y
Supermarine Spitfire FR.Mk. XIV	6S/648206	(RAF) NH904	N1148P
Other Aircraft			
Fairchild C-123B-3-FA Provider	20014	54-565	N123K
Scaled Composites Model 151	001	—	N151SC

Aerial Gunner

USA / Paramount Pictures / 1943 / B&W / 78 minutes

Director: William H. Pine

Cast: Chester Morris, Richard Arlen, Jimmy Lydon, Lita Ward, Dick Purcell, Keith Richards, William Benedict, Olive Blakeney

Synopsis / Aviation Content: Wartime film showing off the USAAF gunnery school has fictional student characters going through training, then on to the Pacific Theater for a typical Hollywood ending. Aircraft featured are the **Lockheed B-34 Lexington**, **North American BT-9** (doubling as Japanese fighters) and **AT-6A Texan** (two were s/n 41-15849 and 41-16270). Some use of newsreel footage to help illustrate aerial battles. Partly filmed at the USAAF's Aerial Gunnery School at Harlingen AAF, Texas. Watch for a brief scene featuring a young Robert Mitchum as a flight sergeant.

Air America

USA / TriStar & Carolco Pictures / 1990 / Color / 112 minutes

Director: Roger Spottiswoode

Cast: Mel Gibson, Robert Downey, Jr., Nancy Travis, David Marshall Grant, Lane Smith, Ken Jenkins

Synopsis / Aviation Content: A humorous adventure story set in 1969 Laos following the exploits of a group of pilots working for a covert CIA airline known as "Air America." The film used the 1979 nonfiction book *The Invisible Air Force: The True Story of the CIA's Secret Airlines*, by British-born journalist Christopher Robbins, as source material. With political undertones and the relatively weak ending aside, a colorful and overall fun movie with a terrific sense of comradery and loyalty between the characters. Remains today a popular viewing choice for aviation fans, filled to the brim with aircraft both flying and non-flying from start to finish. Amazing aerial photography and stunt work; two highlights include many views of the C-123K Provider and a hilltop landing stunt by a Turbo-Porter!

Filming took place in Thailand with the Royal Thai Air Force and Army generously providing up to twenty-one flying period aircraft, many still in active Thai military service, which consisted of the following:

Bell 206B Jet Ranger—one provided in *Air America* colors with code 364.

Bell UH-1H Iroquois—four provided, two in *Air America* colors with codes 1062 and 1174.

Cessna O-1A / O-1E Bird Dog—three provided in original markings, s/n 51-7353, 53-7978 and 56-2563.

Douglas C-47B-10-DK Skytrain—two provided, one was s/n 43-49254 (msn 15070/26515).

Fairchild C-123K Provider—the main aircraft featured in the movie. Four were provided by 602 Squadron from Bangkok. They were stripped of their Thai camouflage back to bare metal with tail codes including 568, 671, 683 and 698. These codes were taken from real C-123 aircraft that actually flew with Air America in the 1960s and are not indigenous to the aircraft used in the film. The C-123 Providers were flown by their Thai aircrews, but then piloted by American Dave Kunz when filming was ready to commence. Eight days were spent filming the supply drop sequences; all the while, the Thai pilots were picking up a few new skills and tips from Dave on handling the C-123. Two likely flyables may have been Thai s/n BL4k-10/18 (s/n 54-698 / msn 20147) and BL4k-16/18 (s/n 54-700 / msn 20149).

Fairchild AU-23A Peacemaker—U.S.-built version of the Swiss PC-6 Turbo-Porter, thirty-six of which were sold to the RTAF in the early 1970s. Four were provided to the film by 202 Squadron, Lopburi, three being repainted in Air America colors with codes 206, 215 and 238, the last of which was AU-23A Thai s/n JTh2-29/19 (s/n 74-2088 / msn 2088). The fourth remained in original Thai camouflage marked as 184.

Schweizer TH-300C—two helicopters in original Thai liveries.

Sikorsky S-58T—one helicopter in original Thai livery.

Background aircraft include a **Lockheed C-130H Hercules** seen at Chiang Mai, and the U.S. Senator arrives in a Royal Air Lao **Hawker Siddeley HS.748** (reg. XW-PNA). A vintage **Bell Model 47J** helicopter (reg. N1134W / msn 3130), was used at the top of the film for the Radio 1080 a.m. traffic report sequence.

Pilots were serving members of the Royal Thai Air Force. Film pilots were Tom Danaher, Mark Hanna, Harry Hauss (Bell 47J), Russell John Kern, David Kunz (C-123K), Frank Lang, David Paris (aerial coordinator), Duncan Prentice (helicopter) and Marc Wolff (aerial unit director / coordinator).

The Royal Thai Air Force also provided the filmmakers with a number of derelicts and wrecks for the high number of crashes and stunts that were performed:

Bell UH-1H Iroquois—one fuselage used for interior filming and the treetop crash, marked as 1062.

Cessna O-1 Bird Dog—one fuselage wreck seen being airlifted by a Sikorsky S-58T.

Fairchild C-123K Provider—fuselage and parts of C-123B-4-FA (s/n 54-569 / msn 20018), used for Downey's "Tango 7" crash-landing sequence, tail marked as 671. This derelict C-123 had previously been used as a saloon by crews at Chiang Mai before its role in the film. The C-123 wreck on fire at the top of the film was a very accurate wood and tin mock-up built by the film crew, which even fooled some of the C-123 mechanics and pilots.

Fairchild AU-23A Peacemaker—Thai aircrews would not allow one of their Turbo-Porters to be used in the high-risk hilltop landing scene, so a hybrid Porter was built from eight derelicts found at an aircraft graveyard in Lopburi. Ten Thai Army mechanics took two weeks to assemble a "new Turbo-Porter" which was nicknamed *Corrosion City*. An eighty-pound truck battery was fitted into the rear fuselage so the aircraft would make an easy three-point landing on the uphill gradient of the runway. The Turbo-Porter rebuild was supervised by Tom Banaher; he also flew the stunt itself, which was photographed by up to six cameras. A second Turbo-Porter wreck was used for the scene where it plows into the back of a C-123 cargo hold. A small Honda engine was fitted to spin a wooden prop and the whole fuselage was then towed at speed into the C-123 fuselage via a retracting cable.

Filmed almost entirely in northern Thailand from September to December 1989. Chiang Mai Intl. was the aerial unit's base of operations for the flying scenes, as well as "Vien Tiane Intl. Airport" for the Senator arrival scene. Mae Hong Son Airport, located in the northernmost tip of Thailand, was the film's main set of "Long Tieng," where the CIA ran their Air America base. Mae Sariang Airfield is forty-six miles south of Mae Hong Son and doubled as the old Japanese airfield of "Tango 7" for the film; this field has since become a sealed strip. The hilltop landing strip was purpose-built for the movie, located around sixty-five miles north of Chiang Mai. Aircraft interiors were filmed at Pinewood Studios, Hertfordshire, England, with a C-123 and Turbo-Porter fuselage.

GPS LOCATIONS

Chiang Mai Intl. Airport, Thailand: N18 46.00 / E098 57.90

Mae Hong Son Airport, Thailand: N19 18.10 / E097 58.50

Mae Sariang Airfield, Thailand: N18 10.90 / E097 55.80

FACTUAL BACKGROUND: AIR AMERICA, INC.

"Anything, Anywhere, Anytime, Professionally" was the slogan for Air America, Inc., a company secretly owned by the CIA from 1950 to 1976 for running covert operations in Southeast Asia, especially during the Vietnam War years. In 1946, Flying Tigers legend Claire L. Chennault founded a civilian airline for providing relief supplies to war-ravaged China using surplus World War II aircraft. The airline was facing financial difficulties by 1950, when the Central Intelligence Agency (CIA) secretly brought out the company as Civil Air Transport (CAT), Inc. The CIA's intention was to maintain a civilian appearance with scheduled flights, all the while using other aircraft in the fleet to fly CIA operations around Asia. From 1950 to 1959, CAT flew covert CIA missions in support of various anti-communist conflicts, including the Chinese Civil War, the Korean War and the First Indochina War. In 1959, CAT was renamed Air America, Inc., and flew passengers, cargo, VIPs, spies, commandos, etc., all over Southeast Asia from Burma to Japan in direct and indirect support of CIA-based operations—the Vietnam War provided the "secret airline" with its biggest business. At its height Air America employed over 11,000 staff and used a large number of both fixed and rotary winged aircraft in its operations. STOL and rough field capable aircraft were the main types desired by Air America; these included large numbers of the Beechcraft 18, Pilatus PC-6 Turbo-Porter, Helio Courier, Fairchild C-123 and C-7 Caribou. Long-term use was made of the ever-faithful Curtiss C-46 and Douglas C-47, and several types were leased from the USAF on an as-needed basis, such as the Lockheed C-130 and Fairchild C-119. Air America's most utilized aircraft overall was the Sikorsky S-58 / H-34 helicopter. An Air America pilot could earn in a week what he normally earned in a month, but the flying was dangerous, with often mountainous terrain, poor navigation aids, and the constant threat of combat situations. After the U.S. pullout from South Vietnam in 1975, the CIA attempted to retain an "airline" presence in Thailand, but this fell through. Air America, Inc., finally shut up shop on June 30, 1976, closing a very colorful chapter in aviation history.

Air Cadet

USA / Universal-International / 1951 / B&W / 94 minutes

Director: Joseph Pevney

Cast: Stephen McNally, Gail Russell, Alex Nicol, Richard Long, Charles Drake

Synopsis / Aviation Content: A group of young cadets join the USAF to train as jet pilots and ultimately gain entry into an aerobatic display team. A classic example of the USAF "the way it was" in the post–World War II years, featuring insightful on-base details and flying scenes of the Lockheed Shooting Star.

Type	msn	Military s/n
Douglas TC-47B-30-DK Skytrain	16158/32906	44-76574
Lockheed P-80A-1-LO Shooting Star	080-1041	44-85018
Lockheed P-80A-1-LO Shooting Star	080-1175	44-85152
Lockheed P-80A-1-LO Shooting Star	080-1283	44-85260
Lockheed P-80B-5-LO Shooting Star	080-1782	45-8568
Lockheed P-80B-5-LO Shooting Star	080-1799	45-8585
Lockheed P-80B-1-LO Shooting Star	080-1810	45-8596
Lockheed P-80B-1-LO Shooting Star	080-1896	45-8682
Lockheed P-80B-1-LO Shooting Star	080-1904	45-8690
Lockheed P-80B-1-LO Shooting Star	080-1906	45-8692
Lockheed F-80C-10-LO Shooting Star	080-2719	49-1892
Lockheed T-33A-1-LO Shooting Star	580-5014	48-369
Lockheed T-33A-1-LO Shooting Star	580-5051	49-901
Lockheed T-33A-1-LO Shooting Star	580-5052	49-902
Lockheed T-33A-1-LO Shooting Star	580-5230	50-377
North American AT-6D-NT Texan	88-17890	42-86109

Background aircraft include a **North American B-25 Mitchell** and several **F-86 Sabres** at one point. The flyover in the opening shot was done with 106 T-6 Texan trainers over Randolph AFB. The C-47B (s/n 44-76574) is seen dropping off the cadets at Williams AFB. AT-6 Texan (s/n 42-86109) was used for studio cockpit filming, as was P-80A (s/n 44-85152) and T-33A (s/n 50-377). P-80B Shooting Star (s/n 45-8690) was used for the off-runway crash sequence. As several AT-6 Texan trainers had dual buzz numbers, and because suffix letters weren't always added, correct original serial numbers could not be determined. Noted buzz numbers include TA-158, TA-409A, TA-438B, TA-536, TA-547, TA-611, TA-774 and TA-970.

Actor Rock Hudson's first on-screen role playing an instructor at Randolph. Future astronaut Gus Grissom makes a brief appearance at a lecture after the cadets arrive at Williams AFB. Some use of models in the crash scenes.

The first part of the picture with the AT-6 Texan trainers was shot at Randolph AFB near San Antonio, Texas. The rest of the film was shot at Williams AFB, Mesa, Arizona, which has operated as a local civilian airport since 1993.

GPS LOCATIONS

Randolph AFB, San Antonio, Texas: N29 31.55 / W098 16.50

Williams AFB, Mesa, Arizona: N33 18.245 / W111 39.55

FACTUAL BACKGROUND: THE SHOOTING STAR SERIES

With service entry in 1945, the Lockheed P-80 Shooting Star has the distinction of being the first operational jet fighter in the U.S. inventory and has since become an iconic image of 1950s military aviation in America. It was designed around a British Goblin engine. The majority of production used the Allison J33-A, with the first flight taking place on January 8, 1944. Lockheed's newly formed "Skunk Works," headed by renowned aircraft designer Clarence "Kelly" Johnson, were responsible for the Shooting Star's development, the company itself having been formed as a direct response to the Axis Powers' Me 262 jet fighter. In 1948 the "P" for Pursuit designation was changed to "F" for Fighter. By the outbreak of the Korean War, the F-80 was considered largely obsolete, but many still fought in the early stages of the war. By stretching the fuselage and adding a second seat, Lockheed had developed the T-33A, which first flew on March 22, 1948, and went on to be a real winner for the USAF and U.S. Navy as a jet trainer. Many were sold to foreign air forces, and some even flew on into the 21st century. The third and final version of the Shooting Star series was the 2-seater, all-weather F-94 Starfire interceptor-fighter, whose first flight was on April 16, 1949. Shooting Star production ran from 1943 to 1959. In that time there were 1,731 F-80 fighters built, 5,921 T-33 trainers, plus 866 by Canada and Japan, plus 854 F-94 fighters for a grand total of 9,372 airframes.

The Acrojets, as seen in the film, were the first USAF jet aerobatic display team, which flew F-80C Shooting Stars out of Williams AFB from early 1949 to late 1950. They were disbanded when the Korean War began.

The Air Circus

USA / Fox Film Corp. / 1928 / B&W / 118 minutes

Directors: Howard Hawks, Lewis Seiler

Cast: Arthur Lake, Sue Carol, David Rollins, Louise Dresser, Heinie Conklin, Charles Delaney

Synopsis / Aviation Content: Two young friends, Lake and Rollins, journey out west to become pilots, whereupon they meet resident aviatrix Carol at a local airfield. A superior film for its day has several well photographed aerial sequences using **Travel Air** and **Swallow** biplanes, some piloted by *Wings* (1927) stunt pilot Dick Grace. Filmed from April to June 1928 in part at Clover Field, Santa Monica, California. Notable as being the first sound-on-film feature to be released, containing a short fifteen minute audio section. No prints of this film are known to exist today.

Air Force

USA / Warner Bros. / 1943 / B&W / 124 minutes

Director: Howard Hawks

Cast: John Ridgely, Gig Young, Arthur Kennedy,

Charles Drake, Harry Carey, George Tobias, Ward Wood, Ray Montgomery, John Garfield, James Brown

Synopsis / Aviation Content: Fictional tale that follows the crew of an early variant B-17 as they fly across the Pacific in the immediate days after Pearl Harbor. Action-packed, escapist formula is a real winner featuring a sharp and well-paced narrative for a picture of this period. Excellent film for B-17 fans includes many angles, close-ups and details of early Flying Fortress bombers simply not seen anywhere else. Remains a period favorite of many aviation film fans to this day.

Type	msn	Military s/n	Film Markings
Boeing B-17B Flying Fortress	2004	38-211	18
Boeing B-17B Flying Fortress	2020	38-261	07
Boeing B-17B Flying Fortress	2031	38-584	10 / 05564 / *Mary Ann*
Boeing B-17B Flying Fortress	2033	39-001	15

More than twelve early Boeing B-17 Flying Fortress bombers were used in the production, which was shot in and around Tampa, Florida. Aerial photography was undertaken by Warner Bros. Chief Pilot Paul Mantz, using up to nine B-17B, C, and D Flying Fortress bombers to depict the journey to Hawaii at the top of the film. Four of the B-17 Fortresses have been identified as listed above, the most important, of course, being the *Mary Ann* herself, painted as No.10 and with false nonexistent s/n "40-5564." Like most of the early B-17 bombers, this aircraft had a relatively short life: delivered to the USAAC on September 7, 1940, it was written off in an accident at Hobbs Field, New Mexico, on October 17, 1943. Most of the B-17B variants as seen in the film were upgraded to B-17C standards with the modified gun (bubble designs removed) installations, which is why they have traditionally been mistaken for the "C" variant.

More than five **Bell P-39D Airacobra** fighters were also hired for the film (identified s/n 41-28345, 41-28347, 41-28378), as well as a **North American AT-6 Texan** (s/n 40-2143). Japanese aircraft were depicted by several **Republic P-43 Lancer** fighters, and the usual **North American T-6 Texan** trainers doubling as "Zero" fighters.

Wide use of stock and newsreel footage in the

film's climax features the Bell P-39, Boeing B-17E, Brewster F2A, Curtiss P-40E, Douglas SBD, TBD, Grumman F4F, Lockheed Hudson, Martin B-26 and Vought SB2U. Some naval scenes also use stock and newsreel footage. A full-scale B-17 mock-up fuselage was built on a soundstage to film aircraft interiors. There was much use of models and miniatures throughout for the B-17 takeoffs and landings; one memorable shot has a model B-17 snagging a fence with its tail wheel! Aerial battles also used models to great effect. The naval battle featured battleship miniatures blown up in Santa Monica Bay, California.

Producer Hal Wallis was forced to film in Florida, as fighters could not be flown on the West Coast in Japanese livery for fear of being shot down. Ground scenes with the B-17 bombers were shot at Drew Army Air Field, Florida, which stood in for Hamilton AFB, California; Hickam Field, Hawaii; Wake Island; and Manila in the Philippines. A derelict **Martin B-18 Bolo** was used for set dressing, as well as some **Bell P-39 Airacobra** aircraft. Filming started on May 18, 1942, and finished on October 26, 1942.

FACTUAL BACKGROUND:
THE EARLY B-17 BOMBERS

The legend of the B-17 Flying Fortress began in the mid–1930s with a series of early variants testing the waters in heavy bomber design and combat capability. The first fledgling variants amounted to only 134 airframes of an eventual 12,731 that would be built. The B-17 prototype first flew on July 28, 1935, as the Boeing Model 299 with civil reg. NX13372. Although a tragic accident saw this prototype written off, Boeing was lucky enough to receive a contract from the USAAC for thirteen Y1B-17 and one Y1B-17A service test aircraft. The gamble proved a winner, and soon Boeing was producing the bomber in an ever-evolving fashion as the B-17B (39 built) in 1939, B-17C (38 built) in 1940, and B-17D (42 built) in 1941. The RAF took delivery of 20 Fortress Mk. I (B-17C) bombers, with the aircraft's combat debut taking place on July 8, 1941, in a raid over Germany. The combat shortcomings of this essentially prewar design meant most of the B, C and D variants were lost in battle, the survivors being restricted from combat for state-

side duties. Lessons learned, the much improved, now "classic look" of the Fortress, with redesigned rear fuselage and tail, began with the B-17E (512 built) in 1941. From there the legend, and numbers, grew as the U.S. entered World War II. The definitive B-17F (3,405 built) and B-17G (8,680 built) refined the design into a winning formula that helped the Allies defeat the Axis powers.

Air Force One

USA / Columbia Pictures / 1997 / Color / 124 minutes

Director: Wolfgang Petersen

Cast: Harrison Ford, Gary Oldman, Glenn Close, Dean Stockwell, Wendy Crewson, William H. Macy, Xander Berkeley

Synopsis / Aviation Content: Terrorists take over the Boeing VC-25A, Air Force One, in midair and hold it for ransom, but fail to realize the determination of the U.S. President to save his family and colleagues. Top-notch action story is, of course, far-fetched but entertaining, featuring a variety of aircraft types—although many are models or CGI created. Highlights for aviation purists will be the climatic in-flight sequence putting a Boeing 747 and Lockheed MC-130 Hercules together.

Type	msn	Civil reg.	Film Markings
Boeing 747-146	19727/54	N703CK	United States of America / 28000

The main aeronautical star here is the real **Boeing 747-100** series airliner hired for the film from American International Airways. The 54th 747 airframe built (msn 19727), it first flew on June 9, 1970, and was delivered to Japan Airlines on June 26, 1970 (reg. JA8103). On November 24, 1982, it joined Japan Asia Airways before being acquired by American Intl. as a cargo carrier on December 22, 1992 (reg. N703CK). In mid–1996 it was selected to play the part of Air Force One and given a $300,000-dollar paint scheme matching that of the actual presidential Boeing aircraft. Once filming started, this movie "stand-in" caused much confusion at airports, with its new livery prompting many radio call-ins to control towers and many locals to ask if the *real* president was in town. After filming, N703CK was sold to Kitty Hawk Interna-

A $300,000 paint scheme and looking the part! Boeing 747–100 N703CK at Los Angeles Intl. for the filming of *Air Force One* in 1996. Photograph: Duncan Stewart.

tional on February 3, 1999, and has subsequently been retired from service and scrapped.

Other real aircraft used were a **Lockheed MC-130 Hercules**, up to six **McDonnell Douglas F-15 Eagle** fighters, several **Bell UH-1H Iroquois**, **Sikorsky UH-60 Black Hawk** helicopters and a Russian **Mil Mi-24 Hind** helicopter for the prison sequence. Background aircraft were the **Boeing KC-135 Stratotanker, Lockheed C-141 Starlifter** and **C-5 Galaxy**.

Models and CGI-created aircraft included a USAF McDonnell Douglas KC-10A Extender tanker, F-15 Eagle, Russian MiG-29 Fulcrum fighters and Air Force One itself.

Some of the armed services involved in filming were the 33rd Fighter Wing, Elgin AFB, Florida; 89th Airlift Wing (Presidential Flight), Andrews AFB, Maryland; 305th Air Mobility Wing, McGuire AFB, New Jersey; 60th Air Mobility Wing, Travis AFB, California; and the 8th Special Operations Squadron, Hurlburt Field, Florida.

Moscow Intl. Airport was actually Los Angeles Intl. Airport, which included a C-5 Galaxy in the background. Ramstein AFB, Germany, was Rickenbacker Airport in Columbus, Ohio, where a lot of night filming took place using the 747 (reg. N703CK). The 747 and MC-130 aerial sequence was filmed near Channel Islands, Oxnard, California, using a B-25 Mitchell camera-plane, which restricted the Boeing airliner to a very slow 200 mph! A full-scale Air Force One interior was constructed on Stage 15 at Sony Pictures Studios, Culver City, California, for the extensive onboard scenes. Principal photography took place from September 16, 1996, to January 17, 1997.

GPS Locations

Rickenbacker Intl. Airport, Columbus, Ohio: N39 48.50 / W082 56.00

Factual Background: Air Force One

Strictly speaking, the term "Air Force One" is a radio call sign assigned to any aircraft which has the U.S. president onboard—whether it be a small Gulfstream jet or large Boeing airliner. However, the term over the years has become a colloquial one used mainly to describe the large airliner-type aircraft most often used by the U.S. president.

The two 747 airliners are a fifth-generation presidential aircraft. The first was a Douglas VC-54C (s/n 42-107451) named *Sacred Cow*; the second a Douglas VC-118 (s/n 46-505) named *Independence*; the third a Lockheed VC-121E (s/n 53-7885) named *Columbine III*; and the fourth were two Boeing VC-137C (s/n 62-6000 and 72-7000). The fifth generation comprises two Boeing 747-2G4B aircraft with the designation VC-25A (s/n 82-8000 / msn 23824/679) and 92-9000 (msn 23825/685). They first flew on May 16 and October 29, 1987, respectively. After extensive modifications to the avionics and airframe for defensive measures, including blast shielding from the electromagnetic pulse of a nuclear detonation, both aircraft began presidential service in the latter part of 1990. They are maintained by the 89th Airlift Wing (Presidential Flight) at Andrews AFB, Maryland. Contrary to popular belief, there is no belly escape pod designed into the aircraft as depicted in the film, but both aircraft do have an aerial refueling capability.

Air Mail

USA / Universal Pictures / 1932 / B&W / 84 minutes

Director: John Ford

Cast: Ralph Bellamy, Gloria Stuart, Pat O'Brien, Slim Summerville, Lilian Bond, Russell Hopton

Synopsis / Aviation Content: Fictional story depicting the challenges and dangers faced by a small airmail company in often adverse weather. This classic, if somewhat dramatically light, aviation picture was one of the first films to use the new studio-based process photography. This meant actors could be placed in mock-up cockpits while previously filmed moving clouds could be projected on a screen behind them. Story written by former navy pilot turned screenwriter Frank "Spig" Wead.

Notable as being the one of the first aviation-themed films for new Hollywood pilot Paul Mantz, who provided his **Stearman C2B** biplane (reg. NC4099 / msn 110), which also served as a camera-plane. Mantz also flew a **Travel Air 16-K** (reg. NC446W / msn 16K-2001) through a hanger at Bishop Airport, California. Western Air Express provided three **Boeing Model 95** aircraft and a **Fokker Model 10** for some scenes. Some parts were also filmed at United (now Bob Hope) Airport, California. Excellent use of miniatures and special effects.

GPS LOCATIONS

Bishop Airport, Bishop, California: N37 22.25 / W118 22.00

United Airport, Burbank, California: N34 12.10 / W118 21.35

The Air Mail

USA / Paramount Pictures / 1925 / B&W / 80 minutes

Director: Irvin Willat

Cast: Warner Baxter, Billie Dove, Mary Brian, Douglas Fairbanks Jr., George Irving

Synopsis / Aviation Content: Silent-era film about risk-taking pilot Baxter, who flies in any weather to get the mail through. Aircraft were **DeHavilland DH.4** and **Fisk** biplanes. Partly filmed in Death Valley, California. Only one half of a single print of this film survives today.

Airplane!

Alternate / International Title: *Flying High!*

USA / Paramount Pictures / 1980 / Color / 88 minutes

Directors: Jim Abrahams, David Zucker, Jerry Zucker

Cast: Robert Hays, Julie Hagerty, Robert Stack, Lloyd Bridges, Peter Graves, Kareem Abdul-Jabbar, Leslie Nielsen, Lorna Patterson, Stephen Stucker

Synopsis / Aviation Content: Slapstick comedy spoof of air-disaster films *Zero Hour!* (1957) and to a lesser extent *Airport* (1970), it was a such a smash hit that it's hard to watch the original dramas and take them seriously. Still funny today and highly regarded as one of the best comedy motion pictures ever released. Some ground scenes used a **Boeing 707-131B** (reg. N6721 / msn 18987/486) of U.S. airline TWA. Flying was done with a scale model—the tail of which does a great shark-fin gag in the opening sequence! A sequel was made titled *Airplane II: The Sequel* (1982), which is set on the space shuttle taking passengers to the moon.

Airport

USA / Universal Pictures / 1970 / Color / 131 minutes

Director: George Seaton

Cast: Burt Lancaster, Dean Martin, Jean Seberg, Jacqueline Bisset, George Kennedy, Helen Hayes, Van Heflin, Maureen Stapleton, Barry Nelson, Dana Wynter, Lloyd Nolan, Barbara Hale

Synopsis / Aviation Content: A large international airport faces a series of aerial emergencies while enduring a ferocious snowstorm. Based on the 1968 novel of the same name by British/Canadian author Arthur Hailey. A timeless classic which set the stage for other disaster films to follow. Not much in the way of *real* aircraft, since most flying scenes are accomplished with miniatures. Some good ground shots, however, of the Boeing 707 airliner.

Type	msn	Civil reg.	Film Markings
Boeing 707-349C	19354/503	N324F	Trans Global Airlines

Boeing 707, N324F, was the only real aircraft hired for the film painted in the livery of fictional "Trans Global Airlines." This aircraft was first flown on June 9, 1966; owners and lease operators included Flying Tigers Line as N324F from 1966; Aer Lingus as EI-ASO in 1969; Qantas as VH-EBZ in 1970; British Caledonian as G-BAWP in 1973; Zambia Airways as 9J-AEC in 1975; Bangladesh Biman as S2-ACG in 1980; and finally Transbrazil as PT-TCS in 1987. It was written off after it crashed while on approach to Sao Paulo, Brazil, on March 21, 1989. The three crew members plus eighteen people on the ground were killed.

Background aircraft include various **Boeing 707** airliners, a **Boeing 727-100** and **Douglas DC-9**. Aircraft interiors were studio mock-ups with some use of models and special effects. The airport scenes, at the fictional Lincoln International Airport, was in reality Minneapolis-St. Paul Intl. Airport in Minneapolis, Minnesota, USA (GPS Location: N44 52.80 / W093 13.10).

Airport 1975

USA / Universal Pictures / 1974 / Color / 102 minutes

Director: Jack Smight

Cast: Charlton Heston, Karen Black, George Kennedy, Efrem Zimbalist, Jr., Susan Clark, Helen Reddy

Synopsis / Aviation Content: The second installment in the *Airport* series sees a midair collision leaving a Boeing 747 without a flight crew and little hope for survival. Putting 1970s clichés and attitudes aside, one of the best air disaster films of the period featuring some outstanding aerial sequences, undoubtedly making it the most action-packed of the four *Airport* movies. A realistic 747 flight deck with detailed scenes of airports and aircraft will definitely make pleasing viewing for aviation fans.

The Beechcraft Baron was used for the midair collision with the Boeing 747. Ironically, it was written off in a real midair collision with a Cessna 180 over Stockton, California, on August 24, 1989. Both pilots were killed.

Boeing 747-123, N9675, was first flown on May 7, 1971, and delivered to first customer American Airlines on May 25, 1971; converted to Special Freighter standard as a 747-123(SF) with delivery on October 1, 1974; to TMA as OD-AGM in 1976; back to American Airlines as N9675 in 1977; to United Parcel Service on September 12, 1984, as N675UP. The aircraft was finally retired by UPS into desert storage at Roswell, New Mexico, in 2005. For *Airport 1975*, the aircraft was painted in the livery of fictional "Columbia Airlines," but retained the American Airlines blue, red and white side strip and original registration. The 747 cost Universal Pictures up to $30,000 per day to hire. There are several shots in the film of actor Charlton Heston actually sitting in the pilot's seat while in-flight. Stock footage of this aircraft was extensively used by Universal in a 1978 television episode of *The Incredible Hulk* starring Bill Bixby.

The T-37 Tweet (s/n 67-14762) became known as the "Hollywood Tweet" to the pilots who flew it in the years after the film was released. It was finally retired to AMARC in Arizona with s/n TE0250 on December 1, 2004.

The Gates Learjet was owned by renowned aviator businessman Clay Lacy.

The massive "jet-helicopter" is a HH-53B Super Jolly Green Giant, the USAF search and rescue version of the USMC CH-53A Sea Stallion (s/n 66-14431) was one of eight HH-53B variants built and was later converted to an MH-53J Pave Low III for special ops. It was written off in 1998: during a post-maintenance flight check, a takeoff was performed with no oil in the gearbox. It quickly seized, the hovering chopper falling to the ground. Damaged beyond repair, it was then used as a

Type	msn	Military s/n	Civil reg.	Film Markings
Beechcraft Baron 95-A55	TC431	—	N9750Y	N9750Y
Boeing 747-123	20390/136	—	N9675	N9675 / Columbia Airlines
Cessna T-37B-CE Tweet	41026	67-14762	—	14762
Gates Learjet 24A	24A-096	—	N1972L	N1972L
Sikorsky HH-53B-SI	65-086	66-14431	—	14431

One of the most recognized jumbo jets on the big screen during the 1970s was American Airlines 747–100 N9675 marked "Columbia Airlines" for *Airport 1975* (1974). Photograph: Howard Chaloner.

ground instructional airframe before being re-tired to AMARC with s/n HC0030 on July 17, 2003. There was another "14431" which was a USMC CH-53A, BuNo. 152397, loaned to the USAF for training with s/n 67-14431, but this along with six others were later returned to the Marines.

Background aircraft include a **Douglas DC-8**, **DC-10** and **Convair CV-580**. Aircraft interiors were studio mock-ups created of the Boeing 747 flight-deck and cabin. Famed Hollywood aviation film company Tallmantz Aviation Inc. provided the aerial logistics and photography for the film. The airport at the start of the film is Washington Dulles International Airport, Virginia (GPS Location: N38 57.20 / W077 26.80). The small, rainy airport also near the top of the movie is Brackett Field, California.

Actor Charlton Heston was a World War II B-25 Mitchell gunner / radio operator with the Eleventh Air Force in the Aleutian Islands during 1944–45.

Airport '77

USA / Universal Pictures / 1977 / Color / 109 minutes

Director: Jerry Jameson

Cast: Jack Lemmon, Lee Grant, Brenda Vaccaro, Joseph Cotten, Olivia de Havilland, Darren McGavin, Christopher Lee, Robert Foxworth, Robert Hooks, George Kennedy, James Stewart

Synopsis / Aviation Content: The third installment in the *Airport* series has an attempted

hijacking of a Boeing 747 by art thieves, as a result of which the aircraft crashes in the Bermuda Triangle. It sinks to the bottom of the Atlantic, where a race against time ensues to rescue the passengers before the aircraft floods. As the *Airport* series of films progressed throughout the 1970s, so did the level of absurdity in the storylines. Still entertaining enough, though with highlights for aviation fans being the U.S. Naval forces in action, namely the Seasprite helicopters and Viking jets.

The main aircraft is a **Boeing 747-123** (reg. N9667 / msn 20106/79), which first flew on September 24, 1970, being delivered to American Airlines on October 8, 1970. It subsequently flew with Braniff Airways from 1978, Citicorp from 1984, National Airlines from 1984, and Air Afrique from 1985, all under the same N9667 registration; to Citicorp as N14937 in 1986; to Air Inter, Luxembourg, as LX-MCV in 1986, then Cargolux and Iran Air; to United Airlines as N157UA on October 8, 1987, until retired into storage in September 1999. It was scrapped and parted out in 2001. For the film it was briefly painted in the fictional markings of "N13S / Stevens Corporation," but retained the American Airlines blue, red and white side stripes.

Identified military aircraft include the **Kaman UH-2A** (BuNo.149036) and **UH-2B Seasprite** (BuNo. 150185), both of naval squadron HSL-31; **Lockheed S-3A Viking** (BuNo. 159749, BuNo. 160125 and BuNo. 160136), all of naval squadron VS-41; a **Sikorsky HH-52A Sea Guardian** (USCG

1408) is also seen. There was one UH-2 Seasprite with an odd s/n 8186, which might be UH-2B BuNo. 150186.

The helicopter in the opening scene is an unidentified **Bell Model 206B Jet Ranger**. Aircraft interiors were studio mock-ups with an extensive use of models and special effects. The airport terminal at the start of the film is Washington Dulles International Airport, Virginia.

Airport '79   see   *The Concorde ... Airport '79*

Airport '80—The Concorde   see   *The Concorde ... Airport '79*

Air Strike

USA / Lippert Pictures / 1955 / B&W / 67 minutes
Director: Cy Roth
Cast: Richard Denning, Gloria Jean, Don Haggerty, William Hudson, Alan Wells, John Kirby
Synopsis / Aviation Content: Very little known about this film except it's set during the Korean War on an aircraft carrier. Only actors Denning and Jean stand out in an otherwise poor production. Most of the aerial action is made up with the usual newsreel and naval stock footage.

Airwolf: The Movie   see   **Section Two (Television): *Airwolf***

Alive

USA / Paramount & Touchstone Pictures / 1993 / Color / 121 minutes
Director: Frank Marshall
Cast: Ethan Hawke, Vincent Spano, Josh Hamilton, Bruce Ramsay, John Haymes Newton, David Kriegel, Kevin Breznahan, Sam Behrens, Illeana Douglas, Jack Noseworthy
Synopsis / Aviation Content: Dramatic survival movie based on the incredible real-life story of passengers on a Uruguayan aircraft that crashed

in the Andes Mountains in 1972. Developed from the 1974 book *Alive: The Story of the Andes Survivors* by British writer Piers Paul Read. A short flying sequence starts the film, and the realism of the subsequent crash is rated as one of the best ever created for a motion picture.

Acquired for a few brief flying shots was **Fairchild-Hiller FH-227D Friendship** (reg. N2784R / msn 573), owned by the South Seattle Community College. Painted to match the original aircraft marked as Fuerza Aerea Uruguaya / 571, it can be seen in a couple of shots intercut with a model aircraft built for specific camera angles not able to be captured using the real aircraft. After filming N2784R was sold overseas to Ecuador as HC-BUF; it was written off on October 28, 1997, when it overshot the runway at Ambato-Chachoan Airport, Ecuador. Ironically this FH-227D (msn 573) was the very next airframe on the production line after the FH-227D that was involved in the actual 1972 crash (msn 572)!

An unidentified Fokker or Fairchild-Hiller Friendship derelict was acquired as the fuselage set piece and filmed on location in Canada. Two **Bell Model 212** helicopters from Vancouver Helicopters, Canada, were provided for the final scene, marked with fictional Chilean Air Force s/n "H-89" and "H-91."

FACTUAL BACKGROUND:
FLIGHT 571

The actual aircraft involved in the incident was a Fairchild-Hiller FH-227D Friendship, the U.S. version of the classic Dutch Fokker F.27 Friendship. At the time of the crash it had been in military service with the Uruguayan Air Force (Fuerza Aerea Uruguaya, s/n T-571 / msn 572) since July 1971. The tragedy occurred on October 13, 1972, in the final phase of a flight from Montevideo, Uruguay, to Santiago, Chile. The search was called off eight days later. Facing extreme cold, high altitudes, avalanches and starvation, the survivors ate the flesh of the deceased in order to stay alive. Two survivors, Nando Parrado and Roberto Canessa, eventually trekked out to civilization over a ten-day period, with the first rescuers arriving at the crash site on December 22, 1972. Of

Fairchild-Hiller FH-227D N2784R painted in the livery of ill-fated Uruguayan Air Force aircraft (s/n 571) for the 1993 film *Alive*. Photograph: Rich Tregear.

the forty-five people onboard Flight 571, twenty-nine perished and sixteen survived. GPS coordinates for the crash site are: S34 45.80 / W070 17.45.

Always

USA / Universal Pictures & United Artists / 1989 / Color / 117 minutes

Director: Steven Spielberg

Cast: Richard Dreyfuss, Holly Hunter, John Goodman, Brad Johnson, Audrey Hepburn

Synopsis / Aviation Content: Romance story developed from the classic World War II film *A Guy Named Joe* (1943), but now set amongst the Montana forests during fire season. A mature, slow-paced storyline ultimately proves unsatisfying, but is worth staying with for the multitude of piston-era, fire-bomber aircraft that provide some riveting flying sequences. The opening shot is a real jaw dropper! A must-see for any PBY Catalina or A-26 Invader fans.

The main attraction is the three A-26 Invaders hired from Lynch Air Tankers, Inc., of Billings, Montana. All three are genuine, operating fire-bomber aircraft and *Lynch STOL 26* conversions with various performance upgrades undertaken by their owner / operator.

N4805E—Delivered to USAAF; to Wood River Oil & Refining Co., Kansas, as N4805E in 1958, after which the company changed its name to Rock Island Oil & Refining Co., Inc., in 1959, and the plane converted to *Rock Island Consort 26*; to Koch Industries Inc., Kansas, in 1970; to Reeder Flying Service, Inc., Idaho, in 1972, and converted to a fire-bomber; to Lynch Air Tankers, Inc., Montana, in 1975, and converted to *Lynch STOL 26*; used in *Always* as "Tanker 58," mainly in a background role; to Grout Aircraft, Washington, in 1993; exported to Air Spray Ltd., Canada, in 2001 as C-GHZM.

N4818E—Delivered to USAAF; to Wood River Oil & Refining Co., Kansas, as N4818E in 1959, after which the company changed its name to

Type	msn	Military s/n	Civil reg.	Film Markings
Consolidated PBY-5A Catalina	1581	BuNo.34027	N9505C	53 / *Fire Eaters*
Douglas A-26B-45-DL Invader	27400	44-34121	N4805E	58 / *Fire Eaters*
Douglas A-26C-35-DT Invader	28650	44-35371	N4818E	59 / *Fire Eaters*
Douglas A-26C-45-DT Invader	29000	44-35721	N9425Z	57 / 59 / *Fire Eaters*
Fairchild C-119F-FA Flying Boxcar	10776	(RCAF) 22111	N8093	N8093

This **A-26 Invader C-GHZM (ex–N4805E), marked as "Tanker 58," played mainly a background role in the 1989 film *Always*. Photograph: Ralph M. Pettersen.**

Rock Island Oil & Refining Co., Inc., in 1959; to Consolidated Air Parts Co., California, in 1968; to Lynch Flying Service, Inc., Montana in 1969, and converted to a fire-bomber; after the company changed its name to Lynch Air Tankers, Inc., in 1973, converted to *Lynch STOL 26*; used in *Always* as "Tanker 59" (Holly Hunter) and as background in some scenes.

N9425Z—Delivered to USAAF; to Atlas Investment Corp., California, in 1960 as N9425Z; to Belcher Aircraft Corp., California, in 1960; to

Central Oregon Aerial Co., Oregon, in 1961, and converted to an air-tanker; to Lynch Flying Service, Inc., Montana, in 1966; after the company changed its name to Lynch Air Tankers, Inc., in 1973, converted to *Lynch STOL 26*; was the main aircraft used in *Always* as "Tanker 57" (Richard Dreyfuss) and "Tanker 59" (Holly Hunter); to Robert Pond, Minnesota, in 1992; to Pond Warbirds LLC (Palm Springs Air Museum), California, in 2001 for display.

The PBY-5A, N9505C, was from SLAFCO of

One of the A-26 aerial tankers of the 1989 Spielberg film *Always* was N4818E, seen here in 2006. Photograph: Ralph M. Pettersen.

"Fire Eaters" logo on A-26 (N4805E) from *Always* (1989). Photograph: Air Spray (1967) Ltd.

Libby Airport near Libby, Montana, where the filmmakers constructed a control tower especially for the film. Afterward, it was retained and built into an actual working tower that still stands today. The Flat Rock, Colorado, training base was actually Ephrata Municipal Airport near Ephrata, Washington.

GPS Locations
Libby Airport, Montana: N48 17.05 / W115 29.30

Ephrata Municipal Airport, Washington State: N47 18.25 / W119 30.55

Moses Lake, Washington, as John Goodman's "Tanker 53." It was a Steward-Davis Super-Catalina civil conversion with up-rated engines, faired-over nose turret, and a reshaped, squared tail. The C-119F, N8093, was hired from Hawkins & Powers Aviation, Inc., of Greybull, Wyoming. It's seen during the "Flat Rock" training scenes still marked in its original RCAF service side-stripe lightning bolt. It was sold when H&P closed up in 2006 to the Hagerstown Aviation Museum, Maryland, and is *still* in its original RCAF livery.

Three unidentified light aircraft were also provided for filming: an **Aeronca 7AC Champion** was used to depict Pete's first solo in the Dreyfuss / Hepburn wheat-field scene. A 1970 **Bellanca 8KCAB Decathlon** was used as Brad Johnson's colorful *Wing N' Prayer* aircraft; this was a development of the 1968 Champion 8KCAB Citabria light aerobatic aircraft. The **Cessna Model 337 Skymaster** was the light twin-boom aircraft seen in a few scenes.

Background aircraft are a **Beechcraft 18**, **Bell 204** (reg. N59887), **Bell 206B Jet Ranger**, **Cessna 340** (reg. N2637Y), **DHC-6 Twin-Otter** (reg. N141Z) and a **North American B-25J Mitchell** (reg. N3675G). Camera-planes were the B-25J, one of the A-26 Invaders, and the PBY Catalina.

The main firebase was filmed at

Amelia

USA-Canada / Fox Searchlight & Avalon Pictures / 2009 / Color / 111 minutes

Director: Mira Nair

Cast: Hilary Swank, Richard Gere, Ewan McGregor, Christopher Eccleston, Joe Anderson, Cherry Jones, Mia Wasikowska

Synopsis / Aviation Content: A look at the life and times of American aviatrix Amelia Earhart from her 1928 Atlantic crossing to her mysterious disappearance over the Pacific Ocean in 1937. Stunning aerial camera work of the Lockheed Electra and a fascinating depiction of Earhart's final moments make this worth see-

Type	msn	civil reg.	Film Markings
Main / Flying Aircraft			
Beechcraft Model E18S	BA-428	ZS-IJO	NR16020
Bleriot XI (replica)	1	N126HM	XI
Bucker Jungmann 1.131-E-2000E3B	439	C-FLAE	C-FLAE
Ford 4-AT-B Tri-Motor	10	N1077	N1077 / Ford
Lockheed Model 12-A Electra Junior	1208	N2072	NR16020
Lockheed Model 12-A Electra Junior	1214	N16085	NR16020
Lockheed Model 12-A Electra Junior	1287	F-AZLL	NR16020
Morane-Saulnier L Parasol (replica)	001	N323SS	—
Background Aircraft			
DeHavilland DH.60M Moth	757	CF-AAJ	CF-AAJ
Douglas C-47A-1-DK Skytrain	12107	ZS-BXF	—
Douglas C-47A-30-DL Skytrain	9581	ZS-GPL	—
Fleet (Finch) Model 16R	92319	C-FDAF	C-FDAF
Stinson V-77 Reliant	77-166	CF-CAJ	CF-CAJ
Waco ATO	A-65	CF-BPM	CF-BPM
Waco YMF-5	F5C-102	C-GZPR	C-GZPR

ing. Too bad the story's heavy focus on her married and personal life tends to crowd out the far more significant story of her aviation achievements. Developed from the 1997 book *East to the Dawn* by American journalist Susan Butler, and the 1989 book *The Sound of Wings* by English writer Mary S. Lovell. Hilary Swank also co-executive produced.

Amelia Earhart's famous aircraft was a Lockheed Model 10-E Electra (reg. NR16020 / msn 1055). Built in 1936, it was modified to carry a 1,250-gallon fuel tank in the main cabin, and was outfitted with various other modifications suitable for a round-the-world flight. In 1988 the FAA permanently reserved the registration NR16020 for Amelia Earhart. The filmmakers were unable to use an original Model 10, so it was decided to settle for the similar but slightly more contoured Model 12 Electra Junior. Two flyable airframes and one non-flyable were then acquired for the part:

N2072—Delivered in 1936 as NC2072 to H.E. Talbot & Co.; subsequently to various (oil) companies in South America from the 1940s into the 1970s; acquired by Joseph Shepard in 1988 for restoration; briefly used in the film with the Canadian film unit piloted by Shepard himself, recognizable by the VOR / ILS antenna directly behind the DF loop above the cockpit.

N16085—Delivered in 1937 as NC16085 to Erle Halliburton, Inc.; many U.S. owners over the ensuing decades; acquired for the film in a non-flying role for ground scenes, the takeoff crash scene, and the hangar repair scene.

F-AZLL—Delivered in 1941 as NC33615 to Sky Kraft Corp.; drafted into U.S. Navy service as the one and only R3O-2 with BuNo. 02947 based in London with the naval attaché; to civil registry in 1944 as G-AGTL for supposed covert ops; sold into France in 1961 as F-BJJY; several minor accidents over the next few years; restored and registered as F-AZLL in 1999; flew in the film with the South African film unit for all African, Middle East, Asian and over-water scenes. In fact, it was used in almost all the flying scenes and is recognizable by the small shark-fin antenna on the aft fuselage spine.

An additional aircraft, a Beechcraft E18S, ZS-IJO, was used as an Electra stand-in for ground scenes in the New Guinea sequence, which is why we only see it from a rear angle.

The small aircraft seen at the top of the film in the first flashback sequence is a French 1914 Morane-Saulnier L Parasol, N323SS, replica owned by Sharon Starks. The yellow biplane Earhart is then flying is a Bucker Jungmann (CASA) 1.131, C-FLAE, of Canadian ownership. It's also seen doing a flypast in the air derby sequence. The 1909 Bleriot XI, N126HM, is a Baslee-built replica used in a childhood flashback sequence during Earhart's solo Atlantic. Earhart takes Mrs. Roosevelt for a ride in a genuine Ford 4-AT-B Tri-Motor, N1077, fully restored and provided by Yellowstone Aviation, Inc. Built in 1927, it's the oldest Tri-Motor still flying.

There were many biplane period aircraft used in background scenes throughout the film. In one hangar scene, shot in South Africa, Earhart and Putnam are around four unidentified DeHavilland DH.82 Tiger Moth biplanes—one silver which flew, one yellow falsely marked as N953Y, one blue and yellow, and one red without wings. The air derby sequence was shot near Toronto, Canada, using a lineup of locally owned aircraft which included an unidentified red Beechcraft Model 17 Staggerwing; a red and yellow DeHavilland DH.60M Moth, CF-AAJ; a yellow Fleet (Finch) Model 16R, C-FDAF; a Stinson V-77 Reliant, CF-CAJ; a red and black Waco ATO, CF-BPM; a yellow Waco YMF-5, C-GZPR; plus one other unidentified. Although the scene was meant to be set in the U.S., the Canadian registration markings were retained. In the scene before Earhart departs on her final journey, shot in South Africa, two Douglas DC-3 aircraft are used as background. ZS-BXF was originally U.S. s/n 42-92320, and also ex–SAAF Dakota Mk. III (s/n FZ572 / 6821). ZS-GPL was originally U.S. s/n 42-23719. Also seen here is a Stampe SV-4 biplane falsely marked as NR417. They are, however, not clearly seen in the finished film.

Cinespace Studios in Toronto built two full-scale, non-flying replicas of Earhart's aircraft. The first is of the Fokker F.VIIb/3m (reg. NX4204) floatplane used in her 1928 Atlantic crossing. Built with turning electric motors, it was used in a hangar scene and later stationary on-water scenes. The takeoffs were filmed in Halifax, Nova Scotia, with a Cessna U206B Stationair (reg. C-FVDG) doing the takeoff run with replica floats producing spray and wake. A CGI Fokker was then superimposed on the Cessna in post-production to complete the illusion of a real Fokker floatplane taking off. The second mock-up was of Earhart's Lockheed Vega 5B (reg. NR7952), used in her 1932 solo Atlantic crossing. It's seen in several Canadian locations that double for the U.S. and Ireland.

Filming took place from April 27 to August 15, 2008, largely in Canada and South Africa. Scenes were shot at Dunnville Airport, Ontario, and various other Canadian locations. Many scenes were shot at Rand Airport, Johannesburg, South Africa, including the Miami, Florida, scene of Earhart and Noonan leaving on their round-the-world flight. Much of the aerial footage was done in South Africa as well using an Aerospatiale AS.350B Ecureuil (reg. ZS-RSS / msn 2373) camera helicopter filming Lockheed Electra F-AZLL over a variety of landscapes.

GPS Locations

Dunnville Airport, Ontario, Canada: N42 52.50 / W079 35.50

Rand Airport, Johannesburg, South Africa: S26 14.40 / E028 09.05

Factual Background: Amelia Earhart

Amelia Mary Earhart (July 24, 1897–July 2, 1937) was a famous American aviator who pioneered many aviation frontiers and records for women. She was also a strong voice in promoting women's careers and rights through her love of aviation. Earhart started flying lessons in January 1921 and became the 16th woman to obtain a private pilot's license. Earhart continued to gain experience in flying, breaking several women's records along the way. On June 17–18, 1928, Earhart became the first woman to fly the Atlantic Ocean west to east, completing the crossing in 20 hours, 40 minutes in a Fokker F.7. Gaining fame and notoriety, she began a lecture tour and wrote books promoting aviation and its future. On May 20–21, 1932, Earhart became the first woman to fly solo the Atlantic Ocean in a single-engined Lock-heed Vega 5B, completing the flight in 14 hours, 56 minutes, for which she was awarded the Distinguished Flying Cross. On August 24–25, 1932, she became the first woman to fly solo nonstop from coast to coast in the United States in 19 hours, 5 minutes. By mid–1936, Earhart, now very much a celebrity, began planning a round-the-world trip. Using a modified Lockheed Electra 10-E (reg. NR16020 / msn 1055), with extra fuel tanks, Amelia Earhart and navigator Fred Noonan departed Miami on June 1, 1937. Flying via South America, Africa, India and Southeast Asia, they arrived in New Guinea on June 29, 1937. The next stage of the journey required careful navigation, as it involved a fuel stop on the tiny Howland Island in a very large Pacific Ocean. Earhart departed New Guinea on July 2, 1937, but for reasons never determined, the Electra's interception of Howland failed. With fuel low, Earhart and Noonan were unable to even establish strong radio contact with the USCG ship *Itasca* on station to assist. Radio contact was eventually lost and nothing more was ever heard from the Electra again. Earhart's disappearance has become one of the great aviation mysteries, sparking theories, speculation and debate that continue to this day.

Previous screen appearances of Earhart have been the fictionalized 1943 RKO film *Flight for Freedom*, starring Rosalind Russel; the 1976 NBC TV movie *Amelia Earhart*, starring Susan Clark; and the 1994 TNT TV movie *Amelia Earhart: The Final Flight*, starring Diane Keaton.

Angels One Five

UK / Associated British-Picture Corp. / 1952 / B&W / 93 minutes

Director: George More O'Ferrall

Cast: Jack Hawkins, Michael Denison, Dulcie Gray, John Gregson, Cyril Raymond, Veronica Hurst

Synopsis / Aviation Content: The story begins in June 1940 and follows the challenges bestowed on a front-line fighter squadron throughout the Battle of Britain. The first postwar film to be made on this historic battle, it was based on the 1943 book *What Are Your Angels Now?* by British author Arthur John Clinton Pelham Groom, a former RAF sector controller during the Battle of Britain. There's a relatively decent amount of Hawker Hurricane content in ground shots, taxiing, takeoffs and formation flying, but disappointingly, no staged combat was filmed with the available aircraft; this was done with special effects, and fairly crude ones at that. The title was originally *Hawks in the Sun*, which was changed to *Angels Fifteen* before finally settling on *Angels One Five*—this term is derived from radio slang meaning "altitude 15,000 feet."

Type	msn	Military s/n
Hawker Hurricane Mk. I	unknown	L1591
Hawker Hurricane Mk. I	W/05422	L1592
Hawker Hurricane Mk. I	unknown	P2617
Hawker Hurricane Mk. IIc	14533	PZ865
Hawker Hurricane Mk. IIc	41H/469290	LF363
Hawker Hurricane Mk. IIc	unknown	(Portugal) 544
Hawker Hurricane Mk. IIc	unknown	(Portugal) 554
Hawker Hurricane Mk. IIc	unknown	(Portugal) 600
Hawker Hurricane Mk. IIc	unknown	(Portugal) 601
Hawker Hurricane Mk. IIc	unknown	(Portugal) 624

A total of ten Hawker Hurricane fighters were acquired for filming, with up to six of them being seen flying together at some points in the film. The three Hurricane Mk. I types (L1591, L1592, P2617) were owned by the RAF and taken out of storage for filming, but were only used for static or taxiing scenes. Hurricane Mk. IIc (LF363) was also owned by the RAF, but in a ready flying condition. Mk. IIc (PZ865) was owned by Hawker Siddeley Aircraft Ltd. and in flying condition with civil reg. G-AMAU. Five Hurricane Mk. IIc types were provided by the Portuguese Air Force (PAF), who flew them up to England from their base at Espinho, fitted with long-range fuel tanks; the trip took three days, from July 13 to July 16, 1951. Aircraft operations were filmed at RAF Kenley from July 20 to 27, 1951. Film markings were: US-B / P2617; US-D / L1592; US-H / L1581; US-N / L1591; US-P; US-R; US-V / T7012 and US-X. Some aircraft are also seen marked as: AV-P / N6547 and AV-X / K1694 in several scenes. Portugal operated the Hurricane fighter from 1943 to 1954, and still had sixty in service at the time of filming. L1591 was also used for cockpit scenes at Elstree Studios, but some sources note s/n Z3687 was possibly used, at the time taken from storage with the RAF.

Also employed in the film was a **Messerschmitt**

Bf 110G-4 with German Wnr.180850—this s/n is seen on the tail fin in the sequence where one of the characters claims it as a trophy. The aircraft was acquired out of Germany by an RAF maintenance unit after World War II. The remains were scrapped after filming finished in 1952. Background aircraft were an **Avro Anson Mk. XII** (from Portugal with s/n 215), two silver RAF **North American Harvard** trainers, and two **Supermarine Spitfire** (s/n K9942, P9444) fighters. Some stock footage of Hurricanes and Spitfires was used, with most of the brief combat sequences accomplished via some fairly basic special effects and miniatures of the German Junkers Ju 88 and Messerschmitt Bf 109.

Mainly filmed at RAF Kenley in Surrey, England (closed 1959: N51 18.20 / W000 05.60), which doubles in the film as fictional RAF Neethley, during the months of July and August 1951. Also used was the wartime operations room at RAF Uxbridge, at the time still a classified "Top Secret" installation. Director O'Ferrall was in the Royal Artillery at Fighter Command HQ during the Battle of Britain, and author Pelham Groom was hired as the film's technical advisor.

Apocalypse Now (Non–Aviation Themed Title)

USA / United Artists / 1979 / Color / 153 minutes
Director: Francis Ford Coppola
Cast: Marlon Brando, Martin Sheen, Robert Duvall, Frederic Forrest, Sam Bottoms, Laurence Fishburne, Albert Hall, Dennis Hopper, Harrison Ford
Synopsis / Aviation Content: Epic Vietnam story about a U.S. Army captain who journeys upriver to assassinate a renegade colonel. Loosely developed from the 1902 novella *Heart of Darkness* by Polish-English writer Joseph Conrad. The ultimate movie for army helicopter fans—the village attack sequence featuring Wagner's *Ride of the Valkyries* as the music score has become not only a classic cinematic scene, but is now synonymous with the UH-1 Huey helicopter.

Director Coppola acquired the following aircraft from Philippines President Ferdinand Marcos: eight-plus **Bell UH-1H Iroquois**, six-plus **Hughes OH-6A Cayuse**, two **Bell OH-58A Kiowa**, one **Cessna O-2A Skymaster**, and five **Northrop F-5 Tiger** (four F-5E and one F-5F—s/n FA-380) fighters. The Hueys and Cayuse choppers were flown by their Philippine Air Force crews and were frequently called off during filming to fight rebels in Northern Luzon, causing nightmarish logistical problems for the filmmakers. Furthermore, different helicopters (and crews) were arriving at the filming location on different days, depending on what other duties the air force had planned. This held up filming again as the new crews had to be instructed on what was required based on the previous day's filming. All helicopters had their Philippine markings removed, making identification of any one machine impossible. One UH-1H Huey wreck was acquired for a crashed chopper burning in a tree. A massive Boeing B-52 tail section mock-up was built for one dramatic shot. The village attack sequence was filmed at Baler on the northeastern coast of Luzon, Philippines; the general GPS location is: N15 45.60 / E121 34.20.

Apollo 13 (Non–Aviation Themed Title)

USA / Universal Pictures / 1995 / Color / 134 minutes

Director: Ron Howard

Cast: Tom Hanks, Bill Paxton, Kevin Bacon, Gary Sinise, Ed Harris, Kathleen Quinlan

Synopsis / Aviation Content: Drama following the true-life incident of the Apollo 13 moon mission. Zero-gravity scenes were shot onboard a NASA Boeing KC-135A-BN Stratotanker, N931NA (USAF s/n 63-7998, msn 18615), which had a scale Apollo spacecraft set built inside the fuselage. Other aircraft include the **Bell UH-1H Iroquois**, **Northrop T-38A(N) Talon** (NASA s/n 920), and two **Sikorsky SH-3 Sea King** helicopters.

Appointment in London

U.S. Title: **Raiders in the Sky**

UK / British Lion Film Corp. / 1953 / B&W / 96 minutes

Director: Philip Leacock

Cast: Dirk Bogarde, Ian Hunter, Dinah Sheridan, William Sylvester, Walter Fitzgerald, Bryan Forbes, Bill Kerr, Charles Victor

Synopsis / Aviation Content: Set in 1943, the story follows an obsessed Lancaster wing commander, played by Bogarde, in his efforts to obtain his 90th mission. The screenplay was co-written by John Wooldridge, who had a friendship with Guy Gibson of Dam Busters fame, a lot of whose personality was put into the main character in the film. Although not attaining the same heights of fame as *The Dam Busters* (1955), this film still has a strong period flavor about it and plenty of the Avro Lancaster, which after all is what we really want to see!

Type	Military s/n	Film Markings
Avro Lancaster B.Mk. I	TW862	IH-S
Avro Lancaster B.Mk. I	TW883	—
Avro Lancaster B.Mk. VII	NX673	IH-B
Avro Lancaster B.Mk. VII	NX679	IH-C
Avro Lancaster B.Mk. VII	NX782	IH-V
DeHavilland DH-82A Tiger Moth	T7187	T7187

Four flyable Lancasters (TW862, NX673, NX679, NX782) were used for filming at RAF Upwood, Cambridgeshire, from June to July 1952. The RAF also provided all aircraft servicing and aircrews for the bombers. All three Lancaster Mk. VII aircraft were later used in *The Dam Busters* (1955). Lancaster Mk. I (s/n TW883) was a non-flyer used for background in airfield scenes. Several Avro Lincoln Mk. II bombers were used as Lancaster "stand-ins," parked far from the camera or in the background during aerial filming. Several shots clearly show filming onboard one of the Lancasters, the unique shots giving some rarely seen views from the cockpit. Four pilots were assigned to the Lancasters from the RAF: Sqn/Ldr D. "Lofty" Hayes (NX782), Flt/Lt George Fletcher (NX679), Fg/Off Reg Wareham (TW862) and Sqn/Ldr Peter Landon (NX673). The Tiger Moth (RAF s/n T7187 / msn 83653) seen in the film was built in 1940 by Morris Motors in England before going to the civilian market as G-AOBX in 1955. Several library file shots are featured of the Focke-Wulf Fw 190, Messerschmitt Bf 109 and German defenses. Interiors for dramatic scenes were filmed at British Lion Studios, Shepperton, Surrey, in August 1952.

GPS LOCATION

RAF Upwood, Cambridgeshire, England (closed 1994): N52 26.20 / W000 07.80

The A-Team (Non–Aviation Themed Title)

USA / 20th Century–Fox / 2010 / Color / 117 minutes

Director: Joe Carnahan

Cast: Liam Neeson, Bradley Cooper, Jessica Biel, Quinton "Rampage" Jackson, Sharlto Copley, Patrick Wilson, Gerald McRaney, Henry Czerny

Synopsis / Aviation Content: High-action, big-screen adaptation of the hugely successful 1980s TV series of the same name, following the exploits of four Special Forces soldiers who become fugitives. Contains the usual high use of helicopters and other aircraft in the action sequences. Real aircraft consist of an **Aerospatiale AS.355 Ecureuil** doubling as a Mexican gunship; a **Bell UH-1H Iroquois** as a Mexican "Ambulancia" helicopter marked as "XA638"; a **Bell 206L Long Ranger** as an army helicopter; a line-up of **Boeing F/A-18 Hornet** fighters that lose their canopies(!); a **Eurocopter EC.130** marked as "D-VKF7"; and a rare **Martin JRM-1 Mars** (reg. C-FLYL / BuNo. 76823 / msn 9267) four-engined seaplane. Nonexistent CGI-created aircraft include a Lockheed-Boeing F-22A Raptor; a Bell-Boeing V-22 Osprey; an amazing Lockheed C-130H Hercules, modeled off a real USMC KC-130T-30, BuNo. 164597; a pair of General Dynamics MQ-9 Reaper UAV drones; an MD-500 helicopter; and a Lockheed AC-130U Spooky II gunship. Filmed from September to December 2009, mostly in Canada.

The Aviator

USA / Warner Bros. / 1929 / B&W / 75 minutes

Director: Roy Del Ruth

Cast: Edward Everett Horton, Patsy Ruth Miller, Johnny Arthur, Lee Moran, Edward Martindel

Synopsis / Aviation Content: Horton plays an apparent flying expert who, once airborne, creates comical mayhem. Excellent aerial stunt work which tragically cost the life of William Hauber, a stunt double whose plane crashed during filming on July 17, 1929. No prints of this film are known to exist today.

The Aviator

USA / Metro-Goldwyn-Mayor & United Artists / 1985 / Color / 97 minutes

Director: George Miller

Cast: Christopher Reeve, Rosanna Arquette, Jack Warden, Sam Wanamaker, Scott Wilson, Tyne Daly

Synopsis / Aviation Content: In 1928, an air-mail pilot reluctantly agrees to fly the daughter of a wealthy businessman, who's also the financial backer of the air-mail company, cross country, but they crash en route in the Nevada Mountains. A hearty, honest movie with good actors and fantastic aerial camera work set against some dramatic backdrops. Based on the 1981 novel by aviation pioneer and writer Ernest K. Gann. One of the best films for Boeing-Stearman action!

Type	msn	Military s/n	Civil reg.
Boeing-Stearman PT-13D-BW Kaydet	75-5659	42-17496	G-BAVN
Boeing-Stearman PT-17-BW Kaydet	75-3047	41-25540	YU-BAI
Boeing-Stearman PT-17-BW Kaydet	75-4775	42-16612	G-AROY
Boeing-Stearman N2S-3 Kaydet	75-7394	BuNo.07790	G-ROAN
Curtiss-Wright 12Q Travelair	2026	—	G-AAOK

While the U.S. air-mail service never flew the Boeing-Stearman, and the first didn't fly till 1934, they were the only practical choice at the time for the filmmakers. The film was actually shot in northwestern Yugoslavia with two Stearman biplanes (G-AROY, G-ROAN), flown out from England by Professional Aviation Services. Unfortunately G-ROAN was damaged the day before filming began in a freak windstorm while parked at Krk Airfield. It was replaced by another Stearman, G-BAVN, trucked out from England. Later a third Stearman, YU-BAI, was added to the filming schedule, acquired from the Belgrade Air Museum.

The crashed Stearman in the film was a wooden mock-up built by the filmmakers. Two **DeHavilland DH.82 Tiger Moth** biplanes were brought in from India for set dressing but were not airworthy during filming. A Curtiss-Wright Travelair, G-AAOK, was provided but doesn't seem to appear in the finished film.

The airstrip used in the movie is Grobnik Airfield (GPS coordinates N45 22.70 / E014 30.60), located a few miles northeast of the town of Rijeka, Yugoslavia (now Croatia). It was an existing air-club strip but had a grass runway added for the film, which strangely ran straight towards the main hangar and a hill beyond! Camera-planes were a Cessna and one helicopter. Actor Christopher Reeve, who held a pilot's license and could fly a Stearman, did an actual takeoff on camera as part of the film.

The Aviator

USA / Warner Bros. / 2004 / Color / 163 minutes
Director: Martin Scorsese
Cast: Leonardo DiCaprio, Cate Blanchett, Kate Beckinsale, John C. Reilly, Alec Baldwin, Alan Alda
Synopsis / Aviation Content: Epic story of the life and times of billionaire businessman, filmmaker and pioneer aviator Howard Hughes from the late 1920s to the flight of the H-4 Hercules in 1947. Although sparse on actual flying aircraft, this portrayal of Hughes's eccentric and tragic life is fascinating from start to finish. Aviation highlights are, of course, the test-flight sequences featuring the Hughes H-1 Racer, the twin-boom XF-11, and the giant "Spruce Goose."

The Lockheed Super Connie was hired from Save A Connie, Inc., and was already painted in a TWA livery. It was CGI-replicated on-screen to make it appear as though there are many parked in the same area. The Sikorsky S-38B was the twin-engined floatplane Hughes picks up Audrey Hepburn (Blanchett) in. It was provided by Unlimited Adventure LLC. Other "real aircraft" included replicas of a **Boeing Model 100**, three **Royal Aircraft factory S.E.5a** (one was N125QB) and six **Fokker D.VII** (one was N1918P) biplane fighters for the *Hell's Angels* sequences. The Boe-

ing biplane is the one Hughes rips the top wing off to create a monoplane.

Since many of the aircraft depicted in the film were not available or simply nonexistent, full-scale replicas, mock-ups and CGI were used to recreate the many and varied aircraft. The main method, however, was the use of large-scale flying models, which were designed and built by Aero Telemetry Corp. of California. They completed models of the Hughes H-1 Racer (18 ft. wingspan / 450 lbs.), the Hughes XF-11 (30 ft. wingspan / 750 lbs.) and the Hughes H-4 Hercules (25 ft. wingspan / 375 lbs.). They also built a scale model of the Sikorsky S-38B floatplane, plus various scale biplanes for the *Hell's Angels* sequences. This sequence also included CGI of a giant Sikorsky S-29 doubling as a German Gotha bomber.

Mock-ups of a Sikorsky S-38 and H-4 Hercules were built for cabin interior filming. Camera-planes were a Beech Model 18 and a B-25J (reg. N8195H), used to capture background imagery for special effects and studio filming. Stock footage was used from Hughes's film *Hell's Angels* (1930), plus newsreel footage of the 1938 Hughes round-the-world trip in the Lockheed Super Electra. Spruce Goose newsreel footage was also used. Principal photography took place in and around Los Angeles from July 7 to November 14, 2003.

Previous on-screen depictions of Howard Hughes have been played by Tommy Lee Jones in the exceptional TV movie *The Amazing Howard Hughes* (1976), Jason Robards in *Melvin and Howard* (1980), Dean Stockwell in *Tucker ... The Man and His Dream* (1988) and Terry O'Quinn in *The Rocketeer* (1991).

FACTUAL BACKGROUND:
HOWARD HUGHES AIRCRAFT

Howard Robard Hughes, Jr. (December 24, 1905–April 5, 1976) owned a large number of aircraft throughout his life and set many aviation records. He became the owner of Trans World Airlines (TWA) in 1939 and his aviation businesses have contributed greatly to the aerospace industry. The Hughes 300 and 500 family of helicopters and the AH-64 Apache attack helicopter are a three of his products. The table below is a list of the most significant aircraft that were in Hughes's collection:

Type	msn	Civil reg.
Fokker D.VII (replica)	6880	N1918P
Lockheed L-1049H Super Constellation	1049H-4830	N6937C
Royal Aircraft Factory S.E.5a (replica)	DE3540	N125QB
Sikorsky S-38	BB414-20	N28V

Type	s/n / rego.	First Flight	Notes
Hughes H-1B Racer	NR258Y	09/13/1935	Set landplane speed record: 567.12 km/hr.
Hughes XF-11-HU	44-70155	07/07/1946	Crashed in Beverly Hills on maiden flight.
Hughes XF-11-HU	44-70156	04/15/1947	Declared obsolete, production canceled.
Hughes H-4 Hercules	NX37602	11/02/1947	Holds record for largest wingspan: 97.51m.
Northrop 2G Gamma	NX13761	1935	Set U.S. transcontinental record: 9.26 hrs. 01/14/1936.
Douglas DC-1	X223Y	07/01/1933	Purchased 1936 for world record attempt, canceled.
Lockheed L-14 Super Electra	NX18973	1938	Set round-the-world record: 71.11 hrs. 07/14/1938.
Boeing SB-307B Stratoliner	NC19904	1938	Purchased for world record attempt, canceled.

Back from Eternity

USA / RKO Radio Pictures / 1956 / B&W / 97 minutes

Director: John Farrow

Cast: Robert Ryan, Anita Ekberg, Rod Steiger, Phyllis Kirk, Keith Andes, Gene Barry, Fred Clark, Beulah Bondi, Cameron Prud'Homme, Jesse White, Adele Mara, Jon Provost

Synopsis / Aviation Content: A direct remake of John Farrow's earlier *Five Came Back* (1939), about a plane crash in a South American jungle infested with headhunting natives. Not as engrossing as the original but still a fascinating scenario. The aircraft on this production was a **Douglas R2D-1** (BuNo. 9993 / msn 1404)— the Model DC-2-142 version built for the U.S. Marine Corps in 1935. Declared surplus in 1944, it entered civilian service with reg. NC39165. It was hired to provide the flying scenes in the film. The post-crash airframe appears to be an unidentified **Douglas DC-3** fuselage, judging by the tail fillet shape.

Bailout at 43,000

UK Title: *Bail Out at 43,000*

USA / United Artists / 1957 / B&W / 78 minutes

Director: Francis D. Lyon

Cast: John Payne, Karen Steele, Paul Kelly, Richard Eyer, Constance Ford, Eddie Firestone

Synopsis / Aviation Content: Test pilot story following the trials and challenges of developing a safe ejection seat system for the **Boeing B-47 Stratojet**. Partly filmed in Imperial County, California.

Battle Hymn

USA / Universal-International / 1957 / Color / 108 minutes

Director: Douglas Sirk

Cast: Rock Hudson, Anna Kashfi, Dan Duryea, Don Fefore, Martha Hyer, Jock Mahoney

Synopsis / Aviation Content: Dramatized version of the true-life events surrounding USAF pilot Dean Hess and his humanitarian efforts to rescue orphaned children in Korea. Based on Hess's 1956 autobiography of the same name. The usual fictionalized "Hollywood" aspects of the script and associated dramatic scenes luckily don't weigh too much on the importance of the real story to be told here. Solid action sequences featuring the F-51D Mustang with the rarely seen C-119 Flying Boxcar making an exciting screen entrance in the latter part of the film.

Fourteen **North American F-51D Mustang** fighters were provided from the 182nd Fighter Squadron of the 149th Fighter Group, Texas ANG, based at Kelly AFB. This fighter group, along with the 167th Fighter Group of the West Virginia ANG, were the very last to fly the F-51 Mustang, with final retirement of the type due by the end of 1956. One F-51D was smashed into a truck and crates for the cameras; the stunt was performed by pilot Ken Slater, who was awarded the aircraft, relatively undamaged, as payment for the stunt. Identified airframes used in the film are Hess's "No. 18," which was an F-51D-30-NA (s/n 44-74960 / msn 122-41500) and an F-51D-25-NA (s/n 44-72739 / msn 122-39198), which was purchased for studio-based filming. It was later acquired by a collector and restored with civil reg. N44727.

Two unidentified AF Reserve **North American T-28A Trojan** aircraft doubled as North Korean "Yak" fighters. One U.S. Army **Cessna L-19A Bird Dog** (s/n 53-7994) and five **Fairchild C-119G Flying Boxcar** transports also make a brief appearance—one of these was a rare Kaiser-built C-119G-50-FA (s/n 53-8093 / msn 196).

Camera-planes were a Douglas A-26 Invader for forward-facing filming, and the Thunderbirds Aerobatic Team's Fairchild C-119 Flying Boxcar for rear-facing filming with the clamshell doors removed. Some battle scenes featured the use of models and miniatures.

Rock Hudson had served in World War II as a naval aircraft ground crewman. He was very impressed with the F-51D Mustang, even more so after Dean Hess took him for a joyride between takes at the Nogales filming location. Twenty-five young South Korean orphans were flown to Arizona especially to take part in the film's final evacuation scene.

Filming began in early March 1956 at Nogales Airport, Arizona, which doubled for K-2 Airfield at Taegu, South Korea. A dirt strip was constructed for the film next to the main runway along with a control tower and buildings. The main airport and runway of Nogales doubled for Kimpo Air Base, South Korea, where the children were evacuated. The sequence with the C-119s was filmed on the main runway in early April 1956. Nearby U.S. Army Fort Huachuca provided the tanks and vehicles for the communist army scenes. Pickup shots and aerial battle scenes with four F-51Ds and two T-28A "Yaks" were filmed at Fort Hood, Texas, in late July 1956.

GPS LOCATIONS

Nogales Airport, Arizona: N31 25.10 / W110 50.90

Fort Hood, Texas: N31 08.20 / W097 43.00

FACTUAL BACKGROUND: KIDDY CAR AIRLIFT

An ordained church minister in Cleveland, Ohio, Dean Hess served in the European Theater during World War II, flying sixty-three combat missions in the Republic P-47 Thunderbolt. Recalled to duty in 1948, he later entered the Korean War in 1950 as a major training a squadron of South Korean pilots on F-51D Mustangs. Hess soon began caring for large numbers of orphaned children who were living around the airfield, and on December 20, 1950, he was a major player in what became known as the "Kiddy Car Airlift." Along with Air Force Chaplin Russell C. Blaisdell and Staff Sergeant Merle Y. Strang, Hess organ-

ized the evacuation of 950 orphans and eighty staff members using fifteen Douglas C-54 Skymasters (five C-119s in the film), before they were overrun by the North Koreans. Lt Colonel Hess, by mid–1951, had flown 250 combat missions before returning to the United Sates. His fighter was an F-51D-30-NA Mustang (s/n 44-74692 / msn 122-41232). Assigned as the film's technical advisor, Dean Hess himself flew Mustang "No. 18" for the movie. The golden football helmet worn by Hudson in the film was the actual one worn by Hess in Korea and is now on display at the USAF Museum in Dayton, Ohio. Hess retired from the USAF in 1969, and he passed away on March 2, 2015.

*Bat*21*

USA / TriStar Pictures & Vision P.D.G. / 1988 / Color / 101 minutes

Director: Peter Markle

Cast: Gene Hackman, Danny Glover, Jerry Reed, David Marshall Grant, Clayton Rohner, Erich Anderson, Joe Dorsey

Synopsis / Aviation Content: A high-ranking officer is shot down over North Vietnam in 1972, with the ensuing rescue becoming a race against time due to the scheduled carpet bombing of the area. Based on the true story published in the 1980 book of the same name by American writer William Charles Anderson, who also co-wrote the screenplay. Superb flying and views of Vietnam-era aircraft make for exciting viewing. Highlights include the rarely seen Malaysian version of the Sea King helicopter.

Filmed in Sabah, Eastern Malaysia, with generous assistance from the Royal Malaysian Air Force and Army. The RMAF provided two **Northrop F-5E Freedom Fighter** aircraft (one was RMAF s/n M29-04 / msn R-1118) and two **Sikorsky S-61A-4 "Nuri"** helicopters (RMAF s/n M23-09, M23-29), which doubled as the USAF HH-3 Jolly Green Giant rescue chopper. The name "Nuri" is Malaysian for "Parrot." A civil **Bell Model 212** was acquired to fly as a military UH-1N Iroquois, and similarly, a **Cessna Model 337** flew as a military O-2A Skymaster spotter plane.

The RMAF operated 42 Sikorsky S-61A-4 Nuri helicopters from 1967. Seen here is s/n M23–09, which was one of two that doubled as USAF Jolly Green Giant rescue choppers for the Vietnam film *Bat*21* (1988). Photograph: M. Radzi Desa.

An interior mock-up and model of a Douglas EB-66C Destroyer was built for the crash scene. Stock footage of the North American F-100 Super Sabre was used in the final air assault. A Bell 206B Jet Ranger was used as a camera helicopter—the shadow of which can be seen in several shots!

FACTUAL BACKGROUND: DOUGLAS EB-66C "BAT-21"

"Bat-21" was a radio call-sign given to a Douglas EB-66C Destroyer (s/n 54-466 / msn 44766) that was escorting a B-52 air strike into North Vietnam on April 2, 1972, when it was downed by a SAM missile. High-ranking navigator Lt Colonel Iceal Eugene Hambleton was the only one of the six crew to eject from the doomed aircraft. Due to his high rank, a full-scale rescue mission was put into action, which saw him finally rescued twelve days later, but not without great cost to U.S. forces. During the lengthy rescue mission a UH-1 Huey, A-1 Skyraider, HH-53 Jolly Green Giant and two OV-10 Broncos were lost, along with most of the crews. Nine other aircraft were so badly damaged by enemy action, most never flew again. While on the ground during his twelve days, Hambleton evaded capture and radioed in enemy positions and targets for air strikes, a feat that earned him several military medals and honors. Hambleton (November 16, 1918–September 19, 2004) had previously served in World War II, then in the Korean War as a B-29 navigator, and had worked on several ballistic missile projects in the 1960s.

Battle of Britain

UK / United Artists / 1969 / Color / 126 minutes

Director: Guy Hamilton

Cast: Harry Andrews, Michael Caine, Trevor Howard, Curt Jurgens, Ian McShane, Kenneth More, Laurence Olivier, Nigel Patrick, Christopher Plummer, Michael Redgrave, Ralph Richardson, Robert Shaw, Patrick Wymark, Susannah York

Synopsis / Aviation Content: Spectacular recreation of the historical 1940 aerial battle between the British RAF and German *Luftwaffe*—the results of which altered the course of World War II and history itself. The screenplay was based on the 1961 book *The Narrow Margin* by Derek Wood and Derek Dempster. The quintessential British aviation film and certainly one of the best aviation films ever made, with over ninety aircraft filling the screen from start to finish. Neither before nor since have so many aircraft acquisitions, along with the necessary aeronautical maintenance and logistical planning, been executed by a film production company. The character stories are kept to a minimum, so the narrative focus is on the development of the battle itself, with plenty of action, history and Merlin engine sound— nowadays a true cult classic amongst the Warbird fraternity!

Thirty-two CASA 2.111 flyable bombers were actually used in the film, with two of them (noted in table) and seventeen Hispano Buchons later brought to the UK and registered in May 1968 for the aerial scenes to be shot over England. Static Buchon (s/n C.4K-111) was also sent to the UK for Pinewood Studios cockpit close-ups, as was a static CASA 2.111B bomber (s/n B.2I-20). Two unidentified **CASA 352L** transports were provided in Spain as Junkers Ju 52 transports, one flying in the opening titles.

The CASA 2.111 doubled for the *Luftwaffe* **Heinkel He 111H / P**. The CASA 2.111 was license-built in Spain from 1940 to 1956, with a total of 236 delivered (130 during World War II); the 2.111B and D variants were built after the war with Rolls Royce Merlin engines. The CASA 352L doubled for the *Luftwaffe* **Junkers Ju 52**. A total of 170 were built in Spain from 1945 to 1952, the "L" variant (sixty-four built) being delivered with Spanish-built engines. The Hispano HA-1112 doubled for the *Luftwaffe* **Messerschmitt Bf 109E**. The Buchon fighter was license-built by Spain from 1951 to 1958 and based on the Bf 109G with the HA-1112-M1L being the final version powered by a Rolls Royce Merlin engine.

Flyable Hispano HA-1112 (Spanish s/n C.4K-159) was the eighteenth Buchon acquired by Spitfire Productions Ltd., but was tragically destroyed when it crashed at Tablada on January 20, 1968, killing pilot Don Federico Iglesias Lanzos. Out of respect, a moment of silence was observed by the film crew

Type	msn	Military s/n	Civil reg.
Flying Aircraft			
CASA 2.111B	025	B.2I-77	G-AWHA
CASA 2.111B	167	B.2I-37	G-AWHB
CCF Hurricane Mk. XII	42012	(RCAF) 5377	G-AWLW
Hawker Hurricane Mk. IIc	41H/469290	LF363	—
Hawker Hurricane Mk. IIc	14533	PZ865	G-AMAU
Hispano HA-1112-M1L Buchon	067	C.4K-31	G-AWHE
Hispano HA-1112-M1L Buchon	129	C.4K-61	G-AWHF
Hispano HA-1112-M1L Buchon	139	C.4K-75	G-AWHG
Hispano HA-1112-M1L Buchon	145	C.4K-105	G-AWHH
Hispano HA-1112-M1L Buchon	166	C.4K-106	G-AWHI
Hispano HA-1112-M1L Buchon	171	C.4K-100	G-AWHJ
Hispano HA-1112-M1L Buchon	186	C.4K-122	G-AWHL
Hispano HA-1112-M1L Buchon	187	C.4K-99	G-AWHM
Hispano HA-1112-M1L Buchon	190	C.4K-126	G-AWHD
Hispano HA-1112-M1L Buchon	193	C.4K-130	G-AWHN
Hispano HA-1112-M1L Buchon	199	C.4K-127	G-AWHO
Hispano HA-1112-M1L Buchon	208	C.4K-144	G-AWHP
Hispano HA-1112-M1L Buchon	220	C.4K-152	G-AWHR
Hispano HA-1112-M1L Buchon	223	C.4K-102	G-AWHK
Hispano HA-1112-M1L Buchon	225	C.4K-159	—
Hispano HA-1112-M1L Buchon	228	C.4K-170	G-AWHS
Hispano HA-1112-M1L Buchon	234	C.4K-169	G-AWHT
Hispano HA-1112-M4L Buchon	40/2	C.4K-112	G-AWHC
Supermarine Spitfire Mk. Ib	WASP.20/2	AR213	G-AIST
Supermarine Spitfire Mk. IIa	CBAF.14	P7350	G-AWIJ
Supermarine Spitfire LF.Mk. Vb	CBAF.1061	AB910	G-AISU
Supermarine Spitfire LF.Mk. Vc	WASP.20/223	AR501	G-AWII
Supermarine Spitfire HF.Mk. IXe	CBAF.IX4494	TE308	G-AWGB
Supermarine Spitfire LF.Mk. IX	CBAF.IX7263	MJ772	G-AVAV
Supermarine Spitfire LF.Mk. IXb	CBAF.IX533	MH415	G-AVDJ
Supermarine Spitfire LF.Mk. IXb	CBAF.IX552	MH434	G-ASJV
Supermarine Spitfire LF.Mk. IXc	CBAF.IX1514	MK297	G-ASSD
Supermarine Spitfire F.Mk. XIVc	6S.432263	RM689	G-ALGT
Supermarine Spitfire PR.Mk. XIX	6S.594677	PS853	—
Supermarine Spitfire PR.Mk. XIX	6S.683528	PM631	—
Taxi Aircraft			
CCF Sea Hurricane Mk. Ib	CCF/41H.4013	Z7015	—
Hawker Hurricane Mk. I	unknown	P2617	—
Hispano HA-1112-M1L Buchon	170	C.4K-107	—
Hispano HA-1112-M1L Buchon	178	C.4K-121	—
Hispano HA-1112-M1L Buchon	194	C.4K-134	—
Hispano HA-1112-M1L Buchon	195	C.4K-135	—
Hispano HA-1112-M1L Buchon	201	C.4K-131	—
Hispano HA-1112-M1L Buchon	235	C.4K-172	—
Supermarine Spitfire Mk. Vb	CBAF.1646	BL614	—
Supermarine Spitfire LF.Mk. XVIe	CBAF.3495	SM411 *	—
Supermarine Spitfire LF.Mk. XVIe	unknown	TB382 *	—
Supermarine Spitfire LF.Mk. XVIe	CBAF.4497	TE311 *	—
Supermarine Spitfire LF.Mk. XVIe	CBAF.4610	TE476 *	—
Supermarine Spitfire LF.Mk. XVIe	CBAF.11470	TE356 *	—
Supermarine Spitfire LF.Mk. XVIe	CBAF.11485	TE384 *	—
Static Aircraft			
CASA 2.111B	150	B.2I-20	—
Hawker Hurricane Mk. IIc	unknown	LF751	—

(Type)	(msn)	(Military s/n)	(Civil reg.)
Hispano HA-1112-M1L Buchon	unknown	C.4K-30	—
Hispano HA-1112-M1L Buchon	unknown	C.4K-111	—
Hispano HA-1112-M1L Buchon	164	C.4K-114	—
Hispano HA-1112-M1L Buchon	unknown	C.4K-154	—
Supermarine Spitfire LF.Mk. Vb	CBAF.2403	EP120	—
Supermarine Spitfire LF.Mk. Vb	CBAF.2461	BM597	—
Supermarine Spitfire LF.Mk. IXc	CBAF.IX1561	MK356	—
Supermarine Spitfire LF.Mk. XVIe	CBAF.4640	RW382	—
Supermarine Spitfire LF.Mk. XVIe	CBAF.4688	SL574	—
Supermarine Spitfire PR.Mk. XIX	6S.585121	PS915 *	—
Supermarine Spitfire PR.Mk. XIX	6S.687107	PM651 *	—
Supermarine Spitfire F.21	SMAF.4338	LA198 *	—

* *Mark Addie* conversions.

prior to the commencement of principal photography. Another flyable Hispano HA-1112 (reg. G-AWHF) was written off when it ground-looped at Duxford on May 21, 1968. It was never repaired and does not appear in the UK-based flying scenes.

Spitfires MJ772 and TE308 were 2-seater Spitfire Tr.Mk. IX conversions.

Various additional aircraft of the above types were also purchased and used for spares, including seven Spitfires: K9942, NH904, PK724, RM694, TB863 (MGM Studios owned), TE184 and TD248. Seven additional Spitfires appear to have been allocated to the film company but not used: LA226, LA255, MJ627, MT847, PK624, PK664 and RW393.

Spitfire BM597 and Hurricane LF751 were used to make molds at Pinewood Studios for the wooden- or steel-frame / fiberglass mock-ups designated for destruction on the airfields. Some had motorcycle engines so they could be filmed taxiing. The finished Spitfire replicas were nicknamed the Spitfire Mk. 68—presumably for the year in which they were built, 1968. A full-size Heinkel mock-up was also constructed for a crashed scene in which the German crew are being cut out of the wreck by RAF ground staff.

The genesis for the *Battle of Britain* began with Polish-born film producer and former World War II Spitfire pilot S. Benjamin Fisz, whose 1965 inspiration for a motion picture based on the historic battle led him to form Spitfire Productions Ltd. with *James Bond* producer Harry Saltzman in order to get the project "off the ground." The most daunting task was to be the acquisition of

so many period fighters in order to portray a genuine feel of authenticity.

All aircraft were located by retired RAF Group Captain Hamish Mahaddie, an aviation film consultant, who began the search for Battle of Britain–era aircraft as far back as early 1966. All German types were supplied by the Spanish Air Force, leaving only the acquisitions of the Spitfire and Hurricane types for Mahaddie. The six Hurricanes came from Canadian Robert Diemert (RCAF), 5377; BoB Memorial Flight, LF363; Hawker Siddeley Aircraft Ltd., PZ865; Shuttleworth Trust, Z7015; and the RAF, P2617 and LF751. The fourteen taxi / static Spitfires were all on loan from various RAF stations by Britain's Ministry of Defence. The twelve flyable Spitfires came from a variety of sources: three from the BoB Memorial Flight, AB910, PS853, and PM631; one from the RAF, P7350 (an actual Battle of Britain veteran); two from Samuelson Film Services, TE308 and MJ772; and six from various museum or private collections: Allen Wheeler, AR213; Shuttleworth Trust, AR501; Rousseau Aviation, France, MH415; Tim Davies, MH434; G.A. Rich, MK297; and Rolls Royce Ltd., RM689. The final count of more than 115 aircraft, including reserves, spare airframes and camera-planes, made "Saltzman's Air Force" (after Producer Harry Saltzman), the 35th largest air force in the world, and certainly one of the most elaborate ever assembled for a motion picture! It took Spitfire Productions a full two years to acquire all the fighters and bombers, with another year of production on top of that.

Reconstruction of the Spitfires and Hurricanes was carried out at RAF Henlow, Bedfordshire, by RAF tradesmen and fitters. The later model Spitfires had their various bubble canopies, clipped wings, pointed tails, props and cannons modified to appear more as the 1940 fighter marks. Such retrofitted Spitfires (see table for listing) were nicknamed the *Mark Addie*—after Mahaddie himself. The final tally for the Spitfire was twelve flyable, seven taxiing and eight static, with an additional six for spares. The Hurricane saw three fly-able, two taxiing and one static. Servicing during production was provided by Simpson's Aero Services of Elstree with RAF crews doing the everyday aircraft line maintenance. Mahaddie located the Hispano Buchons at Tablada AFB in Spain stored in various states of disrepair. After some negotiation, the Spanish Air Force made eighteen flyable, six taxi-capable and four for static display. Several flyable Buchons were later painted as Hurricanes to help fill out the backgrounds in the Polish flying scenes; such conversions were known as the *Hurrischmitt*. Spanish Air Force mechanics were employed for maintenance of the Buchon and CASA 2.111 aircraft in both Spain and the UK. Spain also lent thirty-two CASA 2.111 bombers and two CASA 352L transports to Spitfire Productions free of charge, provided the film company pay for the painting of the aircraft into German colors.

Three Percival Proctor trainers (G-AIAE, G-AIEY, G-ALOK), were to be converted to Junkers Ju 87 Stuka dive-bombers, with G-AIEY actually flying in this configuration. Safety issues surrounding the dive capabilities of the converted aircraft meant they were never used, and Stuka scale replica models were built and filmed instead.

The Buchon and CASA 2.111 aircraft were flown by Spanish Air Force pilots led by Commandante Pedro Santa Cruz. Sixteen pilots including Cruz were also granted leave from the Spanish Air Force to fly for the production in England. The UK Spitfires and Hurricanes were flown by experienced RAF fighter pilots all qualified to flight instructor standards with the rank of either flight lieutenant or squadron leader. Led by Wing Commander George Elliot, each eager applicant was type-certified in one of the Spitfire Tr. Mk. IX trainers. The winners included R.B. Boyd, R.D. Coles, D.J. Curry, J. Homer, R. Lloyd, M.R. Merrett, D.W. Mills, J.M. Preece, D.J. Spink and M.A. Vickers. In addition, four pilots came from the U.S.–based Confederate Air Force, including Wilson "Connie" Edwards, Lloyd Nolen and "Lefty" Gardner.

The film's technical advisers included actual Battle of Britain Luftwaffe Ace General Adolf Galland, RAF Group Captain Peter Townsend, Wing Commander Robert Stanford Tuck, Squadron Leader "Ginger" Lacey, and Luftwaffe pilot Oberst Hans Brustellin.

A B-25J (s/n 44-31508 / reg. N6578D) camera-plane was brought in from the USA and flown by pilot and owner Jeff Hawke. Hawke owned it from 1967 to 1975, and he'd fitted it out for aerial filming with camera mounts in the gun positions in order to cover every possible angle of sky. It was nicknamed the *Psychedelic Monster* after the striped, bright orange markings it was adorned in so pilots could keep track of its position in the sky. Camera operators included famous aerial photographers "Skeets" Kelly and Johnny Jordan. Sud-Aviation SA.318B Alouette II, G-AWAP, was employed as a camera helicopter. Spitfire Mk. IX, TE308 / G-AWGB, was a 2-seater with a camera in the front seat and Buchon, G-AWHC, a 2-seater variant, employed a camera in the rear seat.

The mass Heinkel bomber scenes were filmed over Spain early on in the production, with the thirty-two CASA 2.111s, seventeen Buchons, and a single Spitfire, MH415, brought over from England. Aerial filming then moved to England from May 1968. The seventeen flyable Hispano Buchons and two Spanish CASA 2.111Bs were flown across the English Channel and certified with British civil registrations. In the UK an official segment of airspace, located in three slots of sky over East Anglia, was granted for exclusive use by Spitfire Productions for the complex aerial scenes. Bad weather hampered filming, which put the production over budget. As a result, many sequences were filmed in the skies over Southern France in August 1968 using the B-25 camera-plane, nine Spitfires and three Buchons. They were based out of France's Frejorgues Airport in Montpellier. In the end it took twenty weeks and 5,000 flying hours to capture the forty minutes of aerial action in the final movie. Mechanical problems with the aircraft and changing filming schedules meant some fighters carried up to a dozen different markings throughout the production, some being changed daily depending on requirements. All of these markings, squadron codes and unit badges, on both sides, were fictional in order to avoid glory or blame being assigned to any one real squadron.

Hamish Mahaddie's superb work on restoring these aircraft for the film is now widely accepted as the origin of the Warbird scene as it is known today in the UK and in much of the rest of the world. Many of the Spitfires, Hurricanes and Bu-chons still survive in the care of museums and private owners, including several of the Pinewood Studios–built mock-ups. Air Chief Marshall Hugh Dowding, commander of RAF Fighter Command during the actual Battle of Britain, was eighty-seven years old at the time the film premiered. He had a cataract operation so he could see the finished film. It is said he cried at the screening and friends say the experience gave him another year of life.

Filming began on March 11, 1968, and concluded in late September 1968. The opening airfield inspection scene was shot at Tablada Air Base in Seville, Spain (with twenty-five CASA 2.111 bombers), as were later German scenes including a Berlin Airport recreation with the two CASA 352L transports. Adjoining El Copero Air Base was used for the Bf 109 scenes. The main English airfield location was at Duxford, Cambridgeshire, England. The massive hangar explosion was filmed at Duxford on June 20–21, 1968, totally destroying Hangar 3. The site is readily accessible to tourists today, being the hub of Warbird activities in the UK. The opening French airfield scene was shot on the southwestern edge of Duxford. Other featured airfields are RAF North Weald, Northolt, and Hawkinge. RAF Debden in Essex was used as the flying unit base, leaving the other locations free for filming ground scenes. Building interiors and aircraft mock-ups for the actors were all filmed at Pinewood Studios.

GPS Locations

Duxford Aerodrome, Cambridgeshire (closed 1961): N52 05.50 / E000 07.80

RAF North Weald, Essex (closed 1979): N51 43.20 / E000 09.10

RAF Northolt, London (active): N51 33.10 / W000 25.10

RAF Hawkinge, Kent (closed 1958): N51 06.45 / E001 09.10

RAF Debden, Essex (closed 1975): N51 59.40 / E000 16.50

Tablada Air Base, Seville, Spain (closed 1990): N37 21.10 / W006 00.50

El Copero Air Base, Seville, Spain (active): N37 18.80 / W006 00.00

Factual Background: The Battle of Britain

The historical Battle of Britain began on July 10, 1940, when German Stuka diver-bombers began attacking British shipping interests. It lasted through a long hot summer, finally culminating on September 15, 1940, with a climatic daylight battle over London that resulted in the loss of sixty Luftwaffe aircraft to twenty-six RAF fighters. This date has since come to be known by Great Britain as Battle of Britain Day. The battle officially ended on October 31, 1940.

Aircrews		Aircraft Losses	
RAF / Allied pilots who took part:	2365	Hawker Hurricane:	601
RAF / Allied pilots killed:	446	Supermarine Spitfire:	357
		Other aircraft:	129
Luftwaffe pilots / crews who took part: unknown			
Luftwaffe pilots / crews killed:	3089	RAF Total:	1087
		Heinkel He 111:	246
		Junkers Ju 87:	74
		Messerschmitt Bf 109:	533
		Other aircraft:	753
		Luftwaffe Total:	1606

Battle of Midway   see   *Midway*

Battle Stations

USA / Columbia Pictures / 1956 / B&W / 81 minutes

Director: Lewis Seiler

Cast: John Lund, William Bendix, Keefe Brasselle, Richard Boone, William Leslie, John Craven

Synopsis / Aviation Content: Relatively entertaining movie about the aircraft carrier USS *Franklin* (CV-13) and her days during World War II. Much stock footage of the *Franklin* with some principal photography shot onboard the USS *Princeton* (CV-37). Aircraft include the **Grumman TBM-3S Avenger** and **Vought F4U Corsair**.

Battle Taxi

USA / United Artists / 1955 / B&W / 82 minutes
Director: Herbert L. Strock
Cast: Sterling Hayden, Arthur Franz, Marshall
    Thompson, Leo Needham, Jay Barney, John
    Dennis, Michael Colgan
Synopsis / Aviation Content: During the Korean
    War, a fighter jock sees his transfer to a rescue
    squadron to help boost a shortage of helicopter
    pilots as a non-glamorous "demotion." The only
    aeronautical highlight in this otherwise low-key
    production involves ample and detailed views
    of the rarely filmed Sikorsky H-19 helicopter.
    A definite viewing for helicopter fans, the film
    also provides a rich assortment of file footage
    of various USAF aircraft in action.

Two **Sikorsky SH-19B-SI Chickasaw** (s/n
52-7520, 52-7526), search and rescue helicopters
were provided to the production by the 42nd Air
Rescue Squadron. One H-19 wreck was used for
a crash scene. Also provided to the film were up
to three **Grumman SA-16A-GR Albatross** amphibians, two ANG **North American F-51D
Mustang** fighters, and up to three **Sikorsky H-
5G-SI Dragonfly** helicopters. There's much use
of stock and newsreel footage, some being very
obviously from World War II, plus some USAF
flight-test film. Aircraft here include the Boeing
B-29 Superfortress, Douglas A-26B Invader,
Lockheed F-80 Shooting Star, North American
P-51B Mustang, North Amer-
ican B-45 Tornado, North American F-86 Sabre and Republic
F-84 Thunderjet. Up to fifty
Sikorsky H-19 helicopters took
part in the impressive closing
scene fly-by.

FACTUAL BACKGROUND:
SIKORSKY H-19

The Sikorsky Model S-55 was the first true
multi-role transport helicopter developed for the
U.S. Army (H-19 Chickasaw), U.S. Navy (HO4S)
and USMC (HRS). The prototype YH-19 first
flew on November 10, 1949, with service entry in
1950 in time for the Korean War. The USAF used
the helicopter in the search and rescue role as the

SH-19. Sikorsky manufactured 1,084 for the U.S.
military with additional deliveries as the commercial Model S-55. France, Japan and Yugoslavia
also built examples under license, and Westland
in England built 436 as the Westland Whirlwind.
Two of these were VIP versions assigned to the
Queen's Flight from 1959. The American-built H-
19 was powered by either a Pratt & Whitney Wasp
R-1340 or Wright Cyclone R-1300 radial engine.

Beautiful Dreamer

USA / Imageworks Entertainment Intl. / 2006 /
    Color / 87 minutes
Director: Terri Farley-Teruel
Cast: Brooke Langton, Colin Egglesfield, James
    Denton, Barry Corbin, Elise Jackson
Synopsis / Aviation Content: A newlywed B-24
    pilot loses his memory and identity in a horrific
    bombing mission into Germany. He returns to
    the U.S. after World War II to a different life in
    a different town, until his wife learns of the sit-
    uation and goes searching for him. Certainly a
    beautiful-looking film, but stodgy and slow in
    its development. Warbird fans will love seeing
    the B-24 *Diamond Lil* performing fly-bys, but
    will be shocked out of their seats when they see
    the multitude of "B-24 substitutes" used for
    various aircraft interior and exterior shots! The
    film is dedicated to a real-life B-24 crew and
    their Liberator named *Starduster* that completed
    over thirty missions into occupied Europe.

Type	msn	Military s/n	Civil reg.
Beechcraft C-45G-BH Expeditor	AF-420	51-11863	N11863
Boeing-Stearman N2S-4 Kaydet	75-3420	BuNo.29989	N450WT
Consolidated Liberator Mk. I	18	(RAF) AM927	N24927
Curtiss C-46F-1-CU Commando	22486	44-78663	N53594
North American B-25J-25-NC Mitchell	108-34076	44-30801	N30801

The Commemorative Air Force's Southern
California Wing were the logistics behind the aerial scenes of the picture, with some scenes filmed
at their base at Camarillo Airport, California. The
main aircraft featured is the CAF's rare Consolidated Liberator Mk. I, N24927. It was originally
one of twenty B-24A (s/n 40-2366), variants before being reassigned as an LB-30B Liberator Mk.
I (RAF s/n AM927) and sent to Europe for ASW
duties. It was damaged in Canada during delivery

and ended up being used by Consolidated during the war with civil reg. NL24927. It then had a career with Continental Can Co. as N1503 in 1948–1959; Petroleos Mexicanos as XC-CAY from 1959 to 1967; Confederate Air Force as N12905 from 1967 to 1990; and the renamed Commemorative Air Force from 1990 as N24927. Originally named *Diamond Lil*, it has, since filming, been rebuilt as a B-24A and renamed as *Ol 927*. A full scale B-24 wooden mock-up was also built for a post-crash sequence.

N24927 was used in the film for ground shots and a series of flyovers, mostly with wheels down. Strangely, all close-up exteriors were filmed with a B-25J Mitchell, N30801, including cockpit and upper turret; fuselage interiors were also done using this aircraft. Even stranger, cockpit interiors were filmed using a Fairchild C-82A Packet, the identity of which is a complete mystery! A C-82A cargo hold was even used in one shot as a B-24 interior—try to figure that out. While ground shots used N24927, a glass-nosed Liberator, all CGI sequences of aerial combat had turret-nosed Liberators, and the CGI Messerschmitt Bf 109 fighters are so inaccurate anyone would mistake them for a fictional aircraft.

An unidentified yellow Boeing-Stearman was used in several flying shots with a "41" on the cowling. Background aircraft were a red Boeing-Stearman, N450WT, in several shots at "Kelly Field"—actually Disney Ranch, California; there's a stray shot of the CAF's Curtiss C-46F, N53594 *China Doll*, and a Beechcraft C-45G, N11863, used as set dressing in a few sequences.

The Beginning or the End

USA / Metro-Goldwyn-Mayer / 1947 / B&W / 112 minutes

Director: Norman Taurog

Cast: Brian Donlevy, Robert Walker, Tom Drake, Beverly Tyler, Audrey Totter, Hume Cronyn

Synopsis / Aviation Content: Excellent, dramatized story concerning the development of the atomic bomb and its use against Japan, which ended World War II. Due to the highly sensitive nature at the time about America's "new weapon," many facts and processes were intentionally inaccurate. Written by former naval aviator turned Hollywood screenwriter Frank "Spig" Wead." Aircraft used were the **Boeing B-29 Superfortress** and **Douglas C-47 Skytrain**. Partly filmed at Los Alamos, New Mexico. MGM's Stage 15 in Culver City, of *Thirty Seconds over Tokyo* (1944) fame, was transformed into an indoor set depicting the Pacific island of Tinian. Hollywood pilot Paul Mantz provided the aerial photography, and one of the film's technical advisors was Lt Col Charles W. Sweeney, who flew the B-29 *Bockscar* in the atomic bomb mission to Nagasaki, Japan.

Behind Enemy Lines

USA / 20th Century–Fox / 2001 / Color / 106 minutes

Director: John Moore

Cast: Owen Wilson, Gene Hackman, Gabriel Macht, Joaquim De Almeida, David Keith, Olek Krupa, Vladimir Mashkov

Synopsis / Aviation Content: An F/A-18 is shot down over Bosnia, forcing airman Wilson to evade ground forces and a nasty sniper, while political pressure prevents naval commander Hackman from mounting a rescue. Well-made action film stays on target throughout and has some fantastic action views of the U.S. Navy's F/A-18F Hornet fighter. A highlight is the missile-evading sequence—great pictures and great sound!

Featured aircraft is the U.S. Navy **Boeing F/A-18F Super Hornet**, one of which was loaned from Navy Squadron VFA-122 Flying Eagles and marked as older squadron "VFA-163 / 106." An F/A-18 cockpit mock-up was also built for actor and instrument close-ups. Filmed onboard the carrier USS *Carl Vinson* (CVN-70), as depicted in the film story, with older **F/A-18C / D Hornet** fighters (some from squadron VFA-137 Kestrels). The two Hornet types can be distinguished quickly: the C/D variant has small oval engine air intakes, but the E/F variant has larger, squared intakes.

Background aircraft include the **Grumman EA-6B Prowler, Grumman F-14A Tomcat, Lockheed S-3B Viking** and **Sikorsky SH-60 Seahawk**. Some filming also took place on the carrier USS *Constellation* (CV-64).

Aerial landscapes for backgrounds and flying were filmed by a Clay Lacy Learjet. The French rescue helicopter is a Russian **Mil Mi-17 Hip** (port rear tail rotor), with rear cargo doors removed. The final scene features three **Bell UH-1N Iroquois** helicopters in the over-water and carrier scenes; however, they suddenly become two civil **Bell Model 205A-1** (as gunships, reg. D-HOOK / msn 30206 as "Marines 103"; and reg. D-HAFL / msn 30056) and one Spanish-hired **Bell Model 412** (Hackman) helicopters, in Marines livery, for the final hilltop statue sequence. This was due to an unavoidable logistical problem brought on by filming between the aircraft carriers in the USA and half a world away in Slovakia, having to do with what helicopters were available. Principal photography took place from October 2000 to January 2001.

The Best Years of Our Lives (Non–Aviation Themed Title)

USA / RKO Radio Pictures / 1946 / B&W / 172 minutes
Director: William Wyler
Cast: Myrna Loy, Fredric March, Dana Andrews, Teresa Wright, Virginia Mayo, Cathy O'Donnell, Hoagy Carmichael, Harold Russell
Synopsis / Aviation Content: Classic masterpiece of three World War II veterans and the problems they face adjusting to civilian life. Developed from the 1945 novel *Glory for Me* by American writer MacKinlay Kantor. Aviation content is minimal, with brief but notable scenes at the start and end of the film. The aircraft graveyards are about the most detailed and memorable ever captured for a motion picture!

The top of the film features a civil **Douglas DC-4-1009** (civil reg. NC10201 / msn 42904), of Western Airlines, this one the first of seventy-nine such aircraft built based on the military C-54G. The main characters journey home on an unidentified **Boeing B-17E Flying Fortress**. This film was the first postwar job for famed Hollywood stunt flier Paul Mantz, who flew his new (at the time) B-25H (reg. N1203) camera-plane for the aerial scenes shown in the veterans' view

from the B-17. The mammoth scrap yard included in this sequence is Searcy Field, Stillwater, Oklahoma. All 475 aircraft in this yard were purchased by Mantz himself in February 1946 for just over $55,000! He acquired eleven aircraft for himself and scrapped the rest in 1947. Mostly seen in the film were the seventy-eight B-17 and 144 B-24 bombers. Mantz later said he made back his $55,000 alone from selling the remaining gasoline in the aircraft's fuel tanks. The B-17 used is often credited as being Mantz's own B-17F (s/n 42-3360 / reg. N67974), but the aircraft has the ribbed nose glass of the earlier B-17E variant.

The final scene of Dana Andrews in the scrap yard was shot at Cal-Aero Field, Ontario, California. Of the 1,340 aircraft stored there, only a few of the **Boeing B-17 Flying Fortress** and **Bell P-39 Airacobra** wrecks were shown. Rows of engines and props from B-17 bombers were also included. Identified B-17 Flying Fortress aircraft include 41-24636, 42-3236, 42-3463, 42-5322, 42-5332, 42-5736, 42-5742, 42-29929 and 42-30890. An earlier scene shows a Curtiss C-46, Douglas C-47, C-54 with several Vultee BT-13 trainers in the background.

Biggles: Adventures in Time

UK-USA / Compact Yellowbill & Tambarle / 1986 / Color / 92 minutes
Director: John Hough
Cast: Neil Dickson, Alex Hyde-White, Fiona Hutchison, Peter Cushing, Marcus Gilbert, William Hootkins, Alan Polonsky, Francesca Gronshaw
Synopsis / Aviation Content: An extreme '80s-style movie of the classic aviation character James "Biggles" Bigglesworth, created by Capt. W.E. Johns in 1932. While Neil Dickson is expertly cast in the lead role, the film falls short in its concept—an old-fashioned hero, a science fiction plot, and an inappropriate rock music score—what a mixture! Aeronautically, the biplane scenes aren't bad, with brilliant onboard camera work and low-level, high-speed passes making for well-paced chase sequences. The Jet Ranger helicopter time-traveling back to World War I France is preposterous, but at the same time amusing.

Type	msn	Civil reg.
Avro 504K	R3/LE/61400	G-ADEV
Bell 206B Jet Ranger	854	G-BAKF
Boeing-Stearman PT-17-BW Kaydet	75-4775	G-AROY
LVG C.VI	4503	G-AANJ
(SNCAN) Stampe SV.4C	141	G-BXNW

The Stampe biplane, G-BXNW, was used in the film as Biggles's photographic aircraft with an extra seat for a gunner and was marked as "E6452." This particular Stampe SV.4C was a license-built French version of the original Belgian design. The Stearman, G-AROY, was used in the film as the German villain's fighter with twin machine guns. It belonged to former RAF pilot John Jordan, who actually flew it in the film. This biplane is ex–USAAC (s/n 42-16612 and ex–U.S. civil reg. N56418). The Bell Jet Ranger, G-BAKF, was expertly flown by renowned film helicopter pilot Marc Wolff and was modified, for reasons not explained in the movie, with strange side fittings that seem to be loudspeakers. This helicopter was built in 1972 and belonged to the Helicopter Partnership at the time of filming. The aircraft was later destroyed in an accident on January 9, 1989, when it collided with power lines.

Background aircraft are a World War I–era German LVG (Luft-Verkehrs-Gesellschaft) C.VI biplane, G-AANJ, and a British Avro 504K, G-ADEV, both of the Shuttleworth Collection, Bedfordshire, England, and one additional, unidentified Stampe biplane. A full-scale, non-flying Sopwith Pup replica was built for background set dressing and destroyed during filming in the scene in which Biggles is first introduced. Biplane operations were supervised and performed by SkySport Engineering Ltd. and filmed from Old Warden Aerodrome, Bedfordshire, England. A Boeing 727 airliner is in one brief linking shot.

GPS Location

Old Warden Aerodrome, Bedfordshire, England: N52 05.10 / W000 19.20

The Big Lift

USA / 20th Century–Fox / 1950 / B&W / 119 minutes

Director: George Seaton

Cast: Montgomery Clift, Paul Douglas, Cornell Borchers, Bruni Lobel, O.E. Hasse

Synopsis / Aviation Content: Aircrew Clift and Douglas are assigned to the Berlin Airlift, where they both become involved with two local women. A unique insight into West Berlin at the start of the Cold War and the amount of devastation caused by Allied bombing—much of it still evident in 1949 when this film was shot. Aviation highlights are the amazing C-54 landing approaches across the city that are not only cinematically entertaining but historically important for their depiction of the actual airlift in action.

The main aircraft is the four-engined **Douglas C-54 Skymaster**, many of which are seen throughout the film at what was then called Tempelhof Air Base, West Berlin. Almost all military personnel seen in the film are actual USAF staff on assignment in Berlin at the time—they are credited in a special scene at the end. Background aircraft are the usual **Douglas C-47 Skytrain** transports (one was 43-48251) and a single **Fairchild C-82A Packet** seen in the distance during a radar approach. The C-82A was also used as a camera-plane for C-54 aerial photography. The burning wreck was newsreel footage of C-54G-1-DO (s/n 45-514 / msn 35967), after it crashed during Airlift operations.

Black Hawk Down

USA / Revolution Studios / 2001 / Color / 138 minutes

Director: Ridley Scott

Cast: Josh Hartnett, Ewan McGregor, Tom Sizemore, Eric Bana, William Fichtner, Ewen Bremner, Sam Shepherd

Synopsis / Aviation Content: Factual portrayal of the botched 1993 U.S. Special Forces mission to capture local warlords in Somalia. Based on the 1999 book of the same name by American writer Mark Bowden. Powerful, boldly stylistic shots are captured of the UH-60 Black Hawk helicopters in action, along with the rarely seen A/MH-6 Little Birds, making for some of the best helicopter sequences ever placed on the big screen. This film made the "Black Hawk" helicopter a household name.

Four **Sikorsky MH-60L Black Hawk** and four **McDonnell Douglas AH/MH-6J Little Bird** helicopters were especially flown by the U.S. military to the filming location in Morocco onboard two giant C-5 Galaxy transports. They were provided by the U.S. Army 160th SOAR, the same regiment assigned to the actual operation in 1993, some of the pilots on the film were veterans of that mission as well. The four Little Birds were AH-6J (s/n 84-24319, 89-25354 and 95-25371) with MH-6J (s/n 81-23653). "354" was the most utilized chopper of the four, appearing throughout in multiple scenes. One unidentified, black-painted **Bell UH-1H Iroquois** with red and white rotor blades can also be seen in several shots.

UNCONFIRMED DATA

Two MH-60L mock-ups were built for the post-crash scenes with tail numbers "26365" and "26350." Since neither of these serial numbers match the ones shot down during the actual battle, it seems likely they might have been copied over from two of the Black Hawks supplied for filming—MH-60L (s/n 91-26365), doubling as "Super 61"; and MH-60L (s/n 91-26350), doubling as "Super 64." Both are 160th SOAR serving helicopters.

Background aircraft in the Mogadishu Airport scenes were Moroccan **Lockheed C-130H Hercules** transports, including s/n CNA-OC, CNA-OD, CNA-OF, CNA-OJ and CNA-OS. The derelict airliner seen in one airport scene was an ex–Qantas **Boeing 707-138B** (reg. VH-EBK / msn 18334/229), which had been sold to TAG Aviation as N58937 and then leased from 1983 to the Moroccan Air Force as CN-ANS. By 2001, when the film was shot, it had obviously been grounded for some time.

Kenitra Airbase near Kenitra, Morocco, doubled for Mogadishu Airport, Somalia, where the 160th SOAR had been based during their occupation in 1993. The city of Mogadishu itself was actually the coastal cities of Rabat and Sale, Morocco. Filming took place from March to July 2001.

GPS LOCATION
Kenitra Airbase, Kenitra, Morocco: N34 17.80 / W006 35.70

FACTUAL BACKGROUND: THE UH-60 AND OPERATION GOTHIC SERPENT

The Sikorsky UH-60 Black Hawk has been the helicopter backbone of the U.S. Army since 1979 and is the only helicopter used by all five branches of the U.S. armed forces. It was designed as a twin-engined assault transport to replace the classic UH-1 Huey. The definitive Army versions are the UH-60A and re-engined UH-60L; the U.S. Navy has the SH-60B and from 2000 the MH-60S. The USAF operates a rescue version as the HH-60G, and the USMC flies the Presidential VIP VH-60A with an executive interior. Lastly, the USCG has the HH-60J Jayhawk SAR version.

The Battle of Mogadishu, as it has come to be known, was a part of Operation Gothic Serpent, a U.S. objective to capture political advisors to Somali Warlord Mohamed Farrah Aidid. Aidid had been a part of the 1991 coalition that overthrew the Somali government, resulting in civil disorder and mass famine throughout Somalia. The 160th SOAR (Special Operations Airborne Regiment) provided aerial transport and cover to Delta Force and Army Ranger soldiers. The mission began on October 3, 1993, with nineteen UH-60 Black Hawk and A/MH-6 Little Birds flying to a building in downtown Mogadishu where Aidid's advisors were meeting. Resistance, however, from the 4,000-plus Aidid loyal militia was unexpectedly greater than the 160 strong U.S. Forces could handle, and two Black Hawks were shot down by shoulder-held rocket launchers. The stranded survivors dug in and were unable to withdraw until the following morning of October 4, 1993. Although American objectives had been achieved, nineteen U.S. personnel had been killed.

The first Black Hawk downed was "Super 61" MH-60L (s/n 91-26324), followed by "Super 64" MH-60L (s/n 89-26188), in which pilot Mike Durant was taken prisoner. Three other Black Hawks were damaged during the fighting but not downed—MH-60K (s/n 91-26368) and two UH-60L (s/n 90-26253 and 91-26360).

Blaze of Noon

USA / Paramount Pictures / 1947 / B&W / 90 minutes

Director: John Farrow

Cast: Anne Baxter, William Holden, Sonny Tufts, William Bendix, Sterling Hayden, Howard Da Silva, Johnny Sands

Synopsis / Aviation Content: Four brothers, known as the "Flying McDonald Brothers," tire of the aerial circus routine and all become pioneering mail-plane pilots, each learning the dangers of the career they've chosen. Co-written by former naval pilot turned Hollywood screenwriter Frank "Spig" Wead, based on the 1946 novel of the same name by aviation pioneer and writer Ernest K. Gann. Surprisingly routine given the aeronautical talents and backgrounds of the writers, but the aircraft content should satisfy most aviation fans.

Aerial supervisor and chief pilot was Hollywood flier Paul Mantz, who had at his disposal a selection of aircraft including his own **Boeing Model 100** (reg. N873H / msn 1144); a **Curtiss D Pusher** (likely Mantz's replica reg. N8Y); **Curtiss JN-4 Jenny**; **Douglas DC-3**; **Lockheed Constellation**; three **Pitcairn PA-7 Mailwing** (two might be reg. N54W and N95W), and three **Travel Air 4000** biplanes. The Pitcairn Mailwing aircraft were located and refurbished by Mantz as the film's 1920s–era mail-planes. One of them was flown sixteen times under the Brooklyn Bridge for the final moments in the film. Mantz also located and refurbished the three Travel Air biplanes for the circus aerobatic sequences.

Camera-planes were a Douglas B-23, Vultee BT-13, and Mantz's Stinson L-1 (reg. N63230) and Boeing 100 (reg. N873H). Filmed at Pomona (now Brackett) Airport, California, which stands in for 1926 Newark Airport, New Jersey.

GPS Location

Pomona (Brackett) Airport, California: N34 05.50 / W117 47.00

The Blue Max

UK / 20th Century–Fox / 1966 / Color / 150 minutes

Director: John Guillermin

Cast: George Peppard, James Mason, Ursula Andress, Jeremy Kemp, Karl Michael Vogler

Synopsis / Aviation Content: During the last months of World War I in France, cold and heartless German fighter pilot Peppard will stop at nothing to obtain the coveted Blue Max military decoration. Based on the 1964 novel of the same name by American author Jack D. Hunter. Excellent aerial sequences with replica period aircraft make for one of the best biplane-era films ever made! The film's unique style and action set the stage in fact for a revival of biplane-era motion pictures that would be produced well into the 1970s. Features a striking music score by Jerry Goldsmith.

Type	msn	Civil reg.
Replica Aircraft		
Fokker Dr.I	001	G-ATIY
Fokker Dr.I	002	G-ATJM
Fokker D.VII-65	01	F-BNDF
Fokker D.VII-65	02	F-BNDG
Fokker D.VII-65	03	F-BNDH
Pfalz D.IIIa	PPS/PFLZ/1	G-ATIF
Pfalz D.IIIa	PT.16	G-ATIJ
Royal Aircraft Factory S.E.5a	SEM.7282	G-ATGV
Royal Aircraft Factory S.E.5a	SEM.7283	G-ATGW
Original Aircraft		
Caudron C.277 Luciole	7546/135	G-ATIP
Morane-Saulnier MS.230	1049	F-BGMR
Morane-Saulnier MS.230	1076	F-BGJT
Stampe SV.4C	386	F-BBIT
Stampe SV.4C	1060	F-BAUR

All nine "starring" aircraft were full-scale replicas built especially for the film in 1965. After filming, ex–RCAF pilot Lynn Garrison purchased the nine replicas, plus other aircraft, and retained them in Ireland under the company name Blue Max Aviation Ltd. (See Appendix III.) Most then went on to star in subsequent World War I film productions which had become so popular during this period.

The Fokker Dr.I *Dreidecker* (Triplane) first flew in 1917 and only around 320 were built. It became the definitive World War I German fighter, as it was flown by the renowned fighter ace Manfred von Richthofen, aka the Red Baron. The two for the movie were replicas built by John Bitz GmbH in Munich, West Germany, and were each powered by a 110 hp Oberursal rotary engine. Delivered for filming in September 1965. Re-registered in Ireland as EI-APW (001) and EI-APY (002) in mid–1967.

The Fokker D.VII biplane first flew in 1918 and around 2,000 were mass produced before war's end. The three biplane replicas for the film were built by Rousseau Aviation at Dinard Airport, France. These were used in the majority of German flying sequences and were designated as the "D.VII-65" (presumably for 1965), by Rosseau. Each was powered by a 200 to 210 hp DeHavilland Gipsy Queen engine. Re-registered in Ireland as EI-APT (02), EI-APU (03) and EI-APV (01) in mid–1967.

The pointed-nose Pfalz D.IIIa German biplane first flew in 1917 and around 1,000 were produced. Two were constructed for the film: G-ATIF was built by Personal Plane Services at Booker Field, and G-ATIJ was built by Voiv Bellamy of the Hampshire Aero Club. Both replicas were powered by a vee-inverted 145 hp DeHavilland Gipsy Major 10 Mk. 2 engine and delivered in late 1965 to Ireland. This is the type actor George Peppard is mainly seen flying and crashes midway through the movie. Re-registered in Ireland as EI-ARC (PPS/PFLZ/1) and EI-ARD (PT.16) in mid–1967.

The British Royal Aircraft Factory S.E.5 (Scout Experimental 5) first flew in 1917 and over 5,000 were eventually produced. Two S.E.5a biplane replicas were built by Miles Marine and Structural Plastics Ltd. and were each powered by a 200 hp DeHavilland Gipsy Queen 30 engine. Both were delivered to Ireland in late 1965 for filming. Re-registered in Ireland as EI-ARA (7282) and EI-ARB (7283) in mid–1967.

The Caudron C.277 Luciole, G-ATIP, was a 1930s French-built biplane, which doubled in the film as, firstly, an RAF spotter plane with rear-gunner, marked as "A8590," then as a German spotter plane later in the film. It was re-registered as EI-ARF in mid–1967 after filming.

The Morane-Saulnier MS.230 parasol-wing monoplane, F-BGMR, doubled as the new German prototype Peppard confidently flies in the film's final scene. A French design which first flew in 1929, it was employed by the French air force as a primary trainer with over 1,100 being built. It was re-registered as EI-ARG in mid–1967 after

filming. The second MS.230, F-BGJT, was used as a back-up aircraft; it went to the UK in 1967 as G-AVEB.

The Stampe SV.4C biplanes, F-BAUR and F-BBIT, doubled in the film as both the British S.E.5a and German Fokker D.VII. Both subsequently entered the Blue Max Aviation Collection with Irish reg. EI-AVU and EI-ARE, respectively.

To fill out the backgrounds, **DeHavilland DH-82A Tiger Moth** biplanes with reg. EI-AGP (ex–G-ANDM / msn 82335), F-BMKG, G-AIRI (msn 3761), G-AIRK (msn 82336), G-AMTK (msn 3982), G-ANKK (msn 83590), G-ANKU (msn 85866), and G-ANLD (msn 85990), and a **Stampe SV.4C** with reg. F-BMKQ (ex–G-ATIR / msn 1047), were used to represent either the British S.E.5a or German Fokker D.VII. These are seen throughout the film in the background or during the flying scenes in formation behind the S.E.5a or D.VII replicas. It should be noted that these identifications come from various sources and are not totally confirmed as having actually flown in the movie. Also unconfirmed is the use of a **Caudron C.277 Luciole** registered to Fox Studios as G-ATIO in September 1965 and reported as having been written off during filming by November 1965.

Aerial Supervisor was retired RAF Air Commodore Allen H. Wheeler, with both civilian pilots and pilots from the Irish Air Corps flying the replica aircraft. Credited pilots were Derek Piggott, Ken Byrnes, Tim Clutterbuck, Pat Cranfield, Tim Healey, Peter Hillwood, Joan Hughes, Darby Kennedy, Roger Kennedy, Liam Mulligan and Taffy Rich. Aircraft engineer was Johnny Maher. Stunt pilot Derek Piggott flew one of the Fokker Dr.I Triplane replicas under the viaduct around thirty times to capture the various angles needed. The flock of sheep were placed there on purpose to create a more dynamic scene. The aerial sequences were directed by Anthony Squire. Actor George Peppard acquired his private pilot's license for his role and apparently flew some scenes in the film.

The entire film was shot in Ireland in 1965. The airfield was at Western Aerodrome, Leixlip, near Dublin. The city of Dublin itself doubled as World War I Berlin. The bridge the two Triplanes fly under is the viaduct east of Fermoy, County Cork. The airport at the end of the film is Casement Aerodrome (Baldonnel Aerodrome before 1965) near Dublin. Interior scenes were filmed at Ardmore Studios in Bray, Ireland.

Type	msn	Civil reg.	Film Markings
Aerospatiale SA.341G Gazelle	1066	N37LR	N77GH / 02
Aerospatiale SA.341G Gazelle	1075	N777GH	N77GH / 02
Bell 206B Jet Ranger	2615	N250CA	N250CA / Police
Bell 206B Jet Ranger	2779	N230CA	N230CA / Police
Bell 206B Jet Ranger	2840	N1068A	N1068A / Police
Bell 206B Jet Ranger	3264	N200NP	N200NP
Bell 206B Jet Ranger	3363	N2044C	N2044C / Police
Hughes 500D	129-0624D	N58428	—

GPS Locations

Western Aerodrome, Leixlip, Ireland: N53 21.10 / W006 29.15

Casement Aerodrome, Dublin, Ireland: N53 18.20 / W006 26.80

The Viaduct, Fermoy, Ireland: N52 08.65 / W008 15.40

Factual Background: The Blue Max Medal

The *Pour le Merite* Military Order was introduced by King Frederick II of Prussia in 1740; it was named in French as that language was in use by the Prussian Royal Court at the time. Informally known as the Blue Max during World War I, it was the highest military decoration that could be awarded to German serving personnel. It was abolished near the end of World War I on November 9, 1918, with the abdication of the Kaiser Wilhelm II of Prussia. One notable recipient was Manfred von Richthofen—the Red Baron.

Blue Thunder

USA / Columbia Pictures / 1983 / Color / 105 minutes

Director: John Badham

Cast: Roy Scheider, Warren Oates, Candy Clark, Daniel Stern, Malcolm McDowell, Paul Roebling, David S. Sheiner, Joe Santos

Synopsis / Aviation Content: Police pilot Scheider and partner Stern are assigned to evaluate a new, heavily armed helicopter nicknamed Blue Thunder; however, things turn nasty when they stumble across the sinister scheme for its true purpose. One of the all-time great, if not the greatest of helicopter movies has some incredible aerial action and chase sequences. The sinister appearance of the Blue Thunder helicopter itself is still awesome, even in present-day cinema. The film has since developed a respectable cult following among movie and helicopter fans alike.

The featured helicopter was created from the airframe of the French-designed and -built Aerospatiale SA.341 Gazelle, a 1960s response to a French Army requirement for a lightweight utility helicopter. The prototype first flew on April 7, 1967, and most were built for either the British or French military services. The SA.341G series was the civil commercial version that first flew in 1972, featuring the Turbomeca Astazou IIIA 590 shp turbine engine. The Gazelle is notable as being the first helicopter to incorporate Aerospatiale's distinctive Fenestron ducted-fan tail rotor system, a concept which has featured on several subsequent Aerospatiale products.

Two Gazelle helicopters were converted to Blue Thunder machines for filming. Likely because of the lower time airframe, msn 1075 was the main-use helicopter with msn 1066 a backup in case of mechanical trouble with msn 1075. The histories of these two forever famous helicopters are:

MSN 1066

Built 1973 by Aerospatiale, registered as F-WKQD for testing.

July 31, 1974, to Vought Helicopter Corp., Texas, as N57936.

October 10, 1974, to the Kentucky Gem Cola Co., Kentucky, as N57936.

November 19, 1976, to Continental Flying Service, Inc., Kentucky, as N57936.

December 20, 1976, to L.T. Ruth Coal Co., Kentucky, as N57936.

October 21, 1978, special registration change to N37LR.

August 19, 1981, to Columbia Pictures Industries, Inc., as N37LR.

Converted to Blue Thunder configuration as a stand-by helicopter.

2,371 hours on the airframe at the time of conversion.

November 4, 1983, special registration change to N51BT.

October 25, 1984, to Michael E. Grube, New Mexico Aero Salvage, as N51BT.

June 23, 1994, dismantled and scrapped for parts.

MSN 1075

Built 1973 by Aerospatiale, no French registration issued.

September 24, 1973, to Vought Helicopter Corp., Texas, as N94494.

July 11, 1974, to F.R.B.C. Leasing Corp., Georgia, as N94494.

Registration changed to N777GH with a lease to Holly & Beck.

August 17, 1981, to Moceri Management Co., Michigan, as N777GH.

August 17, 1981, to Columbia Pictures Industries, Inc., as N777GH.

Converted to Blue Thunder configuration as the main-use helicopter.

1,705 hours on the airframe at the time of conversion.

November 4, 1983, special registration change to N52BT.

October 25, 1984, to Michael E. Grube, New Mexico Aero Salvage, as N52BT.

August 16, 1988, dismantled and scrapped for parts.

Both Gazelles were purchased by Columbia Pictures in August 1981 and flown to R.W. Martin, Inc. (Cinema Air, Inc.), at Palomar Airport, Carlsbad, California, to be modified. R.W. Martin was the acting agency for Columbia Pictures and looked after the storage, servicing and conversions of the helicopters. Aviation company The Metal Cage carried out the actual engineering and physical work of converting the two helicopters into Blue Thunder configuration. The entire forward cabin was removed with a new, redesigned flat-plated canopy installed that was fourteen inches wider than the original one. All kinds of "Hollywood props" and fuselage protrusions were added to simulate armor and surveillance gear. The rotary cannon was of wooden construction; it had limited movement and weighed about 225 lbs. It dispensed diffused water to simulate gunfire; gun close-ups with fire coming out were filmed in a studio with a specially built gun prop. Both helicopters retained their original Turbomeca Astazou IIIA turbine engines and flew during filming under standard Gazelle operating parameters except for a restricted Vne (never ex-

The *Blue Thunder* helicopter comes to life for another day of filming. Note the film camera mounted on the tail mast and shattered side window. Photograph: Gary Mason.

ceed) airspeed of 100 knots. The greatest complaints from pilots were the machine's resistance to slow down once up to speed and its tendency to "lean" a bit in flight due to all the modifications. The rumor it was "front heavy" isn't true (this was a scripted line in the film), and overall both helicopters handled fine and the center of gravity was normal.

Both helicopters were marked with a fictional military designation and s/n "OH17A / 25102" and the registration N777GH (the main-use Gazelle), was shortened to "N77GH." After principal filming, Columbia Pictures retained both machines for publicity work and so changed their registrations. N37LR became N51BT and N777GH became N52BT. Subsequent roles for the helicopters were the short-lived *Blue Thunder* (1984) TV series; one was used in the pilot episode for *Mac-Gyver* (1985); one was featured in a television commercial; and both appeared in the TV miniseries *Amerika* (1987) as Russian gunship helicopters.

Up to four Jet Ranger helicopters were painted up in false LAPD Air Support livery, identified as N1068A, N2044C, N230CA and N250CA. N200NP was in Bell factory livery and used for the scene where Scheider auto-rotates onto a building site. The KBLA 8 News helicopter is an unidentified **Aerospatiale AS.350 Ecureuil**. McDowell's armed helicopter in the final scene is a **Hughes 500D**, reg. N58428, gunship conversion owned by JetCopters, Inc. A **Bell Model 205A-1** (likely either N630V or N4774R) can be seen in the background of a few shots at the heliport, and was most likely the one used for the Vietnam flashback sequences.

Blue Thunder pilots were James Gavin, Ross Reynolds and Tom Friedkin. Hughes 500 gunship pilot was Karl Wickman. Other pilots were Harry Hauss, Art Scholl and Peter J. McKernan, Sr., whose company JetCopters, Inc., supplied some of the Bell Jet Ranger choppers. Helicopter mechanic was Ernie Gustafson. Assistance was also provided by the actual LAPD Air Support Division, on whose heliport the film was shot.

Around four Bell Jet Ranger mock-ups were acquired for filming—one was used for the building site crash and another for the high-speed viaduct

Hughes 500D N58428 played the gunship chopper in *Blue Thunder* (1983). It also made appearances in such TV series as *The A-Team* and *Airwolf*. Photograph: Gary Mason.

crash. All General Dynamics F-16 Fighting Falcon fighters and missiles were done with models and special effects. Scaled RC (remote-control), flyable model aircraft of the F-16 fighters, Hughes 500D and Blue Thunder were built for various shots involving explosions. Studio mock-ups were built for Blue Thunder, the Jet Ranger and F-16 fighters. The Blue Thunder mock-up was, for many years, located at MGM Studios, Florida, as a public display item.

Actor Roy Scheider, having hands-on helicopter experience, actually flew the Blue Thunder chopper in some shots under the supervision of aerial director and pilot James Gavin. For safety, these shots were among the last filmed, with cameras mounted in and around the cockpit. Scheider did some takeoffs, hovering and maneuvering around downtown Los Angeles.

The ASTRO Division headquarters was located at the Hooper Memorial Heliport on top of the Piper Technical Center building in central Los Angeles. Several mock hangars, etc., were built for filming on top of this building, but have since been removed. This is the headquarters of the actual LAPD Air Support Division, who provided assistance throughout filming. The terms "ASTRO" (Assistance To Regular Operations) and "Air Support" are used throughout the movie. The "Pinkville Weapons Evaluation Center" was a purpose-built set located in the Mojave Desert sixteen miles West of Edwards AFB. Principal photography took place from January to April 1982.

GPS LOCATIONS

Hooper Memorial Heliport, Los Angeles, California: N34 03.25 / W118 13.80

"Pinkville Weapons Evaluation Center": N34 54.70 / W118 13.20

Bombardier

USA / RKO Radio Pictures / 1943 / B&W / 99 minutes
Director: Richard Wallace
Cast: Pat O'Brien, Randolph Scott, Anne Shirley, Eddie Albert, Walter Reed, Robert Ryan, Barton MacLane
Synopsis / Aviation Content:

Wartime story following the training of a group of bombardiers from cadet level up to a fictional B-17 mission into Japan. Largely a USAAF propaganda picture, it features some excellent training footage and aerial photography of various bomber types. Aircraft are the **Beechcraft AT-11 Kansan**, **Boeing B-17E Flying Fortress** and **Douglas B-18 Bolo**. Some use of footage from earlier films *Test Pilot* (1938), *I Wanted Wings* (1941) and *Dive Bomber* (1941). Filmed from October 12 to December 18, 1942, at Kirkland AAF, Albuquerque, New Mexico. Notable future directors Robert Wise and Robert Aldrich worked on this film in the editing and assistant directing areas.

Bombers B-52

UK Title: **No Sleep Till Dawn**
USA / Warner Bros. / 1957 / Color / 102 minutes
Director: Gordon Douglas
Cast: Natalie Wood, Karl Malden, Marsha Hunt, Efrem Zimbalist Jr., Don Kelly, Nelson Leigh, Robert Nichols, Ray Montgomery, Robert Hover
Synopsis / Aviation Content: A former Korean War aircraft mechanic with a grudge against a fighter pilot finds himself serving in the same B-52 bomber wing six years later, with the pilot taking a keen interest in the mechanic's daughter. A classic period piece offering excellent insight into a working 1950s SAC base, it has all the usual off-duty drama scenes but is worth sticking with. Many backgrounds are filled out with B-47 and B-52 bombers, plus there's excellent aerial footage of an early bare-metal B-52B!

All aircraft were owned and operated by the USAF, with filming taking place at Castle AFB, California. Many Boeing B-47B, B-47E and early B-52 variants are seen on the ramp throughout

Type	msn	Military s/n	Film Markings
Boeing B-47E-115-BW Stratojet	4501124	53-2311	2311
Boeing B-47E-10-DT Stratojet	43666	52-051	2051
Boeing B-52B-25-BO Stratofortress	16852	53-373	3373
Boeing KC-97G-120-BO Stratofreighter	16669	52-2638	22638
North American F-86A-5-NA Sabre	151-632	48-263	12793 / Lucky Lady
Sikorsky SH-19B-SI Chickasaw	55-589	52-7513	27513

the picture, and two B-47E Stratojets (s/n 52-051 and 53-2311) are used in the filming of ground scenes. The star of the movie is of course the B-52 Stratofortress, brand new at the time; s/n 53-373 was the airframe provided to the filmmakers. It was retired in 1966 to MASDC in Arizona. KC-97G (s/n 52-2638) was used for the midair refueling sequence. F-86A (s/n 48-263) was a non-flying airframe used for the opening scenes set in South Korea. The H-19B helicopter was a USAF SH-19B rescue conversion used in the final sequences of the movie. Also seen during the Castle AFB scenes is a very tidy-looking Beechcraft C-45 Expeditor parked behind some hangars during a fight scene.

Bomber's Moon

USA / 20th Century–Fox / 1943 / B&W / 67 minutes

Directors: Edward Ludwig, Harold D. Schuster

Cast: George Montgomery, Annabella, Kent Taylor, Walter Kingsford, Martin Kosleck, Dennis Hoey

Synopsis / Aviation Content: An American pilot is shot down while on a bombing raid over Germany during World War II; he and others then try to evade capture. Mediocre propaganda film was made entirely in a film studio. Models, miniatures and full-scale aircraft mock-up interiors were built to represent the Lockheed Hudson and Messerschmitt Bf 109.

Breaking the Sound Barrier see *The Sound Barrier*

Breaking Through the Sound Barrier see *The Sound Barrier*

The Bride Came C.O.D.

USA / Warner Bros. / 1941 / B&W / 92 minutes

Director: William Keighley

Cast: James Cagney, Bette Davis, Stuart Erwin, Eugene Pallette, Jack Carson, George Tobias

Synopsis / Aviation Content: A wealthy oil tycoon hires down-and-out charter pilot Cagney to kidnap his daughter in order to stop her marrying a bandleader. Hollywood pilot Paul Mantz provided his **Lockheed 9C Orion** (reg. NC12222 / msn 180). Other aircraft are a **Beechcraft Staggerwing; Bellanca Skyrocket / Pacemaker; Cessna; Douglas DC-2** and **Lockheed 5C Vega** (reg. NC19958 / msn 108). Notable for Mantz's first on-screen cameo appearance with a brief speaking part. Filmed in January and February 1941, partly in Death Valley, California. The term C.O.D. is a financial transaction meaning "Collect On Delivery."

A Bridge Too Far (Non–Aviation Themed Title)

UK-USA / Metro-Goldwyn-Mayer / 1977 / Color / 169 minutes

Director: Richard Attenborough

Cast: Dirk Bogarde, James Caan, Michael Caine, Sean Connery, Edward Fox, Elliott Gould, Gene Hackman, Anthony Hopkins, Hardy Kruger, Laurence Olivier, Ryan O'Neal, Robert Redford, Maximilian Schell, Liv Ullmann

Synopsis / Aviation Content: Epic recreation of the September 1944 Allied airborne invasion of Arnham known as Operation Market Garden. Notable for its all-star cast and the highly complex aerial sequence featuring eleven C-47 Dakotas taking off, all towing replica Horsa gliders! Another highlight is the massive paratroop drop sequence.

In the table on the following page, the first four C-47 aircraft were on loan from the Finnish AF (s/n DO-10, DO-12, DO-4, DO-7 respectively), the next three were on loan from the Danish AF (s/n K-687, K-685, K-688 respectively). The last four were purchased and owned by the film company Visionair Ltd. specifically for this movie. N9983Q and N9984Q were purchased from the Portuguese AF (ex-s/n 6171, 6153 respectively). N9985Q and N9986Q were purchased from France's Air Djibouti. C-47A (s/n 42-93096) took part in the actual operation in 1944, dropping paratroops into Holland!

The first, second and fifth AT-16D aircraft were hired from the Netherlands AF (s/n B-64, B-182,

Type	msn	Military s/n	Civil reg.	Film Markings
Douglas C-47A-1-DK Skytrain	12050	42-92268	—	721182 / I-C1
Douglas C-47A-20-DK Skytrain	12970	42-93096	—	314013 / I-C7
Douglas C-47A-30-DK Skytrain	14070/25515	43-48254	—	700318 / I-D1
Douglas C-47A-70-DL Skytrain	19109	42-100646	—	711212 / I-D3
Douglas C-47A-70-DL Skytrain	19200	42-100737	—	823561 / I-C3
Douglas C-47A-70-DL Skytrain	19291	42-100828	—	337185 / I-C6
Douglas C-47A-90-DL Skytrain	20118	43-15652	—	315317 / I-C8
Douglas C-47B-1-DK Skytrain	14365/25810	43-48549	N9986Q	CS
Douglas C-47B-20-DK Skytrain	15770/27215	43-49954	N9985Q	KG411 / CS
Douglas C-47B-40-DK Skytrain	16784/33532	44-77200	N9983Q	KK149 / YS
Douglas C-53D-DO Skytrooper	11675	42-68748	N9984Q	KG637 / YS
Noorduyn AT-16-ND Harvard	14-641	42-12394	—	HF-J
Noorduyn AT-16-ND Harvard	14A-808	43-12509	—	—
Noorduyn AT-16-ND Harvard	14A-1020	43-12721	PH-BKT	HF-L
Noorduyn AT-16-ND Harvard	14A-1184	43-12885	PH-KLU	HF-S
Noorduyn AT-16-ND Harvard	14A-1467	43-13168	—	HF-N
Supermarine Spitfire LF.Mk.IXb	CBAF.IX552	(RAF) MH434	G-ASJV	MH434 / S-AG
Taylorcraft Auster AOP.Mk. III	344	(RAF) MZ231	PH-NGK	RT607

B-118 respectively). The AT-16 (ex–Harvard Mk.IIb) trainers doubled in the film as **Focke-Wulf Fw 190A, Hawker Typhoon** and **Republic P-47 Thunderbolt** fighters! The film markings given in the table are those for the Hawker Typhoon.

Twelve Horsa glider replicas were constructed out of wood at Jaarsma BV near Deventer, The Netherlands, with a few later smashed up for the post-drop landing zone scenes. Camera-planes were an Auster J.1 Autocrat (G-AJDW), two Piper PA.27 Aztecs (G-ASND, G-AWDI), and an Aerospatiale SA.318C Alouette II (G-BDWN). One Lockheed C-130H Hercules (s/n 71-1803 / CH-07) was used for the paratroop drops. One LET L.13 Blanik glider was towed behind a C-47 to film Horsa cockpit views. Filmed at Deelen AFB, The Netherlands, in September 1976. The paratroop drop featured the use of some twenty-five film cameras.

The Bridges at Toko-Ri

USA / Paramount Pictures / 1954 / Color / 103 minutes

Director: Mark Robson

Cast: William Holden, Grace Kelly, Fredric March, Mickey Rooney, Robert Strauss, Charles McGraw, Keiko Awaji, Earl Holliman, Richard Shannon

Synopsis / Aviation Content: In 1952 during the Korean War, top naval reservist Holden wants to quit but stays on for one more mission against an important target in North Korea. Based on the 1953 novel of the same name by American novelist James A. Michener, who was inspired to write the story while a visitor on the USS *Essex* during 1952. Excellent depiction of 1950s naval aviation with many detailed shots of the Grumman F9F Panther and Sikorsky HO3S Dragonfly rescue helicopter, making this one of the best Korean War aviation pictures from the period. One often noted aspect of this film is that actor Mickey Rooney wears a top hat for his role as a rescue pilot.

The aircraft depicted in this film is the **Grumman F9F Panther** of naval squadrons VF-192 and VF-52. The Panther was a straight-wing naval strike-fighter (1,385 built), which served throughout the 1950s, later being replaced by the swept-wing version—the F9F Cougar (1,989 built). The last of the F9F series, a 2-seater trainer TF-9J, wasn't retired until 1974. There were two aspects to the aerial filming portions of this production—the carrier scenes and the overland scenes. The carrier sequences were shot onboard the USS *Oriskany* (CV-34) with F9F Panther squadron VF-192 Golden Dragons during November and December 1953. Carrier launch scenes and over-water flight scenes were completed with the F9F-5 variant of VF-192 while the *Oriskany* was stationed in the Sea of Japan as a "stand-by" measure in the months after the Korean War ended. Mostly seen is F9F-5 BuNo. 125598 (No. 209), which was used as Holden's aircraft for filming, also seen are BuNo. 126000 (No. 21) and BuNo. 126225 (No. 202), with the Golden Dragon emblem of VF-192 plainly visible on the aircraft in the movie. The overland ("feet dry") sequences were shot back in the United States in early 1954 with naval squadron VF-52 Sealancers flying up to twelve Panthers before the cameras. Filming took place with famed Hollywood pilot Paul Mantz, using his B-25 camera-ship, directing the F9F-2 Panthers painted in VF-192 livery over the Chocolate Mountain Gunnery Range at the northern end of Imperial Valley, California. Holden's (No. 209) Panther was flown by VF-52's commanding officer Cmdr. James Holloway, who would later go on to become an admiral and the Chief of Naval Operations from 1974 to 1978. He would also serve as a technical advisor on the hit film *Top Gun* (1986). Some additional shooting apparently took place onboard the aircraft carrier USS *Kearsarge* (CV-33).

Other background aircraft include over a dozen **Douglas AD-4 Skyraider** propeller-driven fighters of VA-195 and silver **McDonnell F2H-3 Banshee** jet fighters of VF-193. The rescue helicopter was the 4-seater **Sikorsky HO3S-1 Dragonfly** of naval squadron HU-1. Rooney's helicopter, in the final scene filmed at Thousand Oaks Ranch, carried BuNo. 123129.

One Panther fuselage was used for studio close-ups, plus one more for a crash scene (likely F9F-5 BuNo. 125939), filmed at the Thousand Oaks Ranch in California. Much use was made of models and miniatures for the final battle, which earned an Academy Award for special effects. A difficult role for William Holden, as his brother Robert Beedle never returned from a Grumman Hellcat mission near Papua New Guinea during World War II. Holden himself served in the USAAF Special Branch making training films with the First Motion Picture Unit.

Brink of Hell   see   *Toward the Unknown*

Broken Arrow

USA / 20th Century–Fox / 1996 / color / 108 minutes

Director: John Woo

Cast: John Travolta, Christian Slater, Samantha Mathis, Delroy Lindo, Bob Gunton, Frank Whaley, Howie Long

Synopsis / Aviation Content: Traitorous USAF pilot Travolta crashes a stealth bomber and holds the nuclear weapons for ransom while co-pilot Slater teams up with a local park ranger in order to stop him. Mostly has helicopter action utilizing civilian Hueys as gunships, with all other military aircraft being accomplished with visual effects and mock-up airframes. Still an okay action yarn, even though the creation of a fictional stealth bomber for the story seems unwarranted.

Although the main aircraft in this film appears to be the Northrop B-2A Spirit, it is in fact, a fictional creation known as the "B-3 Stealth Bomber"—a supposed development of the B-2. A full-scale mock-up was built (marked as "4718"), along with cockpit and various scale models for the flying scenes. Real aircraft flown were three **Bell Model 204** helicopters as military gunships (UH-1C) and one "nuclear rescue" helicopter—an **Agusta 109A Hirundo** (reg. N502RP / msn 7220). The Bell 206B Jet Ranger on the train at the end marked as "N17340" appears to be a mock-up built from a derelict airframe. One shot of an early model NASA **Gates Learjet**. Aerial logistics were provided by Motion Picture Aviation Services, Inc., a company that specializes in providing aircraft and aerial photography to filmmakers.

Broken Journey

UK / General Film Distributors (GFD) / 1948 / B&W / 89 minutes

Directors: Ken Annakin, Michael C. Chorlton

Cast: Phyllis Calvert, Margot Grahame, James Donald, Francis L. Sullivan, Raymond Huntley, Derek Bond, Guy Rolfe, Sonia Holm, Grey Blake, David Tomlinson

Synopsis / Aviation Content: A DC-3 airliner, full of passengers with varying backgrounds, crashes in a remote mountain region, whereupon a large-scale rescue operation ensues. Based in part on the actual crash of a European

Air Transport Service Douglas C-53D-DO Skytrooper (s/n 42-68846 / msn 11773), which went down in the Swiss Alps on November 19, 1946. All twelve onboard survived and were rescued four days later. The film used an unidentified **Douglas DC-3** marked with false reg. "F-XGPI" at the start of the film and a DC-3 derelict for the post-crash sequences. Rescue aircraft include a **Moraine-Saulnier MS.502 Criquet** (reg. F-BBUI / msn 544) and **Potez 43.1** (reg. F-AMPI / msn 3448). Background aircraft include **Douglas DC-3**, **DC-4** airliners and a **Vickers Viking**. Some use of models and miniatures in the flying scenes.

Capricorn One

USA / Sir Lew Grade / 1978 / Color / 118 minutes

Director: Peter Hyams

Cast: Elliott Gould, James Brolin, Brenda Vaccaro, Sam Waterston, O.J. Simpson, Hal Holbrook, Karen Black, Telly Savalas

Synopsis / Aviation Content: Intriguing, pacey story concerning a fake NASA mission to Mars and the attempts to both expose and cover it up. The political conspiracy of budget cuts and profiteering seem more relevant today than ever. Technically, not classed as an aviation film, but the main characters are test pilots and astronauts, and there are enough aeronautical sequences to keep any aviation fan happy. Two notable highlights are a biplane / helicopter chase and a brilliant Jerry Goldsmith music score!

Type	msn	Civil reg.
Boeing-Stearman PT-13D-BW Kaydet	75-5488	N4766V
Hughes 500C	24-0564S	N501WH
Hughes 500C	33-0459S	N9134F
Gates Learjet 24A	24A-096	N464CL

Aerial supervisor was Hollywood pilot Frank Tallman, who acquired a red Boeing-Stearman PT-13D Kaydet, N4766V, for the film's climatic aerial chase. This biplane was originally built as a dual-service variant, both as a USAAF PT-13D (s/n 42-17325) and U.S. Navy N2S-5 (BuNo. 61366). It was declared surplus to military requirements and sold from Hill AFB, Utah, to the Babb Company, California, on July 26, 1949. It then saw life as a crop-duster with Budd Aero Dusters and Baker Aircraft Sales, among several other owners. Tallman piloted the biplane during filming, performing all the required aerial stunt work. This film is notable as being the last major

The Stearman Kaydet N4766V that Frank Tallman flew in *Capricorn One* (1978). Although still retaining an overall red livery, it now sports wheel pants and a white leading edge trim. Photograph: Mike Henniger, www.aerialvisuals.ca.

After the filming of *Capricorn One* (1978), Hughes 500C N501WH was exported overseas. It's seen here in New Zealand as ZK-HXA with Christchurch Helicopters in the early 1990s. Photograph: Tim Douglas-Clifford.

motion picture completed by Tallman before his death in 1978. The Stearman was sold by its owners to Art Scholl in June 1979 and was used extensively on further filming work up until Scholl's death in 1985. N4766V was eventually acquired by the CC Air Corp. of Oxnard in 1990, which holds a large collection of vintage aircraft.

The two Hughes 500C helicopters were supplied by Western Helicopters, Inc., of California as the sinister government "black helicopters." Pilots Karl A. Wickman flew "Gunship No. 1" N501WH and George Nolan flew "Gunship No. 2" N9134F. N501WH was purchased by Western Helicopters on April 1, 1974, and was, for a period, involved in experimental work with Hughes Helicopters for the testing of electronics equipment. In 1979 it was exported to Australia with reg. VH-PXA then New Zealand with reg. ZK-HXA. On May 2, 1989, it suffered a crash in New Zealand and was rebuilt using parts from a Japanese Hughes 500C (reg. JA9052 / msn 6607). It was exported to Australia in 1994 as VH-SHD. The second Hughes, N9134F, was also exported to New Zealand with reg. ZK-HLY in 1978 and

flew until deregistered in 1999. It has since become a museum display item.

UNCONFIRMED DATA

While the identity of N501WH is confirmed from Wickman's logbooks, the use of N9134F, as the second gunship, is not as yet totally confirmed. However, other sighted logbooks show N9134F as having been based at California City Airport, the Aerial Unit base of operations, during the time of filming in early 1977. Other Western owned Hughes 500 helicopters at the time were N500WH (msn 14-0557S); N502WH (msn 25-0702S); N9103F (msn 52-0378S); N9130F (msn 33-0455S) and N9222F (msn 94-0639S). Camera helicopter may have been Western's Bell 205A-1, N6207N (msn 30001).

The unmarked NASA executive jet was a Clay Lacy–owned Gates Learjet 24A, N464CL, flown by Lacy himself for the film. This aircraft was also used in a post-crash scene by digging a shallow ditch in the desert just off the California City Airport runway and wheeling the aircraft into it to create the appearance of a belly landing. When

Also exported to New Zealand was the second Gunship from *Capricorn One* (1978). N9134F became ZK-HLY flying until 1999 before becoming a museum display item as seen here. Photograph: Simon D. Beck.

one is viewing the film, the undamaged nature of the airframe itself can be noted, plus the actors aren't seen to stand or sit on the wings.

Background aircraft are an unidentified blue and white **Bell 206B Jet Ranger** used to transport the astronauts away from the launch pad. The large 3-bladed turboprop transports in the background during this sequence are two **Douglas C-133A Cargomaster** military aircraft with civil reg. N136AB (s/n 54-136 / msn 44706) and N201AB (s/n 56-2001 / msn 45166). Also seen is a **Beechcraft Model 18** and a **Douglas C-47 Skytrain**.

The launch complex and secret "Jackson Airbase" were both filmed at Mojave Airport, California. The astronauts' Learjet escape and subsequent crash was filmed at California City Airport, California. The desert trek, gas station scene and biplane-helicopter chase were filmed north of California City, plus in and around Red Rock Canyon, Kern County, California.

GPS LOCATIONS

Mojave Airport, California: N35 03.20 / W118 08.50

California City Airport, California: N35 09.00 / W118 01.00

Red Rock Canyon, California: (approx.) N35 21.45 / W117 59.15

Captain Eddie

USA / 20th Century–Fox / 1945 / B&W / 107 minutes

Director: Lloyd Bacon

Cast: Fred MacMurray, Lynn Barry, Charles Bickford, Thomas Mitchell, Lloyd Nolan, James Gleason, Mary Philips

Synopsis / Aviation Content: A B-17 crew are forced down in the Pacific Ocean, whereupon passenger MacMurray, while awaiting rescue in a life raft, recounts his earlier life as a World War I fighter ace. Based in part on a true story developed from the 1943 book *Seven Came Through* by World War I ace Eddie Rickenbacker, who was the passenger on the ill-fated B-17. Largely considered an inferior film that turns the many incredible real-life experiences of one-time American "Ace of Aces" Rickenbacker into simple Hollywood escapism. Featured aircraft are a derelict **Boeing B-17 Flying Fortress** with false s/n "42-72032" and **Vought OS2U Kingfisher**. Footage of the Curtiss D Pusher, SPAD VII and Travel Air 2000/4000 (Wichita Fokker) for the World War I scenes comes from the earlier film *Men With Wings* (1938). Some use of miniatures and special effects.

FACTUAL BACKGROUND: AMERICA'S ACE OF ACES

Edward V. Rickenbacker (October 8, 1890–July 27, 1973) was America's top-scoring ace of World War I, whose record was not broken until World War II. He scored twenty-six kills in both a SPAD XIII and Nieuport fighter, being awarded the Medal of Honor and seven Distinguished Service Cross citations. Following several post-war business ventures, Rickenbacker eventually became manager of Eastern Airlines in 1935, a position he would hold for twenty-four years. During his tenure, Rickenbacker would oversee and pioneer, with many other aircraft designers, ways of improving air travel with larger and more reliable airliners. In February 1941, Rickenbacker very narrowly survived a horrific DC-3 crash in Atlanta, Georgia. After a long recovery he became a civilian consultant in the war effort, making recommendations to the military in foreign operations. It was during one of these missions that Rickenbacker had another scrape with death. In October 1942, his B-17D (s/n 40-3089) made a navigational error and was forced to ditch in the Pacific Ocean. For twenty-four days Rickenbacker and the B-17 crew fought starvation, sunburn, dehydration and possible capture by the Japanese. A U.S. spotter plane found them on November 12, 1942. The Vought Kingfisher pilot couldn't fly all the crew out on the small aircraft in one flight, so the survivors lay on the wings while it taxied across forty miles of ocean to the nearest base! After the war, Rickenbacker continued his leadership of Eastern Airlines until 1959, and would then spend the rest of his life as a writer and public speaker. Eddie Rickenbacker died from a stroke in 1973.

Captains of the Clouds

USA / Warner Bros. / 1942 / Color / 113 minutes

Director: Michael Curtiz

Cast: James Cagney, Dennis Morgan, Brenda Marshall, Alan Hale, George Tobias, Reginald Gardiner

Synopsis / Aviation Content: A group of highly competitive Canadian bush pilots enlist in the RCAF Training Corps. A wartime promotional film aimed at getting civilian pilots to enlist, this was the last big-budget color film shot before Pearl Harbor and America's entry into World War II. An energetic performance from Cagney, a light atmosphere, outstanding color aerial photography of the Canadian outback and fantastic views of the RCAF in action make this film a must-see!

The bush plane sequences feature four aircraft, all with floats: a **Fairchild Model 71** (CF-NBP); a **Noorduyn Norseman Mk. I** (CF-AYO)—this was the prototype aircraft which first flew in 1935 and was leased to the film company as Cagney's aircraft marked as "CF-HGO." Two **Waco Cabin** biplanes (CF-GHV, CF-GHY) were also hired.

Featured RCAF aircraft are many of the Canadian-built **Fleet 16B Finch II** (identified RCAF s/n 4666) biplane trainers; the **Lockheed Hudson Mk. III** (identified: AE596 [msn 3951], AE597 [msn 3952] and AE601 [msn 3956]); **North American Harvard Mk. II** (identified RCAF s/n 2505, 2588, 2628, 2689, 3048) and the bare-metal, fixed undercarriage **North American Yale Mk. I** (identified RCAF s/n 3346, 3398, 3399, 3400, 3447). An unidentified **Hawker Hurricane** makes an appearance as a Messerschmitt Bf 109E in the final sequence. Background aircraft include the **Avro Anson Mk. I** (one was RCAF s/n 6538); **Fairy Battle**; a single **Lockheed Model 12 Electra Junior** and the **Northrop A-17A Nomad**.

Cockpit mock-ups were used for interiors, and models for the more dangerous stunts and aerial scenes. Cameo appearance by Air Marshall and former World War I Ace W.A. "Billy" Bishop V.C., it was Bishop who coined the phrase "Captains of the Clouds." The song written for the film became the official song of the RCAF.

Filmed in and around Trout Lake and Jumping Caribou Lake in the North Bays of Ontario. Base locations are at No. 2 RCAF Service Flying School,

Uplands, Ontario; RCAF Manning Depot; RCAF Central Flying School, Trenton, Ontario; and No. 1 RCAF Bombing and Gunnery School, Jarvis, Ontario. City scenes were filmed in Ottawa, Ontario. The Hudson bomber scenes were shot outside the Lockheed plant at Lockheed Air Terminal, Burbank, California.

Casino Royale (Non–Aviation Themed Title) see *James Bond* Series

Catch-22

USA / Paramount Pictures / 1970 / Color / 117 minutes

Director: Mike Nichols

Cast: Alan Arkin, Martin Balsam, Richard Benjamin, Arthur Garfunkel, Jack Gilford, Buck Henry, Bob Newhart, Anthony Perkins, Paula Prentiss, Martin Sheen, John Voight, Orson Welles

Synopsis / Aviation Content: An antiwar satire set in 1944 on a USAAF Mediterranean base, where some of the aircrews' sanity is in question, while others are colluding with the enemy in order to further their own private business ventures. Based on the 1961 novel of the same name by American author Joseph Heller. Classic, hysterical comedy satire gets better with

each viewing, although the second half takes an inexplicable shift to a darker tone. One of the most memorable and highly regarded aviation films, not for the amount of on-screen flying as such, but simply for the incredible feat of assembling so many B-25 bombers and capturing them so well for the big screen—a definite must-see for any aviation film fan!

B-25 Mitchells N1203 and N1042B were camera-planes only and did not have a "starring role," although N1203 was painted up for background with tail code "6A." B-25 N10V was later repainted to serve as Orson Welles's VIP aircraft. The Mitchell with Mexican civil reg. XB-HEY, was a derelict purchased in Mexico to be intentionally destroyed for the film. It's seen as the burning wreck near the start of the film and as a background derelict in other scenes. Eight of the B-25 bombers were later repainted in Mexico to represent the fictional "M&M" Air Force.

The 1943 L-5 Sentinel, N64669, was owned and flown in the film by Frank Tallman for the "Hungry Joe" scene. The aircraft was later fully restored by Sam Tabor and still flies on the Warbird scene today. Film support aircraft were a Consolidated PBY-5A Catalina (reg. N5591V / BuNo. 48446 / msn 1808), a Cessna 310B (reg. N5450A / msn 35650), and a Bell Model 47G-3B-1 (reg. N1399X / msn 6584).

Type	msn	Military s/n	Civil reg.	Film Markings
North American B-25H-5-NA Mitchell	98-21433	43-4432	N10V	6N / *Berlin Express*
North American B-25H-5-NA Mitchell	98-21644	43-4643	N1203	6A
North American B-25J-10-NC Mitchell	108-35217	43-28204	N9856C	6G / *Booby Trap*
North American B-25J-15-NC Mitchell	108-32200	44-28925	N7687C	6F / *Superman*
North American B-25J-20-NC Mitchell	108-32641	44-29366	N9115Z	6M / *Hot Pants*
North American B-25J-20-NC Mitchell	108-33162	44-29887	N10564	6Y / *Luscious LuLu*
North American B-25J-25-NC Mitchell	108-33214	44-29939	N9456Z	6C
North American B-25J-25-NC Mitchell	108-33352	44-30077	N2849G	6Q / *Denver Dumper*
North American B-25J-25-NC Mitchell	108-33768	44-30493	N9451Z	6V / *Dumbo*
North American B-25J-25-NC Mitchell	108-33924	44-30649	N9452Z	6V and 6W
North American B-25J-25-NC Mitchell	108-34023	44-30748	N8195H	6H / *Miss Renee*
North American B-25J-25-NC Mitchell	108-34076	44-30801	N3699G	6K / *Vestal Virgin*
North American B-25J-25-NC Mitchell	108-34098	44-30823	N1042B	6E
North American B-25J-30-NC Mitchell	108-34200	44-30925	N9494Z	6P / *Abominable Snow Man* and *Laden Maiden*
North American B-25J-30-NC Mitchell	108-34307	44-31032	N3174G	6D / *Free, Fast, Ready*
North American B-25J-30-NC Mitchell	108-47455	44-86701	N7681C	6J / *Annzas*
North American B-25J-30-NC Mitchell	108-47597	44-86843	N3507G	6B / *Passionate Paulette*
North American B-25J-35-NC Mitchell	108-47694	45-8843	XB-HEY	6S
Stinson L-5-VW Sentinel	76-560	42-98319	N64669	L

Hollywood aviation personality and pilot Frank Tallman, along with his company Tallmantz Aviation, Inc., were contracted to locate, furnish and fly the aircraft for *Catch-22*. Work began eight months before cameras were due to roll, and fifteen flyable B-25 bombers were located and readied in that time. One more B-25 was acquired in Mexico and additional B-25 parts were purchased as spares plus background set dressing—including a tail section for a scene of a B-25 ditched in the ocean. The B-25 Mitchells had come from all over the USA, each in various states of disrepair when found. Frank Tallman avoided any gutted aircraft or one in which the wings' roots had corroded; anything that required rewiring or had cut hydraulics wasn't purchased. The upper gun turrets on the Mitchells had all been removed when they were sold to civil owners, so new turrets were located from an ordnance firm in New York State. The turrets were fitted to the aircraft on custom mounts designed by Tallman, which even allowed them to turn. Each was positioned on the upper fuselage either at the rear of the aircraft or behind the cockpit to resemble both the B-25D and B-25J variants.

Tallman's airplanes soon became known as the *Catch-22* Air Force. As Tallman observed, they were a fully operational World War II squadron with anywhere from thirteen to eighteen operating aircraft, plus crews and spares.

Tallmantz employee Jim Appleby started a *Catch-22* Air Force training program for the pilot, co-pilot and flight engineer required on each aircraft. Because of the complexities of formation flying planned for the movie, all crews were drafted from a military and/or air tanker background and were high-time pilots in their 40s or 50s. Up to thirty hours of preproduction flight training was given before the move down to Mexico on January 1, 1969. Known B-25 pilots were James Appleby, John Bagley, Jack Bivin, Willis Fritts, Dick Gillespie, Hal Gray, Don Hackett, Danny Johnson, Steward Kunkee, Skip Marsh, Edward Mitrani, Tom Mooney, Don Ornbaum, Frank Pine (N1042B camera-plane), Wendell Reid, Terri Rossi, Frank Tallman (Chief Pilot / Aerial Supervisor) and Forest Watson. Known co-pilots and flight engineers were Wayne Berg, Dale Bradley, Richard Fischer, Jim Harjer, Dan

Hill, Jenner Knight, Mike McDonald, Jack Silva, Jim Speers, Len "Stoney" Stonich, David Viviano, Rick Wilson, Wayne Burtt, and Tallmantz mechanic Bob Siemieniewicz. Other pilot names were Frank Blaha, "Junior" Burchinal, Odel Burton, Les Hall, Marvin Jackson and Charles Rector.

This is probably one of the most dangerous and potentially lethal aerial stunts ever carried out on a motion picture. Thirteen to sixteen of the B-25 aircraft, distributed in four tight groups with wings interlocking, were to take off all together, no more than 100 feet apart. It also had to be repeated up to thirteen times: each shot took so long to set up, daylight would be lost, meaning the same scene would have to be done again the next day. The design of the runway was such that there was always a ninety-degree crosswind with winds ten knots in excess of what the B-25 flight manual stated. As Tallman stated, if anyone at the front had lost a tire or an engine on the takeoff run, there would have been a fire so big at the end of the runway, it wouldn't be out yet!

After three months in Mexico, the *Catch-22* Air Force had logged over 1,500 flight hours and shot fourteen and a half hours of film of which the filmmakers would only use seventeen minutes in the final print! This total includes the use of aircraft in background taxiing, parked shots, and the front-screen projection for the studio cockpit process shots. Tallman observed afterward that somewhere, fourteen and a half hours of the most stunning footage ever shot of the B-25 is sitting in storage.

Second Unit Aerial Director John Jordan was killed when he fell from the tail section of B-25 N1203, while attempting to take continuity stills on May 16, 1969. It was a tragic loss of such a talented aerial cameraman who had worked on so many well-known film productions. After filming concluded in August 1969, thirteen of the seventeen remaining Mitchell aircraft were sold in an auction at Orange County Airport, California, by Tallmantz Aviation, Inc. Many of these aircraft still fly today on the Warbird circuit. Actor Martin Balsam (Col. Cathcart) served as a bomber crewman during World War II.

The entire air base set was scratch-built, in-

A *Catch-22* (1970) B-25 N9451Z (s/n 44–30493) at Orange County Airport. Photograph: James H. Farmer Collection.

A group of B-25 Mitchell bombers being readied for the filming of *Catch-22* (1970) in Mexico. Photograph: James H. Farmer Collection.

cluding the runway, next to a beach northwest of the city of Guaymas, Mexico, on the Gulf of California. The set cost about one million dollars to construct—a big figure in 1969! The buildings were destroyed for the movie, but the remains of the airstrip are still there today, and the area has become a tourist attraction unofficially named Catch-22 Beach. The city locale and street scenes were all shot in Rome, Italy.

GPS Location

Catch-22 airbase and runway: N27 58.50 / W111 06.30

Factual Background: North American B-25 Mitchell

North American produced a total of 9,890 B-25 Mitchell bombers, one of the all-time great medium bombers of World War II, between 1939 and 1945. The prototype NA-40 first flew on January 29, 1939. Most were bomber versions, but two variants were produced as the B-25G / H ground attack model with a "gun nose" in place of the "glass nose." The definitive variant was the B-25J, of which 4,390 were built, and it's this type that carried on in service after the war. From 1950, Hayes Aircraft Co. of Alabama and the

Hughes Tool Co. of California modified a total of 597 B-25J aircraft into the TB-25K, TB-25L, TB-25M and TB-25N pilot and crew trainers. Hayes also upgraded nearly 1,000 B-25J aircraft for an extended service life with upgraded engines, wiring and equipment modifications. The USAF finally retired the Mitchell in 1960. Twelve of the eighteen B-25 aircraft used in *Catch-22* were TB-25N rebuilds.

Ceiling Zero

USA / Warner Bros. / 1936 / B&W / 95 minutes
Director: Howard Hawks
Cast: James Cagney, Pat O'Brien, June Travis, Stuart Erwin, Barton MacLane, Henry Wadsworth, Martha Tibbetts
Synopsis / Aviation Content: Carefree airmail pilot Cagney swaps flights with a friend, who is then killed flying into a severe storm. Cagney, left with a sense of guilt, is desperate to perfect a de-icing system to help pilots in bad weather. Excellently rated drama written by ex–naval aviator turned Hollywood screenwriter Frank "Spig" Wead, based on his 1935 stage play of the same name. Mostly shot in the studio, but some sequences were done at Alhambra Airport, California, with two **Boeing Model 100** biplanes and a Pancho Barnes–owned **Travel Air Racer**. Camera-plane is a Stearman C2B (reg. NR4099), owned and flown by famed Hollywood pilot Paul Mantz.

Central Airport

USA / Warner Bros. / 1933 / B&W / 72 minutes
Director: William A. Wellman
Cast: Richard Barthelmess, Sally Eilers, Tom Brown, Grant Mitchell, James Murray, Claire McDowell, Willard Robertson, Arthur Vinton, Charles Sellon
Synopsis / Aviation Content: After killing his passengers in a crash due to a storm, a guilt-ridden pilot starts a barnstorming career with an attractive female parachutist, only to then have to compete for her affections with his own brother, who's also an aviator. Based on the story *The Hawk's Mate* by Jack Moffitt. The ever-popular Hollywood love-triangle storyline

somewhat stifles some amazingly impressive flying sequences by Hollywood pilot Paul Mantz, this production among his earlier films. In one highlight, Mantz performs a stunt flying sequence involving low, high-speed passes of a moving train. A similar stunt got Mantz kicked out of the USAAC some years earlier, just before he was to graduate!

Type	msn	Civil reg.
Alexander Eaglerock Longwing	207	NC1412
American Eagle A-1	277	NC6969
Fairchild Model 71	675	NC2K
Ford 4-AT-D Tri-Motor	24	NC5578
Pitcairn PA-5	30	NR6708
Stearman C2B	107	NC4011
Stearman C2B	110	NC4099
Travel Air D-4000	1379	NC477N

There are a respectable number of period biplanes seen in this film. The Eaglerock Longwing, NC1412, was used as the runaway aircraft in the air-circus scene, with the American Eagle A-1, NC6969, being the airplane used to crash into it before it runs into a crowd. The Fairchild Model 71, NC2K, is a monoplane design that is crashed and totaled, doubling for the Stearman C2B, NC4011, which blows up in midair in the previous shot. The Ford Tri-Motor, NC5578, is seen at various intervals throughout the film. The Stearman C2B, NC4099, belonged to Paul Mantz; it was used in the parachute sequence and some aerobatic sequences, and also served as the camera-plane for the production. Mantz flew the Travel Air D-4000, NC477N, in the scene where he buzzes a moving train. The Pitcairn PA-5, NR6708, is the sleek-looking biplane with a pair of floats fitted and is used in the climatic rescue at the end of the movie, although much of the storm flying was done with models and a studio mock-up.

There are also various views of other **Ford Tri-Motor** (the crashed one with false reg. NC127H) aircraft, stock footage of the military **Boeing P-12, Fokker C-14, Keystone LB-7,** plus numerous scenes employing special effects and models. Filmed at United Airport, Burbank, Wilson and Los Angeles Metropolitan Airports, California. Watch for a brief scene of future star John Wayne in an uncredited role as a co-pilot.

Chain Lightning

USA / Warner Bros. / 1950 / B&W / 94 minutes
Director: Stuart Heisler
Cast: Humphrey Bogart, Eleanor Parker, Raymond Massey, Richard Whorf, James Brown
Synopsis / Aviation Content: Top B-17 pilot Bogart finds post-World War II life less profitable and is subsequently drawn into a risky job test flying a new high-performance jet aircraft. Much of the flying is done with models and special effects, given the experimental aircraft in the film are fictional creations that didn't actually fly in real life.

Hollywood pilot Paul Mantz was heavily involved with this film (although he goes uncredited). His **Boeing B-17F-50-DL Flying Fortress** (s/n 42-3360 / msn 8296 / reg. N67974) is seen in several airfield scenes during the World War II sequences. The experimental Willis JA-3 aircraft was a full-scale, scratch-built mock-up using Bell P-39 Airacobra components. It was designed, constructed and taxied at high speed by Paul Mantz himself. Wide-angle flying shots of the JA-3 were done with a North American F-86A Sabre.

The light aircraft which is nosed over by a young pilot is a **Stinson Model 108**. Background aircraft include the **Douglas C-47 Skytrain, C-54 Skymaster, Lockheed C-69 Constellation**

and **F-80C Shooting Star** (s/n 49-500, 49-508, 49-510). Much use of period combat footage during the B-17 sequences (one was B-17E s/n 41-9125), plus stock footage of the Messerschmitt Me 163 Komet jet aircraft. The B-17 cockpit was a studio mock-up.

Filmed from April to July 1949 at the Lockheed Air Terminal, Burbank, and San Fernando Valley Airport (later Van Nuys Municipal Airport), California. Screenwriter Vincent Evans was a personal friend of Bogart's and was the bombardier on the famous B-17F *Memphis Belle* during World War II. He also later flew with the *Belle*'s captain, Robert Morgan, on the B-29 Superfortress in the Pacific Theater.

Charter Pilot

USA / 20th Century–Fox / 1940 / B&W / 70 minutes
Director: Eugene Forde
Cast: Lloyd Nolan, Lynn Bari, Arleen Whelan, George Montgomery, Hobert Cavanaugh, Henry Victor, Etta McDaniel
Synopsis / Aviation Content: A charter airline pilot played by Nolan is harassed by a sinister saboteur who is trying to put his company out of business. With war clouds looming in Europe, the theme of sabotage was a strong one during the pre–World War II period and was featured in many aviation related films. Aircraft used

The fictional, non-flyable Willis JA-3 as seen in *Chain Lightning* (1950). It was partly built using Bell P-39 components by film pilot Paul Mantz. Photograph: James H. Farmer Collection.

were a **Ford 4-AT-B Tri-Motor** (reg. NC7121 / msn 35), owned by Hollywood pilot Paul Mantz, who also served as the production's stunt pilot. A **Stinson Model W** (reg. NC12146 / msn 3054), was used in the final scene. Briefly seen is a **Lockheed Model 10 Electra** and stock footage of a **Boeing Model 314** flying boat, the *Yankee Clipper*. The areas around Santa Anita, California, stand in for the country of Honduras in Central America.

China Clipper

USA / Warner Bros. / 1936 / B&W / 88 minutes
Director: Ray Enright
Cast: Pat O'Brien, Beverly Roberts, Ross Alexander, Humphrey Bogart, Marie Wilson, Joseph Crehan
Synopsis / Aviation Content: Fictional story of an obsessed man, played by O'Brien, who sets out to establish a trans-Pacific flying route. Intense, dramatic story of early pioneering airline routes was written by ex–naval aviator turned Hollywood screenwriter Frank "Spig" Wead. Excellent sequences featuring the mammoth Martin Clipper flying boat, including some rare onboard shots.

The 1935 **Martin M-130 Clipper** (reg. NC 14716 / msn 558) flying boat was one of three built by the Glenn L. Martin Co. for Pan American Airways, named *China Clipper*. It made the first trans-Pacific airmail flight from San Francisco to Manila on November 22, 1935. The onboard navigator was Fred Noonan, who would later famously disappear over the Pacific with aviatrix Amelia Earhart in 1937. In 1942, NC14716 would be impressed into U.S. Navy service with BuNo. 48231. Postwar, back in civil airline service, the Clipper flying boat would end its days in a crash in Trinidad on January 8, 1945, killing all twenty-five people onboard.

Also seen in the film were several **Ford 4-AT Tri-Motor** airliners and **Sikorsky S-42 Clipper** flying boats of Pan American, with some filming taking place at Alameda, San Francisco, California. Hollywood stunt pilot Paul Mantz worked on this film but goes uncredited. Notable as being one of actor Humphrey Bogart's earlier films.

China Doll

USA / United Artists / 1958 / B&W / 99 minutes
Director: Frank Borzage
Cast: Victor Mature, Li Hua Li, Ward Bond, Bob Mathias, Johnny Desmond, Stuart Whitman, Elaine Devry, Ann McCrea
Synopsis / Aviation Content: World War II pilot Mature flies "the hump" into China with his crew, but after a night of drinking finds he has "inherited" a young Chinese bride. An above-average romance-drama was filmed in part at Saugus-Newall Airport in California with two **Douglas C-47 Skytrain** transports and several **Vought F4U Corsair** fighters. Stock footage used features the Curtiss P-40E Warhawk and Mitsubishi G3M3 Nell, plus various other clips. The final scene has a **Douglas DC-7C** (reg. N741PA / msn 44883), of Pan American Airlines.

China's Little Devils

USA / Monogram Pictures / 1945 / B&W / 74 minutes
Director: Monta Bell
Cast: Harry Carey, Paul Kelly, "Ducky" Louie, Gloria Ann Chew, Hayward Soo Hoo, Jimmie Dodd, Ralph Lewis
Synopsis / Aviation Content: A group of young Chinese children befriend members of the American Volunteer Group in China. Low-budget story filmed at Iverson Ranch, California, with the wooden Curtiss P-40C Warhawk mock-ups built for the earlier but far more successful Republic Pictures production *Flying Tigers* (1942).

Clear and Present Danger (Non–Aviation Themed Title)

USA / Paramount Pictures / 1994 / Color / 141 minutes
Director: Phillip Noyce
Cast: Harrison Ford, Willem Dafoe, Anne Archer, Joaquim de Almeida, Henry Czerny, Harris Yulin, Donald Moffat, Miguel Sandoval
Synopsis / Aviation Content: Third film adaptation of the popular Tom Clancy novels has Har-

rison Ford fighting South American drug lords; notable for its various aircraft content. In order of appearance are two **Sikorsky MH-60K Black Hawk** helicopters provided by the 160th SOAR Nightstalkers. The drug plane blown up is an **Aero Commander 720** (reg. N825WD / msn 720-850-13). Ford arrives in Bogota on a **Raytheon Hawker 800** falsely marked as "N9747P"; it's later seen again, marked as "N81AB," but replaced by a **Gulfstream II** in the close-ups! Background aircraft on Ford's return to the U.S. is a **Lockheed C-141B Starlifter**. The aircraft carrier is the USS *Kitty Hawk* (CV-63), featuring the **McDonnell Douglas F/A-18 Hornet** and **Grumman E-2C Hawkeye**. The drug lord's helicopter is a **Bell Model 206 Jet Ranger** and the helicopter Ford hires is a twin-engined **Bell Model 412** with a 4-bladed rotor, falsely marked as "HK-37Z."

Cliffhanger (Non–Aviation Themed Title)

Italy-France-USA / TriStar Pictures / 1993 / Color / 113 minutes
Director: Renny Harlin
Cast: Sylvester Stallone, John Lithgow, Michael Booker, Janine Turner, Rex Linn, Caroline Goodall
Synopsis / Aviation Content: Action film set in the high Colorado Mountains, but filmed in Italy using two **Bell Model 205A-1** (reg. D-HOOK / msn 30206 and reg. D-HAFM / msn 30101) helicopters and an **Aerospatiale AS.350 Ecureuil**. The aerial robbery sequence, shot in the U.S., is noteworthy for its use of a **Douglas DC-9-32** (reg. N1295L / msn 47525/631, minus its tail cone!) and a **Lockheed L-1329-23E JetStar** (reg. N680TT / msn 1329-5108).

Close Encounters of the Third Kind (Non–Aviation Themed Title)

USA / Columbia Pictures / 1977 / Color / 129 minutes
Director: Steven Spielberg
Cast: Richard Dreyfuss, Francois Truffaut, Teri Garr, Melinda Dillon, Bob Balaban, Cary Guffey

Synopsis / Aviation Content: Classic, ground-breaking science-fiction epic is the UFO film all others are measured against. It features a significant Warbird and helicopter content, including a brilliant opening scene with a group of lost Grumman Avengers!

Type	msn	Military s/n	Civil reg.
Bell 204B	2196	—	N1304X
Bell 206B Jet Ranger	1557	—	N59642
Bell 206B Jet Ranger	1738	—	N90296
Bell 206B Jet Ranger	2615	—	N250CA *
Bell 206B Jet Ranger	2779	—	N2774L *
Bell 214B-1 Big Lifter	28001	—	N214RM
Grumman F6F-5 Hellcat	A-11631	BuNo.93879	N4994V
Grumman TBM-3 Avenger	3099	BuNo.86280	N86280
Grumman TBM-3 Avenger	3181	BuNo.53119	N33BM
Grumman TBM-3 Avenger	3565	BuNo.53503	N53503
Grumman TBM-3 Avenger	3866	BuNo.53804	N9710Z

* 1980 Special Edition version only.

Five World War II–vintage Grumman aircraft were provided to reenact the return of ill-fated Flight 19, which went missing in the Bermuda Triangle in 1945. In order of on-screen appearance (with listed owners) are TBM-3 N86280 (Thomas Wofford); N9710Z (David Tallichet); Hellcat N4994V (Planes of Fame, as an Avenger "stand-in" parked furthest from camera); N53503 / #82 (Confederate Air Force); and N33BM / #33 (Wilson Edwards). This sequence was filmed on El Mirage Dry Lake Bed, California, on May 17–18, 1977. Serial numbers for the *real* Flight 19 were TBM-1C: BuNo. 45714, 46094, 46325, 73209 and TBM-3: BuNo. 23307, which was lead pilot Lt. Charles ("Frank" in the movie) Taylor's aircraft.

The scenes at Devils Tower, Wyoming (GPS location: N44 35.40 / W104 41.90), made use of four Bell helicopters. The two Bell Jet Rangers, N59642 and N90296, were provided by National Helicopter Service, Inc., of California, who also painted all the choppers in army green liveries. The two Bell "Huey" types were provided by Rocky Mountain Helicopters, Inc., of Utah. The aerial sprayer was a civil-built Bell 204B, N1304X. It was brought new in 1966 by Air America, Inc., and assisted in the infamous evacuations out of Vietnam when Saigon fell on April 29–30, 1975. It later went to Canada as reg. C-GVVI, then Peru where it was written off on May 21, 2011, with reg.

One of four Grumman TBM-3 Avengers N33BM that starred in *Close Encounters of the Third Kind* (1977) as a part of Flight 19, lost in the Bermuda Triangle in 1945. Photograph: Billy Sierra.

The giant Bell 214B-1 N214RM in unmarked U.S. Army livery as seen in *Close Encounters* (1977). Photograph: Harry Wadley.

OB-1891-P. The giant Bell 214B-1 Big Lifter, used in the scene of the detainees being airlifted out, was the very first of seventy Model 214Bs to have been built and assisted with FAA 214B type certification as N49631 in 1975. Tragically, N214RM crashed after an engine failure on June 19, 1985, east of Fresno, California; both pilots onboard were killed.

"Indianapolis Air Traffic Control" was actually Los Angeles Air Route Traffic Control Center, Palmdale, California. One scene cut from the film made use of an ex–Delta Airlines **Convair CV-880** (reg. N8806E / msn 22-00-21) marked as "Air East." Two Bell Jet Rangers, N2774L and N250CA, were provided by Cinema Air, Inc., for the Gobi Desert sequence, a new scene shot for the 1980 Special Edition release.

Closing the Ring

UK-Canada-USA / The Works UK Distribution / 2007 / Color / 118 minutes
Director: Richard Attenborough
Cast: Shirley MacLaine, Christopher Plummer, Mischa Barton, Stephen Amell, Neve Campbell, Pete Postlethwaite, Brenda Fricker, Gregory Smith, Martin McCaan
Synopsis / Aviation Content: An interesting, if drawn-out, romance-drama about an elderly World War II veteran whose past comes back to light when a B-17 Flying Fortress wreck is dug up half a world away in Ireland. Brief appearance by **Boeing B-17G-110-VE Flying Fortress** (s/n 44-85829 / msn 17-8738 / reg. N3193G), owned and operated by the Yankee Air Museum of Ypsilanti, Michigan. Most other B-17 sequences were done with CGI. A brief flyover appearance by a **North American T-6 Texan**.

Cloud Dancer

USA / Blossom Pictures / 1980 / Color / 104 minutes
Director: Barry Brown
Cast: David Carradine, Jennifer O'Neill, Joseph Bottoms, Colleen Camp, Norman Alden, James Callahan, Salome Jens, Albert Salmi, Nina Van Pallandt

Synopsis / Aviation Content: Top aerobatic pilot Carradine competes at national competitions while also trying to restart a past romantic relationship and train a young pilot who earns a living flying illegal drugs. A muddled script with a weak narrative is made up for by excellent, innovative aerobatic sequences with a good variety of light aircraft types that capture the art of flying better than most films in this genre. Director Brown also produced, co-wrote the story and designed the aerial sequences.

Type	msn	Civil reg.
Aerotek-Pitts S-1S Special	1-0056	N31428
Aerotek-Pitts S-2A Special	2159	N31427
North American P-51D-25-NT Mustang	124-44471	N55JL
Piper PA-28R-201T Turbo Arrow III	28R-7703118	N4013Q
Piper PA-28R-201T Turbo Arrow III	28R-7803188	N3707M

The Pitts S-1 (single-seat) and S-2 (two-seat) Special biplane was originally designed by Florida-based Curtis Pitts, with the prototype first flying in 1944. Since then, the aircraft has revolutionized the sport of competitive aerobatics, and has also been very popular as a kit-build or scratch-build among sportsman pilots. Two Pitts biplanes were especially built for this film by Aerotek-Pitts in Afton, Wyoming, to include built-in camera mounts for aerial photography. Pitts N31428 was a single-seat S-1S Special, and N31427 was a two-seat S-2A Special. Actor David Carradine learned how to taxi these aircraft as part of his role for the film. Director Barry Brown, also a pilot with an engineering degree from LIT, invented a special 12g film camera and used these on the Aerotek aircraft. The results are spectacular, and the distorted G-force expressions on the actors' faces are the real thing! Subsequently, Pitts N31427 became reg. N121GR and N31428 became reg. N362JW.

The P-51D Mustang (s/n 44-84615) and two Piper Arrow aircraft are used in several sequences involving drug-running operations. The Mustang was owned and operated by racing pilot Jimmy Leeward. Background aircraft are a **Boeing-Stearman Kaydet, Cessna Model 140** (N2270V), **Cessna Model 172M** (N5274H), **Christen Eagle II** (N2FC / msn 0001), **Cunningham Alan COZY 3** (N89MC / msn 001), **Ford 5-AT-C Tri-Motor** (N414H / msn 74) of Scenic Airlines, **Lake LA-4 Buccaneer, Raytheon A36 Bonanza** (N7131), two **Boeing B-17** fire-bombers, and the U.S. Navy Blue Angels' **McDonnell Douglas A-4F Skyhawk** fleet.

Film pilots were Jimmy Leeward, Walt Tubb, Charlie Hillard and Tom Poberezny, who was also the production's technical advisor and chief pilot. Hillard and Poberezny were part of the then-famous "Red Devils" aerobatic display team, also flying Pitts S-1 biplanes. They first appeared at the 1969 EAA fly-in held in Illinois, and by 1971 consisted of the highly skilled team of Charlie Hillard (N442X / msn 117H), Tom Poberezny (N58J / msn 107) and Gene Soucy (N9J / msn LPS1). The Red Devils thrilled crowds with their aerobatic displays up to 1978, when they retired their aircraft and put them up for display at the EAA museum in Oshkosh, Wisconsin. Well-known sportsman pilots Bill Barber, Leo Loudenslager and Walt Tubb appear as themselves in the film. In fact, the film is dedicated to Walt Tubb, who was killed while performing a spin stunt at an air-show not long after filming was completed.

Filmed in 1978 in Phoenix, Arizona, making use of various aerobatic competition meetings, including those at Falcon Field, Chandler and Deer Valley Airports during April of that year. Actor Joseph Bottoms became so fascinated with sport flying while filming, he gained his pilot's license and even went solo during the production in a Decathlon.

Clouds Over Europe   see
Q Planes

Cock of the Air

USA / United Artists / 1932 / B&W / 80 minutes
Director: Tom Buckingham
Cast: Chester Morris, Billie Dove, Matt Moore, Walter Catlett, Luis Alberni
Synopsis / Aviation Content: In World War I France, American flier Morris pursues a relationship with seductive actress Dove. Makes use of a **Travel Air** biplane doubling as an RFC fighter type. Only notable as having been produced by enigmatic aviator / filmmaker Howard Hughes, who dragged out the mountains of stock footage from his earlier epic *Hell's Angels* (1930) to fill out the few flying scenes in this picture. A similar approach was done for Hughes's other 1932 aviation film, *Sky Devils*.

Command Decision

USA / Metro-Goldwyn-Mayer / 1948 / B&W / 107 minutes
Director: Sam Wood
Cast: Clark Gable, Walter Pidgeon, Van Johnson, Brian Donlevy, Charles Bickford, John Hodiak, Edward Arnold
Synopsis / Aviation Content: Tough commander Gable faces strong opposition from the brass and fellow crews over aircraft losses incurred to bomb a German jet-fighter factory. Based on the 1946 novel and 1947 stage play of the same name by American author and playwright William Wister Haines. Excellent film, but sparse on flying scenes; only two B-17 bombers were actually hired for filming. Many of the aerial sequences used World War II newsreel and documentary footage.

Type	msn	Military s/n	Civil reg.
Boeing B-17F-50-DL Flying Fortress	8296	42-3360	N67974
Boeing B-17G-95-DL Flying Fortress	32483	44-83842	NL1212N

Two civilian-owned Boeing B-17 Flying Fortress bombers were hired for a brief, exterior scene in the middle of the film. B-17F, N67974, was one of seventy-eight obtained by Hollywood pilot Paul Mantz in February 1946 when he purchased the World War II aircraft graveyard at Searcy Field, Stillwater, Oklahoma. It played the background Fortress in the film. It was eventually sold by Mantz, then exported to Bolivia as reg. CP-70. It crashed at La Paz on September 21, 1955. B-17G, NL1212N, was the main aircraft used in the film, marked as 38362 / *Impatient Virgin III*. It had been declared surplus in 1945 and sold onto the civilian market in 1947. Having previously appeared in the film *Fighter Squadron* (1948), it became one of four Fortresses illegally sought by Israel. However, they eventually only acquired three, as NL1212N was impounded in the Azores during transit in 1948. It's generally believed the aircraft ended up in the Dominican Republic.

Most of the B-17 aerial and combat footage was

lifted from the wartime documentary *Target For Today* (1944). Miniatures and special effects were required for a landing sequence involving a crippled Fortress. The final scene features a **Douglas C-47 Skytrain**. Filmed from April to July 1948, mostly at MGM Studios in Culver City, California. The exterior scene with the two B-17 aircraft was shot in May at San Fernando Valley Airport (later renamed Van Nuys Municipal Airport), California. William Wister Haines was an intelligence officer with the Eighth Air Force in England, attaining the rank of lieutenant colonel.

Con Air

USA / Touchstone Pictures / 1997 / Color / 111 minutes

Director: Simon West

Cast: Nicolas Cage, John Cusack, John Malkovich, Steve Buscemi, Ving Rhames, Colm Meaney, Mykelti Williamson, Rachel Ticotin

Synopsis / Aviation Content: A U.S. Marshal C-123K transport is hijacked by notorious criminals while on a prisoner transfer flight, resulting in all the usual high-action fights, shoot-outs and chases. Although the story is overly violent in places, there is an abundance of amazing air-to-air footage of the C-123, Cobra gunships and other aircraft. "Boneyard fans" will enjoy spotting all the various aircraft wrecks in several scenes.

Type	msn	Military s/n	Civil reg.
Beechcraft Expeditor Mk. 3NM	CA-265	(RCAF) 1579	N476PA
Bell 206B Jet Ranger	2615	—	N250CA
Bell 206B Jet Ranger	3025	—	N5739V
Bell AH-1S-BF Cobra	24039	76-22605	N605DB
Bell AH-1S-BF Cobra	24072	77-22734	N2734D
Bell UH-1D-BF Iroquois	5657	66-1174	N313CF
Cessna 152 Aerobat	152-83043	—	N46405
Fairchild C-123B-10-FA Provider	20155	54-706	N94DT
Fairchild C-123B-11-FA Provider	20158	54-709	N709RR
Fairchild C-123B-17-FA Provider	20245	56-4361	—

Of course, the main aeronautical attraction is the Fairchild C-123K Provider that performed all the flying scenes for the filmmakers. Owned in 1996 by Ray Petkow of Nevada as N709RR, the aircraft retained this registration for the movie but gained a blue side-stripe "United States Marshal" logo and nose art painting titled *The Jailbird*. Delivered in 1956 as a C-123B-11-FA to the 302nd

TAW, USAF with s/n 54-709; converted to C-123K standard in the late 1960s; served until retirement to MASDC, Arizona on November 4, 1981, with MASDC s/n CP0064 (later 9C0003); purchased in 1986 by Al Redrick of Classics in Aviation (CIA); to Ray Petkow in 1994, but remained in the care of Al Redrick, who served as flight engineer on the film; in 2003 sold to All West Freight for commercial work in Alaska. N709RR crashed on August 10, 2010, near Denali National Park, Alaska; all three crew members onboard lost their lives, and the airframe was totally destroyed upon impact.

With C-123K, N709RR, being a real aircraft still flying in commercial service, the more dangerous, destructive scenes were shot with two C-123K wrecks made up with in "N709RR / U.S. Marshal" markings.

The first was used for the desert scenes at Wendover AFB, Utah (Lerner Field), where the C-123K noses in during landing and needs to be dug out. It was also used in the later takeoff sequence where the aircraft goes astray through fences and other obstacles. This aircraft was C-123B-17-FA (s/n 56-4361); delivered in 1957 and retired to MASDC on July 12, 1982, with MASDC s/n CP0080 (later MC0003). There it remained until purchased for the film in 1996. The filmcrew gutted the interior and fitted it with a diesel engine, bus transmission and steering wheel so it could be taxied around the Wendover film set by a stunt driver for the various filming requirements.

The second "stand-in" came in the form of C-123B-10-FA (s/n 54-706), which performed the climatic crash into the Sands Hotel and Casino in Las Vegas at the end of the film. Delivered to the USAF in 1956, it was retired to MASDC on April 19, 1982, with MASDC s/n CP0072. In 1995, it was purchased by the Military Aircraft Restoration Corp. with civil reg. N94DT. The filmmakers soon acquired it, and on October 21, 1996, N94DT was launched at speed down a purpose-built railtrack and smashed into the Sands Hotel for the cameras. What remained was sold to the Aviation Warehouse, California, who specialize in aircraft parts for film and television.

The two Bell 206B Jet Rangers are the prison escort helicopters seen at the top of the film. The Beechcraft Expeditor Mk. 3NM was manufactured for the RCAF, delivered in 1952 and retired in 1968. It later went to the U.S. as a Beechcraft Model D18S (reg. N476PA). It flew in the movie marked as *Uncle Bob's Scenic Flights*. The two Cobra Gunships have flat-plate squared canopies, making them the AH-1S variant. Of the 498 "S" airframes built, both were in a batch of 100 that were redesignated as the AH-1P in 1987. They were later converted as TAH-1P helicopter trainers before being sold on the civilian market. UH-1D Huey (reg. N313CF) was delivered in 1966 and later upgraded to UH-1H standards. The Cessna 152 seen landing at "Lerner Field" was an airworthy 1978 Aerobat model.

The drug dealer's private jet, hidden at Lerner Field, is an unidentified **North American (Rockwell) Sabreliner** wreck painted up with the fictional Colombian registration "HK-723," and is destined to be destroyed during filming by a falling crane. Strangely, cockpit shots of this aircraft seem to show that of a Learjet. Lerner Field boneyard wrecks include, among others, the **Boeing-Vertol CH-46 Sea Knight**, **DHC-4 Caribou**, **Douglas C-118 Liftmaster**, **Sikorsky H-34 Choctaw** and **Vickers Viscount**. Wide shots of the Lerner Field boneyard are digital matte paintings. Much use was made of scale models, miniatures and special effects for the C-123K Las Vegas crash sequence.

The airport at the start of the film *The Jailbird* aircraft departs from was Oakland Intl. Airport in San Francisco for the film, but in reality was Salt Lake City Intl. Airport, Utah. The prisoner exchange in the sandstorm was filmed at Ogden-Hinckley Airport, Ogden, Utah, which played Carson City Airport, Nevada, in the film. The fictional Lerner Field, Death Valley, where *The Jailbird* lands, was filmed on the salt flats at the closed-down Wendover AFB, Utah. The C-123K interior was a studio mock-up filmed on Studio 7 at Hollywood Center Studios, California.

GPS LOCATIONS

Salt Lake City Intl. Airport, Utah: N40 47.20 / W111 58.40

Ogden-Hinckley Airport, Utah: N41 11.60 / W112 00.80

Wendover AFB, Utah: N40 43.10 / W114 01.50

FACTUAL BACKGROUND: FAIRCHILD C-123 PROVIDER

Originally the C-123 was designed as an assault glider by the Chase Aircraft Co. designated as the CG-18 Avitruc, which first flew in 1947. The potential for a piston-engined tactical cargo transport was soon realized, with a developed XC-123 prototype flying in 1949. For various political reasons concerning Chase and its majority owner, Kaiser-Frazer Corp., the C-123 production contract was awarded to the Fairchild Aircraft Corp. in Maryland. Chase built five airframes before their contract was canceled, and Fairchild went on to build another 304 C-123B aircraft from 1952 to 1958. Named the Provider, the aircraft saw outstanding service in Vietnam and gained a reputation as a tough and reliable transport aircraft capable of flying in and out of short, rough jungle airstrips. Many were converted as defoliant sprayers for the Agent Orange program. In 1966, the renamed Fairchild-Hiller Corp. began a conversion program for the C-123B, fitting wing-mounted General Electric J85-GE jet-pods with undercarriage upgrades for improved takeoff performance. A total of 183 C-123B aircraft were converted and designated the C-123K, which served until their final retirement in 1982. Since then, many C-123K Providers have made their way onto the civilian scene as cargo transports. All three Providers used for *Con Air* are C-123K conversions. Incidentally, the C-123K Provider has no underfloor cargo area; this was a "plot device" added for the film.

The Concorde ... Airport '79

International Title: *Airport '80—The Concorde*

USA / Universal Pictures / 1979 / Color / 109 minutes

Director: David Lowell Rich

Cast: George Kennedy, Alain Delon, Susan Blakely, Robert Wagner, Sylvia Kristel

Synopsis / Aviation Content: The fourth and final installment in the *Airport* series has a wealthy businessman attempting to destroy the Concorde, which is carrying documents that link him to illegal arms deals. Highly implausible storyline and situations, both in the air and on the ground, make this the least appealing of the

Airport films. The only real highlights are the aerial sequences of ill-fated French Concorde (reg. F-BTSC).

Type	msn	Civil reg.
Aerospatiale / BAC Concorde	203	F-BTSC
Agusta-Bell AB.206B Jet Ranger	8353	F-BUIA
Dassault Mystere-Falcon 20GF	145	F-BPJB
Gates Learjet 25	25-096	N564CL

The Concorde provided for filming was Air France's F-BTSC, the seventh Concorde built; it first flew on January 31, 1975, registered as F-WTSC. It was reregistered as F-BTSC in May 1975 and leased to Air France from January 1976 before being totally purchased in October 1980. Ironically, F-BTSC was the Concorde involved in the fiery crash near Paris on July 25, 2000, triggering the demise of Concorde airline service. The very last flight of a Concorde was by G-BOAF (msn 216), on November 26, 2003. A total of twenty Concorde aircraft were built from 1966 to 1979, with the first prototype maiden flight on March 2, 1969. There were ten built by France's Aerospatiale and ten by Great Britain's BAC, later to become BAe in 1977. Production was split down the middle, each country producing one prototype, one pre-production prototype and eight production aircraft.

The Desault Falcon 20 is a French-designed and -built private jet, F-BPJB, and was marked in the film as "H Industries" as the executive jet to Robert Wagner's character. Other featured aircraft are a **Bell 206B Jet Ranger** (F-BUIA), several French **Dassault Mirage** jet fighters, **Learjet 25** (N564CL), a **McDonnell Douglas F-4 Phantom II** drone conversion (marked as 9420 / 40), and two **McDonnell Douglas F-15A Eagles**. Aircraft interiors were studio mock-ups with a large use of models and special effects for the more dramatic aerial scenes.

Courage Under Fire

USA / 20th Century–Fox / 1996 / Color / 112 minutes
Director: Edward Zwick
Cast: Denzel Washington, Meg Ryan, Lou Diamond Phillips, Michael Moriarty, Matt Damon, Bronson Pinchot, Seth Gilliam, Scott Glenn
Synopsis / Aviation Content: A Medal of Honor is to be posthumously awarded to a female Army Medivac pilot, but the investigating colonel finds there's more to the story than meets the eye. One of the first films to use the 1991 Gulf War as a story setting, this riveting drama features some amazing helicopter work, making it a definite must-see for all Huey fans!

Provided to the filmmakers were up to three ex-military **Bell UH-1H Iroquois** (one was reg. N313CF), two **AH-1S Cobra** (reg. N605DB, N2734D) gunships, and up to two UH-1H Iroquois derelict fuselages for post-crash scenes. The two Fairchild-Republic A-10A Thunderbolt II aircraft appear to be models and special effects. Filming took place in Texas from October 1995 to January 1996.

The Court-Martial of Billy Mitchell

Aka (UK Title): *One Man Mutiny*
USA / Warner Bros. / 1955 / Color / 100 minutes
Director: Otto Preminger
Cast: Gary Cooper, Charles Bickford, Ralph Bellamy, Rod Steiger, Elizabeth Montgomery, Fred Clark, James Daly, Jack Lord, Peter Graves, Darren McGavin
Synopsis / Aviation Content: Relatively slow-paced account of U.S. Army General Billy Mitchell's court-martial for his outspoken views on the armed forces' lack of vision for the development of air power. Featured aircraft were Hollywood stunt pilot Paul Mantz's **DeHavilland DH.4M-1** (reg. N3258 / msn ET-4); **Grumman J2F-6 Duck** (either N67790 or N1196N), doubling as an early Loening amphibian, and a **Standard J-1** (reg. N62505 / msn T4595) biplane. Mantz was also the film's aerial coordinator.

FACTUAL BACKGROUND: BILLY MITCHELL

William Lendrum Mitchell (December 28, 1879–February 19, 1936) is widely regarded as being the father of U.S. military airpower. He attained the rank of brigadier general during World War I in France, commanding American air combat units. Returning to the U.S., he held a high position in the Air Service and began promoting aircraft as the future of military power. His relentless criticisms and views regarding both the Army's and Navy's lack for foresight for air power made Mitchell many enemies in both military and political circles. Mitchell was demoted to colonel in March 1925, and after several fatal accidents of military aircraft, including the airship *Shenandoah*, he further accused the military of an almost treasonable behavior towards the defense of the country. This resulted in President Coolidge's direct order to court-martial Mitchell in November 1925. After a hearing he was found guilty of insubordination and was suspended from active duty for five years. Mitchell instead resigned on February 1, 1926, and spent the last ten years of his life writing about air power. He died in 1936 from a bad influenza infection coupled with a weak heart. His 1925 book *Winged Defense* predicted a coming war with Japan and a surprise attack on Hawaii using aircraft. The subsequent course of history would help vindicate Mitchell, and in 1942 President Roosevelt posthumously elevated his rank to that of major general. Numerous other recognitions would follow, including the naming of the World War II North American B-25 bomber, the "Mitchell," in his honor.

Crimson Romance

USA / Mascot Pictures / 1934 / B&W / 71 minutes

Director: David Howard

Cast: Ben Lyon, Sari Maritza, Erich von Stroheim, Hardie Albright, James Bush, William Bakewell

Synopsis / Aviation Content: During World War I, two loyal friends end up on opposite sides of the war, flying against one another all the while in love with the same woman. Some use of a **Royal Aircraft Factory S.E.5** biplane for scenes with actor Ben Lyon. The rest of the aerial sequences were made up of footage from Howard Hughes's *Hell's Angels* (1930), in which Lyon also starred.

The Crowded Sky

USA / Warner Bros. / 1960 / Color / 105 minutes

Director: Joseph Pevney

Cast: Dana Andrews, Rhonda Fleming, Efrem Zimbalist Jr., John Kerr, Anne Francis, Keenan Wynn, Tony Donahue

Synopsis / Aviation Content: An aerial disaster tale has an Air Force jet trainer, piloted by Zimbalist, colliding with a civilian airliner piloted by Andrews in the skies over the United States. Much of the film is a series of flashbacks depicting the lives of the main characters in the lead-up to the collision, which doesn't happen until the last third of the film.

The provided airliner was a National Airlines **Douglas DC-6B** marked as "Trans States," with the USAF jet a **Lockheed T-33A Shooting Star** falsely marked as "8255." Background aircraft include brief views of a Convair R4Y Samaritan, Lockheed Constellation and several North American F-86H Sabre jets. Ironically, actors Dana Andrews and Efrem Zimbalist, Jr. would reunite for the similar film, *Airport 1975* (1974), but this time Zimbalist would be the airline pilot and Andrews piloting the small plane in distress.

Dakota Harris   see   Sky Pirates

The Dam Busters

UK / Associated British Picture Corp. / 1955 / B&W / 120 minutes

Director: Michael Anderson

Cast: Richard Todd, Michael Redgrave, Ursula Jeans, Basil Sydney, Patrick Barr, Ernest Clark, Derek Farr

Synopsis / Aviation Content: Classic recreation of 617 Squadron's 1943 raid on the Ruhr Dams led by Wing Commander Guy Gibson using a unique bouncing bomb designed by British engineer and inventor Barnes Wallis. An intelligent, true aviation classic whose narrative is conducted in a docudrama style, not only one of the best British war films ever made, but also one of the most famous and enduring in the aviation genre. Based on the 1951 book of the same name by Australian author Paul Brickhill and the 1946 book *Enemy Coast Ahead* by Guy Gibson, V.C. A real crowd-pleaser for the amazing aerial photography of the Lancaster bomber, "The Dam Busters March" score by Eric Coates has since gained significant recognition as an aviation signature theme.

NX673, NX679, NX782 and RT686 were taken out of storage at Aston Down in Gloucestershire and flown for the film by several Avro Lincoln crews from RAF Hemswell. All had been built in 1945 by Austin Motors at Longbridge and saw active duty in the RAF, the last being put into storage in 1953. Three of the Lancasters—NX673, NX679 and RT686—were converted into the "B.Mk. III (Special)" configuration, which was the designation for the Dam Busters Lancasters. A group from A.V. Roe Repair Organisation arrived at Hemswell and modified the aircraft by removing the mid-upper turret, belly radome and bomb-bay doors. They then bolted into place a large bouncing bomb mock-up which was for show only and could not be dropped from the aircraft. The size of the bomb as depicted was larger than the real thing which, in 1954, was still classified by the British government—the finer details of the raid weren't made public until 1963. NX679 was repainted as Guy Gibson's aircraft AJ-G with s/n ED932 for close-up shots; this aircraft was, in fact, briefly part of the actual 617 Squadron in 1945. NX782 retained its original bomb-bay configuration, marked as ZN-G for the training flight scenes made before the raid took place. After filming, the four Lancasters were sold for scrap to British Aluminium Co. on July 17, 1956.

Assigned RAF Pilot / Flight Engineer pairings were: Flt/Lt Ken Souter (*Chief Pilot*) / F/Sgt Jack Worthington; F/Sgt Joe Kmiecik / F/Sgt Duncan "Jock" Cameron; Fg/Off Dick Lambert / Sgt Dennis Wheatley; F/Sgt Ted Szuwalski / Sgt Mike Cawsey and Sgt Eric Quinney / Sgt Bill Parry. Other crew members to serve on the film were: Fg/Off Colin Batchelor (*Navigator*), F/Sgt Miles (*Air Signaler*), Sgt James Fell (*Air Signaler*), Sgt Bill French (*Air Signaler*) and Sgt G.W. Wrightson (*Gunner*).

Type	Military s/n	Film Markings
Avro Lancaster B.Mk. VII	NX673	AJ-P
Avro Lancaster B.Mk. VII	NX679	AJ-G / ED932
Avro Lancaster B.Mk. VII	NX782	ZN-G
Avro Lancaster B.Mk. VII	RT686	AJ-M
DeHavilland Mosquito B.Mk. 35	VR803	VR803
Vickers Wellington T.10	MF628	MF628

UNCONFIRMED DATA

There have been persistent rumors of a "fifth" Lancaster used in the film. A B.Mk. VII (s/n NX739) was borrowed from Boscombe Down, where it was in service for RAF photographic work. It did some aerial filming but served mainly as a standby aircraft in case of mechanical faults to the other four Lancasters. It was supposedly marked as AJ-A.

The Wellington (s/n MF628) bomber briefly seen taking off was originally built in 1944 by Vickers at Blackpool. It was, in 1954, the only airworthy bomber of its kind still flying, and is today preserved at the RAF Hendon Museum. The Mosquito (VR803), briefly seen in a ground scene, was built in 1948 by Airspeed at Christchurch; its subsequent history after the film is unknown. Further scenes of the Wellington and Mosquito made use of archive footage from RAF test films during World War II.

Background aircraft doubling for Lancasters in wide shots are Avro Lincoln bombers, a development of the Lancaster, and a lone Airspeed Oxford (RAF s/n PH462) can also be seen at one point. Aerial unit camera-planes were an RAF Vickers Varsity T.1 (RAF s/n WJ920) and the Wellington bomber (s/n MF628). Actors Richard Todd and Robert Shaw learned the start-up drill for the Lancaster under the supervision of an RAF engineer kneeling out of shot—that is actually Todd in the film starting the engines and taxiing the Lancaster around!

A real Lancaster flight-deck and front section was acquired for studio filming, along with mock-ups of other Lancaster sections for aircraft interior filming. Large-scale models of the Ruhr Dams and surrounding areas were built at Elstree Studios, Hertfordshire, as were scale models of the Lancasters for special effects as required.

Aerial cinematographer Gilbert Taylor served during World War II in the RAF Volunteer Reserve and flew several Lancaster missions as a mid-upper gunner and cameraman filming bombing raids.

Filming began in April 1954 at 617 Squadron's actual home on RAF Scampton, where base exteriors around buildings and hangars were filmed. Lancaster start-up and taxi scenes were shot at RAF Hemswell, with most of the aerial scenes based out of this airfield as well. The actual takeoffs were filmed on the grass runway at RAF Kirton-in-Lindsey to replicate the real wartime grass strip that Scampton had during the war. The Ruhr dams and surrounding areas were, in fact, filmed over Lake Windermere in Cumbria and the Derwent Dam and reservoir in the Derbyshire Valley Peak District; this dam was one of three used by 617 Squadron for practice runs in 1943. The Lancasters were based out of RAF Silloth, Cumbria, in August and September 1954 for the filming of these scenes. Interior sets were built at Elstree Studios; the operations room during the raid was a full-scale replica with measurements taken from the actual room at Grantham, which had been locked up since 1945. The huge water tank was filmed inside the building of Tank No. 2 at the National Physical Laboratory in Teddington and was the actual one used by Barnes Wallis to test his theories in 1942 and 1943. Filming was completed by September 1954. The flood shots at the end were a natural disaster that occurred in the Ruhr Valley, Germany, during the filming schedule; a film crew was dispatched to record it.

GPS Locations

RAF Hemswell, Lincolnshire (closed 1967): N53 24.00 / W000 34.60

RAF Kirton-in-Lindsey, Lincolnshire: N53 28.00 / W000 34.70

RAF Scampton, Lincolnshire: N53 18.20 / W000 33.05

Derwent Dam, Derbyshire: N53 24.30 / W001 44.50

Factual Background: Operation Chastise

The codename for the bouncing bomb was Upkeep and the operation was code named Chastise. The raid took place on the night of May 16–17, 1943, with Wing Commander Guy Gibson leading nineteen Lancaster B.Mk.III (Special) conversions into Germany. Below is a table of the Dams Raid; the film concentrates on the First

Code / military s/n	Take-off Time	Dam Attacked	Bombing Result	Aircraft
AJ-M / ED765/G	—	—	—	First prototype
AJ-C / ED817/G	—	—	—	Second prototype
AJ-Q / ED915/G	—	—	—	Unserviceable—ED825 used
AJ-X / ED933/G	—	—	—	Reserve aircraft
First Wave				
AJ-G / ED932/G	2139	Mohne	Hit—no breach	Returned
AJ-M / ED925/G	2139	Mohne	Miss—overshoot	Shot down during attack
AJ-P / ED909/G	2139	Mohne	Miss—burst short	Returned
AJ-A / ED887/G	2147	Mohne	Hit—no breach	Shot down during return
AJ-J / ED906/G	2147	Mohne	Hit—Dam breached	Returned
AJ-L / ED929/G	2147	Eder	Hit—no breach	Returned
AJ-Z / ED937/G	2159	Eder	Miss—overshoot	Shot down during return
AJ-B / ED864/G	2159	—	—	Crashed en route
AJ-N / ED912/G	2159	Eder	Hit—Dam breached	Returned
Second Wave				
AJ-E / ED927/G	2128	—	—	Shot down en route
AJ-W / ED921/G	2129	—	—	Mission aborted
AJ-K / ED934/G	2130	—	—	Shot down en route
AJ-H / ED936/G	2131	—	—	Mission aborted
AJ-T / ED825/G	2201	Sorpe	Hit—no breach / damaged	(Third prototype) Returned
Third Wave				
AJ-C / ED910/G	0009	—	—	Shot down en route
AJ-S / ED865/G	0011	—	—	Shot down en route
AJ-F / ED918/G	0012	Sorpe	Hit—no breach	Returned
AJ-O / ED886/G	0014	Bever	Hit—no breach	Returned
AJ-Y / ED924/G	0015	—	—	Mission aborted

Wave, with the story unfolding, for the most part, as it did on the actual mission. Note that the Second Wave crew of AJ-Q / ED915 found their Lancaster to have a mechanical fault, forcing them to use the third prototype AJ-T / ED825.

Type	msn	Military s/n	Civil reg.
North American B-25J-35-NC Mitchell	108-47647	44-86893	N6123C
Supermarine Spitfire LF.Mk. Vb	CBAF.2403	EP120	G-LFVB
Supermarine Spitfire LF.Mk. Vb	CBAF.2461	BM597	G-MKVB
Supermarine Spitfire LF.Mk. VIIIc	6S/583793	MV154	G-BKMI
Supermarine Spitfire LF.Mk. IXb	CBAF.IX552	MH434	G-ASJV

Danger in the Skies   see   *The Pilot*

Dangerous Moonlight

U.S. Title: *Suicide Squadron*
UK-USA / RKO Radio Pictures / 1941 / B&W / 94 minutes
Director: Brian Desmond Hurst
Cast: Anton Walbrook, Sally Gray, Derrick De Marney, Cecil Parker, Percy Parsons, Kenneth Kent
Synopsis / Aviation Content: Polish piano virtuoso and fighter pilot Walbrook meets American reporter Gray in Warsaw just as Germany invades, starting World War II. A great example of one of the many films made during this period where the title bears no resemblance to the story premise! Limited aerial action features actual combat footage which includes the Supermarine Spitfire. Filmed at D&P Studios, Denham, Buckinghamshire, England. U.S. prints released in 1942 by Republic Pictures at 82 minutes.

Dark Blue World

Czech Republic-UK / CinemArt / 2001 / Color / 108 minutes
Director: Jan Sverak
Cast: Ondrej Vetchy, Krystof Hadek, Tara Fitzgerald, Oldrich Kaiser, Hans-Jorg Assmann, Charles Dance
Synopsis / Aviation Content: Two Czechoslovakian pilots head to England in 1939 after their country is occupied by Nazi Germany, then join the RAF flying Spitfires. A genuine period atmosphere is created throughout with seamless picture and sound editing that make for pleasing and outstanding flying and dogfight sequences. The film has since developed a respectable cult following among Warbird enthusiasts.

The Czech aircraft in the opening scenes were Czech-built **Aero C-104** biplanes, a postwar license-built version of the German Bucker Bu. 131 Jungmann. The unfortunately silver-clad, no-gun-turreted B-25J was hired from the Flying Bulls, GmbH, Austria. Four flyable Spitfires were hired for filming coming from the Fighter Collection, Duxford (G-LFVB), Historic Flying Ltd., Audley End (G-MKVB), the Air Museum Ltd., North Weald (G-BKMI) and the Old Flying Machine Co., Duxford (G-ASJV).

GB Replicas Ltd. of the UK built several full-scale Spitfire mock-ups for ground scenes. The camera-helicopter for some sequences was a Russian-built Mil Mi-8 Hip. Much use of models and CGI in the flying and dogfight sequences, plus several scale RC flying models of Spitfires. Stock footage and outtakes were used of CASA 2.111Ds, Buchons, Spitfires and Hurricanes from *Battle of Britain* (1969) and B-17s from *Memphis Belle* (1990). Filmed at Hradcany Airport, Ralsko, Czech Republic (GPS Location: N50 37.15 / E014 44.20), which has been closed since 1991.

Darling Lili

USA / Paramount Pictures / 1970 / Color / 137 minutes
Director: Blake Edwards
Cast: Julie Andrews, Rock Hudson, Jeremy Kemp, Lance Percival, Michael Witney, Gloria Paul, Jacques Marin, Andre Maranne
Synopsis / Aviation Content: Musical film about World War I stage performer Andrews, who's really a German spy working under cover in England. Complications set in when she falls for top Allied pilot Hudson. Aerial sequences are sparse but extremely well executed. One highlight is the aerial strafing of a German airfield by Hudson flying a stolen Fokker Triplane! Mainly notable for the six Currie Wot biplanes converted as S.E.5 replicas.

Type	msn	Civil reg.	Film Markings
Currie Wot S.E.5a replica	1590	G-AVOT	A5435
Currie Wot S.E.5a replica	1591	G-AVOU	A4850
Currie Wot S.E.5a replica	1592	G-AVOV	A7001
Currie Wot S.E.5a replica	1593	G-AVOW	A5202
Currie Wot S.E.5a replica	1594	G-AVOX	A6262
Currie Wot S.E.5a replica	1595	G-AVOY	A1313

The Currie Wot was a small 1937 aerobatic biplane design that sold widely in the home-built category. Six of these fuselages were converted into 4/5 scale replicas of the **Royal Aircraft Factory S.E.5** biplane fighter of World War I by Slingsby Sailplanes Ltd. at Kirkbymoorside, Yorkshire, in 1967. They were designated by the company as the Slingsby Type 56 S.E.5a and were all powered by a 115 hp Lycoming O-235-C2A engine. Re-registered in Ireland with reg. EI-ARH / EI-ARM, in mid–1967 they were based out of Casement Aerodrome, Dublin, for filming.

Other aircraft used were two **Miles S.E.5a** replicas, two **Fokker Dr.I Triplane** replicas, three **Fokker D.VII-65** replicas, two **Pfalz D.IIIa** replicas and a **Caudron C.277**. The German and British airfields were both located at Western Aerodrome, Leixlip near Dublin, Ireland. See under *The Blue Max* (1966) for details on all these replicas and locations. Several mock-ups were built for airfield dressing, stunt performances and destruction.

Filmed in Belgium, France, Ireland and Paramount Studios, California, from mid–1967 into 1968. Aerial sequences were supervised by renowned second unit director Anthony Squire, who also did the aerial sequences for *The Sound Barrier* (1952) and *The Blue Max* (1966). All Currie Wot S.E.5a replicas were later used for a 1969 Cliff Robertson production titled *I Shot Down Richthofen, I Think*. However, this production was never completed and never released.

The Dawn Patrol

Television Title: ***Flight Commander***
USA / First National Pictures / 1930 / B&W / 108 minutes
Director: Howard Hawks
Cast: Richard Barthelmess, Douglas Fairbanks Jr., Neil Hamilton, William Janney, James Finlayson, Clyde Cook
Synopsis / Aviation Content: During World War I, Royal Flying Corps commander Hamilton is under strict orders to push new, inexperienced pilots into combat, which divides him from his fellow airmen. Highly regarded as one of the first true classics of the genre to explore the stress and futility of war, it was unfortunately, at the time of its release, overshadowed by another aviation film—the more bombastic *Hell's Angels* (1930). The aerial footage is outstanding, featuring mostly Travel Air 2000 / 4000 biplanes doubling as both British and German types. It subsequently provided much footage for later Hollywood productions, including the 1938 remake. The story is based on an original outline penned by American writer John Monk Saunders that would win him the Academy Award for Best Story in 1931.

More than thirty-eight aircraft were acquired for filming, which consisted for the British forces of four non-flying French **Nieuport 28C-1** biplanes for ground scenes; eight **Travel Air 2000 / 4000** (seven were reg. NC2743, NC3621, NC4419, NC477M, NC4835, NC688K and NR4419) biplanes dressed as Nieuports for the flying scenes; two **Thomas-Morse S-4C Scout** biplanes for set dressing and crash scenes; with two **Travel Air 4-U Speedwing** biplanes for other sequences. For the German aircraft there were the **Travel Air 2000 / 4000** biplanes reconfigured as the German Fokker D.VII, nicknamed as "Wichita Fokkers"; two static, original **Pfalz D.XII** biplanes for ground shots; and five **Curtiss JN-4 Jenny** and two **Standard J-1** (reg. NC2627, NC2629) biplanes dressed as German fighters for background and destruction sequences. Also provided were three **AEG Biplanes**; two **Boeing C-W** biplanes; five **Great Lakes Model 2T-1** (reg. NC542K, NC543K, NC544K, NC841H and NC842H); two **Laird Swallow J-5** (one was reg. NC8730); two **Orenco** biplanes; one **Sopwith Snipe**; and one **Waco Taperwing** (reg. NC719E). Three observation balloons were also purchased.

Several Travel Airs and a J-6 Stearman (reg. NC656K) biplane were used as camera-planes, with Howard Hawks, a former World War I fighter pilot, flying some of these aircraft himself to ensure he captured the right angles. One Travel Air (reg. NC477M) crash-landed after being damaged by an exploding JN-4 Jenny, detonated on the ground by the film crew just as it overflew the charge-laden aircraft. Chief pilot was Leo Nomis, and other studio-employed pilots were Robbie Robinson, Rupert McAllister, Frank Tomick, Ira Reed, Leon Hayes, Roy Wilson, Roscoe Turner, Garland Lincoln, Pancho Barnes and Roy Minor.

Filming took place from February 20 to April 14, 1930, at the northwest end of San Fernando Valley, with the British airfield being in the Triunfo Canyon area. The concluding scene was filmed over a rail line near Van Nuys, California.

FACTUAL BACKGROUND: JOHN MONK SAUNDERS

Born on November 22, 1897, Saunders was a screenwriter and novelist known for writing well-crafted character stories exploring human emotions. A flight instructor in the Air Service during World War I, he sought combat experience but never got it, which dogged him the rest of his life. Best known for writing the stories of legendary aviation films *Wings* (1927) and *The Dawn Patrol* (1930), the second earning him an Academy Award for Best Story. Was married to *King Kong* (1933) actress Fay Wray. He committed suicide in Florida on March 11, 1940. Saunders wrote either the screenplay or story for *Wings* (1927), *The Legion of the Condemned* (1928), *The Dawn Patrol* (1930 / 1938), *The Last Flight* (1931), *The Eagle and the Hawk* (1933), *Ace of Aces* (1933), *Devil Dogs of the Air* (1935), *West Point of the Air* (1935) and *Conquest of the Air* (1936; also director).

The Dawn Patrol

USA / Warner Bros. / 1938 / B&W / 103 minutes
Director: Edmund Goulding
Cast: Errol Flynn, Basil Rathbone, David Niven, Donald Crisp, Melville Cooper, Barry Fitzgerald, Carl Esmond
Synopsis / Aviation Content: A remake of the 1930 original reshot with a new director, cast and scriptwriter, but retaining the original 1930 story and the same aerial / combat footage. The updated and newly shot dramatic scenes greatly improve the pace and themes of the story, largely thanks to Flynn and Niven's outstanding performances. But avid fans of Howard

Hawks still regard the original as the better of the two.

With the original film's aerial footage already available, it remained only to film and insert new ground scenes and a few flying shots. The British scenes were shot with four **Garland-Lincoln LF-1 / LF-2** Nieuport 28 converted replicas and several **Thomas-Morse S-4C Scout** biplanes doubling as Nieuport 28 fighters in taxi and takeoff scenes. The German scenes were done with several **Travel Air 2000 / 4000** "Wichita Fokker" biplanes doubling as the Fokker D.VII and two genuine **Pfalz D.XII** as static aircraft. Filmed from August to September 1938 at the Warner Bros. Ranch near Calabasas, California.

Death Flies East

USA / Columbia Pictures / 1935 / B&W / 65 minutes
Director: Phil Rosen
Cast: Conrad Nagel, Florence Rice, Raymond Walburn, Geneva Mitchell, Robert Allen, Oscar Apfel, Miki Morita, Purnell Pratt
Synopsis / Aviation Content: A now largely forgotten film has one notable claim to fame as the first-ever "airliner disaster" movie, a plotline which was later brought to the fore with *Thirteen Hours by Air* (1936) and refined into an almost stand-alone genre with *The High and the Mighty* (1954) two decades later. American Airlines provided a **Douglas DC-2-120** (reg. NC14283 / msn 1316) to the film studio for the flying scenes. This aircraft was delivered in 1934 to American; in 1940 it went to Indian Airlines as VT-AOR, then into RAF service in 1941 as a DC-2K with s/n DG470. It was written off in a non-fatal accident in Pakistan on November 11, 1943. Aircraft interiors and flight-deck scenes were created in a studio.

Decision Against Time   see The Man in the Sky

Desperate Journey

USA / Warner Bros. / 1942 / B&W / 107 minutes
Director: Raoul Walsh

Cast: Errol Flynn, Ronald Reagan, Nancy Coleman, Raymond Massey, Alan Hale, Arthur Kennedy

Synopsis / Aviation Content: An RAF Fortress Mk. I (with the turrets of a B-17B) crashes in Nazi Germany while on a secret bomb mission, with the five surviving crew evading capture in the hope of getting back to England. A very refreshing fantasy action yarn made purely for entertainment is an absolute must-see with just the right mix of drama, action and comedy, not to mention all the usual Errol Flynn heroics! Max Steiner's rousing score keeps perfect pace with the spot-on script and direction. Just a pity it's lumbered with such a downbeat title.

Featured aircraft are a Boeing B-17B Flying Fortress accomplished with models and a large-scale interior mock-up for studio filming; Messerschmitt Bf 109 and Junkers Ju 87 Stuka models and studio mock-ups (the Stuka in close up is actually an AT-6 Texan!); a 1934 tri-motor **Stinson Model A** doubling as a Junkers Ju 52 in one brief taxiing shot; and a **Lockheed Hudson Mk. III** (RAF s/n T9386 / msn 414-2421) during the finale. Notably, this Hudson is the very first of 427 Mk. III airframes built for the RAF, this one being delivered on September 9, 1940. For reasons unknown it was retained in Canada during delivery and by 1941 appears to have been back at Lockheed in California, where filming took place.

Destination Tokyo see *Pilot #5*

Devil Dogs of the Air

USA / Warner Bros. / 1935 / B&W / 85 minutes
Director: Lloyd Bacon
Cast: James Cagney, Pat O'Brien, Margaret Lindsay, Frank McHugh, John Arledge, Helen Lowell
Synopsis / Aviation Content: Show-off civilian pilot Cagney joins the USMC, driving his superiors to distraction, but slowly learns the values of teamwork and respect in the service. Based on the story *Devil Dogs* by former World War I flight instructor John Monk Saunders. An overall well made and highly regarded film among

aviation buffs for its capture of mid–1930s naval aviation, featuring several soon to become obsolete biplane types.

Featured aircraft are a **Travel Air D-4000** (reg. NC406N / msn 1337) marked as *Tommy O'Toole / World's Greatest Aviator*; **Stearman C2B** (reg. NR4099 / msn 110) doubling for a Vought O2U-1 in aerial stunt sequences and flown by Hollywood stunt pilot Paul Mantz; USMC sequences feature the **Boeing F4B-3** biplane fighter (BuNo. A-8894); **Curtiss OC-1 Falcon** biplane; the single **Curtiss RC-1 Kingbird** transport (BuNo. A-8846); **Ford RR-4 Tri-Motor** staff transport (BuNo. A-8840); **Loening OL-9** amphibian; **Vought O2U-1 Corsair** biplane (BuNo. A-7938, A-7939) and **Vought O3U-6 Corsair** biplane. Some full-scale mock-ups were built of the Travel Air and O2U-1 for studio photography. Filmed at NAS San Diego, California and at sea during the U.S. Navy's 1934 fleet exercise off the San Diego coast onboard the aircraft carrier USS *Saratoga* (CV-3).

GPS LOCATION

NAS San Diego, California: N32 42.00 / W117 12.45

Diamonds Are Forever (Non–Aviation Themed Title) see *James Bond* Series

Die Another Day (Non–Aviation Themed Title) see *James Bond* Series

Die Hard 2 (Non–Aviation Themed Title)

Alternate Title: *Die Hard 2: Die Harder*
USA / 20th Century–Fox / 1990 / Color / 124 minutes
Director: Renny Harlin
Cast: Bruce Willis, Bonnie Bedelia, William Atherton, Reginald VelJohnson, Franco Nero, William Sadler, John Amos, Dennis Franz, Art Evans, Fred Dalton Thompson
Synopsis / Aviation Content: The first sequel in the hugely successful *Die Hard* series has terror-

ists holding Washington Dulles Intl. Airport for ransom until a detained comrade on an incoming flight is released. Developed from the 1987 novel *58 Minutes* by American author Walter Wagner. A far-fetched scenario has even more far-fetched situations, but with so much top-notch action, all that doesn't really seem to matter. A good line-up of various aircraft from start to finish makes for great viewing—*Yippie Ki Yay!*

Type	msn	Civil reg.
Aerospatiale AS.350B Ecureuil	1227	N300CE
Boeing 747-121	19657/37	N473EV
Fairchild C-123B-11-FA Provider	20158	N709RR
Lockheed L-1011-500 Tristar	193Y-1184	N755DL

The Squirrel helicopter doubled as the *WNTV Night-Time News* chopper for the 747 wing stunt. The Boeing 747 was provided by Evergreen Intl. Airlines. It was first delivered to Pan American on April 29, 1970, as N753PA; after eighteen years of service, it then went to CNA in 1988, then to TWA in the same year. Evergreen acquired it on July 13, 1989, as N473EV and converted the aircraft into a Special Freighter (SF). The 747 was retired in 1997 and finally scrapped at Marana, Arizona, in 2001. The aircraft was used in ground taxi scenes for the wing-fight sequence. The C-123K (s/n 54-709) was provided by owner Al Redick and featured dummy jet-pods to represent a somewhat fictional all-jet version of the aircraft. It's only seen landing and in ground taxi scenes, with a model used for the actual flying sequences. The L-1011 Tristar, ex–Delta Airlines, was used in the final scene marked as NEA.

Two **Bell Model 204** helicopters double as military helicopters. Much use is made of models, including the Boeing 727, Douglas DC-8, Lockheed L-1011 Tristar and McDonnell Douglas F-4 Phantom II. Filmed from November 28, 1989, to April 6, 1990, at numerous airport locations including Los Angeles Intl. Airport; Stapleton Intl. Airport, Colorado; Grant County Airport, Washington; Alpena County Regional Airport and Kincheloe AFB, both in Michigan.

Dive Bomber

USA / Warner Bros. / 1941 / Color / 127 minutes
Director: Michael Curtiz
Cast: Errol Flynn, Fred MacMurray, Ralph Bellamy, Alexis Smith, Robert Armstrong, Regis Toomey, Allen Jenkins
Synopsis / Aviation Content: U.S. Navy flight surgeon Flynn and squadron leader MacMurray

One of the many Grumman F3F-2 naval fighters, BuNo. 1039, employed to fill out the background at NAS San Diego for the 1941 film *Dive Bomber*. Photograph: James H. Farmer Collection.

Grumman F3F-2 fighters on the ramp at NAS San Diego for *Dive Bomber* (1941). The date on the clapperboard says March 20, 1941. Photograph: James H. Farmer Collection.

strive to solve the problems of blackouts in dive-bomber pilots. What was really made as a prewar Hollywood "preparedness film" is now an insightful and wonderful look back at U.S. naval aviation in the period before the Pearl Harbor attack. Excellent, sharp color photography covers many (even then) obsolete naval aircraft types not seen in detail anywhere else, making this a true classic for any naval aviation fan. Based on a story and co-written by former naval aviator turned Hollywood screenwriter Frank "Spig" Wead.

The main aircraft provided were numerous examples of the **Curtiss SBC-4 Helldiver** biplane; **Grumman F3F-2 / -3** biplane (including BuNo. 0967, 0978, 0984, 0988, 1030, 1039, 1451); **Naval Aircraft Factory N3N-1 / -3 Canary** biplane (including BuNo. 0701, 1978, 2590, 2717) and **Vought SB2U-2 Vindicator** (including BuNo. 1333, 1381). Of noticeable absence were more modern types like the Douglas SBD Dauntless and Grumman F4F Wildcat, which are believed to have been kept out of filming for security reasons.

A **Lockheed Model 10 Electra** was used in the high-altitude test sequence, and a **Ryan ST-A** makes an appearance doubling as an RAF fighter prototype. Background aircraft include the **Brewster F2A Buffalo, Consolidated PBY Catalina, Consolidated PB2Y Coronado, Curtiss SOC Seagull, Douglas TBD-1 Devastator, North American SNJ-3** (one was BuNo. 6786), **Northrop BT-1** and **Vought OS2U Kingfisher**.

Full-scale aircraft mock-ups from *Test Pilot* (1938) and *Flight Command* (1940) were used for crash scenes and studio filming. Miniatures for special effects built of the F3F-2, SB2U-2 and TBD.

Filmed in February and March 1941 at NAS San Diego, California, with the opening carrier scenes filmed onboard the carrier USS *Enterprise* (CV-6), off the San Diego coast. The aerial scenes were supervised by Hollywood pilot Paul Mantz, who flew a Travel Air biplane doubling as an N3N-3 in some stunt sequences.

GPS LOCATION

NAS San Diego, California: N32 42.00 / W117 12.45

Dr. No (Non–Aviation Themed Title)

see   ***James Bond* Series**

Dr. Strangelove or: How I Learned to Stop Worrying and Love the Bomb

UK / Columbia Pictures / 1964 / B&W / 93 minutes

Director: Stanley Kubrick

Cast: Peter Sellers, George C. Scott, Sterling Hayden, Keenan Wynn, Slim Pickens

Synopsis / Aviation Content: A classic, antiwar satire swings between a frantic American war room, the crew of a strategic bomber, and a paranoid USAF general who has initiated an attack on the USSR. Loosely based on the 1958 novel *Red Alert* by British author Peter George, who also co-wrote the screenplay. The film's success overshadowed the similar, equally well made, but dramatically themed *Fail-Safe* (1964). Featured aircraft is the **Boeing B-52 Stratofortress**, a full-scale, mock-up flight-deck section of which was built for onboard scenes. The opening title sequence of a B-52 (with a Boeing KC-135A Stratotanker) is file footage. B-52 miniatures were used later on with back projection footage of the Arctic filmed from a French *l'Institut Geographique National* Boeing B-17G-100-VE Flying Fortress (s/n 44-85643 / msn 17-8552 / reg. F-BEEA)—the shadow of which can be seen in several shots substituting that of the B-52—oh dear, but at least they're both Boeing products!

Dragonfly Squadron

USA / Allied Artists Pictures / 1954 / B&W / 82 minutes

Director: Lesley Selander

Cast: John Hodiak, Barbara Britton, Bruce Bennett, Jess Barker, Gerald Mohr, Chuck Connors, Harry Lauter, Pamela Duncan

Synopsis / Aviation Content: Fighter pilot Hodiak is sent to South Korea to train pilots for combat. The base doctor turns out to be the husband of a woman Hodiak almost married a year earlier, until she learned that her husband, whom she thought had been killed in action, was still alive. Second-rate film suffers from poor production standards and makes wide use of wartime stock footage, especially from World War II.

Featured aircraft are the **Curtiss C-46A Commando**; **North American F-51D Mustang** (one was s/n 44-84935 / msn 124-44791 / Buzz No. FF-935; two others were FF-539, FF-640); **Republic P-47D Thunderbolt** as Russian Yak fighters; and the **Vultee BT-13 Valiant**. The editing of the stock footage blatantly mixes shots of the A-35, P-80 and F-84, all intended to represent the F-51D! Filmed at Iverson Ranch in Chatsworth, California, representing South Korea. It was apparently filmed, but not released, using the Monogram 3-D system. Of notable interest was USAF Colonel Dean Hess (see under *Battle Hymn* (1957), hired as the technical supervisor, who actually trained the first South Korean pilots on the F-51 Mustang in the early stages of the Korean War.

Drop Zone

USA / Paramount Pictures / 1994 / Color / 97 minutes

Director: John Badham

Cast: Wesley Snipes, Gary Busey, Yancy Butler, Michael Jeter, Corin Nemec, Kyle Secor, Luca Bercovici

Synopsis / Aviation Content: U.S. Marshal Snipes goes undercover amongst the parachute fraternity in order to flush out the skydiving criminals who nabbed his prisoner while on an airliner flight. This entertaining film has several things going for it—a sunny, idyllic Florida setting and some expert aerial parachuting supervised by veteran Hollywood parachutist B.J. Worth—the stunts and photography are crystal clear and expertly performed. Also a small treat for the light aircraft fan. The aeronautical highlights would have to be the PC-6 Turbo-Porter and original DC-3A airliner. Certainly worth the price of admission even if only to see Yancy Butler—what a gal!

The Boeing 747-146 Jumbo Jet was provided by American International Airways marked as "PAC Atlantic Pacific," with a small "hole" added to the rear fuselage to simulate the hijackers' escape route while in-flight. This aircraft initially flew on May 26, 1972, and was delivered to Japan Airlines as JA-8112 on June 14, 1972. It served JAL

Type	msn	Civil reg.	Film Markings
Bell 206B Jet Ranger III	3167	N57BL	N57BL
Boeing 747-146	20528/191	N704CK	PAC Atlantic Pacific
Cessna 172	29697	N6497B	N6497B
Cessna 172P	172-75046	N54743	N54743
Cessna 175	55151	N9351B	N9351B
Cessna 180D	180-50971	N6471X	N6471X
Cessna 182A	34007	N6007B	N6007B
Cessna 182A	34420	N3720D	N3720D
Cessna 182Q	182-67013	N97200	N97200
Douglas DC-3A	4126	N129H	Vector Skydiving
Douglas C-47A-65-DL Skytrain	19054	N3239T	U5 / 2100591 / *Tico Belle*
Fairchild-Hiller PC-6/B1-H2 Turbo-Porter	2001	N346F	N346F / *Crazy Flamingo*
Rockwell 114 Commander	14399	N5854N	N5854N

until joining AIA as N704CK on June 23, 1993. On February 3, 1999, it went to Kitty Hawk International before finally being withdrawn from service on February 10, 2006, by that time registered as N40489.

The white Douglas DC-3A, N129H, is an original passenger version with the single side entry door and was originally delivered with reg. NC33647 to United Airlines. The C-47 in D-Day stripes was N3239T, named *Tico Belle*, and was provided by the Valiant Air Command Museum in Florida.

The worn-out Fairchild-Hiller Turbo-Porter was N346F; it's significant to note that this airframe was the very first Porter built by Fairchild at Hagerstown, Maryland, in 1966. It was one of ten (Pilatus msn 604 through 613) kitsets supplied to them from parent manufacturer Pilatus in Switzerland before local U.S. production got underway.

Fairchild went on to build another forty-six for the civilian market and thirty-six for the USAF, who sold them to the Thai Air Force. N346F was provided to the film production by U.S. parachuting company Freefall Express, Inc.

The seven Cessnas and one Rockwell 114 are used as background aircraft in the various airfield scenes; some are derelict. Unidentified aircraft include two **DeHavilland-Canada DHC-6 Twin Otter** aircraft, a **North American T-6 Texan**, and a **T-28 Trojan**, amongst several other light aircraft types. Filmed in and around Miami and Key Largo, Florida, from March 14 to June 7, 1994. The small airstrip is Sugarloaf Key Airport, Key West, Florida (GPS Location: N24 38.90 / W081 34.45).

The Dubious Patriots   see *You Can't Win 'Em All*

The Eagle and the Hawk

USA / Paramount Pictures / 1933 / B&W / 68 minutes

Director: Stuart Walker

Cast: Fredric March, Cary Grant, Jack Oakie, Carole Lombard, Guy Standing, Forrester Harvey

Synopsis / Aviation Content: A World War I pilot suffering from extreme mental and physical fatigue commits suicide, so his gunner / observer flies his body into combat for a "proper burial." Based on the story by former World War I flight instructor John Monk Saunders. Filmed in California with a **DeHavilland D.H. 9** owned by Garland Lincoln, who was one of the stunt pilots; a **Curtiss P-1 Hawk** doubling as a German type; and several non-flying **Nieuport 28** biplane fighters. Many of the combat sequences are made up with footage from *Wings* (1927), *Lilac Time* (1928) and *The Dawn Patrol* (1930).

Eagle Squadron

USA / Universal Pictures / 1942 / B&W / 109 minutes

Director: Arthur Lubin

Cast: Robert Stack, Diana Barrymore, Jon Hall, Eddie Albert, Nigel Bruce, Evelyn Ankers, Leif Erickson

Synopsis / Aviation Content: Three American pilots go to England to join the fight against Germany, forming part of the first U.S. Eagle

Squadron in the RAF. What could have become a timely, highly regarded salute to the American pilots flying with the RAF instead sinks into a B-grade action yarn involving fictional "Bf 109 Leopard" prototypes and a commando raid into Germany. Filmed in California with a full-scale Supermarine Spitfire and Messerschmitt Bf 109 wooden mock-ups along with a **Lockheed 12 Electra Junior** as an RAF transport. Footage obtained from England of the **Supermaine Spitfire Mk. IIa** and **Mk. Vb** of No. 71, 27 and 222 Squadrons. Also appearing is a **Westland Lysander** and a **Vickers Wellington** as a German bomber(?).

Eagles of the Fleet see *Flat Top*

Empire of the Sun

USA / Warner Bros. / 1987 / Color / 153 minutes
Director: Steven Spielberg
Cast: Christian Bale, John Malkovich, Miranda Richardson, Nigel Havers, Joe Pantoliano, Leslie Phillips, Masato Ibu
Synopsis / Aviation Content: Epic story of a young British boy separated from his parents when the Japanese invade Shanghai and his subsequent survival in an internment camp. Based on English novelist J.G. Ballard's 1984 semi-autobiographical novel of the same name. Not technically an aviation film, but the consistent themes of flying and aircraft throughout the story make it worthy of inclusion. Actual aviation scenes are sparse, but incredibly pow-

erful on-screen—the P-51 Mustang attack is a now classic sequence among Warbird fans. Features a haunting, surreal John Williams music score.

Three flyable North American P-51D Mustang fighters were required for filming. Pilots were Ray Hanna, his son Mark Hanna, and Hoof Proudfoot. Aerial Coordination was by John "Jeff" Hawke and James Good.

G-HAEC—Commonwealth Aircraft Company–built Mustang PR.22 delivered to the RAAF with s/n A68-192; flew with Australian civil reg. VH-FCB from 1958; went to the Philippines in 1969 as PI-C651; obtained by Ray Hanna in 1976 and restored in Hong Kong with reg. VR-HIU; imported to the UK by Hanna as G-HAEC with The Old Flying Machine Co. (OFMC); sold to Robert Davies in 1997; exported to Germany as D-FBBD in 2011. Destroyed in an accident at Duxford, England, on July 10, 2011.

G-PSID—Delivered to the USAAF; sold into civilian ownership in 1957 and saw several operators with multiple reg. N6171C, N3350, N166G and then to The Fighter Collection in the UK as G-PSID; to France as F-AZFI in 1988; crashed in June 1998. This was the P-51D that Ray Hanna flew during filming and the one he did the famous "fly-by wave" from.

N51JJ—Delivered to the USAAF; to the RCAF as a Mustang TF.Mk. IV (s/n 9568); sold into civilian use as N6340T in 1957; exported to the UK, it joined The Fighter Collection as N51JJ, later becoming G-BTCD; sold to The Old Flying Machine Co. (OFMC) in 1999. It sill flies today.

The North American T-6G Texan trainer dou-

Type	msn	Military s/n	Civil reg.	Film Markings
Flying Aircraft				
CAC Mustang PR.Mk. 22	192-1517	(RAAF) A68-192	G-HAEC	592 / *Missy Wong from Hong Kong*
Nord 3400	37	unknown	G-ZARA	2
North American P-51D-20-NA Mustang	122-31514	44-63788	G-PSID	599 / *Tugboat*
North American P-51D-25-NA Mustang	122-39608	44-73149	N51JJ	583 / *My Dallas Darlin'*
North American SNJ-5 Texan	88-17667	BuNo.90669	F-AZBL	3-189
North American T-6G-NH Texan	182-54	51-14367	F-AZBK	3-217
North American T-6G-NH Texan	182-736	51-15049	F-AZAS	3-281
Static Aircraft				
North American T-6G-NH Texan	182-72	51-14385	—	3-158
North American T-6G-NH Texan	182-387	51-14700	—	—

North American P-51D Mustang G-HAEC (ex–RAAF A68–192), painted as *Missy Wong from Hong Kong* for the Steven Spielberg film *Empire of the Sun* (1987). Photograph: Derek Ferguson.

bled for the **Mitsubishi A6M Zero** and all were located for the film in France. Amicale Jean-Baptiste Salis (AJBS) provided F-AZBK and F-AZAS, while Aero-Retro provided F-AZBL, which is a composite airframe, also containing parts from T-6G airframes (msn 182-182 and 182-183). All three were converted to "Zero" configuration in 1986 with new msn: SMA2-669 (F-AZBL), SMA2-367 (FAZBK) and SMA2-049 (F-AZAS). Chief Zero pilot was Tom Danaher. T-6G (s/n 51-14700) was the derelict "Zero" in the field seen near the top of the film. It has since been restored with reg. G-TOMC, by Beech Restorations in England.

The very brief shots of the Japanese "spotter plane" seen on the internment camp airfield is a very rare ex–French Army observation aircraft—a Nord 3400 (reg. G-ZARA), flown by its owner to Spain from Coventry for background set dressing.

Several ⅓-scale flyable Mustang and Zero remote-control models were also used in the film, as was a similar RC flyable B-29 Superfortress model. Early CGI was used to create the Japanese bombers over Shanghai and the atomic bomb explosion. The "abandoned Zero" scene was shot at RAF Bovingdon, Hertfordshire, England. The in-

ternment camp / airfield was filmed on a purpose-built set near Jerez de la Frontera in Spain.

The Eternal Sea

USA / Republic Pictures / 1955 / B&W / 103 minutes

Director: John H. Auer

Cast: Sterling Hayden, Alexis Smith, Dean Jagger, Ben Cooper, Virginia Grey, Richard Crane

Synopsis / Aviation Content: Biographical film following the military career of naval commander John Madison Hoskins from World War II through to the Korean War. Film story written by renowned author and scriptwriter William Wister Haines. A notable picture, as Hoskins was one of the earliest naval aviators; earning his wings in 1925, he attained the rank of air officer on the USS *Ranger* (CV-4) during 1941–1942. He lost his right foot in the Battle of Leyte Gulf in 1944, and despite this disability, went on to become the commanding officer of the USS *Princeton* (CV-37). Promoted to rear admiral, Hoskins was one of the leading proponents in developing U.S. naval aviation into the jet age.

Filmed partly onboard the USS *Kearsarge* (CV-33) in 1954 off the Californian coast with various views of the **Douglas AD-4 Skyraider**, **Grumman F9F Panther** and a **Piasecki HUP-2 Retriever**. Background aircraft on land are a Boeing C-97 Stratofreighter and a Douglas C-54 Skymaster. Much of the film uses documentary and stock footage, including the Douglas AD-Skyraider, R4D-6 Skytrain, Grumman F6F Hellcat, F9F Panther, North American SNJ and Vought F7U Cutlass.

Executive Decision

USA / Warner Bros. / 1996 / Color / 134 minutes
Director: Stuart Baird
Cast: Kurt Russell, Halle Berry, John Leguizamo, Oliver Platt, Joe Morton, David Suchet, Steven Seagal
Synopsis / Aviation Content: A top U.S. Army assault team boards a Boeing 747 in-flight after it has been hijacked by terrorists plotting to cause widespread destruction on the U.S. east coast with an on-board chemical weapon. Routine, "paint-by-numbers" action yarn does have some unique aerial action sequences, including a cargo-converted F-117A for the in-flight 747 boarding scene—all fictional, of course!

The main aircraft used was a Boeing 747-269B, N707CK, marked as the fictional "Oceanic Airlines" for the flying scenes in the film. It was originally built in 1978 and delivered as 9K-ADA to Kuwait Airways, whom it served with until 1995, when it was purchased by American Intl. Airways as N707CK. In 1999 it was converted to Special Freighter (SF) standards with Kitty Hawk, Kalitta Air and Airfreight Express until scrapped in 2004 after service with Ocean Airlines as S2-ADT (Bangladesh). The final crash scene was filmed at Mojave Airport, California, with a due-to-be-scrapped Boeing 747-121, ex–France F-GIMJ, marked up as "Oceanic Airlines / N707CK." Originally delivered to Pan Am in 1970 as N754PA, it was then converted to a freighter in 1988 for Luxembourg's Cargolux as LX-FCV before going to

France's Corsair in 1991 as F-GIMJ. It had returned to the U.S. by the mid–1990s and was in storage at Mojave Airport when it was acquired for the film.

The small aircraft Kurt Russell is learning to fly at the top of the film is a **Beechcraft Bonanza** with fictional reg. "N2TS." Filming location for this sequence was above Chino Airport, California, but the ground scenes were shot at Van Nuys Airport in Burbank, California. Background aircraft are various makes of Beechcraft, Cessna and Piper, plus a Bell 206B Jet Ranger.

Military aircraft appearances are a **Bell UH-1H Iroquois** (background), **Boeing-Vertol CH-47 Chinook**, **Grumman E-2 Hawkeye**, **Grumman F-14A Tomcat** (four from squadron VF-84 Jolly Rogers), **Lockheed F-117A Nighthawk** and a **Sikorsky UH-60 Black Hawk**. The civilian executive jet is a **British Aerospace BAe.125**. Much use of models and special effects in the aerial scenes.

Eyes of the Skies   see   Mission Over Korea

Fail-Safe

USA / Columbia Pictures / 1964 / B&W / 112 minutes
Director: Sidney Lumet
Cast: Henry Fonda, Dan O'Herlihy, Walter Matthau, Frank Overton, Edward Binns, Larry Hagman, Fritz Weaver
Synopsis / Aviation Content: Excellent, high-tension drama concerning a group of U.S. bombers accidentally deployed to attack Russia and the futile attempts to stop them. Based on the popular 1962 novel of the same name by American authors Eugene Burdick and Harvey Wheeler. Aircraft are stock footage (Dept. of Defense declined to take part in filming) of the **Convair B-58A Hustler** bomber, named in the film as the "Vindicator." The bomber interior scenes were filmed inside a commercial airliner cockpit that, in reality, is very different from the separated crew stations onboard a B-58. There are also very brief shots of various other Cold War U.S.

Type	msn	Civil reg.	Film Markings
Boeing 747-121	19658/47	F-GIMJ	N707CK / Oceanic Airlines
Boeing 747-269B	21541/332	N707CK	N707CK / Oceanic Airlines

fighters throughout, such as the F-86 Sabre, F-104 Starfighter and F-102 Delta Dagger. The film's serious nature was overshadowed by Columbia's other, more popular and satirical Cold War film *Dr. Strangelove*, also released in 1964.

Fate Is the Hunter

USA / 20th Century–Fox / 1964 / B&W / 106 minutes

Director: Ralph Nelson

Cast: Glenn Ford, Nancy Kwan, Rod Taylor, Suzanne Pleshette, Jane Russell, Wally Cox, Nehemiah Persoff, Mark Stevens

Synopsis / Aviation Content: An airliner crashes after takeoff, killing all passengers onboard. Pilot error is the suspected cause, but the long-time friend of the ill-fated flight's captain isn't so sure. Based in part on the 1961 biography by renowned aviation pioneer and writer Ernest K. Gann, who was so disappointed by the finished film he tried to have his name removed from the credits. In fact, the title is the only thing the movie has in common with the book!

In fairness, this film isn't all that bad; the "detective story" following the accident becomes more intriguing as the story progresses. The only drawback is that, in the final moments of the test flight finale, most aviation fans will probably guess the cause of the crash before Glenn Ford does!

Aircraft manufacturers and airlines during the early 1960s were quite sensitive about seeing aerial disaster films produced featuring their products being mangled across the big screen. Consequently, for this production, a fictional airliner was built from a **Douglas DC-6B** and falsely marked as "N819CA," then "N319CA," with "Consolidated Airlines" written down the side. It was essentially a DC-6 fuselage with swept jet airliner wings and two jet engines mounted, of all places, on the rear stabilizers. The end result is a rather unconvincing, clumsy-looking aircraft. The post-crash sequence was so well recreated on the Fox Studios backlot that overhead flying aircraft were mistakenly reporting in a downed airliner. Models were used to depict the in-flight crash sequence.

The World War II flashback sequence was

The heavily modified DC-6B as seen in *Fate Is the Hunter* (1964), photographed here on the Fox Studios backlot next to an ex–*Tora!* fiberglass P-40. Photograph: James H. Farmer Collection.

This derelict Mosquito bomber was featured in *Fate Is the Hunter* in 1964. It was photographed here in January 1970 at Whiteman Air Park, California. Photograph: James H. Farmer Collection.

filmed at Whiteman Air Park in San Fernando Valley, California, with a **DeHavilland Mosquito**, **Douglas A-26B Invader**, **C-54 Skymaster**, **Fairchild UC-61 Argus**, **North American AT-6 Texan** and **B-25 Mitchell**. Some use of scale models for the mountain flying sequences.

time of filming in June 1953, in non-flying condition, being used as an engine test-bed by a civilian owner. It was then stored until 1981, whereupon the fighter was returned to flying status first as N42354, then N47DG, and in 2006 to the UK as G-CDVX.

Fighter Attack

USA / Allied Artists Pictures / 1953 / Color / 80 minutes

Director: Lesley Selander

Cast: Sterling Hayden, J. Carrol Naish, Joy Page, Kenneth Tobey, Arthur Caruso, Frank DeKova

Synopsis / Aviation Content: Routine formula story of a fighter pilot during World War II who is shot down but continues the fight with the help of Italian locals. Not much flying, with most footage taken from the 1947 William Wyler documentary *Thunderbolt*. Filmed in California with three aircraft: two background **Vultee BT-13 Valiant** trainers doubling as the P-47, and a **Republic P-47G-10-CU Thunderbolt** (s/n 42-25068 / msn 21953). Converted as a TP-47G two-seater it was, at the

Fighter Squadron

USA / Warner Bros. / 1948 / Color / 96 minutes

Director: Raoul Walsh

Cast: Edmond O'Brien, Robert Stack, John Rodney, Tom D'Andrea, Henry Hull, James Holden

Synopsis / Aviation Content: Reckless fighter ace O'Brien creates problems for his superiors but learns the weight of responsibility once made commander of his own group. The story is loosely based on the earlier World War I aviation classic, *The Dawn Patrol* (1930), but updated to England in 1943. Many sequences featuring the mighty P-47 Thunderbolt, or Jug as it's affectionately known.

Sixteen **Republic P-47D Thunderbolt** fighters were provided from the Air National Guard

118th Fighter Bomber Group at Nashville, Tennessee—four each from the 105th FBS, 158th FBS, 128th FBS and 156th FBS. Eighteen pilots were assigned the role of flying the P-47 fighters for the film, among them Major Leroy Gover. Gover was a World War II fighter ace with 257 combat missions, seventeen claims and seven confirmed kills; he also saw extensive service in Europe in the P-47. He was the perfect choice as the film's chief pilot but uncredited technical advisor. The credited technical advisor was Major Joseph Perry, who did liaison work for the film studio. Two additional P-47 fighters were also later acquired for a total of eighteen Thunderbolts. Actual serial numbers were painted out, but three of the Thunderbolts have been identified as P-47D-30-RE (s/n 44-20990 / msn 6398)—Major Gover's personal aircraft; P-47D-30-RA (s/n 44-33311 / msn 4272); and P-47D-40-RA (s/n 44-90437 / msn 5582). Combat footage was used from the William Wyler documentary *Thunderbolt* (1947)—all P-47 aircraft hired for the film were painted in the same colors as those used in that production—the 12th AF, 57th Fighter Group with large two-digit fuselage numbers.

Eight **North American P-51D Mustang** fighters of the 195th FS–146th FG, California ANG were painted as opposing German Messerschmitt fighters. The **Boeing B-17G-95-DL Flying Fortress** (s/n 44-83842 / msn 32483 / reg. NL1212N) was the natural metal Fortress seen at the start of the film. It was one of four B-17 bombers that would later be sought and acquired by the Israeli Air Force.

Hollywood pilot Paul Mantz provided his B-25H camera-plane (reg. N1203). One death occurred during filming when Lt Avary Mikell was forced to bail out of a disintegrating P-47 during a practice flight. He parachuted into Lake Huron without incident but drowned in the chilly waters before a rescue boat could reach him.

P-47 takeoffs, landings, base scenes and mass flying scenes were shot at Oscoda AFB, Oscoda, Michigan (as an English field) from May 27 to June 9, 1948. Nearby Lake Huron doubled as the English Channel. The German airfield was at San Fernando Metropolitan Airport (Van Nuys Airport from 1957), California—filming there took place from June 16 to June 25, 1948. The filmmakers also used this airport as a base of operations to stage the aerial dogfights between the P-47 and "German" P-51D fighters, including the B-17 sequence.

Six of the eight California ANG P-51D Mustangs doubling as German Messerschmitt Bf 109 fighters for the 1948 film *Fighter Squadron*. Photograph: James H. Farmer Collection.

GPS LOCATIONS

Oscoda AAFB, Oscoda, Michigan (Wurtsmith AFB from 1953): N44 27.15 / W083 23.00

San Fernando Metropolitan (Van Nuys) Airport, California: N34 12.35 / W118 29.25

FACTUAL BACKGROUND: THE JUG

Republic's P-47 Thunderbolt was the largest single-engined fighter of its time and one of the main fighter aircraft employed by the USAAF in both the European and Pacific theaters of World War II. An impressive 15,685 airframes (including prototypes) were produced from the Republic Aviation Corp. plants in Farmingdale, New York, and Evansville, Indiana, from 1941 to 1945. The vast majority were the definitive P-47D variant, of which 12,608 were built in both the "razorback" fuselage and "teardrop" canopy versions. Suitable for the ground attack role and developing a reputation as a very tough and reliable fighter, it earned the nickname Jug, short for Juggernaut. In the post–World War II years the P-47 was downgraded to stateside ANG service until finally retired in 1953. Republic would later enter the jet age, continuing their *Thunder* series with the F-84, F-105 and (under Fairchild-Hiller) A-10 Thunderbolt II.

The Final Countdown

USA / United Artists / 1980 / Color / 98 minutes
Director: Don Taylor
Cast: Kirk Douglas, Martin Sheen, Katharine Ross, James Farentino, Ron O'Neil, Charles Durning
Synopsis / Aviation Content: Science fiction tale of a modern-day U.S. aircraft carrier encountering an eerie storm at sea and inadvertently time-traveling back to December 6, 1941, just before the Japanese attack on Pearl Harbor. The crew then faces the dilemma of should we or shouldn't we intervene? A strong story premise that advertises itself well but doesn't quite sustain a motion picture length; in this case the story falls well short of providing a satisfying out-

come, leading one to ask why they bothered to make the film at all. There is, however, excellent carrier footage throughout, with many naval aircraft types in action. F-14 Tomcats and Japanese Zeros dogfighting—you won't believe it until you see it!

The two Harvards are Japanese "Zero" conversions first used for *Tora! Tora! Tora!* (1970) and were at this time owned by the Confederate Air Force's Tora Group. Zero pilots were Mack Sterling, Archie Donahue, Charles Hutchins and Tom Gregory. Prominently featured throughout are three SH-3A Sea Kings from naval squadron HS-9 which, by 1979, had all been upgraded to SH-3H standards.

The carrier, both on film and in real life, was the USS *Nimitz* (CVN-68), then stationed as part of the Atlantic fleet out of Norfolk, Virginia. Featured naval aircraft and squadrons which took part in filming off the *Nimitz* are the **Chance Vought RF-8G Crusader** (VFP-63), **Grumman A-6E Intruder** (VA-35), **Grumman EA-6B Prowler** (VAQ-134), **Grumman E-2B Hawkeye** (VAW-112), **Grumman F-14A Tomcat** (VF-41, VF-84), **Lockheed S-3A Viking** (VS-24) and **LTV A-7E Corsair II** (VA-82, VA-86). Background aircraft seen at the naval station are the **Grumman S-2 Tracker, Lockheed C-141A Starlifter** and a **North American A-5 Vigilante** under tow.

For the F-14A vs. Zero dogfight, the Zeros were flying at full throttle and the Tomcats were at stall speeds with wings fully extended. Watch closely for a brief moment where an F-14 almost stalls into the ocean before the pilot guns the throttle and pulls up, just avoiding a splash into the drink! Aerial photography was provided by a Tallmantz Aviation, Inc., B-25J (reg. N1042B). Stock footage was used from *Tora! Tora! Tora!* (1970) for the final battle scene.

As the USS *Nimitz* was based in the Atlantic; all carrier filming took place there during the

Type	msn	Military s/n	Civil reg.	Film Markings
CCF Harvard Mk. 4 (Zero)	CCF4-117	(RCAF) 20326	N15799	AI-113
CCF Harvard Mk. 4 (Zero)	CCF4-199	(RCAF) 20408	N15797	AI-114
Sikorsky SH-3A-SI Sea King	61-069	BuNo.148995	—	8995
Sikorsky SH-3A-SI Sea King	61-084	BuNo.149010	—	9010
Sikorsky SH-3A-SI Sea King	61-134	BuNo.149717	—	9717

ship's September 1979–May 1980 cruise. The naval base in the opening scene was NAS Key West, Florida, which stood in for the Pearl Harbor naval base. Aerial sequences were shot over the ocean nearby and used NAS Key West as their operating base. The final scene was shot on Pier 12 at Norfolk, Virginia, where the *Nimitz* was based. The only real Pacific filming location was the Arizona Memorial in Pearl Harbor, where the USS *Kitty Hawk* stood in for the *Nimitz* in the film's closing sequence.

GPS Location

NAS Key West, Florida: N24 34.45 / W081 41.25

Fire Birds

Aka: *Wings of the Apache*

USA / Buena Vista Pictures / 1990 / Color / 85 minutes

Director: David Green

Cast: Nicolas Cage, Tommy Lee Jones, Sean Young, Bryan Kestner, Dale Dye, Mary Ellen Trainor

Synopsis / Aviation Content: The U.S. Army goes to war against South American drug cartels with Cage the leading student in an Apache helicopter training program initiated to combat the cartel's defenses. Aimed solely at a youth market; the only real aeronautical highlights are the many and varied views of the AH-64 Apache and OH-58 Kiowa. A definite must-see for any fan of army helicopters, but the temptation to push the fast-forward button between aerial scenes may prove too much for some viewers. Co-produced and story co-written by well-known Hollywood military advisor Dale Dye, who also has a supporting role.

A wide array of U.S. Army rotary-winged aircraft were used, with the **Bell OH-58D Kiowa Warrior** (mainly s/n 88-0295 / msn 43151); one **Bell UH-1H Iroquois** briefly doubling as an enemy cargo helicopter; two **Bell AH-1 Cobra** gunship helicopters in the opening sequence; numerous **McDonnell Douglas AH-64A Apache** gunship helicopters—the stars of the film—are seen throughout; and one **Sikorsky UH-60A Black Hawk** support helicopter. The enemy hel-

icopter was a **Hughes 500D** as the fictional "Scorpion." The jet fighter was a Swedish built **SAAB J 35F Draken** piloted by Skip Holmes. Filmed from October 1989 to January 1990 at Fort Hood, Texas, and Fort Huachuca, Arizona.

GPS Locations

Fort Huachuca, Arizona: N31 33.60 / W110 20.60

Fort Hood AAF, Texas: N31 08.55 / W097 43.20

Factual Background: McDonnell Douglas AH-64 Apache

Regarded as the premier attack helicopter against which all others are compared, the AH-64 Apache first flew as five YAH-64A prototypes from Hughes Helicopters on September 30, 1975. A production contract followed, which saw a total of 939 AH-64A helicopters built from 1982 to 1996. Early on in production, Hughes was taken over by McDonnell Douglas in 1984, and then in 1997 Boeing became the prime contractor. Around this time Boeing began remanufacturing the Apache into the definitive AH-64D Apache Longbow. Around 600 "A" airframes have been upgraded with new General Electric T700 engines, new electronics and a mast-mounted Longbow fire-control radome built by Northrop Grumman. Including export versions, around 1,200 Apache attack choppers have been built in total. This includes sixty-seven of the Apache AH.Mk. 1 variant built by Westland helicopters of England from 1998 to 2004 for the British Army, but featuring Rolls Royce engines. The Apache began its military service with the U.S. Army in 1984.

Firefox

USA / Warner Bros. / 1982 / Color / 120 minutes

Director: Clint Eastwood

Cast: Clint Eastwood, Freddie Jones, David Huffman, Warren Clarke, Ronald Lacey, Stefan Schnabel, Nigel Hawthorne

Synopsis / Aviation Content: Retired top pilot Eastwood returns to the job to infiltrate the USSR and steal a top secret military jet—the MiG-31 Firefox. Based on the 1977 novel of the same name by Welsh author Craig Thomas. Since the Firefox was a fictional aircraft, all flying was done with the aid of special effects, which unfortunately are nowadays looking very dated. A popular film at the time of its release and one that today remains fair viewing for the intriguing Cold War storyline.

The helicopter in the opening scene is a twin-engined SAR, **Sikorsky HH-53C-SI Super Jolly Green Giant** (USAF s/n 69-5795 / msn 65-274); it was later upgraded to MH-53J Pave Low III standards around 1986.

The star attraction is the fictional Mikoyan-Gurevich MiG-31 Firefox, a twin-engined, Mach-6 prototype fighter of the USSR. A full-scale mock-up was built for filming, consisting of a metal framework with plywood panel coverings. A VW automobile engine was installed, chain-linked to the back wheels for taxiing scenes. A functional mock-up cockpit was also built for close-ups, as were other aircraft parts to represent the second Firefox in the hangar scenes. Two remote-control flying Firefox models were built, but these didn't look convincing on-screen and were subsequently dropped from filming.

Six miniature Firefox models were also constructed for special effects photography by industry technician John Dysktra's company, Apogee Inc. Other Russian aircraft models include the Mil Mi-24 Hind, Tupolev Tu-16 Badger and Tu-154 airliner. The Russian helicopter cockpit in the Arctic scene was the *Blue Thunder* (1983) mock-up. High-speed landscapes were filmed from a Clay Lacey Learjet using a special camera to speed up the vision. Flashback sequences used Vietnam combat footage. Filmed in Vienna, Austria (standing in for the USSR), Van Nuys Airport, California (Firefox hangar scenes), and at Thule AFB, Greenland (Arctic refueling scenes).

Actor Clint Eastwood later became a recreational flyer, obtaining his helicopter pilot's license.

FACTUAL BACKGROUND: THE REAL MiG-31

A Russian supersonic interceptor-fighter, the Mikoyan-Gurevich MiG-31 Foxhound is a twin-engined development from the earlier MiG-25

Foxbat—it first flew on March 6, 1964, and 1,190 were later built. The developed MiG-31 first flew on September 11, 1975, and around 500 were built. Entering service in 1982, the fighter proved to be a top-performing aircraft. One of the inspirational factors in the story of Firefox is the true-life defection of a Russian pilot, Viktor Belenko. Landing his MiG-25 Foxbat in Japan on September 6, 1976, he was granted asylum by the U.S. government. His Foxbat fighter, an aircraft never before seen by western observers, was dismantled and studied at length by U.S. personnel, who then shipped the parts back to Russia inside packing crates.

The First of the Few

U.S. Title: *Spitfire*
UK / General Film Distributors (GFD) / 1942 / B&W / 118 minutes
Director: Leslie Howard
Cast: Leslie Howard, David Niven, Rosamund John, Roland Culver, Anne Firth, David Horne, J.H. Roberts, Derrick De Marney
Synopsis / Aviation Content: Outstanding, enlightening biographical film about aeronautical engineer R.J. Mitchell, the designer and developer of England's famous World War II fighter, the Supermarine Spitfire. Not much actual flying and largely studio-based, but an excellent film for its time, featuring some unique footage of RAF airfields in action and including a few real-life RAF pilots as background actors. A fine music score by English composer William Walton, who subsequently arranged a stand-alone musical piece titled "Spitfire Prelude and Fugue" from the film's score. Producer, director and actor Leslie Howard's last starring role; he was killed on June 1, 1943, when German fighters shot down his civilian (KLM) flight over the Bay of Biscay.

Featured aircraft are **Supermarine Spitfire Mk. II / Mk. V** (identified are s/n P8256, P8664), fighters of No. 501 Squadron; an early Spitfire variant doubled as the original prototype marked with RAF s/n K5054. There are also various views of the **Supermarine S.5 / S.6** floatplane racers. Newsreel footage was utilized of the Curtiss CR-

3, Macchi M.12, Supermarine Sea Lion racer plus Model S.4, S.5, S.6 racers, the actual Spitfire prototype and various German gliders. World War II combat footage was used of the Spitfire and German Heinkel He 111 in action. Some use of miniatures for special effects including mock-up cockpits of the Supermarine S.4 / 5 / 6, Spitfire and Messerschmitt Bf 109E.

U.S. prints were cut down to 90 minutes and released in 1943 by RKO Radio Pictures under the title *Spitfire*. The different title, run time, year of release and distributor have meant this version is often mistaken for a different movie altogether.

Airfield scenes were filmed on location at RAF Ibsley, Hampshire, England, where pilots and aircraft were on active duty; often filming was halted while they were scrambled to fly off into combat. Today the airfield is a series of quarry lakes.

GPS Location

RAF Ibsley, Hampshire (closed 1947): N50 52.75 / W001 46.60

Factual Background: The Supermarine Type 300

The origin of the legendary Spitfire goes back to 1931, when the Air Ministry issued Specification F.7/30, requesting a replacement for the Bristol Bulldog fighter. Supermarine Aviation Works (a subsidiary of Vickers-Armstrong since 1928), responded with the Type 224, a bulky, open-cockpit monoplane, which first flew in 1934. Failing to generate any interest, Supermarine's chief designer, R.J. Mitchell, and his team set about a radical redesign based on their famous Schneider Trophy–winning seaplane racers. The result was the Type 300, with an enclosed cockpit, streamlined fuselage, retractable undercarriage, a new 990hp Rolls Royce V-12 engine, plus a uniquely designed, elliptical wing of thin cross-section. This gave the fighter a higher top speed over other contemporary fighters of the time. By March of 1935, now with backing from Supermarine, Rolls Royce, the Air Ministry (under new Specification F.37/34) and RAE Farnborough, Mitchell began construction of the first prototype. On March 5, 1936, at Eastleigh Airport in Hampshire, the first Supermarine Type 300 Spitfire, with RAF s/n K5054, made its maiden flight.

Pilot Joseph "Mutt" Summers was at the controls. All parties concerned with the project knew straight away they were onto a winner: the Air Ministry on July 3, 1936, ordered 310 of the Spitfire Mk. I into production; this was later increased to 510 airframes. The V-12 engine, which powered the new fighter, came to be known as the Merlin, and between it and the Spitfire, a legend was born! Tragically, the father of the spitfire, R.J. Mitchell, died from cancer on June 11, 1937, and never saw his design enter service. The prototype, K5054, crashed during flight tests on September 4, 1939—three days after World War II began. Service entry was with the RAF in August 1938, and the fighter would be developed through twenty-nine major marks and fifty-nine subvariants, with production not ceasing until well after the war in 1948. In total over 22,000 Spitfire and Seafire naval variants would be built, more than any other British aircraft type during World War II.

Five Came Back

USA / RKO Radio Pictures / 1939 / B&W / 75 minutes

Director: John Farrow

Cast: Chester Morris, Lucille Ball, Wendy Barrie, John Carradine, Allen Jenkins, Joseph Calleia, C. Aubrey Smith, Kent Taylor, Patric Knowles, Elisabeth Risdon, Casey Johnson

Synopsis / Aviation Content: A passenger aircraft is forced down in a remote South American jungle, where the passengers and crew face continuous hardships, including headhunting natives, as they repair the aircraft and attempt to fly out. Excellent drama for its period and one of the best prewar civil aviation–themed films, it would later be remade by director Farrow as *Back From Eternity* (1956). The film used the infamous aircraft failure **Capelis Model XC-12** (reg. NX12762 / msn 1) as the central aircraft. Named the *Silver Queen*, it was used for ground scenes both on location and in the studio. It had been purchased by RKO Pictures from its manufacturer in 1938 just for this picture, but would go on to greater fame in *Flying Tigers* (1942) and a few others. One takeoff scene was done with a "stand-in" Lockheed Electra shot from a distance in a cloud of dust. Flying scenes were a miniature model and special effects—the model Capelis would be used again in subsequent film productions that also employed the real Capelis aircraft.

Flat Top

UK Title: *Eagles of the Fleet*

USA / Monogram Pictures / 1952 / Color / 83 minutes

Director: Lesley Selander

Cast: Sterling Hayden, Richard Carlson, William Phipps, John Bromfield, Keith Larsen, William Schallert, Todd Karns

Synopsis / Aviation Content: In 1952 during the Korean War, group commander Hayden recalls his days fighting the Japanese during World War II. Seemingly designed to incorporate the widely used and nowadays very familiar color newsreel footage gathered during World War II of naval aircraft and ships in the Pacific Theater. The footage features numerous types including the Curtiss SB2U Helldiver, Douglas SBD Dauntless, Grumman F4F Wildcat, F6F Hellcat, TBM Avenger and Vought F4U Corsair fighters. Mainly shot onboard the carrier USS *Princeton* (CV-37), with brief shots of the **Grumman F9F-2 Panther**. Retitled for the UK release, as it was felt the colloquial aircraft carrier term "flat top" was not well known enough outside the United States.

Flight

USA / Columbia Pictures / 1929 / B&W / 110 minutes

Director: Frank Capra

Cast: Jack Holt, Lila Lee, Ralph Graves, Alan Roscoe

Synopsis / Aviation Content: The story of two marine pilots, Holt and Graves, as they go through training, then into combat in Nicaragua, which is partly based on an actual incident. Notable for its well-crafted aerial scenes of early naval aviation, up to twenty-eight aircraft were supplied to the filmmakers by the U.S. Marines at NAS San Diego where filming took place. Featured aircraft are the **Consolidated NY**

biplane trainer and up to nine **Curtiss OC-2 Falcon** biplanes of USMC squadrons VO-8M and VO-10M. Actor Jack Holt was terrified of flying, and to the annoyance of director Capra, he refused to stand up in the gunner's position during an aerial sequence so he could be seen on camera. It was later learned Holt had been playing with his ripcord and had accidentally deployed his chute while sitting in the aircraft; had he stood up he would have been dragged out!

Flight

USA / Paramount Pictures / 2012 / Color / 138 minutes

Director: Robert Zemeckis

Cast: Denzel Washington, Don Cheadle, Kelly Reilly, John Goodman, Bruce Greenwood, Melissa Leo

Synopsis / Aviation Content: An accomplished airline pilot's chronic alcohol addiction is brought to light after he heroically crash-lands his aircraft due to mechanical failure. Commanding performances and a compelling premise (including a scene where the pilot is pouring a drink while talking on the interphone to his passengers!) are weakened by a plot development which doesn't quite deliver that emotional next level you expect from a drama of this caliber. An eye-popping crash sequence with accurate flight-deck visuals make for very convincing viewing.

Type	msn	Civil reg.
Cessna 172C	172-49361	N1661Y
McDonnell Douglas MD-82	49261/1153	N16807
McDonnell Douglas MD-82	49468/1409	N442AA
McDonnell Douglas MD-88	49532/1338	N901DL
McDonnell Douglas MD-88	49810/1588	N937DL

The featured aircraft is, more-or-less, the twin-engined **McDonnell Douglas MD-88**, described here as a fictional "JR-88" airliner of fictional airline "South Jet Air" with fictional reg. "NC 1983MC." Former Continental Airlines MD-82, N16807, was the airframe used for interior cabin and flight-deck scenes; both were separated sections which were mounted on gimbals to simulate flying. Former American Airlines MD-82, N442AA, and former Delta Airlines MD-88, N901DL, were retired airframes used for the crash scenes in the field and later scenes inside a hangar. MD-88, N937DL, was in service with Delta Airlines and was provided for the brief pre-crash ground scenes. Large use of CGI for the crash sequences and general airport background scenes. The winglets were a film add-on, as the MD-88 never had these in real life. Aircraft wrecks, parts and mock-ups were provided by Scroggins Aviation of Nevada. The Cessna in later scenes is a Model 172C falsely marked as "N1661YG."

Flight Angels

USA / Warner Bros. / 1940 / B&W / 74 minutes
Director: Lewis Seiler
Cast: Virginia Bruce, Dennis Morgan, Wayne Morris, Ralph Bellamy, Jane Wyman
Synopsis / Aviation Content: Airline pilot Morgan is grounded with an eye condition and ends up in a job teaching air hostesses, but soon longs to be back in the air testing a new prototype he'd been working on with fellow pilot Morris. A B-grade picture, it was one of many to focus on the "air hostess" theme, but this one is notable for the inclusion of several early, prewar DC-3 airliners provided by American Airlines.

The first was a **Douglas DST-144** (reg. NC 16002 / msn 1496), named *Flagship Illinois*. This aircraft would be drafted into the USAAF as a C-49E (s/n 42-56103), and would later be operated post–World War II by Airborne Transport and disappear in the so-called Bermuda Triangle on December 28, 1948. The second was a **Douglas DST-144** (reg. NC16005 / msn 1499), named *Flagship Tennessee*. This aircraft was later drafted into the USAAF as a C-49E (s/n 42-56092) and is known today as the oldest surviving DC-3 airframe, with reg. N133D. Both of these DST airliners were among the very first batch of DC-3 aircraft delivered to launch customer-based American Airlines in 1936. A third was **Douglas DC-3-178** (reg. NC17333 / msn 1919), another American Airlines aircraft.

The experimental prototype was a **Lockheed Model 12-A Electra Junior** (reg. NX17342 / msn

1216), owned at the time by the Lang Transportation Co. The aircraft served in the RCAF from 1940 to 1944 with s/n 7653. It then went back to the U.S. with several subsequent owners including Sperry Gyroscope Co. and Gulf Oil Corp. Registered in 1960 as N505, its ultimate fate is unknown.

Background aircraft include a **Boeing Model 247** (reg. NC13330 / msn 1712) in the opening titles; **Lockheed Vega**; and a **Stinson Model SM-8**. Filmed largely at Grand Central Air Terminal in Glendale, California. Some use of models and miniatures in several DC-3 and Lockheed Model 12 flying sequences. Actor Wayne Morris acquired an interest in flying while making this film and became a naval pilot in 1942. He later flew the F6F Hellcat, downing seven Japanese aircraft and becoming a World War II fighter ace. He earned four Distinguished Flying Cross medals and two Air Medals.

Flight Command

USA / Metro-Goldwyn-Mayer / 1940 / B&W / 116 minutes
Director: Frank Borzage
Cast: Robert Taylor, Ruth Hussey, Walter Pidgeon, Paul Kelly, Sheppard Strudwick, Red Skelton, Nat Pendleton, Dick Purcell
Synopsis / Aviation Content: New naval pilot Taylor joins the "VF-8 Fighting Hellcats," only to experience a string of events that see him having trouble fitting into the squadron. Regular film bogs down in the second half with melodramatics, but has an exciting finale. Superior aerial footage and, like other prewar preparedness flicks, this is a "time capsule" for the nearly obsolete lineup of aircraft the U.S. Navy flew in the pre–Pearl Harbor period. Excellent sequences of the Grumman F3F.

Aircraft featured are around eighteen **Grumman F3F-2** biplane fighters of squadron VF-6 with two aircraft, BuNo. 1028 (msn 426) and 1029 (msn 427), loaned to the filmmakers for certain scenes; a single **Curtiss SBC-4 Helldiver** as a target tug; a **Ryan ST-A** (reg. NC17344 / msn 144); and the sole **Sikorsky XPBS-1** (BuNo. 9995 / msn 4400). Partial full-scale mock-ups were built of the F3F-2 and Consolidated PBY Catalina, plus the Seversky SEV-S2 mock-up built for *Test Pilot* (1938) doubles as the fictional "Brewman" fighter. Oscar-nominated for special effects in 1942, which included miniatures of the F3F-2 and PBY.

Aerial stunts were performed by Hollywood pilot Paul Mantz, who goes uncredited. Filmed from August 19 to October 10, 1940, at NAS San Diego, California, and onboard the aircraft carrier USS *Enterprise* (CV-6). While filming the landing sequence on the *Enterprise*, Mantz's camera-plane is visible in the back of one shot circling above the carrier.

GPS LOCATION

NAS San Diego, California: N32 42.00 / W117 12.45

Flight Commander see *The Dawn Patrol* (1930 version)

Flight for Freedom

USA / RKO Radio Pictures / 1943 / B&W / 102 minutes

Director: Lothar Mendes

Cast: Rosalind Russell, Fred MacMurray, Herbert Marshall, Eduardo Ciannelli, Walter Kingsford

Synopsis / Aviation Content: Heavily fictionalized account of aviatrix Amelia Earhart's disappearance, which, for this film, makes the proposition she was working for the U.S. Navy on a secret mission. A mixture of aircraft are a **Ryan S-C** marked as "No. 16"; a **Brown B-2** racer marked as "No. 5"; likely a **Stearman C2B** biplane; a **Lockheed Electra** (reg. NR16056 / msn 1070); a **Lockheed 8D Altair**; and a **North American O-47** cockpit section for studio filming. Stock footage used of the Brewster F2A Buffalo; Douglas TBD Devastator; SBD Dauntless; Ford Tri-Motor; and Grumman F4F Wildcat.

Flight from Ashiya

USA / United Artists / 1964 / Color / 100 minutes

Director: Michael Anderson

Cast: Yul Brynner, Richard Widmark, George Chakiris, Suzy Parker, Shirley Knight, Eiko Taki

Synopsis / Aviation Content: Three Air Rescue Service aircrew, each with their own personal tragedies, must fly into a Pacific storm to rescue a raft full of Japanese shipwreck survivors. Based on the 1959 novel of the same name by American writer Elliott Arnold. While there are some excellent views of the Grumman Albatross, the film doesn't actually play out as well as it advertises, being more of a romance story than a rescue drama. Ashiya is the name of an air base on the southwestern side of Japan that was a major hub of operations for U.S. forces during the Korean War.

Type	msn	military s/n	civil reg.
Douglas C-47A-25-DK Skytrain	13510	42-93582	JA5025
Douglas R4D-4	6349	BuNo.07003	JA5040
Grumman SA-16A-GR Albatross	G-334	51-7245	—
Sikorsky SH-19B-SI Chickasaw	55-535	52-7495	—

The main featured aircraft is the Grumman SA-16A Albatross, two of which were provided by the 36th Air Rescue Service (ARS), who were based out of Tachikawa, Japan, from 1952 to 1972. They were both repainted to represent aircraft of the 39th ARS, which actually flew from Ashiya on rescue missions during the Korean conflict. The identified SA-16A Albatross (s/n 51-7245) later went to the USCG as a UF-1G with s/n 7245; it was later upgraded to UF-2G standard, then redesignated as an HU-16E in 1962. After retirement from military service it was sold onto the civilian market with reg. N70262.

The Douglas aircraft are seen in a World War II flashback sequence, but still bear their postwar Japanese civilian registrations during filming! JA5025 was originally a C-47A with the USAAF; it went to Philippine Air Lines in 1954 as PT-C55, then to Japan as JA5025. The second, JA5040, was a factory-impressed PanAm DC-3A, civilian reg. NC34956, put into U.S. Navy service as an R4D-4 (BuNo. 07003); it was struck off in 1956 with civilian reg. N2087A. It then went to Japan as JA5040. It crashed at Sendai, Japan, on May 10, 1963.

The USAF Sikorsky SH-19B appears in a flashback sequence concerning a snow rescue. A stock shot of a PanAm Boeing 707 airliner was also used. There's some use of models and miniatures. Filmed on the USAF air force bases at Tachikawa and Kadena in Japan.

FACTUAL BACKGROUND: GRUMMAN ALBATROSS

Building on its success with the G-21 Goose and G-73 Mallard, the Grumman Aircraft Engineering Corp. developed the G-64 Pelican in response to an armed forces need for an amphibious search and rescue utility aircraft. First flown as two XJR2F-1 prototypes on October 1, 1947, this resourceful amphibian would remain in production until 1961 for a total of 466 delivered. The USAF was the first customer for the now re-named Albatross, taking delivery of 305 of the SA-16A variant from 1949. The U.S. Navy ordered 107 as the UF-1 and five as the UF-1T; the U.S. Coast Guard twenty-six as the UF-1G; eleven were exported as the UF-2S; and the RCAF took delivery of ten as the CSR-110 in 1960. Some of these figures are slightly misleading, as inter-service "exchanges" before and after delivery, not to mention conversions, meant some aircraft had a multitude of designations and serial numbers! For example Albatross msn G-90 was ordered as a USAF SA-16A (s/n 51-017), but was delivered as a U.S. Navy UF-1 (BuNo. 149836), was later sent to the USCG with s/n 1017, then redesignated as an HU-16C in 1962 before going to the civilian registry as N7026C. From 1956, many Albatrosses were upgraded with wider wings, a broader tail and other improvements as the SA-16B, UF-2 and UF-2G. In 1962, all aircraft were redesignated as HU-16A (SA-16A), HU-16B (SA-16B), HU-16C (UF-1), HU-16D (UF-2) and HU-16E (UF-2G). U.S. Navy retirement of the Albatross was in 1976, and the last U.S. Coast Guard HU-16E in 1983. The Albatross has enjoyed an ongoing civilian career, being very popular with private owners looking to build flying "motor homes."

Flight of the Intruder

USA / Paramount Pictures / 1991 / Color / 113 minutes

Director: John Milius
Cast: Danny Glover, Willem Dafoe, Brad Johnson, Rosanna Arquette, Tom Sizemore
Synopsis / Aviation Content: Frustrated by futile bombing of pointless targets during the Vietnam War, A-6 pilot Johnson conspires to fly an unauthorized mission into Hanoi to destroy a major munitions dump. Based on the 1986 novel of the same name by former Intruder pilot Stephen Coonts. Excellent A-6 footage and colorful aerial action throughout, but like many aviation films of this type, it doesn't stack up so well when the film is "on the ground." Very realistic Vietnam-era backdrops created for the carrier and jungle crash sequences.

Type	msn	Military s/n	Civil reg.
Douglas AD-4N (A-1D) Skyraider	7797	BuNo.126997	N409Z
Douglas AD-6 (A-1H) Skyraider	10838	BuNo.139606	N39606
Grumman A-6A-GR Intruder	I-87	BuNo.151784	—
Grumman A-6A-GR Intruder	I-167	BuNo.152619	—
Grumman A-6A-GR Intruder	I-310	BuNo.155584	—
Grumman A-6E-GR Intruder	I-528	BuNo.158792	—
Grumman A-6E-GR Intruder	I-619	BuNo.161107	—

The two Skyraiders were privately owned War-birds. All five A-6 Intruder aircraft were hired from VA-165 at NAS Whidbey Island, Washington. Most at some point carried the livery and markings of the fictional A-6 "VA-196 / Devil 505 / BuNo.151686." Carrier background aircraft are six **McDonnell Douglas F-4S Phantom II** fighters—two flyable; several **Vought-LTV A-7 Corsair II** fighters, all flyable; a non-flying **Douglas A-3 Skywarrior**; and several **Kaman SH-2 Seasprite** helicopters.

The film production had three major aeronautical / location requirements:

- **A-6 Filming**—Although all A-6 aircraft were of the "E" variant by design or conversion, they were retrofitted back to the "A" variant of 1972 by removal the various modern aerials and electronics packages. Three Intruders were ferried, along with a Douglas C-9 Skytrain of spares and personnel, out to Travis Field in Savannah, Georgia, where the coastal backdrop would serve as the Vietnam landscape. Clay Lacy's Learjet was employed as the camera-plane for the shoot, which lasted from September 25 to October 8, 1989, in the skies over Savannah. As many as six sorties a day were flown at low level and higher altitudes to capture the general flying sequences for the film.

- **Hawaii Filming**—Three VA-165 squadron A-6 Intruders were flown out to Hawaii for further A-6 filming, including air-to-air shots against various Hawaiian backgrounds that serve as Vietnam settings. One aircraft (BuNo. 158792) was fitted with onboard cameras for in-flight A-6 point-of-view shots. Clay Lacy again provided his Learjet as a camera-plane. The A-6 base of operations was at NAS Barber's Point, which also doubled in the film as a fictional Navy base in the Philippines. Also joining the Hawaii shoot were two veteran Warbirds—A-1 Skyraiders (reg. N409Z and N39606), were shipped to Hawaii from Long Beach in September 1989. Once re-assembled at Honolulu Intl. Airport, they served as background in some NAS Barber's Point ground sequences. The aircraft were then based out of Lihue Airport on Kauai, where the final scene of the film was being shot on a nearby plateau. This sequence required an A-6 wreck to be set up while the Skyraiders did low passes, dropping dummy bombs. The **Sikorsky SH-3 Sea King** in the rescue sequence was provided by the U.S. Navy in Hawaii and doubled as a USAF Jolly Green Giant rescue helicopter marked as "7146." Hawaiian logistics took place from October 13 to November 13, 1989.
- **Aircraft Carrier Filming**—VA-165's Intruders were then flown onto the USS *Independence* (CV-62), off the coast of San Diego, for the carrier scenes. Also present for these scenes were A-7 Corsairs of VA-122 out of NAS Lemoore, painted in period-1972 colors. Six F-4S Phantoms and a single A-3 Skywarrior were also on the carrier as background set dressing. The A-6 Intruders carried fictional BuNo. 151105, 151107 and 151187. Daily carrier operations such as catapult launches were filmed and cut into the movie. One sequence used a **Grumman C-2A Greyhound** (BuNo. 162165) to depict Willem Dafoe's arrival. The *Independence* accepted 108 film crew members onto its decks for the eight-day filming period, the logistics of which lasted from November 27 to mid–December 1989.

During pre-production, actors Brad Johnson, Willem Dafoe and Danny Glover did an A-6 training course at NAS Whidbey Island, covering cockpit procedures and equipment. All three actors also clocked actual A-6 flying time. Cockpit scenes were filmed at Paramount Studios using real A-6 components, including parts of A-6A BuNo. 152933. Six ⅕ scale A-6 models were built, with some smaller F-4 and MiG-17 Fresco models also required. Models were also built of the Hanoi cityscape for the bomb run sequence.

Factual Background: Grumman A-6 Intruder

The A-6 is a twin-engined, carrier-based attack aircraft designed to replace the Douglas A-1 Skyraider in the air-to-ground attack role. The significance of the A-6 was that it had the ability for day-night, all-weather missions. The prototype YA2F-1 (eight built) first flew on April 19, 1960, and after its acceptance by the U.S. Navy, manufacturer Grumman Aircraft Engr. Corp. delivered a further 872 production aircraft from its plant in Calverton, Long Island, up to 1991. Production variants are the 2-seater A-6A (480 built), ECM version EA-6 (15 built), 4-seater ECM version EA-6B Prowler (170 built) and advanced 2-seater A-6E (207 built). Service entry was in 1963, and wide use was made of this aircraft during the Vietnam War. Up to 240 A-6A aircraft were later converted to A-6E standard, and another ninety were converted to KA-6D flying tankers. Retirement of the 2-seater version occurred in 1997, and the 4-seater EA-6B Prowler to be retired from the USMC in 2019.

Flight of the Living Dead

U.S. DVD Title: *Flight of the Living Dead: Outbreak on a Plane*

Alternate DVD Title: *Plane Dead*

USA / Imageworks Ent. Intl. & Pacific Ent. Group / 2007 / Color / 94 minutes

Director: Scott Thomas

Cast: David Chisum, Kristen Kerr, Kevin J. O'Connor, Derek Webster, Raymond Barry, Dale Midkiff, Erick Avari, Richard Tyson

Synopsis / Aviation Content: Three scientists are transporting a patient on a commercial airliner who's infected with a mysterious disease which is ultimately unleashed. A virtually straight-to-DVD zombie flick with all the usual zombie-killing gags won't be to every viewer's

Type	msn	Military s/n	Civil reg.	Film Markings
Fairchild C-82A-15-FA Packet	10059	44-23015	N6887C	Arabco Oil Co.
Fairchild C-82A-20-FA Packet	10075	44-23031	N4833V	Arabco Oil Co.
Fairchild C-82A-25-FA Packet	10080	44-23036	N53228	Arabco Oil Co.
Fairchild R4Q-1 Packet	10549	BuNo.126580	—	The Phoenix
North American O-47A	25-554	38-284	N4725V	The Phoenix
Tallmantz Phoenix P-1	1	—	N93082	The Phoenix

taste. Makes use of a CGI-created Boeing 747-200 airliner (sometimes with a -400 upper deck and cockpit!), sporting false reg. "N239CK." Aircraft interiors, of course, were filmed in a studio mock-up. Also featured is a CGI creation of a Grumman F-14A Tomcat.

The Flight of the Phoenix

USA / 20th Century–Fox / 1965 / Color / 136 minutes

Director: Robert Aldrich

Cast: James Stewart, Richard Attenborough, Peter Finch, Hardy Kruger, Ernest Borgnine, Ian Bannen, Ronald Fraser, Christian Marquand, Dan Duryea, George Kennedy, Gabriele Tinti, Alex Montoya

Synopsis / Aviation Content: A twin-boom Fairchild "Skytruck" crashes in the Sahara Desert, whereupon the survivors attempt to create a new airplane—the Phoenix—from the wreckage. Based on the 1964 novel of the same name by English author Elleston Trevor. One of the most intelligent and brilliantly made aviation films ever put together, tragically marred by the death of veteran Hollywood stunt pilot Paul Mantz during production. The largely forgotten Fairchild C-82 Packet cargo transport has since become so synonymous with this film that one is rarely mentioned or written about without the other! Features an outstanding cast lineup plus a dynamic music score by Frank DeVol.

Four C-82 aircraft were required to depict the single aircraft seen in the film. They were provided by Long Beach–based company Steward-Davis, Inc., who held the C-82 type certificate and provided the filmmakers with all C-82 expertise including a flight crew. This consisted of former USAF C-82 pilot Earl Bellotte and Steward-Davis employees Bob Thayer and either Ted Whaley or Don Dinoff.

N6887C—The flying aircraft seen at the top of the movie. It had been in commercial service with Steward-Davis as a Jet Packet 1600 since 1958 and had done much lease work in both the United States and South America. Aerial shots with N6887C were shot by Tallmantz's B-25H camera-plane N1042B in early July 1965 over Imperial Valley, California. After filming, Steward-Davis converted the Packet into a "Flying Repair Station" for work up and down the U.S. West Coast. On May 11, 1970, it was impounded in Hermosillo for an illegal flight into Mexican airspace, and the owners were unable to reclaim it. The local authorities donated N6887C to the city of Hermosillo in 1983 where it stayed, on display in a local park, until scrapped in late 2005.

N4833V—Fuselage only used as the main outdoor set located in the sand dunes near Yuma, Arizona with the wings and booms held in storage. N4833V had been on the civil market since 1955 and was potentially a sprayer aircraft at some point before being picked up by Steward-Davis in 1961. After filming it was reunited with it's wings and booms then stored until scrapped in 1970–71.

N53228—Fuselage only used at 20th Century–Fox Studios for the night-work scenes. The aircraft had been in service with the USAF up to 1957 doing experimental work with the Fairchild Aircraft Corp. and has the distinction of being the very last C-82A retired by the USAF. It flew with The Master Equipment Co. in Wyoming as a pesticide sprayer until sold to Steward-Davis in 1961. After filming it was stored, along with N4833V, until scrapped in 1970–71.

UNCONFIRMED DATA

A fourth Steward-Davis owned C-82A was cut up for the cockpit and cargo hold interior scenes. Although its identity remains a mystery, it seems most likely to be one of two possibilities, either reg. N7884C (s/n 44-23013), an airframe then being

Jet-Packet 1600 N6887C in Arabco Oil Co. livery for *The Flight of the Phoenix* (1965). The jet-pack was removed for filming. Photograph: Edward Bertschy.

Derelict at Long Beach Airport in the late 1960s is C-82A N53228 (s/n 44–23036), one of three fuselages used in *The Flight of the Phoenix* (1965). This one was used at Fox Studios for the exterior night scenes in the film. Still evident on the wings and booms are the markings from its USAF days. Photograph: Bruce Orriss.

held in storage; or reg. N5116B (s/n 44-23045), a derelict previously obtained from an aircraft dealer in Florida.

An electrically operated C-82 "Skytruck" model was constructed and filmed in a mock-up sandstorm during the opening titles by industry special effects veterans L.B. Abbott and Howard Lydecker. Actor James Stewart, at the time this film was made, was a brigadier general in the USAF Reserve and a highly respected member of the aviation community. He had served during World War II as an instructor on AT-6, AT-9 and B-17 bombers and flew twenty combat missions into Germany on B-24 Liberators as the CO of the

703rd Bomb Squadron. Actors Hardy Kruger and George Kennedy were both recreational pilots.

Three different aircraft were required to bring the makeshift Phoenix to life on screen. Tallmantz Aviation, Inc., were the principal aeronautical contractors for the film, providing the aerial logistics, aerial filming and construction of the Phoenix P-1 airplane.

The first was the non-flying Phoenix that is seen being built throughout the film. It was components of a USMC Fairchild R4Q-1 (BuNo. 126580) acquired from the scrap yard of Allied Aircraft Co., Phoenix, Arizona. The R4Q-1 Packet was the USMC version of the C-119C Flying Boxcar, a type which had flown extensively with the Marines in Japan before its retirement in 1959. This Phoenix mock-up is the one Jimmy Stewart does the engine start and taxiing sequences in; it was also used with C-82A fuselage N53228 for the night-work scenes on a soundstage in Los Angeles. Components included two booms, engine nacelle assemblies with stabilizers and main wings. The longer engine nacelle and exhaust stack design make it obvious that this is an R4Q-1 (C-119C) variant.

The second and most famous of the three Phoenix replicas was the real-flying Tallmantz Phoenix P-1.

Registered in the experimental category as N93082 and built by Tallmantz Aviation, Inc., a company run by Hollywood stunt pilot veterans Paul Mantz and Frank Tallman, it was conceived by veteran aircraft designer Otto Timm. The fuselage was a steel framework covered by wooden bracing with a plywood skin covering; it utilized Beechcraft C-45 Expeditor wings and a T-6 Texan Wasp R-1340 engine and cowling, plus many other T-6 components. The P-1 was 45.5 feet long, had a wingspan of 42.5 feet, and had an empty weight of 4,550 lbs. During filming on July 8, 1965, the Phoenix P-1 was doing multiple passes before the cameras when, on the third pass, Mantz's descending approach into the filming area was too steep and the aircraft's skids struck the ground. The impact jarred the airframe to the point of structural failure, causing the aircraft to violently break-up, killing Paul Mantz, aged 61. Veteran stuntman Billy Rose, sitting behind Mantz, was thrown clear and survived. The cause of the accident came down to a combination of factors and events—(1) the aircraft was relatively underpowered and difficult to control, with structural faults possibly aggravated by a previous hard landing; (2) the high desert air temperatures at the filming location lessened aircraft performance; and (3) the pilot's judgment was allegedly impaired due to possible alcohol intoxication, a finding that was heavily disputed by friends and colleges who knew Mantz. The official accident report by the Civil Aeronautics Board was released in 1967 and cited structural problems and likely alcohol impairment in its findings.

The third and final Phoenix replica was a swiftly converted North American O-47B, N4725V, of the Air Museum (now Planes of Fame) in California. It was acquired to complete the oil camp flypast sequence not filmed before Mantz crashed. Sold onto the civilian market in 1947, the O-47A saw service with many owners doing a variety of aerial duties, including crop-spraying and seafood transportation. In 1953, it had an engine upgrade, changing the designation to O-47B. It was purchased by the Air Museum in 1961, and its film appearance as the Phoenix taking place in November 1965, with pilot and Warbird collector Wally McDonnell at the controls. Changes made to the aircraft included a modified open cockpit, a fabricated rear tail assembly, and fake skids. N4725V was returned to original configuration in 1966. A landing mishap in 1982 wrecked the aircraft, the remains are still held by Planes of Fame to this day.

Principal photography took place from April 26 to August 13, 1965, almost completely in and around Imperial County, California. Cast and crew were based at nearby Yuma, Arizona. Second unit aerial photography was based out of Yuma Intl. Airport during July 1965 with a Tallmantz B-25 (N1042B) camera-plane, the Tallmantz Phoenix P-1 (N93082) and the C-82A (N6887C). The main wreckage set piece was built in the sand dunes of Buttercup Valley at the southern end of Imperial Valley; this location was also where the Tallmantz Phoenix crashed. The airstrip in the opening shot and the oil camp oasis at the end were both mocked-up sets built close to Pilot Knob Hill located near Yuma. In-flight C-82 interior scenes were filmed at Fox Ranch in Malibu, with night scenes shot on Stage 6 at 20th Century–Fox Studios, California.

GPS LOCATIONS

Arabco Oil Airstrip: (approx.) N32 44.50 / W114 47.80

Buttercup Valley, Imperial County, California: N32 43.70 / W114 53.00

FACTUAL BACKGROUND: FAIRCHILD C-82 PACKET

A twin-engined, twin-boom aircraft by Fairchild designer Armand Thieblot, the C-82 Packet was the first practical, purpose-built cargo aircraft for the USAAF, with a rear-loading, truck-bed height fuselage deck. Most pure cargo transport aircraft since have featured the same direct in-loading style, whether from the front or back of the fuse-lage. The prototype XC-82 first flew on September

Type	msn	Military s/n	Civil reg.	Film Markings
Fairchild C-119F-FA Flying Boxcar	10955	(RCAF) 22130	N15501	H0180-H
Fairchild R4Q-2 Packet	10876	BuNo.131691	—	*Phoenix*
Fairchild R4Q-2 Packet	10885	BuNo.131700	N3267U	H0180-H
Fairchild R4Q-2 Packet	10891	BuNo.131706	—	*Phoenix*

10, 1944, with 220 C-82A and three North American C-82N variants built from 1945 to 1948. Service entry was 1945 and retirement in 1955, though its more able descendant, the C-119 Flying Boxcar, had a longer and more successful career. The Packet's subsequent civilian service was limited, mainly due to poor single-engine performance and the lack of a widespread need for a carrier of out-sized cargoes. In 1956, Steward-Davis devised a dorsal-mounted J30-W and J-34-WE Jet-Pak to boost performance under the brand names Jet Packet and Skytruck, but sales remained limited. The Packet saw limited service across the United States and in many Latin American countries, but by the end of the 1970s this unique aircraft had faded away, with only a small handful remaining in Alaska.

Flight of the Phoenix

USA / 20th Century–Fox / 2004 / Color / 113 minutes

Director: John Moore

Cast: Dennis Quaid, Giovanni Ribisi, Tyrese Gibson, Miranda Otto, Hugh Laurie, Tony Curran, Kirk Jones, Jared Padalecki, Scott Michael Campbell, Jacob Vargas, Kevork Malikyan

Synopsis / Aviation Content: Actionized remake of the 1965 classic of the same name, but now set in the Gobi Desert, Mongolia, with a few character and scripting changes to bring the story up to date. While there's no doubting the brilliant photography, CGI special effects, and stunning filming locations, the original and more faithful version of Elleston Trevor's gripping survival story is still regarded as the superior of the two. Aeronautical changes see the use of a Fairchild C-119 instead of the C-82, with simply the most spectacular film ever shot of the grand old Flying Boxcar in the very twilight of her career! Co-produced by William Aldrich, who had a bit part in the original version directed by his father Robert Aldrich.

C-119G, N15501, was the flying aircraft in the film seen in the opening titles, oil-camp scene and takeoff. Originally built as one of thirty-five C-119F Flying Boxcars for the RCAF from 1952, they were all upgraded to "G" standard before their final retirement in 1967. RCAF s/n 22130 had been retired in 1965 and exported back to the U.S. as N15501 in 1968. It was 1975 when Wyoming-based Hawkins & Powers Aviation, Inc., purchased the C-119G for various cargo duties. Fitted with a dorsal Steward-Davis J34-WE Jet-Pak, the aircraft served H&P up until 1989, when it was grounded and placed in storage. It was 2003 when N15501 was cast for the "leading role" in the new *Phoenix* film and given a complete overhaul at its Greybull home, acquiring the fictional registration "H0180-H" and Amacore Co. logos. In one of the most intriguing stories in modern aviation, N15501 was flown across the U.S., across the Atlantic, and down the African coast to Namibia for the filming of the movie's aerial sequences. A rare and outstanding feat for a vintage aircraft like the Boxcar! On December 8, 2003, Captain Bob West, pilot Steve Dunn and engineer Jim Hederman left their Wyoming base, arriving in Walvis Bay, Namibia, on December 20, 2003. N15501 then flew some of most spectacular aerial sequences ever seen in a motion picture. The aircraft returned to the U.S. in June 2004 and has since been maintained in airworthy condition. In 2006, Hawkins & Powers closed their business, and N15501 was sold to an aircraft collector in Arizona.

The USMC version of the C-119F was the R4Q-2, one of which (BuNo. 131700) was used as the main desert wreck set piece in the film. Serving with the USMC from 1953, it was retired into storage in 1975 and sold onto civilian ownership in 1980. Acquiring registration N3267U, it was sold in 1988 to Comutair of Nebraska, who flew it mainly in Europe. It appears to have been abandoned at Nairobi Airport in Kenya at some point, which is where it was located and acquired for the

Fairchild C-119G N15501 was restored to flying condition for the Namibian shot remake of *Flight of the Phoenix* (2004). Photograph: Ulrich Stulle.

new *Phoenix* film. N3267U was used in the aftermath crash sequences, in which it was buried up to its roof in sand, and all subsequent scenes up to where the survivors detach the main wings and slide them together. From this point, the Phoenix replicas (see below), are used, with only the bare fuselage of N3267U required as a background. Interior cockpit and cargo hold scenes were filmed using the fuselage of Fairchild R4Q-1 BuNo. 131691.

Two derelict R4Q-2 aircraft (BuNo. 131691 and BuNo. 131706) were purchased from Southwest Alloys of Tucson, Arizona, each to be made into a specific Phoenix replica for filming requirements.

• The first Phoenix mock-up was an on-set "continuity version," which could be built up or dismantled, depending on filming requirements—basically, it was a replica used to film the actors constructing the Phoenix. This was accomplished with the wings and starboard boom of Fairchild R4Q-1 BuNo. 131691.
• The second *Phoenix* came from Fairchild R4Q-1 (BuNo. 131706) for the final climactic escape scene, and featured a working radial engine with a V-8 dragster vehicle attached underneath for propulsion. The whole replica could reach speeds of up to 60 mph and is seen in the film doing the engine start sequence and in the wide shots during the final chase sequence.
• A third, partly built Phoenix was made for the close-up shots of the actors riding the aircraft

as it attempts takeoff in the final chase sequence. Constructed from the starboard boom and wings of N3267U, it was mounted on a mobile truck-trailer unit so actor close-ups could be obtained while keeping a live moving background. All N3267U parts and the two Phoenix replicas were scrapped at some point after filming.

Camera-planes were an Aerospatiale AS.350B (ZS-HKJ) helicopter and an Aero Commander 500S (ZS-NRO). A large-scale, cable-mounted C-119 model was built for the crash sequence by the Design Setters, Inc. Two flyable, remote-control Phoenix models were built by London Models of Johannesburg, South Africa. Many aeronautical sequences were done with CGI.

Filming took place in Namibia, Africa, which doubled for the Gobi Desert, from November 10, 2003, to February 28, 2004. The airstrip was purpose-built for the film at Rossing Mountain, nineteen miles east of Swakopmund, featuring a working runway with support buildings and compound. The main desert wreck location was six miles south of Swakopmund in a vast sand dune area. The final takeoff was shot in the same area and also south of Walvis Bay somewhere along cliff faces on the Kuiseb River. C-119 aerial operations were based out of Walvis Bay Airport.

GPS Locations—Namibia
Amacore Airstrip: S22 32.10 / E014 48.05
Main crash site: S22 46.10 / E014 34.45

FACTUAL BACKGROUND:
FAIRCHILD C-119 FLYING BOXCAR

The C-119 is a more refined and powerful version of the earlier Fairchild C-82 Packet, the most obvious change being the newly relocated, streamlined flight deck. A fleet of 1,185 aircraft were built from 1948 to 1955; service entry was 1949, and the C-119 saw action in Korea and Vietnam with the USAF. The name "Flying Boxcar" stemmed from a nickname given to the C-82—its internal capacity being equal to that of a railroad boxcar. The official name of Packet appears to have remained with the USMC version—the R4Q-1 (C-119C) and R4Q-2 (C-119F). Fifty-two were converted as gunships in Vietnam from 1968 to 1973 as the AC-119G Shadow and AC-119K Stinger, the latter featuring two wing-mounted jet-pods. The final version was twenty-four C-119L conversions, which saw the use of three-bladed props instead of the traditional four-bladed ones. The Air National Guard took the C-119L up to its final retirement in 1975. Many have since found their way onto the civilian market as cargo carriers and fire-bombers. One foreign air force, Taiwan, didn't retire their C-119G Boxcars until 1997.

Flightplan

USA / Buena Vista Pictures / 2005 / Color / 98 minutes

Director: Robert Schwentke

Cast: Jodie Foster, Peter Sarsgaard, Sean Bean, Kate Beahan, Michael Irby, Assaf Cohen, Erika Christensen

Synopsis / Aviation Content: In-flight thriller about a grieving widow who awakes on a plane to find her young daughter missing and the passengers and crew not believing she ever boarded the flight with the child in the first place. The aircraft is a fictional, mammoth airliner called the "E-474," a double-deck jumbo modeled strongly after the Airbus A-380, the large size being suitable for the missing-person plot of the film. Many of the interior sets used real aircraft components such as seats, gallies, etc.

Fly Away Home

Original Title: *Flying Wild*

USA / Columbia Pictures / 1996 / Color / 107 minutes

Director: Carroll Ballard

Cast: Jeff Daniels, Anna Paquin, Dana Delany, Terry Kinney, Holter Graham, Jeremy Ratchford

Synopsis / Aviation Content: A young girl living with her estranged father adopts a batch of orphaned geese chicks and uses her father's ultralight aircraft to teach them to migrate. Loosely based on actual bird migration experiments carried out by Canadian inventor William Lishman with his own ultralight aircraft in the late '80s and early '90s. His findings and story were published in the 1995 book *Father Goose*.

Good family film features some stunning aerial photography of the Canadian landscape with two ultralight aircraft: a 1978 **Easy Riser Ultralight** (reg. C-IBYE / msn WAL 001), which first appears as an unpowered hang-glider. This is the actual ultralight used by Lishman during his migration experiments and was piloted, in part, by him during the film. The other was an A-frame **Cosmos Trike Ultralight** with "goose" painted wings and a mock-up goose head. Filmed from July 17 to October 19, 1995, in Ontario, Canada. One sequence was filmed at Niagara Falls AFB, New York, where there are brief glimpses of the Boeing KC-135R; General Dynamics F-16; and Lockheed C-130 and C-5. The film's original title was *Flying Wild*, which wasn't changed until just before release, so some teaser trailers and promotional material retain this title.

Flyboys

USA / Metro-Goldwyn-Mayer / 2006 / Color / 133 minutes

Director: Tony Bill

Cast: James Franco, Martin Henderson, David Ellison, Jennifer Decker, Jean Reno, Tyler Labine, Abdul Salis, Tim Pigott-Smith, Philip Winchester

Synopsis / Aviation Content: A fictionalized story based on the real-life World War I French fighter squadron, the Lafayette Escadrille, which was made up of volunteer American pilots. A film that unfortunately performed quite poorly at the box office, but with this and its minor aviation historical inaccuracies aside (one being that the Nieuport 17 was withdrawn before the Fokker Dr.I entered service), it really isn't too bad a movie in terms of its entertainment value. Nine replica fighter aircraft flew before the cameras, with much help from CGI artists! Dedicated direction from Tony Bill and a soaring music score by Trevor Rabin.

Type	msn	Civil reg.
Baslee Nieuport 17	No. 001	N117TB
Baslee Nieuport 17	No. 002	N117DD
Baslee Nieuport 17	No. 003	N117KP
Baslee Nieuport 17	No. 004	N117MR
Fokker Dr.I Triplane	PFA/238-12654	G-BVGZ
Fokker Dr.I Triplane	002	N78001
Nieuport 17	LCNC 1967	N1290
Nieuport 17	PFA/121-12351	N1977
Sopwith 1-1/2 Strutter	RA003	N4088H

The Nieuport 17 was a French-designed and -built fighter which first flew in January 1916 and was in service by March of the same year. Airdrome Aeroplanes, run by Robert Baslee in Missouri, built the four Baslee Nieuport replicas for the film company in a record fifty-two days starting in January 2005. They can be distinguished from the other two Nieuports by their slightly swept-back wings. All four were registered to Electric Television Holdings, Inc., the company behind the production. The other two Nieuport 17 fighters were also replicas: N1290 was hired from Kermit Weeks (Fantasy of Flight), and N1977 was hired from Bob Gauld-Galliers and John Day, being registered as G-BWMJ in the UK. Two full-scale Nieuport 17 mock-ups were built in the Czech Republic for background scenes; both had electric motors to spin their props and both were later destroyed for the film.

The German Fokker Triplane first flew in July 1917 and is most famous as being the aircraft of Manfred von Richthofen—The Red Baron. In all, 320 aircraft were built, but none survive today. Both versions used in the film were replicas, with the principal aircraft, G-BVGZ, hired from the Real Airplane Co.; this was also the one painted black in some scenes. N78001 was hired briefly from Rob Lamplough for a strafing sequence and was normally registered G-ATJM in the UK. It

was one of two triplanes originally built for *The Blue Max* (1966).

The British-designed 2-seater Sopwith Strutter first flew in April 1916 and was the first British fighter to feature propeller-synchronized machine guns. The one used in the film, N4088H, was a replica hired from Ken Kellett of Florida. The 2-seat design fit in with several sequences scripted in the film.

U.S. aerial coordinator was Michael Patlin. UK aerial coordinators were Ray Hanna and Sarah Hanna. Pilots included Nigel Lamb (chief pilot), Alister Kay (safety pilot), Brian Brown, John Day, Bob Gauld-Galliers, Andrew King, Ken Kellett, Taff Smith, Anna Walker, Douglas Gregory, Robb Metcalfe, Desmond Penrose, Rob Millingship and Andy Sefton. Engineers were Mike Fenton, Nev Gardener, Paul Nicholls, Dave Proctor, Jean Michel Munn and Tom Solomon. The film was dedicated to pilot Ray Hanna, who died soon after filming on December 1, 2005. Director Tony Bill is a recreational pilot and owns several light aircraft types.

Background aircraft were a **Bristol E fighter** and a 1909 **Bleriot** supplied by the Shuttleworth Collection, as well as a scale replica S.E.5a. The German Gotha bomber was only partly built, with the rest being a CGI creation, as was the British Handley-Page bomber. The German zeppelin was a large-scale model. The main airfield set was built at RAF Halton, where location filming took place from May to July 2005. Special effects mock-ups were filmed with green screens at Elstree Studios in the UK.

The Fly Boys

UK / DVD Title: **Sky Kids**

USA / Dark Coast Pictures / 2008 / Color / 118 minutes

Director: Rocco Devilliers

Cast: Jesse James, Reiley McClendon, Stephen Baldwin, Tom Sizemore, J. Todd Adams, Dallen Gettling, Jennifer Slimko

Synopsis / Aviation Content: Two school kids accidentally become trapped in the back of a Mafia drug-running Twin-Beech and have to take control of the doomed aircraft after the pilots jump out. Although some of the villainous characters' motives are a little intense, considering the young age group at which the movie is aimed, the story is well crafted and directed with twists and turns along the way. There's fantastic aerial photography and an entertaining depiction of the youngsters flying. Some of the highlights are a daring highway landing and an absolutely mind-blowing skydiving sequence!

Type	msn	Civil reg.
Aerospatiale AS.350BA A-Star	2130	N410JC
Beechcraft Expeditor Mk. 3NM	CA-265	N476PA
Cessna 172G	172-53829	N3660L

The main aerial attraction is the Beechcraft Model D18S, owned and flown by pilot Skip Evans. The aircraft was originally one of 133 Expeditor Mk. 3NM navigation trainers for the RCAF; with s/n 1579 it was delivered to the RCAF on January 22, 1953, and retired from service and struck off on July 19, 1968, for sale to the civilian market. It flew with the Hamilton Aircraft Co. of Tucson, Arizona, until being acquired in 1986 by Skip Evans, who has maintained it to an airworthy standard ever since. The highway landing scene was filmed along a four-mile stretch of road between Mesquite and St. George, Utah. Skip Evans flew N576PA down to seventy knots, narrowly bobbing over the carefully placed and spaced eighteen stunt vehicles and a single large semi truck.

The drug-dealers' Aerospatiale helicopter, N410JC, was provided by Jet Copters, Inc., of Van Nuys, California. Cessna 172G, N3660L, had a brief appearance when the two kids were playing around in various airplanes. The twin-engined light aircraft in the final scene is an unidentified **Cessna 310**. Background aircraft include a **Beechcraft A36 Bonanza**, a **Piper PA-28 Archer**, and a **Piper PA-31 Navajo**. The airfield was Mesquite Airport, Mesquite, Utah (GPS Location: N36 49.90 / W114 03.50), and the township scenes were filmed in nearby St. George, Utah.

Flying Blind

USA / Paramount Pictures / 1941 / B&W / 69 minutes
Director: Frank McDonald

Cast: Richard Arlen, Jean Parker, Nils Asther, Marie Wilson, Roger Pryor, Eddie Quillan, Dick Purcell, Grady Sutton, Kay Sutton
Synopsis / Aviation Content: A young couple running a "honeymoon" air charter business flying to Las Vegas are forced to crash land in the wilderness with foreign Axis spies onboard. One of many such airliner films made during the prewar period is notable as being the last before America's entry into World War II. Filmed in part at Alhambra Airport, California, with a **Lockheed Model 12-A Junior Electra** (reg. NC17376 / msn 1220). This aircraft was likely later used in *Casablanca* (1942) before being drafted into military service as a UC-40D (s/n 42-57504) in 1942. It was written off soon after when it taxied into a parked aircraft. The famous model of the Capelis XC-12 was used for the crash scene of the Lockheed Electra. Other aircraft are a **Boeing Model 247**, a **Douglas DC-2**, and a **Lockheed Model 14 Super Electra**.

The Flying Doctor

Australia-UK / 20th Century–Fox / 1936 / B&W / 92 minutes
Director: Miles Mander
Cast: Charles Farrell, Mary Maguire, James Raglan, Joe Valli, Margaret Vyner, Eric Colman
Synopsis / Aviation Content: An Australian doctor heads to the outback, where he sets about acquiring his pilot's license in order to reach his patients. Aircraft content is unknown, but the film is notable as being the first Australian feature film with sound and the first aviation-themed feature film to be produced in Australia. Although the financial backers are Fox Studios, it doesn't appear to have been released in the USA. Released in the UK by General Film Distributors (GFD) in 1937. The concept was later developed in Australia as the TV series *The Flying Doctor* (1959), then as the smash-hit TV series *The Flying Doctors* (1985–1991).

The Flying Fleet

USA / Metro-Goldwyn-Mayer / 1929 / B&W / 100 minutes

Director: George W. Hill

Cast: Ramon Novarro, Ralph Graves, Anita Page, Edward Nugent

Synopsis / Aviation Content: The story of five naval pilots beginning with their academy training and concluding with a disastrous attempt to fly from California to Hawaii. One of the last silent-era films features some great early naval aircraft sequences thanks to the U.S. Navy's full cooperation in making the picture. Featured aircraft are the **Boeing F2B-1** (one was BuNo. A-7429); **Douglas T2D-1** twin-engined torpedo-bomber; **Consolidated NY-2** (one was BuNo. A-7493) trainer; **Curtiss F6C-3 Hawk** biplane; **Loening OL-3** amphibian biplane; and **Vought O2U-1 Corsair** (BuNo. A-7817) as a camera-plane. Excellent period views of the Pensacola Naval Training Academy in Florida and the Navy's large base at NAS San Diego, California. But the real treat here for aviation fans are the detailed views of the aircraft carrier USS *Langley* in action with haphazard aircraft takeoffs and landings. Based on a story by ex–naval aviator turned Hollywood screenwriter Frank "Spig" Wead—this film being the first of many such naval aviation–themed motion pictures to his credit. Music and sound were later added for subsequent releases of the film.

Flying Fortress

UK-USA / Warner Bros. / 1942 / B&W / 109 minutes (U.S. release: 68 minutes)

Director: Walter Forde

Cast: Richard Greene, Carla Lehman, Betty Stockfeld, Donald Stewart, Basil Radford

Synopsis / Aviation Content: A less-than-average wartime production effort of a careless pilot who goes to England, joins a B-17 squadron, then learns of the horrors of war. Although the film is hampered with a weak plot, the views of early B-17 operations in England do make this worthy of viewing, especially for Flying Fortress fans.

When filming began in September 1941, the B-17 Flying Fortress had not yet made its mark on aviation history—the thousands of B-17F and B-17G variants that would pound Germany were still some time away. During late 1941, there was only the under-armed B-17C, twenty of which were being operated by the RAF as the **Fortress Mk. I**. Around five or six of these were made available to the filmmakers, three of which were RAF s/n AN518, AN530 and AN536 (U.S. s/n 40-2043, 40-2066 and 40-2076 respectively). Ground, taxi, takeoff and formation scenes were all shot, giving good views of this rarely photographed B-17 variant. Filmed on location with No. 90 Squadron, RAF Polebrook, England. Studio scenes were filmed at Teddington Studios, Middlesex, England.

Flying High!   see   Airplane!

Flying Leathernecks

USA / RKO Radio Pictures / 1951 / Color / 121 minutes

Director: Nicholas Ray

Cast: John Wayne, Robert Ryan, Don Taylor, Janis Carter, Jay C. Flippen, William Harrigan

Synopsis / Aviation Content: Hard squadron commander Wayne butts heads with subordinates in this World War II drama set on Guadalcanal in the Pacific. Tiresome arguing and drama throughout, with the only relief being some excellent Grumman Hellcat sequences including takeoffs and formation shots. Aviation legend Howard Hughes was a prime backer in the making of this film.

Grumman F6F-5 Hellcat fighters of VMT-2 at MCAS El Toro and **Vought F4U-4 Corsair** fighters of VMF-232 were employed for filming on location at MCAS Camp Pendleton from November 1950 to February 1951. Other aircraft were a **Consolidated PBY-6A Catalina**, which was destroyed in the recreation of a Japanese attack, plus many derelict F6F Hellcat fighters were used to depict destroyed aircraft on the airfield. A **North American SNJ Texan** was converted to a Japanese Zero look-alike. A large use of stock newsreel footage of actual aircraft in combat included the Grumman TBF Avenger, Grumman F6F Hellcat, Vought F4U Corsair and Douglas

C-54 Skymaster. Paul Mantz was the aerial supervisor, providing his B-25H camera-plane, N1203, for the aerial sequences.

Flying Tigers

USA / Republic Pictures / 1942 / B&W / 101 minutes

Director: David Miller

Cast: John Wayne, John Carroll, Anna Lee, Paul Kelly, Gordon Jones, Mae Clarke, Addison Richards, Chester Gan

Synopsis / Aviation Content: World War II drama set in Burma and China has pilot Wayne leading a squadron of the American Volunteer Group (AVG), better known as the Flying Tigers. An excellent but relatively shallow look at the combat efforts of the AVG; contains plenty of action and tight pacing with actual combat footage. Notable as being one of the best known of films to feature the P-40, even though most were only full-scale mock-ups! This is actor John Wayne's first wartime role.

The film was shot soon after America's entry into World War II. Due to the war effort, P-40 fighters were not available for Hollywood hire, so the studio commissioned Hollywood special effects team Howard and Theodore Lydecker to construct six full-scale Curtiss P-40C Warhawk wooden mock-ups. All had electric motors to drive the propeller and wheels for startup and taxi shots, with the cockpits built slightly larger for better camera access to the actors. The mock-ups were extensively used throughout filming, and the Lydecker Bros., along with their other effects work on this film, gained an Academy Award nomination.

The twin-engined cargo transport at the end of the film was the one and only **Capelis Model XC-12** (reg. NX12762 / msn 1), a privately built 1933 prototype which failed to generate any buyer interest. It had been purchased in 1938 by RKO Pictures for the film *Five Came Back* (1939), and subsequently appeared in a number of other productions throughout the 1940s. It was an airworthy aircraft but had to be grounded for insurance reasons, so all the flying shots were accomplished with a scale Capelis model.

Footage of newly built Curtiss P-40 fighters was shot at the Curtiss plant in Buffalo, New York, while the aircraft were being flight-tested. These are the high-speed P-40 takeoffs seen in the finished film. Stock newsreel footage from the Spanish Civil War and Japanese aircraft types over China were used in the battle sequences. Airfield location scenes were shot on Paramount Ranch outside of Hollywood, California.

Flying Wild   see   Fly Away Home

Forever Young

USA / Warner Bros. / 1992 / Color / 102 minutes

Director: Steve Miner

Cast: Mel Gibson, Jamie Lee Curtis, Elijah Wood, Isabel Glasser, George Wendt, Joe Morton, Nicolas Surovy, David Marshall Grant

Synopsis / Aviation Content: Gibson plays a 1939-era test pilot who volunteers to undergo an experiment in "suspended animation," only to be forgotten about until 1992, when two kids stumble upon his forgotten capsule in a military warehouse. Mainly of the romance / science fiction genre, the story has a promising and interesting premise that unfortunately all too quickly runs out of credibility. Warbird fans will enjoy the prominently featured Planes of Fame–owned B-25J bomber, plus the astonishing array of "eye candy" at a locally filmed airshow.

The story begins with a test flight of what appears to be the North American NA-40 (B-25) prototype, reproduced here as a full-scale mock-up filmed at Moonpark, California, along with a **Vultee BT-13 Valiant** in the background. The prototype of the B-25 bomber, by the way, did in fact first fly in 1939. The red biplane, which does a flyby in a dream sequence, is Planes of Fame's **Boeing-Stearman N2S-2 Kaydet** (BuNo. 3558 / msn 75-1335 / reg. N61445). The brief scene with a helicopter is a **Bell Model 206B Jet Ranger** (reg. N250CA / msn 2615), this particular one having made many film appearances over the years.

The finale makes use of a **North American B-25J-25-NC Mitchell** (s/n 44-30423 / msn 108-33698 / reg. N3675G), hired from Planes of Fame in Chino, California. After serving as a TB-25J trainer in the USAF, it was sold onto the civilian market as N3675G on July 30, 1959; Air Museum creator Ed Maloney picked it up in 1965, and its been in their (now Planes of Fame) care ever since. N3675G also made an appearance in *1941* (1979) and later in *Pearl Harbor* (2001), as one of the Doolittle B-25 bombers.

The airshow sequences were filmed at Los Alamitos Army Airfield in Long Beach, California, with background aircraft including the **Bell UH-1H Iroquois, AH-1 Cobra**; **Bell OH-58A Kiowa**; **Boeing-Stearman Kaydet**; **Curtiss P-40N Warhawk**; **Douglas A-1 Skyraider**; **Gates Learjet**; **Grumman Avenger, Goose**; **Lockheed P-38J Lightning** (N38BP); **North American AT-6 Texan, P-51D Mustang**; **Sikorsky UH-60A Black Hawk** and **Vought F4U Corsair**.

GPS LOCATION

Los Alamitos Army Airfield, California: N33 47.35 / W118 03.15

For the Moment

Canada / John Aaron Productions / 1993 / Color / 120 minutes

Director: Aaron Kim Johnston

Cast: Russell Crowe, Christianne Hirt, Wanda Cannon, Scott Kraft, Peter Outerbridge, Sara McMillan, Bruce Boa, Katelynd Johnston

Synopsis / Aviation Content: In 1942, an Australian pilot undergoes aerial combat training in Canada, where he begins an affair with a local married woman whose husband is overseas fighting. Routine romance drama made better by the inclusion of some World War II period Canadian trainer types, especially the Tiger Moth, Anson and Crane (Bobcat). Released in the U.S. in 1996.

Featured aircraft were, in large part, provided and furnished by the Commonwealth Air Training Plan Museum in Brandon, Canada. Seen at various points throughout the film are the **Avro Anson** (RCAF s/n 12477, 12125); **Bristol Blenheim** (RCAF s/n 9059); **Cessna Crane Mk. I** (RCAF s/n 8656), the Canadian designation for the Cessna AT-8 Bobcat; **DeHavilland DH.82 Tiger Moth** (RCAF s/n 1138, 4188) and a **North American Harvard Mk. II** (s/n 2557 / msn 66-2290 / reg. CF-MGZ), which is seen in the suicide scene. The serial numbers on some aircraft maybe "representative" only and not be the aircraft's actual serial number. A **Douglas A-26C-45-DT Invader** (s/n 44-35661 / msn 28940 / reg. C-FCBK) was provided by Canadian company Air Spray, Ltd., for the beach flyby scene, doubling as a Douglas A-20 Havoc (according to the film's dialogue). Normally, it flew as an aerial tanker (Tanker 11) in forest fire operations, but was written off in Alberta on August 12, 2004. Other aviation companies who assisted with aircraft were Arcot Aviation Ltd. and the Reynolds Museum of Alberta, plus the Red River Tiger Moth Group.

Filmed in large part at Brandon Municipal Airport, Manitoba, Canada, which is the location of the Commonwealth Air Training Plane Museum. Many of the hangars and aircraft, along with much expertise, were provided to the filmmakers by the museum, which retains many historic aircraft. Other locations were in and around the local town of Brandon.

GPS LOCATION

Brandon Municipal Airport, Manitoba, Canada: N49 54.30 / W099 56.60

For Your Eyes Only (Non–Aviation Themed Title)   see   James Bond Series

From Russia with Love (Non–Aviation Themed Title)   see   James Bond Series

Full Metal Jacket (Non–Aviation Themed Title)

USA-UK / Warner Bros. / 1987 / Color / 112 minutes

Director: Stanley Kubrick

Cast: Matthew Modine, Adam Baldwin, Vincent D'Onofrio, R. Lee Ermey, Dorian Harewood, Kevyn Major Howard

Synopsis / Aviation Content: Set during the Vietnam War, the story follows a USMC platoon from boot camp training to battlefield. Three civilian **Westland Wessex Mk. 60** helicopters were used for filming—flying was G-AYNC (msn WA739), owned by the Sykes Group and marked as "EM18"; two static examples were G-AWOX (msn WA686), as "EM17" and G-AZBY (msn WA740), as "EM16." Seventeen Westland Wessex Mk. 60 helicopters were built, with most initially owned by Bristow Helicopters Ltd. of the UK for offshore oil rig work. The Westland Wessex is based on the U.S.-built Sikorsky H-34 Choctaw.

Fury in the Sky see *Ladies Courageous*

Gallant Journey

USA / Columbia Pictures / 1946 / B&W / 85 minutes

Director: William A. Wellman

Cast: Glenn Ford, Janet Blair, Charles Ruggles, Henry Travers, Jimmy Lloyd, Charles Kemper, Arthur Shields, Robert DeHaven

Synopsis / Aviation Content: A biographical film following the life and times of American aviation pioneer John Montgomery (1858–1911), who on August 28, 1883, made the first manned, controlled, and heavier-than-air flight inside the United States using a glider. He was also an inventor and professor at Santa Clara College. Montgomery, was killed in 1911 after crashing in his glider named *The Evergreen*. The film features some magnificent aerial photography. Former World War I fighter pilot Wellman also produced and co-wrote the screenplay.

Director Wellman hired the Radioplane Company to construct replica Montgomery Gliders, which, like that of the original inventor himself, were launched from balloons after being elevated to altitude. The glider replicas were built from lightweight metals, as opposed to the original

wooden construction; they also utilized modern fabrics, had larger wingspans for greater lift, and featured a rudder for safety. Glider pilots were Paul Tuntland, Don C. Stevens, and Hollywood pilot Paul Mantz, who was hired to supervise filming. During one occasion Tuntland's glider failed to release from the balloon it was using to gain altitude and it wasn't until 16,000 feet that he managed to free the glider! He subsequently gently descended to the assigned 4,000-foot altitude for filming. Principal photography took place in California from March 4 to June 1, 1946.

A Gathering of Eagles

USA / Universal Pictures / 1963 / Color / 116 minutes

Director: Delbert Mann

Cast: Rock Hudson, Rod Taylor, Mary Peach, Barry Sullivan, Henry Silva, Robert Lansing, Kevin McCarthy, Richard Anderson, Leora Dana, Leif Erickson

Synopsis / Aviation Content: A B-52 commander played by Hudson must push his crews to pass an operational readiness test imposed by a visiting Strategic Air Command general. Produced and co-written by Sy Bartlett, who co-created the similarly themed aviation classic *Twelve O'Clock High* (1949), exploring the pressures of command. Former SAC commander General Curtis LeMay used his influence to allow unprecedented access to real B-52 SAC bases and facilities for the filmmakers. Some good views of the B-52 Stratofortress in action, including takeoffs and landings.

Filmed mainly at Beale AFB, north of Sacramento, California, which stood in for the film's fictional 904th Strategic Air Wing at Carody AFB near San Francisco. Aircraft are numerous **Boeing B-52 Stratofortress** bombers, both of the long- and short-tailed variant. Identified are B-52E-85-BO (s/n 56-642 / msn 17325) and B-52G-90-BW (s/n 57-6516 / msn 464221); the **Boeing KC-135A Stratotanker** (one was s/n 58-0095 / msn 17840); **Lockheed T-33A Shooting Star** (buzz nos. TR-271, TR-280, TR-873); **Sikorsky SH-19 Chickasaw**; and a **Douglas C-47 Skytrain** in the background.

GPS LOCATION
Beale AFB, California: N39 08.40 / W121 26.10

God Is My Co-Pilot

USA / Warner Bros. / 1945 / B&W / 90 minutes
Director: Robert Florey
Cast: Dennis Morgan, Raymond Massey, Andrea King, Alan Hale Sr., Dane Clark, Richard Loo
Synopsis / Aviation Content: Aging stateside flight instructor Morgan is told he's too old for combat but manages to convince superiors to let him fly in the China-India-Burma Theater. Providing many and varied views of several World War II types, especially the P-40 Warhawk, the film is most notable for its brilliant aerial sequences. Based on the 1943 autobiography of the same name by fighter ace Robert L. Scott, Jr.

Aircraft provided to the filmmakers were fifteen-plus **Curtiss P-40E / F Warhawk** fighter variants of the 544th Single-Engine Flight Training Squadron at Luke AAF, Arizona; eighteen-plus **North American B-25C / D / G Mitchell** bombers from the 952nd Transition Group from Mather Field, California; eighteen-plus **North American AT-6 Texan** trainers used as Japanese "Zero" look-alikes; one **Douglas C-47 Skytrain**; and one **Republic P-43 Lancer**. All these aircraft were stationed for filming at a Luke auxiliary airfield southwest of the main Luke AAF, Arizona. The fifty or so aircraft was the largest number provided to a film studio during World War II.

Three mock-up P-40 fighters from *Flying Tigers* (1942) were used at Warner Bros. Calabasas Ranch, California, for the "Kunming Airstrip" scenes. Cockpit sections were used of a **Naval Aircraft Factory N3N** as a Boeing P-12 and a **Vought SB2U-1** from *Dive Bomber* (1941) as a "Zero." Cockpit sections were also used of a Boeing B-17, Curtiss P-40, Douglas C-47 and Republic P-43. There's also stock footage of the Boeing B-17 from *Air Force* (1943), as well as the P-12, Boeing-Stearman PT-13/-17, Curtiss C-46, Douglas O-3 and Martin B-26. There's some use of scale models and special effects.

One tragic, on-set death occurred during filming when an AT-6 trainer clipped a B-25 bomber during an aerial sequence, killing the pilot in the trainer; the B-25 landed safely. Hollywood pilot Paul Mantz was involved in the aerial photography, which took place from August 1944. Robert Scott was the film's technical advisor and flew many of the P-40 sequences himself.

FACTUAL BACKGROUND:
ROBERT L. SCOTT, JR.

Georgia-born Robert Lee Scott, Jr. (April 12, 1908–February 27, 2006) was best known for his autobiographical book *God Is My Co-Pilot*, which he wrote in a hotel room after returning to the United States from the China-India-Burma Theater during World War II. In the book, Scott recounts his experiences fighting the Japanese with the Flying Tigers. He flew 388 combat missions, shooting down thirteen enemy aircraft to become one of America's top scoring aces at that time. He held various commands in the U.S. and Europe during and after the war and continued to publish books on military themes. Scott had attained the rank of brigadier general by the time of his retirement in 1957. Although the film version of the book makes several liberal "Hollywood" changes, it still proved very popular and made Robert Scott a household name at the time of its release.

GoldenEye (Non–Aviation Themed Title)
  see   *James Bond* Series

Goldfinger (Non–Aviation Themed Title)
  see   *James Bond* Series

The Great Air Robbery

USA / Universal Film Manufacturing Co. / 1919 / B&W / duration unknown
Director: Jacques Jaccard
Cast: Ormer Locklear, Allan Forrest, Ray Ripley, Francelia Billington, Carmen Phillips, Tom London
Synopsis / Aviation Content: Top pilot Larry Cassidy (Locklear) pursues an aerial group of thieving pirates known as the "Death's Head Squadron." This silent-era film is highly notable as being the first successful, feature-length avi-

ation film to be released, and is crammed with spectacular aerial stunt work performed by Hollywood newcomer Ormer Locklear, who also has the leading role! The film was shot very quickly in the second half of July 1919, in part at legendary film producer Cecil B. DeMille's own airfield—aptly named DeMille Field No. 1—in Los Angeles. Aircraft were **Curtiss JN Jenny** biplanes, also owned by DeMille. The daredevil stunts and overall success of this film, along with Ormer Locklear's next ill-fated feature, *The Skywayman* (1920), would gain him the unique title of "Hollywood's first stunt man."

The Great Santini

Original Release Title: *The Ace*
USA / Orion Pictures & Warner Bros. / 1979 / Color / 115 minutes
Director: Lewis John Carlino
Cast: Robert Duvall, Blythe Danner, Michael O'Keefe, Stan Shaw, Lisa Jane Persky, Julie Anne Haddock, Brian Andrews
Synopsis / Aviation Content: In 1962, a USMC fighter pilot, played by Duvall, has been very successful in his military career, but off duty is an abusive father and husband at home. Based on the 1976 novel of the same name by American author Pat Conroy, the story of which is a memoir of Conroy's own childhood as the son of a strict fighter pilot father. Filmed at MCAS Beaufort in South Carolina, with various views of the **McDonnell Douglas F-4 Phantom II** in action. The variant used was the F-4J, which didn't enter service until 1966. In 1962 the USMC would have been flying the F-4B. Aerial sequences were filmed by Clay Lacy flying his Learjet camera-plane. Warner Bros. originally released the film on cable television and to airlines as *The Ace*. However, when very favorable reviews came back, it was released theatrically and retitled *The Great Santini*. Duvall's character was based on Conroy's father, Donald "The Great Santini" Conroy, who was a World War II veteran, as well as a member of the famous Black Sheep Squadron during the Korean War, and completed two tours during the Vietnam War in the A-4 Skyhawk.

The Great Waldo Pepper

USA / Universal Pictures / 1975 / Color / 107 minutes
Director: George Roy Hill
Cast: Robert Redford, Bo Svenson, Bo Brundin, Susan Sarandon, Geoffrey Lewis
Synopsis / Aviation Content: In the barnstorming days of 1926, Redford plays a carefree pilot providing joy rides for locals before a tragic accident sees him barred from flying. He then heads to Hollywood to try a career stunt flying in the movies. The director, former fighter pilot George Roy Hill, also produced and wrote the story, apparently based on an idea pitched to him some years earlier by Frank Tallman, the film's aerial supervisor. Excellent biplane-era film was one of the last "big movies" for longtime Hollywood aviation company Tallmantz Aviation, which provided a large number of vintage aircraft and pilots for the production. Remember, all the jaw-dropping stunts and crashes here are the real thing—no mock-ups or miniatures were used!

Tallmantz Aviation, Inc., provided all aeronautical expertise, up to fourteen vintage aircraft, and twelve pilots including Frank Tallman himself and well-known aerobatic pilot Art Scholl. Other pilots employed on the movie were James S. Appleby (at the time Tallmantz's chief pilot), Howard Curtis, John Kazian, Frank Pine (at the time Tallmantz's vice-president), Audrey Saunders, Wayne Berg, Mike Dewey, Thomas G. Mooney, Frank Price and Ralph Wiggins. Director George Roy Hill was a transport pilot during World War II and a fighter pilot flying Corsairs during the Korean War.

Two **Standard J-1** biplane-era aircraft were acquired, one was marked *The Great Waldo Pepper*, as Redford's aircraft, with the other used later on for the aerial circus scenes. One was reg. N2825D / msn 1582, which had been restored by renowned aircraft designer Otto Timm and Paul Mantz for *The Spirit of St. Louis* (1957); the other Standard J-1 was either N2826D or N62505. Two similar **Curtiss JN-4 Jenny** biplanes were acquired (likely N6898 and N2062), with one marked as *Capt. Axel Olsson*. One Jenny was later painted silver as *Cinegraph Studios*, as the film company camera-plane. All four aircraft were later marked as *Dillhoefer Flying Circus* numbers 20, 22, 24 and 27.

The spritely, aerobatic aircraft marked as *Ernst Kessler* is a **Bucker Bu.133 Jungmeister** (reg. N87P / msn 1015), imported to the U.S. in 1961 and upgraded from its old radial engine to a 200 hp Lycoming in a streamlined fuselage. Originally built in Germany in 1939 as a military trainer, it was owned and flown in the film by aerobatic pilot Frank Price.

The fictional prototype aerobatic monoplane named the *Stiles Skystreak*, performing outside loops, was a converted **DeHavilland-Canada DHC-1 Chipmunk T.Mk. 10** (RAF s/n WG427 / msn DHB/F/370). It was built in 1951 and eventually flew in Australia with civilian reg. VH-GEB as a Sasin-Aerostructures SA-29 Spraymaster single-seat crop-duster conversion. Exported to the U.S. in 1972 as reg. N7DW, it was flown for the film by aerobatic pilot Art Scholl.

The three fighters used in the final scenes on the "movie set" were a black **Fokker DR.1 Triplane** (reg. N5523V / msn DB1), a replica owned by Tallmantz as Kessler's fighter; a **Sopwith Camel F.1** (reg. N8997 / msn TM-10) replica built for the film by Tallmantz in 1974, with a red cowling that enabled it to double as Redford's fighter; and a **Thomas-Morse S-4B** (reg. N38923 / msn 1), also a replica owned by Tallmantz, with a green cowling and doubling as Olsson's fighter, which is "shot down." A background biplane marked as "A5202" is a Currie-Wot S.E.5a replica originally built for the film *Darling Lili* (1970).

Two **DeHavilland DH.82 Tiger Moth** biplanes were crashed by Frank Tallman for the cameras. The first plummets into a lake while doubling as Olsson's Curtiss JN-4, and the second, also doubling as a Curtiss JN-4, is crashed during a carnival scene. Two aircraft were lost to the production before it even began filming. The first was a **Garland-Lincoln LF-4** (reg. N12237 / msn 3), which crashed during landing at Piru, California, on January 15, 1974, due to a strong crosswind and a wet airstrip. The pilot was Frank Pine, who walked away unhurt. The second was a **Pawkett-Nieuport 28** replica (reg. N2SR / msn 002), which crashed at Newhall, California, on January 21, 1974. The pilot this time was Frank

Tallman, and the crash was the result of a rudder pedal that had failed, causing the aircraft spiral in. Tallman suffered minor injuries, and George Roy Hill shut the film down until he recovered. The Thomas-Morse biplane was then employed to cover the loss of these two aircraft.

Filmed mostly in Elgin, Texas, with some scenes filmed at Zuehl Field (GPS Location: N29 29.70 / W098 09.40), outside San Antonio, Texas. The "movie set" set, where the final dogfight is staged, was built outside Piru, California, where filming took place in early 1974. The altitude flying scenes were filmed in Florida, where large billowy clouds helped create a more plausible backdrop.

The Green Berets (Non–Aviation Themed Title)

USA / Warner Bros.—Seven Arts / 1968 / Color / 142 minutes

Directors: John Wayne, Ray Kellogg

Cast: John Wayne, David Janssen, Jim Hutton, Aldo Ray, Raymond St. Jacques, Bruce Cabot, Jack Soo, George Takei, Patrick Wayne, Luke Askew, Irene Tsu

Synopsis / Aviation Content: An outdated and heavily pro-war account of the U.S. Army's Special Forces, known as the "Green Berets," in Vietnam. Based on the 1965 novel of the same name by American author Robin Moore. Actor John Wayne wrote to President Lyndon B. Johnson requesting military assistance in the making of this film and got it! Army helicopter fans will enjoy the many and varied views of the UH-1 Huey, which also features a rocket firing sequence and a simulated crash with a UH-1B wreck. Featured aircraft include the **Bell UH-1B / -1C / -1D** (one was s/n 65-9651) / **-1H Iroquois; AH-1 Cobra; Boeing-Vertol CH-47B Chinook** (one was s/n 66-19137); **DeHavilland-Canada U-6A Beaver; C-7A Caribou; Douglas AC-47D Spooky; Hiller OH-23G Raven** (s/n 64-15279) and **Lockheed C-130 Hercules** (one with Fulton recovery gear). Filmed from August to December 1967 in and around Fort Benning and Lawson AAF, Georgia (GPS Location: N32 20.30 / W084 59.35), which stands in for the movie settings of Fort Bragg and Vietnam itself—note the native pines as opposed to tropical foliage!

The Grim Game (Non–Aviation Themed Title)

USA / Famous Players-Lasky Corp. (Paramount Pictures) / 1919 / B&W / 50 minutes

Director: Irvin Willat

Cast: Harry Houdini, Thomas Jefferson, Ann Forrest, Augustus Phillips, Tully Marshall, Arthur Hoyt

Synopsis / Aviation Content: An innocent man is wrongfully imprisoned for murder but soon escapes in pursuit of the true criminals, who also hold his fiancée. Designed as a film to highlight the talents of famed escapologist and magician Harry Houdini, it's notable as being the first Hollywood film to feature an unscripted midair collision, which occurred over Santa Monica on May 31, 1919. The two **Curtiss JN-4 Jenny** biplanes collided while stunt man Robert Kennedy was performing an air-to-air transfer via rope ladder. The two aircraft spun to within 200 feet of the ground before they separated and made controlled crash landings without loss of life. The incident quickly made headlines, with Houdini promoting himself as having been the stunt man on the end of the ladder!

The Guardian

USA / Touchstone, Beacon Pictures / 2006 / Color / 133 minutes

Director: Andrew Davis

Cast: Kevin Costner, Aston Kutcher, Neal McDonough, Melissa Sagemiller, Clancy Brown, Sela Ward

Synopsis / Aviation Content: Veteran U.S. Coast Guard rescue swimmer Costner takes a coaching position training rookies, one of whom shows greater potential above the rest. An interesting new angle for an aviation-themed film, with the story centered around the rarely featured USCG branch of the U.S. armed forces. Outstanding aerial photography of the HH-60J Jay Hawk helicopter, including an end credit roll featuring aerial photography outtakes not seen in the film.

Type	msn	military s/n	USCG s/n
Lockheed HC-130H Hercules	382-4993	83-0007	1705
Lockheed HC-130H Hercules	382-4999	83-0506	1707
Lockheed HC-130H Hercules	382-5002	83-0507	1708
Sikorsky HH-60J-SI Jay Hawk	70-1565	BuNo.163808	6008
Sikorsky HH-60J-SI Jay Hawk	70-1585	BuNo.163814	6014
Sikorsky HH-60J-SI Jay Hawk	70-1705	BuNo.163823	6023
Sikorsky HH-60J-SI Jay Hawk	70-1789	BuNo.163830	6030
Sikorsky HH-60J-SI Jay Hawk	70-1955	BuNo.163821	6034
Sikorsky HH-60J-SI Jay Hawk	70-2283	BuNo.164825	6042

Additional Jay Hawk helicopters used for minor scenes were USCG s/n 6010, 6029, plus others not identified. One former Navy SH-60B Seahawk was rebuilt as a training unit airframe and appears with USCG s/n 6096. Background aircraft are a couple of USCG **Aerospatiale HH-65 Dolphin** helicopters, a single **Dassault-Breguet HU-25A Guardian** jet, and a USAF **Boeing B-52H Stratofortress** in one distant wide shot at Barksdale AFB. An HH-60J mock-up was built for studio filming marked with nonexistent USCG s/n 6000. The HC-130H Hercules can be seen in the background throughout the film. A total of forty-two HH-60J Jay Hawks were delivered to the USCG from 1989 to 1996. Most were upgraded to MH-60T standard from 2007.

Coast Guard (CG) Air Station Elizabeth City, North Carolina, doubled for CG Air Station Kodiak, Alaska, for the base and hangar scenes. Kodiak itself was filmed for background and additional shots. Many of the training scenes were filmed at Barksdale AFB, Louisiana.

GPS LOCATIONS

CG Air Station Elizabeth City, North Carolina: N36 15.40 / W076 10.30

CG Air Station Kodiak, Alaska: N57 44.25 / W152 30.35

Gunbus

UK Alternate Title / U.S. Title: **Sky Bandits**

UK / J&M Entertainment & London Front / 1986 / Color / 105 minutes

Director: Zoran Perisic

Cast: Scott McGinnis, Jeff Osterhage, Ronald Lacey, Miles Anderson, Valerie Steffen, Ingrid Held, Nicolas Lyndhurst, Keith Buckley

Synopsis / Aviation Content: In 1917, two American outlaws are captured, and as punishment are sent to the Great War in Europe, where they accidentally end up pilots in the Air Service! A comedy-adventure yarn that's more fantasy than anything else, with metal-clad airships and fictional aircraft that, of course, can only fly with the help of visual effects. Similar in style to other box office failures released during this period, *Biggles* (1986) and *Sky Pirates* (1986). The title comes from the World War I Vickers F.B.5 Gunbus, which is played in the film by a flyable **Airco DH.2** replica (reg. G-BFVH / msn WA4). Various other period aircraft and replicas are seen throughout, but only in background and non-flying roles.

A Guy Named Joe

USA / Metro-Goldwyn-Mayer / 1943 / B&W / 120 minutes

Director: Victor Fleming

Cast: Spencer Tracy, Irene Dunne, Van Johnson, Ward Bond, James Gleason, Lionel Barrymore, Barry Nelson, Esther Williams, Don DeFore

Synopsis / Aviation Content: World War II pilot Tracy is killed in action, then returns from the dead to offer spiritual guidance to a young flyer who also just happens to fall for Tracy's former girlfriend. This supernatural romance was a refreshing change of pace from the usual World War II propaganda films and was a success at the box office, becoming one of the most popular motion pictures of its time. A film that just seems to improve with age, a must-see for all aviation fans. Developed and remade in 1989 by Universal Pictures as *Always*.

The majority of the actors' scenes (including exteriors) were actually shot indoors at MGM Studios in Culver City utilizing two **Lockheed P-38E / F Lightning** fighters, two **North American B-25B / C Mitchell** bombers (one was s/n 40-2295) and a **Vultee BT-13 Valiant**, all trucked to the studio in parts. Once the aircraft were set up, pre-filmed backgrounds were projected to create the illusion of an actual airfield.

A second unit film crew was deployed to a series of airfields in Florida to film scenes of the **North American B-25B / C / D Mitchell** bombers and **Lockheed P-38E / F Lightning** fighters. Several aerobatic sequences were shot with a P-38 in addition to a base attack scene. Also seen are a **Douglas C-47 Skytrain** and a **Lockheed C-60A Lodestar**. **Martin B-26 Marauder** bombers from MacDill AAF, Florida, double as Japanese "Betty" bombers, and four **North American P-51A Mustang** fighters double as German "Bf 109" fighters in several sequences. Another film unit was sent to Luke AAF, Arizona, to film **Vultee BT-13 Valiant** trainers (three were s/n 42-42406, 42-42559, 42-42599). Dorina first arrives in a **Fairchild PT-19A Cornell** marked in an RAF livery and later in a **Lockheed Electra Junior**. There's some use of B-25, B-26 and P-38 scale models for several combat scenes.

Filming had begun in February 1943 but didn't conclude until November of that year, mostly due to a serious motorcycle accident Van Johnson had in March. Filming was suspended until he recovered and could return to work.

Hanover Street

USA-UK / Columbia Pictures / 1979 / Color / 109 minutes

Director: Peter Hyams

Cast: Harrison Ford, Lesley-Ann Down, Christopher Plummer, Alec McCowen, Richard Masur, Michael Sacks

Synopsis / Aviation Content: Forbidden love story between an American pilot and the wife of a high-ranking British officer, set in England during World War II, with London's Hanover Street being their secret meeting place. A slow-moving romance drama that only gets better in the second half when Ford and Plummer are shot down behind enemy lines. The assemblage of five B-25 Mitchell bombers is the aeronautical highlight.

The five B-25 Mitchell bombers were all ferried from the United States in 1978 by renowned aircraft pilot and businessman John "Jeff" Hawke and were painted up in period livery upon arrival in the UK. N86427 and N9494Z came from John Hawke's Visionair Intl., Inc.; N9115Z, N9455Z and N7681C came from David Tallichet's Military Aircraft Restoration Corp. (MARC). The Mitchells were all left to various fates in Europe

Type	msn	Military s/n	Civil reg.	Film Markings
North American B-25J-20-NC Mitchell	108-32396	44-29121	N86427	151724 *Brenda's Boys* / 151451 *Miami Clipper*
North American B-25J-20-NC Mitchell	108-32641	44-29366	N9115Z	151645 *Marvellous Miriam*
North American B-25J-25-NC Mitchell	108-33485	44-30210	N9455Z	151863 *Big Bad Bonnie*
North American B-25J-30-NC Mitchell	108-34200	44-30925	N9494Z	151632 *Gorgeous George-Ann* / *Thar She Blows*
North American B-25J-30-NC Mitchell	108-47455	44-86701	N7681C	151790 *Amazing Andrea*

after filming concluded—N86427 was abandoned in Spain after it was damaged during the filming of the movie *Cuba* (1979); N9115Z ended up in the RAF Hendon Museum; N9455Z eventually made it back to the U.S.; N9494Z went to various UK owners, including Aces High Ltd., as G-BWGR; and N7681C ended up in France until destroyed by fire in 1990. All five Mitchells were former USAF TB-25N trainer conversions, and three (N9115Z, N9494Z and N7681C) were ex–Tallmantz *Catch-22* (1970) film veterans.

The camera-plane was a Piper PA-23 Aztec (reg. N9990Q). Mention should be made that USAAF B-25 Mitchell bomber groups were never stationed in England during World War II, instead serving mainly in the Pacific or Mediterranean Theaters.

Filming took place at two RAF airfields. The first was Little Rissington in Gloucestershire, where most of the flying scenes were staged from. The second was Bovingdon in Hertfordshire, where a World War II base was recreated for the B-25 ground and taxi scenes. Various scenes were also filmed at Elstree Studios, Hertfordshire, England.

GPS Locations

RAF Little Rissington, Gloucestershire (closed 1994): N51 52.00 / W001 42.00

RAF Bovingdon, Hertfordshire (closed 1972): N51 43.60 / W000 32.70

Hawks in the Sun   see   *Angels One Five*

Heartbreak Ridge (Non–Aviation Themed Title)

USA / Warner Bros. / 1986 / B&W / Color / 125 minutes

Director: Clint Eastwood

Cast: Clint Eastwood, Marsha Mason, Everett McGill, Moses Gunn, Eileen Heckart, Bo Svenson

Synopsis / Aviation Content: A typically '80s-style Eastwood picture sees him train undisciplined Marines into fighting soldiers. Many Marine aircraft types seen, such as the **Bell UH-1H, UH-1N Iroquois, AH-1 Cobra, Boeing-Vertol CH-46 Sea Knight, Lockheed KC-130 Hercules** (including BuNo. 149816, 160019), and **Sikorsky CH-53 Sea Stallion**.

Hell Bent for Glory   see   *Lafayette Escadrille*

Hell Divers

USA / Metro-Goldwyn-Mayer / 1931 / B&W / 109 minutes

Director: George W. Hill

Cast: Wallace Beery, Clark Gable, Conrad Nagel, Dorothy Jordan, Marjorie Rambeau, Marie Prevost

Synopsis / Aviation Content: Two aerial gunners, Beery and Gable, are aggressive rivals in the air and off-duty, until one of them is marooned on a Pacific island. Based on the story by ex–naval aviator turned Hollywood screenwriter Frank "Spig" Wead, it's among the first of many films that would be centered around naval aviation during the 1930s. Features early navy carrier operations in the Caribbean during 1931 with excellent coverage of the Curtiss Helldiver—after which the film was titled.

Featured aircraft include up to eighteen **Curtiss F8C-4 Helldiver** biplane dive-bombers (two were BuNo. A-8425 and A-8438) of squadron VF-1B; the **Martin T4M-1 / TG-1** biplane torpedo-bombers of squadron VT-2B; and the **Boeing F4B-2** biplane fighters of squadron VF-6B. Some miniatures were built of the F8C and USN dirigibles for special effects sequences. Filmed at NAS San Diego, California; Guantanamo Bay, Cuba; Panama; and onboard the carrier USS *Saratoga* (CV-3) from June 26 to August 7, 1931. Aerial cameraman Charles Marshall spent eleven weeks on the USS *Saratoga* filming various power-dives in the Curtiss biplanes. He would later recall the experience as one of best thrills of his life.

GPS Location

NAS San Diego, California: N32 42.00 / W117 12.45

Hell in the Heavens

Alternate Title: *The Ace*
USA / Fox Film Corp. / 1934 / B&W / 79 minutes
Director: John G. Blystone
Cast: Warner Baxter, Conchita Montenegro, Russell Hardie, Herbert Mundin, Andy Devine, Arno Frey
Synopsis / Aviation Content: A British and German pilot during World War I face off in the skies over Europe, each equally as fearful as the other. Based on the play *The Ace* by Herman Rossman. Featured aircraft are several vintage **Nieuport 28** fighters and a **Garland-Lincoln LF-1**.

Hell's Angels

USA / United Artists / 1930 / B&W / 127 minutes
Director: Howard Hughes
Cast: Ben Lyon, James Hall, Jean Harlow, John Darrow, Lucien Prival, Frank Clarke, Roy Wilson
Synopsis / Aviation Content: Two American brothers, Lyon and Hall, while studying in England join the Royal Flying Corps and become World War I fighter pilots. A massive epic in its day that took three years to film at a then-staggering budget of four million dollars, with every aspect of production overseen by an obsessive Howard Hughes. This film made Jean Harlow an overnight star (she replaced the earlier Greta

Nissen when Hughes re-shot the picture with sound) and Hughes a big-time Hollywood celebrity, bringing him fame and a healthy financial return. Aeronautically, the film features some rare aircraft types, such as the one and only Sikorsky S.29 and some very dramatic onboard camera angles of the pilots while actually flying. The aerial footage would later be reused in several other Hollywood pictures throughout the 1930s.

During 1927, Hughes assembled a team of aviation experts to scour the United States for period biplane aircraft for his World War I epic. The final count was more than forty aircraft, which were all restored and made ready for filming, along with over eighty pilots and numerous other mechanics and ground staff. Known aircraft types consisted of at least two **Curtiss JN-4 Jenny** biplanes doubling as British Avro 504 trainers; seven or more **Fokker D.VII** biplane fighters; three or more **Royal Aircraft Factory S.E.5** biplane fighters; the unique **Sikorsky S.29-A** (civil reg. NC2756 / msn 1), doubling as a giant German Gotha G.V bomber biplane; five plus **Thomas-Morse S-4C Scout** biplane fighters doubling as the British Sopwith Camel; and numerous **Travel Air 2000 / 4000** biplanes doubling as German Fokker D.VII biplanes, nicknamed the "Wichita Fokker" by their crews. An Airco (DeHavilland) DH.4 was acquired as an aerial camera-plane.

When the aerial sequences started filming in early 1928, the eccentric Hughes acquired his pilot's license and then fired his director, Luther Reed, taking control of the movie himself. He even crashed a Thomas-Morse biplane at Caddo Field, Van Nuys, while performing a stunt his pilots refused to do! Loss of aircraft and pilots became synonymous with the *Hell's Angels* shoot—three S.E.5 and one Fokker biplane were lost before filming even started. Pilot Ross Cook wrote off an S.E.5, crashing it through a fence while at Santa Paula. The first pilot killed was Al Johnson, who flew into power lines in his Curtiss Jenny after taking off from Glendale Airport. A second pilot, C.K. Phillips, was killed while attempting a dead-stick landing in an S.E.5 after running out of fuel. Three further Fokker D.VII biplanes were damaged beyond repair in forced landings, and another pilot,

Al Williamson, was forced to bail out of a Fokker D.VII after the propeller spun off its shaft. Williamson landed safely but the Fokker was lost. Numerous air-to-air close misses were also reported, some being seen in the final cut of the film during the air battles. The final fatality was mechanic Phil Jones, who failed to bail out of the giant Sikorsky S.29-A (NC2756, doubling as a German Gotha), before it crashed while performing a dangerous spin-stunt which went wrong. An additional Curtiss JN-1 Jenny was converted to a mock-up Gotha to complete the stunt sequence.

In one of the longest location shoots in film history, Hughes spent over four long months in Oakland, California, with 100 crew members and over forty aircraft simply waiting for the correct cloud formations required for the final air battle. With the development of sound entering motion pictures around 1929, Hughes recalled his cast and hired a new director, James Whale, to reshoot the dramatic scenes with sound, incorporating dialogue. The aerial scenes were also reedited to feature sound as well. These aspects of the *Hell's Angels* filming were expertly dramatized in Martin Scorsese's biographical Howard Hughes epic *The Aviator* (2004).

Up to eight filming locations were established during filming. The main location was Caddo Field in Van Nuys, which doubled as the Allies' main airfield. The British Flying School sequences were shot at Inglewood Field, now Los Angeles Intl. Airport. The German airfield was filmed at Chatsworth, north of San Fernando Valley. Other airfields were in San Diego; Oakland in San Francisco; March Field in Riverside; Encino, Glendale and Santa Cruz, all in California. The zeppelin sequence was filmed in a large hangar at Ross Field in Arcadia, California, and required up to three thirty-foot-long zeppelin models to complete the dramatic action sequence. Studio-based (silent) scenes were done under the direction of Luther Reed between October 1927 and January 1928 at Metropolitan Studios in Hollywood.

Hell's Horizon

USA / Columbia Pictures / 1955 / B&W / 80 minutes
Director: Tom Gries

Cast: John Ireland, Marla English, Bill Williams, Hugh Beaumont, Larry Pennell, Chet Baker
Synopsis / Aviation Content: A formula story set during the Korean War features stock vision of the **Boeing B-29 Superfortress** plus a derelict B-29 fuselage for studio-based interior filming.

Hers to Hold

USA / Universal Pictures / 1943 / B&W / 94 minutes
Director: Frank Ryan
Cast: Deanna Durbin, Joseph Cotten, Charles Winninger, Ludwig Stossel, Nella Walker, Gus Schilling
Synopsis / Aviation Content: A young woman takes a "Rosie-the-Riveter" job at a B-17 assembly plant to be near a pilot she has a crush on. Easygoing romantic film was shot on Lockheed-Vega's Burbank, California, B-17 assembly line in early 1943. Featured aircraft are the **Boeing B-17F Flying Fortress**, including the B-17F-25-VE (s/n 42-5846 / msn 17-6142), named *Tinkertoy*, which went to Europe with the 381st BG. It was lost on December 20, 1943, after a head-on collision with a German Bf 109 fighter.

The High and the Mighty

USA / Warner Bros. / 1954 / Color / 141 minutes
Director: William A. Wellman
Cast: John Wayne, Claire Trevor, Laraine Day, Robert Stack, Jan Sterling, Phil Harris, Robert Newton, David Brian, Paul Kelly, Sidney Blackmer, Julie Bishop, Gonzalez Gonzalez, John Howard
Synopsis / Aviation Content: Wayne and Stack play pilots on a fully loaded DC-4 passenger flight from Hawaii to San Francisco which develops an engine fire at the "point of no return." A true aviation classic that brought the "air disaster genre" back to the box office after it had been made largely redundant during the war years. Screenplay by pioneer aviator and writer Ernest K. Gann from his 1952 novel. Gann was a DC-4 captain on the Hawaii-U.S. routes after World War II. The catchy theme music by Dimitri Tiomkin won an Academy Award for Best Score.

Type	msn	Military s/n	Civil reg.	Film Markings
Boeing B-17G-110-VE Flying Fortress	17-8746	44-85837	—	2855
Douglas C-54A-10-DC Skymaster	10315	42-72210	N4726V	Topac
Douglas C-54B-1-DC Skymaster	10538	42-72433	N4665V	Topac

Two DC-4 aircraft were hired from Transocean Airlines of Oakland, California, in 1953, both of them ex-military C-54 cargo transports. C-54A, N4726V, was only used for the maintenance bay area scene at the top of the film. Ironically, this aircraft was lost in an accident that almost entirely mirrors the one depicted in the film! On March 28, 1964, while flying from Hawaii to Los Angeles with nine people onboard, N4726V radioed it had a No. 2 engine fire 700 miles west of San Francisco. Nothing more was heard from the aircraft or crew, and no wreckage was ever found. The DC-4 was registered at the time to Facilities Management Corp. The second C-54B, N4665V, was the more widely used aircraft in the film. It featured in the terminal scenes with the passengers waiting to board, as well as taxi and takeoff shots, all daylight flying scenes, plus the terminal scene at the end of the movie. Twelve flights were made with N4665V for aerial photography from November 16 to 30, 1953, with Transocean pilots Captain Bill Keating and Captain Bill Benge serving as technical advisor. A Douglas DC-4 interior mock-up was built at MGM Studios in California. Night flying and stormy exterior flying shots of the DC-4 and PB-1G used miniatures and special effects.

The search and rescue aircraft was a B-17G (s/n 44-85837), converted to a United States Coast Guard PB-1G (BuNo. 82855), seventeen of which served with the USCG from 1946 to 1959. It's seen briefly in the film for ground scenes and a short taxi shot.

One derelict Douglas DC-3 tail section was acquired for the flashback sequence. Background aircraft include at least three **Curtiss C-46 Commando** and one **Douglas DC-4** airliner conversions at Oakland, plus a **Martin PBM Mariner** and **Sikorsky HO4S-3G** (**HH-19G**) in the USCG scenes.

Filmed from November 1953 to February 1954. Oakland Intl. Airport, California doubled for Honolulu Intl. Airport in the opening scenes. The DC-4 takeoff was shot along Oakland's Runway 28L. Runway 28R was used for the night landing scenes. A purpose-built set was constructed at Grand Central Air Terminal, Glendale, California, for the closing scenes, which doubled for San Francisco Intl. Airport. The USCG Air Station was most likely one located in the San Francisco area.

GPS LOCATIONS

Oakland Intl. Airport, San Francisco, California: N37 43.50 / W122 13.00

Grand Central Air Terminal, Glendale, California (closed 1959): N34 09.80 / W118 17.20

High Barbaree

USA / Metro-Goldwyn-Mayer / 1947 / B&W / 91 minutes

Director: Jack Conway

Cast: Van Johnson, June Allyson, Thomas Mitchell, Marilyn Maxwell, Cameron Mitchell, Claude Jarman Jr.

Synopsis / Aviation Content: A downed Catalina pilot, played by Johnson, recalls his earlier life and loves while stranded somewhere in the Pacific Ocean during World War II. Based on the 1945 novel of the same name by American authors James Norman Hall and Charles Nordhoff. Not much flying but some excellent, albeit brief, views of a rarely seen PBN-1 Nomad and some eye-popping aerial action with a Stinson L-1!

The main featured aircraft is a **Naval Aircraft Factory PBN-1 Nomad** (BuNo. 02838), playing the part of the downed Catalina named *High Barbaree*. The PBN-1 is a slightly modified version of the PBY-5 Catalina, 156 of which were built by the Naval Aircraft Factory, with most being sent to Russia. Some, as in the film, were fitted with an enlarged forward gun turret. BuNo. 02838 was subsequently retained by MGM Studios after filming, and the fuselage remained at its Culver City backlot until scrapped in 1970. Library footage was also used of a **Consolidated PBY-5 Catalina** marked as "101" for some flying scenes. Other aircraft were a **Ryan ST-A** (reg. NC16039 /

The chopped-up remains of the PBN-1 Nomad BuNo. 02838, used for the filming of *High Barbaree* in 1947. Seen here on the MGM Studios back lot in the late 1960s. Photograph: James H. Farmer Collection.

msn 128) monoplane and a **Stinson L-1 Vigilant** (s/n 40-3102 / reg. N63230), as a pre–World War II observation aircraft marked as "NX63287." Chief pilot was Hollywood stunt flyer Paul Mantz, who also owned and flew the Stinson L-1 seen in the film.

High Flight

UK / Columbia Pictures / 1957 / Color / 102 minutes

Director: John Gilling

Cast: Ray Milland, Anthony Newley, Bernard Lee, Helen Cherry, Kenneth Haigh, Leslie Phillips, Kenneth Fortescue

Synopsis / Aviation Content: A group of new cadets begin a course to become RAF pilots, among them an undisciplined member whose father saved the life of the group's new wing commander during World War II. Notable for its insight into Cold War–era RAF training and operations. Some very good views of the Vampire and the Hunter, and an excellent low-level sequence with a Piston Provost. The film's title is taken from RCAF-serving American pilot and poet John Gillespie Magee Jr.'s famous and often quoted poem. Magee was killed in a midair collision near RAF Cranwell on December 11, 1941. Composer Eric Coates, of *The Dam Busters* (1955) fame, wrote the film's title theme, "The High Flight March."

Featured aircraft include the **Taylorcraft Auster AOP.Mk. 5** (s/n TW462 / msn 1800), which at the time of filming was owned on the civil register as G-AOCP; **DeHavilland DH.115 Vampire T.Mk. 11** (s/n XE937, XH318); **Hawker Hunter F.Mk. 4** (s/n WV333, WV366); **Percival P.56 Provost T.Mk. 1** (s/n WW446); and **Vickers Valetta T.Mk. 3** (s/n WG266). Background aircraft include the **Avro Vulcan**; **Bristol Sycamore** helicopter; **Fairey F.D.2**; **Fairey Ultra-light Helicopter**; and **Vickers Valiant**.

Released in the U.S. in 1958, but only in black & white and cut to 89 minutes. Filmed in part at RAF Cranwell in Lincolnshire, England, with several real RAF Vampire and Hunter squadrons.

GPS Location

RAF Cranwell, Lincolnshire: N53 02.00 / W000 29.35

High Road to China

USA / Warner Bros. / 1983 / color / 105 minutes
Director: Brian G. Hutton
Cast: Tom Selleck, Bess Armstrong, Jack Weston, Wilford Brimley, Robert Morley, Brian Blessed
Synopsis / Aviation Content: Hard-living pilot Selleck is hired by well-to-do Armstrong in order to locate her father and claim an inheritance. Intrepid adventures across Asia ensue, but mostly without an audience, as box office performance showed. Varied scenes of two Stampe SV.4 biplanes hired from Bianchi Aviation Film Services of Booker Field in England.

Type	msn	Civil reg.	Film Markings
Stampe SV.4C	120	G-AZGC	G-EOHE / *Dorothy*
Stampe SV.4C	376	G-AZGE	G-EQHF / *Lillian*

Stampe G-AZGC was later modified as a fictional "villainous" biplane with a black livery and twin machine guns. Filmed mostly in Yugoslavia with additional scenes completed in England.

The original plan was to make the picture in the Rocky Mountains in the U.S., and Vernon Homert of Ypsilanti, Michigan, was hired to build six Bristol F.2 Fighter replicas. Two flyables were completed (one was reg. N47CH), along with one static example, before the filming plan was changed to a European location with Stampe biplanes. The three Bristol replicas were subsequently sold off, with one of them going to Planes of Fame in Chino, California.

The Hindenburg

USA / Universal Pictures / 1975 / B&W / Color / 125 minutes
Director: Robert Wise
Cast: George C. Scott, Anne Bancroft, William Atherton, Roy Thinnes, Gig Young, Burgess Meredith, Charles Durning, Richard A. Dysart
Synopsis / Aviation Content: Story of the famous airship's fateful last flight, for dramatic purposes, takes the viewpoint of sabotage as the

The film star that never was. One of three replica Bristol F.2 Fighter aircraft built for the Tom Selleck adventure film *High Road to China* (1983) that had their roles canceled in favor of using Stampe biplanes. This one is now part of the Planes of Fame collection in Chino, California. Photograph: James H. Farmer Collection.

cause of the crash. Based on the 1972 investigative book by Michael M. Mooney. Filmed using a twenty-five-foot long model and various full-scale airship set pieces built at Universal Studios, California. Brief glimpse of a **Hispano HA-1112-M1L Buchon** (Spanish s/n C.4K-31 / msn 67 / reg. N109ME), as a Messerschmitt Bf 109. Another Buchon and a Nord 1002 are in the background. Exteriors were filmed at the massive airship hangars at MCAS Tustin, California (closed 1999; GPS location: N33 42.20 / W117 49.40). Notably, one of the first disaster-themed motion pictures made concerning airships was the Cecil B. DeMille film *Madam Satan* (1930), which depicted an airship disaster seven years before the actual *Hindenburg* incident.

FACTUAL BACKGROUND: A FEW FACTS ON THE HINDENBURG

The most famous of all airships, the *Hindenburg* was named after Germany's last President before Adolf Hitler took power, Paul von Hindenburg, who held office from 1925 to 1934. The airship was built from 1931 to 1936 (reg. D-LZ129 / msn LZ129) by Luftschiffbau Zeppelin and remains the largest aircraft ever to fly, with a length of 804 ft., width of 135 ft. and gas capacity of 7,062,100 cubic feet. Empty weight is 130 tons; it could lift 112 tons, giving it a gross weight of 242 tons, and could travel at speeds up to 70 knots. The very flammable hydrogen was used as the lifting gas; most U.S. airships used nonflammable but less effective helium gas. The first flight was on March 4, 1936, and the *Hindenburg* completed eighteen Atlantic round trips—ten to the USA and eight to Brazil. The nineteenth Atlantic voyage of the airship left Frankfurt, Germany, on May 3, 1937, with ninety-seven souls onboard (61 crew, 36 passengers) and arrived at NAS Lakehurst, New Jersey, on May 6, 1937. At 7:25 p.m. local time, for reasons never determined, the rear of the airship suddenly caught fire, and the entire airframe was engulfed in just thirty-seven seconds. Twenty-two crew,

thirteen passengers and one ground crewman died in the inferno, which has become one of the most iconic news events of the 20th century. Actual footage of the disaster is included in the climax of this film.

The Hunters

USA / 20th Century–Fox / 1958 / Color / 108 minutes

Director: Dick Powell

Cast: Robert Mitchum, Robert Wagner, Richard Egan, May Britt, Lee Philips, John Gabriel, Stacy Harris, Victor Sen Young, Candace Lee

Synopsis / Aviation Content: In 1952 during the Korean War, Mitchum plays a major leading a group of F-86 fighters, who has to deal not only with the Communist MiG fighters but members of his own squadron. Based on the 1956 novel of the same name by former Korean War F-86E fighter pilot James Salter. Tense, dramatic dogfight sequences are well photographed, making this one of the best Sabre Jet movies, a must-see for all F-86 enthusiasts!

As many as seventy-two **North American F-86F Sabre** jet-fighters were provided from the 3525th Combat Crew Training Wing (CCTW) at Williams AFB (forty-eight Sabres) and 3600th CCTW at Luke AFB (twenty-four Sabres), both in Arizona. The table below lists fifteen of the Sabres identifiable throughout the film. The first digit of their serial numbers was changed to a "1" to supposedly reflect the earlier F-86E variant.

Type	msn	military s/n	Film Markings / Buzz Numbers
North American F-86F-30-NA Sabre	191-178	52-4482	14482 / FU-482
North American F-86F-30-NA Sabre	191-430	52-4734	14734 / FU-734
North American F-86F-30-NA Sabre	191-723	52-5027	15027 / FU-027
North American F-86F-30-NA Sabre	191-803	52-5107	15107 / FU-107
North American F-86F-30-NA Sabre	191-836	52-5140	15140 / FU-140
North American F-86F-35-NA Sabre	191-940	52-5244	13244 / FU-244
North American F-86F-35-NA Sabre	191-966	52-5270	15270 / FU-270
North American F-86F-26-NH Sabre	193-114	52-5385	15385 / FU-385
North American F-86F-26-NH Sabre	193-142	52-5413	15413 / FU-413
North American F-86F-26-NH Sabre	193-154	52-5425	15425 / FU-425
North American F-86F-26-NH Sabre	193-211	52-5482	15482 / FU-482
North American F-86F-26-NH Sabre	193-227	52-5498	15498 / FU-498
North American F-86F-26-NH Sabre	193-245	52-5516	15516 / FU-516
North American F-86F-26-NH Sabre	193-253	52-5524	15524 / FU-524
North American F-86F-26-NH Sabre	193-256	52-5527	12527 / FU-527

Sabre 14482, for the most part, flew as Saville's (Robert Mitchum) aircraft; Sabre 14734 flew as Pell's (Robert Wagner) aircraft; Sabre 15027 flew as Dutch's (Richard Egan) aircraft; Sabre 15425 flew as Corona's (John Gabriel) aircraft. 52-5482 (as 51-5482) doubled as Mitchum's F-86 for studio cockpit close-ups. One F-86 wreck was also acquired for Mitchum's crash scene, filmed in California. In one scene, drop tanks were to be seen jettisoned before the Sabres entered into a dogfight. This was accomplished via pneumatic air guns blowing off fake fiberglass tanks; however, the high pressure of the air guns disintegrated the tanks as they blew off. Several of the larger pieces fell to earth and apparently killed more than one farm cow! Aluminum tanks were then ordered to be used to ensure a more realistic jettison sequence.

Eight **Republic F-84F Thunderstreak** fighters from the 3600th Combat Crew Training Wing (CCTW) at Luke AFB, Arizona, were painted as North Korean MiG-15 fighters, two as the ominous Korean ace *Casey Jones* / 7-11. They were retired to Davis-Monthan AFB soon after and had all been scrapped before the film was even released!

A **Douglas C-54G-10-DO Skymaster** (s/n 45-579 / msn 36032), makes a brief appearance at the beginning of the film. Note the serial number 0-50579 has the extra "0" added for the 5-digit call-sign requirement and the "0-" at the front of the serial number to denote "over 10 years old"; neither of these would have been present in the 1952 time frame of the film. An interesting contrast here, considering the amount of trouble gone to in the renumbering of the F-86 Sabres.

Background aircraft are a **Douglas C-47 Skytrain** and a **Sikorsky H-19B Chickasaw**. Cameraplanes were a Boeing KB-50 Superfortress (for the mass formation with contrails filmed over Arizona); a Lockheed C-130A Hercules (s/n 56-496); a Lockheed T-33A Shooting Star (s/n 51-8572); and one of the North American F-86F Sabres. Stock footage was used of a North American F-100 Super Sabre crash at Edwards AFB and Fairchild C-119 Flying Boxcar paratroop operations. Outstanding model and miniature effects by Hollywood special effects technician L.B. Abbott.

The opening scene was filmed at Luke AFB, Arizona, which doubled for Itami AFB, Japan, along with various other aircraft takeoff shots etc.; the North Korean MiG taxi shots were also

Several of the eight Republic F-84F Thunderstreak fighters doubling as North Korean MiG-15 jets for *The Hunters* (1958). Photograph: James H. Farmer Collection.

Some of the ground crew in front of the "Casey Jones" MiG (F-84F) during the filming of the Korean War F-86 movie *The Hunters* (1958). Photograph: Edward Bertschy.

filmed here. Filmed mainly from January to March 1958, at Luke AFB Auxiliary Field #1 (also known as Wittman Field), which stood in for Suwon K-13 Air base, South Korea. The field was complete with tents, sandbag revetments, rice paddies and two-dimensional painted flats as background hangars. Aerial sequences were filmed in the skies above West Palm Beach, Florida, from March to May 1958, in order to obtain large, puffy cumulus clouds as backgrounds. Ground scenes behind enemy lines were filmed at 20th Century–Fox Ranch in Malibu, California.

GPS Locations
Luke AFB, Arizona: N33 32.30 / W112 22.25
Luke Aux Field #1 (Wittman Field), Arizona: N33 42.80 / W112 31.30

Independence Day (Non–Aviation Themed Title)

USA / 20th Century–Fox / 1996 / Color / 139 minutes
Director: Roland Emmerich
Cast: Will Smith, Bill Pullman, Jeff Goldblum, Mary McDonnell, Judd Hirsch, Robert Loggia, Randy Quaid, Margaret Colin

Synopsis / Aviation Content: Hugely successful science fiction tale of alien invasion set the stage for a whole run of alien-themed movies that were still being made over a decade afterward. Notable for the interesting and varied content of military and civilian aircraft types throughout.

Flyable aircraft provided to the film included a **Boeing-Stearman N2S-3 Kaydet** (BuNo. 38138 / msn 75-7759 / reg. N68405), as Russ Casse's red crop-duster. The "Welcome Wagon" military helicopter was a **Sikorsky S-64E Skycrane** (reg. N4035S / msn 64-099), marked as "201" and provided by the Siller Bros.; it was accompanied by two **Bell Model 204** helicopters. "Marine One" was a **Sikorsky S-61N** (reg. N15456 / msn 61-826), also from the Siller Bros.; the First Lady's helicopter was a **Bell 206B Jet Ranger** (reg. N25AJ / msn 2842). Two LAPD Jet Rangers were also hired for this sequence. Some use of the **McDonnell Douglas F/A-18 Hornet** in several shots; the helicopter borrowed by Will Smith was a **Bell UH-1H Iroquois**.

Originally built as a Stearman N2S-3 Kaydet, BuNo. 38138, for the U.S. Navy, this biplane was famously used as Russ Case's red Stearman in the blockbuster sci-fi film *Independence Day* (1996). Photograph: Michael Mason.

Models, miniatures and mock-ups consisted of an AWACS Boeing E-3A Sentry; Boeing 747 as "Air Force One" with two McDonnell Douglas F-15 Eagle fighters; the *Black Knights* aircraft are McDonnell Douglas F/A-18 Hornet fighters, which came as several full-scale mock-ups and as cockpit sections for actor close-ups; Northrop-Grumman B-2A Spirit; Mikoyan MiG-25 Foxbat aircraft for the Russian base shot. The El Toro sequences were filmed at Wendover Airport, Utah, with three Lockheed C-130H Hercules, one Northrop F-5, one General Dynamics F-16 and one McDonnell Douglas F/A-18 mock-up airframe. Foreign Air Force scenes were also filmed on the salt flats at Wendover using the T-38, F-16 and F/A-18 mock-ups—the F-16 in the background carries RAF s/n WS690, a Gloster Meteor serial number! Mock-ups were provided by the Producers Air Force of California.

Indiana Jones Series (Non–Aviation Themed Title)

USA / Paramount Pictures / Color
Synopsis / Aviation Content: Very entertaining adventure series created by filmmakers George Lucas and Steven Spielberg stars Harrison Ford in the title role. All films feature a number of unique and rare aircraft types that help reflect the time period.

RAIDERS OF THE LOST ARK (1981 / 111 MINUTES)

Type	msn	Civil reg.	Film Markings
Short S.45A Solent Mk. 3	S.1295	N9946F	Pan American
Waco UBF-2	3692	N13075	OB-CPO

Indy escapes Peru in a 1933 Waco UBF-2 biplane fitted out with floats and provided to the film by owner and pilot Hank Strauch. The fictional "CPO" in the registration is an in-joke to the Lucasfilm *Star Wars* character C-3PO. The aircraft was flown by airline pilot Fred Sorenson, who actually plays the Waco's pilot "Jock" in the movie. The flying boat Indy boards is a Short Solent Mk. 3, one of six converted from the Seaford Mk. I (RAF s/n NJ203) military flying boat for civilian use. It flew as G-AKNP from 1949 and in the Pacific as VH-TOB from 1951. In 1953, it went to the United States as N9946F; its last flight was on July 25, 1958. It was purchased derelict by Rick and Randy Grant in 1976; only one engine operated when it was hired by the *Raiders* film crew in 1980–81, which is the one seen starting in the film. Solent flying shots were done using a model at Industrial Light & Magic studios. The DC-3 seen during the map montage was taken from the 1973 Peter Finch film, *Lost Horizon*. The German "Flying Wing" aircraft was a movie mock-up and never actually existed as a real aircraft; it was built at Elstree Studios in England and shipped out to Tunisia for filming.

INDIANA JONES AND THE TEMPLE OF DOOM (1984 / 114 MINUTES)

Type	msn	Civil reg.	Film Markings
Ford 5-AT-B Tri-Motor	34	N9651	Lao Che Air Freight

The 1929 Tri-Motor was first delivered to Transcontinental Air Transport as NC9651 and flew the "Coast to Coast" route from Clovis to Los Angeles. It had long since passed into private ownership by the time of filming in September 1983. The Shanghai airport sequence was filmed at Hamilton Army Air Field, Novato, California.

The aerial shots of the Tri-Motor's engines cutting out were filmed from N9651 over the Mammoth Mountains, Mono County, California. A scale model was used for some flying shots and the crash.

INDIANA JONES AND THE LAST CRUSADE (1989 / 122 MINUTES)

Type	msn	Civil reg.	Film Markings
Douglas C-47B-35-DK Skytrain	16688/ 33436	G-ANAF	NC170GP
Pilatus P-2.05	36	F-AZCD	—
Pilatus P-2.05	37	F-AZCC	—
Stampe SV.4C	360	G-AWXZ	D-EKVY

The DC-3C, ex–C-47B (s/n 44-77104 / RAF KP220) Indy departs for Venice in was hired from Air Atlantique and filmed at Baginton-Coventry Airport, Warwickshire, England. The two fighters that chase the biplane are Pilatus P-2 combat trainers, a Swiss-built aircraft which first flew in 1945; in all, fifty-six were built between 1945 and 1950. F-AZCC is ex–Swiss AF s/n U-117, and F-AZCD is ex–Swiss AF s/n U-116—it later went to the U.S. as N6145U. Both were painted in German colors for the film. The German biplane is a 2-seater Stampe SV.4, of which 940 were built by Stampe et Vertongen in Antwerp, Belgium, and under license in France and Algeria; the prototype first flew in 1933. The biplane / fighter chase was staged in and around an abandoned airfield in Majocar, Spain, under the supervision of pilot Tony Bianchi and his company Personal Plane Services Ltd. A second Stampe SV.4C (reg. G-BHFG / msn 45) was used as a standby aircraft only, but never appears in the finished film. A

mock-up Stampe was built for studio filming with Harrison Ford and Sean Connery. The German Airship marked as "D-138" was a model.

INDIANA JONES AND THE KINGDOM OF THE CRYSTAL SKULL (2008 / 117 MINUTES)

Type	msn	Civil reg.	Film Markings
Douglas DC-3	2169	N26MA	NC33673 / Pan American
PZL-Mielec An-2	1G22331	N87AN	N48550 / Pan American

The DC-3 was hired from Californian owner Skip Evans. The biplane Indy and Mutt travel to Peru in was a PZL-Mielec An-2, a Polish-built version of the famous Russian biplane, the Antonov An-2 "Colt." Filming of the Peruvian airport was at Eagle Field, Dos Palos, California, in October 2007. CGI creations were completed of the North American F-86 Sabre and a Russian Antonov An-12 "Cub." The Area 51 sequence was shot at Deming AFB, New Mexico.

International Squadron

USA / Warner Bros. / 1941 / B&W / 85 minutes
   Directors: Lothar Mendes, Lewis Seiler
Cast: Ronald Reagan, Olympe Bradna, James Stephenson, William Lundigan, Joan Perry
Synopsis / Aviation Content: A new American pilot, played by Reagan, joins the RAF in England. Apparently based on ex-aviator Frank "Spig" Wead's original 1935 stage play *Ceiling Zero*. Notable only for having used two **Ryan ST** monoplanes, a **Brown B-2** racer and a **Travel Air Mystery** racer (reg. NR613K), all disguised as Supermarine Spitfire fighters! Filmed partly at the Lockheed Plant in Burbank, California, with brand-new **Lockheed Hudson** bombers in some scenes. Hollywood pilot Paul Mantz flew for the film, which also made use of his **Boeing Model 100** (reg. N873H), doubling as a Gloster Gladiator.

Iron Eagle

USA-Canada / TriStar Pictures / 1986 / Color / 117 minutes

Director: Sidney J. Furie

Cast: Louis Gossett Jr., Jason Gedrick, David Suchet, Tim Thomerson, Larry B. Scott

Synopsis / Aviation Content: An F-16 pilot is shot down over an unnamed, hostile Middle Eastern country, whereupon the pilot's teenage son takes it upon himself to mount a daring rescue. Strictly aimed at a youth market and containing many far-fetched situations; there are, however, some rewarding views of the F-16 Fighting Falcon and rarely seen IAI Kfir expertly flown by their Israeli pilots. Also contains some excellent stunt work by aerobatic pilot Art Scholl in a Cessna Aerobat! Followed by *Iron Eagle II* (1988).

Due to conflicts with the script, the USAF would not partake in the film, so the producers were forced to film overseas in Israel. Use of Israeli **General Dynamics F-16A / F-16B Fighting Falcon** aircraft as USAF fighters and Israeli-built **IAI Kfri** (U.S. designation: **F-21A**) fighters—doubling as enemy MiG-23 aircraft—was granted under strict rules. All F-16 aircraft had their original bands and serial numbers masked out. Israeli pilots and ground crew served as background doubles, although filming of any one person was strictly forbidden for security reasons. Several times during filming, all aircraft were scrambled to fly off for actual strikes against southern Lebanon, leaving the filmmakers with an empty air base. Filming took place at Hatzerim Israeli Air Base (N31 14.30 / E034 40.00), west of Beersheba, Israel, from June to August 1985. Also located at Hatzerim was the Israeli Air Force Museum, which doubles in the film as a U.S. air base hangar containing a **Douglas A-4 Skyhawk** and original **Hawker Hunter FGA.Mk. 9**.

The IAI Kfri (Hebrew for "Lion Cub"), is a multi-role combat fighter built by Israel Aircraft Industries and based on the French Dassault Mirage IIIC fighter. Over 220 have been built since its first flight in June 1973. The U.S. Navy leased twelve of the F-21A Kfir to fly as adversary aircraft in combat training.

U.S.-based scenes feature a daring airplane-motorbike race using a **Cessna 150M Aerobat** (reg. N9828J / msn A150-0637), a **Champion 8KCAB Citabria** (reg. N1230E), and an unidentified **Piper PA-22 Tomahawk**. A **Lockheed T-33A Shooting Star** is seen landing in the background in one shot. Other sequences shot in the U.S. were at Camarillo and Van Nuys Airports, California. The latter is used for the final scene with a VIP **Boeing VC-137** and several **Lockheed C-130 Hercules** in the background.

There's some use of models and miniatures in the dogfight and aerial (Boeing KC-135A Stratotanker) refueling sequences.

Iron Eagle II

Canada-Israel / TriStar Pictures / 1988 / Color / 105 minutes

Director: Sidney J. Furie

Cast: Louis Gossett Jr., Mark Humphrey, Stuart Margolin, Alan Scarfe, Sharon H. Brandon, Maury Chaykin, Colm Feore

Synopsis / Aviation Content: "Chappy" Sinclair (Gossett) finds himself back in hostile skies leading a joint American-Soviet mission to destroy the nuclear plant of an unnamed Middle Eastern country. First sequel in the *Iron Eagle* series is still firmly aimed at a youth-culture market, but there are some excellent views of the F-16 and F-4 in action, thanks to superb aerial photography by Clay Lacy; otherwise just a standard '80s-style action yarn. Followed by *Aces: Iron Eagle III* (1990).

The filmmakers again traveled to Israel to make this film, receiving generous support from the Israeli Air Force. Provided were three **General Dynamics F-16A Fighting Falcon**, several **IAI Kfir** fighters, and two **McDonnell Douglas F-4E Kurnass** (Hebrew for "Heavy Hammer"), doubling as the Soviet "MiG-25" fighter. Aircraft markings and serial numbers were masked out, but some of the F-16 fighters retained the Star of David Israeli insignia. Also provided were two Israeli **Lockheed C-130 Karnaf** (Hebrew for "Rhino") transports (s/n 102, ex–U.S. 71-1374; and s/n 311, ex–U.S. 63-7870), and a **Boeing 707-320C** as a soviet VIP aircraft. Filmed mainly at Ramat David Air Base (N32 40.00 / E035 11.00), located near Haifa, Israel.

Chappy's aviation museum at "Fowler AFB, Arizona," is actually the Israeli Air Force Museum at

Hatzerim Israeli Air Base near Beersheba and includes examples of the **Britten-Norman BN-2 Islander, DeHavilland DH.82A Tiger Moth, Douglas A-4E Skyhawk** (s/n 893 / BuNo. 150090 / msn 13143), **Fokker S.11 Instructor,** and **Nord 2501 Noratlas.**

Some F-16 and Kfir aerial combat footage was reused from the first film. A model of a Boeing B-52 Stratofortress and Tupolev Tu-95 Bear was created to depict these bombers in flight. A model of a C-130 *Karnaf* was also created for a crash sequence.

Iron Eagle III   see   *Aces: Iron Eagle III*

Iron Eagle IV

Alternate / Video Title: **Iron Eagle on the Attack**
Canada / Trimark Pictures / 1995 / Color / 96 minutes
Director: Sidney J. Furie
Cast: Louis Gossett Jr., Jason Cadieux, Joanne Vannicola, Max Piersig, Karen Gayle, Ross Hull
Synopsis / Aviation Content: In the fourth installment of the *Iron Eagle* series, "Chappy" (Gossett) is now running a flight school for troubled youth, some of who stumble upon a criminal plot by USAF officers in transporting toxic waste. Although the least favored of the *Iron Eagle* series, it does give a good close-up look at many Canadian aircraft, both military and civilian. This film had a limited cinema release, with most distribution straight to the home video market.

Type	msn	Military s/n	Civil reg.
Bell 206L Long Ranger	45116	—	C-FHJK
CCF Harvard Mk. 4	CCF4-27	(RCAF) 20236	C-FGUY
CCF Harvard Mk. 4	CCF4-223	(RCAF) 20432	C-FHWU
CCF Harvard Mk. 4	CCF4-242	(RCAF) 20451	CF-ROA
Cessna Model 150	unknown	—	C-GTTG
Lockheed CC-130H Hercules	382-4994	130334	—
Percival P.57 Sea Prince T.Mk. 1	P57-31	(RAF) WF133	C-GJIE
Piper J-3 Cub	unknown	—	CF-ALI
Waco YMF-5	F5030	—	C-GKLH

The main aircraft featured were the three yellow Harvard Mk. 4 trainers owned and operated by Hannu Halminen of Roaero Ltd. in Oshawa,

Canada. The Waco YMF was the biplane seen in the opening scene with one of the Harvards. The CC-130H was used as the secret cargo transport, but the interior appears to be that of a DeHavilland-Canada DHC-5 Buffalo with the oval windows. The Bell 206L is a private civilian helicopter doubling as a USAF OH-58 Kiowa. Additional aircraft seen are a Cessna Model 150, a rare Percival Sea Prince, and a Piper J-3 Cub as a sprayer aircraft.

Background aircraft are the **Bell CH-136 Kiowa** helicopter, several **Canadair CC-109 Cosmopolitan** transports, several **Canadair CF-116A / D** jet fighters, and a **Boeing-Stearman PT-17 Kaydet** biplane.

Some aerial combat footage reused from *Iron Eagle* (1986) and *Iron Eagle II* (1988). Filmed from October 31 to December 9, 1994, at Oshawa-Kirby Airport (GPS Location: N43 55.40 / W078 53.70) and CFB Downsview (GPS Location: N43 44.35 / W079 28.00), both a part of Toronto, Ontario, Canada. CFB Downsview closed in 1996.

I Shot Down Richthofen, I Think Production canceled; for details, see: **Darling Lili**

Island in the Sky

USA / Warner Bros. / 1953 / B&W / 105 minutes
Director: William A. Wellman
Cast: John Wayne, Lloyd Nolan, Walter Abel, James Arness, Andy Devine
Synopsis / Aviation Content: During World War II, an Air Transport Command C-47 piloted by Wayne is forced down in remote Labrador, Canada, while on a ferry flight to Europe. Sharp aerial photography and excellent detail shots of the C-47 by cinematographer William Clothier make for top viewing, one of the best C-47 / DC-3 movies! Screenplay by renowned pioneer aviator, adventurer and writer Ernest K. Gann from his 1944 novel of the same name and based on a true-life incident involving a Consolidated C-87 Liberator Express transport.

Four **Douglas DC-3 / C-47 Skytrain** transports were acquired for filming—three ex–TWA from storage at Muskegon County Airport, Michigan—DC-3-209 (msn 1969 / reg NC

17323); DC-3-277C (msn 2245 / reg NC15591) and DC-3B-202 (msn 1924 / reg NC17314), and one leased from Alaska Airlines—C-47B-1-DK (msn 14323/25768 / s/n 43-48507 / reg N91014). Transocean Airlines of Oakland, California were awarded the contract to service and pilot the aircraft for the production. NC15591, built in 1940, saw service with Ozark Airlines after filming, it's now on display at Boeing's Museum of Flight in Seattle. NC17314 was impressed into military service in 1942 as a C-84-DO Skytrain, USAAF s/n: 42-57511, going back to TWA service in 1944; it crashed on February 1, 1959 in Texas. All three were ferried from Michigan to California from December 17, 1952 by Transocean pilots led by Capt Frank Kennedy. The fourth (N91014), was leased from Wien Alaska Airlines, it served with the U.S. Navy (BuNo.17265) during World War II then as a DC-3C with Wien Alaska from 1946–1953. None of the DC-3s appear to have been correctly painted for the time period of the film, most were covered in roughly blotched over sections of silver paint with the previous Arctic red trim retained and looked very faded. Some still had "United States Air Force" stencilled on the side—a name change, which would not come about until late 1947. Film markings were: 1043, 1045, 1046 and 1048.

Filmed January to March, 1953 around Donner Lake, east of Sacramento in the Sierra-Nevada Mountain Range, California. The DC-3 crash site was located off Truckee Airport, California (GPS Location: N39 19.10 / W120 08.21), where all aircraft were stationed during the filming schedule. On February 6, 1953 Capt Kennedy's logbook records Ernie Gann, himself a veteran pilot, nosing over DC-3 NC17314 in the snow at Truckee. It was back flying by February 9. Camera-ship was a Beechcraft C-45.

It's a Mad, Mad, Mad, Mad World (Non–Aviation Themed Title)

USA / United Artists / 1963 / Color / 154 minutes
Director: Stanley Kramer
Cast: Spencer Tracy, Milton Berle, Sid Caesar, Buddy Hackett, Ethel Merman, Mickey Rooney, Dick Shawn, Phil Silvers, Terry-Thomas, plus many, many more.
Synopsis / Aviation Content: Mega-comedy fea-

turing mega-stars of the time has a brief but very well-executed stunt by Hollywood pilot Frank Tallman—flying his Tallmantz-owned **Beechcraft AT-11-BH Kansan** (s/n 42-37444 / msn 4037 / reg. N63158) through a billboard sign! The sign was constructed near Orange County Airport from lightweight materials. Even so, the aircraft was still damaged by the stunt, but made a safe landing. The twin-Beech was also used in a hangar fly-through filmed at Santa Rosa Airport, California. The rickety biplane is Hollywood pilot Paul Mantz's 1917 **Standard J-1** (reg. N2825D / msn 1582), which takes off from Twenty-Nine Palms Airport, California. What also makes this title noteworthy is the fact that Tallmantz founders Paul Mantz and Frank Tallman are both credited during the opening titles, just about the only time their names appeared together on the big screen!

I Wanted Wings

USA / Paramount Pictures / 1941 / B&W / 135 minutes
Director: Mitchell Leisen
Cast: Ray Milland, William Holden, Wayne Morris, Brian Donlevy, Constance Moore, Veronica Lake, Harry Davenport
Synopsis / Aviation Content: One of the best-known American "war preparedness" films follows the training of three cadets from different backgrounds as they learn to fly at a USAAC flight training school in Texas. Highly regarded for its thoughtful and imaginative flying sequences. These aspects of the film were largely overlooked at the time by the screen presence of newcomer actress Veronica Lake, who stole the show and subsequently became one of the most famous actresses of the 1940s. Truly fantastic aerial sequences featuring the rarely seen fixed undercarriage BT-9 trainer, along with some detailed footage of the AT-6 Texan. Based on the 1937 autobiographical book of the same name by aviation personality Beirne Lay, Jr., describing his own experiences of pilot training at Randolph Field in 1932–1933. However, many of the events and characters were fictionally created and shaped into a story by several Hollywood screenwriters, including former naval pilot Frank "Spig" Wead.

Featured aircraft are **Boeing Y1B-17 Flying Fortress** bombers of the 2nd BG, using stock footage filmed during the production of *Test Pilot* (1938); **Boeing B-17B Flying Fortress** bombers of the 19th BG and 32nd BS; early **Curtiss P-40** fighters; **Douglas B-18 Bolo** bombers; excellent shots of the **North American BT-9 / AT-6 Texan** trainers; and a **Northrop A-17** in the final scene. Filmed at Kelly Field and Randolph AAF, San Antonio, Texas, and at March AAF in Riverside, California, starting in the summer of 1940. These locations gave the filmmakers access to 1,160 aircraft, 1,050 cadets, 450 officers and 2,543 enlisted men. The chief pilot was Hollywood pilot Paul Mantz, who supplied his Boeing Model 100 (reg. N873H) as a camera-plane.

The miniature and special effects work earned an Academy Award, particularly for the new process photography technique developed especially for this film, which consisted of projecting previously shot footage against a studio background with the subject in front. Models were used of the AT-6, B-17 and P-40 aircraft. A full-scale Boeing B-17B mock-up fuselage was constructed for onboard flying sequences. The film's premier was held at Randolph Field, Texas, in early 1941.

Actress Veronica Lake later earned her private pilot's license in 1946. Actor William Holden joined the USAAF during World War II, making documentaries for the war effort. Actor Wayne Morris served as a navy pilot, becoming an F6F Hellcat ace in the Pacific Theater. Actors Brian Donlevy and Ray Millard were both USAAF flight instructors during World War II. While making *I Wanted Wings* in 1940, Milland was almost killed when he spontaneously decided to attempt a parachute jump from an aircraft being used on the film that was on a test flight. Just as he was about to dive out, the pilot ushered him back into the plane, as the engine had begun sputtering. Upon returning to the ground, Milland discovered he had only been wearing a fake movie-prop parachute assigned to him by the costume department!

James Bond Series (Non–Aviation Themed Title)

UK-USA / EON Productions / Color
Synopsis / Aviation Content: British novelist Ian Fleming's 1953 creation of international spy James Bond—007 inspired one of the most prestigious and longest-running film series in cinema history. Many aircraft have been used in these films over the years, a few performing some incredible aerial stunt work. The table below lists all major aircraft appearances, plus all identified and unidentified background aircraft from each film. Best known Bond aircraft include the autogyro *Little Nellie* from *You Only Live Twice* (1967), the Bede Micro-jet from *Octopussy* (1983), and the red AB.206B Jet Ranger helicopter from *For Your Eyes Only* (1981).

DR. NO (BOND #1 / 1962 / 111 MINUTES / SEAN CONNERY)

Background / unidentified: Boeing 707-321 (PanAm livery)

FROM RUSSIA WITH LOVE (BOND #2 / 1963 / 118 MINUTES / SEAN CONNERY)

Type	msn	s/n or Civil reg.	Remarks
Hiller Model UH-12C	WH6003	N780ND	Seen at SPECTRE HQ and in finale

Background / unidentified: Boeing 707-321 (PanAm livery).

GOLDFINGER (BOND #3 / 1964 / 111 MINUTES / SEAN CONNERY)

Type	msn	s/n or Civil reg.	Remarks
AT(E)L.98 Carvair	10273/7	G-ASDC	C-54A ex–USAF 42-72168 / plus one other
Hiller Model UH-12E4	2070	G-ASAZ	Goldfinger's helicopter as NASAZ
Lockheed L-1329 JetStar 6	1329-5023	N711Z	Auric Enterprises Inc. and USAF VC-140B
Piper PA-28-140 Cherokee	28-20068	N6056W	Pussy Galore's Flying Circus
Piper PA-28-150 Cherokee	28-1658	N5781W	Pussy Galore's Flying Circus
Piper PA-28-180 Cherokee	28-1400	N7489W	Pussy Galore's Flying Circus
Piper PA-28-180 Cherokee	28-1613	N7641W	Pussy Galore's Flying Circus
Piper PA-28-235 Cherokee	28-10264	N8729W	Pussy Galore's Flying Circus

Background / unidentified: Brantly B-2B, Cessna O-1 Bird Dog (several at Fort Knox), two Douglas C-47 Skytrains

THUNDERBALL (BOND #4 / 1965 / 129 MINUTES / SEAN CONNERY)

Type	msn	s/n or Civil reg.	Remarks
Avro Vulcan B.1A	—	(RAF) XA913	Ground shots / plus three others
Avro Vulcan B.1A	—	(RAF) XH506	Flying shots
Bell Model 47J-2A Ranger	3302	N1190W	Floats fitted
Boeing B-17G-95-DL Flying Fortress	32426	N809Z	Ex-USAF 44-83785 /Fulton retrieval system
Sikorsky HH-52A-SI Seaguard	62-069	(USCG) 1388 N4341Q	Later to civil reg.

Background / unidentified: Boeing C-97 Stratofreighter (paratroop drop).

YOU ONLY LIVE TWICE (BOND #5 / 1967 / 116 MINUTES / SEAN CONNERY)

Type	msn	s/n or Civil reg.	Remarks
Brantly B-2B	445	G-ASXE	Mr. Osato's helicopter as OS7241, landing inside volcano
Brantly B-2B	449	G-ATFH	Mr. Osato's helicopter as OS7241, landing on office building rooftop
Kawasaki-Vertol KV-107/II-2	4004	JA9503	Picks up car via magnet
Meyers 200D	308	N2907T	Marked as OS7429
Sud-Aviation SA.313B Alouette II	1679	JA9007	Arrival at the ninja school
Wallis WA.116 Agile	B.203	G-ARZB	Autogyro named *Little Nellie*

Background / unidentified: four Kawasaki-Bell Model 47G-3, two Lockheed C-130 Hercules.

ON HER MAJESTY'S SECRET SERVICE (BOND #6 / 1969 / 140 MINUTES / GEORGE LAZENBY)

Type	msn	s/n or Civil reg.	Remarks
Agusta-Bell AB.204B	3002	HB-XCG	White livery, side-mounted exhaust
Agusta-Bell AB.204B	3209	HB-XCQ	White livery, side-mounted exhaust
Agusta-Bell AB.204B	3211	LN-ORZ	White livery, side-mounted exhaust
Agusta-Bell AB.206B Jet Ranger	8013	HB-XCF	Red and white livery
Morane-Saulnier MS.760A Paris	69	HB-PAA	Marked as J-4117

DIAMONDS ARE FOREVER (BOND #7 / 1971 / 119 MINUTES / SEAN CONNERY)

Type	msn	s/n or Civil reg.	Remarks
Bell 206A Jet Ranger	174	N209D	Leads attack on oil rig
Boeing 707-330B	19315/ 545	D-ABUL	Lufthansa Airlines

Background / unidentified: Beechcraft Bonanza (parachute drop), two Bell Model 205 (as USMC UH-1 Iroquois); four Hughes 500C (three as USMC OH-6 Cayuse).

LIVE AND LET DIE (BOND #8 / 1973 / 121 MINUTES / ROGER MOORE)

Type	msn	s/n or Civil reg.	Remarks
Bell 206A Jet Ranger	657	JDFH-03	Provided by the Jamaica Defense Force
Cessna Model 140	12361	N77029	Plus two others for stunt work
Douglas C-50B-DO Skytrain	4110	N340EL	Ex-USAF 41-7704, damaged for film
IAI 1124N Sea Scan	152	4X-CJC	Mr. Big's private jet

Background / unidentified: Boeing 747-121 (PanAm livery), various light aircraft types (N4651E, N5305Z, N8854E, N9519M).

THE MAN WITH THE GOLDEN GUN (BOND #9 / 1974 / 125 MINUTES / ROGER MOORE)

Type	msn	s/n or Civil reg.	Remarks
Hawker Hunter F.6	8798	N-202	Nose section only
Republic RC-3 Seabee	105	N87545	Amphibian. Mock-up destroyed for film

The Spy Who Loved Me (Bond #10 / 1977 / 125 minutes / Roger Moore)

Background / unidentified: Bell 206 Jet Ranger, Westland Sea King HAS.2 (Royal Navy), Westland Wessex HU.5 (Royal Navy).

Moonraker (Bond #11 / 1979 / 126 minutes / Roger Moore)

Type	msn	s/n or Civil reg.	Remarks
Bell 206B Jet Ranger	1557	N59642	Marked as N5364W, Drax Airlines
Handley-Page HP.137 Jetstream 1	209	N5VH	Marked as Apollo Airways

Background / unidentified: Aerospatiale/BAC Concorde (F-BVFD), Bell 206 Jet Ranger (France double for N59642), Boeing 707-320, 727-200C, 747-100, Lockheed L-188 Electra (Drax Air Freight), various airliners at LAX, California.

For Your Eyes Only (Bond #12 / 1981 / 127 minutes / Roger Moore)

Type	msn	s/n or Civil reg.	Remarks
Agusta-Bell AB.206B Jet Ranger	8339	G-BAKS	Marked as Universal Exports
Cessna A185F Skywagon	185-02279	N3357S	Marked as SX-JKR / Kerkyra Charter
PZL-Swidnik Mi-2 Hoplite	525-523-038	SP-SAP	Marked as 8P-8AP. Gogol's helicopter

Octopussy (Bond #13 / 1983 / 130 minutes / Roger Moore)

Type	msn	s/n or Civil reg.	Remarks
Aerospatiale AS.365C1 Dauphin	5023	G-BGNM	Marked as 06 and later as 51
Bede BD-5J Acrostar	001	N70CF	"Micro-jet," a real flying aircraft
Beechcraft C-45G-BH Expeditor	AF-222	N75WB	Ex-USAF 51-11665, marked as VN75WB

Background / unidentified: Armstrong-Whitworth AW. 660 Argosy E.1 (s/n XR137), British Aerospace BAe.

125 CC.1, DeHavilland Devon C.2 (s/n WB531), several General Dynamics F-111 Aardvarks, nose section of Hawker Hunter F.6 (s/n N-202), Sud-Aviation SA.316B Alouette III (Khan's helicopter), Westland Whirlwind HAR.10 (s/n XP339).

Never Say Never Again (1983 / 137 minutes / Sean Connery)

Non–EON Productions remake of *Thunderball*, not counted as an "official" Bond film.

Background / unidentified: Aerospatiale/BAC Concorde (G-AXDN, doubles for B-1B in bomb load sequence), Bell 206 Jet Ranger, Boeing KC-135A Stratotanker, Lockheed C-130H Hercules, MBB Bo.105 (marked as U.S. Navy), McDonnell Douglas DC-10 (BCAL livery). Rockwell B-1B Lancer (model only).

A View to a Kill (Bond #14 / 1985 / 131 minutes / Roger Moore)

Type	msn	s/n or Civil reg.	Remarks
Aerospatiale AS.355 F1 Ecureuil 2	5063	F-GDMS	Zorin's helicopter
Airship Industries Skyship 500	1214/02	G-BIHN	Marked as: Zorin Industries

Background / unidentified: MBB Bo.105 (Russian helicopter / 06). Airship Industries Skyship 6000 (model only).

The Living Daylights (Bond #15 / 1987 / 130 minutes / Timothy Dalton)

Type	msn	s/n or Civil reg.	Remarks
Bell UH-1H-BF Iroquois	13560	G-HUEY	Ex–U.S. Army 73-22077 / medical chopper
Fairchild C-123B-6-FA Provider	20059	N3836A	Ex-54-610, C-130 stand-in for aerial stunts
Hawker Harrier T.4A	212034	(RAF) ZB602	VTOL RAF fighter
Lockheed C-130K-LM Hercules	382-4274	(RAF) XV306	Paratroop jump

Background / unidentified: BAe Nimrod MR.2, Boeing 727-2B6, 767-200, Dassault-Dornier Alpha Jet, Fouga CM.170 Magister, Lockheed C-130H-LM Hercules (Moroccan AF as Russian / 18), North American OV-10 Bronco, Rockwell 680 Turbo Commander (plus model).

Licence to Kill (Bond #16 / 1989 / 133 minutes / Timothy Dalton)

Type	msn	s/n or Civil reg.	Remarks
Aerospatiale HH-65A Dolphin	6270	(USCG) 6574	Coast Guard helicopter
Aerospatiale AS.350B Ecureuil	1531	XA-MUA	Sanchez's helicopter
Cessna 172P Skyhawk	172-75046	N54743	Stolen by Sanchez at airfield
Cessna A185F Skywagon	185-04318	N6964N	Drug-runners' floatplane
Gates Learjet 35	35-034	N37TA	Drug-runners' plane
Piper PA-18-150 Super Cub	unknown	XB-LOX	Crop-duster aircraft

Background / unidentified: Beechcraft Model 18, Beechcraft B-55 Baron (XB-DTF), Grumman E-2C Hawkeye, various Cessna and Piper light aircraft in airfield scenes.

Goldeneye (Bond #17 / 1995 / 130 minutes / Pierce Brosnan)

Type	msn	s/n or Civil reg.	Remarks
Cessna 172P Skyhawk	172-76119	N96816	CIA plane lent to Bond
Eurocopter EC.665 Tiger	PT.1	F-ZWWW	Helicopter stolen off navy ship
Pilatus PC-6/ B2-H2 Turbo-Porter	735	(Swiss) HB-FFW	Russian livery— in opening scene

Background / unidentified: Aerospatiale AS.355 Ecureuil 2 (gunship helicopter at dish), Bell UH-1H-BF Iroquois (three Puerto Rico National Guard), Boeing 757-236 (British Airways livery), Robinson R-22 Beta (Russian / 22). Mikoyan-Gurevich MiG-29 Fulcrum (CGI only).

Tomorrow Never Dies (Bond #18 / 1997 / 119 minutes / Pierce Brosnan)

Type	msn	s/n or Civil reg.	Remarks
Aero L-39ZA Albatros	5321	unknown	Marked as 28/08, flying scenes
Aero L-39ZO Albatros	232337	G-OTAF	Marked as 28/02, flying scenes
Aero L-39ZO Albatros	731002	G-BWTS	Marked as 28/02, ground scenes
Aero L-39ZO Albatros	731013	G-BWTT	Marked as 28/08, ground scenes
Sikorsky MH-53J Pave Low III	65-335	70-1625	USAF heavy lift helicopter

Background / unidentified: Aerospatiale AS.355 Ecureuil 2 (Carver's helicopter), AS.565 Panther, ATR-72, two British Aerospace BAe.125-400B, two BAe.146-200QC, Boeing 737 (Sabena livery), Eurocopter EC.135, Fairchild C-123K-FA Provider (parachute jump), McDonnell Douglas F-15E Strike Eagle. Mikoyan-Gurevich MiG-23 Flogger (CGI models only)

The World Is Not Enough (Bond #19 / 1999 / 125 minutes / Pierce Brosnan)

Type	msn	s/n or Civil reg.	Remarks
Aerospatiale AS.355 F1 Ecureuil 2	5201	G-BPRJ	Marked as King Industries / saw blades
CASA C-212-100 Aviocar	TC-9-92	F-GOGN	Cargo aircraft

Background / unidentified: Aerospatiale AS.365N Dauphin (marked as King Industries), Bell 206 Jet Ranger (two in balloon sequence), Eurocopter EC.135 (M's white helicopter).

Die Another Day (Bond #20 / 2002 / 132 minutes / Pierce Brosnan)

Type	msn	s/n or Civil reg.	Remarks
Antonov An-124-100 Ruslan	19530501005	UR-82007	Giant cargo plane in the final scene
MD Helicopters MD 600N	RN023	N511VA	Seen at the end of the final scene
MD Helicopters MD 900 Explorer	900-00010	N9208V	Marked as CU-H13
Mil Mi-8T Hip	105103	D-HOXQ	Marked as P-71

Background / unidentified: Boeing 747-436 (British Airways livery), Boeing-Vertol Chinook HC.2 (five RAF as U.S. Army CH-47).

Casino Royale (Bond #21 / 2006 / 144 minutes / Daniel Craig)

Type	msn	s/n or Civil reg.	Remarks
Boeing 747-236B	21831/440	G-BDXJ	Skyfleet S570, marked as N88892

Type	msn	Civil reg.	Remarks
DeHavilland DHC-6-300 Twin Otter	647	N300WH	Floatplane
MD Helicopters MD 600N	RN042	N451DL	MI6 helicopter

Background / unidentified: Bell 206 Jet Ranger, several Airbus and Boeing airliners in airport sequence.

QUANTUM OF SOLACE (BOND #22 / 2008 / 106 MINUTES / DANIEL CRAIG)

Type	msn	s/n or Civil reg.	Remarks
Bell 205A-1	30289	N205SF	Black gunship helicopter
Bombardier Challenger 604	5505	G-OCSC	Greene's jet to Austria
Douglas DC-3	2169	N26MA	Marked as CP265, stunt flying scenes
Douglas C-47A-50-DL Skytrain	10035	N12BA	Ex-USAAF 42-24173. Marked as CP265, ground scenes
Gulfstream V	517	HB-IMJ	Greene's jet to Bolivia
SIAI-Marchetti SF.260TP	703/62-006	N260TP	Black turbo prop fighter

Background / unidentified: British Aerospace BAe.125-800A (N803RK), Piper PA-28 Cherokee, Rockwell Aero Commander (HP-668), various executive and private aircraft in airport sequence.

SKYFALL (BOND #23 / 2012 / 143 MINUTES / DANIEL CRAIG)

Type	msn	s/n or Civil reg.	Remarks
AgustaWestland AW.101 Merlin	50012	G-17-510	UK Class B reg., flying
AgustaWestland AW.159 Wildcat	478	ZZ408	Replicated as three choppers on screen

SPECTRE (BOND #24 / 2015 / 148 MINUTES / DANIEL CRAIG)

Type	msn	s/n or Civil reg.	Remarks
Aerospatiale SA.365 N2 Dauphin 2	6393	G-LCPL	Flying, Blofeld's helicopter

Type	msn	Civil reg.	Remarks
Britten-Norman BN-2B-26 Islander	2272	G-BUBP	Flying, marked as: OE-FZO
Britten-Norman BN-2B-21 Islander	2301	G-CZNE	Flying, marked as: OE-FZO
MBB Bo.105 CBS-4	S-598	N133EH	Flying, Chuck Aaron aerobatic chopper opening scene

Background / unidentified: Aerospatiale AS.350 Ecureuil, BAe.146, Britten-Norman BN-2A Islander wrecks (G-AWVY / 48; G-BAXD / 359; N721BN / 435; 1072; G-RAPA / 2115; G-BKOK / 2174), Hughes 500E.

Jet Alert   see   *Jet Attack*

Jet Attack

Alternate Title: ***Jet Alert***
UK Title: ***Through Hell to Glory***
USA / American International Pictures (AIP) / 1958 / B&W / 69 minutes
Director: Edward L. Cahn
Cast: John Agar, Audrey Totter, Gregory Walcott, James Dobson, Leonard Strong, Nicky Blair, Victor Sen Yung, Joseph Hamilton
Synopsis / Aviation Content: During the Korean War, three jet pilots are shot down behind enemy lines, where they link up with friendly locals to instigate an escape plan. Low-budget production was originally released as a second bill alongside another war film, *Suicide Battalion*, made by the same production company. Produced with limited assistance from the California Air National Guard using the **North American F-86F-25-NH Sabre** (s/n 51-13192, 51-13214, 51-13218, 51-13233, 51-13238, 51-13335) and **Republic F-84E Thunderjet** (s/n 49-2031, 49-2085, 49-2306). Other aircraft are a **Bell H-13E Sioux**, **Lockheed F-94C Starfire**, and **North American B-25 Mitchell**. Much use of aerial combat stock footage.

Jet Over the Atlantic

USA / Inter-Continent Films / 1959 / B&W / 95 minutes
Director: Byron Haskin

Cast: Guy Madison, Virginia Mayo, George Raft, Ilona Massey, George Macready, Anna Lee, Margaret Lindsay, Venetia Stevenson

Synopsis / Aviation Content: A convicted killer is being extradited back to the United States on an airliner across the Atlantic when the pilots are rendered unconscious from the gas bomb of a suicidal passenger. Their only hope of survival is the killer, who has a pilot's license. Various views of a rare British-built airliner, the Bristol Britannia.

Although the title promotes a "jet" as the featured aircraft, it's actually a British-built **Bristol 175 Britannia Series 302** (reg. XA-MEC / msn 12918), a medium to long-range turboprop airliner. Technically, a turboprop can be described as a "jet-prop," but the title is still a little misleading. The aircraft itself was built at Bristol's Belfast plant and delivered to Mexico's *Aeronaves de Mexico* airline on November 1, 1957, with reg. XA-MEC; its previous British test reg. was G-ANCB. In Mexican service, XA-MEC was first named *Montezuma*, then *Tenochtitlan* and finally *Acapulco*, and served on the Mexico City-to-New York route. XA-MEC was written off on July 9, 1965, when it made a belly landing at Tijuana after the undercarriage failed to lock; there were no fatalities, but the damage to the aircraft was so severe it was subsequently scrapped. Eighty-five Bristol Britannia aircraft were built from 1952 to 1960, with sixty-two for civilian operators and twenty-three for the RAF. The first flight was on August 16, 1952, with service entry in 1957. Some Britannias were still flying into the 1990s.

Aerial shots of the airliner made use of stock footage of a BOAC Britannia and even a Boeing Model 377 Stratocruiser doubling as a Britannia! Aircraft interiors were a studio-built set filmed in Mexico City. Some aircraft scenes were gathered at Mexico City Intl. Airport doubling as Madrid, Spain, with San Francisco Intl. Airport doubling as New York.

Jet Pilot

USA / Universal-International / 1957* / Color / 108 minutes

Director: Josef Von Sternberg

Cast: John Wayne, Janet Leigh, Jay C. Flippen, Paul Fix, Hans Conried, Richard Rober, Roland Winters, Ivan Triesault

Synopsis / Aviation Content: All-American fighter ace Wayne falls for attractive Russian female pilot Leigh after she seemingly defects to a U.S. air base. Plenty of F-86 Sabres and a scattering of other early 1950s period aircraft, including the Bell X-1, in sharp color certainly make entertaining viewing for the aviation enthusiast. The final escape sequence from Siberia is especially a highlight.

Type	msn	Military s/n	Film Markings
Bell X-1-BE	unknown	46-062	—
Boeing B-50A-5-BN Superfortress	15726	46-006	6006
Convair B-36B-15-CF Peacemaker	unknown	44-92065	065
Lockheed F-94A-1-LO Starfire	780-7001	49-2479	FA-479
North American F-86A-5-NA Sabre	151-513	48-144	FU-144
North American F-86A-5-NA Sabre	151-516	48-147	FU-147
North American F-86A-5-NA Sabre	151-529	48-160	FU-160
North American F-86A-5-NA Sabre	151-549	48-180	FU-180
North American F-86A-5-NA Sabre	151-559	48-190	FU-190
North American F-86A-5-NA Sabre	151-566	48-197	FU-197
North American F-86A-5-NA Sabre	151-577	48-208	FU-208
North American F-86A-5-NA Sabre	161-229	49-1235	FU-235
North American F-86A-5-NA Sabre	161-279	49-1285	FU-285
Northrop XF-89-NO Scorpion	unknown	46-678	—
Northrop F-89A-NO Scorpion	unknown	49-2438	FV-438

The Bell X-1 and Boeing B-50A double for a Russian Tupolev Tu-4 *Bull* with parasite fighter. The X-1 is the actual one that broke the sound barrier in 1947 and is even flown in the film by Chuck Yeager himself. The sequence was shot on May 12, 1950, at Edwards AFB and was the X-1's last flight before retirement. Chuck Yeager also flew some of the F-86 aerial sequences. The Convair B-36B appears briefly in a night flying sequence. F-94A (Buzz No. FA-479) is used when Wayne and Leigh go on a training mission. Many F-86 Sabres were provided to the film company for the opening scenes; s/n 48-160 and 48-180, however, were used extensively for Wayne and Leigh's aerial sequences later in the film. Two were also painted to represent a pair of Russian MiG fighters. The XF-89 prototype was the black-colored aircraft a Russian commander arrives in; it was lost in a fatal crash a short time after filming on February 22, 1950. The F-89A is used in the ground-launched ejector-seat sequence.

Two unidentified **Lockheed T-33A-LO Shooting Star** trainers appear as fictional Russian "Yak-12" fighters marked as "2" and "6." Background aircraft include the **Boeing B-29 Superfortress**, **Douglas C-47 Skytrain** and **North American AT-6 Texan**.

Filmed mainly at Edwards AFB and at George AFB, both located in California. Notable are the watered down tarmacs to depict the wetter, cooler climate of either Alaska or Siberia. The snow scenes were filmed at Eielson AFB in Alaska and used an F-86A fighter group stationed there.

* Pioneering aviator and filmmaker Howard Hughes was behind this motion picture, which he shot from December 1949 to May 1950, with final pick-up shots being done in May 1953. For various reasons, Hughes did not release the film until 1957, by which time many of the aircraft featured had either been developed further or retired altogether, making the film seem quite outdated.

Jet Storm

Reissue Title (UK): *Killing Urge*
UK / British Lion Film Corp. / 1959 / B&W / 99 minutes
Director: Cy Endfield
Cast: Richard Attenborough, Stanley Baker, Mai Zetterling, Hermione Baddeley, Bernard Braden, Diane Cilento, Barbara Kelly, David Kossoff
Synopsis / Aviation Content: A man boards a London-to-New York flight carrying a bomb in order to take revenge on another passenger who killed his daughter in a car accident. One of the early "bomb on a plane" film scenarios, it mostly plays out with in-depth coverage of the passengers' reaction to facing death. Strangely, and for no known reason, a Russian Aeroflot **Tupolev Tu-104B** jet was chosen as the featured airliner. One reason may have been that western aircraft manufacturers and airlines didn't want their aircraft, i.e., the new 707, DC-8 and Comet 4, being used in an air disaster movie. The year 1959 was, of course, the dawning of the passenger jet age, and operators were

keen to maintain high public confidence in the new technology. The scenes of the passengers boarding the flight at the top of the movie used a **Vickers V.806 Viscount** (reg. G-AOYM / msn 262), in close-up. Aircraft interiors were completed in a film studio with the usual fictional spacious cabin and split-level areas. One of the first motion pictures for renowned British aviation film technical advisor and pilot Captain John Crewdson.

Johnny in the Clouds   see *The Way to the Stars*

Journey Together

UK / RKO Radio Pictures / 1945 / B&W / 91 minutes
Director: John Boulting
Cast: Richard Attenborough, Jack Watling, David Tomlinson, Sid Rider, Stuart Latham
Synopsis / Aviation Content: A young air cadet's dream of being a pilot is dashed as he fails to make the grade and instead is forced to settle for navigation. A refreshing approach to the usual "training orientated" film, with an excellent presentation of the process towards earning one's wings. Aircraft featured are an **Avro 652 Anson, DeHavilland DH.82 Tiger Moth**, **North American AT-6 Texan, Boeing-Stearman PT-17 Kaydet, Avro 691 Lancaster**, and **Douglas A-20 Havoc**. Filmed at RAF Methwold, Norfolk, England, and Falcon Field, Mesa, Arizona. Produced by the RAF Film Unit toward the end of World War II, when the pressure on personnel and equipment was declining, allowing for better production values in films.

Jungle Patrol

USA / 20th Century–Fox / 1948 / B&W / 71 minutes
Director: Joseph M. Newman
Cast: Kristine Miller, Arthur Franz, Ross Ford, Tommy Noonan, Gene Reynolds, Richard Jaeckel
Synopsis / Aviation Content: During World War

II, USO showgirl Miller arrives at a remote New Guinea airstrip, where she witnesses pilots of a fighter squadron being killed one-by-one defending the island. Not much action or flying, but regarded as a well-crafted drama. Several **Curtiss P-40N Warhawk** fighters were hired for filming. The usual use of scale models and stock footage for the combat scenes.

Keep 'Em Flying

USA / Universal Pictures / 1941 / B&W / 86 minutes

Director: Arthur Lubin

Cast: Bud Abbott, Lou Costello, Martha Raye, Carol Bruce, William Gargan, Dick Foran

Synopsis / Aviation Content: Abbott & Costello comedy fare has them enlist in a USAAC training school with manic results! Many World War II period trainer aircraft on display with the aerial stunt work, including a hangar fly-through, being a highlight.

Most of the ground scenes featured the **Stearman PT-13 Kaydet** primary trainer, as did the interior studio scenes for cockpit close-ups. The Stearman the comedy pair have to bail out of at the end of the film was PT-13B Kaydet s/n 41-842. The background monoplanes are **Vultee BT-13 Valiant** trainers. "Jinx Roberts's" stunt aircraft is a **Stearman C3MB** (reg. NC6486 / msn 172); it was used for ground scenes and the nosed-over crash scene.

Paul Mantz was chief pilot on the film. His **Boeing Model 100** (reg. NX873H / msn 1144) doubled both as the Stearman C3 (NC6486) and as a PT-13 Kaydet marked "85." In the latter livery he performed the aerial stunts and spectacular hangar fly-through. This one-take stunt was flown by the film's military technical advisor Major Robert L. Scott (a future fighter ace; see: *God Is My Co-Pilot* [1945]), as the military forbade civilian pilot Mantz to perform such an action on army property. Stock footage was used of the Boeing P-26, Boeing Y1B-17, Douglas C-47, Martin B-10, Northrop A-17 and Vultee BT-13. Filmed at Cal-Aero Academy, Ontario, California from September 5 to October 29, 1941. This airfield is now known as Chino Airport.

Killing Urge   see   Jet Storm

Ladies Courageous

Reissue Title: *Fury in the Sky*

USA / Universal Pictures / 1944 / B&W / 88 minutes

Director: John Rawlins

Cast: Loretta Young, Geraldine Fitzgerald, Diana Barrymore, Anne Gwynne, Evelyn Ankers, Phillip Terry, David Bruce, Richard Fraser

Synopsis / Aviation Content: The story of the Women's Auxiliary Ferrying Squadron, who delivered aircraft from the factory to the front line. Based on the 1941 novel *Looking for Trouble* by American journalist Virginia Spencer Cowles. Filmed from July to November 1943, featuring the **Boeing B-17F / G Flying Fortress; Consolidated B-24 Liberator; Curtiss P-40 Warhawk; Douglas A-20 Havoc, A-24, C-47 Skytrain; Lockheed Hudson, P-38 Lightning; Martin B-26 Marauder; North American AT-6 Texan, B-25 Mitchell, P-51B / C Mustang; Republic P-47 Thunderbolt; and Vultee BT-13 Valiant**.

The Lady Takes a Flyer

USA / Universal-International / 1958 / color / 94 minutes

Director: Jack Arnold

Cast: Lana Turner, Jeff Chandler, Richard Denning, Andra Martin, Chuck Connors, Reta Shaw, Alan Hale Jr., Jerry Paris, Dee J. Thompson, Nestor Paiva

Synopsis / Aviation Content: Lighthearted story about a couple who hastily marry, only to discover starting a family and ferrying World War II bombers don't always mix. Fun movie, if a little thin on aircraft and flying, its saving grace being the energetic performances of the cast and terrific views of the U.S. Navy storage yard at Litchfield Park in Arizona.

The opening scenes were filmed at the Lockheed Air Terminal in Burbank, California, with a borrowed USAF **Boeing B-17G-110-BO Flying Fortress** (s/n 43-39356 / msn 10334), sporting the fictional civilian N-number "N39356"—the

N simply having been painted on at the start of the serial number. Several light aircraft, including a Beechcraft Bonanza V35 and Cessna Model 120, are also visible. The Lockheed plant is also in the background with a number of L-1049 Super Constellation airliners parked out front. The aircraft auction scene was shot at Litchfield Park, Arizona, the main featured aircraft being the **Consolidated PB2Y-1 Privateer**. Background aircraft include the **Fairchild R4Q-1 Packet**, **Grumman F8F Bearcat**, and **North American SNJ Texan**. Other featured aircraft seen throughout are the **Douglas C-47B Skytrain** (s/n 43-16138 / msn 20604), **North American B-25J Mitchell**, and **P-51D Mustang**.

Lafayette Escadrille

Alternate Title: *With You in My Arms*
UK Title: *Hell Bent for Glory*
USA / Warner Bros. / 1958 / B&W / 93 minutes
Director: William A. Wellman
Cast: Tab Hunter, Etchika Choureau, Marcel Dalio, David Janssen, Paul Fix, Veola Vonn
Synopsis / Aviation Content: A young American goes to France during World War I to join the American volunteer squadron known as the Lafayette Escadrille, whereupon he also meets and falls in love with a local French girl. Notable as being famed director Wellman's last motion picture, much of which is based on his own experiences as a fighter pilot in France during World War I. See under *Wings* (1927) for a short biography of Wellman.

Hollywood pilot Paul Mantz was heavily involved in the flying logistics with the film crew based out of Santa Maria Airport, California, between October 1956 and May 1957. Aircraft included two **Bleriot XI Penguin** replicas (one was reg. N6683C / msn 1); one **Garland Lincoln LF-1** as a Nieuport replica (reg. N12237 / msn 3); one **Royal Aircraft Factory S.E.5a**; one **Sopwith Camel F.I** (reg. N6254 / msn 3); a **Nieuport 28** replica (reg. N4728V / msn 512); and a **Thomas-Morse S-4B Scout** replica (reg. N38923 / msn 1), marked as "N1801."

Much use was made of stock footage from Wellman's *Men With Wings* (1938) for many of the aerial sequences. Wellman's son, Bill Wellman Jr., plays his own father in the film, and watch for a young Clint Eastwood in a minor role as one of the American pilots.

FACTUAL BACKGROUND:
THE LAFAYETTE ESCADRILLE

Founded during World War I in April 1916 as the Escadrille Americaine, this squadron of the French Air Service was created to cater to the numbers of American volunteer pilots who were eager to assist the French in the war against Germany. The name was changed in December 1916 to Lafayette Escadrille after Germany complained that a supposedly neutral country appeared to be taking part in the war as an ally of France. Altogether 265 American volunteer pilots flew in not only the Lafayette Escadrille, but in other French flying units. When the U.S. entered World War I, the squadron was transferred to the United States Army Air Unit as the 103rd Pursuit Squadron in February 1918 which it remained as until wars end in November that same year.

The Last Flight of Noah's Ark

USA / Walt Disney Productions / 1980 / Color / 97 minutes
Director: Charles Jarrott
Cast: Elliott Gould, Genevieve Bujold, Ricky Schroder, Vincent Gardenia, Tammy Lauren, John Fujioka, Yuki Shimoda
Synopsis / Aviation Content: An exceptional family film concerning a vintage, cargo-converted B-29 bomber that crashes on a remote Pacific island, whereupon the survivors fabricate a raft from the wreckage in order to sail home. Fan-

Type	msn	Military s/n	Civil reg.
Flyable Aircraft			
Boeing B-29-95-BW Superfortress	13681	45-21787	N91329
Boeing-Stearman PT-13D-BW Kaydet	75-5510	42-17347	N121R
Derelict Aircraft			
Boeing B-29-75-BW Superfortress	10881	44-70049	—
Boeing B-29-60-BA Superfortress	unknown	44-84084	—
Boeing B-29A-65-BN Superfortress	11589	44-62112	—
Boeing B-29A-70-BN Superfortress	11699	44-62222	—

tastic details of a rare civilian Superfortress in action both on the ground and in the air. Receiving a largely low-key reception at the time of its release, this film is something of a lost treasure for all audiences, especially B-29 fans! Story written by aviation pioneer and author Ernest K. Gann.

The featured aircraft is a World War II Boeing B-29 Superfortress, the one in the film having a very distinctive history, as one of only two B-29 bombers to fly on the U.S. civilian register. It was diverted to the U.S. Navy as a P2B-1S (BuNo. 84029) in 1947; flew from 1950 to 1956 with the NACA (s/n 137), as a mothership to the Douglas Skyrocket experimental jet, earning the B-29 the nickname *Fertile Myrtle*. On the civilian market it was purchased by the Ace Smelting Co., Arizona, in 1960; sold to Allied Aircraft Sales, Arizona, as N91329 in 1965; then to the American Air Museum Society, Oakland, in 1969; and was leased to Disney productions for the flying scenes in the film. Both the registration and *Fertile Myrtle* nose art can be seen in the movie. The B-29 was sold to Kermit Weeks (Fantasy of Flight), Florida, in 1984 as N29KW; it was subsequently dismantled for museum display.

The brief white-and-red stunt-plane flyby at the top of the film was a Joe Hughes Super Stearman conversion, N121R, originally built as a standardized dual-service Kaydet having two serial numbers: USAAF PT-13D (s/n 42-17347) and U.S. Navy N2S-5 (BuNo. 61388). During filming, the biplane lost its landing gear while performing a stunt and had to make a belly landing at nearby Edwards AFB.

Four derelict B-29 bombers were located for use at the U.S. Navy's China Lake facility in the Mojave Desert in California. Two (s/n 44-70049, 44-84084) were shipped to Hawaii—one as the beach wreck and the other as an actual oceangoing raft for daylight scenes shot off Waikiki Beach. Both were returned to China Lake upon completion of filming. The two others (s/n 44-62112, 44-62222) were sent to Disney Studios in Burbank, California—one was broken up for B-29 interior scenes, and the other was rigged as a raft for nighttime ocean scenes shot in the studio's giant outdoor tank. The Pima Air & Space Mu-

seum in Arizona acquired some components from both these aircraft after filming.

The airfield at the top of the film is El Mirage Airport located in the Mojave Desert near Victorville, California. Some B-29 aerial shots were filmed over San Francisco. The island setting is the secluded Allerton Beach located on the south shore of the island of Kauai, Hawaii. Ocean scenes were shot off Kauai and also Waikiki Beach, Oahu, Hawaii, with the assistance of the U.S. Coast Guard.

GPS LOCATIONS

El Mirage Airport, California: N34 37.40 / W117 36.20

Allerton Beach, Kauai, Hawaii: N21 53.30 / W159 30.15

Lawrence of Arabia (Non–Aviation Film Title)

UK / Columbia Pictures / 1962 / Color / 222 minutes

Director: David Lean

Cast: Peter O'Toole, Alec Guinness, Anthony Quinn, Jack Hawkins, Omar Sharif, Jose Ferrer, Anthony Quayle, Claude Rains, Arthur Kennedy

Synopsis / Aviation Content: Epic, timeless film following the life and exploits of British soldier T.E. Lawrence, notable here for its brief use of two **DeHavilland DH.82A Tiger Moth** biplanes. G-ANNF (msn 83028) and G-ANLC (msn 85154). They were converted by Film Aviation Services Ltd. for delivery to Jordan in 1961 as World War I German Rumpler C.IV biplanes. Another Tiger Moth (RAF s/n T7438), was modified as a Fokker D.VII fighter, but was never sent abroad. Location support aircraft for cast and crew were a DeHavilland DH.104 Dove 1B (reg. G-ARBH / msn 4196) and Douglas C-47B (reg. JY-ABR / msn 14660/26105).

The Legion of the Condemned

USA / Paramount Pictures / 1928 / B&W / 80 minutes

Director: William A. Wellman

Cast: Gary Cooper, Fay Wray, Barry Norton, Lane Chandler, Francis McDonald, George Wood

Synopsis / Aviation Content: Silent-era film follows American pilot Cooper delivering his former lover Wray behind enemy lines on a dangerous spy mission. Story written by American writer and former World War I flight instructor John Monk Saunders, who also wrote the screenplay with former World War I French fighter ace Jean De Limur. Saunders and director Wellman, fresh off the success of their film *Wings* (1927), made this picture utilizing the mountains of leftover aerial footage and combat sequences from that film. Notable as being one of the first leading roles for actor Gary Cooper, who had a bit part in *Wings*. No prints of this film are known to survive today. (Non–Aviation Themed Title)

Licence to Kill see *James Bond* Series

Lilac Time

USA / First National Pictures / 1928 / B&W / 80 minutes

Directors: George Fitzmaurice, Frank Lloyd (uncredited)

Cast: Colleen Moore, Gary Cooper, Burr McIntosh, George Cooper, Cleve Moore, Kathryn McGuire

Synopsis / Aviation Content: Silent-era film follows closely on the heels of the hugely successful *Wings* (1927), about a French girl who falls for an RFC pilot staying near her father's farmhouse. Based on a 1917 Broadway stage play by Jane Murfin and Jane Cowl, which was in turn adapted from a book by Guy Fowler. Filmed in California with around fifteen aircraft, most being **Waco Model 10** biplanes doubling as World War I fighters. *Wings* stunt flyer Dick Grace was the chief pilot on the film and hired a group of other stunt pilots who collectively became known as the "buzzards." One of them, Frank Baker, was killed during production while performing an aerial stunt before the cameras. The film is notable for its original aerial sequences, with Grace performing several of his trademark crashes before the cameras.

The Lion Has Wings

UK / United Artists Corp. / 1939 / B&W / 76 minutes

Directors: Adrian Brunel, Brian Desmond Hurst, Michael Powell, Alexander Korda [uncredited]

Cast: Merle Oberon, Ralph Richardson, June Duprez, Flora Robson, Robert Douglas, Anthony Bushell, Brian Worth

Synopsis / Aviation Content: A docudrama begun by producer Alexander Korda only days after World War II began with Germany. It was designed to convince the British government of the value of cinema for propaganda purposes and the British public of the preparedness of the RAF. Essentially, Korda hoped to keep the British film industry alive during the war years. A heavily censored (Britain's secret radar installations are not seen) but important film which showcases a pre–Battle of Britain RAF with views of many already obsolete aircraft types in service.

Aircraft were early British types including the **Avro 652 Anson**; **Bristol Bulldog** biplane; **Fairey Battle**; **Hawker Fury** biplane and **Hurricane**; **Supermarine Spitfire Mk. IA** fighters from No. 74 Squadron and **Vickers Wellington** bombers from No. 149 Squadron. German types featured are stock footage of the Focke-Wulf Fw 200 Condor, Heinkel He 51, He 111 and Junkers Ju 52.

Filmed in less than a month during September 1939; the three directors shot simultaneously, which allowed for such a short production period. Active airfields were RAF Hornchurch in Essex and RAF Mildenhall in Suffolk. Interiors were filmed at Denham Studios in Buckinghamshire. It was edited and printed in about four weeks, then released in the UK and many other countries before the end of 1939. U.S. prints were released in January 1940.

Live and Let Die (Non–Aviation Themed Title) see *James Bond* Series

The Living Daylights (Non–Aviation Themed Title) see *James Bond* Series

The Lost Squadron

USA / RKO Radio Pictures / 1932 / B&W / 79 minutes

Director: George Archainbaud

Cast: Richard Dix, Mary Astor, Robert Armstrong, Dorothy Jordan, Joel McCrea, Erich von Stroheim, Hugh Herbert, Ralph Ince

Synopsis / Aviation Content: A group of veteran World War I pilots go to Hollywood, where each is eventually killed performing aerial stunts for films. An interesting premise given that the story was written by Dick Grace, a top Hollywood stunt pilot at the time. Grace also performed several on-screen crashes for the film, which featured the **Nieuport 28**, **Thomas-Morse S-4C Scout**, and **Travel Air** biplanes.

Mad Max 2 (Non–Aviation Themed Title)

U.S. Title: **The Road Warrior**

Australia / Warner Bros. / 1981 / Color / 94 minutes

Director: George Miller

Cast: Mel Gibson, Bruce Spence, Mike Preston, Max Phipps, Vernon Wells, Emil Minty

Synopsis / Aviation Content: This successful futuristic car chase movie features a unique flying machine—a heavily modified autogyro flown by a character aptly named the "Gyro Captain." It was hired for the film from Australian owner and pilot Gerry Goodwin and is based on the American Bensen Aircraft Corp. Autogyro designed by Dr. Igor Bensen as a kit set for amateur construction. The aircraft was not required to be on the Australian civil register at the time, so it carries no registration, and since it was virtually scratch-built from the frame up, it also has no factory build number. Concerning the custom construction, Goodwin says, "The gyro I built was based on the Bensen gyro with the only dimension taken being the nine-degree rake in the mast; all other dimensions was [sic] developed by me. Every component except the VW engine was hand-built by myself, and I do mean every component, from rotor blades, propeller, rotor head, control stick and airframe." Goodwin's unique version included a twin tail configuration also developed in Australia. The Bensen Aircraft Corp. built autogyros in North Carolina from 1953 to 1988. *Mad Max* producer Byron Kennedy, a recreational helicopter pilot, was killed on July 17, 1983, when his Bell 206B Jet Ranger (reg. VH-KMX / msn 3172) crashed at Lake Burragorang west of Sydney. This helicopter was used as the aerial photography camera-ship on *Mad Max 2*, often doubling as the autogyro in point-of-view shots.

The Bensen Autogyro design heavily modified by owner and pilot Gerry Goodwin before it had its movie make-up applied for *Mad Max 2* (1981), which included centerfolds from adult magazines stuck to the tail fin! Photograph: Gerry Goodwin.

Mad Max Beyond Thunderdome

(Non–Aviation Themed Title)

Australia / Warner Bros. / 1985 / Color / 110 minutes

Directors: George Miller, George Ogilvie

Cast: Mel Gibson, Tina Turner, Helen Buday, Frank Thring, Bruce Spence, Robert Grubb

Synopsis / Aviation Content: Third installment in the *Mad Max* series showcases a now rare and very strange-looking agricultural / utility aircraft known as the **Transavia PL-12 Airtruk**. Two were used for the film.

PL-12 reg. VH-IVH (msn G353), was purchased by the film producers but crashed during the delivery flight on November 14, 1984. Although not confirmed, this aircraft may have been used in static ground shots for actor close-ups. VH-IVH was later repaired and sold, but was written off in another crash on August 2, 1988. The actual flying aircraft seen in the finished film was PL-12 reg. VH-EVY (msn 1248), rented from owner and pilot Rod Venables. Its flying career later ended in a minor crash on February 7, 1988; the aircraft then went on static display at the Air World Museum in Wangaratta, Australia. Transavia manufactured 118 PL-12 Airtruks from 1965 to 1985, with VH-EVY being delivered in 1972 as the 48th airframe built overall.

The Malta Story

UK / The J. Arthur Rank Organisation / 1953 / B&W / 103 minutes

Director: Brian Desmond Hurst

Cast: Alec Guinness, Jack Hawkins, Anthony Steel, Muriel Pavlow, Renee Asherson, Flora Robson

Synopsis / Aviation Content: Photo reconnaissance pilot Guinness has an unexpected stopover on Malta in 1942, where he soon becomes involved in the fight to defend the island and its people. A well-crafted film, especially the film editing, it has many unique views of Malta as it was in the early 1950s, plus some excellent scenes featuring the classic Spitfire.

Four **Supermarine Spitfire Mk. XVI** fighters were used for filming—three were the low-back, bubble canopy version (s/n RW352, TE178 and TE241), and one (Guinness's photo reconn.), was

Seen here in 1995 at the Air World Museum collection in Australia is Transavia PL-12 Airtruk VH-EVY that was owned and piloted by Rod Venables for *Mad Max Beyond Thunderdome* (1985). Photograph: Henk Geerlings.

a classic high-back Mk. XVI (s/n TB245). All had the clipped wings of later Spitfire variants. The bomber was a **Vickers Wellington T.Mk. 10** (either s/n HF626 or NB113), and the large biplane was a **Fairy Albacore Mk. I** torpedo bomber. Much use was made of wartime film footage and models in many of the aerial sequences. Location filming took place on the Mediterranean island of Malta itself from October through December 1952, capturing unique shots of island life and buildings during this period. Of special interest to aviation fans is Malta's infamous Spitfire graveyard, which provided many derelict fighters of the type for set dressing. Production was completed at Pinewood Studios in England.

The Man in the Sky

Alternate Title: *Test Pilot*
U.S. Title: *Decision Against Time*
UK / Metro-Goldwyn-Mayer / 1957 / B&W / 87 minutes
Director: Charles Crichton
Cast: Jack Hawkins, Elizabeth Sellars, Jeremy Bodkin, Gerard Lohan, Walter Fitzgerald, John Stratton, Eddie Byrne, Donald Pleasence
Synopsis / Aviation Content: A company test pilot played by Hawkins refuses to bail out after an in-flight emergency, opting instead to attempt a rescue of the company's only, uninsured cargo aircraft. Fantastic shots of the rarely seen British-built Bristol Freighter is a real treat for fans of the type. Hawkins's excellent performance, magnificent black and white photography and flying sequences make for an exciting and well-crafted aviation film.

The star, of course, is a **Bristol Type 170 Wayfarer Mk. IIA** (reg. G-AIFV / msn 12781), hired from Silver City Airways—a British air-ferry company well known for its use of the type. First registered to the Bristol Aeroplane Co. on October 11, 1946, it went to India with Dalmia Jain Airways on November 28, 1946, as VT-CID. It returned to the UK in 1949 and was upgraded to **Mk. 21 Freighter** standard by Bristol before going to Silver City Airways on June 19, 1953. During filming at Wolverhampton Airport on May 15, 1956, G-AIFV damaged its nose, under-

carriage and wings when it overshot the runway during a simulated emergency landing.

After repairs it returned to service with Silver City and was later named *City of Manchester* in 1958. G-AIFV was withdrawn from use on October 19, 1961, and was scrapped at Lydd Airport in May 1962.

Bristol Type 170 Freighter Mk. 21 (reg. G-AIFM / msn 12773) can briefly be seen in a hangar in the background. There appears to have been a third Bristol Freighter, possibly a Mk. 31, used in filming and doubling for G-AIFV in the aerial scenes. This aircraft is evident in the engine-out flying scenes, as it suddenly has a dorsal tail fillet, painted-out blotches under the wings (perhaps to hide the registration?), and a lighter colored side-stripe. It may have been acquired to complete these scenes after G-AIFV was damaged in the runway overshoot. Actor Jack Hawkins, in preparation for his role, visited the Bristol plants at Filton and Western-Super-Mare, receiving three days' cockpit instruction from Bristol test pilot Ronnie Ellison. Filming took place at Wolverhampton Aerodrome, Wolverhampton, Staffordshire, England (N52 30.90 / W002 15.70), with interiors completed at MGM Studios, Borehamwood, Hertfordshire, utilizing an excellent Bristol Freighter mock-up that included engines that could simulate an in-flight fire.

FACTUAL BACKGROUND: BRISTOL TYPE 170 FREIGHTER

The Type 170 was a British-designed and -built aircraft resulting from the need for a dedicated cargo freighter with easy, front-end loading via clamshell doors. The prototype first flew on December 2, 1945, at Bristol's Filton plant. Various versions were produced, the main ones initially being the Mk. I Freighter and Mk. II Wayfarer passenger version. The 1948 Mk. 21 was a Freighter version with engine upgrade. The definitive variant was the 1950 Mk. 31 Freighter with upgraded engines, dorsal tail fillet, and many other improvements—ninety were built with some earlier airframes being upgraded to this standard. In all, 214 Bristol Freighters were rolled out from 1945 to 1958; the last version was the Mk. 32 Superfreighter with extended nose doors. Pakistan and New Zealand were the largest military operators, with England's Silver City Airways and New Zealand's SAFE Air Ltd. being the most prominent civilian operators. A few Freighters were still flying in Canada as late as 1988.

Man Mad   see   *No Place to Land*

The Man with the Golden Gun

(Non–Aviation Themed Title)   see *James Bond Series*

A Matter of Life and Death

U.S. Title: *Stairway to Heaven*
UK / Eagle-Lion Distributors Ltd. / 1946 / B&W / Color / 104 minutes
Directors: Michael Powell, Emeric Pressburger
Cast: David Niven, Kim Hunter, Raymond Massey, Roger Livesey, Robert Coote, Marius Goring, Richard Attenborough
Synopsis / Aviation Content: Comical romance story about a Lancaster pilot who is killed, but heaven "misplaces" his death; while waiting on Earth, he falls in love, which complicates things further. A top-notch, entertaining film uses a model of an Avro Lancaster for the flying scenes and a scaled mock-up for onboard scenes. Also seen is a real **DeHavilland DH.98 Mosquito** bomber. Released in the U.S. in 1946 through Universal Pictures.

The McConnell Story

UK Title: *Tiger in the Sky*
USA / Warner Bros. / 1955 / Color / 107 minutes
Director: Gordon Douglas
Cast: Alan Ladd, June Allyson, James Whitmore, Frank Faylen, Robert Ellis, Willis Bouchey, Sarah Selby, Gregory Walcott, Frank Ferguson
Synopsis / Aviation Content: Entertaining, biographical story following the life and times of Korean War fighter ace Captain Joseph C. McConnell. Little aeronautical content in the first half of the film, but some great views of the F-86 Sabre and other period aircraft in the second half.

The small aircraft in the opening scene is a **Piper J-3 Cub**; a Boeing Stearman can be seen in the background. Piper Cubs are also seen at the air cadet school, Douglas C-47 Skytrain transports are used throughout the movie, and Republic P-47 Thunderbolts can be seen in one post–World War II ramp scene. McConnell trains in a **Lockheed F-80C Shooting Star** fighter; identified are s/n 47-556, 49-432, 49-656 and 49-786. Korean combat scenes use the **North American F-86F Sabre**; identified are s/n 51-13192, 51-13214, 51-13238, 51-13297, and 51-13298, plus one unidentified marked as "2203 / FU-03." **Republic F-84G Thunderstreak** fighters double as North Korean MiG-15 fighters, and three **Sikorsky H-19 Chickasaw** helicopters were provided for a rescue scene; identified are SH-19A (s/n 51-3882) and SH-19B (s/n 51-3947). Also seen are several Lockheed T-33A Shooting Star trainers in some scenes. World War II B-17 combat scenes used footage from the 1944 documentary *Memphis Belle*, plus there's additional stock footage of the Messerschmitt Me 163 Komet jet aircraft.

Factual Background: Top Korean Ace

New Hampshire born Joseph C. McConnell (January 30, 1922–August 25, 1954) was at first a B-24 navigator (B-17 bombers for the film), in Europe during World War II before attaining his dream as a fighter pilot in 1948. Captain McConnell went on to become the top American ace of the Korean War shooting down sixteen MiG-15 fighters in his F-86 Sabre. He remains the all-time top scoring American jet ace to this day. McConnell was killed at Edwards AFB, California on August 25, 1954, after a hydraulic failure in the fifth built F-86H Sabre (s/n 52-1981), the cause was later attributed to a missing bolt.

Memphis Belle

USA-UK / Warner Bros. / 1990 / Color / 103 minutes
Director: Michael Caton-Jones
Cast: Matthew Modine, Eric Stoltz, Tate Donovan, D.B. Sweeny, Billy Zane, Sean Astin, Harry Connick, Jr., Reed Edward Diamond, Courtney

Gains, Neil Giuntoli, David Strathairn, John Lithgow

Synopsis / Aviation Content: A fiction-based-on-fact recreation of the twenty-fifth and final mission of the U.S. Eighth Air Force B-17F *Memphis Belle* in 1943. Several changes were made here, for the sake of "cinematic excitement," that significantly differ from actual events—the main one being the final mission for the real *Belle* was to a light target in France, not a heavily defended Bremen. Additionally, the characters are fictional, and not based, to any large extent, on the original crew. Contains some weak dialogue in parts, but without doubt the best B-17 footage ever put on film, with the famous bomber featured from start to finish either on the ground, in the background, taxiing or flying. A highlight is almost certainly the taxi and takeoff sequence accompanied by an outstanding George Fenton music score. Crank up the home theater!

The film markings for the B-17 bombers in the above table were the main ones carried in accordance with the script. The same aircraft also carried various other markings throughout filming to depict B-17 aircraft from different squadrons: N17W was also DP-X; F-AZDX also DP-O; F-BEEA also DF-Q, DP-H and G-BEDF also DF-B *My Zita*, DF-U *Baby Ruth*, DF-O *Gee Whiz*, DF-X *C Cup*, and as DF-A *Memphis Belle* for the final landing sequence. Additional codes include DF-H and ZQ-T. Names include *Black Eyed Pea, Buckaroo, Clooney Baby, Gee Whiz, Hot Lips, Lady Jane, Mama's Boys, Mary Lou, Sweet Dreams* and *Vacillating Virgin*.

B-17F N17W was a *Tora! Tora! Tora!* (1970) veteran, and like B-17G N3703G was brought out to England from the USA. N17W was owned by Bob Richardson of Seattle, and N3703G was owned by David Tallichet's Military Aircraft Restoration Corp. in California. F-ASZD and F-BEEA had previously been in service with I'Institut Geographique National (IGN), based in France for survey work, and were preserved as such with the IGN/Forteresse Toujours Volante Assoc. G-BEDF was with the B-17 Preservation Trust Ltd. and was already based at Duxford, one of the film's locations. B-17G F-BEEA crashed during filming at Binbrook on July 25, 1989, while taking off on Runway 21. All ten onboard survived, but the aircraft was written off.

B-17 pilots were N17W: Bob Richardson and Donald Clark; N3703G: David Tallichet; F-AZDX: Andre Domine; F-BEEA: Jean-Pierre Gattegno; and G-BEDF: Keith Sisson and Alan Walker. Technical consultants were B-17 historians Roger Freeman, Tommy Garcia and Bruce Orriss.

The C-47A G-DAKS seen in the background at the top of the film was owned by Aces High U.S., Inc. The Old Flying Machine Co., headed by chief pilot Ray Hanna and son Mark, amassed a total of three Hispano Buchons and seven P-51D Mustang fighters with a crew of fifteen available pilots. The Hispano Buchons G-BOML and G-HUNN were *Battle of Britain* (1969) veterans, and along with Buchon D-FEHD, doubled for the Luftwaffe **Messerschmitt Bf 109G**. P-51D Mustangs N314BG and N1051S were flown as background aircraft only without movie markings; the

Type	msn	Military s/n	Civil reg.	Film Markings
Boeing B-17F-70-BO Flying Fortress	4896	42-29782	N17W	DF-X *C-Cup*
Boeing B-17G-85-DL Flying Fortress	32187	44-83546	N3703G	DF-A *Memphis Belle*
Boeing B-17G-85-VE Flying Fortress	17-8246	44-8846	F-AZDX	DF-S *Mother & Country*
Boeing B-17G-100-VE Flying Fortress	17-8552	44-85643	F-BEEA	DF-U *Baby Ruth*
Boeing B-17G-105-VE Flying Fortress	17-8693	44-85784	G-BEDF	DF-M *Windy City*
CAC Mustang PR.Mk. 22	192-1517	(RAAF) A68-192	G-HAEC	AJ-A *Ding Hao*
Douglas C-47A-75-DL Skytrain	19347	42-100884	G-DAKS	—
Hispano HA-1112-M1L Buchon	170	C.4K-107	G-BOML	—
Hispano HA-1112-M1L Buchon	213	C.4K-40	D-FEHD	15
Hispano HA-1112-M1L Buchon	235	C.4K-172	G-HUNN	14
North American P-51D-20-NA Mustang	122-38675	44-72216	G-BIXL	AJ-L *Miss L*
North American P-51D-25-NA Mustang	122-39232	44-72773	G-SUSY	AJ-C
North American P-51D-25-NA Mustang	122-39599	44-73140	N314BG	—
North American P-51D-25-NA Mustang	122-39608	44-73149	N51JJ	AJ-S *Candyman, Moose*
North American P-51D-25-NA Mustang	122-40417	44-73877	N167F	AJ-N *Cisco*
North American P-51D-25-NT Mustang	124-48124	45-11371	N1051S	—

Boeing B-17 Flying Fortress F-BEEA (s/n 44–85643), painted as *Baby Ruth* for the 1989 film *Memphis Belle*. This aircraft crashed during takeoff on July 25, 1989; there were no fatalities, but the B-17 was written off. Photograph: Derek Ferguson.

other five Mustangs were painted olive-drab with white prop spinners and "AJ" markings. G-HAEC came from the Old Flying Machine Co.; G-BIXL was provided by Robs Lamplough at Duxford; G-SUSY came from Charles Church (Spitfires) Ltd.; N314BG came from Warbirds of GB Ltd.; N51JJ was provided by the Fighter Collection at Duxford; N167F was provided by the Scandinavian Historic Flight; and N1051S came from Myrick Aviation based in Florida.

Fighter pilots were P-51: Stephen Grey, Reg Hallam, Peter John, Hoof Proudfoot, Anders Saether and Rolf Meum; Buchon: Walter Eichorn, Mark Hanna (aerial coordinator) and Ray Hanna (chief pilot). Other pilots were Chris Bevan, Paul Chaplin, Rob Dean, Peter Jarvis, Carl Schofield and Brian Smith.

Camera-planes were an ex–Tallmantz B-25J, N1042B, at the time operated by Aces High U.S., Inc. A second camera-plane was a Grumman TBM-3E Avenger (BuNo. 91110 / reg. N6827C), operated by the Old Flying Machine Co. after N1024B broke down. Some scenes were shot from a helicopter piloted by Marc Wolff and Peter Thompson.

Five 1:6 scale B-17F Flying Fortress models were built for the more dangerous landings and crashes by Model Effects Ltd. of Watford. Two actually flew under remote control, and each weighed about 100 lbs. Three static models were built for

North American P-51D Mustang G-HAEC painted as "AJ-A *Ding Hao*" for filming on the B-17 motion picture *Memphis Belle* (1989). Photograph: Derek Ferguson.

various taxi and crash shots, each weighing around 300 lbs. Many background B-17 bombers were painted 2-D flats. A zoom-in shot at the start of the takeoff sequence features the scale models (foreground), flyable B-17 aircraft (on runway), and a 2-D flat (background), creating the illusion of up to ten Fortresses in one shot!

A full-scale mock-up B-17 tail section and two Percival P.66 Pembroke skeletal airframes were used to depict a crashed and burning Fortress. A full-scale B-17 fuselage mock-up was built for the interior scenes of the *Memphis Belle*, filmed at Pinewood Studios, Buckinghamshire. Any section could be removed or altered to gain camera access from any angle. The mock-up was later an attraction at Warner Bros. Movie World in Australia.

The main airfield set was at RAF Binbrook, Lincolnshire, where ground scenes with the actors, the dance scene, and aircraft preparations were filmed. The control tower at the top of the film was purpose-built, and the background church steeple in the plough field scene was a wooden mock-up. Some scenes were also filmed at the Imperial War Museum at Duxford, Cambridgeshire; all aerial sequences with aircraft were based out of this location.

GPS Locations

RAF Binbrook, Lincolnshire (closed 1988): N53 26.70 / W000 12.25

Duxford Aerodrome, Cambridgeshire: N52 05.50 / E000 07.80

Factual Background: The Real *Memphis Belle*

Rolling off the assembly line at the Boeing plant in Seattle, the real *Memphis Belle* was delivered as a B-17F-10-BO (s/n 41-24485 / msn 3170), to the USAAF in 1942. Assigned to the 91st BG, 324 BS at Bassingbourn, north of London, the Fortress commenced operations on November 7, 1942. Captain Robert K. Morgan named the aircraft after his wartime girlfriend, Ms. Margaret Polk, from Memphis, Tennessee. The B-17F completed twenty-five missions, flying almost 149 hours and dropping over sixty tons of bombs, with the last sortie to Lorient, France, on May 17, 1943. The *Memphis Belle* and her crew then re-turned to the U.S. on a wartime promotional tour and the aircraft has since become the most legendary of all the B-17 Flying Fortresses to serve in World War II. An award-winning documentary was produced about the B-17 and its crew in 1944 by filmmaker William Wyler; titled *The Memphis Belle: A Story of a Flying Fortress*, it was the inspiration for the 1990 feature film co-produced by his daughter Catherine Wyler. Many of the crew's combat dialogue recorded in the documentary was written into the film script for the actors. The aircraft itself was retired to a boneyard at Altus Field, Oklahoma, on August 1, 1945. It was rescued from the scrapper by the City of Memphis for $350 and flown home on July 17, 1946. Over the years, it slowly deteriorated outside, until finally it was placed inside a purpose-built enclosure in 1987. In late 2005, the *Belle* was transferred to the USAF Museum, Dayton, Ohio, for long-term preservation and display.

Men of the Fighting Lady

USA / Metro-Goldwyn-Mayer / 1954 / Color / 79 minutes

Director: Andrew Marton

Cast: Van Johnson, Walter Pidgeon, Louis Calhern, Dewey Martin, Keenan Wynn, Frank Lovejoy, Bert Freed, Lewis Martin, George Cooper, Dick Simmons

Synopsis / Aviation Content: Set during the Korean War, the film follows the trials and hardships experienced by a naval flight crew as they attempt to knock out a railroad target. Above-average production values plus some good views of several period naval fighter types, make this one of the better Korean War period aviation films. Based on the short stories "The Forgotten Heroes of Korea" by James A. Michener and "The Case of the Blind Pilot" by Commander Harry A. Burns. Not to be confused with the similarly titled 1944 William Wyler documentary *The Fighting Lady*, detailing the service of the USS *Yorktown* (CV-10) during World War II.

Filmed onboard the aircraft carrier USS *Oriskany* (CV-34) using **Grumman F9F-5 Panther** fighters of naval squadron VF-192 Golden Dragons.

The same aircraft and squadron were also employed for another Korean War film, *The Bridges at Toko-Ri* (1954). One scene used actual footage of the spectacular July 23, 1951, crash of pilot George Duncan's F9F-5 Panther, which snapped apart on the end of the carrier USS *Midway*; the pilot survived with minor injuries. This crash was also used in several later film productions, including *Midway* (1976), where it stood in for an SBD Dauntless! Some additional scenes were filmed onboard the USS *Princeton* (CV-37), also featuring the F9F Panther. Other aircraft include the **Douglas AD-1 Skyraider**, **North American FJ Fury**, and **Sikorsky HO3S Dragonfly**.

Men with Wings

USA / Paramount Pictures / 1938 / Color / 105 minutes
Director: William A. Wellman
Cast: Fred MacMurray, Ray Milland, Louise Campbell, Andy Devine, Lynne Overman, Porter Hall, Walter Abel, Kitty Kelly
Synopsis / Aviation Content: Big-scale fictional story following the development of flight from 1903 to 1938 as seen from the viewpoint of two young fliers, MacMurray and Milland. Notable as the first major aviation-themed film to be shot in full color, the final product falls way short of its epic goals and has been tagged as "Wellman's Aerial Colossus" and "Paramount's Cavalcade of the Air." Still a must-see for aviation and movie fans alike for the large lineup of vintage aircraft and outstanding aerial sequences.

Type	msn	Civil reg.
Boeing Model 100	1143	N872H
Boeing Model 100	1144	N873H
Boeing Model 247	1948	NC13362
Curtiss D Pusher (replica)	101	N8Y
Fokker D.VII	504/17	N6268
Garland-Lincoln LF-1	512	NX10415
Garland-Lincoln LF-2	1466	NR75W
Lockheed Vega 5B	100	NC48M
SPAD VII	S-248	N4727V
Stearman C2B	110	NR4099

By 1938 stunt pilot Paul Mantz had established himself as the leading Hollywood go-to guy for aviation requirements in motion pictures. His company, United Air Services in Burbank, could provide filmmakers with a selection of aircraft, pilots and film equipment. When *Men With Wings* began pre-production, Mantz got the job of aerial supervisor and acquired many biplane-era aircraft for the film. It was, in fact, the largest aviation motion picture made without military assistance since *Hell's Angels* (1930) and helped kick-start Mantz's famed aircraft collection.

The two Boeing Model 100 biplanes, N872H and N873H, double as U.S. Army P-12 fighters; the Boeing Model 247, NC13362, plus two others were loaned from Western Airlines as the fictional "Falconer bomber." The 1911 Curtiss D Pusher was a replica originally built by Billy Parker for the film *West Point of the Air* (1935). The genuine Fokker D.VII, N6268, was located in a Los Angeles garage and restored to flying condition. The two Garland-Lincoln LF biplanes, NX10415 and NR75W, are Nieuport 28 replicas originally built in 1932. Mantz's Vega 5B, NC48M, doubles as the Falconer aircraft named *Miss Patricia*. The SPAD VII, N4727V, was found in Imperial Valley and restored to flying condition; it doesn't appear in the final film but was used in promotional stills. The Stearman C2B, NR4099, doubles as a 1930s U.S. Army fighter. Also acquired for the film were up to three **DeHavilland DH.4** biplanes; a genuine **Nieuport 28**, either N8539 or N4728V; two **Thomas-Morse S-4 Scout** biplanes; and up to six **Travel Air 2000/4000** "Wichita Fokker" biplanes as Fokker D.VIII fighters.

Background aircraft include several Buhl LA-1 Bull Pups, Curtiss JN-4 Jennies, and a North American NA-50. Several mock-ups and aircraft simulations were also built. Mantz utilized two Stearmans (reg. NR4099 and NR6259) and his Lockheed Sirius 8A (reg. NC117W) as camera-planes. Aerial filming was based out of Van Nuys Airport, California, starting in February 1938; the epic shoot, including dramatic scenes, lasted until September that year.

Midway

International Title: **Battle of Midway**
U.S. Video Title: **The Battle of Midway**
USA / Universal Pictures / 1976 / Color / 126 minutes
Director: Jack Smight

Cast: Charlton Heston, Henry Fonda, James Coburn, Glenn Ford, Hal Halbrook, Toshiro Mifune, Robert Mitchum, Cliff Robertson, Robert Wagner, Robert Webber, Ed Nelson, James Shigeta, Christina Kokubo, Edward Albert

Synopsis / Aviation Content: An insightful enough recreation of the June 1942 battle for the Pacific atoll of Midway, which saw the Japanese carrier fleet decimated. Produced in a similar style to the earlier film *Tora! Tora! Tora!* (1970), but not as grand in scale, largely due to an overuse of stock and newsreel footage, plus a "soap opera" approach to the characters' personal stories. An unexpected box-office smash hit in its day, which seems more likely a reflection on the mood in a post–Vietnam America than a result of the film's mediocre production values, including only a limited amount of newly shot aerial footage.

Type	msn	Military s/n	Civil reg.
Consolidated PBY-6A Catalina	2069/127	BuNo.63998	N16KL
Douglas A-24A-DE Banshee	2350	42-60817	N15749
Grumman FM-2 Wildcat	5804	BuNo.86746	N6290C
Grumman FM-2 Wildcat	5835	BuNo.86777	N90541
Grumman J2F-6 Duck	unknown	BuNo.33549	N1214N

Japanese carrier shots used several **North American T-6 "Zero"** and **Vultee BT-13 "Val"** replicas first converted and flown for *Tora! Tora! Tora!* (1970), which by this film were leased back to the filmmakers from private owners or museum collections.

The unmarked Catalina, N16KL, was hired from the American Air Museum Society of San Francisco and was originally one of 175 New Orleans–built PBY-6A variants with the taller tail. It had served in the Danish Navy with s/n L-863 from 1957 to 1972. N16KL was written off in Texas on October 13, 1984, after a simulated water landing mishap. The brief shots of Douglas A-24A, N15749, were film stock completed for *Tora!* but not used until this film. The two FM-2 Wildcats were both in private ownership and used for filming on the USS *Lexington* (CV-16); N6290C featured the *Felix the Cat* artwork. The Grumman Duck biplane is a background aircraft in one Charlton Heston scene.

Studio close-ups of actors in aircraft made use of a **Vultee BT-13 Valiant** fuselage doubling for the Douglas TBD Devastators of ill-fated Torpedo Squadron 8 (VT-8). A **Douglas SBD-5 Dauntless** fuselage (BuNo. 28536 / msn 3883) was accurately used for later dive-bombing scenes. Background projection in both cases was, inaccurately, Vought SB2U Vindicator footage from *Dive Bomber* (1941).

A Consolidated PBY Catalina fuselage section was also used in the studio, as were the FM-2 Wildcat fighters.

The Midway filmmakers didn't recreate the battle from scratch but used footage from previ-

This **Douglas SBD-5 Dauntless, BuNo. 28536, was used for studio cockpit filming in the 1976 film** *Midway*. **It was subsequently restored to airworthy condition as N670AM and flew in the 1988 TV miniseries** *War and Remembrance*. **Photograph: James H. Farmer Collection.**

ous Hollywood films and actual wartime documentaries. Most of the action sequences involving the Japanese attacks and aircraft were lifted from *Tora! Tora! Tora!* (1970). These scenes included the amazing pre-dawn carrier launch of the Japanese bombers and fighters, some formation flying, and aerial combat footage, and the attacks on Midway Island used scenes from the airfield bombings in *Tora!* The P-40 takeoff and B-17 crash were also used. The opening title sequence of the B-25 Doolittle Raid were lifted from the Spencer Tracey film *Thirty Seconds Over Tokyo* (1944). The Grumman Hellcats taking off from Midway Atoll were taken from the John Wayne film *Flying Leathernecks* (1953). Many of the Vought Vindicator flying shots were from *Dive Bomber* (1941). Aerial combat wide shots and several explosions (one a Heinkel He 111, no less!) came from *Battle of Britain* (1969), and a few naval shots came from *Away All Boats* (1956). The Japanese fleet departing their homeland used shots from the Japanese film *I Bombed Pearl Harbor* (1960). Actual wartime combat shots were used from newsreel footage, plus the documentaries *The Battle of Midway* (1942) and *The Fighting Lady* (1944).

The major problem with intercutting stock footage and newsreel shots is the unavoidable inconsistency in aircraft types and quality of image. *Midway* made wide use of such material with almost every type of World War II naval fighter or bomber being shown at some point—including two types not entering combat until after the Battle of Midway, the Grumman F6F Hellcat and Vought F4U Corsair. The television version, extended by forty minutes, features a Lockheed C-130 Hercules doubling at one point for a Japanese Kawanishi H8K2 "Emily" with cockpit close-ups shot in a Catalina painted in Japanese colors! The final scene of Charlton Heston taking to the air has him climb into a Douglas Dauntless, take off in a Grumman Avenger, fight in a Douglas Dauntless, approach the carrier in a Curtiss Helldiver, and crash back on deck in a Grumman Panther!

Various exterior scenes were shot at Terminal Island Naval Base, NAS Long Beach, NAS Point Mugu, Fort MacArthur—all in California—and NAS Pensacola, Florida. The carrier scenes for both the U.S. Navy and Japanese Navy made use of the USS *Lexington* (CV-16), with two FM-2 Wildcats and a handful of "Zero" and "Val" replicas for the Japanese sequences.

FACTUAL BACKGROUND: TURNING POINT IN THE PACIFIC

The Battle of Midway was unique in that it was the first naval battle in history where the opposing ships never came into visual contact with each other. The battle started at 4:30 a.m., June 4, 1942, with Vice Admiral Nagumo launching naval aircraft against the U.S. base on Midway Atoll, located in the mid–Pacific Ocean. One priceless asset the commander of the U.S. forces, Admiral Nimitz, had was the ability to read the Japanese naval codes. The Americans entered the battle with an accurate understanding of the Japanese strategic plan. During the battle, an entire squadron, VT-8, of the USS *Hornet* was lost to Zero fighters, with only one survivor, Ensign George Gay, ditching and later rescued. After this tragic loss, the Douglas TBD Devastator naval bomber was withdrawn from service. Midway ended on June 7, 1942, with U.S. forces having devastated the Japanese Navy, destroying four of their carriers—*Kaga, Akagi, Soryu* and *Hiryu*—and the cruiser *Mikuma.* The American forces lost the carrier USS *Yorktown* (CV-5), plus the destroyer USS *Hammann.* Although it didn't win the Pacific War for the U.S., it did mark the beginning of the end for Japan. Admiral Yamamoto's prediction that Japan would hold dominance in the Pacific for only six months after Pearl Harbor was proven correct almost to the day.

U.S. Navy Strength	Japanese Navy Strength
3 aircraft carriers	4 aircraft carriers
50 support ships (approx.)	157 support ships (approx.)
360 aircraft	261 aircraft

U.S. Navy Losses	Japanese Navy Losses
1 aircraft carrier sunk	4 aircraft carriers sunk
1 destroyer sunk	1 cruiser sunk
153 aircraft lost	261 aircraft lost
307 personnel killed	3057 personnel killed

Mission Over Korea

UK Title: *Eyes of the Skies*
USA / Columbia Pictures / 1953 / B&W / 85 minutes
Director: Fred F. Sears

Cast: John Hodiak, John Derek, Audrey Totter, Maureen O'Sullivan, Harvey Lembeck, Richard Erdman, William Chun, Rex Reason, Richard Bowers

Synopsis / Aviation Content: At the start of the Korean War in 1950, a new Army spotter-plane pilot is overly keen to get involved in combat, including arming his aircraft with a bazooka, but must be kept in check by his more experienced superior. Pretty much typical in style of the war films made during this period but it does, at least, take a fresh stance in grounding the story around the rarely explored service of the observation pilot. A definite must-see for any fan of observer or light aircraft types.

Type	msn	Military s/n	Civil reg.
Stinson L-5-VW Sentinel	—	42-98119	—
Stinson L-5-VW Sentinel	76-121	42-98496	N9838F
Stinson L-5G-VW Sentinel	—	45-35025	—
Stinson L-5G-VW Sentinel	76-3597	45-35035	N3232S

Four Stinson L-5 Sentinel aircraft were used in filming. Two were the L-5 variant, s/n 42-98119 and 42-98496, the latter going to the U.S. civil market as N9838F. The other two were the L-5G variant, s/n 45-35025 and 45-35035. S/n 45-35025 was actually the last L-5G delivered to the U.S. Army; subsequent aircraft completed were offered for sale directly onto the civilian market, with s/n 45-35035 becoming reg. N3232S. Two additional L-5 Sentinel aircraft were destroyed during filming. The army took delivery of 3,590 L-5 Sentinels from 1941 to 1945, with active service lasting beyond the Korean War. Aircraft surviving past 1962 were redesignated as the U-19. The film was shot in Japan and South Korea with background aircraft including the **Curtiss C-46D Commando**, **Douglas C-47 Skytrain**, **Lockheed F-80C / T-33A Shooting Star**, and four **North American F-51H Mustang** fighters doubling as North Korean "Yak 9" fighters.

Moonraker (Non–Aviation Themed Title)
see   *James Bond* **Series**

Mosquito Squadron

UK / United Artists / 1969 / Color / 87 minutes
Director: Boris Sagal

Cast: David McCallum, Suzanne Neve, Charles Gray, David Buck, David Dundas

Synopsis / Aviation Content: Indirect, and inferior, sequel to *633 Squadron* (1964) sees RAF Mosquito squadrons assigned the mission of bombing a chateau containing not only a German rocket plant but British POWs being used as human shields. New footage of the classic Mossie includes some aerial scenes and a wide range of airfield ground scenes, but much of the flying, crashes and action scenes are rehashed film stock from the earlier *633 Squadron* production.

Type	Military s/n	Civil reg.	Film Markings
Flying Aircraft			
DeHavilland Mosquito T.Mk. III	RR299	G-ASKH	HJ898 / HT-G
DeHavilland Mosquito B.Mk. 35	RS709	G-ASKA	unknown
DeHavilland Mosquito B.Mk. 35	RS712	G-ASKB	RF580 / HT-F
DeHavilland Mosquito B.Mk. 35	TA634	G-AWJV	HT896 / HT-G and HJ516 / HT-C
Ground / Studio Aircraft			
DeHavilland Mosquito B.Mk. 35	TA719	G-ASKC	HT-G
DeHavilland Mosquito B.Mk. 35	TJ118	—	—

All Mosquito B.Mk. 35 aircraft had been TT.Mk. 35 target-tug conversions with No. 3 CAACU at Exeter in Devon, and three were *633 Squadron* (1964) movie veterans. The flying Mosquitos were RR299 from Hawker Siddeley Aviation Ltd.; RS709 from the Skyframe Museum in Staverton; RS712 owned by T.G. Mahaddie; and TA634 owned by the City of Liverpool Corp.

TA719 was loaned from the Skyframe Museum for the crash at the end of the film, shot outside at MGM-British Studios. It was later recovered by the museum even though the staged-fire damage was quite extensive. When Skyframe closed in 1978, TA719 was transferred to the Imperial War Museum at Duxford, where it was later restored. The dismembered remains of TJ118 were still at MGM-British Studios in 1967–68 after being used for *633 Squadron*, and so were again set up for the cockpit scenes. The four Mossie pilots were: "Taffy" Rich (ex–RAF); aerobatics pilot Neil Williams; BOAC test pilot "Dizzy" Addicott; and Hawker Siddeley test pilot Pat Fillingham. Chief aeronautical advisor was RAF Air Commodore Allen Wheeler. Two **Avro 652A Anson** aircraft appear in the final scene returning the POWs. Camera-plane was an Avro Shackleton MR.Mk. 3 with RAF s/n WR972.

Filmed at RAF Bovingdon and MGM-British Studios, Borehamwood, both in Hertfordshire, England. The German "Chateau Charlon" was actually Minley Manor in Hampshire, England.

GPS LOCATIONS

RAF Bovingdon, Hertfordshire (closed 1972): N51 43.60 / W000 32.70

Minley Manor, Hampshire: N51 18.90 / W000 49.30

Murphy's War (Non–Aviation Themed Title)

UK / London Screen—Paramount Pictures / 1971 / Color / 102 minutes
Director: Peter Yates
Cast: Peter O'Toole, Sian Phillips, Philippe Noiret, Horst Janson, John Hallam, Ingo Mogendorf
Synopsis / Aviation Content: Irish sailor O'Toole is hell-bent on destroying the German submarine that sank his ship. Two **Grumman J2F-6 Duck** floatplanes were used for filming, both being provided by Tallmantz Aviation, Inc., California. Company owner and renowned Hollywood stunt pilot Frank Tallman acquired J2F-6 reg. N67790 (BuNo. 33587) and reg. N1196N (BuNo. 36976) in late 1969; Tallman also flew these aircraft during filming. His amazing piloting and the fantastic sequences captured have since made the Grumman Duck synonymous with this motion picture. Both aircraft were painted with a dark blue livery and carried fictional markings "RN/MS Mount Kyle." The Grumman Duck that is blown up was merely a mock-up made from various spare parts. Filming took place from February to July 1970 in the Orinoco River area of Venezuela.

UNCONFIRMED DATA
Some sources also quote a third Duck being used, J2F-6 (reg. N1214N / BuNo. 33549), of Tallmantz Aviation, Inc., but no solid proof has emerged that Tallman ever owned this aircraft or that it was even used in the film.

Never Say Never Again (Non–Aviation Themed Title) see *James Bond* **Series**

Night Plane from Chungking

USA / Paramount Pictures / 1943 / B&W / 69 minutes
Director: Ralph Murphy
Cast: Robert Preston, Ellen Drew, Otto Kruger, Steven Geray, Tamara Geva, Soo Yong, Victor Sen Yung, Ernst Deutsch, Allen Jung
Synopsis / Aviation Content: A small civilian Chinese airliner is known to be carrying an Axis spy on a flight to India but is shot down by Japanese fighters; the stranded survivors then try to figure out just who the spy is. Notable film in that it uses RKO Pictures non-flying **Capelis Model XC-12** (reg. NX12762 / msn 1) painted in Chinese markings for filming on a Hollywood backlot. Equally well known is the RKO Pictures–built Capelis miniature model used for the flying shots. Five **Ryan SC** monoplanes double as Japanese Zero fighters in footage used from the earlier film *Wake Island* (1942).

1941 (Non–Aviation Themed Title)

USA / Universal & Columbia Pictures / 1979 / Color / 118 minutes
Director: Steven Spielberg
Cast: Dan Aykroyd, Ned Beatty, John Belushi, Lorraine Gary, Murray Hamilton, Christopher Lee, Tim Matheson, Toshiro Mifune, Warren Oates, Robert Stack, Treat Williams
Synopsis / Aviation Content: Epic comedy parodying the fear and paranoia of Japanese invasion on the West Coast of the United States in the days after Pearl Harbor. Aviation highlights are the P-40 flying sequences and the B-17

Long Beach Airport scenes. Much use was made of models and special effects for the more complex aerial dogfight scenes. The film was disliked by American audiences, but was a smash hit on the international market—including Japan.

Type	msn	Military s/n	Civil reg.
Beechcraft C-45H-BH Expeditor	AF-701	52-10771	N403SE
Boeing B-17G-85-DL Flying Fortress	32155	44-83514	N9323Z
Curtiss Kittyhawk Mk. I (P-40E)	15376	(RAF) AK905	N40PE
Curtiss Kittyhawk Mk. I (P-40E)	18723	(RAF) AK979	N151U
Curtiss Kittyhawk Mk. I (P-40E)	18815	(RAF) AL171	N62435
North American B-25J-1-NC Mitchell	108-24356	43-4030	N3339G
North American B-25J-20-NC Mitchell	108-32782	44-29507	N3698G
North American B-25J-25-NC Mitchell	108-33698	44-30423	N3675G
North American SNJ-2 Texan	65-1999	BuNo.2010	N52900
North American SNJ-2 Texan	65-2000	BuNo.2011	N55729
North American SNJ-2 Texan	65-2009	BuNo.2020	N87613
North American SNJ-2 Texan	65-2014	BuNo.2025	N61563
North American SNJ-2 Texan	65-2021	BuNo.2032	N60734
North American SNJ-2 Texan	65-2026	BuNo.2037	N66082
North American SNJ-2 Texan	65-2028	BuNo.2039	N62382
North American SNJ-2 Texan	65-2029	BuNo.2040	N52033
North American SNJ-2 Texan	79-3988	BuNo.2553	N58224
North American SNJ-2 Texan	79-3997	BuNo.2562	N65370

The Beechcraft C-45H was an airworthy aircraft but never flew in the film. The shots of it taxiing around uncontrollably were filmed on the airstrip at Indian Dunes, Ventura County, California, with Warbird pilot Steve Hinton at the controls. This aircraft was remanufactured in 1952 from a Beechcraft AT-11 (s/n 41-27372 / msn 1217) to C-45H standards and served with the USAF until 1958. It flew with various civilian operators as reg. N8076E, N139 and N4, then N403SE. It retained the prewar USAAC film livery after being in *1941*. The aircraft tragically crashed after take off on October 17, 1982, at Taft, California, due to being overloaded and unbalanced for a group parachute jump. All fourteen onboard were killed. A Beechcraft 18 derelict was acquired for studio filming with the actors and a later tar-pit crash scene.

The Boeing B-17G, N9323Z, was hired from the Confederate Air Force and dressed as a prewar B-17E variant with ribbed glass nose, red and white rudder, etc. These scenes were filmed at the southern end of Long Beach Airport, California, along with three North American B-25J Mitchell bombers—N3339G and N3675G from Planes of Fame, and N3698G owned by "Junior" Burchi-

nal. As a point of interest, N3339G was originally General D.D. Eisenhower's VIP transport during World War II. There were also six North American SNJ-2 Texan trainers hired from Skytypers, Inc., California. All ten known West Coast–based aircraft are listed above, but which are the exact six involved in filming is unknown. A rudderless Douglas DC-3 can be seen in the background in one shot.

"Wild Bill's" P-40 was actually played by three different fighters—N40PE (Rudy Frasca) was used for studio cockpit close-ups with John Belushi; N151U (Tom Camp) was used for the gas station / army outpost (Indian Dunes) scenes; and N62435 (John Paul) was used in the Grand Canyon scenes. The P-40 street crash was done with a fiberglass mock-up left over from *Tora! Tora! Tora!* (1970). Much use was made of scale models for the P-40 / Beech 18 boulevard chase sequence. A rather lengthy production period ran from October 23, 1978, to May 16, 1979.

No Highway in the Sky

UK / 20th Century–Fox / 1951 / B&W / 98 minutes

Director: Henry Koster

Cast: James Stewart, Marlene Dietrich, Glynis Johns, Jack Hawkins, Janette Scott, Kenneth More

Synopsis / Aviation Content: An eccentric aeronautical engineer has limited time to convince the crew that the aircraft they're traveling on has a serious design flaw in the tail section. The story eerily resembles the later real-life crashes of the DeHavilland Comet airliner caused through metal fatigue. Based on the 1948 novel *No Highway* by popular English author Nevil Shute.

Type	Military s/n	Civil reg.
Avro Lancaster B.Mk. VII	(RAF) NX636	—
Gloster GA.2A	(RAF) TX145	—
Handley Page Halifax C.Mk. VIII	(RAF) PP296	G-AJNW

The fictional Rutland Reindeer airliner was originally created from the fuselage of a Handley Page HP.70 Halifax. After service as a cargo transport in the RAF, Halifax PP296 was sold to Westminster Airways Ltd. on April 27, 1949, with civilian reg. G-AJNW. It subsequently completed 116 tanker missions for the Berlin Airlift and returned to England on April 26, 1950. Its owner then became Westminster Airways Servicing Ltd., who extensively converted it into the Rutland Reindeer with false civil reg. "G-AFOH" on behalf of the filmmakers. The final conversion was a strictly non-flying behemoth with a tricycle undercarriage, larger wings, a single tail with two separate sets of elevators, and a bubble flight-deck canopy. The conversion and filming took place at Blackbushe Airport, Hampshire, England. The giant Reindeer film-prop was scrapped in December 1950.

Also seen at various intervals is a rare Gloster GA.2A (RAF s/n TX145); an Avro Lancaster (RAF s/n NX636); and a **DeHavilland Venom FB.Mk. 1**. Live action aircraft interiors and aircraft model miniatures were filmed at Denham Studios, Buckinghamshire, England.

Before becoming a writer, Nevil Shute (full name Nevil Shute Norway) was a pioneering aircraft designer and co-founded the British aircraft company Airspeed Ltd. in 1931, their most famous product being the Airspeed AS.10 Oxford. The company was absorbed into DeHavilland in 1951.

No Place to Land

Alternate Title (UK): **Man Mad**

USA / Republic Pictures / 1958 / B&W / 77 minutes

Director: Albert C. Gannaway

Cast: John Ireland, Mari Blanchard, Gail Russell, Jackie Coogan, Robert Middleton, Douglas Henderson, Bill Ward

Synopsis / Aviation Content: A grimly toned drama set in the late 1950s amongst a community of crop-duster pilots, each competing for agricultural flying work. Filmed in Imperial Valley, California, the film offers a unique insight into American rural life during this period. Aircraft are a **Stearman C3R** biplane

(reg. N794H / msn 5036) and a **Boeing-Stearman PT-13D Kaydet** (reg. N4826V / msn 75-5247), originally a dual service designated trainer both as a USAAF PT-13D (s/n 42-17084) and a U.S. Navy N2S-5 (BuNo. 61125). This biplane was involved in a crash in July 1966 but appears to have been restored, and was subsequently re-registered as N10KP.

No Sleep Till Dawn   see   Bombers B-52

Octopussy (Non–Aviation Themed Title) see **James Bond Series**

On an Island with You

USA / Metro-Goldwyn-Mayer / 1948 / Color / 107 minutes

Director: Richard Thorpe

Cast: Esther Williams, Peter Lawford, Ricardo Montalban, Jimmy Durante, Cyd Charisse, Xavier Cugat

Synopsis / Aviation Content: A Grumman TBM pilot is hired to act as technical advisor on a film set, only to fall in love with the production's leading lady, played by the stunning Esther Williams. A light, romantic comedy with idyllic Florida settings (standing in for Hawaii), it has a few scenes with several Grumman types.

Type	msn	Military s/n	Civil reg.
Grumman J4F-2 Widgeon	1323	BuNo.32969	N66432
Grumman TBM-1C Avenger	unknown	BuNo.46122	N9394H

The twin-engined J4F-2 Widgeon, N66432, was one of 131 J4F-2 amphibians for the U.S. Navy, with this airframe declared surplus in 1946. It was sold in 1947 to Florida Air Company; another owner was Island Airways, Florida, in 1949. N66432 eventually went to Kodiak Airways in Alaska in 1953, and in 1956 had a Mansdorf conversion with Lycoming R-680 radials and a modified bow. It was sold in 1959 to R&S Aircraft Sales in Washington State; another owner acquired N66432 in 1961, and it crashed soon after. The TBM-1C Avenger, N9394H, was owned and operated by Paul Mantz Air Services, a company started by Hollywood stunt flyer Paul Mantz. In 1954 he used this aircraft for experimental air-tanker work, and it's believed to have been written off in a crash at some point afterward.

On Her Majesty's Secret Service

(Non–Aviation Themed Title)   see

James Bond Series

On the Threshold of Space

USA / 20th Century–Fox / 1956 / Color / 98 minutes

Director: Robert W. Webb

Cast: Guy Madison, Virginia Leith, John Hodiak, Dean Jagger

Synopsis / Aviation Content: An Air Force doctor pushes himself and his marriage to the limits in pursuit of obtaining valuable aeronautical test data. Many impressive views of the various experiments conducted by the USAF during the 1950s, including ejection seats, rocket-sleds and high-altitude balloons. Provided to the filmmakers was a **Boeing B-47 Stratojet**, two **Lockheed T-33A Shooting Star** trainers, and several **Sikorsky SH-19B Chickasaw** (s/n 53-4450, 53-4452) helicopters. Background aircraft include the **Boeing B-50 Superfortress**, **KC-97 Stratofreighter**, **Convair C-131 Samaritan**, and **Fairchild C-123 Provider**. Partly filmed at Eglin AFB, Florida. Actor John Hodiak (Major Ward Thomas) suddenly died near the end of filming, so his final scenes could not be shot.

One Man Mutiny   see   The Court-Martial of Billy Mitchell

One of Our Aircraft Is Missing

UK / British First National Films Ltd. / 1942 / B&W / 98 minutes

Directors: Michael Powell, Emeric Pressburger

Cast: Godfrey Tearle, Eric Portman, Hugh Williams, Bernard Miles, Hugh Burden, Emrys Jones

Synopsis / Aviation Content: A Wellington bomber crew is forced to bail out over Nazi-occupied

Holland, with the locals helping the crew evade capture while they develop an escape plan. The opening scenes were filmed at RAF Marham, Norfolk, with several **Vickers Wellington Mk. Ic** bombers of No. 115 Squadron. The final scene has massive **Short Stirling Mk. I** bombers of No. 7 Squadron filmed at RAF Oakington, Cambridgeshire. One Wellington fuselage was sent to Denham Studios in Buckinghamshire for aircraft interior scenes. Use of models in the crash and bomb run sequences. Excellent photography throughout and edited by David Lean, who would later go on to establish himself as one of the all-time great film directors.

The One That Got Away

UK / The Rank Organisation / 1957 / B&W / 106 minutes

Director: Roy Baker

Cast: Hardy Kruger, Colin Gordon, Michael Goodliffe, Terence Alexander, Jack Gwillim, Andrew Faulds, Julian Somers, Alec McCowen

Synopsis / Aviation Content: Dramatized version of the true-life events concerning the persistent escape attempts by captured German pilot Oberleutnant Franz von Werra. A tight script and excellent performance by Kruger keeps the film on track throughout. Based on the 1956 book by Kendal Burt and James Leasor. Kruger crashes at the start of the film in a Messerschmitt Bf. 109E, accomplished with a scale model for the crash and a full-scale replica for the post-crash scene, evident in part from the canopy, which hinges open the wrong way! Kruger later attempts an escape from an English airfield in a **Hawker Hurricane Mk. IIc** (s/n LF363 / msn 41H/469290), provided by the RAF, which doesn't fly in the film but is used in an extensive ground scene. Interiors were filmed at Pinewood Studios, Buckinghamshire, England.

FACTUAL BACKGROUND: FRANZ VON WERRA

Franz Xaver Baron von Werra (July 13, 1914– October 25, 1941), was the only German POW of World War II to successfully escape from Allied internment and return to fight in the war. He joined the Luftwaffe in 1936, and when war broke out, he scored a total of eight aerial victories and five aircraft on the ground before being shot down over Kent, England, on September 5, 1940. His subsequent escape attempts unfold very much the same as depicted in the film—the country lane getaway taking place on October 7, 1940, and the tunnel escape on December 20, 1940. In January 1941, von Werra was shipped to Canada for internment, but escaped again by jumping out a train window on January 21, 1941. Crossing the border into a neutral United States, von Werra, with the help of the German consul, was able to cross the border into Mexico. He traveled through Latin and South America, departing via Brazil, and made it back to Germany on April 18, 1941, whereupon Hitler awarded him the Ritterkreuz des Eisernen Kreuzes (Knight Cross of the Iron Cross). Deployed to the Russian Front, von Werra raised his aerial combat score to twenty-one by July 1941. On October 25, 1941, while over the North Sea on a practice flight, von Werra disappeared without a trace, likely due to an engine failure.

Only Angels Have Wings

USA / Columbia Pictures / 1939 / B&W / 121 minutes

Director: Howard Hawks

Cast: Cary Grant, Jean Arthur, Richard Barthelmess, Rita Hayworth, Thomas Mitchell, Allyn Joslyn

Synopsis / Aviation Content: Cary Grant plays the manager of a small airfreight business in South America who makes life-threatening decisions by sending pilots into unfavorable mountainous weather. One of Hawks's finest films; he came up with the story after meeting a real-life couple running a similar business in Mexico. Not much actual flying, but what there is features some genuinely incredible stunt work by Hollywood pilot Paul Mantz in a Curtiss-Wright 6B and Ford Tri-Motor.

The first aircraft seen in the film is a rare corrugated-skinned 1928 **Hamilton H-47 Metalplane**, around twenty-one of which were built by the Hamilton Metalplane Co. of Milwaukee,

Wisconsin. It carried the fictional registration "F-ADD." The aircraft used in the clifftop mesa scene was supposed to be Paul Mantz's Lockheed Vega 5B (reg. NC48M / msn 100), but it suffered a ground accident when a tire ran into a rut while filming on December 13, 1938, at the Saint George, Utah, location. The scene, and other flying scenes, were then completed with a **Curtiss-Wright 6B** (formerly a **Travel Air 6000B**), marked as "F-LTM." The aerobatic aircraft Grant tests out is a **Boeing Model 40** biplane falsely marked as "F-THD." The three-engined aircraft in the final sequence is a **Ford Tri-Motor 4-AT-B** (reg. NC7121 / msn 35), especially purchased for the film by Columbia Pictures, with Paul Mantz performing an impressive controlled spin in the giant aircraft. The final crash sequence was accomplished by using a mocked-up Fokker Tri-Motor, which was launched off a ramp into the ground. Both Tri-Motor types were falsely marked as "F-HLI." Almost all aircraft were marked with fictional "Barranca Airways Ltd." logos for the film.

The aviation sequences are, unfortunately, brief, with much of the film taking place in a local bar. Most of the takeoffs and landings were done with very good models and miniatures, which earned a 1940 Academy Award Nomination for Special Effects. Filmed from December 20, 1938, to March 24, 1939, mainly in Hollywood. This film later inspired the popular but short-lived 1982 TV Series *Tales of the Gold Monkey*.

Operation Dumbo Drop (Non–Aviation Themed Title)

USA / Walt Disney Pictures / 1995 / Color / 108 minutes

Director: Simon Wincer

Cast: Danny Glover, Ray Liotta, Denis Leary, Doug E. Doug, Corin Nemec, Tcheky Karyo, Dinh Thien Le

Synopsis / Aviation Content: In 1968 during the Vietnam War, soldiers Glover and Liotta are assigned a mission to acquire and deliver an elephant to appease a strategically located village. Based on true events, the film conveys high-end production values, but is strangely pitched to a family audience, many of whom will have no concept or understanding of the Vietnam War setting. An aeronautically significant film for several sequences featuring the ever-reliable Fairchild C-123K Provider. Filming took place in Thailand during 1994 with assistance from the Royal Thai Air Force (RTAF), who provided **Fairchild C-123B-4-FA Provider** BL4k-1/16 (s/n 54-576 / msn 20025), in a limited capacity it seems, for an airbase scene. Almost all C-123 filming, including the flying and ground shots, were actually done stateside in Florida, with **Fairchild C-123B-3-FA Provider** (s/n 54-565 / msn 20014 / reg. N123K), flown by Dave Kunz, who had also worked with the RTAF on the earlier *Air America* (1990), also using the C-123. Aircraft interior filming was likely completed onboard a C-123K derelict in Thailand. The opening title sequence features a **Bell UH-1H Iroquois** and briefly a **Bell AH-1 Huey-Cobra**.

Operation Haylift

USA / Lippert Pictures / 1950 / B&W / 73 minutes
Director: William Berke
Cast: Bill Williams, Ann Rutherford, Tom Brown, Jane Nigh, Joe Sawyer, James Conlin, Tommy Ivo
Synopsis / Aviation Content: A U.S. rancher's brother returns to USAF service to assist airdrops to the thousands of stranded cattle caught in a record snow blizzard. Dramatized story based on the severe 1949 blizzards of northern Nevada that saw the USAF provide up to thirty **Fairchild C-82A Packet** cargo transports for airdrops of hay into isolated areas. The film employed the same aircraft type, specifically C-82A-30-FA (s/n 44-23050 / msn 10094), provided by the 316th Troop Carrier Group performing low-level passes and flying shots for the filmmakers. All other footage of C-82 Packets came from newsreel stock footage, including some great snippets of hay bales being loaded and airdropped. Filmed in Ely, Nevada—one of the airfields used in the actual operation. Brief glimpses of several light aircraft types including an **ERCO Ercoupe Model 415-C**

(reg. NC93365 / msn 688), Berlin Airlift Douglas C-47 Dakotas, and a brief shot of a C-54 Skymaster. Actor Joe Sawyer, who also produced and co-wrote the screenplay, played real-life stockman George Swallow, who organized the actual Operation Haylift. Swallow himself served as technical advisor to the film.

Outbreak (Non–Aviation Themed Title)

USA / Warner Bros. / 1995 / Color / 127 minutes
Director: Wolfgang Petersen
Cast: Dustin Hoffman, Rene Russo, Morgan Freeman, Donald Sutherland, Cuba Gooding Jr., Kevin Spacey
Synopsis / Aviation Content: A deadly virus wreaks havoc in a quiet rural town, but the military knows more about the disease than it's letting on. Contains some excellent helicopter chase sequences. African scenes were shot on Kauai, Hawaii, with a **Bell Model 206 Jet Ranger**, a **Douglas C-47A Skytrain** (reg. N99131 / s/n 42-100486), both as U.S. military aircraft, then later a **Bell Model 206L Long Ranger** and a **Bell Model 204**, both marked as Zaire AF. The town of Ferndale, California, stood in for Cedar Creek, filming for which West Coast Helicopters, Inc., provided three **Bell Model 204** and one **Hughes 500D**, all marked as U.S. Army gunship choppers. The news helicopter is a former **Bell OH-58A Kiowa** (s/n 70-15448 / msn 40999 / reg. N38FA), marked as "KPIX 5." The "Sandman" cargo plane is a **Fairchild C-123B-3-FA Provider** (s/n 54-565 / msn 20014 / reg. N123K). Also seen are glimpses of a **Lockheed C-130H Hercules** and file footage of a Boeing E-3C Sentry.

Pacific Adventure   see   Smithy

Passenger 57

USA / Warner Bros. / 1992 / Color / 84 minutes
Director: Kevin Hooks
Cast: Wesley Snipes, Bruce Payne, Tom Sizemore, Alex Datcher, Bruce Greenwood, Elizabeth Hurley, Robert Hooks
Synopsis / Aviation Content: Aviation security expert Snipes has his hands full when he inad-

vertently boards an airliner transporting a captured terrorist who has other plans about the destination. Aviation highlights are the many and varied views of the Lockheed Tristar with one of the film's characters commenting: "Biggest damn Cessna I ever saw!"

Type	msn	Civil reg.	Film Markings
Bell Model 206B Jet Ranger II	1792	N62FH	AIA
Lockheed L-1011-1 Tristar	193A-1087	N330EA	Atlantic International / AIA

The *real* star here is the Lockheed L-1011 Tristar provided to the film company by Eastern Airlines. N330EA first flew on August 5, 1974, and was delivered to Eastern from Lockheed's Palmdale plant on June 30, 1975. It was stored in November 1990 to fly again for the film in 1991–1992, painted in a fictional "Atlantic International" livery. On September 15, 1992, it was sold to Peru with reg. OB-1504 until being withdrawn from use on April 25, 1997, and subsequently broken up at Mojave Airport in California for spares.

Much location filming took place at Orlando-Sanford Intl. Airport, Florida (GPS Location: N28 46.35 / W081 14.50).

Pearl Harbor

USA / Touchstone Pictures / 2001 / Color / 177 minutes
Director: Michael Bay
Cast: Ben Affleck, Josh Hartnett, Kate Beckinsale, Cuba Gooding, Jr., Tom Sizemore, Jon Voight, Colm Feore, Mako, Alec Baldwin
Synopsis / Aviation Content: Dramatized version of the 1941 attack by Japan on the U.S. Fleet at Pearl Harbor, which triggered the war in the Pacific. Aeronautically speaking, an exceptional film with a fine blend of real Warbird aircraft and special effects seamlessly blended together with a crackling sound mix to boost. The love-triangle formula, which has plagued aviation films right back to *Wings* in 1927, draws out the story's duration resulting in a film that lasts longer than the actual raid itself! This, in part, is made up for by a genuine period atmosphere

Film star Lockheed L-1011 Tristar N330EA photographed at Miami Intl. in 1992 for the film *Passenger 57* (1992). Photograph: Adriaan Lengkeek.

and dazzling production values. With ever-rising production costs and the evolution of CGI effects, *Pearl Harbor* will be notable as one of the last motion pictures to feature such a wide range and high number of "real flying aircraft"— those are actual Zeros, by the way, not replicas!

The three "Kate" conversions are based on the three-seater **Nakajima B5N2 (Navy Type 97)** torpedo-bomber codenamed "Kate" by the Allies. The four "Val" conversions are based on the two-seater **Aichi D3A1 (Navy Type 99)**, fixed undercarriage dive-bomber codenamed "Val" by the Allies. The Hispano HA-1112-M1L Buchon doubled for the Luftwaffe **Messerschmitt Bf 109E**.

"Kate" and "Val" pilots were Gene Armstrong, Will Bonefas, Gary D. Hudson, William E. Powers, James A. Ryan and John Storrie. U.S.-based pilots were Thomas L. Camp, Matt R. Dickson, Kevin Eldridge, James W. Gavin, John Hinton, Steve Hinton (chief pilot), Graig Hosking, Gary Hubbard, Bill Klaers, Kevin La Rosa, Bruce Lockwood, John Maloney, Matthew S. Mauch, Mike McDougall, Matt Nightingale, Robert W. Nightingale, Randy Peters, Alan Preston, Alan Purwin (aerial coordinator), Tony Ritzman, Carl Scholl, Mark Siebert, Dirk Vahle and Alan Wojciak. England-based (Battle of Britain) pilots were Roger Bailey, Guy Black, Charlie Brown, Nick Grey, Tony Haigh-Thomas, Peter Kynsey, Robert Lamplough, Dave McKay, Andy Sephton, Carl Shofield and aerial coordinator Stephen Grey.

Type	msn	Military s/n	Civil reg.	Film Markings
Tennessee Sequences				
Boeing-Stearman N2S-2 Kaydet	75-1335	BuNo.3558	N61445	*McCawley Crop Dusting*
U.S. Forces				
Curtiss Kittyhawk Mk. I (P-40E)	15404	(RAF) AK933	N94466	302
Curtiss P-40N-5-CU Warhawk	28954	42-105192	N85104	—
Curtiss P-40N-15-CU Warhawk	30158	42-106396	N1195N	—
Curtiss P-40N-30-CU Warhawk	32824	44-7084	N999CD	306
Douglas DC-3-313	2169	—	N26MA	90385 / 17265
Douglas C-47A-65-DL Skytrain	18949	42-100486	N99131	90395
Japanese Forces				
Mitsubishi A6M2-21 Zero	3869	X-133	N712Z	AI-157
Mitsubishi A6M3-22 Zero	3858	unknown	N553TT	AI-112
Mitsubishi A6M5-52 Zero	5357	61-120	N46770	61-120 / AI-120
CCF Harvard Mk. 4 (Kate)	CCF4-83	(RCAF) 20292	N2047	AI-302
North American SNJ-5 Texan (Kate)	88-15757	BuNo.43766	N3242G	BI-313
North American SNJ-5 Texan (Kate)	88-16686	BuNo.84875	N3725G	AI-356
Vultee BT-13A Valiant (Val)	74-2307	41-11297	N67208	AI-257
Vultee BT-13A Valiant (Val)	74-6656	41-22578	N56336	EI-231
Vultee BT-13A Valiant (Val)	74-7356	41-22926	N56478	—
Vultee BT-15 Valiant (Val)	74A-11513	42-42171	N67629	AI-201
Battle of Britain Sequences				
CCF Sea Hurricane Mk. Ib	CCF/41H.4013	Z7015	G-BKTH	Z7015 / 7-L
CCF Hurricane Mk. XIIa	72036	(RCAF) 5711	G-HURI	Z7381 / XR-T
Hispano HA-1112-M1L Buchon	120	C.4K-77	N700E	—
Supermarine Spitfire LF.Mk. Vb	CBAF.2403	EP120	G-LFVB	AR3185 / RF-M
Supermarine Spitfire LF.Mk. Vb	CBAF.2461	BM597	G-MKVB	AR352 / RF-C
Supermarine Spitfire LF.Mk. Vc	WASP.20/223	AR501	G-AWII	AR4474 / RF-Y
Supermarine Spitfire LF.Mk. VIIIc	6S.583793	MV154	G-BKMI	AR654 / RF-T
Doolittle Raiders				
North American B-25J-10-NC Mitchell	108-35217	43-28204	N9856C	02203 / *Whirling Dervish*
North American B-25J-20-NC Mitchell	108-32474	44-29199	N9117Z	02267
North American B-25J-25-NC Mitchell	108-33698	44-30423	N3675G	02261
North American B-25J-30-NC Mitchell	108-47501	44-86747	N8163H	02249 / *Ruptured Duck*

The Stearman biplane, N61445, in the opening sequence was provided by Planes of Fame and piloted by the film's chief pilot, Steve Hinton. The four P-40 fighters are seen flying together during the "Mitchell Field" sequence shot at NAS Point Mugu. N94466 and N1195N came from the Warhawk Air Museum; N85104 from Planes of Fame; and N999CD from Palm Springs Air Museum—this aircraft was a rare dual-control TP-40N. All fighters were extensively used in Hawaii for the aerial dogfight scenes. N26MA is an original DC-3-313 model delivered in 1939 as NC21781 and features the single port side passenger door. Owned by Paralift, Inc., it had a black painted nose and was used at the Van Nuys location for the Hawaiian departure and Doolittle returnee scene at the end. C-47A, N99131, was hired from GENAVCO Air Cargo as a background aircraft used at the Ford Island, Hawaii, location as a U.S. Navy R4D-1. Nearly twenty P-40 replicas were built from wood and foam for the airfield attack sequences. One R4D-1 (C-47) replica was built and destroyed during filming on Ford Island, Hawaii.

Three authentic Mitsubishi A6M Zeros were used in this film. N712Z was recovered from Babo Airfield, Indonesia, in 1991 and rebuilt to A6M3-22 standard; it was hired from the Commemorative Air Force. N553TT came from LGT Aviation, Inc., and had also been recovered from Babo Airfield in 1991. N46770 is a Planes of Fame hire and flies with its original Nakajima Sakae radial engine. It was captured by U.S. Marines on Saipan in 1944 and returned to the USA for tests before being acquired by Planes of Fame in the 1950s, known then as the Air Museum.

All seven "Kate" and "Val" replicas are *Tora! Tora! Tora!* (1970; see entry for details) conversions now owned and operated by the Commemorative Air Force. N67629, however, was owned by Planes of Fame and was taken out of storage and restored to airworthy condition for the film. "Val" N56336 crashed during filming at Ford Island on April 17, 2000. Pilot Gene Armstrong suffered only minor injuries, but the aircraft was written off. "Val" N56478 was only used on the USS *Lexington* (CV-16) in Texas for the Japanese preparation and takeoff scenes and was not shipped to Hawaii. One Zero, three "Kates" and two "Vals"

from the Hawaii shoot made up the rest of the aircraft in these sequences.

Camera-planes included, among several helicopters, a North American T-28D Trojan (s/n 51-3626 / msn 174-164 / reg. N5015L), with a painted Japanese tail for point-of-view shots.

The two Hurricanes were both in airworthy condition but were only used for ground filming. G-BKTH came from the Shuttleworth Trust and G-HURI from the Fighter Collection. The airworthy Hispano HA-1112, N700E, was shipped over from Planes of Fame in the U.S.; although it didn't have specific film markings, it did have a Luftwaffe livery. Four flying Spitfires were used for aerial shots, hired from the Fighter Collection (G-LFVB); Historic Flying Ltd. (G-MKVB); Shuttleworth Trust (G-AWII); and the Air Museum Ltd. (G-BKMI, with 4-bladed prop). Two replica Spitfires were used in ground scenes—one was a Mk. VIII replica with a 4-bladed prop painted as a second "RF-M." This is the shot-up Spitfire Ben Affleck inspects when he first arrives. Spitfire FR.Mk. XIV, NH904, from Palm Springs Air Museum, was painted up in film markings as another "RF-M" but was dropped from filming when more authentic Battle of Britain period Spitfires were located. Camera-plane was a Douglas A-1D Skyraider (BuNo. 126922 / reg. G-RAID) from the Fighter Collection.

Although most of the USS *Hornet* carrier scenes were actually filmed on the retired USS *Lexington* (CV-16) in Texas, permission was granted from the U.S. Navy to fly the four Mitchells off a real operating carrier—the USS *Constellation*. This was done off San Diego in September 2000 with the takeoff shots mixed in with the ones done onboard the *Lexington*. Some carrier deck prep-shots were also filmed on the *Constellation*. Two of the B-25 bombers names, *Ruptured Duck* and *Whirling Dervish*, were actual names carried by two of Doolittle's Mitchells in 1942. Aircraft were hired from Aero Trader (N9856C), Bill Klasers (N9117Z), Planes of Fame (N3675G), and Palm Springs Air Museum (N8163H).

Although set in Hawaii, much of the film was shot in and around Los Angeles, with filming from April to September 2000. The childhood (Kaydet) and B-25 China crash scenes were filmed at Disney's Golden Oak Ranch, Newhall,

California. "Mitchell Field," Long Island, was located at active Naval Base Ventura County (NAS Point Mugu up to 2000), California, where Runway 09/27 was used for the P-40 game of "chicken." The red and white hangars also doubled for Hawaii later on in the P-40 gun alignment sequence and romance scenes. The Doolittle B-25 preparation scenes and practice takeoffs were done at MCAS Tustin, California, in and around the giant blimp hangars. The hangar coffins, Hawaiian departure, Doolittle returnee and nurses' medal sequences were all filmed at the Air National Guard hangars at Van Nuys Airport, California. The two hangars were both demolished in 2002. Hawaiian locations were filmed in the actual Pearl Harbor area itself. The majority of the airfield scenes—P-40 fighters, DC-3 blowing up, strafing, the dud bomb, etc.—were all filmed on the tarmac outside the large red and white control tower on Ford Island in the middle of Pearl Harbor; those are Hangars 37, 79 and 54 in the background. The later airfield sequences, getting the P-40 aircraft ready, and taking off, were filmed outside Hangar 54 at the southern end of Ford Island. Most of the aerial chase sequences were filmed over Ford Island; the red and white control tower is the actual one from World War II. Active Wheeler AAF was used early on in the film as "mechanics' row," and again during some of the low-level aerial chase sequences. Hawaiian ship locations used the U.S. Naval inactive fleet moored in Pearl Harbor for many of the massive explosions, the retired USS *Missouri* appeared in the pre-attack on-deck scenes, and permission was granted to film the sunken USS *Arizona* memorial for the closing montage. The Japanese aircraft carrier scenes and Doolittle takeoffs were filmed on the retired USS *Lexington* (CV-16), moored at Corpus Christi, Texas. Many ship interiors were filmed on the retired USS *Texas* moored at La Porte, Texas. A purpose-built roll-over gimble set of the USS *Oklahoma* and parts of other ships were built in the giant film studio water tank in Baja, Mexico. Tokyo wide shots were actually a steel mill in Gary, Indiana, on the shores of Lake Michigan. Battle of Britain sequences were filmed at Badminton House in Gloucestershire, England, with aerials shot off the coast of Lydd in Kent. Cockpit shots were done on Stage 2, Disney Studios, and

in a gimble-mounted P-40 replica in the parking lot of what was Marineland, Rancho Palos Verdes, California.

GPS LOCATIONS

Naval Base Ventura County, California: N34 07.15 / W119 07.15

MCAS Tustin, California (closed 1999): N33 42.20 / W117 49.40

Van Nuys Airport, California: N34 12.35 / W118 29.25

Ford Island, Pearl Harbor, Hawaii (closed 1999): N21 21.70 / W157 57.70

Wheeler Army Airfield, Hawaii: N21 29.00 / W158 02.15

Badminton House, Gloucestershire, England: N51 32.70 / W002 16.70

FACTUAL BACKGROUND: PEARL HARBOR DEFENDERS

A swarm of 351 Japanese aircraft attacked Pearl Harbor on December 7, 1941. During this time, a few U.S. Army Air Force pilots managed to get their fighters airborne over Oahu. Two pilots in particular achieved some outstanding victories against the Japanese aggressors. Second Lieutenants George Welch and Kenneth Taylor raced to Haleiwa Airfield and took off in two Curtiss P-40B fighters. Welch got #160 and Taylor #316; both airplanes were of the 15th Pursuit Group. During the course of the battle Welch shot down three "Vals" and a Zero, with Taylor claiming two "Vals" and damaging two more. Both pilots received the Distinguished Service Cross for their actions, and Welch was honored by President Roosevelt at a special White House ceremony. Other pilots able to score aerial victories on the day were Lieutenants Harry Brown (1 kill), Phillip Rasmussen (1 kill), Lewis Sanders (1 kill) and Gordon Sterling (1 kill). Additional pilots were also airborne, flying either P-40B or P-36A fighters. Welch went on to work as a test pilot for North American Aviation and flew the maiden flight of the XP-86 prototype (s/n 45-59597) that evolved into the famed F-86 Sabre. On October 12, 1954, George Welch was killed when the F-100A Super Sabre (s/n 52-5764) he was flying failed to pull out of a 7G dive near Edwards AFB. Kenneth Taylor served in the military up to 1967, retiring as a brigadier general. He passed away on November 25, 2006, in Tucson, Arizona. For details on the Pearl Harbor attack itself, see under: *Tora! Tora! Tora!* (1970).

The Perfect Storm (Non–Aviation Themed Title)

USA / Warner Bros. / 2000 / Color / 130 minutes
Director: Wolfgang Petersen
Cast: George Clooney, Mark Wahlberg, Diane Lane, John C. Reilly, William Fichtner, John Hawkes, Allen Payne, Mary Elizabeth Mastrantonio, Karen Allen
Synopsis / Aviation Content: The true-life story following the crew of the fishing boat *Andrea Gail* and its sinking during the massive storm that hit North America in October 1991. Based on the 1997 book of the same name by Sebastian Junger. Features several extended sequences of an Air National Guard **Lockheed KC-130 Hercules** and **Sikorsky HH-60 Black Hawk** helicopter trying to midair refuel in the storm. Although almost entirely done with CGI and studio mock-ups, the sequences nonetheless still look very real.

Pilot #5

Alternate Titles: ***Destination Tokyo, Skyway to Glory***; ***The Story of Number 5***
USA / Metro-Goldwyn-Mayer / 1943 / B&W / 71 minutes
Director: George Sidney
Cast: Franchot Tone, Marsha Hunt, Gene Kelly, Van Johnson, Alan Baxter, Dick Simmons
Synopsis / Aviation Content: Wartime studio propaganda story about a group of American pilots, and one pilot in particular played by Tone, on the island of Java with but a single fighter aircraft between them to strike back at an advancing Japanese aircraft carrier located off the coast. Budget quickie produced on the MGM studio backlot using models and mock-ups of the Seversky SEV-S2 built for *Test Pilot* (1938). The Seversky mock-ups here suitably double as the Republic P-43 Lancer. Some scenes filmed at the Cal-Aero Academy, Ontario, California, today known as Chino Airport.

The Pilot

U.S. Video Title: ***Danger in the Skies***
USA / Summit Feature Distributors / 1980 / Color / 97 minutes
Director: Cliff Robertson
Cast: Cliff Robertson, Diane Baker, Frank Converse, Dana Andrews, Milo O'Shea, Edward Binns, Gordon MacRae, Jennifer Holton
Synopsis / Aviation Content: A highly skilled airline pilot, played by Robertson, is concealing one problem which is slowly consuming his professional and personal life—alcoholism. Dated production values don't really seem to matter in this effectively told story of high drama. Based on the novel of the same name by American author and scriptwriter Robert P. Davis, who also wrote the screenplay. Vintage airliner fans will enjoy the many and varied views of a real DC-8 in action, which includes cockpit scenes and many aerial sequences. This film is highly regarded for its accurate depiction of flight procedures and airport operations, largely thanks to the direction of Cliff Robertson, who is himself a licensed pilot.

The featured aircraft is a **Douglas DC-8-21** (reg. N8021U / msn 45594/35) in United Airlines livery, but carrying the fictional titles of "North American" Airlines. Delivered to United on January 21, 1960, N8021U remained in passenger service with the airline up until 1974, when it was placed in desert storage. It was subsequently converted to freight standards as a DC-8-21F and entered service with General Air Services, Inc., in 1981 as N580JC. The aircraft was eventually scrapped in 1986. Also seen is **Douglas DC-8-54AF** (reg. N8041U / msn 45675/200), which doubles for N8021U in some scenes. This aircraft was delivered to United Airlines as an "All Freight" airliner on March 28, 1964. Robertson's private aerobatic aircraft is a **Pitts S-2A Special** (reg. N9CC). Also seen are a **Piper J3C** (reg. N3628N) and a **Stearman Kaydet** crop-duster. Filmed in the Palm Beach area of Florida.

Plane Dead   see   Flight of the Living Dead

Power Dive

USA / Paramount Pictures / 1941 / B&W / 68 minutes

Director: James Hogan

Cast: Richard Arlen, Jean Parker, Helen Mack, Roger Pryor, Don Castle, Cliff Edwards, Billy Lee, Thomas Ross, Louis Jean Heydt

Synopsis / Aviation Content: Two brothers, one a test pilot and the other a designer, have developed a new secret aircraft made from plastic, but have a falling-out when they both fall for the same woman. Standard love-triangle subplot for an otherwise interesting aviation film featuring some rare vintage aircraft types. Main aircraft were a **Phillips 1-B Aeroneer** (reg. NX16075 / msn 1), a 1936 prototype built for the USAAC as a primary trainer but not put into production. It was subsequently sold to MGM Studios for film work. The "plastic prototype" is a **Greenleaf (Player) CT-6A** (reg. NX19994 / msn 1), a 1940 wooden prototype of geodetic construction. Other aircraft include the **Boeing Model 247**; **Cornelius LW-1 Freewing** (reg. N13706 / msn LW-1); **Fokker Model 8 Super Universal** (reg. NC9724 / msn 826); **Kinner K Sportster** (reg. NC218Y / msn 22); **Luscombe Model 8**; **Piper J-4F Cub Coupe** (reg. NC30992); **Piper J-5 Cub Cruiser** (reg. NC30087 and NC33403); **Stearman C2B** (reg. NC4099 / msn 110); and **Waco EQC-6** (reg. NC15716 / msn 4391). Filmed in part at Metropolitan Airport, Van Nuys, California, where actor Richard Arlen also ran his own real-life flying school named Arlen-Probert Flying Service.

The Purple Heart

USA / 20th Century–Fox / 1944 / B&W / 99 minutes

Director: Lewis Milestone

Cast: Dana Andrews, Richard Conte, Farley Granger, Kevin O'Shea, Donald Barry, Trudy Marshall, Sam Levene

Synopsis / Aviation Content: A U.S. wartime propaganda film following the hardships experienced by eight downed airmen after a raid on Japan. A timely (as propaganda pieces usually

are), intelligently made film by Hollywood kingpin producer Daryl F. Zanuck, based on the then recent revelations of Japanese atrocities, including the trial and execution of several of the "Doolittle Raiders" captured in 1942. Aircraft were miniatures of the North American B-25 Mitchell and a mock-up interior using the fuselage of a **Lockheed Hudson**.

The Purple Plain

UK / The Rank Organization / 1954 / Color / 97 minutes

Director: Robert Parrish

Cast: Gregory Peck, Win Min Than, Brenda De Banzie, Bernard Lee, Maurice Denham, Lyndon Brook

Synopsis / Aviation Content: In Burma during 1945, a burnt-out Mosquito pilot finds a new lease on life when he must rescue his crew after a crash landing behind enemy lines. Based on the 1947 novel of the same name by English author Herbert E. Bates. Not much aerial action, but still enough to rank this film among the few featuring the classic Mosquito.

Three **DeHavilland DH.98 Mosquito** fighter-bombers were used in the making of this film. Variants were one **PR.Mk. 34**, a **T.Mk. 4** and a **T.Mk. III**—this one was later destroyed for a crash scene. Background aircraft were an **Avro 652A Anson** (one RAF s/n TX181) and **North American Harvard**. Aerial footage was shot using an RAF Short Sunderland. Filmed on an airbase at Negombo, Ceylon (later Sri Lanka). Some combat shots were done with special effects and models.

The Pursuit of D.B. Cooper

USA / Universal Pictures / 1981 / Color / 100 minutes

Director: Roger Spottiswoode

Cast: Robert Duvall, Treat Williams, Kathryn Harrold, Ed Flanders, Paul Gleason, R.G. Armstrong, Nicolas Coster, Cooper Huckabee

Synopsis / Aviation Content: A hijacker extorts $200,000 in cash and then jumps from a Boeing 727 airliner; he's subsequently pursued cross-country by the airline's insurance agent. Light-hearted, fictional adaptation of the true-life hijacking of a Northwest 727 in 1971 by an unknown offender who went by the alias of Dan B. Cooper. The film was developed from the 1979 novel *Free Fall* by American poet J.D. Reed, which itself was based on the same hijacking event. Some generally good views of the 727, including an actual re-enactment of the famous parachute jump made by Cooper from the rear air-stairs of a 727 airliner. Art Scholl's Stearman biplane chase is also worthy of mention.

Type	msn	Civil reg.
Boeing 727-51	19122/319	N105RK
Boeing 727-173C	19504/527	N690WA
Boeing-Stearman PT-17-BW Kaydet	75-2793	N56949

Two Boeing 727 airliners were provided to the film production. The first, 727-173C, N690WA, was used for the in-flight scenes with fictional livery "Northern-Pacific." It first flew on June 26, 1967, and was delivered to operator World Airways on July 12, 1967. N690WA would subsequently be leased to various airlines in Japan, Yemen and Afghanistan. In 1998 it would go to Kitty Hawk Aircargo as N704A and several other freight operators before being placed in storage at Kingman, Arizona, in March 2008 and scrapped in October 2009. The second Boeing 727, N105RK, was used for the ground sequences. It first flew on September 19, 1966, with delivery to Northwest Airlines as N476US on September 28, 1966. It became N105RK in 1978 after being sold to McDonald's owner Ray Kroc to transport his baseball team, the San Diego Padres. In September 1981 it would go to Thunderbird Airways as N727TA, then to Avianca, Colombia, in 1984 as HK-315 and HK-3803, among other registrations. It then came back to the United States in 1995 as N11415 with Air Taxi Intl. in Florida before being scrapped in November 1998.

A biplane chase takes place which involves the use of a Boeing-Stearman PT-17, N56949, which originally had USAAF s/n 41-25304; renowned aerobatic pilot Art Scholl flew this sequence. Other aircraft include a **Bell Model 206B Jet Ranger** and in one scene an **Embraer EMB 110P1 Bandeirante** (either N107CA or N108CA), an

Israeli-built **IAI Westwind** jet, and a **Lockheed L-1329 Jetstar**. Filmed on location in Oregon, Wyoming and Arizona, including at the famous Davis-Monthan AFB storage yard, with numerous piston-engined giants including the Douglas C-47 Skytrain, C-54 Skymaster, Lockheed C-121 Super Constellation, and P-2 Neptune, along with a few Sikorsky H-34 and H-37 helicopters.

Clay Lacy provided one of his Learjet cameraplanes for the air-to-air photography. Four professional parachutists—Jerry Meyers, Bill Edwards, Dean Westgaard and Carl Boenish—were hired to perform the risky parachute jump from the back of the 727 airliner. This is slightly ironic as it proves that Cooper himself, although jumping at night and in adverse weather conditions, might have actually survived the jump!

Factual Background: Who was D.B. Cooper?

On November 24, 1971, a middle-aged man purchased an airline ticket at Portland Intl. Airport, Oregon, on Northwest Airlines Flight 305 to Seattle, Washington. He signed his name as Dan Cooper. The aircraft, a Boeing 727-51 (reg. N467US / msn 18803/137), departed Portland at 3:07 p.m. local time. Once in the air, the man announced to the crew that he had a bomb in his briefcase and demanded $200,000 in cash and several parachutes. The 727 landed at 5:47 p.m. at Seattle-Tacoma Airport, where all his demands were met and the thirty-six passengers onboard released. The airliner then took off again at 7:34 p.m. on a southerly track with only Cooper and the flight crew onboard. Ordering them to remain in the cockpit, Cooper then disappeared to the rear of the aircraft. Using the 727's unique rear-stair entry/exit hatch design, Cooper was able to open it in-flight without disrupting the aircraft's flight profile to any significant degree. At approximately 8:13 p.m. Cooper jumped from the airliner with one of the parachutes and the money and was never seen or heard from again. The 727 landed at Reno, Nevada, at 11:02 p.m. It is believed Cooper jumped in the area around Lake Merwin, Ariel, Washington, but extensive searches of this area turned up no trace of the hijacker or the money. In 1978, a hunter located a 727 place card from N467US in bush six miles south of

Lake Merwin. Then, in 1980, a young boy unearthed almost $6,000 of the ransom money twenty miles southwest of Ariel. There have been many suspects as to who Cooper actually was, but no positive proof has ever emerged. It is generally agreed upon, however, that he appears to have had a working knowledge of aircraft and parachute operations and may have had a military background. The mystery of D.B. Cooper has since become something of an American folklore legend! He has in no small way firmly established himself in the realms of popular culture, being the subject of films, TV show episodes, documentaries, books, radio shows and songs.

After three copycat hijackings in 1972 on 727 airliners, a simple, spring-loaded paddle device was added to the rear air-stairs, which prevents them from being lowered in-flight. Named the "Cooper vane," "Dan Cooper switch" or "D.B. Cooper device," it operates by locking the stairs shut during increased airflow (flying) and unlocking them with decreased airflow (on ground). Several airlines with 727 aircraft simply bolted the air-stairs shut altogether to prevent any further copycat hijackings.

Pushing Tin

USA / 20th Century–Fox / 1999 / Color / 119 minutes

Director: Mike Newell

Cast: John Cusack, Billy Bob Thornton, Cate Blanchett, Angelina Jolie, Jake Weber, Kurt Fuller, Vicki Lewis

Synopsis / Aviation Content: Comedy-drama about a game of one-upmanship that develops between two New York air traffic controllers—the straight and level Cusack and the laid-back cowboy Thornton. Mildly entertaining film is kept afloat mainly by the star quality of the cast. Features some good air traffic control sequences and a scattering of various airliners in action. Can't really say much else.

Q Planes

U.S. Title: **Clouds Over Europe**

UK / Columbia Pictures / 1939 / B&W / 82 minutes

Directors: Tim Whelan, Arthur B. Woods [uncredited]

Cast: Laurence Olivier, Ralph Richardson, Valerie Hobson, George Curzon, George Merritt, Gus McNaughton

Synopsis / Aviation Content: A light-hearted adventure has secret agent Richardson and test pilot Olivier team up to solve a mysterious case of vanishing aircraft. Innocent, fun prewar film has little flying, but what there is shows some good views of the Tiger Moth and the rarely seen Airspeed Envoy. Mostly kept interesting through Richardson's charismatic performance.

Type	msn	Civil reg.
Airspeed AS.6 Envoy	33	G-ADBA
DeHavilland DH.82 Tiger Moth	3101	G-ABTB
DeHavilland DH.82A Tiger Moth	3544	G-AESA
DeHavilland DH.82A Tiger Moth	3624	G-AESC
DeHavilland DH.89A Dragon Rapide	6340	G-AENN

The Airspeed Envoy was owned and operated by North Eastern Airways (NEA) and flew in the film in both instances as the experimental prototype marked as "E97" and "E131." It was drafted into RAF service during World War II with s/n P5778. Five DeHavilland Tiger Moth biplanes were used in the search sequence with the three identified listed above. All were later put into RAF service with s/n BD152 (G-AEZC), BD153 (G-ABTB) and BD161 (G-AESC). The Dragon Rapide is seen arriving at the airfield just before the first test flight. It was later impressed into RAF service with s/n W6455. Interiors were filmed at Denham Studios, Buckinghamshire, England; some use of models and miniatures. Both actors Laurence Olivier and Ralph Richardson became Royal Navy pilots during World War II, which was declared only a few months after this film was released.

Quantum of Solace (Non–Aviation Themed Title) see James Bond Series

Race for the Yankee Zephyr

U.S. Title: *Treasure of the Yankee Zephyr*

Australia-New Zealand / Hemdale & Pact / 1981 / B&W / Color / 105 minutes

Director: David Hemmings

Cast: Ken Wahl, Leslie Ann Warren, Donald Pleasence, George Peppard, Bruno Lawrence

Synopsis / Aviation Content: Two down-and-out deer hunters stumble upon the wreckage of a gold bullion–packed C-47, the *Yankee Zephyr*, lost since World War II. Villainous competition soon shows up, hence the "race." An all-round exciting film with many aerial stunts, a definite must-see for all helicopter fans; the once-proud C-47 wreck is a highlight as well. Filmed in Queenstown, New Zealand, with an outstanding Brian May music score that keeps everything moving along!

Type	msn	Civil reg.
Bell 206B Jet Ranger III	3092	ZK-HSA
Cessna U206G Stationair	U206-03525	ZK-EFI
Douglas C-47A-20-DK Skytrain	13099	ZK-BEU
Hughes Series 300	15-0025	ZK-HGD
Hughes Series 300C	113-0258	ZK-HHQ
Hughes Series 500C	46-0811S	ZK-HKM
Hughes Series 500D	29-0460D	ZK-HMB

The C-47 *Yankee Zephyr* herself was a 1944 Oklahoma City–built Douglas C-47A-20-DK Skytrain (s/n 42-93212 / msn 13099), delivered to the RNZAF as NZ3518. Military service ended in 1946, but it was retained as an instructional airframe. From 1954 to 1970, the aircraft flew as a DC-3C (reg. ZK-BEU) with New Zealand's National Airways Corp. In 1963, it was given a "Skyliner"-style conversion with larger passenger windows along the fuselage. From 1970 to 1979 it flew with Mount Cook Airlines, finally being sold to Alpine Helicopters Ltd. as a livestock freighter. In 1980, ZK-BEU was purchased by the filmmakers and painted in military colors as "69 / 1-7689." Some ground shots were filmed at Queenstown Airport and a few flying shots done over nearby mountains before the aircraft was broken up and placed on a beach for the wreckage scenes. Large float bags were used for on-lake filming and the fuselage was strengthened with an interior wooden framework. The C-47 was broken up after filming—the rear fuselage was sunk in Lake Wakitipu and the forward fuselage was sent to RNZAF Wigram in Christchurch for future display.

All helicopters were owned and operated by Alpine Helicopters Ltd. Bell Jet Ranger, ZK-HSA,

Looking worse for wear on a Queenstown lakefront is C-47A ZK-BEU (s/n 42–93212), converted as a World War II wreck that's hiding crates of gold bullion for the 1981 film *Race for the Yankee Zephyr*. Photograph: Simon D. Beck.

Hughes 300 ZK-HGD was modified to shoot actor close-ups for *Race for the Yankee Zephyr* (1981). It survives today with a private collector in New Zealand. Photograph: Simon D. Beck.

was brand-new at the time, playing George Peppard's transport. Hughes 300, ZK-HHQ, was painted up to represent the luckless deer hunters' worn-out machine. Flying close-ups with the actors were filmed in a mock-up using parts from Hughes 300, ZK-HGD, which had previously been written off in a crash. The two Hughes 500 choppers, ZK-HKM (red) and ZK-HMB (blue), are seen during the opening title sequence. The Cessna Stationair, ZK-EFI, was provided by Mount Cook Airlines for Peppard's arrival scene.

The tank-buggy was part-built with the canopy of a derelict Hughes 300. Filming took place from October 13, 1980, to February 28, 1981, entirely on location in and around Queenstown, New Zealand. The supposedly remote C-47 crash site was actually filmed on the lakefront of Queenstown's Botanic Gardens!

Raiders in the Sky   see
Appointment in London

Raiders of the Lost Ark   see
Indiana Jones **Series**

Rambo: First Blood Part II (Non–Aviation Themed Title)

USA / TriStar Pictures / 1985 / Color / 97 minutes

Director: George P. Cosmatos

Cast: Sylvester Stallone, Richard Crenna, Charles Napier, Steven Berkoff, Julia Nickson, Martin Kove

Synopsis / Aviation Content: Second installment in the Rambo series sees the title character return to Vietnam to rescue POWs. Filmed entirely in and around Acapulco, Mexico, with assistance from the Mexican Air Force. Base scenes were filmed at Pie de la Cuesta AFB near Acapulco (GPS location N16 54.55 / W099 59.00); Rambo arrives in a **Bell 206B Jet Ranger**; base aircraft are three Mexican AF **Pilatus PC-7 Turbo-Trainer** aircraft; the black jet is a **Rockwell 1121 Jet Commander** (possibly the Israeli version: IAI 1121 Commodore Jet); the black helicopter is a **Bell Model 212** (possibly also repainted as the "Russian" Model 212 later in film); an **Aerospatiale SA.330J Puma** doubles as a Russian "Mil

Mi-24 Hind." A derelict **Bell UH-1H Huey** is the burning wreck in the final scene.

Rambo III (Non–Aviation Themed Title)

USA / TriStar Pictures / 1988 / Color / 101 minutes

Director: Peter MacDonald

Cast: Sylvester Stallone, Richard Crenna, Marc de Jonge, Kurtwood Smith, Spiros Focas

Synopsis / Aviation Content: Third film in the series has Rambo assisting locals in Russian-occupied Afghanistan. Two helicopters were converted by U.S. company The Metal Cage to look like Russian military types. **Aerospatiale SA.330J Puma** (reg. N3263U / msn 1501), from Petroleum Helicopters, Inc., was the large "Mil Mi-24 Hind" look-alike marked first as "42," then "45." **Aerospatiale SA.341G Gazelle** (reg. N58283 / msn 1015), was the smaller gunship. Partly filmed in Israel with a brief flyby of four Dassault Mirage III fighters.

Reach for the Sky

UK / The Rank Organisation / 1956 / B&W / 135 minutes

Director: Lewis Gilbert

Cast: Kenneth More, Muriel Pavlow, Lyndon Brook, Lee Patterson, Alexander Knox

Synopsis / Aviation Content: Biographical film following the life and times of Douglas Bader, who lost both legs in an air accident but went on to become an RAF fighter ace in the Battle of Britain. Based on the 1954 book of the same name by Australian author Paul Brickhill. Riveting, classic aviation film made all the better by Kenneth More's charismatic performance as Bader. Sharp views of period biplane aircraft and classic British fighters; the Hurricane fighter scramble sequence is one highlight.

The British Science Museum provided Avro 504K (s/n D7560), which was used for background only. The Shuttleworth Trust provided

U.S. company The Metal Cage converted this Aerospatiale Puma N3263U and Gazelle N58283 as Russian military helicopters for *Rambo III* (1988). Photograph: The Yoak Collection.

Type	msn	Military s/n	Civil reg.	Film Markings
Flying Aircraft				
Avro 504K	unknown	(RAF) D7560	—	—
Avro 504K	R3/LE/61400	(RAF) H5199	G-ADEV	E3404
Avro 621 Tutor I	—	(RAF) K3241	G-AHSA	R2511
Bristol F.2B Fighter	7575	(RAF) D8096	G-AEPH	D8096
Hawker Hurricane Mk. IIc	41H/469290	(RAF) LF363	—	T4125
Spartan Arrow	78	—	G-ABWP	G-ABWP
Supermarine Spitfire LF.Mk. XVIe	unknown	(RAF) RW352	—	RA617 / QV-P / QV-S
Supermarine Spitfire LF.Mk. XVIe	unknown	(RAF) SL574	—	RV214 / QV-R
Supermarine Spitfire LF.Mk. XVIe	unknown	(RAF) TE358	—	AR251 QV-X
Supermarine Spitfire LF.Mk. XVIe	CBAF.IX4590	(RAF) TE456	—	TE425 / PD-S
Static Aircraft				
Bristol Bulldog IIA	7446	(RAF) K2227	G-ABBB	K2496, K2494
Hawker Hurricane Mk. I	unknown	(RAF) P2617	—	T4107
Hawker Hurricane Mk. IIc	unknown	(RAF) LF378	—	V5276
Supermarine Spitfire LF.Mk. XVIe	unknown	(RAF) RW345	—	TA614
Supermarine Spitfire LF.Mk. XVIe	unknown	(RAF) SL745	—	TR627 / QV-T
Supermarine Spitfire LF.Mk. XVIe	unknown	(RAF) TB293	—	RV415 / QV-U
Supermarine Spitfire LF.Mk. XVIe	unknown	(RAF) TB885	—	R1247 / QV-V
Supermarine Spitfire LF.Mk. XVIe	CBAF.11414	(RAF) TE288	—	AR251 / QV-X / ZD-S
Supermarine Spitfire LF.Mk. XVIe	unknown	(RAF) TE341	—	VT151 / ZD-S / QV-S

Avro 504K, G-ADEV and Bristol F.2, G-AEPH. The Avro 504K is seen in the opening scene and is the aircraft Bader goes solo with the Bristol F.2 as background only, mainly seen during the new recruit inspection scene. Both also flew as camera-planes for filming. Avro 621 Tutor, G-AHSA, flew a few times but suffered an engine failure and was subsequently stored and is not seen in the finished film. It was purchased by the Shuttleworth Trust after filming for restoration. The rare Spartan Arrow, G-ABWP, is background only. The Bristol Bulldog IIA, G-ABBB, was non-flying but used in close-up shots as "K2496," then as "K2494" in one shot *after* Bader's crash. Pinewood Studios built a replica Bristol Bulldog for location background and studio cockpit shots as "K2494," which was then broken up for the crash scene as "K2496."

Purists will quickly point out all Spitfire fighters were the LF.Mk. XVIe version, a late war type which didn't fly until 1944 and featured the bubble canopy (from 1945). There were no actual classic line Battle of Britain–era Spitfires flying during production in 1955, so for the director it was the Mk. XVI or no Spitfires at all! Four were flyable (from 3 Civil Anti-Aircraft Co-operation Unit—CAACU at Exeter) and six were trucked into Kenley for static background set dressing.

S/n TE288 was then rumored to have been shipped to Pinewood for cockpit flying shots. Spitfire Mk. XVIe s/n TB863 is also noted as being used for studio filming; this was an MGM Studios–owned airframe purchased after retirement from the RAF.

Only *one* Hawker Hurricane (RAF s/n LF363) flew at all in the movie, coming from RAF Waterbeach Station Flight. Two other Hurricanes were brought in as static background—P2617 and LF378. Some sources quote Hurricane L1592 as also being used. One Hurricane mock-up was built, marked as "R7141." The squadron code used was "SD," but squadron letters were changed throughout filming. All Hurricane footage was intercut with stock footage from the earlier British film *Angels One Five* (1952), so the final cut saw an impressive number of fighters.

Much use of actual wartime film to depict advancing German aircraft, use of gun-camera footage in dogfights, and a large use of models to depict formation and crash shots.

All airfield location scenes throughout the movie were filmed at RAF Kenley, where buildings and sets were built on one corner of the airfield from August to September 1955. The Bulldog crash scene, however, was filmed at Denham near Pinewood Studios. Aircraft cockpit shots, in-

Now preserved at the Air Force Museum of New Zealand in Christchurch, New Zealand, this Spitfire Mk. XVIe was once used as background set dressing in the British film *Reach for the Sky* (1956). Photograph: Simon D. Beck.

teriors, etc., were all filmed at Pinewood Studios, Buckinghamshire, England, from October to November 1955.

GPS LOCATION

RAF Kenley, Surrey, England (closed 1959): N51 18.15 / W000 05.50

FACTUAL BACKGROUND: SIR DOUGLAS BADER

Douglas Bader (February 21, 1910–September 5, 1982), was a double amputee RAF fighter ace of World War II renowned for his dedication to other amputees and the disabled. He joined the RAF in 1928; his first flight was in an Avro 504 on September 13 that year, and his first solo flight on February 19, 1929. While performing low-level aerobatics in a Bristol Bulldog IIA (RAF s/n K1676), on December 14, 1931, Bader crashed when his wingtip caught the ground and dug in. As a result of the accident, both his legs had to be amputated. After a long recovery period in which he gained the use of artificial limbs, Bader got

back into flying in 1932 but was refused re-entry into RAF service. When World War II broke out, a desperate RAF accepted him back. He subsequently earned the rank of squadron leader, flying Hawker Hurricanes; he scored eleven kills, one probable and four damaged during the Battle of Britain. He was soon promoted wing commander flying Spitfires and had accumulated twenty-two kills by the time he was shot down over France on August 9, 1941. After several escape attempts from German POW camps and threats of taking away his artificial limbs, the Germans sent Bader to the notorious "escape proof" Colditz Castle on August 18, 1942, where he remained until liberated by U.S. forces on April 15, 1945. Bader returned to England, where he led a victorious 300-aircraft flypast over London in June 1945, later leaving the RAF as a group captain in 1946. He was knighted in 1976 as Sir Douglas Bader for the outstanding public work he had dedicated himself to in the services of other amputees and the disabled. Sir Douglas flew for the last time on June 4, 1979, having accumulated a lifetime total of

5,744 hours and 25 minutes. He died from a heart attack in 1982 and remains today one of Britain's best-known war heroes.

The Red Baron   see   *Von Richthofen and Brown* (1971)

The Red Baron

Germany-UK-USA / Niama-Film GmbH / 2008 / Color / 101 minutes

Director: Nikolai Muellerschoen

Cast: Matthias Schweighofer, Lena Headey, Til Schweiger, Volker Bruch, Joseph Fiennes

Synopsis / Aviation Content: German-made film shot in the English language following the last two years in the life of famous World War I air ace Manfred von Richthofen from 1916 to 1918. There's beautiful photography and stunning visual effects, but a failure to deliver any kind of emotional punch or offer the audience any insight into how Richthofen evolved into a winning ace. Fantastic aircraft detail, such as moving engine valves and flexing wings during the dogfights, do at least create some form of realism for aviation film fans.

Full-scale mock-ups and brilliant CGI visual effects were created to depict the German forces, which included the **Albatros D.III** and **D.V** biplane fighters in the earlier parts of the film and the famous **Fokker Dr.I** triplane fighter in the latter parts of the film. One flyable Fokker Dr.I replica (reg. G-ATJM / msn 002) was used for some sequences. British aircraft were the **Royal Aircraft factory S.E.5** fighter; **R.E. 8** fighter with gunner; **Handley Page Type O** twin-engined bomber; and the **Sopwith F.1 Camel**. The German trainer seen taxiing into a haystack during a garden party sequence was, in real life, a three-quarter-scale flyable replica of an American **Curtiss JN-4 Jenny** biplane with Czech reg. OK-FUL-28.

FACTUAL BACKGROUND: MANFRED VON RICHTHOFEN

Manfred Albrecht von Richthofen (May 2, 1892–April 21, 1918) was a German World War I fighter pilot whose eighty confirmed aerial victo-

ries made him that period's most famous air ace. His name and posthumous nickname, the Red Baron, have become an aviation legend, and he's today firmly embedded in popular culture the world over as the ace of aces. Richthofen joined the German Army Air Service (Luftstreikrafte) in May 1915 as an observer. In March 1916 he began pilot training and flew an Albatros C.III. His first aerial victory was on September 17, 1916, and his tally steadily grew while he was flying the Albatros D.II, D.III, D.V or Halberstadt D.II. In January 1917 he was awarded the highest German military honor that could be bestowed—the *Pour le Merite* or Blue Max medal. By June, Richthofen was commander of his new fighter wing, which came to be known as the Flying Circus because of the brightly colored aircraft and use of tents and trains for mobility on the war front. On July 6, 1917, he sustained a serious head injury while in combat with British fighters, which grounded him for over a month and required several surgeries to remove bone splinters. Richthofen subsequently suffered ongoing headaches and nausea after returning to duty. By now, Richthofen had acquired his signature fighter, a bright red Fokker Dr.I triplane marked as "425/17." This aircraft would become synonymous with the Red Baron legend, although Richthofen would only make nineteen of his eighty kills in this fighter. On April 21, 1918, von Richthofen was pursuing a Sopwith Camel at low level when he was hit and mortally wounded by a single .303 bullet. He managed a landing in a field north of the village of Vaux-sur-Somme, France, his aircraft intact. Australian soldiers reached the site just as Richthofen died, and his aircraft was later dismantled for souvenirs. Debate continues to this day over just who killed the Red Baron. Traditionally the kill has been attributed to Canadian pilot Arthur "Roy" Brown, who made an attacking pass of Richtohofen's triplane at the time he was shot, but many now agree he was killed by a single round fired from the ground. Brown never officially claimed the kill.

Red Eye

USA / Dreamworks Pictures / 2005 / Color / 85 minutes

Director: Wes Craven

Cast: Rachel McAdams, Cillian Murphy, Brian Cox, Jack Scalia, Jayma Mays

Synopsis / Aviation Content: Engaging thriller about a hotel manager on a late-night flight who becomes entangled in the plot to assassinate a high-profile guest staying in her hotel. While the film itself is well crafted, someone didn't do his homework on the aircraft types! The interior of the airliner is a double aisle Boeing 767, but the exterior traveling shots jump between an Airbus A320 and Boeing 727, 737 and 777 airliners. The airline "Fresh Air" does in fact exist as a Nigerian-based airline, but is a fictional representation in this motion picture. Filmed in both Los Angeles and Miami from November 2004 to January 2005.

Red Tails

USA / 20th Century–Fox / 2012 / Color / 125 minutes

Director: Anthony Hemingway

Cast: Nate Parker, David Oyelowo, Tristan Wilds, Ne-Yo, Elijah Kelley, Andre Royo, Cliff Smith, Marcus T. Paulk, Cuba Gooding Jr., Terrence Howard

Synopsis / Aviation Content: The real-life story depicting the service of African American pilots, known as the Tuskegee Airmen, flying for the USAAF as the 332nd Fight Group in Italy during 1944. The red-colored stabilizers of their fighters earned them the nickname Red Tails. Although the characters and some situations are fictionalized, it's difficult to determine whether the intention here is for an adolescent war adventure or a historical drama focused on the fighter group's challenges to overcome racial prejudice and prove their worth—the end result seems to go neither way. Limited use of real P-40 and P-51 aircraft, but they're hard to spot amongst the CGI, which, along with

the sound design, is top-notch, especially the Me 262 sequences. The 332nd FG story has previously been explored in the 1995 television movie *The Tuskegee Airmen*.

The B-17G, F-AZDX, named *Pink Lady*, was provided by French owner IGN/ Fortresse Toujours Volante Association and is a *Memphis Belle* (1990) film veteran, having flown in that production marked as *Mother and Country*. The P-40M, G-KITT, was a Kittyhawk Mk. III for the RCAF (s/n 840), and was hired from UK-based Hanger 11 Collection. P-40N, F-AZKU, was a recently restored aircraft by Amicale Jean-Baptiste Salis, having previously been registered in Australia as VH-KTI. C-47A, N147DC, was hired from Aces High Ltd. in the UK and is a veteran of many film and TV productions. Old Flying Machine Co. film veteran P-51D, G-HAEC, came from owner Robert Davies; N167F came from Joda LLC of the United States, and F-AZAB from Baudet/JCB Aviation in France. Several full-scale mock-ups of the P-40, P-51 and Stuka dive-bomber were created. A large-scale use of CGI visual effects depicting the P-40, P-51, B-17, Messerschmitt Bf. 109 and Me 262 jet fighter, most of which are very well done and accurate, to the point that it's difficult to pinpoint the real aircraft in the action. Flying scenes were filmed at Milovice Airport in the Czech Republic (GPS: N50 14.10 / E014 55.20) from April through May 2009. Also filmed in Italy, Croatia, England, and San Rafael, California.

The Rescue (Non–Aviation Themed Title)

USA / Touchstone Pictures / 1988 / Color / 93 minutes

Director: Ferdinand Fairfax

Cast: Kevin Dillon, Marc Price, Ned Vaughn, Christina Harnos, Ian Giatti, Charles Haid, Edward Albert, James Cromwell

Type	msn	Military s/n	Civil reg.	Film Markings
Boeing B-17G-85-VE Flying Fortress	17-8246	44-8846	F-AZDX	—
CAC Mustang PR.Mk. 22	192-1517	(RAAF) A68-192	G-HAEC	AI-4
Curtiss P-40M-10-CU Warhawk	27490	43-5802	G-KITT	A3-1, -3, -7
Curtiss P-40N-5-CU Warhawk	29677	42-105915	F-AZKU	—
Douglas C-47A-75-DL Skytrain	19347	42-100884	N147DC	2100884 / D
North American P-51D-25-NA Mustang	122-40417	44-73877	N167F	A2-9
North American P-51D-30-NA Mustang	122-40967	44-74427	F-AZAB	AI-7

Synopsis / Aviation Content: A group of Air Force brats cross enemy lines in an attempt to rescue their fathers from a North Korean prison camp before they are executed. Fantastic coverage of the Royal New Zealand Air Force with many aircraft types in action; the highlight, of course, is the vintage **Bristol Type 170 Freighter Mk. 31M** (ex-reg. G-AMPJ / msn 13134), originally delivered as one of twelve Freighters for the RNZAF from 1951, this one with RNZAF s/n NZ5910. It was for a time based in Singapore during the RNZAF's involvement in the Malayan conflict; NZ5910 was retired from military service in 1977. At the time of filming it was operated by civilian New Zealand company Hercules Airlines Ltd. as ZK-EPF. Leased to the production, EPF was painted in a fictional North Korean livery as "101," the Korean markings translating as "Chosun Civil Air." After filming was completed in 1987, it was then sold to Trans-Provincial Airlines of Canada as C-GYQY. It crashed and was written off on June 21, 1988. Featured RNZAF aircraft are the **Bell UH-1H Huey**, **Lockheed C-130H**, **P-3K**, and **McDonnell Douglas A-4K Skyhawk**. The air base is RNZAF Whenuapai located in Auckland, New Zealand. The North Korean prison was built in Queenstown, New Zealand, where much of the aerial filming with the Bristol Freighter took place.

Rescue Dawn

USA / Metro-Goldwyn-Mayer / 2006 / Color / 126 minutes
Director: Werner Herzog
Cast: Christian Bale, Steve Zahn, Jeremy Davies, Marshall Bell, Brad Carr, Francois Chau
Synopsis / Aviation Content: Dramatized film of the true-life story concerning U.S. Navy pilot Dieter Dengler and his remarkable escape from a Pathet Lao POW camp in 1966. An engaging and passionately made film that unfortunately did little to boost public awareness of Dengler's incredible experience. Most of the aerial action is in the film's first ten minutes, which is well-crafted considering there were no actual Skyraider aircraft the filmmakers could call upon. In addition, there are some good Huey helicop-ter scenes at the end. Developed from director Herzog's earlier 1997 documentary *Little Dieter Needs to Fly*. The film's title is Dengler's individual "authenticator code," assigned to him in the event of being shot down.

The U.S. Naval aircraft are depicted in the film as the **Douglas A-1H Skyraider**, with serial numbers also in the A-1H range; the actual aircraft Dengler (BuNo. 142031 / msn 11511) and his squadron flew were the later A-1J variant. With no actual aircraft of this type available during production, all sequences were accomplished with models, mock-ups and CGI creations. The crashed Skyraider in the rice paddy appears to be the tail section of an unidentified civilian type painted in Skyraider markings "AK / 37543." The Thai Air Force provided several **Bell UH-1H Iroquois** helicopters for the various jungle search sequences and flyovers. The helicopter at the end when Dengler is picked up is a **Bell 212** with Thai s/n 2209 (msn 30555). Background aircraft are several **Fairchild-Hiller AU-23A Peacemaker** utility aircraft. Filmed in Thailand from August 22 to October 17, 2005, with the assistance of 203 Squadron based out of Lopburi, who provided the Bell helicopters.

The Right Stuff

USA / Ladd Company, Warner Bros. / 1983 / B&W / Color / 185minutes
Director: Philip Kaufman
Cast: Charles Frank, Scott Glenn, Ed Harris, Lance Henriksen, Scott Paulin, Dennis Quaid, Sam Shepard, Fred Ward, Kim Stanley, Barbara Hershey, Veronica Cartwright, Pamela Reed
Synopsis / Aviation Content: The true story behind the birth of the U.S. Space Program from Chuck Yeager's breaking of the sound barrier to the pioneering astronauts of Project Mercury. Developed from the 1979 book of the same name by Tom Wolfe. An entertaining, often underrated film is a well-made look at this unique period in American aviation and space history. Although there's a various assortment of period aircraft throughout, many are only seen in fleeting glances. Highlights include the re-enactment of Yeager's historic feat in 1947

and a thrilling, Oscar-winning music score by Bill Conti.

Type	msn	Military s/n	Civil reg.
Bell UH-1D-BF Iroquois	4738	65-9694	N72376
Boeing B-29A-60-BN Superfortress	11547	44-62070	N529B
Canadair Silver Star Mk. 3	T33-273	(RCAF) 21273	N12413
Canadair Silver Star Mk. 3	T33-456	(RCAF) 21456	N333MJ
Hawker Hunter F.Mk. 51	41H-680262	(Denmark) E-403	N72602
Lockheed F-104G Starfighter	683-2026	63-13243	—
Lockheed-Fokker F-104G Starfighter	683D-8002	63-13269	—
North American F-86F-30-NA Sabre	191-835	52-5139	N86F
Sikorsky H-34G.II	58-1097	(W.Germ) 80+32	N8292

The Bell UH-1H, N72376 (a UH-1D conversion), was provided from the FBI for the Gus Grissom ceremony painted in NASA colors. B-29, N529B, was provided by the Confederate Air Force, having been registered as N4249 up to 1981. It would go on to become a star attraction for the CAF, named *Fifi*, and remains the only flying B-29 in existence. Most scenes in the film see N529B performing ground and taxi shots, with models making up most of the flying scenes. The funeral flybys were performed by five Lockheed T-33A Shooting Star trainers, three of which remain unidentified, from the California ANG 144th FIS. The other two, N12413 and N333MJ, were provided by Flight Systems International (FSI), Inc., and are both ex–RCAF Silver Star Mk. 3 variants, the Canadair-built version of the T-33A Shooting Star. The imported British Hawker Hunter doubled as the Douglas D-558-II Skyrocket in the Scott Crossfield scenes. It originally served in the Danish AF (s/n E-403) before being imported into the U.S. in the 1970s with civil reg. N72602. On January 8, 2000, the aircraft suffered a loss of power on approach to land at Chino Airport, forcing the pilot to eject just before the aircraft force landed, causing significant damage. The airframe has since been broken up. For the climatic Yeager NF-104A sequence, two Lockheed F-104G Starfighter jets were used from the 69th TFTS at Luke AFB, Arizona. This squadron trained West German pilots using their own F-104G fighters up to 1983. The first was Lockheed-built F-104G (s/n 63-13243 / German code 2021), and the second was a Fokker-built F-104G (s/n 63-13269 / German code 2328). The flying was performed by German AF Oberstleutnant Heinrich Thueringer and Lt Col Robert Patterson

of the USAF. Both jets were sold to Taiwan in 1983; "13243" crashed in 1990, killing the Taiwanese pilot. F-86F Sabre, N86F, was provided by Flight Systems International (FSI), Inc., and carried false buzz number FU-849. It was piloted in the film by Skip Holm and Chuck Yeager himself. The USMC Sikorsky HUS-1 Seahorse for the Gus Grissom recovery scene was an ex–West German Army Sikorsky H-34G.II (s/n 80+32). It was imported into the U.S. in the early 1970s as a civilian Sikorsky S-58E registered N51881, then N8292. It was provided to the film by Crane Helicopter Services of Fremont, California. Soon afterward N8292 was exported to Canada as C-GQCJ.

For the carrier scenes there are two **McDonnell Douglas A-4M Skyhawk II**, including BuNo. 160245; four **Sikorsky SH-3G Sea King**, including BuNo. 149720 and 149919; and two **Vought A-7C Corsair II**, including BuNo. 156752. Background aircraft comprise one **Beechcraft T-34**, two **Bell UH-1H Iroquois**, one **Boeing EC-135**, one **Convair F-106B Delta Dart**, one **Lockheed C-130 Hercules**, two **Northrop T-38A Talon** trainers and a number of **T-33A Shooting Star** trainers in various scenes.

Derelict aircraft sections acquired for various interior and cockpit scenes included one B-29 (Pima Air & Space Museum), three T-33A, and three F-104D (including 57-1330, all from Davis-Monthan AFB). Wooden mock-ups were built of the Bell X-1 (s/n 46-062, 46-063) and X-1A (s/n 48-1384) at Van Nuys Airport, California.

Camera aircraft were Art Scholl's DHC-1 Chipmunk (reg. N13Y), Clay Lacy's Learjet, Tallmantz Aviation's B-25J (reg. N1042B), and a hired Hughes 500. Stunt pilots were Art Scholl and Clay Lacy. General Chuck Yeager was the production technical adviser and makes a cameo appearance as a patron named "Fred" in the saloon sequences.

Some Bell X-1 sequences used actual footage of the rocket-plane from 1947, as the FAA would not certify B-29, N529B, to fly with the wooden mock-ups in the bomb-bay due to concerns wind buffet would tear the film prop apart. The takeoff shot on Yeager's historic day in 1947 uses stock footage of a B-50 Superfortress rather than the historically correct B-29. Much NASA stock footage was used of rockets and training. Large-scale use of mock-ups and models for the dramatic flying shots include the B-29, X-1, X-1A and NF-104A.

Filming took place from March 1982 to January 1983, mainly in the San Francisco area. Hamilton AFB, just outside of San Francisco, was used for sound stage work, mock NASA locations, and filming of the aircraft interior and cockpit scenes. Filming also took place at Edwards AFB from May to June 1982. The older South Base was used for the earlier X-1 sequences and the main base for the later scenes including the NF-104A. Pancho Barnes's Happy Bottom Riding Club saloon was recreated in the Mojave Desert. The carrier scenes were shot on the USS *Coral Sea* (CV-43) off the Californian coast in July 1982.

GPS LOCATIONS

Hamilton AFB, California: N38 03.50 / W122 30.80

Edwards AFB, California: N34 55.00 / W117 53.30

FACTUAL BACKGROUND: SPEED RECORDS AND THE MERCURY PROGRAM

Chuck Yeager broke the sound barrier over Edwards AFB on October 14, 1947, flying the Bell X-1 (s/n 46-062), named *Glamorous Glennis* after his wife. The mothership was B-29-96-BW (s/n 45-21800).

Mach 2 (twice the speed of sound) was attained by Scott Crossfield on November 20, 1953, in the Douglas D-558-II Skyrocket (Hawker Hunter in the film), which was dropped from a U.S. Navy P2B-1S (B-29-95-BW, s/n 45-21787), BuNo. 84029. Yeager beat Crossfield's record,

going Mach 2.44 on December 12, 1953, in the Bell X-1A (s/n 48-1384). As depicted in the film, Yeager lost control but regained it after losing 51,000 feet of altitude and landed without further incident. He wasn't so lucky while testing the Lockheed NF-104A (s/n 56-0762 / msn 183-1050) on December 10, 1963. In a power zoom climb above Edwards AFB the aircraft faltered at 104,000 feet and Yeager was forced to eject, parachuting to the ground but sustaining facial burns.

Project Mercury was the United States' first manned space program, which ran from 1959 to 1963 with the intent of putting an astronaut into orbit around the Earth. Seven military test pilots who were considered to have the "Right Stuff" were chosen from a pool of 110 in April 1959 and consequently became known as the Mercury 7. Six of these pilots flew Mercury missions from 1961 to 1963. Donald "Deke" Slayton (played by Scott Paulin) was grounded in 1962 due to an irregular heartbeat. Although Chuck Yeager (played by Sam Shepard) was in the running, he was not selected. The Carpenter and Schirra missions, though detailed in Wolfe's book, are not depicted in the film.

The Road Warrior see *Mad Max 2*

The Rocketeer

International Titles: ***Rocketeer, The Adventures of the Rocketeer***

USA / Buena Vista Pictures / 1991 / Color / 108 minutes

Director: Joe Johnston

Cast: Bill Campbell, Jennifer Connelly, Alan Arkin, Timothy Dalton, Paul Sorvino, Terry O'Quinn, Ed Lauter, James Handy

Synopsis / Aviation Content: In 1938, a racing pilot played by Campbell finds a stolen rocket-pack in his hangar and soon finds himself pursued by the FBI, the Mob, and Nazi agents, all trying to get their hands on it. Based on the 1982 graphic novel created by Dave Stevens, the film is a homage to 1930s matinee serials that unfortu-

Astronaut	Callsign	Launch Date	Portrayed in Film By
Alan Shepard	*Freedom 7*	May 5, 1961	Scott Glenn
Virgil "Gus" Grissom	*Liberty Bell 7*	Jul. 21, 1961	Fred Ward
John Glenn	*Friendship 7*	Feb. 20, 1962	Ed Harris
Scott Carpenter	*Aurora 7*	May 24, 1962	Charles Frank
Walter Schirra	*Sigma 7*	Oct. 3, 1962	Lance Henriksen
Gordon "Gordo" Cooper	*Faith 7*	May 15, 1963	Dennis Quaid

nately has too much talking and not enough rocketeering. There are, however, some fantastic aerial sequences with a number of classic period aircraft. The inclusion of pioneering aviator Howard Hughes as the rocket-pack's designer is one highlight, as is the Standard J-1 biplane rescue sequence.

Type	msn	Civil reg.
Flying Aircraft		
Brown B-2 (replica)	T-2	N255Y
Granville Gee Bee Z (replica)	T-4	NR77V
Great Lakes 2T-1A	199	N312Y
Ryan ST-A	128	NC16039
Standard J-1	T4595	N62505
Travel Air R Mystery Ship (replica)	RB0001	NR614K
Background Aircraft		
Bird BK	1002	N9739
Fleetwings F-4 Sea Bird	1	NC16793
Stinson SM-8A	M-4277	NC469Y
Waco Cabin Biplane	4440	NC16233

The Granville Gee Bee Z, NR77V, is the yellow and black racer seen in the opening sequence, and is a replica of the original racer built in 1931 that won the Thompson Trophy. This one was built and flown in 1978 by Bill Turner and Ed Marquart and features a slightly longer fuselage and wider wings for better handling. The four aircraft seen in the air race sequence are a Brown B-2 monoplane, N255Y—red marked as "33," it was a 1972-built replica by Bill Turner based on the original 1934 air racer named *Miss Los Angeles*; a Great Lakes 2T-1A, N312Y—red biplane; a silver metal Ryan ST-A, NC16039—a 1936-built monoplane; and a red and black Travel Air R monoplane, NR614K—a replica built in 1971 by Jim Younkin based on the original 1929 air racer. The light-colored biplane flown by the clown that the Rocketeer rescues is a Standard J-1, N62505, once owned by Tallmantz Aviation, Inc., and is a veteran of several motion pictures.

Background aircraft seen throughout the airfield sequences are a Bird BK, N9739—red biplane; a rare Fleetwings F-4 Sea Bird, NC16793—silver amphibian with high-mounted engine; a Stinson SM-8A, NC469Y—purple high-wing monoplane; and a Waco Cabin Biplane, NC16233—white with red trim. Several other unidentified period aircraft were also used, including a yellow DeHavilland DH.82 Tiger Moth.

Models and replica mock-ups built for the film were a Ford Tri-Motor; a Pitcairn-Cierva PCA-2 Gyroplane (as flown by Howard Hughes in the film); Hughes H-1 Racer; a model of the Hughes H-4 Hercules; a non-flying black and white Gee Bee Z replica marked as "NA73 / 5" for the final scene; and a large, 12-foot-long model depicting a fictional German airship named *Luxembourg* with false reg. "D-LZ130."

Filmed from September 19, 1990, to January 22, 1991. The main airfield set was constructed at Santa Maria Public Airport, California—a former World War II army airfield used for P-38 training. The hangar built for the film has subsequently become part of the Santa Maria Museum of Flight and features several props and items from the film.

GPS Location

Santa Maria Public Airport, California: N34 53.70 / W120 27.30

Sabre Jet

USA / United Artists / 1953 / Color / 96 minutes

Director: Louis King

Cast: Robert Stack, Coleen Gray, Richard Arlen, Julie Bishop, Leon Ames, Amanda Blake, Reed Sherman, Michael Moore, Lucy Knoch

Synopsis / Aviation Content: A thoughtful, if emotionally distant, look at the trials experienced by the wives and partners of F-86 Sabre jet pilots during the Korean War. The only real highlight is the many ramp views of the F-86 Sabre and F-80 Shooting Star. Television prints were screened in black and white.

Filmed on the apron and taxiways at Nellis AFB, Nevada, which doubles for Itazuke AFB, Japan, using numerous **North American F-86E / F-86F Sabre** and **Lockheed F-80C Shooting Star** variant fighters. One shot (by mistake?) features a landing by a **Republic F-84E Thunderjet** amongst a group of F-80 fighters. Positively identified Sabres include F-86E s/n 51-12978, 51-12989, 51-12991, 51-13017 (with false buzz number "FU-060"), 51-13019, 51-13022, 51-13023, 51-13027, 51-13048, 51-13064, 51-13067, and F-

86F s/n 51-12948 and 51-12969. Some F-86 Sabres were painted as North Korean MiG-15 fighters. Some identified F-80C Shooting Stars include s/n 47-181, 47-182, 47-184, 47-188 and 47-203. Stock footage of Boeing B-29 Superfortress bombers, but very poor use of combat stock footage, which appears to be mainly World War II vintage featuring piston-engined fighters and B-17 bombers being shot down!

The Sea Shall Not Have Them

UK / Eros Films / 1954 / B&W / 91 minutes
Director: Lewis Gilbert
Cast: Michael Redgrave, Dirk Bogarde, Anthony Steel, Nigel Patrick, Bonar Colleano
Synopsis / Aviation Content: In the autumn of 1944, a British bomber crew on a secret mission is forced to ditch in the North Sea with rescue attempts being hampered at every turn. Interesting film has good performances, but suffers slightly due to the lower production values of the period. Features some detailed views of the rarely seen Supermarine Sea Otter. Based on the 1953 novel of the same name by English author John Harris with a classically British music score by Malcolm Arnold.

The British bomber is a **Lockheed Hudson** with a real, disused airframe submerged in the ocean for the brief post-crash sequence. The British seaplane is a single-engined **Supermarine Sea Otter Mk. I** (RN s/n JM909), the last of Supermarine's biplane amphibians and the last biplane of any type to enter RAF service. The prototype first flew in August 1938, and 290 were built between 1943 and 1946, entering air-sea rescue service with RAF Coastal Command in late 1943. Designed as a Supermarine Walrus replacement, the aircraft can quickly be distinguished from its predecessor by the forward, rather than aft, facing Bristol engine. Background aircraft are a **Short S.45 Seaford I** (RAF s/n NJ201) and a **Short S.45A Solent 3** (RAF s/n WM759). The **Avro Lancaster**, marked as IH-V / NX782, is a file shot taken from an earlier film, *Appointment in London* (1953). As a note of interest, the pilot picked up by the Sea Otter was played by German actor Anton Diffring, who famously went on to play the "German officer" in many subsequent war films.

Six Days Seven Nights

USA / Touchstone Pictures / 1998 / Color / 101 minutes
Director: Ivan Reitman
Cast: Harrison Ford, Anne Heche, David Schwimmer, Jacqueline Obradors, Temuera Morrison
Synopsis / Aviation Content: Lighthearted romance comedy about an unlikely couple—bush pilot Ford and city girl Heche—crash landing on a deserted island with only each other for company. Great sequences of the sturdy DHC-2 Beaver in flight, plus excellent close-ups in the beach wreck scenes.

The main aircraft is a **DeHavilland-Canada L-20A-DH Beaver** (s/n 58-2075 / msn 1408), this one originally delivered to the U.S. Army in 1959. After retirement, it featured civilian reg. N9823F for a while before going to Ken Spray, Inc., of Idaho as N9251Z in 1991. It was hired from Ken Spray in 1997, being marked for the film as "F-0318 / Harris Air Freight." Actor Harrison Ford is type-rated on the Beaver and actually flew in a few sequences on film. After filming, the aircraft went to Canada in 1998 as C-GHAF in float configuration and subsequently crashed in 2003, killing all three people onboard. A second DHC-2 used for beach wreck scenes was registered as N1799F (msn 799). It was rebuilt after the film to flying condition with reg. N67DN.

Another DHC-2 Beaver wreck was obtained for the beach and lagoon "crash" scenes; plus, what appears to be a set of Beaver float pontoons was also acquired for filming in a river sequence. One **North American AT-6 Texan** wreck was obtained as a crashed World War II Japanese floatplane. The search helicopter was a **Bell Model 205A.**

Filmed in and around the island of Kauai, Hawaii, from July to August 1997. Also filmed at Lihue Airport on Kauai featuring Aloha Airlines Boeing 737-200 airliners along with many background private and commuter aircraft, including a **Hughes 500D.**

633 Squadron

UK-USA / United Artists / 1964 / Color / 91 minutes

Director: Walter E. Grauman

Cast: Cliff Robertson, George Chakiris, Maria Perschy, Harry Andrews, Donald Houston, Michael Goodliffe, John Meillon, John Bonney, Angus Lennie

Synopsis / Aviation Content: RAF Mosquitos are sent on a daring mission against a German fuel plant located in a Norwegian Fjord. Based on the 1956 novel of the same name by British author Frederick E. Smith. This quintessential Mosquito film is also highly regarded as one of the best British aviation films. Superb views of the classic Mossie with sound to match; highlights include a start-up sequence featuring many Mosquito angles and close-ups. The film was a timely undertaking, as the Mosquito had just retired from RAF service, saving the production from expensive rebuilds, spares procurement and mock-up construction—several complete aircraft were simply destroyed during filming! Composer Ron Goodwin's unforgettable music score has since become a classic war and aviation theme.

Over 7,600 of DeHavilland's "wooden wonder" were built, with the Mosquito B.Mk. 35 being the last glass-nosed bomber version for the RAF. All nine used in the film had, by 1963, been converted to **Mosquito TT.Mk. 35** target-tugs in service with No. 3 CAACU at Exeter in Devon. The two Mk. III Mossies were also with No. 3 CAACU. Notably, the last official flyby before the RAF retired the Mosquito was performed on May 9, 1963, by six aircraft: TW117, RS709, RS712, TA634, TA639 and TA719. Five of these immediately went on to fly in *633 Squadron*, with TA634 later appearing in *Mosquito Squadron* (1968). Of the flying Mossies, TW117 and TA639 were loaned to the film by the RAF and retained their RAF serial numbers for flying. RS709, RS712 and TA719 were owned by and civilian registered to Mirisch Films Ltd., the company making the movie. TA719 was actually re-engined with two zero-time Rolls Royce Merlins and was used to fly all the low-level fjord scenes. The new Merlins provided a clear safety margin in the narrow valleys and surrounding cliffs around Lake Morar in the west of Scotland.

The TT.Mk. 35 featured the entry hatch on the belly of the fuselage and had a V-shaped windscreen, as opposed to the Mk. III, which had a

Type	msn	Military s/n	Civil reg.	Film Markings
Flying Aircraft				
DeHavilland Mosquito T.Mk. III	—	TW117	—	HR155 / HT-M
DeHavilland Mosquito B.Mk. 35	—	RS709	G-ASKA	HR113 / HT-D and HJ898 / HT-G
DeHavilland Mosquito B.Mk. 35	—	RS712	G-ASKB	RF580 / HT-F
DeHavilland Mosquito B.Mk. 35	—	TA639	—	HJ682 / HT-B
DeHavilland Mosquito B.Mk. 35	—	TA719	G-ASKC	HJ898 / HT-G
Miles Messenger Mk. 2A	6378	—	G-AKBO	—
Nord 1002 Pingouin II	188	—	F-BFYX	14
Nord 1002 Pingouin II	264	—	F-BGVU	—
North American B-25J-25-NC Mitchell	108-34136	44-30861	N9089Z	N908
Taxi / Ground Aircraft				
DeHavilland Mosquito T.Mk. III	—	TV959	—	MM398 / HT-P & HT-A
DeHavilland Mosquito B.Mk. 35	—	RS718	—	HJ662 / HT-C HJ898 / HT-G
DeHavilland Mosquito B.Mk. 35	—	TA642	—	HJ898 / HT-G
DeHavilland Mosquito B.Mk. 35	—	TA724	—	HJ862 / HT-B & HT-R
Studio Aircraft				
DeHavilland Mosquito B.Mk. 35	—	RS715	—	—
DeHavilland Mosquito B.Mk. 35	—	TJ118	—	—

side entry hatch and flat-faced windscreen. The four TT.Mk. 35 Mossies had their glass noses painted over with dummy machine guns added in order to replicate the Mosquito FB.Mk. VI variant depicted in the film.

Mossie TV959 was used at RAF Bovingdon for exterior cockpit shots, and the tail section can be seen on Bovingdon field in one scene. RS718 and TA724 were background aircraft at Bovingdon and later destroyed for the film—RS718 in an undercarriage failure sequence and TA724 by driving it into a fuel truck. TA642 was destroyed for the final scene by burning it in a field outside at MGM-British Studios. Mossies RS715 and TJ118 were cut up for interior cockpit scenes at MGM-British Studios in Hertfordshire. The wings of TJ118 can be seen on jacks at the start of a German strafing sequence at Bovingdon Field.

The Miles M.38 Messenger was a 1942 RAF liaison aircraft. The one used in the film (in the opening sequence) was a Mk. 2A, a post–World War II civil version built in limited numbers. The French built Nord 1002 Pingouin II (French: *Penguin*), is a post–World War II license built version of the 1934 German built Messerschmitt Bf 108 Taifun (German: *Typhoon*). These two aircraft were painted in military colors and flew in the film as Messerschmitt Bf 109 fighter stand-ins. Both Nords went to the U.S. after filming as N107U (msn 264; crashed en route) and N108U (msn 188; FAA lists as "88"). The B-25J flew in the UK with its U.S. registered number and served as both the film's camera-plane and also in a cameo appearance as a fictional RAF transport.

The technical advisor was Group Captain T.G. Mahaddie, who was also tasked with gathering the Mosquito aircraft together from the RAF. Captain John Crewdson's Film Aviation Services Ltd. provided the pilots, which were Crewdson himself, Flt Lt John "Jeff" Hawke, Sqn Ldr Graham "Taffy" Rich, Capt. Peter Warden, and Flt Lt Chick Kirkham. Mossies TW117 and TA719 were used for the pilots' type-rating course. John Hawke and Michael Caiden flew the Nords with Neville Browning flying the Miles aircraft. Much use was made of 1:48 scale models for the combat action and crash sequences. Director Walter Grauman was a USAAF B-25 pilot during World War II. Actor Cliff Robertson was a sportsman pilot who owned several aircraft, including a Tiger Moth and Spitfire (MK923).

Filmed on location at RAF Bovingdon, Hertfordshire, England. The flying shots were done in the Glencoe Highlands, Scotland, which also doubled for the Norwegian fjords in the attack sequences. Interiors and cockpit scenes were filmed at MGM-British Studios, Borehamwood, Hertfordshire, England. Filming began late July 1963 and continued until September that same year.

GPS Location

RAF Bovingdon, Hertfordshire (closed 1972): N51 43.60 / W000 32.70

Sky Bandits   see   *Gunbus*

Sky Bride

USA / Paramount Pictures / 1932 / B&W / 78 minutes

Director: Stephen Roberts

Cast: Richard Arlen, Jack Oakie, Robert Coogan, Virginia Bruce, Tom Douglas, Louise Closser Hale, Harold Goodwin, Charles Starrett

Synopsis / Aviation Content: A reckless barnstorming pilot causes the death of a fellow flyer and swears to never fly again, until he's called upon to rescue a young boy. Stunt pilot Leo Nomis was killed before cast and crew when a spin stunt went wrong at Metropolitan Airport in Los Angeles. He was a veteran stunt flyer of *The Dawn Patrol* (1930), *Hell's Angels* (1930) and *The Lost Squadron* (1932). This film also featured other notable stunt pilots such as Frank Clarke and Dick Grace.

Sky Devils

USA / United Artists / 1932 / B&W / 90 minutes

Director: A. Edward Sutherland

Cast: Spencer Tracy, William Boyd, George Cooper, Ann Dvorak, Billy Bevan, Yola d'Avril

Synopsis / Aviation Content: A comedy set during World War I in which supposed flyers Tracy and Cooper will do anything to avoid the draft. Filmed at Metropolitan Airport, Van Nuys,

California, with several **Thomas-Morse S-4 Scout** biplanes. Notable as having been produced by enigmatic aviator and filmmaker Howard Hughes, who dragged out mountains of stock footage from his earlier epic *Hell's Angels* (1930) to fill out the flying scenes. A similar approach was done for Hughes's other 1932 aviation film *Cock of the Air*. (Non–Aviation Themed Title)

Skyfall   see   *James Bond* Series

Skyjacked

Television Title: **Sky Terror**
USA / Metro-Goldwyn-Mayer / 1972 / Color / 100 minutes
Director: John Guillermin
Cast: Charlton Heston, Yvette Mimieux, James Brolin, Claude Akins, Jeanne Crain, Susan Dey, Roosevelt Grier
Synopsis / Aviation Content: A disturbed Vietnam vet played by Brolin hijacks a 707 flight and forces it to fly to Russia. Probably one of the better entries in the air-disaster genre provides some tense moments, but the overall result falls somewhat flat. Based on the 1970 novel *Hijacked* by American author David Harper. Some fantastic views of the Boeing 707, both taxiing and in-flight, with colorful, sharp aerial photography to boot. And who else but Heston has the style to light a pipe before gunning the four giant Pratt & Whitney engines!

Generously provided to the filmmakers was a Series 300C Boeing 707, N374WA, of U.S. airline World Airways, which is extensively used throughout the film both on the ground and in air-to-air filming. This 707 first flew on August 9, 1963, and was delivered to World Airways on August 20 the same year. It then went to Saudi Airlines as HZ-ACF in August 1973; then to TAAG Angola as D2-TAG in July 1978; re-registered with Angola as D2-TOG in May 1980; to Angola Air Charter in 1988; and finally scrapped at Manston, England, in 1991.

Five North American F-100C Super Sabre fighters double as Russian MiG fighters for one sequence. These aircraft came from the Air National Guard's 150th TFW and 188th TFS, and were filmed over northern New Mexico and Colorado. S/n 54-1753 was used as a standby fighter with only four of the "MiG doubles" ever seen in the film at any one time.

There are several shots of actor Charlton He-

Five F-100C Super Sabre fighters were provided by the New Mexico ANG to double as Russian MiGs for the 1972 film *Skyjacked*. Photograph: James H. Farmer Collection.

Type	msn	Military s/n	Civil reg.
Boeing 707-373C	18583/346	—	N374WA
North American F-100C-1-NA Super Sabre	214-045	54-1753	—
North American F-100C-5-NA Super Sabre	217-064	54-1803	—
North American F-100C-25-NA Super Sabre	217-304	54-2043	—
North American F-100C-25-NA Super Sabre	217-317	54-2056	—
North American F-100C-25-NA Super Sabre	217-345	54-2084	—

ston in the pilot's seat during aerial photography with the 707. The camera-plane was Tallmantz Aviation's rarely used Douglas A-26C Invader (s/n 44-35505 / reg. N4815E). Filmed in part at Oakland Intl. Airport, San Francisco, California.

Sky Pirates

Alternate Title: **Dakota Harris**
Australia-USA / Roadshow Entertainment / 1986 / Color / 89 minutes
Director: Colin Eggleston
Cast: John Hargreaves, Meredith Phillips, Max Phipps, Bill Hunter, Simon Chilvers, Alex Scott, David Parker, Adrian Wright
Synopsis / Aviation Content: A World War II C-47 pilot gets caught up in a wild adventure while transporting a mysterious cargo. From high adventure to science fiction, some time traveling, then sharks and the supernatural, this picture appears to have been influenced by every single Spielberg production made up to the mid–'80s! The only aeronautical attributes are some varied scenes of several Aussie Warbird types and an interesting aerial C-47 wing-walking stunt!

P-51 Mustang VH-BOB and VH-AUB are both ex–RAAF Australian built Mustangs delivered during 1947 and sold onto the civilian market in 1958. VH-AUB was owned by Aussie Warbird collector Col Pay. Dakota VH-DAS was non-flying and used in a mock-up crash scene marked as "6903007." VH-PWM is ex–RAAF s/n A65-21 and served as the flying aircraft in the film doing the wing-walk stunt; it later went to New Zealand as reg. ZK-AMR with Fieldair Freight Ltd. VH-MMF is ex–RAAF s/n A65-41 and was another non-flying example marked as "6903077 / B5." The Grumman Mallard was a privately operated aircraft in Australia at the time of filming.

The B-25J was hired from Aero Heritage, Inc., of Melbourne, Australia, with former U.S. reg. N8196H. Filming with these aircraft took place from May to June 1984.

Sky Riders

USA / 20th Century–Fox / 1976 / Color / 93 minutes
Director: Douglas Hickox
Cast: James Coburn, Susannah York, Robert Culp, Charles Aznavour, Harry Andrews, John Beck
Synopsis / Aviation Content: The wife and children of a wealthy industrialist are kidnapped by terrorists and held for ransom in a mountaintop monastery; a daring aerial rescue ensues, utilizing hang-gliders. Great locations and fantastic flying sequences filmed over the picturesque Meteora Monasteries in Greece add interest to this otherwise routine action yarn. Appearances by a **Bell 206B Jet Ranger**, **Canadair CL-215**, and a **Sud-Aviation SA.316B Alouette III** (reg. SX-HAC / msn 1509) helicopter.

Sky Terror see *Skyjacked*

The Skywayman

USA / Fox Film Corp. / 1920 / B&W / duration unknown
Director: James P. Hogan
Cast: Ormer Locklear, Louise Lovely, Sam De-Grasse, Ted McCann, Jack Brammall
Synopsis / Aviation Content: A former World War I pilot returns home with amnesia, and his girlfriend then hatches a plan to restore his memory. Silent-era film features the old barnstorming favorite, the **Curtiss JN-4 Jenny** biplane, performing a myriad of aerial stunts. No known prints of this film survive today, but the movie is immortalized as the one that claimed the life of Hollywood's first stunt man, Ormer Locklear. Locklear and fellow stunt flyer Milton Elliot were killed on August 2, 1920, near

Type	msn	Military s/n	civil reg.
CAC Mustang Mk. 21	1429	(RAAF) A68-104	VH-BOB
CAC Mustang Mk. 21	1432	(RAAF) A68-107	VH-AUB
Douglas C-47-DL Skytrain	6051	41-38668	VH-DAS
Douglas C-47A-1-DK Skytrain	11970	42-92196	VH-PWM
Douglas C-47A-10-DK Skytrain	12540	42-92709	VH-MMF
Grumman G-73 Mallard	J-22	—	VH-LAW
North American B-25J-30-NC Mitchell	108-47545	44-86791	VH-XXV

DeMille Field while performing a stunt in a Jenny which failed to pull out of a spin. As was often the case in those days, candid drama of any kind captured in camera was quickly capitalized on, and the grim, fiery spin into the ground was boldly used in final release prints and marketed as such! The stunt flying performed by Locklear, including his previous film *The Great Air Robbery* (1919), helped cement the extensive role aircraft would play in future film productions.

Skyway to Glory　see　*Pilot #5*

Slattery's Hurricane

USA / 20th Century–Fox / 1949 / B&W / 87 minutes
Director: Andre De Toth
Cast: Richard Widmark, Linda Darnell, Veronica Lake, John Russell, Gary Merrill, Walter Kingsford
Synopsis / Aviation Content: Former navy pilot Widmark enjoys the chauffeur piloting lifestyle until he enters into an adulterous affair, then discovers he's smuggling drugs. He attempts to redeem himself by flying into an approaching hurricane to provide valuable weather updates. Based on a story created by American author Herman Wouk, who later adapted it into a novel published in 1956. Aircraft were the **Consolidated-Vultee PB4Y-2M Privateer** of weather reconnaissance Squadron VP-23 filmed in Miami, Florida, at Master Field, which was a part of NAS Miami. Also used was a privately owned **Grumman G-73 Mallard** (reg. N2975 / msn J-39) amphibian. There's a brief shot of an American Airlines DC-6 doubling as a MATS C-54! Notably, the U.S. Navy was so proud of the finished film, they previewed it to guests onboard one of their giant Lockheed XR6O-1 Constitution cargo plane prototypes while flying over New York.

Smithy

U.S. Title: *Pacific Adventure*
UK Title: *Southern Cross*

Australia / Columbia Pictures / 1946 / B&W / 118 minutes
Director: Ken G. Hall
Cast: Ron Randell, Muriel Steinbeck, John Tate, Joy Nichols, Nan Taylor, John Dunne, Alec Kellaway, John Dease, Marshall Crosby
Synopsis / Aviation Content: Biographical film following the pioneering achievements of Australian aviator Charles Kingsford-Smith during the late 1920s and early 1930s. The main aircraft that Smithy used for his record flights was the *Southern Cross*, a three-engined **Fokker F.VIIb/3m** (reg. NC1985 / msn 4954). In something of a rarity in aviation films, this original aircraft actually played itself in the final film!

Initially built for an Arctic expedition in 1926 by Australian George Hubert Wilkins, the Fokker was then sold to Kingsford-Smith after a crash in Alaska, registered with U.S. reg. NC1985. Kingsford-Smith furnished the aircraft for his record flight attempt from the United States across the Pacific Ocean to Australia. After this historic feat, the *Southern Cross*, as the Fokker had come to be named, was re-registered in Australia as G-AUSU in July 1928, and VH-USU from April 1931. Smithy donated the *Southern Cross* to Australia in September 1935, and it was put on public display. It was brought out of retirement in 1945 and restored to flying condition for the motion picture by RAAF mechanics. The aircraft flew in the film with its VH-USU reg., as opposed to the more correct "1985" U.S. registration. The *Southern Cross* made its last flight in 1950 and was then stored before going back on public display from 1958. The aircraft now resides in a purpose-built memorial hangar near Brisbane Airport. The tri-motor Fokker F.VII was built as an airliner by Dutch aircraft manufacturer Fokker from 1924 to 1932.

Other aircraft are an Australian-built **Commonwealth CA-13 Boomerang**, which doubles as Kingsford-Smith's Lockheed Altair *Lady Southern Cross*; a **Bristol Tourer** (reg. G-AUDX); and a **Consolidated B-24J Liberator** seen in a flashback scene at the top of the film.

Released in the U.S. at 95 minutes in 1947 as *Pacific Adventure* with all Australian references deleted, including scenes with former Australian

Prime Minister W.M. Hughes, who played himself in the film. An Australian television miniseries was produced in 1985 titled *A Thousand Skies*, starring John Walton as Kingsford-Smith.

FACTUAL BACKGROUND: AUSTRALIA'S PIONEER AVIATOR

Charles Edward Kingsford-Smith (February 9, 1897–November 8, 1935), also known by his nickname Smithy, was an early Australian pioneering aviator who set numerous aviation records in the Pacific and South Pacific regions. Kingsford-Smith became a pilot in the Royal Flying Corps in 1917 but was soon shot down and sustained injuries, losing a large part of his left foot. He transferred to the new Royal Air Force in April 1918. After World War I, Smithy continued flying in England and did barnstorming in the U.S. before returning to Australia in 1921. He became one of Australia's first airline pilots in 1921, flying for West Australia Airways. The following pioneering flights and records were made by Charles Kingsford-Smith:

First Trans-Pacific Flight (East-West)

Oakland, California, May 31, 1928—Brisbane, Australia, June 9, 1928.
Fokker F.VII *Southern Cross* with Charles Ulm, James Warner, Harry Lyon.
Made two stops, in Hawaii and Fiji.

First Trans-Australia Flight

Melbourne to Perth in August 1928 in the *Southern Cross*.

First Trans-Tasman Flight

Sydney, Australia, September 10, 1928—Christchurch, New Zealand, September 11, 1928.
Fokker F.VII *Southern Cross* with Charles Ulm, H.A. Litchfield, T.H. Williams.

England to Australia Air Race

1930—won it, setting a new record of 10.5 days.

First Trans-Pacific Flight (West-East)

Brisbane, Australia, October 21, 1934—Oakland, California, November 4, 1934.
Lockheed Altair *Lady Southern Cross* (VH-USB), with Patrick Taylor.
Made two stops, in Fiji and Hawaii.

In 1931 Kingsford-Smith purchased an Avro Avian, which he named *Southern Cross Minor*. He also made the first commercial flight between Australia and New Zealand in 1933. The pioneering aviator disappeared, along with copilot Tommy Pethybridge, over the Sea of Burma on November 8, 1935, while attempting an England-to-Australia speed record in the *Lady Southern Cross*. No trace of the flight was ever found except for an undercarriage strut widely believed to be from his aircraft.

Snakes on a Plane

USA / New Line Cinema / 2006 / Color / 105 minutes
Director: David R. Ellis
Cast: Samuel L. Jackson, Julianna Margulies, Nathan Phillips, Rachel Blanchard, Flex Alexander, Kenan Thompson, Keith Dallas
Synopsis / Aviation Content: FBI Agent Jackson must escort a witness from Hawaii to Los Angeles to testify against a gangster who's placed a large number of venomous snakes on their plane in order to stop them from reaching court. There's enough crowd pleasing, snake-killing gags to make you forget about the ludicrous plot, and yes, as usual, the pilots get killed, leaving no one to fly the plane. Aircraft is a Boeing 747-400 airliner created in a film studio for interiors and CGI effects for in-flight shots.

Soldiers of Fortune   see   *You Can't Win 'Em All*

Soldiers of the Air   see   *Thunder Birds*

Solo

Australia-New Zealand / Greg Lynch Film Distributors / 1978 / Color / 96 minutes
Director: Tony Williams
Cast: Vincent Gil, Lisa Peers, Martyn Sanderson, Davina Whitehouse, Maxwell Fernie, Perry Armstrong
Synopsis / Aviation Content: This largely forgotten film is an interesting but slow romance drama about a passing female backpacker who starts

a relationship with a local forestry patrol pilot. Contains some outstanding aerial photography and piloting with a **Cessna 172M Skyhawk** (reg. ZK-DXO / msn 172-65417) owned by Geyserland Airways, plus a **DeHavilland DH.82A Tiger Moth** (reg. ZK-BCZ / msn DHNZ155) owned and flown by pilot Bill Dittmer. This particular Moth (s/n NZ1475) was one of many built in New Zealand by DeHavilland as trainers for the RNZAF. Struck off military charge in 1956, it entered civil ownership in 1957. Actors Vincent Gil and Martyn Sanderson both took basic flying lessons prior to filming. Filmed in February and March 1977, mainly around the forests of Tokoroa in the North Island of New Zealand, it's a definite must-see for any Tiger Moth fan—if you can locate a copy.

SOS Pacific

Alternate Title (U.S.): *S.O.S. Pacific*
UK / The Rank Organisation / 1959 / B&W / 90 minutes
Director: Guy Green
Cast: Richard Attenborough, Pier Angeli, John Gregson, Eva Bartok, Eddie Constantine, Gunnar Moller, Jean Anderson
Synopsis / Aviation Content: After a civilianized Catalina is forced to ditch in the Pacific Ocean, the survivors take refuge on a nearby island, where they soon discover all is not what it seems. This highly rated but rare drama features a **Consolidated PBY-5A Catalina** (BuNo. 48397 / msn 1759), provided by wealthy industrialist Thomas W. Kendall, and registered as N5593V. Kendall purchased the amphibian from NAS Litchfield Park, Arizona, in 1956, and after providing it to the film, he converted it into a luxury flying yacht in 1959. He then set off with his family on a round-the-world trip. During a stopover at the mouth to the Gulf of Aqaba off Saudi Arabia on March 23, 1960, the Catalina was attacked by Saudi Bedouins who mistook them for Israeli commandos. In the panic, they tried to take off, but the Cat ran aground in some shallows. Kendall and his fam-

ily were taken to Jedda as detainees but were eventually released with help from an American ambassador. N5593V was unable to be salvaged and remains where it went aground over fifty years ago. Filmed in the Canary Islands, Spain, which doubles for the Pacific in the film.

The Sound Barrier

U.S. Titles: *Breaking the Sound Barrier; Breaking Through the Sound Barrier*
UK / British Lion Film Corp. / 1952 / B&W / 118 minutes
Director: David Lean
Cast: Ralph Richardson, Ann Todd, Nigel Patrick, John Justin, Dinah Sheridan, Joseph Tomelty, Denholm Elliott
Synopsis / Aviation Content: A fictional film concerning an English aircraft manufacturer's attempts to break the sound barrier at any cost to man or machine. Although not an accurate account of the events that led to the breaking of the sound barrier by the UK, there are plenty of period British aircraft in a sharp black and white film with lots of jet noise!

Type	msn	Military s/n	Civil reg.
Avro 652A Anson Mk. I	—	(RAF) N9948	—
DeHavilland DH.82A Tiger Moth	3861	(RAF) N6548	G-AHRM
DeHavilland DH.106 Comet 1	06002	—	G-ALZK
DeHavilland DH.106 Comet 1	06004	—	G-ALYR
DeHavilland DH.113 Vampire NF.10	13005	(RAF) WP232	—
Supermarine Attacker F.1	unknown	(RAF) WA485	—
Supermarine Type 517 Swift	unknown	(RAF) VV119	—

The Avro Anson is seen briefly at the top of the film as a staff transport. Tiger Moth G-AHRM was used as Denholm Elliott's training aircraft, and a wreck was later substituted for the crash scene. Early Comet 1 G-ALZK was the second Comet prototype built and is used for the Egypt departure scene. Comet 1 G-ALYR is briefly seen in the Egypt arrival scene; this aircraft was damaged beyond repair in Calcutta in 1953 and scrapped. The twin-seater Vampire, WP232, was used in the UK-to-Egypt travel sequence. Supermarine Attacker WA485 was a 1946 British naval fighter design used in the film as the fictional 901 prototype. In all, 183 were built and served from 1951 to 1954. They featured a tail-wheel undercarriage design that made carrier operations impractical, hence their short service life. The Supermarine Type 517 Swift, VV119, was a 1948 prototype and the first British fighter to feature swept wings and tail; 197 were built, with service from 1954 into the 1970s. It was used in the film as the second 902 prototype named *Prometheus*—the Greek mythological figure who brought fire to mankind.

Background aircraft are a **DeHavilland DH.89 Dragon Rapide**, **Douglas DC-3**, **Gloster Meteor III**, **Handley-Page Hermes**, and a group of **Hawker Sea Fury FB.11** fighters (one was s/n VW560). A late-model **Supermarine Spitfire**, with clipped wings, was used for the opening sequence.

The aerial unit director was Anthony Squire. One of the technical advisors was renowned British test pilot and World War II ace John Cunningham, who flew one of the original DH.108 test aircraft (*see below*), which was the first British aircraft to break the sound barrier. Camera-planes were an Avro Lancaster and Vickers Valetta.

Filming took place at Chilbolton Aerodrome, Chilbolton, Hampshire, England (GPS location: N51 08.40 / W001 26.50), a former World War II airfield used as a test facility by Supermarine from 1947 to 1957. Filming also took place at actual DeHavilland and Hawker factories. Interiors and cockpit scenes were filmed at Shepperton Studios, Surrey, England.

FACTUAL BACKGROUND: THE BRITISH EFFORT TO BREAK THE SOUND BARRIER

The speed of sound was first broken by American pilot Chuck Yeager in the Bell X-1 (s/n 46-062) above Edwards AFB, California, on October 14, 1947. British attempts at breaking the sound barrier had begun in 1942 with the Miles M.52, but the project was abandoned. Tests continued with three DeHavilland DH.108 Swallow experimental aircraft, the sound barrier finally being broken by John Derry on September 9, 1949, in DH.108 (RAF s/n VW120). An earlier DH.108 (RAF s/n TG306) was lost due to structural failure over the Thames Estuary on September 27, 1946, during high-speed tests. The pilot, Geoffrey DeHavilland Jr., the son of famed aircraft manufacturer Geoffrey DeHavilland, was

killed instantly. It's this event on which the film is loosely based. Renowned British aviator John Cunningham then took over as chief test pilot.

Southern Cross see *Smithy*

The Spirit of St. Louis

USA / Warner Bros. / 1957 / Color / 135 minutes

Director: Billy Wilder

Cast: James Stewart, Murray Hamilton, Patricia Smith, Bartlett Robinson, Marc Connelly, Arthur Space, Charles Watts

Synopsis / Aviation Content: Accurate, in-depth story of pioneer aviator Charles Lindbergh's 1927 nonstop trans-Atlantic flight. Spectacular aerials with amazing, flyable Ryan NYP replicas and a convincing, passionate performance from Stewart, make this one of the favorites for many aviation enthusiasts. A true, timeless classic with just the right mix of humor and drama that keeps you watching right to the end. Based on the Pulitzer Prize–winning 1953 book of the same name written by Lindbergh himself.

Type	msn	Civil reg.	Film Markings
Curtiss JN-4 Jenny	396	N5391 *	—
Curtiss JN-4C Canuck	1898	N10389 *	—
Curtiss JN-4D Jenny	400	N2821D *	—
Curtiss JN-4D Jenny	47502	N6899 *	—
DeHavilland DH.4M-1	ET-4	N3258	110 / U.S. Air Mail
Ryan B-1 Brougham	153	N7206	N-X-211
Ryan B-1 Brougham	156	N7209	N-X-211
Ryan B-1 Brougham	159	N7212	N-X-211
Standard J-1	1582	N2825D	—
Standard J-1	1598	N2826D	—

* Likely used but not confirmed.

Hollywood pilot Paul Mantz and his company Paul Mantz Air Services of Santa Ana, California, acquired and modified two Ryan NYP replicas from original 1927 Ryan B-1 airframes. Reg. N7206 was purchased from an employee at the McDonnell Aircraft factory in St. Louis, Missouri, and reg. N7212 came from an owner in Moscow, Idaho, where it had been used to ferry hunters into nearby mountains. Both aircraft were completely rebuilt and completed in *Spirit* fashion, then sent to Europe for the French countryside scenes. They were transported there by the USAF in a Douglas C-124C Globemaster II (s/n 51-5196). Mantz also acquired six 220-hp Wright J5 Whirlwind engines, which were rebuilt into four zero-time engines for the replicas (including the third aircraft), with a spare just in case. N7206 is now preserved with the Missouri Historical Society in Missouri. N7212 is now with the Cradle of Aviation Museum in New York.

A third replica, reg. N7209, was purchased derelict from a private owner by pilot W.H. "Hank" Coffin and film actor James Stewart. It was restored to flying condition by Coffin and his team of mechanics in Pacoima, California, and used for the U.S. coastal scenes filmed from a Beechcraft AT-11 and Stinson L-1 camera-plane. Actor James Stewart actually flew N7209 on occasion to help get himself into the role of Lindbergh. He spent many hours leaning out the side windows just as the pioneer aviator had done, which gave him an insight into just how Lindbergh moved and flew. In 1959, Stewart donated this *Spirit* replica to the Henry Ford Museum in Michigan, where it remains to this day.

For safety, each of the three replicas had the original forward-looking cockpit position retained, which was then covered over with a metal plate to resemble the actual *Spirit* when filming commenced. Also built for the film's studio-based scenes of Stewart in the cockpit was a nine-tenth scale mock-up of the *Spirit* that could be suspended and rocked around to simulate flying.

UNCONFIRMED DATA

One source quotes Ryan B-1 Brougham (reg. N7671 / msn 163), as being converted for use in the film but there's no subsequent evidence for this. There's a chance, it might have been acquired as parts for the studio-based mock-up but this is only speculation.

Paul Mantz Air Services also provided additional vintage biplane aircraft for the production. Stewart's mail plane seen near the top of the picture was Mantz's own DeHavilland DH.4, N3258, marked as "110 / U.S. Air Mail."

Mantz also acquired two Standard J-1 biplanes for the scenes of Lindbergh's early life. Both were completely rebuilt, with Mantz employing the tal-

ents of renowned aircraft designer Otto Timm, who, incidentally, gave Charles Lindbergh himself his first airplane ride in Lincoln, Nebraska, in 1921. Both aircraft remained with Mantz afterward and appeared in many subsequent motion pictures. Rumor has it Lindbergh visited Timm while these restorations were underway and during that visit Lindbergh actually flew N2825D. The Standards were used in the film, firstly in the scene where Stewart is teaching the priest to fly; then one was painted blue and marked as "Fly with Bud Gurney." Both were used in the circus stunt sequence marked as "Daredevil Lindbergh" and "Capt. Gurni."

Up to four Curtiss JN-4 Jenny biplanes were provided by Mantz for various scenes. Firstly, all four were used in the scene where Stewart purchases his first airplane; then one appears in the montage of Stewart offering various rides marked as "Sky Rides Spectacular! Safe!" Finally, all four are seen in the Brooks Army Airfield sequence. Although Mantz owned in his collection the four Jennys listed above, the actual use of these aircraft in the film remains unconfirmed. The JN-4C Canuck is the Canadian-built version.

Period newsreel footage of Lindbergh's return to New York was used at the end of the picture. Some use of airplane models and miniatures in certain scenes. Filmed from August 1955 to May 1956 in and around the coast of California, which doubled as the United States' eastern seaboard. The takeoff scene was shot near Santa Maria Airport, California, which doubled for Roosevelt Field, New York, using *Spirit* replica N7209. Also filmed in various parts of France, including Paris, plus Ireland and Newfoundland in Canada.

In 1967, a fourth Ryan NYP replica was built for the 40th anniversary of the Lindbergh flight, to be held at the Paris Airshow. Construction was under the supervision of Frank Tallman at Tallmantz Aviation, Inc. It was registered as N1967T (msn TM-3), and first flew on April 24, 1967, named *Spirit 2*. Although often mistaken for one of the film's aircraft, it is, of course, not. This fine replica aircraft was destroyed in a fire in 1978.

FACTUAL BACKGROUND:
THE SPIRIT OF ST. LOUIS

Charles Augustus Lindbergh (February 4, 1902–August 26, 1974) completed his pioneering feat

The replica Ryan NYP seen here is most likely not a star of the 1957 film *The Spirit of St. Louis* but a replica built in 1967 by Tallmantz for the 50th anniversary of the flight. It was registered as N1967T. Photograph: James H. Farmer Collection.

in a modified 1927 Ryan monoplane, which was a special design developed from the 1926 Ryan M-1 and 1927 Ryan B-1 Brougham aircraft then in production. Lindbergh's aircraft carried the Ryan Aeronautical Co. construction number 30. It was named *Spirit of St. Louis* in honor of Lindbergh's financial backers from St. Louis, Missouri. The most distinguishing feature was the sealed-off front windscreen and aft-moved cockpit. This was done in order to house the massive 450 gallons of fuel required for the trip, the tanks of which had to be manually changed by Lindbergh hourly in order to keep the aircraft balanced. Lindbergh departed on his pioneering trip from Roosevelt Field, Long Island, New York, on May 20, 1927, at 7:52 a.m. local time. He arrived at Le Bourget Aerodrome in Paris on May 21, 1927, at 10:22 p.m. local time—a total flight duration of 33 hours 30 minutes 29.8 seconds. Lindbergh had not slept in fifty-five hours. The Ryan NYP (New York-Paris), as it was known, first flew on April 28, 1927, and last flew on April 30, 1928. It now rests at the Smithsonian National Air and Space Museum in Washington, D.C. Lindbergh died from cancer in 1974 and is buried on the island of Maui, Hawaii.

Spitfire   see   *The First of the Few*

The Spy Who Loved Me (Non–Aviation Themed Title)   see   *James Bond* Series

Stairway to Heaven   see   *A Matter of Life and Death*

The Starfighters

USA / Parade Releasing Organization / 1964 / Color / 78 minutes

Director: Will Zens

Cast: Robert Dornan, Richard Jordahl, Shirley Olmsted, Richard Masters, Robert Winston, Steve Early, Ralph Thomas, Carl Rogers

Synopsis / Aviation Content: A nowadays much-forgotten film concerning a young fighter pilot training on the F-104 Starfighter and his father's insistence he follow in his footsteps and become a bomber pilot. Very low production values (was it shot in 16mm?), bad acting and lounge-room music for a score, but it does actually have one thing going for it—a wealth of superb footage displaying the F-104 both on the ground and in the air. Obviously of great interest to F-104 fans, if you can find a copy.

Ground, taxi, takeoff, midair refueling, target practice and flying scenes were all filmed using the **Lockheed F-104 Starfighter** based out of George AFB, Victorville, California. Much of the footage looks like it was opportunistic, simply filmed during daily base operations, as opposed to aircraft being provided to the filmmakers as such. Noted buzz numbers include those for F-104A: FG-735 (56-0735); F-104C: FG-902 (56-0902), FG-904 (56-0904), FG-908 (56-0908), FG-909 (56-0909), FG-911 (56-0911 or 57-0911), FG-921 (57-0921), FG-925 (56-0925 or 57-0925), FG-932 (56-0932), FG-938 (56-0938), and the two-seater F-104D: FG-331 (s/n 57-1331). A two-seater was provided to the filmmakers in order to shoot onboard material and gather air-to-air shots. Other featured aircraft were a **Boeing KC-135A Stratotanker** and a **Kaman HH-43B Huskie** (s/n 59-1580 / msn 61) base rescue helicopter. Director Will Zens, who also produced and wrote the screenplay, served as a test pilot during World War II with the USAAF.

Stealth

USA / Columbia Pictures / 2005 / Color / 121 minutes
Director: Rob Cohen
Cast: Josh Lucas, Jessica Biel, Jamie Foxx, Sam Shepard, Joe Morton, Richard Roxburgh
Synopsis / Aviation Content: In the near future, naval aviation takes a leap forward with the introduction of an "artificial intelligence"–based stealth fighter, which, for better or worse, soon develops a mind of its own.

Racy film has much action and pace, but most of the aviation scenes are fictionally based and CGI-created, making this better suited to a science fiction audience rather than an aviation one.

The fictional stealth fighter aircraft were, firstly, the "F/A-37 Talon," which were three service test aircraft flown by the main characters. The design is loosely based on the real-life 1999 Northrop-Grumman "Switchblade" prototype proposal, featuring forward-sweeping wings. The other is the "UCAV EDI" (Unmanned Combat Aerial Vehicle—Extreme Deep Invader), a smaller, more agile stealth design flown by a computer with call sign "Tinman." Several full-scale mock-ups of

these rather convincing fictional aircraft were built and filmed on actual aircraft carriers. The film props were so real-looking, in fact, several members of the military and some media even reported they were new prototype fighters doing flight trials with the Navy! The last fictional aircraft was the Russian "Sukhoi Su-37 Terminator," based on the real-life Sukhoi Su-30 Flanker.

Although set on board the USS *Abraham Lincoln* (CVN-72), filming also took place onboard two other carriers—the USS *Carl Vinson* (CVN-70) and USS *John C. Stennis* (CVN-74), both of which doubled for the *Lincoln* in the finished film. Background aircraft were the **Boeing F/A-18 Hornet**, **Grumman E-2 Hawkeye**, and **Sikorsky SH-60 Seahawk**. The North Korean helicopters are firstly a **Eurocopter BK.117** marked as "163," and for the final scene, a **Mil Mi-8MTV-1 Hip** (reg. ER-MHZ / msn 96078), marked as "148" and provided by Heli-Harvest Ltd. of New Zealand. Background flying scenes were filmed with a Clay Lacey Learjet. Mainly filmed at Fox Studios in Sydney, Australia, during 2004.

The Story of Number 5   see Pilot #5

Strategic Air Command

USA / Paramount Pictures / 1955 / Color / 120 minutes
Director: Anthony Mann
Cast: James Stewart, June Allyson, Frank Lovejoy, Barry Sullivan, Alex Nicol, Bruce Bennett, Jay C. Flippen, James Millican, James Bell, Rosemary DeCamp
Synopsis / Aviation Content: Baseball star and ex–B-29 pilot Stewart is recalled to duty with the newly formed Strategic Air Command (SAC) to fill a gap in experienced bomber crews. Lengthy ground scenes are luckily made up for by a good cast and an exciting aerial climax. Aerial photography of the B-36 and B-47 bombers are incredible in widescreen, with the B-36 engine fire and crash sequence an excellent highlight. A definite must-see for all aviation fans. Story and screenplay co-written by Eighth Air Force veteran and renowned aviation writer Beirne Lay, Jr.

Type	msn	Military s/n	Civil reg.
Boeing XB-47-BO Stratojet	15972	46-065	—
Boeing B-47B-50-BW Stratojet	450371	51-2318	—
Convair B-36H-10-CF Peacemaker	222	51-5702	—
Convair B-36H-35-CF Peacemaker	286	51-5734	—
Douglas DC-3A-197B	2005	—	N18939

XB-47 (s/n 46-065) was the prototype B-47 that Stewart is shown in a closed hangar. For no apparent reason, it appears the "6" has been stenciled on the tail as a "9" to read "9065." This aircraft had been retired in 1954 and subsequently displayed at Palm Beach AFB, Florida, then scrapped. However, it is noted that the aircraft was dismantled for display, so whether it is the actual 46-065 isn't confirmed. B-36H (s/n 51-5702) was used to film Stewart's first orientation flight. B-36H (s/n 51-5734) was Stewart's assigned B-36 aircraft. B-47B (s/n 51-2318) was Stewart's bomber in the final scene. N18939 was used in the phony airbase raid at Carswell AFB and was owned at the time by Central Airlines. Note: this aircraft is an original DC-3A airliner with the starboard passenger door. It was first delivered to United Airlines with reg. NC18939.

Identified background aircraft are a B-47B-45-BW (s/n 51-2299 / msn 450352), B-47B-50-BW (s/n 51-2321 / msn 450374), B-47B-50-BW (s/n 51-2336 / msn 450389), B-36H-15-CF (s/n 51-5708 / msn 234), B-36H-25-CF (s/n 51-5721 / msn 260) and B-36J-1-CF (s/n 52-2216 / msn 357). Background aircraft include the **Boeing C/KC-97, Beechcraft C-45 Expeditor, Douglas C-124 Globemaster II, North American B-25 Mitchell, Lockheed T-33A Shooting Star,** and **Sikorsky HH-19.**

A B-36H studio mock-up was created for bomber interior scenes, which used real B-36 components including a real Peacemaker cockpit section. Aerial unit supervisor was Hollywood pilot Paul Mantz, filming from his B-25H camera-plane, reg. N1203. The B-36 scenes were shot at Carswell AFB, Texas, from April 1954, and the B-47 scenes were filmed at MacDill AFB, Florida.

GPS Locations

Carswell AFB, Texas: N32 46.15 / W097 25.55
MacDill AFB, Florida: N27 51.10 / W082 30.20

FACTUAL BACKGROUND: STRATEGIC AIR COMMAND

With World War II over and the new threat from an emerging Soviet Union and other Eastern Bloc countries, the USAAF was reorganized into three major commands on March 21, 1946: Air Defense Command (ADC), Tactical Air Command (TAC) and Strategic Air Command (SAC). SAC was in charge of America's long-range bomber force, all its nuclear capabilities and associated support requirements. The command really started to come into its own when General Curtis LeMay took control in 1948. Under his leadership SAC adopted new technology in the form of the jet engine, longer-range bombers, air-to-air refueling, strategic reconnaissance, and the development of the ballistic nuclear missile. Its role in defending the continental United States grew more important in the ever-evolving nuclear chess game with Russia. Bomber crews were on round-the-clock standby and a Boeing EC-135 command post was constantly airborne from 1961 to 1990. Following the collapse of the Soviet Union, SAC was disestablished on June 1, 1992, during a major restructuring by the USAF. For forty-six years SAC had been the iconic image of a Cold War America, with unlimited abilities to devastate any country in the world from U.S. home bases. Front line bombers were the Boeing B-29 / B-50 Superfortress (1946–1954), Convair B-36 Peacemaker (1948–1958), Boeing B-47 Stratojet (1950–1965), Boeing B-52 Stratofortress (1954–1992), Convair B-58 Hustler (1960–1969) and Rockwell B-1 Lancer (1985–1992). Major support aircraft included the Boeing KC-97 and KC-135 Stratotanker series (1951–1992) and the various Boeing RC/EC-135 reconnaissance and command aircraft.

Stunt Pilot

USA / Monogram Pictures / 1939 / B&W / 61 minutes
Director: George Waggner
Cast: John Trent, Marjorie Reynolds, Milburn Stone, Jason Robards Sr., Pat O'Malley, George Meeker
Synopsis / Aviation Content: The second in a

series of four feature films released in 1939 adapted from the Hal Forrest aviation comic strip *Tailspin Tommy* published from 1928 to 1942. In this story, Tommy must discover who is sabotaging aircraft being used for a World War I film production—it later turns out to be the director! A notable film solely for the large number of vintage aircraft provided by Hollywood stunt pilot Paul Mantz, most of which he had recently acquired for the Wellman air-epic *Men With Wings* (1938).

Featured aircraft include a **Boeing Model 247**; **Douglas DC-2 / DC-3** of TWA Airlines; **Fokker D.VII** (reg. N6268 / msn 504/17); **Lincoln-Garland LF-1** (as Nieuport 28); **Nieuport 28** (either N8539 or N4728V); **Royal Aircraft Factory S.E.5e** (likely N4488); **Ryan ST-A** (reg. NC16037 / msn 128); **SPAD VII** (reg. N4727V / msn S-248); **Stearman C3B** (reg. NC3357), plus two others; **Thomas-Morse S-4 Scout**; and **Travel-Air 2000/4000** "Wichita Fokker" conversions as Fokker D.VII biplanes. Some footage was also used from the Howard Hughes film *Hell's Angels* (1930).

The complete Tailspin Tommy series are *Tailspin Tommy* (1934; 12-part serial), *Tailspin Tommy in the Great Air Mystery* (1935; 12-part serial), and the feature films *Mystery Plane* (March 8, 1939), *Stunt Pilot* (July 1, 1939), *Sky Patrol* (September 12, 1939) and *Danger Flight* (November 1, 1939).

Such Men are Dangerous (Non–

Aviation Themed Title)

USA / Fox Film Corp. / 1930 / B&W / 83 minutes

Director: Kenneth Hawks

Cast: Warner Baxter, Catherine Dale Owen, Hedda Hopper, Claud Allister, Albert Conti, Bela Lugosi

Synopsis / Aviation Content: Drama about a wealthy financier who fakes his own death after his new wife runs out on him. Not an aviation film in the slightest, but worthy of inclusion here because this film is renowned for having the worst-yet air accident in film history. On January 2, 1930, while shooting a brief aerial sequence two miles off Redondo Beach, California, two Stinson aircraft collided in midair, killing ten of the film crew. Those onboard were the director Kenneth Hawks (brother of legendary director Howard Hawks), assistant director Max Gould, cameraman George Eastman, three other cameramen, two property men, and Stinson pilots Hal Rhouse and Ross Cooke.

Suicide Squadron   see *Dangerous Moonlight*

The Survivor

Australia / Greater Union Organisation (GUO) / 1981 / Color / 99 minutes

Director: David Hemmings

Cast: Robert Powell, Jenny Agutter, Joseph Cotten, Angela Punch-McGregor, Peter Sumner, Lorna Lesley, Ralph Cotterill

Synopsis / Aviation Content: A supernatural thriller with Powell playing an airline captain who is "seemingly" the only survivor after his aircraft crashes into a residential area after take-off. Based on the 1976 novel of the same name by English author James Herbert. Confusing and muddled story development hinder what otherwise might have been exciting movie. The airliner is a full-scale mock-up of a Boeing 747-200 front and tail section along with real aircraft parts to fill out the rest of the wreckage in the crash scenes. The crash sequence itself was filmed in a suburb of Adelaide, South Australia, using the 747 mock-up tail section. The explosion and rescue sequences were among the most ambitious undertakings in Australian film up to that point. Pre-crash cockpit scenes actually show that of a Boeing 727, and the passenger cabin is a studio-built set. Other aircraft are a float-fitted **Bell 206 Jet Ranger** and **Cessna 172N** (reg. VH-IMW / msn 172-68532). Filmed in part at South Australia Film Corp.'s Norwood Studios and at RAAF Edinburgh, South Australia. Some prints and home video releases are trimmed down by up to twenty minutes.

Tail of a Tiger

Alternate Title: *Tale of a Tiger*
U.S. Video Title: *The Young Flyers*
Australia / The Producers' Circle / 1984 / Color /
79 minutes
Director: Rolf de Heer
Cast: Grant Navin, Gordon Poole, Caz Leder-
man, Peter Feeley, Gayle Kennedy, Walter Sullivan, Basil Clarke, Norm Gobert
Synopsis / Aviation Content: In Sydney, Australia,
a young boy with a passion for aviation stum-
bles upon a derelict Tiger Moth biplane and
decides to rebuild it with the help of its elderly
owner. Not a great deal of flying, and there's a
little too much made of a dispute with a local
bully, but all told, a rewarding family film that
will likely trigger nostalgic memories for many
older viewers who had a youthful aviation interest. The final scene is fantastic, a must-see for
all Tiger Moth enthusiasts.

Type	msn	Military s/n	Civil reg.
DeHavilland DH.82A Tiger Moth	82186	(RAAF) A17-684	VH-BIN
DeHavilland DH.82A Tiger Moth	85829	(RAF) DE969	VH-BVB
DeHavilland DH.82A Tiger Moth	DHA428	(RAAF) A17-387	VH-ASC
DeHavilland DH.82A Tiger Moth	DHA802	(RAAF) A17-637	VH-SSI
DeHavilland DH.82A Tiger Moth	DHA861	(RAAF) A17-714	VH-DFJ
DeHavilland DH.82A Tiger Moth	DHA1014	(RAAF) A17-579	VH-GVA

The principal Tiger Moth used in this film was
a white and silver colored DH.82A, VH-GVA,
owned and flown by the film's aerial coordinator
Ray Vuillermin. This aircraft was originally built
by DeHavilland-Australia in 1942 and delivered
to the RAAF with s/n A17-579. It continued in
service after World War II in a trainer role until
sold onto the civilian market in 1958 to the
McKenzie Flying School, Moorabbin, as VH-
GME. It then went to Goulburn Valley Aero Club
in the 1960s as VH-GVA. The aircraft was used
for wing-walking from the late 1980s and was still
flying into the 2000s. The second most prominently featured Tiger Moth was VH-ASC, hired
from Red Baron Scenic Flights in Sydney. This
aircraft was provided painted up in a red Fokker
Triplane livery to imitate the "Red Baron" and
was used for a comical attack sequence. Four
other Tiger Moth biplanes were used in several
dream sequences; these were VH-BIN, VH-BVB,
VH-SSI and VH-DFJ. All were originally built as

military trainers for the RAAF. The derelict Tiger
Moth rebuilt during the film was a private restoration project. Filmed in and around the Balmain
area of Sydney, Australia.

Tail Spin

USA / 20th Century–Fox / 1939 / B&W / 84
minutes
Director: Roy Del Ruth
Cast: Alice Faye, Constance Bennett, Nancy
Kelly, Joan Davis, Charles Farrell, Jane Wyman,
Kane Richmond
Synopsis / Aviation Content: The story of three
women played by Faye, Bennett and Kelly, who
are all pilots, and their participation in the 1938
Cleveland National Air Race. Excellent produc-
tion values with plenty of crashes. Screenplay
by former naval aviator turned Hollywood
screenwriter Frank "Spig" Wead. Featured air-
craft include a 1934 **Brown B-2 Racer** (reg.
NX255Y); 1938 **Chester Goon** (reg.
NX93Y); 1932 **Chester Jeep** (reg.
NR12930); 1938 **Keith Rider R-6**
(reg. NX96Y); 1938 **Marcoux-Bromberg Jackrabbit** (former 1936 Keith
Rider R5 / reg. NX264Y); 1935 **Ryan
ST-A** (reg. NC16039 / msn 128) and
a 1932 **Wedell-Williams Model 44 Racer** (reg.
NR536V / msn 104), marked as "Lester Special /
No. 92." The technical director was Hollywood
stunt pilot Paul Mantz.

The Tarnished Angels

USA / Universal International / 1957 / B&W /
91 minutes
Director: Douglas Sirk
Cast: Rock Hudson, Robert Stack, Dorothy Mal-
one, Jack Carson, Robert Middleton, Alan
Reed, Alexander Lockwood, Chris Olsen
Synopsis / Aviation Content: Disillusioned, former World War I fighter ace Stack flies cheap
barnstorming stunts at rural airshows while
reporter Hudson, doing a story on him, is
shocked by his uncaring attitude towards his
family. Based on the 1935 novel *Pylon* by American author William Faulkner. A bold film that's
centered more on the dramatic scenes than the

flying, but does contain several very well crafted air racing sequences. A grand representation of vintage aircraft but not all are period accurate for the 1932 setting.

Type	msn	Civil reg.	Film Markings
Cessna Model C-37 Airmaster	363	NC18037	101
Culver Dart	GG-11	NC20993	2 / *Matt Ord's Blade*
Culver Dart GK	GK-48	NC20944	1 / *Matt Ord's Blade*
Davis D-1-K	510	NC151Y	9
DeHavilland DH.60GM Gipsy Moth	117	NC916M	17
Fairchild Model 22C-7D	916	NC14339	7-11
Fairchild PT-19A Cornell	—	N48672	—
Fleet Model 2	333	NC748V	22
Phillips CT-2 Skylark	101	NC19989	89
Stinson SM-8A Junior	4098	NC930W	—
Vultee V-1AD Special	25	NC16099	NC158
Waco GXE	1149	NC4008	66

Robert Stack's biplane was a 1929 DeHavilland Gipsy Moth, NC916M, marked as "17"; the crashed example was a mock-up built by the set department. The crash of the young pilot was in a 1938 Culver Dart G, NC20993, marked as "2," and Stack's final flight at the end was in a 1938 Culver Dart GK, NC20944, marked as "1." Mock-ups of both aircraft were used as post-crash wrecks. The large, single-engined airliner seen in the final scene was a 1933 Vultee V-1AD, NC16099, marked with false reg. "NC158."

Other aircraft used in the air race sequences were NC151Y / 9, NC14339 / 7-11, NC748V / 22, NC19989 / 89 and NC4008 / 66. Static background aircraft were NC18037 / 101, NC930W and N48672. The film's technical advisor was Hollywood flyer Hank Coffin, who owned the Gipsy Moth, NC916M, and the Waco GXE, NC4008, which carried the name *Hank's Crank*.

The camera-plane was a modified Convair L-13 spotter plane. Filmed on a large field outside San Diego, California (standing in for the film's Depression-era Louisiana setting), where a scratch-built hangar and carnival was especially set up for the film. Originally titled *Pylon*, the film actually premiered first in the UK in November 1957, then the U.S. in January 1958.

Task Force

USA / Warner Bros. / 1949 / B&W / Color / 116 minutes
Director: Delmer Daves

Cast: Gary Cooper, Jane Wyatt, Wayne Morris, Walter Brennan, Julie London
Synopsis / Aviation Content: Historical story of naval airman Cooper's rise through the ranks from the advent of the aircraft carrier USS *Langley* in 1922 up to his discharge in 1949. Very much an "educational film" with fictional characters, it's an informative but lengthy insight into naval aircraft development. Highlights are the use of Paul Mantz's early aircraft collection; the last quarter of the film is screened in color.

Type	msn	Civil reg.
Boeing Model 100	1143	N872H
DeHavilland DH.4-4M-1	ET-4	N3258
Orenco Model F Touriste	45	N2145

As well as flying them, Hollywood pilot Paul Mantz provided three of his vintage aircraft for the film. The Boeing Model 100 biplane doubled as a Curtiss F8C-2 Helldiver variously marked as "I-FI," "UF-2" and "UF-7" in the scenes of Cooper requalifying aboard the USS *Saratoga*. The DeHavilland DH.4-4M-1 was seen landing on the airstrip at the start of the movie. A rare Orenco Model F doubled as a Vought VE-7SF Bluebird biplane in the early *Langley* scenes. It was marked as "2-F-16" and was intercut with actual footage from the period as the U.S. Navy forbade landings on its carriers by out-of-date aircraft. Also acquired for filming in the later World War II scenes was an unidentified **Douglas SBD Dauntless**, a **Grumman FM-2 Wildcat**, and a Douglas TBD Devastator mock-up. The closing scene flyover was performed by **Grumman F9F Panther** and **North American FJ-1 Fury** jets. A large use of period archival footage included the Douglas TBD-1 Devastator, Douglas SBD Dauntless, Grumman F4F Wildcat, F6F Hellcat, TBF Avenger, Martin T4M/TG torpedo bomber biplane and Vought SB2U Vindicator. Brief battle scenes and B-17 footage were also used from the previous Hollywood film *Air Force* (1943).

Filmed onboard the Essex-class carrier USS

Antietam (CV-36), over a twenty-four-day period at the end of 1948 and start of 1949. A hundred tons of film equipment, 117 crew members, 18 actors, the SBD Dauntless, FM-2 Wildcat and Boeing Model 100 worked around the carrier's daily air operations off the southern California coast. The escort carrier USS *Bairoko* (CVE-115), moored at North Island, San Diego, doubled as the USS *Langley* in the early scenes with Cooper learning to land on a carrier. Filming also took place at NAS San Diego, California.

Terminal Velocity

USA-Canada / Buena Vista Pictures / 1994 / Color / 102 minutes

Director: Deran Sarafian

Cast: Charlie Sheen, Nastassja Kinski, James Gandolfini, Christopher McDonald, Suli McCullough, Hans R. Howes

Synopsis / Aviation Content: Arizona-based pro parachutist Sheen seemingly loses a female client on a jump gone wrong, which subsequently gets him involved in a major Russian crime plot. Routine action yarn, but luckily has plenty of eye candy for the aviation buff, which just gets better as the film progresses! Good views of the Beechcraft 18 and the final fight scene has some absolutely fantastic aerial stunt work with a Fairchild C-123K and Waco biplane.

The Beechcraft Model 18, N476PA, is a former RCAF Expeditor Mk. 3NM (s/n 1579) owned and operated by Skip Evans; it's marked in the film as "Desert City Paracenter." Cessna 182A, N4837D, is the mysterious aircraft which shadows Sheen for a period of time. The Fairchild C-123B Provider, N546S, is the large, white twin-engined cargo aircraft used in the final sequence. It's a C-123K conversion with two wing-mounted J85 jet-pods. After retirement to AMARC with s/n CP0045 on January 29, 1980, it was later purchased by a civil operator as N546S. The shots of the C-123K landing in the final scene are outtakes from the earlier Mel Gibson film *Air America* (1990)—note the change from a white livery to a bare metal one and the absence of engines in the auxiliary wing pods. The Waco UPF-7, N30136, was the black biplane with silver stripping which follows the C-123K in the final scene. It was owned by James Franklin, a famous American airshow and aerobatic (Waco) pilot.

The Bell Jet Ranger, N48991, is the news chopper seen at the start marked as "KAZS 6." The Bell Long Ranger, N3388H, was used later in the film in the night chase sequence using a searchlight. The Bellanca, Cessna and Piper aircraft listed above were used for background, seen at various points throughout the film.

Filmed around Tucson, Arizona, the location made large use of the city's aviation scrap yards. In one early scene in which a rocket sled is being built, background and derelict aircraft include the **Convair C-131 Samaritan, Douglas C-54 Skymaster** and **C-118 Liftmaster, Lockheed P-2 Neptune, RC-121 Warning Star**, and a **Sikorsky H-34 Choctaw**.

Much of the second half of the film takes place at Pinal Airpark (formerly Marana Air Park), thirty miles northwest of Tucson, Arizona, which is a major civilian airliner scrap yard and is also home to several Warbird types. Some civilian airliners seen are the **Boeing 707, 727, 747-200, Lockheed L-1011**, and **McDonnell Douglas DC-10**. Warbird types (listed above) include the Boeing B-17G Flying Fortress (N207EV),

Type	msn	Military s/n	Civil reg.
Main Aircraft			
Beechcraft Expeditor Mk. 3NM	CA-265	(RCAF) 1579	N476PA
Cessna 182	A34937	—	N4837D
Fairchild C-123B-6-FA Provider	20064	54-615	N546S
Waco UPF-7	5533	—	N30136
Background Aircraft			
Bell 206B Jet Ranger	1826	—	N49661
Bell 206L-1 Long Ranger	45568	—	N3388H
Bellanca 7KCAB Citabria	612-77	—	N333JS
Boeing B-17G-95-DL Flying Fortress	32426	44-83785	N207EV
Canadair Silver Star Mk. 3	T33-98	(RCAF) 21098	N99184
Cessna 182A	51076	—	N4976D
Curtiss P-40K-5-CU Warhawk	21133	42-9749	N293FR
Douglas DC-3A-197	1910	—	NC16070
Lockheed C-121A-LO Constellation	749-2601	48-609	N494TW
Lockheed P-2E Neptune	526-5383	BuNo.131502	N202EV
Piper PA-32-300 Cherokee	32-40625	—	N4254R
North American T-28B Trojan	200-313	BuNo.138242	N242J

Fairchild C-123K Provider N546S as seen in the 1994 action film *Terminal Velocity*. Photographed here at Kingman Airport, Arizona in the mid–1990s. Photograph: Gerard Helmer.

Canadair Silver Star Mk. 3 (N99184, *The Red Knight*), Curtiss P-40K Warhawk (N293FR), Douglas DC-3A (NC16070), Lockheed C-121A Constellation (N494TW), P-2E Neptune (N202 EV), North American T-28C Trojan (N242J), an unidentified Sikorsky CH-54 Tarhe, and a second Waco UPF-7 biplane, many of which are part of the Evergreen Heritage Collection.

GPS LOCATION
Pinal Airpark, Marana, Arizona: N32 30.35 / W111 19.30

FACTUAL BACKGROUND: THE TERM "TERMINAL VELOCITY"
The title comes from a branch of physics called fluid dynamics, and it means that a free-falling object, such as a parachutist, will only accelerate up to a certain point, and will then continue at a constant speed. As a falling object accelerates due to gravity, the atmospheric drag increases, and so decreases acceleration, resulting in a constant speed being achieved—the terminal velocity. The terminal velocity will vary directly with the ratio of weight to drag. An opening parachute greatly increases the upward force of drag and so greatly decreases the terminal velocity, as gravity remains constant, resulting in a soft landing. The terminal velocity of a falling parachutist is between 120 to 130 mph.

Terminator Salvation (Non–Aviation Themed Title)

USA / Columbia Pictures / 2009 / Color / 110minutes

Director: McG

Cast: Christian Bale, Sam Worthington, Moon Bloodgood, Helena Bonham Carter, Anton Yelchin

Synopsis / Aviation Content: Fourth film in the Terminator series is set after a nuclear war with survivors fighting the Terminator robots and using several classic aircraft types along the way. Seen in some degree of detail are the **Bell UH-1H Iroquois** (and never has the old Huey been in such demand!), **Bell-Boeing CV-22 Osprey, Fairchild-Republic A-10 Thunderbolt II, Hughes AH-6 Little Bird, Lockheed C-130H Hercules,** and **Sikorsky UH-60 Black**

Hawk. Live aerial action was photographed with A-10 Warthogs of the 355th Fighter Wing, Davis-Monthan AFB, Tucson, Arizona, and helicopters of the 58th SOW, Kirkland AFB, New Mexico.

Test Pilot

USA / Metro-Goldwyn-Mayer / 1938 / B&W / 118 minutes

Director: Victor Fleming

Cast: Clark Gable, Myrna Loy, Spencer Tracy, Lionel Barrymore, Samuel S. Hinds, Marjorie Main

Synopsis / Aviation Content: A daredevil pilot played by Gable test flies anything that will leave the ground, not realizing those he leaves behind suffer the anguish of his risky, outlandish flying. Based on a story written by former naval pilot turned screenwriter Frank "Spig" Wead. A strong production team, cast and excellent aerial sequences make this one of the best aviation films of the period. Highlights include genuine footage from the 1937 Thompson Trophy air race and the first big-screen appearance of the famed B-17 Flying Fortress.

Type	msn	Military s/n	Civil reg.
Boeing Model 100	1144	—	N873H
Boeing Y1B-17 Flying Fortress	1973	36-149	—
Boeing Y1B-17 Flying Fortress	1974	36-150 / No. 60	—
Boeing Y1B-17 Flying Fortress	1975	36-151 / No. 80	—
Boeing Y1B-17 Flying Fortress	1976	36-152 / No. 50	—
Boeing Y1B-17 Flying Fortress	1977	36-153	—
Boeing Y1B-17 Flying Fortress	1978	36-154 / No. 81	—
Boeing Y1B-17 Flying Fortress	1979	36-155 / No. 10	—
Boeing Y1B-17 Flying Fortress	1980	36-156 / No. 51	—
Boeing Y1B-17 Flying Fortress	1981	36-157	—
Boeing Y1B-17 Flying Fortress	1982	36-158 / No. 82	—
Boeing Y1B-17 Flying Fortress	1983	36-159 / No. 52	—
Boeing Y1B-17 Flying Fortress	1984	36-160	—
Boeing Y1B-17 Flying Fortress	1985	36-161 / No. 89	—
Douglas DC-3A-197	1983	—	NC18111
Marcoux-Bromberg Special (Keith Rider R-3)	A1	—	NR14215
Ryan ST-A	128	—	NC16039
Schoenfeldt Firecracker (Keith Rider R-4)	—	—	NR261Y
Seversky SEV-S2	43	—	NR70Y

The aircraft in the opening sequence is the genuine Seversky SEV-S2, NR70Y, doubling as the fictional "Drake Bullet / NR23655" racer, filmed at Union Air Terminal in Burbank, California. The sole 1937 SEV-S2 was a modified version of the Seversky P-35 fighter built as a racer with a 950 hp Pratt & Whitney R-1830. It won the 1937 Bendix Trophy while flying to Cleveland for filming and would come in second in 1938, then first again in 1939. Gable's aerobatic sequence was filmed with a Ryan ST-A, NC16039. Tracy arrives in Kansas on a Douglas DC-3A, NC18111, of United Airlines.

The air race sequence was filmed at the 1937 Thompson Trophy race in Cleveland, Ohio, where genuine footage was gathered, and six of the nine aircraft were retained after the race for the filming of specifically scripted sequences. Three of these racers were the Seversky SEV-S2, NR70Y, marked as "NR28555"; a Marcoux-Bromberg Special, NR14215, marked as "NR32727" (both numbers are seen on the miniatures); and a Schoenfeldt Firecracker, NR261Y, marked as "NR201Y." Paul Mantz's Boeing Model 100, N873H, is briefly seen in a short montage sequence before the race.

The Drake / U.S. Army prototype is a **Northrop A-17A** filmed at March Field, Riverside, California. Also filmed at March Field (and Langley Field, Virginia), were the B-17 sequences. A dozen brand-new production Boeing Y1B-17 Flying Fortress bombers were delivered to the 2nd Bomb Group in May 1937, just in time for filming. The film's climatic flight test was carried out using Y1B-17 No. 51 (s/n 36-156), a 20th Bomb Squadron aircraft, although the takeoff shot is of No. 52 (s/n 36-159). The subsequent crash sequence was accomplished with a full-scale mock-up using parts from a surplus **Douglas DC-2**. The thirteen Y1B-17 bombers were, within months after filming, posted overseas and would all be written off by mid–1943 in the Pacific Theater.

Background aircraft are a **Boeing Model 247**, **Consolidated PBY-3 Catalina** flying boats, **Douglas B-18 Bolo** bombers, **Grumman F2F / F3F** fighters, and many **Northrop A-17A** aircraft.

The Drake Company's home airfield is, in reality, Ryan Air Terminal at Lindbergh Field, San

Diego, California. Hollywood pilot Paul Mantz was credited as second unit director in charge of the flying sequences. A Douglas B-18 was used as a camera-plane in the Y1B-17 sequences, and Mantz's Lockheed Sirius 8A, NC117W, for gathering studio background scenes. Some use of miniatures including the SEV-S2, A-17A, Y1B-17 and various Thompson racing aircraft.

GPS LOCATIONS

Union Air Terminal (Bob Hope Airport), Burbank, California: N34 12.10 / W118 21.35

March Field, Riverside, California: N33 53.30 / W117 15.20

Lindbergh Field (San Diego Intl.), San Diego, California: N32 44.00 / W117 11.40

Test Pilot see *The Man in the Sky*

Thirteen Hours by Air

Alternate Title: *13 Hours by Air*
USA / Paramount Pictures / 1936 / B&W / 77 minutes
Director: Mitchell Leisen
Cast: Fred MacMurray, Joan Bennett, ZaSu Pitts, John Howard, Bennie Bartlett, Grace Bradley, Alan Baxter, Brian Donlevy, Ruth Donnelly, Fred Keating
Synopsis / Aviation Content: An odd group of passengers, each with his or her own assorted past, are thrown together after their airliner, piloted by MacMurray, is forced to land in remote mountains during a storm. A well-crafted film that's virtually the pioneer of the "airline disaster film," which in subsequent years would almost evolve into a stand-alone genre. United Airlines generously loaned one of their new Boeing 247 airliners for use, as well as making many other facilities available to the studio; the United logo is therefore prominently seen throughout the film.

The aircraft is a **Boeing Model 247** (reg. NC13342 / msn 1724), with some exterior airport scenes filmed at Alhambra Airport, California. The aircraft was originally delivered to Na-

tional Air Transport as NC13342 on July 17, 1933; it then went to United Airlines on May 1, 1934; upgraded to 247D standards July 7, 1935; leased to Western Air Express; to Pennsylvania Central Airlines in December 1939; impressed into USAAF service as a Boeing C-73 (s/n 42-68373) on July 11, 1942; to Mexico in August 1944 as XA-DEZ, with several subsequent owners and carriers; written off at Veracruz, Mexico, on August 26, 1950. A miniature Boeing 247 model was built for special effects flying sequences and a full-scale studio mock-up was built for aircraft interior scenes.

Thirty Seconds Over Tokyo

USA / Metro-Goldwyn-Mayer / 1944 / B&W / 138 minutes
Director: Mervyn LeRoy
Cast: Van Johnson, Robert Walker, Spencer Tracy, Phyllis Thaxter, Tim Murdock, Scott McKay, Gordon McDonald, Don DeFore, Robert Mitchum, John R. Reilly, Horace McNally
Synopsis / Aviation Content: Exceptional story of the planning, build-up, execution and aftermath of the unique Doolittle Raid against Japan in early 1942. A huge box-office success at the time and all-round classic aviation film tells the story from the point of view of Captain Ted Lawson (based on his 1943 book of the same name), who flew the seventh B-25 in the raid. Brilliantly made with many views of the B-25. One highlight is the practice takeoffs at Eglin, which used the actual airstrip created for the Doolittle Raiders in 1942. The only surprise for first-time viewers might be how little screen time actor Spencer Tracy (as Doolittle) has, despite his prominently marketed part in the film.

Almost twenty **North American B-25D Mitchell** bombers were hired from the 952nd B-25 Transition Group at Mather Field, California. The North American plant at Mines Field repainted the aircraft and readied them for filming. Eglin B-25 Mitchells included B-25D-NC (s/n 41-29754), which flew as the *Ruptured Duck* and performed most of the short takeoffs; B-25D-1-NC (s/n 41-29911); B-25D-5-NC (s/n 41-

30137); and B-25D-15-NC (s/n 41-30475). For the MGM sound-stage work, B-25D-20-NC (s/n 41-30694) as the *Ruptured Duck* was used, along with B-25D-1-NC (s/n 41-29911) and other airframes with fictional s/n 41-13729 and 41-3010.

Six distant **Vultee BT-13 Valiant** and **Douglas SBD Dauntless** aircraft double as Japanese fighters. Background aircraft at NAS Alameda are **Consolidated PBY-5A Catalina** flying boats and **Douglas SBD Dauntless** dive bombers. There's a brief flyby of a **North American P-51 Mustang**. The transport aircraft at the end is a **Douglas C-47A-25-DK Skytrain** (s/n 42-93577 / c/n 13504) with false tail number "193577."

Doolittle Raider participants Lt. Ted Lawson and Lt. Dean Davenport both worked on the film as technical advisors. Lt. Davenport, in fact, performed the B-25 short takeoff re-creations and much of the low flying—who better than an actual Doolittle Raider! Both miniatures and actual archival footage were used to help recreate the takeoff scenes on the USS *Hornet*.

Largely filmed at Eglin Main Field, Florida. The takeoff practices were shot at Eglin Auxiliary Field #9 (Hulburt Field) where actual Doolittle training was undertaken eighteen months earlier. Mines Field, Los Angeles, and Alameda NAS, San Francisco, were also used for filming. Low-level flying was filmed in the Gulf of Mexico off the Florida coast, and the ports of Los Angeles and Oakland were used for Tokyo—the large column of black smoke was an actual fuel-oil fire in Oakland spontaneously captured by the film crew. The deck of the USS *Hornet* was created indoors on MGM's Stage 15 at Culver City, California, where more than three B-25 bombers were trucked in for the carrier deck and engine start scenes. The studio doors were opened at each end while the bombers were doing their engine runs.

GPS Locations

Eglin Main Field, Florida: N30 29.00 / W086 31.10

Hulburt Field (Eglin Auxiliary Field #9), Florida: N30 25.40 / W086 41.20

NAS Alameda, San Francisco, California: N37 47.10 / W122 19.05

Factual Background: The Doolittle Raiders

The Doolittle Raid, named for the mission's leader Lt. Col. James H. Doolittle, took place on April 18, 1942, when sixteen B-25B Mitchell bombers were launched off the USS *Hornet*. Their target was industrial centers in Japan, after which they were to fly on to China to be sheltered by local resistance fighters. Eighty crew members volunteered for the daring mission—69 survived the raid (with 6 injured), 3 were killed in action, and 8 were taken as POWs. Of these captives, 4 of them survived the war, 1 died and 3 were executed.

North American B-25B Mitchell—Doolittle Aircraft		
U.S. s/n	*msn*	*Aircraft Fate*
40-2242	62B-2911	Wheels-down landing on airstrip near Vladivostok, Siberia.
40-2247	62B-2916	Abandoned over China near Poyang.
40-2249	62B-2918	Abandoned over China near Chuchow.
40-2250	62B-2919	Abandoned over China near Chuchow.
40-2261	62B-2930	Ditched in ocean off China coast near Shangchow, Lawson's B-25.
40-2267	62B-2936	Ditched in ocean off China coast near Shangchow.
40-2268	62B-2937	Abandoned over China near Ningpo.
40-2270	62B-2939	Abandoned over China near Chuchow.
40-2278	62B-2947	Abandoned over China near Chuchow.
40-2282	62B-2951	Abandoned over China near Shanghai.
40-2283	62B-2952	Abandoned over China near Chuchow.
40-2292	62B-2961	Crash landed in China near Ningpo.
40-2297	62B-2966	Abandoned over China near Shangjoa.
40-2298	62B-2967	Ditched in ocean off China coast near Nangchang.
40-2303	62B-2972	Abandoned over China near Poyang Lake.
40-2344	62B-3013	Abandoned over China near Tien Mu Shen; Doolittle's B-25.

This Is a Hijack

USA / The Fanfare Corp. / 1973 / Color / 90 minutes

Director: Barry Pollack

A colorful livery on this 1978 shot of Boeing 737–200Adv N463GB as was seen in the now largely forgotten 1973 film *This is a Hijack*. Photograph: Aris Pappas.

Cast: Adam Roarke, Neville Brand, Jay Robinson, Lynn Borden, Dub Taylor, Milt Kamen

Synopsis / Aviation Content: A gambler with a serious accumulation of debts hijacks a private jet, demanding a one-million-dollar ransom. Notable as being one of the few motion pictures to feature the Boeing 737 in a leading role. The type used was a **Boeing 737-293** (reg. N463GB / msn 19308/40), which first flew on June 28, 1968, and was delivered to Air California on July 10, 1968. During filming, the airliner retained its Air California livery and registration. N463GB remained with this operator for nineteen years before going to American Airlines in 1987, Braniff in 1988 as N504BN, and finally to Airmark Aviation in 1991. By 1995, the 737 had been broken up. Filmed in part at Mojave Airport, California.

Those Magnificent Men in Their Flying Machines

Full Title: *Those Magnificent Men in Their Flying Machines or How I Flew from London to Paris in 25 Hours 11 Minutes*

USA / 20th Century–Fox / 1965 / Color / 132 minutes

Director: Ken Annakin

Cast: Stuart Whitman, Sarah Miles, James Fox, Alberto Sordi, Robert Morley, Gert Frobe, Jean-Pierre Cassel, Irina Demick, Eric Sykes, Terry-Thomas, Red Skelton

Synopsis / Aviation Content: Epic comedy fare set in 1910, when a British newspaper tycoon offers a substantial reward to the first man to arrive in Paris from London via air. This motion picture valiantly succeeds in a genre where many others often fail—the big-budget comedy. Still lovingly remembered today for its charm, wit, incredible undertaking of period aircraft construction, and graceful aerial photography. It may seem difficult to believe, but most featured aircraft, flying and non-flying, are period accurate and based on actual designs that were serious aviation ventures. Some of the highlights to be enjoyed in this delightful film are Gert Frobe's ditching into the English Channel and the Terry-Thomas aerial encounter with a train!

Fourteen aircraft placings were scripted in the film's story, with the non-flying aircraft only making brief or background appearances. Placings 7, 8 and 11 are assigned in unknown order to aircraft numbers 3, 10 and 13, which are not seen in the finished film.

Placing / Nationality	Type	Status	Aircraft No. / Film Markings
1 / England	Antoinette IV	Flying replica	8 / *Antoinette*
2 / England	Avro IV Triplane	Flying replica	12 / *Avro*
3 / USA	Bristol Boxkite	Flying replica	7 / *The Phoenix Flyer*
4 / England	Picat Dubreuil	Non-flying replica	4 / *HMS Victory*
5 / England	Dixon Nipper	Non-flying replica	5 / *The Little Tiddler*
6 / Germany	Eardley Billing Tractor Biplane	Flying replica	11
7 / England	—	—	—
8 / England	—	—	—
9 / Japan	Eardley Billing Tractor Biplane	Flying replica	1
10 / Italy	Phillips Multiplane	Non-flying replica	—
	Passat Ornithopter	Non-flying replica	*The Busy Bee*
	Lee Richards Annular Biplane	Non-flying replica	—
	Vickers Type 22 Monoplane	Flying replica	2
11 / France	—	—	—
12 / France	Santos-Dumont Demoiselle	Flying replica	9
13 / Scotland	Blackburn Type D Monoplane	Flying original	6 / *Wake Up Scotland*
14 / England	Walton Edwards Rhomboidal	Non-flying replica	14

Retired RAF Air Commodore Allen H. Wheeler, a former test pilot and expert on early aviation, was contracted as the film's technical advisor, supervising the development, construction and on-set management of up to fourteen flying machine types. It was decided to scratch-build five types that would be flyable on camera—the Antoinette IV, Avro IV Triplane, Bristol Boxkite, Eardley Billing Tractor Biplane and Santos-Dumont Demoiselle. Three examples of each type were constructed, two as flyables and one for ground and studio filming. A sixth, Vickers Type 22 Monoplane, was a previously built flying replica but was modified for filming. Six regular pilots were hired (Tim Clutterbuck, Peter Hillwood, Joan Hughes, Derek Piggott, Taffy Rich and Allen Wheeler himself), plus up to fourteen mechanics were on set to oversee maintenance. Six non-flyable replicas were built for background and comical scenes—the Picat Dubreuil, Dixon Nipper, Phillips Multiplane, Passat Ornithopter, Lee Richards Annular Biplane and Walton Edwards Rhomboidal.

Two original aircraft used were a 1912 **Blackburn Type D Monoplane** (reg. G-AANI / msn 9 / BAPC.5), which flew as the Scotsman's aircraft, identifiable by the half cowling over the engine with the number "6" on the tail; and a 1910 **Deperdussin Monoplane** (reg. G-AANH / msn 43 / BAPC.4), for background. Both were provided by the Shuttleworth Collection at Old Warden Aerodrome.

The 1908 Antoinette IV was a French mono-plane design easily recognizable on screen, having *Antoinette* written on the nose. Two flyables were built by the Hants & Sussex Aviation Co. at Portsmouth Aerodrome, each with an 85 hp De-Havilland Gipsy I engine. Due to the wing design, the Antoinette IV takes off and lands at a very horizontal attitude; landing necessitates a forward boom below the propeller to assist in guiding the airplane in the rollout. Problems encountered during filming included loosening of the rigging and bracing wire due to the unsprung undercarriage, lateral control issues, and wing performance problems requiring a leading edge modification and the addition of ailerons. After filming, Antoinette No. 1 went to Fairoaks Airfield, Surrey; No. 2 to Geneva, Switzerland; and No. 3 (static airframe) may have gone to Jean-Baptiste Salis, France.

Only one original British Avro IV Triplane was ever built, and it first flew in September 1910. For the film two flyable replicas were constructed by John Habin and Peter Hillwood of the Hampshire Aero club, recognizable on screen as the three-winged design with *Avro* stamped on the nose. The engine was a 90 hp DeHavilland Cirrus II, generating much more power than the original 1910 35 hp Green engine. Its robust structure, reliable engine and dampened undercarriage made this airplane an excellent workhorse during filming with few ongoing problems. The first Triplane still flies today (reg. G-ARSG / msn TRI.1) with the Shuttleworth Trust at Old Warden, assigned BAPC No. 1. The second Triplane went to John

The replica 1910 Avro IV Triplane G-ARSG is maintained in airworthy condition with the Shuttleworth Trust. This aircraft is flown by the dastardly Englishman Terry-Thomas in *Those Magnificent Men in Their Flying Machines* (1965). Photograph: Steven Jefferson via the Shuttleworth Collection.

Habin. The third static airframe built for ground filming was exported to Dinard, France.

The 1910 British Bristol (Biplane) Boxkite played the American entry in the film as *The Phoenix Flyer*. It was a close development of the 1909 French Henry Farman Biplane, an aircraft so widely copied the design became known as the "Farman Type." Three replicas were built for the film by F.G. Miles Engineering Co. Ltd. of Shoreham, the first flight being made on May 5, 1964, by company owner George Miles at Ford Aerodrome. It was built almost exactly the same as the original aircraft since the Bristol Aircraft Co. still had all the drawings and photographs. The initial

engine was a 65 hp Rolls Royce Continental A.65, which was later changed to a 90 hp C.90 model. Carburetor icing and engine overheating were early problems but were later cured, and throughout filming the Boxkite performed well. Boxkite No. 1 (reg. G-ASPP / Miles msn BM.7279) still flies today with the Shuttleworth Trust at Old Warden, assigned BAPC No. 2. Boxkite No. 2 (Miles msn BM.7280) was exported to Australia in 1970 for static display, and the non-flyable Boxkite No. 3 (Miles msn BM.7281) went to the Bristol City Museum for display, assigned BAPC No. 40.

The German and Japanese entries are based on

One of the most recognized flying replicas from *Those Magnificent Men in Their Flying Machines* (1965) was the 1910 Bristol Boxkite. This one still flies today with the Shuttleworth Trust, registered as G-ASPP. Photograph: Steven Jefferson via the Shuttleworth Collection.

the unique 1911 Eardley Billing Tractor Biplane. Equipped with wings from a Voisin, it was originally a scratch-built design by Eardley Billing, the operator of the Lane Gliding School at Brooklands during this period. Only one flyable replica was built for the film by British light aircraft advocate Harold Best-Devereux at Stapleford Airfield, using a 65 hp Rolls Royce Continental A.65, which was later changed to a 90 hp C.90 model, the same as on the Boxkite. Serving two roles—Germany and Japan—on screen, the fuselage was adorned with a decorated fabric covering for scenes with the Japanese entry. Problems facing this replica included directional control, trimming and the loosening of rigging and bracing wires—these shortcomings were worked on throughout the production period, but could only be marginally improved before the picture was finished. It was exported to the Berlin Transport Museum in Germany after filming. Two static non-flying airframes were also built due to the extensive ground stunts, studio filming and multitude of crash scenes required with this aircraft type.

The nimble 1908-era Santos-Dumont Demoiselle played the Frenchman's entry in the film marked with the number 9. It was a lightweight monoplane design originally built by the French-Brazilian aviation pioneer Alberto Santos-Dumont. Two flyable and one static airframe were built for the film by Doug Bianchi, owner of Personal Plane Services Ltd. at White Waltham Airfield. The two flyables were firstly powered by a 30 hp VW Ardem engine but these proved to be underpowered. A 50 hp engine was then installed, the wings extended two feet, and a lighter female pilot, Joan Hughes, was given the job of flying the replica. The results meant the Demoiselle was one of the most airworthy replicas used in the movie. Afterward Demoiselle No. 1 (msn PPS/DEM/1) went to the Berlin Transport Museum in Germany, assigned BAPC No. 194. No. 2 (msn PPS/DEM/2) was exported to Australia, assigned BAPC No. 116, and No. 3 (msn PPS/DEM/3) was sold to one Captain Ronnie Jude in the UK.

The Italian's race entry was the 1910 Vickers Type 22 Monoplane marked with the number 2.

Aircraft builder and pilot Harold Best-Devereux moments after completing the first flight of his Eardley-Billing Tractor Biplane replica for *Those Magnificent Men in Their Flying Machines* (1965). This airplane would serve as both the German and Japanese entries in the movie. Photograph: Harold Best-Devereux Collection.

Although designed by Vickers, from a Bleriot design of 1910, it was never actually built until Doug Bianchi of Personal Plane Services Ltd. completed a replica of it in 1960 from original drawings! Purchased by 20th Century–Fox in 1964, it was extensively modified with a 75 hp Continental A.75 engine and a strengthened fuselage. After filming, this unique airplane was exported to a car museum in New Zealand, where it remains to this day.

Construction of six non-flying replicas was undertaken, with all being based on actual early aviation designs. The Picat Dubreuil is seen marked as No. 4 *HMS Victory*, piloted by a British naval officer, and features a ship's anchor for braking. The Dixon Nipper was a tail-first design seen in the film marked as No. 5 *The Little Tiddler*. It was built by the Denton Partners with a wooden mock engine hiding a small electric motor to turn a propeller and is comically depicted flying to Scotland in the film. The film's Italian entrant made use of three designs before settling on his final race aircraft. First seen during the black and white sequence at the start is a 1904-era Phillips Multiplane built for the movie by Doug Bianchi at Personal Plane Services Ltd. Next he tried the Passat Ornithopter, named *The Busy Bee*, a fat cigar-shaped design also built by Personal Plane Services with two sets of flapping wings! The flapping was generated using a 16 hp motorcycle engine. It is now at the Old Rhinebeck Aerodrome Museum in New York. The Italian then tried the 1910-era Lee Richards Annular Biplane, the replica here built by the Denton Partners, and is seen in the balloon-duel scene in which it gets shot down. It's now at the Newark Air Museum assigned BAPC No. 20. The mammoth Walton Edwards Rhomboidal replica was built by Airgeneers Ltd. at Staverton aerodrome. It is briefly seen in the film bouncing into the air marked as aircraft No. 14.

There's some use of special effects and models in the later aerial scenes, especially over Paris, where permission for actual flying with the replicas was not granted to the filmmakers. A DeHavilland Tiger Moth was employed on set to help pilots rehearse the various flying sequences. The jet flyby at the end is a group of English Electric Lightnings.

The primary film set was constructed at Booker Airfield, High Wycombe, Buckinghamshire, England, and featured a windmill (with attached café), motor racing circuit, hangars and a fake sewage pond. It was fashioned after Brooklands race track, where pioneering test flights were actually flown by early aviators. The Dover, Calais and Paris arrival scenes were also filmed at Booker with 2,000 period-dressed extras for crowd scenes. Special effects and shots of the actors flying the static replicas were filmed at Pinewood Studios, also in Buckinghamshire.

GPS LOCATION
Booker Airfield, High Wycombe, Buckinghamshire, England: N51 36.60 / W000 48.30

The Thousand Plane Raid

Alternate Title: **The 1000 Plane Raid**
USA / United Artists / 1969 / Color / 93 minutes
Director: Boris Sagal
Cast: Christopher George, Laraine Stephens, J.D. Cannon, Gary Marshall, Michael Evans, Gavin MacLeod
Synopsis / Aviation Content: Tension and drama ensue amongst B-17 squadrons when a plan is devised to use 1,000 planes against a top-priority German target. Just three B-17 bombers were used by the studio to tell the "1,000 plane" raid story, a top-rated film among B-17 fans. Based on the 1965 nonfiction book *The Thousand Plan* by English author Ralph Barker.

Type	msn	Military s/n	Civil reg.	Film Markings
Boeing B-17F-70-BO Flying Fortress	4896	42-29782	N17W	23613 / *Can Do*
Boeing B-17G-85-DL Flying Fortress	32166	44-83525	N83525	25053 / *Balls of Fire*
Boeing B-17G-90-DL Flying Fortress	32325	44-83684	N3713G	124485 / *Bucking Bronco*

B-17G N17W was leased from Aircraft Specialties, Inc., Arizona and later appeared in the films *Tora! Tora! Tora!* (1970) and *Memphis Belle* (1990). It was at this time being used as a sprayer aircraft by Aircraft Specialties. B-17G N83525 was leased from Tallmantz Aviation, Inc., California, and is notable as being the last B-17 held at Davis-Monthan when Tallmantz acquired it in 1968. It had, like so many other civilian Forts, been a DB-17P drone director in USAF service. B-17G N3713G was leased from the Air Museum at Chino, California, having just been used in the TV Series *12 O'Clock High* (1964–1967). It too was previously a DB-17P drone director before being retired from the USAF in 1959. It was N3713G that did the low-level buzz of the airfield, which was performed six times for the cameras.

Camera-planes were Tallmantz Aviation's B-25 aircraft N1042B and N1203. Large amounts of combat footage were used from the 1944 documentary *The Memphis Belle* and the famous Paul Mantz crash landing was again used from *Twelve O'Clock High* (1949). Author Ralph Barker was an RAF Radio Operator / Gunner during World War II.

Filming of airfield and flying scenes took place at Santa Maria Airport, north of Los Angeles, California, in January 1968. The landscape greenery and coastal areas nearby served as wartime England. Studio filming took place at MGM Studios with a B-17G (s/n 44-83387) cockpit section.

Through Hell to Glory   see Jet Attack

Thunder Across the Pacific   see The Wild Blue Yonder

Thunderball (Non–Aviation Themed Title)   see *James Bond* Series

Thunder Birds

Alternate Title (Subtitle): *Soldiers of the Air*
USA / 20th Century–Fox / 1942 / Color / 78 minutes
Director: William A. Wellman
Cast: Gene Tierney, Preston Foster, John Sutton, Jack Holt, Dame May Whitty, George Barbier, Richard Haydn, Reginald Denny
Synopsis / Aviation Content: USAAF flight instructor Foster and RAF cadet Sutton are both infatuated with local Arizona girl Tierney, which can only lead to professional conflict.

What seems a routine film is actually a wartime propaganda piece designed to promote the USAAF's training and enlistment programs. Excellent color photography of Arizona locations and the many primary training aircraft types on an actual and active wartime airfield make this a must-see, especially for Stearman fans.

Filmed from March to July 1942 at the real Thunderbird Field (where the picture's title came from), near Phoenix, Arizona, featuring many of the **Boeing-Stearman PT-17 Kaydet** primary trainers then in use by the USAAF. Hollywood pilot Paul Mantz performed the aerial stunt flying in his **Boeing Model 100** (reg. N873H / msn 1144), which doubles in the film as the classic yellow and blue-colored Stearman trainer for all non-army, off-base stunt flying scenes. This aircraft is identifiable by its more rounded, flat-topped tail, as opposed to the Stearman's more pointed tail. Background aircraft include the **North American AT-6 Texan** and **Vultee BT-13 Valiant**.

Thunderbird Field was built in three months in early 1941 and was backed by several Hollywood investors and celebrities, including actors James Stewart, Cary Grant and Henry Fonda, to aid in the anticipated war effort. After the war, the field quickly became surplus to requirements and was closed. The site survives today as the Thunderbird School of Global Management.

GPS LOCATION
Thunderbird Field, Glendale, Arizona (closed 1946): N33 37.20 / W112 10.80

Thundering Jets

USA / 20th Century–Fox / 1958 / B&W / 73 minutes
Director: Helmut Dantine
Cast: Rex Reason, Dick Foran, Audrey Dalton, Barry Coe, Buck Class, Robert Dix, Lee Farr
Synopsis / Aviation Content: An air force squadron leader must evaluate how his pilots react to the pressures of high altitude flying in the newest jet fighters. Filmed at Edwards AFB, California, with several **Lockheed T-33A Shooting Star** trainers.

Tiger in the Sky see *The McConnell Story*

Tomorrow Never Dies (Non–Aviation Themed Title) see *James Bond Series*

Top Gun

USA / Paramount Pictures / 1986 / Color / 105 minutes

Director: Tony Scott

Cast: Tom Cruise, Kelly McGillis, Val Kilmer, Anthony Edwards, Tom Skerritt, Michael Ironside, John Stockwell, Barry Tubb, Rick Rossovich, Tim Robbins, Clarence Gilyard Jr., Whip Hubley, James Tolken, Meg Ryan

Synopsis / Aviation Content: "Rock 'n' roll" style picture about naval pilots competing for the prized trophy at America's leading fighter tactics school, known as Top Gun. This film made the F-14 Tomcat naval fighter a living legend with moviegoing audiences worldwide. Fantastic aerial photography captured a realism and look never before seen on film. The movie, and its soundtrack featuring the hit song *Danger Zone*, became a pop-culture phenomenon that arguably remains the most recognized and commercially successful aviation film ever made!

Three unidentified **Northrop F-5E Tiger II** and one **F-5F Tiger II** USAF fighter aircraft were painted black with red tail emblems to act as the fictional "unseen / unfeeling" enemy MiG-28 fighters. The F-5F was the 2-seater buzzed by Maverick in the opening encounter where Goose takes a Polaroid photo. Three unidentified **McDonnell Douglas A-4F Skyhawk** fighter aircraft were used as the aggressor aircraft against the F-14 Tomcats in the Miramar and Fallon training sequences.

Type	msn	Military s/n
Grumman F-14A-100-GR Tomcat	284	BuNo.160665
Grumman F-14A-100-GR Tomcat	300	BuNo.160681
Grumman F-14A-100-GR Tomcat	313	BuNo.160694
McDonnell Douglas C-9B Skytrain II	47584/696	BuNo.159114
Sikorsky SH-3A Sea King	61-160	BuNo.149894
Sikorsky HH-3F Pelican	61-629	(USCG) 1467

Five U.S. Pacific Fleet F-14 squadrons and their aircrews were involved in the filming of *Top Gun*, each noted here with their two-letter tail codes: VF-1 Wolfpack (NE); VF-51 Screaming Eagles (NL); VF-111 Sundowners (NL); VF-114 Aardvarks (NH) and VF-213 Blacklions (NH).

The opening montage and later carrier scenes were filmed on the USS *Enterprise* (CVN-65) and feature Tomcats from squadrons VF-114 and VF-213. Actual 3-digit squadron numbers seen in the film include 101, 203, 205, 210 and 515. Two unidentified F-14 Tomcats from these squadrons were given fictional markings "104" and "114" for the closing carrier scenes in order to match those earlier seen in the film at Miramar.

Squadrons VF-1, VF-51 and VF111 were used in filming at NAS Miramar and Fallon. Actual 3-digit squadron numbers seen in the film include 105, 112, 203, 211 and 301. Three Tomcats from VF-51 and VF-111 (as noted in the table) were painted with the fictional markings of Maverick / Goose (160665), Maverick / Merlin (160694) and Iceman / Slider (160681). Use of fictional squadron numbers "104" and "114" were used by all three aircraft at various times. F-14A BuNo. 160694 had several camera mounts built into the fuselage by Grumman Aerospace Corp. for "onboard" camera angles.

UNCONFIRMED DATA

Other F-14A Tomcats used in the film may have been BuNo. 160685, 160695 and 160925, but these remain unconfirmed.

Background aircraft seen during the carrier opening sequence are the **Grumman A-6 Intruder** and **Vought F-8 Crusader**. The airliner Goose's family arrives in is a C-9B Skytrain II passenger transport, BuNo. 159114, the U.S. Navy version of the Douglas DC-9 commercial airliner. Thirty-three C-9B aircraft have been in navy service since 1973. The U.S. Coast Guard chopper that recovers Maverick after his crash is one (USCG 1467) of forty HH-3F Pelican helicopters, an SH-3 Sea King derivative but featuring an amphibious hull design based on the USAF HH-3E Jolly Green Giant variant. The chopper that lands on the carrier at the end of the film with the downed pilots is an SH-3A Sea King, BuNo. 149894, which by the time of filming had been brought up to SH-3H standards with upgraded avionics and equipment.

Maverick's control tower buzz was done at Miramar with permission from the Navy, and apparently was the first time it had been done at this base. Eager pilots drew straws—the privilege going to the film's F-14 aerial coordinator LCDR. Lloyd "Bozo" Abel. The camera-plane was a Learjet 25, N564CL, owned by Clay Lacy. Large-scale F-14 and MiG-28 (F-5) models were used for the flat spin and destruction sequences.

Tragically, veteran pilot Art Scholl was killed on September 16, 1985, while filming background projection shots for Maverick's flat-spin sequence. With a camera mounted on his Pitts S-2A, N13AS, Art put his aircraft into a spin to capture the shot but failed to recover from the maneuver, the aircraft plummeting into the Pacific Ocean. His body and the aircraft were never recovered; the film is dedicated to his memory.

Filming on the USS *Enterprise* (CVN-65), took place from August 3 to 7, 1985. The ship was located at the time seventy miles off the coast of San Diego. Ship interiors were filmed on the USS *Ranger*. Ground scenes were shot at the actual Top Gun school itself—NAS Miramar, San Diego, California—from June 26 to the end of July 1985. Aerial scenes over the desert were filmed out of NAS Fallon in Nevada from August 15 to 26, 1985. The graduation scene around the swimming pool was filmed at NAS North Island, San Diego, California. Cockpit shots were done with F-14 mock-ups inside a hangar at Burbank Airport, California.

GPS LOCATIONS

NAS Miramar, California: N32 52.10 / W117 08.25

NAS Fallon, Nevada: N39 25.35 / W118 42.25

FACTUAL BACKGROUND: THE TOMCAT AND TOP GUN SCHOOL

The F-14 Tomcat is a twin-engined, 2-seater, swing-wing naval interceptor fighter holding a frontline position with the U.S. Fleet from 1972 to 2006. Its first carrier deployment was on the USS *Enterprise* in 1974. Grumman Aerospace

Corp. built a total of 712 F-14 fighters at its plant in Calverton, Long Island, from 1970 to 1992, with the prototype YF-14A first flying on December 21, 1970. A dozen YF-12A test aircraft were built, followed by 625 of the production F-14A variant from 1971 to 1987—79 of these were delivered to Iran before 1979. The Pratt & Whitney TF30 engines, however, were not always as reliable, or as powerful, as the Navy would have liked, and so the F-14A(Plus) was developed with the General Electric F110. A total of 38 new-built aircraft and 48 F-14A Tomcats were converted to this standard from 1987 to 1990. The final variant was the F-14D Super Tomcat with digital avionics upgrades; 37 were built from 1990 to 1992, after which production was canceled. An additional 19 were converted from the F-14A variant as the F-14D(R). The evolution of the multi-role F/A-18 Super Hornet and the high maintenance of the F-14 saw the aircraft phased out of frontline naval service, the official retirement ceremony taking place on September 22, 2006, and the very last flight the following month on October 4. All Tomcats in the *Top Gun* film are of the F-14A variant.

"Top Gun" is the popular name for the United States Navy Fighter Weapons School founded at NAS Miramar on March 3, 1969. Its goal is to improve air combat tactics among naval pilots, which had been found to be relatively poor in the skies over Vietnam. Also known as "Fightertown U.S.A.," Miramar at first trained F-4 Phantom II crews and soon became a center of excellence in fighter doctrine, tactics and training. There is no "Top Gun trophy"—its inclusion in the film was a dramatic license taken on the part of the filmmakers. In the 1970s and 1980s the F-14 Tomcat and F/A-18 Hornet became the primary naval aircraft flown by students. Top Gun instructors flew the A-4 Skyhawk, T-38 Talon, F-5 Freedom Fighter and the F-16 Fighting Falcon as aggressor aircraft simulating the Soviet MiG opponents. In 1996, Top Gun training was transferred to NAS Fallon in Nevada and was officially named the United States Navy Strike Fighter Tactics Instructor (SFTI) program. More emphasis is now placed on multi-mission capabilities, with not only air-to-air combat but air-to-ground strike tactics on the syllabus.

Top of the World

USA / United Artists / 1955 / B&W / 90 minutes
Director: Lewis R. Foster
Cast: Dale Robertson, Evelyn Keyes, Frank Lovejoy, Nancy Gates, Paul Fix
Synopsis / Aviation Content: An "over the hill" jet pilot is reassigned to Alaska in order to help with the new Operation Deep Freeze project being run by the USAF. Little here on offer other than a few views of the rarely seen F-82 Twin Mustang and excellent aerial photography by cinematographer William H. Clothier.

Aircraft featured are four **Boeing SB-17G Flying Fortress** SAR conversions; seen prominently is a **Cessna LC-126A** (s/n 49-1953 / msn 7354); two **Douglas LC-47 Skytrain** aircraft with skis; several **North American F-82 Twin Mustang** reconn. fighters; and possibly a **Waco G-4C Hadrian** glider. Background aircraft were a fleet of Convair B-36 Peacemaker bombers (closing shot) and a Douglas C-54 Skymaster. Some use of the Fulton-recovery system is also seen, although much of it studio-created. The film must have been shot prior to June 1953, as the F-82 had been retired by this time. Filmed in part at Ladd AFB, Alaska, using Paul Mantz's B-25H (reg. N1203) camera-plane.

Tora! Tora! Tora!

USA-Japan / 20th Century–Fox / 1970 / Color / 139 minutes
Directors: Richard Fleischer, Toshio Masuda, Kinji Fukasaku
Cast: Martin Balsam, Joseph Cotten, E.G. Marshall, James Whitmore, Jason Robards, Soh Yamamura, Tatsuya Mihashi, Takahiro Tamura, Eijiro Tono, Koreya Senda
Synopsis / Aviation Content: Epic recreation, as told from both sides in the conflict, of the Japanese attack on the U.S. Fleet at Pearl Harbor, Hawaii, on December 7, 1941. The screenplay used the 1963 publication *Tora! Tora! Tora!* by American historian Gordon W. Prange and the 1967 book *The Broken Seal* by Hungarian-born historian Ladislas Farago as source material. In terms of aircraft numbers, required materiels, filming logistics and locations, the largest aviation film ever carried out by the United States, comparable in scale only to the UK's 1969 epic *Battle of Britain*. More than fifty-two T-6 Texan and BT-13 Valiant trainers were modified into Japanese fighters, and another sixteen-plus aircraft were also acquired to depict the U.S. Forces; an aircraft carrier was required to ship all the aircraft, spares and film crew out to Hawaii. A major film unit in Japan also built large sets and used a number of aircraft. The results are a spectacular array of aerial action sequences, including a stunning pre-dawn carrier takeoff scene that has been reused in many subsequent productions. A definite must-see with a suspenseful music score by composer Jerry Goldsmith.

The fifteen "Zero" conversions are based on the single-seater **Mitsubishi A6M2 (Navy Type**

Type	msn	Military s/n	Civil reg.	Film Markings
Boeing B-17F-70-BO Flying Fortress	4896	42-29782	N17W	—
Boeing B-17G-85-DL Flying Fortress	32204	44-83563	N9563Z	—
Boeing B-17G-105-VE Flying Fortress	17-8683	44-85774	N621L	—
Boeing B-17G-110-VE Flying Fortress	17-8738	44-85829	N3193G	—
Boeing B-17G-110-VE Flying Fortress	17-8749	44-85840	N620L	—
Boeing-Canada Canso A (PBY-5A)	22022	(RCAF) 9793	N6108	24-P-4 / -9
Boeing-Stearman PT-13D-BW Kaydet	75-5497	42-17334	N6692C	NC34307
Consolidated PBY-5A Catalina	1733	BuNo.48371	N5589V	—
Consolidated PBY-5A Catalina	1764	BuNo.48402	N5592V	—
Consolidated PBY-5A Catalina	1939	BuNo.46575	N5586V	—
Consolidated PBY-5A Catalina	1955/13	BuNo.46591	N5587V	—
Consolidated PBY-5A Catalina	1993/51	BuNo.46629	N5595V	—
Curtiss Kittyhawk Mk. I (P-40E)	18723	(RAF) AK979	N5672	20-15P
Curtiss Kittyhawk Mk. I (P-40E)	18796	(RAF) AL152	N1207V	27-15P
Douglas A-24A-DE Banshee	2350	42-60817	N15749	S.9
North American B-25J-25-NC Mitchell	108-33753	44-30478	N9754Z	—

(Type)	(msn)	(Military s/n)	(Civil reg.)	(Film Markings)
U.S.-Built "Zero" Fighter Conversions				
CCF Harvard Mk. 4	CCF4-16	(RCAF) 20225	N15796	125
CCF Harvard Mk. 4	CCF4-23	(RCAF) 20232	N2048	AI-101
CCF Harvard Mk. 4	CCF4-104	(RCAF) 20313	N15795	122
CCF Harvard Mk. 4	CCF4-117	(RCAF) 20326	N15799	124
CCF Harvard Mk. 4	CCF4-153	(RCAF) 20362	N15798	110
CCF Harvard Mk. 4	CCF4-158	(RCAF) 20367	N9097	129
CCF Harvard Mk. 4	CCF4-171	(RCAF) 20380	N7757	123
CCF Harvard Mk. 4	CCF4-199	(RCAF) 20408	N15797	121
CCF Harvard Mk. 4	CCF4-215	(RCAF) 20424	N7754	130
CCF Harvard Mk. 4	CCF4-241	(RCAF) 20450	N4447	126
CCF Harvard Mk. 4	CCF4-264	(RCAF) 20473	N296W	127
North American SNJ-5 Texan	88-14446	BuNo.51698	N7986C	111
Japanese-Built "Zero" Fighter Conversions				
North American T-6G Texan	unknown	(JASDF) 52-0030	—	—
North American T-6G Texan	unknown	(JASDF) 72-0158	—	—
North American T-6G Texan	unknown	(JASDF) 72-0175	—	—
U.S.-Built "Kate" Torpedo-Bomber Conversions				
CCF Harvard Mk. 4	CCF4-20	(RCAF) 20229	N1264	AI-315
CCF Harvard Mk. 4	CCF4-83	(RCAF) 20292	N2047	316
North American SNJ-4 Texan	88-13171	BuNo.27675	N7062C	312
North American SNJ-5 Texan	88-15757	BuNo.43766	N3242G	AI-313
North American SNJ-5 Texan	88-16686	BuNo.84875	N3725G	314
North American SNJ-5 Texan	88-17652	BuNo.90654	N6438D	317
North American SNJ-5 Texan	88-17780	BuNo.90712	N7130C	311
North American SNJ-5 Texan	121-41736	BuNo.90950	N3239G	301
North American T-6G-NI Texan	168-113	49-3009	N2819G	—
Japanese-Built "Kate" Torpedo-Bomber Conversions				
North American T-6G-NH Texan	182-271	(JASDF) 72-0151	N6522	—
North American T-6G-NH Texan	182-307	(JASDF) 72-0159	N6524	—
North American T-6G-NH Texan	182-362	51-14675	N6526	—
North American T-6G-NH Texan	182-366	51-14679	N6529	—
North American T-6G-NH Texan	182-393	51-14706	N6520	—
U.S.-Built "Val" Dive-Bomber Conversions				
Vultee BT-13 Valiant	54A-308	40-917	N63163	AI-246
Vultee BT-13A Valiant	74-1414	41-1306	N54865	AI-235
Vultee BT-13A Valiant	74-2819	41-10502	N65837	AI-236
Vultee BT-13A Valiant	74-6656	41-22578	N56336	AI-231
Vultee BT-13A Valiant	74-6991	41-22771	N2200S	AI-234
Vultee BT-13A Valiant	74-7356	41-22926	N56478	AI-230
Vultee BT-13B Valiant	79-1220	42-90263	N56867	AI-244
Vultee BT-13B Valiant	79-1703	42-90626	N63227	AI-233
Vultee BT-15-VU Valiant	74A-11513	42-42171	N67629	AI-232
unknown variant	unknown	unknown	N18102	AI-245

0) fighter, codenamed "Zeke" but better known as the "Zero." The fourteen "Kate" conversions are based on the three-seater **Nakajima B5N2** (**Navy Type 97**) torpedo-bomber, codenamed "Kate" by the Allies. The ten "Val" conversions are based on the two-seater **Aichi D3A1** (**Navy Type 99**) fixed undercarriage dive-bomber, codenamed "Val" by the Allies.

The Boeing-Canada-built Canso A (PBY-5A Catalina) was hired from Steward-Davis, Inc., of Long Beach, California, and marked in the film as "24-P-4" and "24-P-9." The Boeing-Stearman

Steward-Davis at Long Beach converted ten Vultee Valiant trainers into Japanese dive-bombers for the 1970 film *Tora! Tora! Tora!* Pictured here in 1972 is N18102, which is something of a mystery machine. No known records of this conversion seem to have survived telling of its original identity or ultimate fate. Photograph: Ron Dupas via 1000aircraftphotos.com.

California-based aviation company Steward-Davis, Inc., owned this Catalina N6108 used in Hawaii during the filming of *Tora! Tora! Tora!* during 1969. Photograph: James H. Farmer Collection.

was hired from Murrayair Ltd. of Honolulu. It was a standardized Kaydet, having both a USAAF / U.S. Navy designation and serial number: PT-13D / N2S54217334 / BuNo. 61375. Built as a Model E75 with a Lycoming engine, it received a post–World War II upgrade to PT-17 (Model A75N1) standards with a Continental engine, which it carried during filming. The tail reg. "NC34307" is based on a civil Meyers OTW-160 biplane which encountered the Japanese attack

force on the actual day in 1941. The two P-40 fighters were hired from Californian-based private owners. N5672N was ex–RCAF s/n 1064, owned by Gil Macy, marked as "20-15P." N1207V was ex–RCAF s/n 1082, owned by A. Woodson, marked as "27-15P"; this was also a former Tallmantz-owned P-40. Another ex–RCAF P-40E (s/n AK933 / msn 15404 / reg. N94466) was also hired, but was soon reclaimed by its owner John Paul when he discovered it was being stripped for spares. The Douglas A-24A, N15749, was filmed, but the scenes were cut from the final print; the footage was later used in the motion picture *Midway* (1976). Steward-Davis handled the furnishing and preparation of this aircraft, which was flown by Steward-Davis pilot Don Dinoff.

The single B-17F and four B-17G bombers were hired from Aircraft Specialties Co. of Mesa, Arizona, who also provided the B-17 crews and aircraft maintenance crews for the entire *Tora* air force. Three Forts were air-tankers in the U.S. forest fire force; Aircraft Specialties purchased another two from Bolivia in December 1968 as N620L and N621L (ex-reg. CP-620 and CP-621). All were hired from January to May 1969 for filming during the forest fire off-season. Filming took place in the skies over Wheeler AFB, Oahu, after the Forts had been flown out from Oakland, California. The B-17 cockpit shots were filmed at Fox Studios with B-17 s/n 44-83387—the same one used for *Twelve O'Clock High* (1949) and *The 1000 Plane Raid* (1969), among others. B-17 pilots were Bill Benedict, George Burnett, Don Clark, Don Fletcher, William Groomer, David Haines, Allen Mosley, Gary Pylant, Sam Steele and James Stumpf.

Veteran pilot Jack Canary was hired as technical advisor to the film and placed in charge of acquiring the Texans and Valiants for conversion to Japanese replicas. Ten "Val" conversions were completed by Steward-Davis, Inc., of Long Beach, California, at a cost of $18,000 per aircraft. A fuselage plug was added aft of the cockpit to lengthen the aircraft, various fiberglass wing fillets and wheel pants were added, and the original 450 hp R-985 Wasp Junior was replaced with a 600 hp R-1340 radial engine. Steward-Davis also built

100 fiberglass torpedoes for the "Kate" conversions and 400 weighted plastic bombs. Cal-Volair, also of Long Beach, California, did the majority of the conversions—twelve "Zero" fighters were modified mostly from the Canadian Harvard Mk. 4 at a cost of $12,000 each. Little modification was required except for a redesigned canopy and rounded wingtips. Cal-Volair's toughest task was the nine "Kate" torpedo-bombers, which cost $23,000 per conversion. Two plugs were added to the base Harvard / Texan airframe, adding over seven feet to the fuselage length, which then had a BT-13 tail section bolted on with a redesigned and lengthened canopy. Fake cowl flaps, fiberglass fillets, and a retractable tail wheel finished off the modification. Although all the conversions were initially given tail codes after completion (see table above), these were removed before filming in order to avoid any continuity problems arising during the editing process.

Twenty-one additional Japanese Defense Force T-6G "Zero" and "Kate" replicas were converted in Japan for the Japanese preparation sequences. Apart from the eight flyable "Zero" and "Kate" conversions (listed in the table), there were also thirteen additional, non-airworthy "Zero" / "Kate" basic conversions for background scenes, some with folding wings. Ten of the thirteen identified Japanese Defense Force serial numbers are 52-0028, 52-0035, 52-0058, 52-0117, 52-0137, 6163 (ex–BuNo. 84819), 6166 (ex–BuNo. 85060), 6176, 6183 (ex–BuNo. 112359) and 6212 (ex–BuNo. 90944). "Zero" conversions were completed by the Kawasaki Aircraft Co. at Oita Airport on Kyushu, Japan, and the "Kate" conversions by the C. Itoh Aircraft Maintenance Co. at Chofu Airport near Tokyo, Japan. Conversion kits were supplied from Cal-Volair in the U.S.

Japanese Aircraft Basic Modification List

Zero	Kate	Val
Modified canopy	Modified lengthened canopy	P&W R1340-AN-1 engine upgrade
Modified wheel fairings	16-inch forward fuselage extension	Modified canopy
Modified fuselage gun wells	7-foot aft fuselage extension	26-inch fuselage extension
Modified tail section	BT-13 tail section added	38-inch fiberglass wing extensions
Fiberglass rounded wingtips	Fiberglass wingtips	Fiberglass wing fillets / dorsal fillet
Large prop spinner added	Fake cowl flaps / exhausts	Fiberglass wheel pants
Dummy drop tank	Retractable tail wheel	Fake cowl flaps / dive brakes
Some with arrestor hook	Working torpedo rack	Working bomb rack / arrestor hook
Some with 3-bladed propeller		Some with 3-bladed propeller

A line-up of *Tora!* Harvard and Valiant conversions after their return from filming in Hawaii. Photograph: James H. Farmer Collection.

Hawaiian filming employed a high number of experienced T-6 pilots from both military and civilian backgrounds led by Lt. Col. Arthur P. Wildern (USAF Ret.) and Capt. George Watkins (USN). In alphabetical order, they were James Ashford, Coy Austin, Joe Beno, Burton Berglund, LeRoy Bruflat, Robert Bumgarner, Louis Cislo, Dennis Clark, Ralph Clark, Greg Corliss, Ken Costa, Art Daegling, John Darby Jr., Don Dinoff (aerial coordinator), Guy Davis, Henry Davis, William Doak, Warren Dukes, George Duncan, Clinton Effinger, Frank Eger Jr. (crashed N2819G during filming), Henry English, Padraic Evans, Fred Farrell, Paul Gillcrist (*Yorktown* takeoff), Frank Hall, William Klopp, Peter Krueger, William Lacy, Dean Laird, Ira Lewey, James Loughmiller, David MacArthur, Robert Maguire, Robert Mayock, John McDaniel, Kenneth Milam, Lewis Mitchell, E.R. Modzelewski, John O'Neil Jr., Lucien Parish, W.H. Ritzmann, Alfred Seol, Guy Strong (killed during filming), Jerry Thompson, Joe Tully, Carl Ward, Eugene Williams and James Williamson.

B-25J N9754Z was destroyed for the film after being retrofitted with a single tail configuration to resemble a Douglas A-20 Havoc. It can briefly be seen in the shot in which the crippled Zero nose-dives through the roof of a hangar. The aircraft had been in a derelict state at Honolulu International Airport. Five engineless, derelict Consolidated PBY-5A Catalina hulks were prepared by Steward-Davis, Inc., to be destroyed in the film's final scenes on Ford Island. They were painted and made ready at Long Beach before being shipped out to Hawaii. Four of the known film markings are "24-P-3," "24-P-5," "24-P-6" and "24-P-7." These five Catalinas were originally part of a fleet of thirteen all purchased by American businessman Thomas Kendall on September 6, 1956, from a sale at NAS North Island, San Diego, California. Kendall intended to convert them to "flying yachts" with luxury interiors, but only three conversions were carried out, and the rest remained in storage at Orange County Airport. Steward-Davis acquired five of these Catalinas on July 21, 1964, and moved them to their Long Beach facility. They were all deregistered with the FAA on October 11, 1968, as "permanently retired from service" when Fox Studios acquired them for shipment to Hawaii. PBY-5A N5587V was noted as derelict at Ford Island in 1969.

Thirty fiberglass P-40 mock-ups were built for destruction. Casts were taken off P-40 N1207V, with the fiberglass sections bolted around a steel framework. T-6 landing gears were used for main wheels with original P-40 tail wheels; several were motorized (with Allison engines, no less!)

Steward-Davis provided up to five engineless PBY-5A Catalina hulks to be destroyed during the Ford Island scenes of *Tora! Tora! Tora!* Photograph: James H. Farmer Collection.

and remote controlled for taxiing purposes. One fiberglass Vought OS2U Kingfisher mock-up was built and mounted on the *Arizona* replica; it was destroyed during the battleship sequences. Several B-17D "2-D flats" were painted for distant background scenes.

Tragically, chief Japanese replica pilot Jack Canary was killed on August 19, 1968, at Summit Station, Pennsylvania, while ferrying one of the BT-15 aircraft, N355H, to Long Beach for conversion. A second pilot, Guy Strong, was killed when his BT-13 "Val," N63227, crashed on January 13, 1969, in Hawaii while practicing dive-bombing maneuvers. One "Kate," N2819G, was lost in Pearl Harbor itself during filming due to a fuel problem; the pilot survived. An unplanned incident with one of the B-17s occurred in March 1969. B-17G N620L radioed they were coming into Wheeler AFB for an emergency landing on one wheel. Film crews quickly set up along the runway and captured the entire incident on film. Studio scenes were later scripted to fit in around the hastily filmed shot. N620L suffered only minor damage and was soon back in flying status. P-40E N5672N ground-looped during filming, requiring the replacement of the landing gear, propeller and engine. This was not a good outcome for its owner, as he had modified it for his own require-

ments with a P-40N canopy and 4-bladed propeller—he received it back after filming in P-40E configuration. A motorized P-40 mock-up went astray during a big scene at Wheeler AFB and careened into a flight-line of other P-40 mock-ups, sending stunt men running. The unplanned incident was filmed on several cameras from various angles and virtually all of the incident made it into the final edit. One now famous shot captures a runaway prop spinning off a motorized mock-up and cartwheeling across the tarmac.

Filming in Hawaii finished in May 1969. All aircraft combined had accumulated 4,000 hours' flying time and had burned around 135,000 gallons of fuel. Wreckage of the B-25J, five PBY Cats and P-40 mock-ups were scrapped in Hawaii. Catalina N6108 flew on for many years until lost in the Pacific Ocean during a ferry flight to New Zealand in mid–January 1994. It was registered as N5404J at the time; the crew were later rescued. The five B-17 Forts continued in forest-fire service. N620L crashed in July 1973, and N621L in July 1975; the remaining aircraft are in museums. Both P-40 Warhawks survive and are in museums. Fox Studios auctioned off all the U.S. Japanese replicas in February 1971 for between $2,000 and $5,000 each. Many are maintained in flying condition to this day, performing Pearl Harbor reenactments on the U.S.

Warbird circuit. The best known of these is the Tora Group, first established in 1972 with four Zeroes, one Kate and one Val. The whereabouts of one "Val," however, N18102, remains a mystery to this day—its history and FAA records seemingly lost, its ultimate fate has never been determined.

The aircraft carrier USS *Yorktown* (CV-10) was converted into the Japanese carrier *Akagi* for the dramatic launch of up to thirty-one U.S. Japanese replicas. It was filmed off the San Diego coast on December 3 and 4, 1968, under beautiful soft pre-dawn light with carrier qualified, off-duty U.S. Naval pilots. The USS *Yorktown* was then used to transport the Japanese replicas, A-24A, two P-40 Warhawks, P-40 mock-up components and five PBY derelicts to Hawaii for filming beginning January 20, 1969. The action was mainly filmed on location in Hawaii at Pearl Harbor Naval Base itself with full-size replica sections of the battleships *Arizona* and *Tennessee*. The main airfield was NAS Ford Island, where the film's on-location "studio"—Hangar 79—was based for P-40 mock-up final assembly, final aircraft mods and set-dressing, etc. The lines of P-40 mock-ups were blown up at Wheeler AFB and the PBY Catalinas at NAS Ford Island. The two P-40 fighters take off from Waiele Gulch Field, an abandoned World War II airstrip located in a gully next to Wheeler AFB. The hangar blown up by the "kamikaze Zero" in the final moments of the battle was a hangar at NAS Barber's Point, due for demolition at the time. The U.S.-built Japanese replica aircraft were based and maintained at NAS Barber's Point with the larger aircraft, such as the B-17s, based at Wheeler AFB. Nearby Hickham AFB was still in use at the time, but was not available to the filmmakers because of Vietnam War logistics.

GPS Locations—Hawaii

Pearl Harbor (NAS Ford Island): N21 21.70 / W157 57.70

Wheeler AFB: N21 29.00 / W158 02.15

Waiele Gulch Field: N21 28.10 / W158 02.25

NAS Barber's Point: N21 18.25 / W158 04.15

A three-quarter-scale replica of the carrier *Akagi* and battleship *Nagato* was built on the beach of Ashiya AFB near Fukuoka on the Japanese island of Kyushu. Many of the Japanese planning scenes take place on the *Nagato* set. The *Akagi* carrier set was used for the pre-dawn deck and engine start shots with the Japanese-built replicas. This scene then cuts to the USS *Yorktown* carrier scenes (as described above) for the actual takeoffs.

GPS Location—Japan

Ashiya Beach, Kyushu: N33 53.50 / E130 39.20

Factual Background: December 7, 1941

An assault force of 351 Japanese aircraft, led by Lt. Cmdr. Mitsuo Fuchida, began takeoff at 0615 hours, December 7, 1941. At 0753 hours Fuchida radioed: "*Tora! Tora! Tora!*" (which translates from Japanese to *Tiger! Tiger! Tiger!*), indicating to Admiral Yamamoto and the Japanese Task Force that their approach to Oahu had been a success—the U.S. military forces have been caught unaware. Two waves attacked Pearl Harbor, inflicting heavy losses—the first wave of 183 aircraft attacked from 0750 hours until 0920 hours. The second wave, of 168 aircraft, attacked from 0905 hours until 0945 hours. The entire assault lasted just under two hours and saw the demise of the battleship and the birth of airpower as the decisive tool of war. The Japanese lost nine Zeros, five Kates and fifteen Vals for a total of twenty-nine

Group	Aircraft	Mission
First Wave Attack Formation		
First Group	89 Nakajima B5N2 Kate	Torpedo / bomb battleships
Second Group	51 Aichi D3A1 Val	Dive-bomb airfields
Third Group	43 Mitsubishi A6M2 Zero	Strafe airfields / harbor
Second Wave Attack Formation		
First Group	54 Nakajima B5N2 Kate	Bomb airfields
Second Group	78 Aichi D3A1 Val	Dive-bomb battleships
Third Group	36 Mitsubishi A6M2 Zero	Strafe airfields / harbor

U.S. Casualties		Japanese Casualties	
Navy / Marines	2107	Aircrew	55
Army	233	Sub crew	130
Civilians	48		
Total:	2388	Total:	185
Wounded:	1109	Captured:	1

aircraft. The U.S. lost 169 aircraft with a further 150 damaged. Although twenty-one U.S. naval vessels were severely damaged, eighteen were salvaged and repaired. Only three were written off, the *Oklahoma, Arizona* and *Utah*—the last two becoming memorial sites to the fallen. For details on the Welch and Taylor P-40 dogfights, see under: *Pearl Harbor* (2001).

Toward the Unknown

UK Title: *Brink of Hell*
USA / Warner Bros. / 1956 / Color / 115 minutes
Director: Mervyn LeRoy
Cast: William Holden, Lloyd Nolan, Virginia Leith, Charles McGraw, Murray Hamilton, James Garner
Synopsis / Aviation Content: Korean War pilot Holden, traumatized from his time as a POW, returns to Edwards AFB in an effort to rebuild his former life as a test pilot. A true aviation classic simply because of the high number of historic aircraft types seen throughout the picture, a real look back at the way things were in the USAF during the 1950s. Screenplay by World War II Eighth Air Force veteran and aviation writer Beirne Lay Jr.

The main aircraft featured is the **Martin XB-51** prototype jet-bomber, a large three-engined design which first flew on October 28, 1949. Two prototypes were built, with s/n 46-685 and 46-686, but no production contract was awarded; both aircraft were subsequently based at Edwards as test vehicles for the USAF. It was 46-685 that was used in the film as the fictional, ill-fated Gilbert XF-120. It later crashed on March 25, 1956, at El Paso, killing the pilot while on its way to film extra footage of the aircraft flying in clouds. Its counterpart, 46-686, had crashed some years before on May 9, 1952, during low-level aerobatics.

Filmed entirely at Edwards Air Force Base in California with a multitude of period aircraft. Those noticeably featured are the **Bell X-2** (s/n 46-674); **Boeing B-50 Superfortress**; **Convair C-131B Samaritan** (s/n 53-7790); **Convair XF-92A** (s/n 46-682) as a YF-102 in the opening crash scene; **Convair F-102A Delta Dagger**,

Douglas X-3 Stiletto (s/n 49-2892) parked on apron; **Lockheed F-94C Starfire** (one was s/n 51-5642) in an aerial drag-chute scene; **North American F-100C Super Sabre** (s/n 53-1572), used as the XF-120 chase plane; and **Sikorsky H-19B Chickasaw** (s/n 52-7564).

Noted background aircraft include the Beechcraft C-45 Expeditor; Boeing B-47 Stratojet; Convair B-36 Peacemaker; Douglas B-66 Destroyer; Douglas C-47 Skytrain; Fairchild XC-120 Packplane; Lockheed T-33A Shooting Star; McDonnell F-101 Voodoo; North American F-86 Sabre and F-86D Sabre Dog (s/n 50-462) and Republic F-84 Thunderjet / Thunderstreak. Stock vision of the Boeing B-50 and Bell X-2 were extensively used, and numerous other Edwards AFB activities were also cut into the film.

During filming, General Holtoner, head of Edwards flight testing, took actor William Holden through the sound barrier in a TF-86F Sabre in return for a drive in Holden's new 12-cylinder Ferrari. Holtoner got the car over 120 mph down Edwards' main runway!

Transformers (Non–Aviation Themed Title)

USA / Dreamworks SKG & Paramount Pictures / 2007 / Color / 143 minutes
Director: Michael Bay
Cast: Shia LaBeouf, Megan Fox, Josh Duhamel, Tyrese Gibson, Rachael Taylor, Anthony Anderson, Jon Voight
Synopsis / Aviation Content: Big-screen CGI / live action film developed from the cartoon series of the same name. Large undertaking of military aircraft; featured with some degree of detail is the **Bell-Boeing CV-22B Osprey** (s/n 02-0025, 04-0027); **Fairchild-Republic A-10A Thunderbolt II** (one was s/n 79-0139); **Lockheed AC-130U Spooky II** gunship; **Lockheed-Boeing F-22A Raptor** (s/n 91-4006) and a **Sikorsky MH-53M Pave Low IV**, both as Decepticons. Background and brief appearances are the Bell UH-1H Iroquois; Boeing VC-25A (Air Force One); C-17A Globemaster III (s/n 03-3121); E-3B Sentry; Lockheed C-130H Hercules; F-117A Nighthawk; F-16 Fighting Falcon; Sikorsky UH-60 Black Hawk /

SH-60 Seahawk and a civilian Eurocopter variant. Filmed at Holloman AFB, Alamogordo, and White Sands Missile Range, both in New Mexico.

Transformers: Revenge of the Fallen (Non–Aviation Themed Title)

USA / Dreamworks SKG & Paramount Pictures / 2009 / Color / 144 minutes

Director: Michael Bay

Cast: Shia LaBeouf, Megan Fox, Josh Duhamel, Tyrese Gibson, John Turturro, Ramon Rodriguez

Synopsis / Aviation Content: This massive sequel outdoes the original in digital effects, but of interest here is the multitude of U.S. military aviation hardware. There's some real eye candy here for the aviation fan if you can catch it amongst all the action. Featured in order of appearance is the **Sikorsky UH-60M Black Hawk**; **Boeing AH-64D Longbow Apache**; many **Boeing C-17A Globemaster III** (including s/n 87-0025 (YC-17A), 96-0003, 03-3121), with some excellent footage of these magnificent aircraft in action; a **Lockheed P-3C Orion** (with piston engine sound, no less!); the **Sikorsky MH-53M Pave Low IV** makes another appearance as a Decepticon; **Boeing F/A-18 Hornet** naval fighters; **Boeing-Vertol CH-47 Chinook**; and several Eurocopter types.

The Smithsonian National Air and Space Museum sequence features in a background role a space shuttle; McDonnell Douglas F-4 Phantom II; Grumman A-6A Intruder (BuNo. 154167); Boeing Model 307 Stratoliner; Air France Concorde (reg. F-BVFA); Boeing Dash-80; Learjet 24; Junkers Ju 52 (reg. D-ADLH); the atomic B-29 bomber *Enola Gay*; Republic P-47D Thunderbolt; Curtiss P-40 Kittyhawk; Vought F4U Corsair; Republic F-105 Thunderchief; and a **Lockheed SR-71A Blackbird** in a pivotal role as an elderly Decepticon called Jetfire, who uses an undercarriage strut for a walking stick!

In what can only be described as one of the most jarring transitions in cinema history ... who would have guessed the Smithsonian's backyard is, in fact, AMARC at Davis-Monthan AFB in Tucson, Arizona! The reason for this boggles the mind, but the visuals of all the Lockheed C-130E Hercules (including s/n 63-7880, 70-1265) and C-141 Starlifter (one was s/n 65-9414) transports are quite impressive.

The final (full on!) battle features a multitude of aircraft: **Lockheed-Boeing F-22A Raptor** as the Decepticon Starscream; General Atomics MQ-1 Predator; Jordanian UH-60 (crashed with reg. IY-RSD); more F/A-18 Hornets; Lockheed-Martin F-16C / D Fight Falcon fighters (likely stock footage); U.S. Marine UH-1N Twin Huey; AH-1W HueyCobra; Boeing E-3B Sentry; Rockwell B-1B Lancer (s/n 86-0122, likely stock footage); Fairchild A-10A Warthog and Bell UH-1H Iroquois. Many were CGI created or enhanced for the film.

Transformers: Dark of the Moon
(Non–Aviation Themed Title)

USA / Paramount Pictures / 2011 / Color / 154 minutes

Director: Michael Bay

Cast: Shia LaBeouf, Josh Duhamel, John Turturro, Tyrese Gibson, Rose Huntington-Whitley, Patrick Dempsey, Frances McDormand, John Malkovich, Ken Jeong

Synopsis / Aviation Content: The Autobots are back once more fighting for humanity's survival against the evil Decepticons, and again there are plenty of eye-popping visual effects and military hardware for aviation fans. Main featured aircraft are a **Gulfstream G450** (reg. N4500X / msn 4004) which, in reality, is owned by director Michael Bay; three **Bell UH-1H Iroquois** helicopters owned and operated by NASA (reg. N416NA; reg. N418NA / s/n 65-12876 / msn 5209; reg. N419NA / s/n 65-9708 / msn 4752); a **Bell Model 429** (reg. N429NA / msn 57009); a single shot of a Chicago Police–operated **Bell 206L Long Ranger** (reg. N911YY / msn 52047); and up to half a dozen **Bell-Boeing CV-22B Osprey** (one was s/n 05-0030 / msn D1011) tilt-rotor aircraft provided by the USAF.

Background aircraft are a Boeing-Vertol CH-47D Chinook (likely s/n 92-00292 / msn M-

3433); several Boeing AH-64D Longbow Apache helicopters; several General Atomics MQ-1 Predator drones; and two Sikorsky UH-60L Black Hawk helicopters, all seen at the Autobot headquarters. There are also a vintage British Aircraft Corp. BAC.111-400 (likely reg. N97GA / msn 117); two Gulfstream V/G550 (one is reg. N517QS), jets and a Lockheed C-130H Hercules seen elsewhere in the movie.

CGI created aircraft include the Bell-Boeing CV-22B Osprey, including a fictional 4-engined version; Boeing F/A-18 Hornet fighters; and a Decepticon as a Lockheed-Martin F-22A Raptor. Space shuttle *Discovery* makes a brief appearance, CGI-enhanced with some sort of extra fuel tank. Watch for an excellent cameo appearance by Astronaut Buzz Aldrin.

Treasure of the Yankee Zephyr see   Race for the Yankee Zephyr

True Lies (Non–Aviation Themed Title)

USA / 20th Century–Fox / 1994 / Color / 141 minutes
Director: James Cameron
Cast: Arnold Schwarzenegger, Jamie Lee Curtis, Tom Arnold, Bill Paxton, Tia Carrere, Art Malik
Synopsis / Aviation Content: A clever, very entertaining action yarn, about a family man leading a double life as a spy, makes excellent use of various aircraft types throughout. First seen is a brief appearance by a **Bell 206 Jet Ranger** (reg. N830RC / msn 1801); Juno's private jet is a **Gulfstream II** (reg. N315TS / msn 220); the terrorists helicopter is a strangely marked **Aerospatiale AS.350 B2 Ecureuil** (reg. N5774J / msn 1384); the rescue helicopters are a **Bell 206L-3 Long Ranger** (reg. N16EA / msn 51067) and a hefty **Bell 212** (reg. N2768N / msn 30973); the Marine jet fighters are two **McDonnell Douglas AV-8B Harrier II** jump-jets of Marine Squadron VMA-223. Serial numbers are BuNo. 162946 (msn 68), which had the starring role and BuNo. 164126 (msn 202). The limo-helicopter chase was filmed along the Old Seven Mile Bridge in the Florida Keys.

Turbulence

USA / Metro-Goldwyn-Mayer / 1997 / Color / 100 minutes
Director: Robert Butler
Cast: Ray Liotta, Lauren Holly, Brendon Gleeson, Hector Elizondo, Rachel Ticotin, Jeffrey DeMunn
Synopsis / Aviation Content: A serial killer being transported on a commercial airliner breaks free and kills, among others, the crew, leaving, as usual, no one but the air hostess to fly the plane. Highly unlikely scenarios are exploited for sensationalism and there are enough aeronautical goofs to fill a jumbo jet! One of the lesser examples of the "air disaster genre" that became so popular during the 1990s. Two straight-to-video sequels followed: *Turbulence 2: Fear of Flying* (1999) and *Turbulence 3: Heavy Metal* (2001).

Featured aircraft is a **Boeing 747-238B** (reg. N614FF / msn 20534/195), provided to the production by Tower Air and painted with false reg. "N644FF." First flying on July 27, 1972, this aircraft was delivered to Qantas as VH-EBE on August 10, 1972, and served with them until 1986; to People Express as N609PE in 1986, then Continental in 1987; registration changed to N10024 in 1991; to Tower Air as N614FF in 1994; to Continental Micronesia as N14024 in 1997; placed into storage at Mojave Airport, California, in 2003; destroyed with explosives for a TV documentary in 2008.

Twelve O'Clock High

USA / 20th Century–Fox / 1949 / B&W / 127 minutes
Director: Henry King
Cast: Gregory Peck, Hugh Marlowe, Gary Merrill, Millard Mitchell, Dean Jagger, Robert Arthur, Paul Stewart, John Kellogg, Bob Patten
Synopsis / Aviation Content: A psychological drama about a B-17 bomb group commander's assignment to up the morale of a hard-luck squadron and the subsequent effect it has on him. A massive box office hit in its time and highly regarded by many as the best aviation

film ever made, certainly an American cinema classic. Although it can be a little sparse on aircraft scenes in some places, there are fantastic views of the B-17 Flying Fortress both on the ground and flying. Based on the 1948 novel of the same name by Eighth Air Force veterans Beirne Lay Jr. and Sy Bartlett, both of whom also developed and wrote the screenplay. Definite required viewing for all aviation fans, no excuses! Later developed into a TV series as *12 O'Clock High* (1964–1967).

The USAF gave invaluable support to the production, providing B-17 aircrews and twelve flyable **Boeing B-17G Flying Fortress** bombers—six from storage at Eglin AFB, Florida, four more from the Mobile Air Depot at Brookley AFB, Alabama. A few of the latter were mildly radioactive, having been used at Bikini Atoll as cloud sampling drones in July 1946. The last two bombers were acquired from storage at Roswell AFB, New Mexico.

B-17G-90-DL (s/n 44-83592), was flown solo by Hollywood stunt pilot Paul Mantz in the famous belly landing scene shot at Ozark AAF in June 1949. The aircraft was one of the radioactive Brookley Fortresses but was declared safe for Mantz, as he was only to be flying it for a short period of time. Mantz received a fee of $2,500 and the controlled crash has since become a classic aerial stunt that's been used repeatedly in subsequent films and television shows. B-17G-80-DL (s/n 44-83387) was taken from storage at Pyote, Texas, for use as a studio mock-up for aircraft interior scenes. It was retained afterward by the studio and used in subsequent aviation films and television shows.

UNCONFIRMED DATA

With 44-83592 being confirmed as starring in the film, its history can be applied to other aircraft with similar movements prior to filming. It appears that the 3202nd Maintenance and Supply Group at Eglin completed the conversions and painting of the B-17s selected for the movie during March–April 1949. Using this piece of information the following serial numbers are a known listing of 3202nd assignments during this time, of which any number could have been used in the movie: 44-8142; 44-83486; 44-

83513; 44-83519; 44-83610; 44-83660; 44-83662; 44-83684; 44-85546; 44-85682 and 44-85815.

Wartime stock footage was used for the aerial battles of B-17 bombers in action over Europe. Paul Mantz provided his B-25H (reg. N1203) camera-plane for the air-to-air scenes of the B-17 bombers. Actor Gary Merrill (Col. Keith Davenport) was a USAAF air crewman during World War II. Screenwriter Sy Bartlett was a major with the Eighth Air Force in England and later Guam in the Pacific. Screenwriter Beirne Lay Jr. joined the USAAC in 1932 as a pilot, then later became a writer and wrote about his flying experiences in *I Wanted Wings*, which became a 1941 film. He returned to active duty with the USAAF (flew combat in the B-24) during World War II, helping to form the Eighth Air Force in England and attaining the rank of lieutenant colonel.

Principal photography took place from April 17 to July 1, 1949, at two airfields in proximity to each other. The (abandoned since 1945) Ozark AAF, Alabama, was where the opening scenes of the derelict runway at "Archbury" were shot. The lawns and area were then cleaned up to depict a working wartime English base where the B-17 takeoffs, landings and apron scenes were filmed. Duke Field (Eglin Auxiliary Field #3), Florida, was where the film's main buildings and set pieces were located for the on-base ground scenes. A few B-17 bombers were flown in for background. Duke was an outlying field to the main Eglin AFB, Florida.

GPS LOCATIONS

Ozark AAF (Cairns AAF since 1959), Alabama: N31 16.50 / W085 42.70

Duke Field (Eglin Aux. Field #3), Florida: N30 38.60 / W086 31.30

20,000 Men a Year

USA / 20th Century–Fox / 1939 / B&W / 84 minutes

Director: Alfred E. Green

Cast: Randolph Scott, Preston Foster, Margaret Lindsay, Mary Healy, Robert Shaw, George Ernest

Synopsis / Aviation Content: An experienced pilot

played by Scott becomes a flight instructor. Later, one of his students is reported overdue while flying over the Grand Canyon. Story by former naval aviator turned Hollywood screenwriter Frank "Spig" Wead. A prewar preparedness film designed to promote the newly formed Civilian Pilot Training Program. Hollywood flyer Paul Mantz was chief pilot and provided his **Stearman C2B** (reg. NX4099 / msn 110) and **C3B** (NC6491 / msn 190) biplanes for the film. Filmed in part at Monrovia Airport, California, and around the Grand Canyon in Arizona.

Uncommon Valor (Non–Aviation Themed Title)

USA / Paramount Pictures / 1983 / Color / 105 minutes

Director: Ted Kotcheff

Cast: Gene Hackman, Robert Stack, Fred Ward, Reb Brown, Randall "Tex" Cobb, Patrick Swayze

Synopsis / Aviation Content: Very 1980s-style film about a father's attempts to rescue his MIA son from a Laos POW camp. Some very good helicopter action throughout will be of interest to rotary wing fans. The training camp scenes in the U.S. made use of three **Bell 206B Jet Ranger** helicopters (reg. N230CA / msn 2779; reg. N250CA / msn 2615; reg. N5736L / msn 3102). The Laos POW camp was filmed in Lumahai Valley, Kauai, Hawaii, with two **Bell 212** choppers marked as "2167" and "6051," plus one **Bell 206B Jet Ranger** marked as "102." Two **Bell UH-1H Iroquois** wrecks were obtained for background set dressing and crash scenes; one had a fake Bell 212 engine cowling attached, as seen in the opening sequence. The private jet at the airport was a **Hawker Siddeley HS.125 Series 400** (reg. N5594U / msn 25219).

United 93

USA-UK-France / Universal Pictures / 2006 / Color / 111 minutes

Director: Paul Greengrass

Cast: David Alan Basche, Richard Bekins, Susan Blommaert, Ray Charleson, Christian Clemen-son, Khalid Abdalla, Lewis Alsamari, David Rasche, Chip Zien, Denny Dillon, Rebecca Schull, Gregg Henry

Synopsis / Aviation Content: Harrowing, realistic account of the heroism onboard the United Airlines Boeing 757 that prevented it from reaching its target in Washington, D.C., on September 11, 2001. Filming took place onboard a retired former MyTravel Airways **Boeing 757-225** fuselage (reg. G-MCEA / msn 22200/20), using hand-held cameras at Pinewood Studios, Buckinghamshire, England, from October to December 2005. Although actors portray many of the passengers, some of the cast are the actual airline ground employees playing themselves from that infamous day. Not to be confused with the similar Fox Television movie *Flight 93*, also released in 2006.

FACTUAL BACKGROUND:
9/11 AIRLINERS

Aircraft Type: **Boeing 757-222**

Delivered: June 28, 1996

Airline: United Airlines

Flight / Route: Flight 93 / Newark to San Francisco

Registration: N591UA

MSN / Line number: 28142 / 718

Timeline: 08:42—departs Newark Intl., New Jersey. 10:03—crashes in a field near Pittsburgh, Pennsylvania.

Aircraft Type: **Boeing 757-223**

Delivered: May 8, 1991

Airline: American Airlines

Flight / Route: Flight 77 / Washington to Los Angeles

Registration: N644AA

MSN / Line number: 24602 / 365

Timeline: 08:20—departs Washington Dulles Intl., Washington. 09:37—crashes into Pentagon building, Washington D.C.

Aircraft Type: **Boeing 767-222**

Delivered: February 23, 1983

Airline: United Airlines

Flight / Route: Flight 175 / Boston to Los Angeles

Registration: N612UA

MSN / Line number: 21873 / 41

Timeline: 08:14—departs Logan Intl., Boston.

09:03—"second plane," hits Building 2 (South Tower). 09:59—South Tower collapses.

Aircraft Type: **Boeing 767-223ER**

Delivered: April 13, 1987

Airline: American Airlines

Flight / Route: Flight 11 / Boston to Los Angeles

Registration: N334AA

MSN / Line Number: 22332 / 169

Timeline: 07:59—departs Logan Intl., Boston. 08:46—"first plane," hits Building 1 (North Tower featuring mast). 10:29—North Tower collapses.

View from the Top

USA / Miramax Films / 2003 / Color / 87 minutes

Director: Bruno Barreto

Cast: Gwyneth Paltrow, Christina Applegate, Mark Ruffalo, Candice Bergen

Synopsis / Aviation Content: Romance-comedy fare of a young woman's aspirations to become an international flight stewardess. Brief scenes filmed at Laughlin-Bullhead Intl. Airport, Nevada, with a rarely seen 1952 **Martin 404** vintage airliner (reg. N636X / msn 14135), provided by Jeff Whitesell's Airliners of America. Filmed from December 2000 to March 2001 for a late 2001 release, the film suffered various delays and recuts due to the sensitivities surrounding the terrorist attacks of September 11, 2001. It was finally released in mid–2003. *Airport* series star George Kennedy makes a brief cameo appearance.

A View to a Kill (Non–Aviation Themed Title) see *James Bond* Series

Von Richthofen and Brown

UK Title: *The Red Baron*

USA / United Artists / 1971 / Color / 96 minutes

Director: Roger Corman

Cast: John Phillip Law, Don Stroud, Barry Primus, Corin Redgrave, Karen Huston, Hurd Hatfield, Stephen McHattie, Brian Foley

Synopsis / Aviation Content: German ace Man-

fred von Richthofen and American pilot Roy Brown face off in the skies over France in 1918. Lower production values are made up for by outstanding aerial sequences and camera angles. Still a must-see for any biplane fan, although the many historical factual errors may make some of the more purist of aviation fans cringe.

Six **Currie Wot S.E.5a** replicas made up the RAF fighters—see under *Darling Lili* (1970) for details. Also used were the two *Blue Max* **Miles S.E.5a** replicas. German forces made use of one **Fokker Dr. I** replica, three **Fokker D.VII-65** replicas, one **Pfalz D.IIIa** replica, and a **Caudron C.277**—see under *The Blue Max* (1966) for details on all these aircraft. **DeHavilland DH.82A Tiger Moth** and **Stampe SV.4C** biplanes made up many of the background aircraft for both sides. The *Blue Max* filming location at Western Aerodrome, Leixlip, Ireland; was used for the airfield scenes; leftover mock-ups and sets were also used from the earlier film *Darling Lili* (1970).

Tragically, one of the *Blue Max* S.E.5a replicas, EI-ARA, crashed on September 15, 1970, killing pilot Charles Boddington, a veteran pilot of both *The Blue Max* and *Darling Lili* film shoots. The very next day, a Stampe biplane also crashed after a bird strike. Pilot Lyn Garrison and actor Don Stroud walked away with moderate injuries.

Unfortunately, built-up modern-day areas can be seen in many of the backgrounds during the dogfight sequences. Biplane models were blown up at Edwards Air Force Base, California, during post-production for many of the action sequences.

The War Lover

UK / Columbia Pictures / 1962 / B&W / 105 minutes

Director: Philip Leacock

Cast: Steve McQueen, Robert Wagner, Shirley Anne Field, Gary Cockrell, Michael Crawford

Synopsis / Aviation Content: An overconfident B-17 pilot, who's enjoying the war, clashes with his cool-headed copilot over the risks he takes while commanding his aircraft and crew. Magnificent B-17 sequences featuring a lot of detail plus some striking camera angles; a worthy film for the most avid of Fortress fans. One highlight is a memorable B-17 low-level pass through an RAF airfield! Based on the 1959 novel of the same name by American author John Hersey.

Type	msn	Military s/n	Civil reg.
Boeing B-17G-85-DL Flying Fortress	32204	44-83563	N9563Z
Boeing B-17G-95-DL Flying Fortress	32452	44-83811	—
Boeing B-17G-95-DL Flying Fortress	32518	44-83877	N5232V
Boeing B-17G-95-DL Flying Fortress	32524	44-83883	N5229V

Renowned pilot / businessman John Crewdson and his company, Film Aviation Services Ltd., located, restored and operated the three flyable B-17 bombers for the film. N9563Z was purchased in Arizona; N5229V and N5232V were purchased from Love Field in Texas, where they had been in storage since 1957. All three were owned by Aero American Corp. of Tucson, Arizona. The plans were overhauled in Arizona with retro-fitted turrets and updated radio and navigation equipment. Crewdson and his pilots then left Tucson on September 23, 1961, and arrived at the filming location in England on October 8. Their epic journey across the Atlantic was plagued by mechanical problems, foul weather and problems with authorities. This all later became the subject of a book titled *Everything but the Flak* by Martin Caiden, who was the co-pilot on N9563Z.

S/n 44-83563 (N9563Z) was a VB-17G staff transport in the Philippines post–World War II and supposedly carried Generals MacArthur and Eisenhower. It entered the civilian market in 1959 and was purchased by Columbia Pictures in 1961 from Aero American Corp. in Tucson. It flew in the film as the main B-17, named *The Body*, with false s/n "127762." It would later fly in *Tora! Tora! Tora!* (1970) and become a major aircraft on the American Warbird scene. S/n 44-83877 (N5232V) and 44-83883 (N5229V) were both PB-1W search and rescue Fortresses with the U.S. Navy as BuNo. 77240 and 77243 respectively. These aircraft flew in the film with false s/n "127741" and "127749," and were both scrapped in England upon completion of filming during early 1962. B-17G (s/n 44-83811 / ex-reg. NL5014N) has the distinction of being one of three B-17 bombers acquired by Israel after World War II and actually bombed Cairo in a raid on July 14, 1948. It was later sold to an American operator as N9814F, then impounded for smuggling arms in 1958 and broken up at Lydda Airport in Israel. The derelict was purchased by John Crewdson in mid–1961 on behalf of Columbia Pictures for fuselage interior shots. The fuselage was also used for exterior scenes of the crashed Fortress, *House of Usher*, filmed at RAF Bovingdon. Nose art and markings on the Forts were changed regularly to make it appear there were many more than just

Two of the three B-17 Flying Fortress bombers, N5229V and N5232V, ferried across the Atlantic to England for the 1962 film *The War Lover*; both were scrapped after filming. The third B-17 was N9563Z, which survives on the Warbird scene today. Photograph: James H. Farmer Collection.

three aircraft; names included *Alabama Wham-mer, Angel Tread, The Body, Chug Pug, Erector Get, Expendable VI, Hellcat Annie, House of Usher* and *Round Trip Ticket.*

Tragically, Mike Reilly, one of the British para-chutists hired to perform the bail-out sequence, was drowned in the English Channel after becom-ing entangled in his parachute lines. Reilly was the chairman of the British Parachuting Associa-tion with four international championships. The camera-plane was a B-25J (s/n 44-30861 / reg. N9089Z), also purchased from Aero American Corp. in Arizona. Newsreel combat footage was used during action sequences, as well as footage from *Twelve O'Clock High* (1949), especially Paul Mantz's famous B-17 belly landing stunt. Some models and miniatures were created for aircraft explosions.

The ground, taxi and takeoff scenes were filmed at RAF Bovingdon, Hertfordshire, En-gland, from October 23 into November 1961. The spectacular low-pass sequence was flown by John Crewdson over this airfield. RAF Manston, Kent, England, was used as a base for the over-water fly-ing scenes. Interiors were filmed at Shepperton Studios, Surrey, with B-17 fuselage s/n 44-83811.

GPS Locations

RAF Bovingdon, Hertfordshire (closed 1972): N51 43.60 / W000 32.70

RAF Manston, Kent (closed 1999): N51 20.70 / E001 20.40

The Way to the Stars

U.S. Title: *Johnny in the Clouds*
UK / Rank Organisation / 1945 / B&W / 109 min-utes
Director: Anthony Asquith
Cast: Michael Redgrave, John Mills, Rosamund John, Douglass Montgomery, Renee Asherson, Stanley Holloway
Synopsis / Aviation Content: The story of an RAF base named Halfpenny, as seen through the eyes of a young lady who falls for both a British and American pilot stationed there. Written by former RAF flight lieutenant Ter-ence Rattigan, based on his 1942 play *Flare Path*, and Captain Richard Sherman of the

USAAF. A significant film in that it was the only such wartime-produced picture to capture a real, working USAAF unit in an overseas the-ater. Aircraft are the **Boeing B-17G Flying Fortress** bombers of the 384th BG; **Bristol Blenheim Mk. II** bombers; **Douglas Boston** bombers; and **Hawker Hurricane** fighters. Filmed in part at RAF Catterick, North York-shire, England. The UK title is taken from the RAF Latin motto *Per ardua ad astra*. The U.S. title is from an ode to RAF pilots by John Pudney titled *For Johnny*. Released in the U.S. through United Artists and cut to 87 min-utes.

GPS Location

RAF Catterick, North Yorkshire (closed 1994): N54 22.00 / W001 37.10

West Point of the Air

USA / Metro-Goldwyn-Mayer / 1935 / B&W / 89 minutes
Director: Richard Rosson
Cast: Wallace Beery, Robert Young, Lewis Stone, Maureen O'Sullivan, Russell Hardie, Rosalind Russell, James Gleason, Henry Wadsworth
Synopsis / Aviation Content: An Army sergeant urges his son to pursue a career as an Army pilot at the Army's central air training school in Texas known as "West Point of the Air." Excellent footage captured of period USAAC trainer aircraft along with mass takeoffs and formation flights. Story co-written by former World War I flight instructor John Monk Saun-ders, with a script co-written by former naval aviator turned Hollywood screenwriter Frank "Spig" Wead.

Featured aircraft are a 1911 **Curtiss D Pusher** (reg. N8Y / msn 101) replica built by Billy Parker in 1934 under direction from Hollywood pilot Paul Mantz, who was the technical director on the film; many 1927 **Consolidated PT-3** trainer biplanes; **Douglas (Northrop) BT-1** dive-bombers; a **Lockheed 5B Vega** (reg. NC48M / msn 100); and a **Stearman C3** biplane. Filmed from November 1934 to January 1935 at Ran-dolph AAF near San Antonio, Texas.

GPS LOCATION

Randolph AFB, San Antonio, Texas: N29 31.55 / W098 17.15

We Were Soldiers (Non–Aviation Themed Title)

USA / Paramount Pictures / 2002 / Color / 137 minutes

Director: Randall Wallace

Cast: Mel Gibson, Madeleine Stowe, Greg Kinnear, Sam Elliott, Chris Klein, Keri Russell

Synopsis / Aviation Content: The true story of the major battle between U.S. soldiers and the NVA in La Drang Valley, Vietnam, in 1965 led by Lt. Col. Hal Moore as played by Gibson. Two **Bell UH-1B**, four **UH-1H Iroquois**, one **Boeing-Vertol CH-47 Chinook**, two **Douglas A-1 Skyraiders** and one UH-1H wreck were used in filming. Stock footage of Grumman A-6A Intruders came from *Flight of the Intruder* (1991). CGI creations were seen of the Douglas A-4 Skyhawk, McDonnell-Douglas F-4 Phantom II and North American F-100 Super Sabre.

The Wild Blue Yonder

UK Title: *Thunder Across the Pacific*

USA / Republic Pictures / 1951 / B&W / 98 minutes

Director: Allan Dwan

Cast: Wendell Corey, Vera Ralston, Forrest Tucker, Phil Harris, Walter Brennan, William Ching, Ruth Donnelly, Harry Carey Jr., Penny Edwards

Synopsis / Aviation Content: Subtitled "The Story of the B-29 Superfortress," this, even then, outdated film follows the combat development of the B-29 from China into the Pacific. It features the usual love triangle scenario of two bomber crewmen interested in the same woman. Filmed at March AFB, California, using **Boeing B-29A Superfortress** bombers of the 22nd BG just returned from the Korean War. A B-29-35-MO fuselage (s/n 42-65401) was also used for studio filming of aircraft interiors and to recreate the crash in the finale, the tail marked as "26314." Several **Douglas C-47 Skytrain** (one was s/n 43-48096) transports are visible in the background. Much use of stock wartime footage that includes the B-29 bombing Japan and North American P-51D Mustang fighters in action. The final shot depicts large numbers of the **Convair B-36 Peacemaker**.

The Wild Geese (Non–Aviation Themed Title)

UK / Rank Film Organization / 1978 / Color / 134 minutes

Director: Andrew V. McLaglen

The well-known C-47 Dakota ZS-UAS that appeared in *The Wild Geese* (1978) with actor Roger Moore at the controls. It was later lost in an accident in 1988 killing all onboard. Photograph: Peter Wonfor via the Dakota Association of South Africa.

Cast: Richard Burton, Roger Moore, Richard Harris, Hardy Kruger, Stewart Granger, Jack Watson

Synopsis / Aviation Content: Burton is hired to lead a group of mercenaries into Africa to rescue a political leader being held captive. An entertaining film with several great leading and supporting British actors also features some aviation sequences pivotal to the story. The large transport used to get the group into Africa is a **Lockheed L-100-20** (reg. ZS-GSK / msn 382E-4385), a civilian version of the Lockheed C-130 Hercules military transport. Sold to Safair Freighters of South Africa, it was named *Boland*, which can be seen written on the side of the aircraft. The small twin-engined attack aircraft appears to be a **Cessna 310** with Swaziland registration 3D-ABN. The Dakota in the final sequence is a **Douglas C-47-DL Skytrain** (s/n 41-38695 / msn 6154 / reg. ZS-UAS), provided by United Air of South Africa. It was a DC-3C with a Viewmaster conversion evident from the modified passenger windows. After filming, it was named *The Wild Goose* in honor of its starring role. ZS-UAS crashed near Hennenman, South Africa, on April 12, 1988, after a fire broke out in the right fuel boost pump; all twenty-four onboard were killed.

Wild in the Sky

USA / American International Pictures (AIP) / 1972 / Color / 87 minutes

Director: William T. Naud

Cast: Brandon De Wilde, Keenan Wynn, Tim O'Connor, Richard Gautier, Robert Lansing, Georg Standford Brown, James Daly

Synopsis / Aviation Content: Three radical antiwar activists decide to hijack an air force bomber and use its nuclear payload to destroy Fort Knox. A muddled comedy featuring to some degree the **Boeing B-52 Stratofortress**. Very few further details.

Wing and a Prayer

USA / 20th Century–Fox / 1944 / B&W / 97 minutes

Director: Henry Hathaway

Cast: Don Ameche, Dana Andrews, William Eythe, Charles Bickford, Sir Cedric Hardwicke

Synopsis / Aviation Content: Fictional story of "Carrier X" sent on a decoy mission to avoid enemy contact in order to bluff the Japanese in the leadup to the Battle of Midway. Sharp, clear operational footage obtained of life and duties on an aircraft carrier during wartime.

Filmed onboard the USS *Yorktown* (CV-10) during a shakedown cruise off the U.S. east coast from April to June 1943. The main aircraft featured is the **Grumman TBF-1 Avenger** and **Grumman F6F-3 Hellcat**, with amazingly detailed shots captured of both aircraft. Also featured to an extent is the **Curtiss SB2C Helldiver**, which were on carrier evaluation trials when filming was underway. The aircraft failed its initial carrier trials during this cruise. Three **Grumman F4F Wildcat** fighters were painted as Japanese Zeros for the air battles. One Grumman Avenger doubled for a Japanese torpedo bomber in the final battle. A few brief shots of the Douglas SBD Dauntless are included in what appears to be stock footage.

Two actual crashes were caught on film during production—the first was a Curtiss SB2C, which stalled into the ocean after takeoff, and the second was a Grumman Hellcat in a landing accident. One Grumman Avenger was loaned to Fox Studios for cockpit close-ups and for the scene of a ditched Avenger, which was filmed in a giant studio water tank. Battle scenes featured special effects miniatures of both ship and aircraft, plus newsreel footage of actual combat.

Winged Victory

USA / 20th Century–Fox / 1944 / B&W / 130 minutes

Director: George Cukor

Cast: Lon McCallister, Jeanne Crain, Edmond O'Brien, Jane Ball, Mark Daniels, Jo-Carroll Dennison

Synopsis / Aviation Content: A group of young cadets join the Army's air training program, going through the tough course to make them pilots—some get their wings, some don't. Based on the 1943 Broadway stage play of the same name by Moss Hart, who would also adapt the screenplay for the film version. Big budget "recruitment production" from Hollywood kingpin Daryl F. Zanuck, making a high use of film and military resources, seemed relevant in early 1943 when the play was conceived, but by the film's premiere in December 1944, it was almost outdated. A since forgotten film, it's now sought after for its content of the B-24 Liberator bomber—an aircraft not often seen in aviation films.

Featured aircraft were up to twenty-seven **Consolidated B-24 Liberator** bombers; fifty-five **Vultee BT-13 Valiant** trainers (one was s/n 42-89464); numerous **Cessna AT-8 / AT-17 Bobcat** trainers; and several **Curtiss P-40 Warhawk** fighters in the background. Filmed from June 15 to September 25, 1944, at many Californian Army airfields, including Stockton, Fort MacArthur and Hamilton. The production used up to 3,000 Army personnel during the course of filming. Notably, this mammoth film premiered at Grauman's Chinese Theater in Hollywood on December 26, 1944, and was attended by several aircraft industry legends, such as Donald Douglas, Jack K. Northrop, Howard Hughes and J.H. Kindelberger from North American.

Wings

USA / Paramount Pictures / 1927 / B&W / 141 minutes

Director: William A. Wellman

Cast: Clara Bow, Charles "Buddy" Rogers, Richard Arlen, Jobyna Ralston, Gary Cooper

Synopsis / Aviation Content: Two friends rival each other for the same girl just as they are shipped overseas to serve in World War I as fighter pilots with the Air Service. Hugely successful in its time and still highly regarded today for its aesthetics and originality. It was the first film to win a Best Picture Oscar in 1929 (the category then known as "Most Outstanding Production"), and began former World War I fighter pilot William A. Wellman's career as a film director. The aerial footage was extremely well executed and set the benchmark for others to follow, largely thanks to the persistence of

director Wellman and his aerial photographer Harry Perry. Story written by American writer and former World War I flight instructor John Monk Saunders. Actor Gary Cooper became an overnight star with his brief appearance as a pilot.

Generous help was provided by the USAAC, who made around 300 pilots and 220 aircraft available to the filmmakers. The USAAC considered the production good public relations and flying experience for their pilots. Aircraft included the **Airco (DeHavilland) DH.4** British-designed bomber biplane, some of which came from the 11th, 90th and 96th Bomb Squadrons; **Curtiss P-1 Hawk** biplanes of the 17th, 27th, 94th and 95th Pursuit Squadrons, some doubling as the German Fokker D.VII; **Fokker D.VII** biplanes, playing of course German fighters; **Royal Aircraft Factory S.E.5** biplanes playing the British fighters; several **SPAD S.VII**, a French-designed biplane; **Martin MB-2 (NBS-1)** twin-engined biplane bombers of the 11th and 96th Bomb Squadrons; **Thomas-Morse (Boeing) MB-3A** scout fighters of the 43rd Pursuit Squadron, with some doubling as SPAD S.VII fighters; **Vought VE-7 Bluebird** biplanes from the 1st Pursuit Group; and a series of balloons from the First Balloon Company, Scott Field, Illinois.

Some aircraft were fitted with remote control cameras, being used to film the actors while actually flying in a second cockpit behind the pilot. Actor Richard Arlen had served as a pilot in the Royal Flying Corps. in Canada during World War I, and Charles "Buddy" Rogers learned to fly during production, with both lead actors doing their own flying on many occasions. Stunt pilot Dick Grace intentionally crashed up to two SPAD and two Fokker D.VII fighters for the film, and one army pilot was killed in a separate off-camera flying incident.

Principal filming began in late July 1926 and continued through to April 1927 at the U.S. Army's Kelly Field, Brook Field and Camp Stanley near San Antonio, Texas. The production was troubled by weather and the technical limitations around shooting the aerial battles, the production schedule then ballooning out for both the filmmakers and the military. This in turn resulted in the U.S.

Congress's banning the USAAC from any further use of "public resources" in making motion pictures.

FACTUAL BACKGROUND: WILLIAM A. WELLMAN

William Augustus Wellman, born February 29, 1896, was one of America's premier film directors, most famous for his groundbreaking film *Wings* (1927). During World War I, Wellman went to Europe and joined the French Foreign Legion, who assigned him to the N.87 *escadrille* in the Lafayette Flying Corps as a pilot in Nieuport 17 and 24 biplane fighters. With three confirmed kills and five probable, Wellman earned the French *Croix de Guerre* medal and two palms, but was later shot down and suffered an injury to his leg, which left him with a slight limp for the rest of his life. After the war, Wellman returned to the States and taught combat tactics with the U.S. Army Air Service in San Diego. Often flying to Hollywood during weekends, he came to know actor Douglas Fairbanks, who introduced him to a new and fledgling movie industry. First working as an actor, Wellman then turned to directing, and after the huge success of *Wings* in 1927, went on to make many films mainly in the action/drama genre, cementing himself as one of the great Hollywood directors. Wellman would make many more aviation pictures in subsequent years, including *The Legion of the Condemned* (1928), *Young Eagles* (1930), *Central Airport* (1933), *Men With Wings* (1938), *Thunder Birds* (1942), *This Man's Navy* (1945), *Gallant Journey* (1946), *Island in the Sky* (1953), *The High and the Mighty* (1954) and *Lafayette Escadrille* (1958), which he directed, produced, co-wrote and narrated. Wellman died from leukemia on December 9, 1975.

Wings for the Eagle

USA / Warner Bros. / 1942 / B&W / 84 minutes
Director: Lloyd Bacon
Cast: Ann Sheridan, Dennis Morgan, Jack Carson, George Tobias, Russell Arms, Don DeFore, Tom Fadden, John Ridgely
Synopsis / Aviation Content: A romance drama centered around a married couple who work in an aircraft plant during World War II. Wartime propaganda picture with a love triangle (can't they ever think of anything else?) as the central story. Filmed in January and February 1942 at the Lockheed aircraft plant in Burbank, California, and at the Curtiss-Wright plant in Buffalo, New York. Featured aircraft include the **Lockheed Hudson** and **P-38 Lightning**. Notable for its rare glances inside a wartime assembly plant.

The Wings of Eagles

USA / Metro-Goldwyn-Mayer / 1957 / Color / 110 minutes
Director: John Ford
Cast: John Wayne, Dan Dailey, Maureen O'Hara, Ward Bond, Ken Curtis
Synopsis / Aviation Content: The story of real-life naval aviator Frank "Spig" Wead, excellently played by Wayne. Wead passionately promoted military aviation first as a pilot, then as a successful Hollywood screenwriter after an accident fractured his neck. A gallant film tribute from famous director John Ford that unfortunately feels somewhat superficial and bounces from comedy to drama in a jarring fashion. The flying scenes are limited; the best, seen at the start of the film, are performed by Hollywood stunt pilot Paul Mantz (who goes uncredited), in his **Standard J-1** (civilian reg. N2826D / msn 1598), marked as "A-109." Other aircraft include brief glimpses of a **Douglas DC-3**, **Grumman TBF Avenger**, **F6F Hellcat**, and **Vought F4U Corsair**. Battle sequences make much use of period newsreel film footage.

FACTUAL BACKGROUND: FRANK "SPIG" WEAD

Born on October 24, 1895, Wead was a 1916 graduate of the U.S. Naval Academy and served during World War I on board a minelayer in the North Sea. After the war he became interested in naval aviation and trained as a pilot at NAS Pensacola, Florida, where he graduated on April 17, 1920. He actively promoted the future of military aviation through air racing with the U.S. Army and speed competitions. Lt. Wead led a navy team that won the 1923 Schneider Trophy in a Curtiss CR-3. Tragedy struck in April 1926 when Wead tripped on the stairs in his house, breaking his neck. Whilst recovering in the hospital, Wead began a writing career, which eventually led him to write screenplays for Hollywood and strike up a friendship with director John Ford. Wead served on several aircraft carriers during World War II until a heart scare cut short his active duty; he was discharged from the U.S. Navy on July 21, 1944, going into retirement. He died from natural causes On November 15, 1947. Ford later made a film about Wead titled *The Wings of Eagles* (1957) starring John Wayne. Wead either wrote the story or screenplay for *The Flying Fleet* (1929), *Hell Divers* (1931), *Dirigible* (1931), *Air Mail* (1932), *West Point of the Air* (1935), *Storm over the Andes* (1935), *Ceiling Zero* (1936), *China Clipper* (1936), *Test Pilot* (1938), *Tail Spin* (1939), *20,000 Men a Year* (1939), *I Wanted Wings* (1941), *Dive Bomber* (1941), *International Squadron* (1941), *The Beginning or the End* (1947) and *Blaze of Noon* (1947).

Wings of the Apache   see   *Fire Birds*

Wings of the Navy

USA / Warner Bros. / 1939 / B&W / 89 minutes
Director: Lloyd Bacon
Cast: George Brent, Olivia DeHavilland, John Payne, Frank McHugh, John Litel, Victor Jory
Synopsis / Aviation Content: Two brothers compete to be the better naval pilot, all the while both are also courting the same lady. A big-budget, prewar "preparedness film" has an all-too-often conventional Hollywood story but above-average flying scenes thanks to the multitude of naval aircraft, especially the much-loved Catalina. Highly regarded as one of the must-see pre–World War II military aviation films.

Aircraft featured in some detail were the then new **Consolidated PBY-1 / -2 / -3 Catalina** flying boats of Navy Squadrons VP-7, VP-9, VP-11 and VP-12; **Boeing F4B-4** biplanes; **Boeing-Stearman N2S Kaydet** biplanes; the **Grumman J2F Duck** in the background; extensive scenes of the **Naval Aircraft Factory N3N Canary** biplane

trainer; the **North American NJ-1** advanced trainer; **Vought O3U-6** and **SBU-1 Corsair** naval types. The fictional experimental biplane was a **Grumman F3F-1**, which was also seen as a scale model in the dive scene. There's some excellent footage depicting naval ground operations of the Canary and Catalina. A detailed, studio-based, wooden Catalina replica was built for interior filming. Filmed from July to September 1938 at both NAS San Diego, California, and NAS Pensacola, Florida. Hollywood pilot Paul Mantz was the aerial director and provided his Lockheed 8 Sirius, NC117W, as a camera-plane.

GPS LOCATIONS
NAS San Diego, California: N32 42.00 / W117 12.45
NAS Pensacola, Florida: N30 21.10 / W087 19.00

FACTUAL BACKGROUND: THE CATALINA

Without a doubt, the most famous flying boat / amphibian aircraft ever built. A grand total of 3,282 of the type were produced from 1934 to 1945, more than all other seaplane types from the period put together! A unique airplane, it had a large, straight-through wing mounted above the fuselage via a center pylon. The wing housed all the fuel, which allowed for very long flight durations, excellent for over-water patrol missions. The prototype first flew as the Consolidated Model 28, XP3Y-1 on March 21, 1935. Its unique potential was soon realized and the U.S. Navy took delivery starting from 1936 of 60 PBY-1, 50 PBY-2, 66 PBY-3 and 33 PBY-4 Catalina flying boats. The PBY-5 appeared in 1940; 1,175 were built, along with 156 from the Naval Aircraft Yard as the PBN-1 Nomad. Boeing of Canada produced 307 as the PB2B-1 / -2. An amphibious version, as the definitive PBY-5A, first flew in 1941; 828 were built, followed by 175 as the PBY-6A, 55 by Boeing Canada as the Canso A, and 369 by Canadian-Vickers as the PBV-1A. The RAF was a large user, acquiring 698, and RCAF had up to 245. The USAAF / USAF utilized 296 Catalinas designated as the OV-10 in the observation role. The last PBY-6A was retired from U.S. military service in 1957. In a civilian role, the Catalina proved its worth in the firefighting arena, serving into the 1990s. Many were modified and up-graded, such as the Stewart-Davis Super Cat, Bird Innovator and Super Canso 1000.

Without Orders

USA / RKO Radio Pictures / 1936 / B&W / 64 minutes

Director: Lew Landers

Cast: Sally Eilers, Robert Armstrong, Frances Sage, Charley Grapewin, Vinton Hayworth, Ward Bond, Frank M. Thomas, May Boley

Synopsis / Aviation Content: Regular love-triangle story between a pilot, hostess and hot-shot young pilot. The concluding scene of the hostess landing the airliner began a long history of such scenarios in aviation disaster films. The featured aircraft is a **Boeing Model 247D** (reg. NC2666 / msn 1946); it was first registered as NX12272 for testing; then to N92Y for export to Germany, but the sale was canceled and it was sold to Phillips Petroleum Co. as NC2666; exported to Canada in 1939 as CF-MBR, then into RCAF service in 1940 (s/n 7635); back to civilian service in 1942 as CF-BVZ, then back to the U.S. after World War II as NC41819; its final fate is unknown. Other aircraft include a **Ryan ST-A** (reg. NC14956 / msn 112) and **Pasped Skylark W-1** (reg. NC14919). Filmed partly at Grand Central Air Terminal in Glen-dale, California, and Salt Lake City Airport, Utah, from mid- to late 1936.

With You in My Arms   see
Lafayette Escadrille

The World Is Not Enough

(Non–Aviation Themed Title)   see
James Bond Series

X-15

USA / United Artists / 1961 / Color / 107 minutes
Director: Richard Donner
Cast: David McLean, Charles Bronson, Ralph Taeger, Brad Dexter, Kenneth Tobey, James

Gregory, Mary Tyler Moore, Patricia Owens, Lisabeth Hush, Stanley Livingston

Synopsis / Aviation Content: An almost documentary approach is taken in this account of the USAF- and NASA-run X-15 program and the toll it takes on the pilots and their families. Almost half the film is aerial action with great views of the X-15 itself and the giant B-52 carrier aircraft. Some excellent views of Edwards AFB operations and equipment. Much of the footage was shot by NASA and USAF photographic crews on actual test flights. Narration by screen legend and USAFR Brig. Gen. James Stewart.

Type	msn	Military s/n
Boeing B-52A-1-BO Stratofortress	16493	52-003
Boeing RB-52B-10-BO Stratofortress	16498	52-008
Lockheed YF-104A-1-LO Starfighter	183-1010	55-2964
North American F-100F-15-NA Super Sabre	243-239	56-3963
North American X-15A-NA	240-2	56-6671
North American X-15A-NA	240-3	56-6672

Largely filmed at Edwards AFB, California, using the real aircraft from the actual X-15 program. These are the second and third X-15 experimental aircraft: 56-6671 and 56-6672. The two B-52 bombers were converted to X-15 carrier aircraft with a pylon fitted under the starboard wing; they were redesignated as the NB-52A, 52-003, and NB-52B, 52-008, for the program. The NB-52B was retained by NASA as a test aircraft, logging over 1,000 missions by the time of its retirement in 2005. The YF-104A, 55-2964, was one of seventeen service test aircraft later upgraded to F-104A standard, some of which were sent to NASA as chase planes. The F-100F, 56-3963, was a 2-seater trainer version of the F-100D. The crash sequence uses file footage of an actual, fatal mishap of North American F-100C-20-NA Super Sabre (s/n 54-1907 / msn 217-168), which was filmed crashing at Edwards AFB on January 10, 1956, killing the pilot. Also seen is a **Piasecki H-21 Workhorse** in several shots. Models and special effects were used for some upper atmosphere scenes.

FACTUAL BACKGROUND:
THE X-15

Of all the "X-Plane" types built by the USAF, U.S. Navy and NASA, perhaps the most prolific would have to be the three Bell X-15A-NA rocket-powered aircraft. Their origins go back as far as 1952, when the NACA (the former entity to NASA) decided to explore aircraft flight characteristics at very high speeds and altitudes—going to the edge of space. The first of three aircraft began construction in September 1956 and was rolled out in October 1958. They were given serial numbers 56-6670 through 56-6672 and made, between them, a total of 199 flights from June 8, 1959, to October 24, 1968. The most powerful engine used by the X-15 program was the 57,000 lbs. Reaction Motors, Inc., Thiokol XLR-99-RM rocket engine. X-15 (s/n 56-6670) is on display at the National Air and Space Museum, Washington, D.C. S/n 56-6671 was converted to the X-15A-2 in 1964 for further tests and is on display at the USAF Museum, Dayton, Ohio. S/n 56-6672 crashed in 1967, killing pilot Major Michael Adams. Astronaut Neil Armstrong was one of twelve test pilots to fly the X-15, logging seven flights.

A Yank in the RAF

USA / 20th Century–Fox / 1941 / B&W / 94 minutes

Director: Henry King

Cast: Tyrone Power, Betty Grable, John Sutton, Reginald Gardiner, Donald Stuart, Morton Lowry

Synopsis / Aviation Content: An American pilot ferries bombers to England for the paychecks but joins the RAF after meeting an old girlfriend and is soon drawn into the more savage aspects of the conflict. A superior film for its time; there are many glances at early wartime aviation, a highlight being the British Spitfire.

The film opens with a batch of **North American Harvard Mk. II** trainers being delivered to the RCAF, identified aircraft are RCAF s/n 3027, 3817. All Canadian, U.S. or English airfields involving the Lockheed Hudson bomber were shot at the Lockheed Air Terminal in Burbank, California, where the bomber was being produced; some can be seen parked without props fitted. The batch in the film were **Lockheed Hudson Mk. V** bombers for RCAF / RAF delivery; iden-

tified are RAF s/n AM870 and AM888. Hudson flying scenes were done off the California coast. The Oxnard, California, area doubles for Holland.

The RAF flying sequences were shot in England and directed by Major Herbert Mason, M.C., using the **Supermarine Spitfire Mk. I / Mk. V** fighters of 602 Squadron—two were RAF s/n R6627 and R6629. These scenes, ground and aerial formations, were shot in and over Glasgow with a film crew from 20th Century–Fox.

Full-scale studio mock-ups were built in the U.S. of the Hudson bomber, Spitfire and Messerschmitt Bf 109. There's much use of special effects and miniatures (including the Junkers Ju 87 Stuka) in the combat sequences. The production was filmed from April to August 1941.

You Came Along

USA / Paramount Pictures / 1945 / B&W / 103 minutes

Director: John Farrow

Cast: Robert Cummings, Lizabeth Scott, Don DeFore, Charles Drake, Julie Bishop, Kim Hunter, Robert Sully, Helen Forrest

Synopsis / Aviation Content: Three World War II P-38 pilots return to the U.S. on a war bond tour, during which one of them becomes romantically involved with the female tour director, little knowing just how short the relationship will be. Touching story which features a fair amount of period aircraft, including the **Beechcraft C-45 Expeditor**, **Boeing B-17F Flying Fortress**, **Douglas C-47 Skytrain**, three **Lockheed P-38J / L Lightning** fighters, **North American AT-6 Texan**, and **Vultee BT-13 Valiant**.

You Can't Win 'Em All (Non–Aviation Themed Title)

Alternate / Original Title: *The Dubious Patriots*

U.S. Video Title: *Soldiers of Fortune*

UK / Columbia Pictures / 1970 / Color / 97 minutes

Director: Peter Collinson

Cast: Tony Curtis, Charles Bronson, Michele

Mercier, Patrick Magee, Gregoire Aslan, Fikret Hakan, Salih Guney

Synopsis / Aviation Content: In 1922, two U.S. soldiers, Curtis and Bronson, are hired by a Turkish governor to escort his three daughters and a shipment of gold, little realizing just how difficult their job is going to get. Action yarn was filmed in Turkey and Yugoslavia during 1969. Notable for its use of two **Currie Wot S.E.5a** replicas, reg. EI-ARI (msn 1591) and EI-ARJ (msn 1592), hired out of the Blue Max Aircraft Collection in Ireland. Pilots were *Blue Max* veteran Derek Piggott and pilots Charles Boddington and Lewis Benjamin.

You Gotta Stay Happy

USA / Universal-International Pictures / 1948 / B&W / 100 minutes

Director: H.C. Potter

Cast: Joan Fontaine, James Stewart, Eddie Albert, Roland Young, Willard Parker, Percy Kilbride, Porter Hall

Synopsis / Aviation Content: Runaway bride Fontaine meets up with air-freight pilot Stewart, and they soon fall for each other while on a cargo flight across the U.S. A lighthearted romance comedy that isn't a classic but remains entertaining throughout, with some great C-47 sequences. The main aircraft is a **Douglas C-47-DL Skytrain** (s/n 41-38720 / msn 6179 / reg. NC86551) marked "Payne Air Lines" and roughed up for the film as an ex–CBI Theater transport. This aircraft was delivered to the USAAF on January 11, 1943, and declared surplus on October 8, 1945; flew in civilian service with, among other owners, Leeward Aeronautical Services, Inc., as NC86551—the reg. it kept during filming; to Canada in 1951 as CF-GEH; CF-QBI in 1957; then C-FQBI in 1979. Now withdrawn from use. Background aircraft are typical piston-era types such as the **Curtiss C-46, Douglas DC-3, DC-6, Convair 240**, and a **Lockheed L-749 Constellation** in the closing scene. The leather jacket worn by James Stewart appears to be his personal one, as it's marked with a patch from the 703rd Bomb Squadron, which Stewart commanded in England during World War II, flying B-24 Liberators.

You Only Live Twice (Non–Aviation Themed Title) see *James Bond Series*

Young Eagles

USA / Paramount Pictures / 1930 / B&W / 70 minutes

Director: William A. Wellman

Cast: Charles "Buddy" Rogers, Jean Arthur, Paul Lukas, Stuart Erwin, Virginia Bruce, Gordon DeMain

Synopsis / Aviation Content: Allied fighter pilot Rogers gets romantic with secret German spy Arthur in this World War I "talkie" from *Wings* (1927) director William Wellman and star Buddy Rogers. The film also makes use of *Wings* footage for the aerial combat scenes, not to mention *Wings* stuntman Dick Grace, who crashes a SPAD biplane before the cameras for good measure. Some use of **Travel Air 2000/4000** and **Waco** biplanes doubling as German fighters. Based on the short stories "The One Who Was Clever" and "Sky High" by Elliott White Springs. Dissatisfied with the studio's final edit on the film, Wellman requested and was granted cancellation of his Paramount studio contract.

The Young Flyers see *Tail of a Tiger*

Zeppelin

UK / Warner Bros. / 1971 / Color / 97 minutes

Director: Etienne Perier

Cast: Michael York, Elke Sommer, Peter Garsten, Marius Goring, Anton Diffring, Andrew Keir

Synopsis / Aviation Content: Michael York plays a World War I British spy onboard a metal German zeppelin headed for England. An often underrated film which is actually quite pacy and entertaining. Much use of models and mock-ups for the zeppelin itself. The main aeronautical feature is the six **Currie Wot S.E.5a** replicas (see: *Darling Lili* (1970) for details), loaned from Roger Corman's *Von Richthofen and Brown* film, also in production in Ireland at the same time. Notable film for the tragic accident which occurred when an S.E.5a replica (reg. EI-ARB) collided with an Alouette II camera helicopter (reg. G-AWEE) off Wicklow Head, Ireland, on August 18, 1970. Four people were killed: pilots Jim Liddy and Gilbert Ghomat, director Burch Williams, and renowned aerial cameraman Skeets Kelly.

Zero Hour!

USA / Paramount Pictures / 1957 / B&W / 81 minutes
Director: Hall Bartlett
Cast: Dana Andrews, Linda Darnell, Sterling Hayden, Elroy "Crazylegs" Hirsch, Geoffrey Toone, Jerry Paris, Peggy King, Carole Eden
Synopsis / Aviation Content: A former World War II pilot, who hasn't flown for ten years, must take the controls of a stricken airliner after the crew contract severe food poisoning. Devel-

oped from the 1956 CBC TV movie *Flight into Danger* written by British/Canadian novelist Arthur Hailey. The featured aircraft is a **Douglas DC-4** (**C-54B Skymaster**), with the interior completed as a studio mock-up. Ludicrously, stock footage was used in some instances of a Convair CV-240 and Douglas DC-3 doubling for the DC-4! Stock footage was also used of combat sequences from several World War II films, notably *A Yank in the RAF* (1941) and *Eagle Squadron* (1942).

Hailey adapted his screenplay from *Zero Hour!* into the 1958 co-authored novel *Runway Zero-Eight*, which itself was turned into the 1971 TV movie titled *Terror in the Sky*, starring Doug McClure. The rights to *Zero Hour!* were later purchased and made into the hugely successful comedy *Airplane!* in 1980, which parodies the storyline and even uses the main character's name of "Ted Stryker."

Section Two—Selected Television Series and TV Movies

All entries in this section are television-based, aviation-themed productions, which include TV series, TV miniseries, and TV movies; titles are listed in alphabetical order under those subheadings. While literally dozens and dozens of aviation-themed television productions have been made since the 1950s, the author has, for practicality reasons, only selected those most notable for their aviation content. Other well-known but generally short-lived aviation-themed TV series include: *Navy Log* (1955–1958), *Flight* (1958–1959), *The Blue Angels* (1960–1962), *Ripcord* (1961–1963), *San Francisco International Airport* (1970–1971), *Chopper One* (1974) *Air America* (1998–1999), *LAX* (2004–2005) and *Pan Am* (2011–2012).

Many aviation related television series were short-lived for a variety of reasons; one of the more prevalent of these was the huge expense of hiring the aircraft involved. It will be noted in the selection of series below that many shows only lasted one or two seasons before being canceled. Many of the longer-running television series, such as *12 O'Clock High* (1964–1967), actually had very little flying, relying on stock footage, which helped hold down the budgets and flying expenses. Some series like *Baa Baa Black Sheep* (1976–1978) and *Tales of the Gold Monkey* (1982–1983) filmed all their flying sequences over a short period to acquire a "film library" of shots, which could then be utilized later on when required. Additional aircraft were only hired on an "as required" basis. Aside from the high number of military-

themed television series over the years, it's interesting to note that many of the more successful shows were helicopter-based stories such as *Whirlybirds* (1957–1960) and *Airwolf* (1984–1987). Audiences, it seems, had a stronger fascination with rotary-winged aircraft. Also, the helicopter was a much more practical choice of flying machine for storylines of crime and high drama in television chase scenes, etc. Around the mid–1980s, costs of television production rose dramatically, and aviation-themed series, which of course were saddled with the expense of hiring aircraft, all but disappeared. Many of the aviation television series listed here, such as *Sky King* (1951–1958) and *Airwolf* (1984–1987), have in subsequent years become cult classics among their initial viewing audiences.

Selected TV Series

Airline

UK / Yorkshire Television / Color / 1982 / 1 season of 9 episodes
Regular Cast: Roy Marsden, Richard Heffer, Sean Scanlan, Polly Hemingway, Terence Rigby
Synopsis / Aviation Content: Roy Marsden stars

Type	msn	Military s/n	Civil reg.	Film Markings
Douglas C-47A-40-DL Skytrain	9914	42-24052	G-BHUA	—
Douglas C-47A-75-DL Skytrain	19347	42-100884	G-DAKSG-A	GHY / *Vera Lynn*
Douglas C-47A-85-DL Skytrain	19975	43-15509	G-BHUBG-A	GIV / *Alice*

as Jack Ruskin, a former RAF pilot struggling to start his own airline, Ruskin Air Services, in post–World War II England. Short-lived series employed two DC-3 aircraft, both provided by Aces High Ltd. at Duxford Aerodrome, UK.

DC-3C (reg. G-DAKS) did most of the flying in the show, with reg. G-BHUB playing the second Ruskin aircraft. G-BHUA was a third DC-3 used on occasion. Also seen at some point in the series was a **North American Harvard AT-6C-NT Texan** (s/n 41-33573, msn 88-12044, reg. G-BGOV), falsely marked as "FX291." Filming took place at Rufforth Airfield near York and at Duxford Aerodrome, Cambridgeshire, UK, with aviation company Aces High Ltd. providing the DC-3 aircraft and flying logistics. One episode, filmed on the island of Malta in April 1981, also used DC-3 aircraft, reg. C-FITH (s/n 43-15762), N535M (s/n 43-16092), N565 (s/n 43-4913), plus one other unidentified. Several DC-3 wrecks were also acquired for crash scenes. Camera-planes were two Piper PA-23 Aztec aircraft with reg. G-BBAV and G-AYZO.

Airwolf

USA / Universal Television / Color / 1984–1987 / 4 seasons totaling 79 episodes
Regular Cast: Jan-Michael Vincent, Ernest Borgnine, Jean Bruce Scott, Alex Cord, Deborah Pratt
Synopsis / Aviation Content: An action series concerning Cold War–style espionage missions, using a highly sophisticated helicopter. The star, of course, was a **Bell Model 222A** (reg. N3176S / msn 47085), twin-engined light executive helicopter. It was owned and operated by JetCopters, Inc., at Van Nuys, California. After the series concluded, it was sold overseas to Germany with reg. D-HHSD and flew as an air ambulance. It crashed on June 6, 1992, during a thunderstorm; all three onboard were killed. Universal Studios also built a static mock-up with lights, gadgets and a working rotor-head for all the non-flying close-up scenes with the cast. Other regular helicopter appearances were a **Bell 206B Jet Ranger** (reg. N2044C / msn 3363), marked "Santini Air"; several **Hughes**

500C / D helicopters, often playing gunship roles (four were reg. N58428 / msn 129-0624D; reg. N8673F / msn 87-0184D; reg. N9267F / msn 115-0778S; reg. N9276F / msn 18-0254D), and a **Sikorsky H-19D Chickasaw** (reg. N91AS / msn 55-646). Much use of stock vision depicting military types, both U.S. and Russian, in action. The series nowadays has a reasonable cult following of fans. The feature-length pilot episode was later re-edited and rereleased on domestic formats, aimed at more mature audiences, as a stand-alone feature titled *Airwolf: The Movie*.

Baa Baa Black Sheep

TV Movie Pilot Title: *The Flying Misfits*
Second Season Title: *Black Sheep Squadron*
USA / Universal Television / Color / 1976–1978 / 1 TV movie and 2 seasons totaling 35 episodes
Regular Cast: Robert Conrad, Simon Oakland, Dana Elcar, James Whitmore Jr., Dirk Blocker, W.K. Stratton, Jeff MacKay, Red West
Synopsis / Aviation Content: A group of "misfit" pilots are assigned to Marine Squadron VMF-214 under the watchful eye of their commander, played by Robert Conrad. Based on the factual book of the same name by USMC fighter ace Gregory "Pappy" Boyington, who commanded such a squadron (actually named "The Black Sheep Squadron") during World War II. The series never achieved any real success; the title was changed in the second season, with a number of female nurses added to broaden audience appeal. Still not rating, however, it was canceled at the end of season two. The show's wide use of the Vought Corsair and other vintage Warbird types, including some of the Japanese *Tora!* replicas, means the series has since attained cult status among Warbird fans.

Most of the Corsairs came from private owners on the U.S. west coast. Corsair reg. N3440G, had a back seat added, unofficially designated as a TFG-1D. Corsair reg. N33693, only made one flight for the TV series. Planes of Fame at Chino, California, supplied the B-17, N3713G, for some episodes. Tallmantz Aviation, Inc., supplied the Duck, N1214N; Zero replica, N15796; and Val

Type	msn	Military s/n	Civil reg.
U.S. Forces			
Boeing B-17G-90-DL Flying Fortress	32325	44-83684	N3713G
Grumman J2F-6 Duck	unknown	BuNo.33549	N1214N
North American B-25J-1-NC Mitchell	108-24356	43-4030	N3339G
North American B-25J-25-NC Mitchell	108-34076	44-30801	N3699G
Vought F4U-1A Corsair	3884	BuNo.17799	N83782
Vought F4U-4 Corsair	unknown	BuNo.97359	N97359
Vought F4U-7 Corsair	unknown	BuNo.133693	N33693
Vought F4U-7 Corsair	unknown	BuNo.133714	N33714
Vought FG-1D Corsair	3367	BuNo.92106	N6897
Vought FG-1D Corsair	3393	BuNo.92132	N3466G
Vought FG-1D Corsair	3694	BuNo.92433	N3440G
Vought FG-1D Corsair	3890	BuNo.92629	N62290
Japanese Forces			
CCF Harvard Mk. 4 (Zero)	CCF4-16	(RCAF) 20225	N15796
CCF Harvard Mk. 4 (Zero)	CCF4-171	(RCAF) 20380	N7757
CCF Harvard Mk. 4 (Zero)	CCF4-264	(RCAF) 20473	N296W
North American SNJ-4 Harvard (Kate)	88-13171	BuNo.27675	N7062C
North American SNJ-5 Harvard (Kate)	88-17652	BuNo.90654	N6438D
Vultee BT-13A Valiant (Val)	74-7356	41-22926	N56478
Vultee BT-13B Valiant (Val)	79-1220	42-90263	N56867

replica, N56867. Challenge Publications of California supplied their B-25J, N3699G; Zero replicas, N7757 and N296W; Kate replica, N6438D; and Val replica, N56478. Planes of Fame provided their B-25J, N3339G, and a Corsair, N83782. Kate replica, N7062C, was provided by a private owner.

Tallmantz Aviation, Inc., of Santa Ana, California, under the direction of co-founder Frank Tallman, was charged with gathering the required aircraft for the TV series, plus providing all aerial logistics during filming. Well-known Hollywood pilot Jim Gavin was hired as second unit director in charge of directing the aerial sequences. Filming was done very quickly in order to save costs; the footage would be spread throughout each episode, and additional aircraft were brought in as required. The camera-plane was Tallmantz's B-25J (reg. N1042B) plus a North American T-28B Trojan. The then sixty-four-year-old Gregory "Pappy" Boyington himself was employed on the series as a technical advisor. There's much use of stock newsreel footage from World War II that

Low flyby of a Corsair at Indian Dunes during the production of the TV series *Baa Baa Black Sheep* **(1976–1978). Photograph: James H. Farmer Collection.**

The outdoor set of *Baa Baa Black Sheep* (1976–1978) at Indian Dunes as two Japanese "Val" replicas make a flyby in a mock attack on the airfield. Photograph: James H. Farmer Collection.

has been nicely blended into the newly shot aerial sequences.

The aerial unit was based out of Van Nuys and Oxnard Airports, California. Over-water scenes were shot off the coast of Ventura, California, near the Channel Islands. The Black Sheep airfield television set was built at the Newhall Land & Farming Co. airstrip at Indian Dunes, Ventura County, California, which also doubles for Japanese airstrips when required (GPS location: N34 25.45 / W118 38.20).

Blue Thunder

USA / Columbia Television / Color / 1984 / 1 season of 11 episodes

Regular Cast: James Farentino, Sandy McPeak, Dana Carvey, Dick Butkus, Bubba Smith, Ann Cooper

Synopsis / Aviation Content: This short-lived series, which followed in the wake of the popular motion picture of the same name, used both Blue Thunder Gazelle conversions—N51BT and N52BT. Much use was also made of aerial footage and stunts taken from the movie. See under: *Blue Thunder* (1983) in **Section One: Feature Films** for more details on these aircraft.

Chopper Squad

Australia / Reg Grundy Productions / Color / 1976–1979 / 1 TV movie (1976) and 2 seasons totaling 26 episodes (1978–1979)

Regular Cast: Dennis Grosvenor, Robert Coleby, Eric Oldfield, Jeanie Drynan, Kerri Eichhorn, Graham Rouse, Tony Hughes

Synopsis / Aviation Content: Drama series following the adventures of a helicopter surf rescue crew on Sydney's northern beaches. An action-packed show in its day, this is one TV series helicopter fans will savor for the many views of the Jet Ranger. The stand-alone TV movie, broadcast in late 1976, made use of a local Airfast-owned yellow and white **Bell 206A Jet Ranger** (reg. VH-UHC / msn 067), fitted with large floats and marked "Surf Rescue." The subsequent TV series, which didn't premiere until over a year later, made use of a blue and white **Bell 206B Jet Ranger II** (reg. VH-FHF / msn 1926), also fitted with floats and marked "Surf Rescue." This chopper was an actual surf rescue helicopter sponsored by the Bank of New South Wales and was marked "Wales Rescue" when not engaged in filming. Helicopter interiors were filmed with a Bell Jet Ranger fuselage salvaged from a crash.

The Flying Doctors

Australia / Crawford Productions / Color / 1985–1992 / 1 miniseries and 7 seasons totaling 221 episodes

Regular Cast: Liz Burch, Robert Grubb, Lenore Smith, Peter O'Brien, Rebecca Gibney, Terry Gill, Maurie Fields, Val Jellay, Pat Evison

Synopsis / Aviation Content: Drama series based around outback Australia's Royal Flying Doctor Service features regular views of the GAF Nomad utility aircraft. The main aircraft was a **Government Aircraft Factory (GAF) N22B Nomad** (reg. VH-MSF / msn N22B-69), which was an actual serving aircraft with the Royal Flying Doctor Service out of Broken Hill in Australia. The registration call sign "Mike Sierra Foxtrot" was frequently written into the show's dialogue. It first flew on February 13, 1978, and was delivered to the Flying Doctor Service the same year, serving up until 1995. It subsequently flew with several Australian operators until exported to Malaysia in 2005 registered as 9M-LLI. A second Nomad was acquired by Crawford Productions for general ground shots and onboard filming. This was, in fact, the first Nomad prototype (reg. VH-SUP / msn N2-01), which made the type's maiden flight on July 23, 1971. When the production finished in 1992, the aircraft went into storage awaiting restoration. The Nomad was a popular utility aircraft, with 172 airframes built from 1971 to 1984 at the GAF factory in Melbourne, Australia.

JAG

USA / Paramount Television / Color / 1995–2005 / 10 seasons totaling 227 episodes

Regular Cast: David James Elliott, John M. Jackson, Catherine Bell, Patrick Labyorteaux, Karri Turner, Scott Lawrence, Trevor Goddard, Tracey Needham

Synopsis / Aviation Content: A legal drama series set within the confines of the U.S. Navy following the cases of a naval lawyer, known as a JAG (Judge Advocate General). Much stock footage of naval aircraft carriers and aircraft, especially the ever-popular F-14 Tomcat. The show was dropped by NBC after poor ratings but was picked up by CBS Television, where it found popularity.

The GAF Nomad prototype VH-SUP as seen in storage in 2008, still with its on-screen livery as VH-MSF used for the hugely popular Australian TV series *The Flying Doctors* (1985–1992). Photograph: Nigel Daw / South Australian Aviation Museum.

The Pathfinders

UK / Thames Television / Color / 1972–1973 /
1 season of 13 episodes

Regular Cast: Robert Urquhart, Jack Watling,
Julian Orchard

Synopsis / Aviation Content: Drama series following the lives of a Lancaster Pathfinder
squadron during World War II. Aerial footage
was filmed of **Avro Lancaster B.Mk. I** (RAF
s/n PA474), with much use of flyable RC Lancaster models, studio mock-ups and stock
footage. Filmed at ex–RAF West Malling, Kent,
England.

Sky King

USA / NBC Television / B&W / 1951–1959 / 4
seasons totaling 72 episodes

Regular Cast: Kirby Grant, Gloria Winters, Ron
Hagerthy, Ewing Mitchell, Monte Blue, Chubby
Johnson, Norman Ollestad, Gary Hunley

Synopsis / Aviation Content: "From out of the
clear blue of the western sky comes ... Sky
King!" stated the opening announcement to
this classic TV series about Arizona rancher
Schuyler "Sky" King and his adventures in an
airplane named *Songbird*. A pioneering TV
series well known for the use of several Cessna
twin types, it inspired a whole generation of
kids to want to be pilots. Originally based on a
radio-serial broadcast from 1946 to 1954.

Type	msn	Civil reg.
Cessna UC-78B-CE Bobcat	6117	N67832
Cessna 310B	35548	N5348A
Cessna 310D	39117	N6817T

The show's original aircraft, from 1951 to 1956,
was an ex–USAAF UC-78B Bobcat, N67832,
which was based on the Cessna Model T-50 and
was built in 1943 with s/n 43-32179. Declared
surplus in 1946, it was sold onto the civilian market where it found its way into the ownership of
Hollywood pilot Paul Mantz in 1950. It was
Mantz who supplied the aircraft to the TV series
and who was also employed as the aerial supervisor from 1951 to 1952. Mantz sold N67832 in
1954. From 1956 to 1959, a newly manufactured
Cessna 310B, N5348A—the second Model 310
built—was provided to the show by Cessna themselves. Both aircraft used for the series were
named *Songbird*, a name which has subsequently

The famous *Songbird* from the 1950s TV series *Sky King*. This is the second aircraft that was used, a brand-new Cessna 310B N5348A. Photograph: Larry Westin.

become a nickname for the Cessna 310 due to its association with the series. A static test airframe was also provided by Cessna for studio-based interior flying scenes with the actors. The third aircraft was a 1960 built Cessna 310D, N6817T, which was not featured in the series as such, being solely used for publicity shots and promotional work in series reruns. It was, strangely enough, marked *Songbird III* in some promo stills. Cessna N67832 was on sold to several private owners and appears to have eventually been broken up. Cessna N5348A also went on to several private owners before it crashed on August 4, 1962, near Delano, California. N6817T has been restored and is still flying. ABC Television broadcast the series from season two, and CBS Television broadcast reruns from 1959 until 1966.

Spencer's Pilots

USA / CBS Television / Color / 1976 / 1 half season of 11 episodes

Regular Cast: Christopher Stone, Todd Susman, Gene Evans, Margaret Impert, Britt Leach

Synopsis / Aviation Content: A short-lived action drama series concerning aviation employer Spencer Parish and his pilot employees becoming involved crime fighting, rescues and in-flight emergencies around California. Extensive use of light aircraft throughout, including both fixed and rotary winged types. Featured on a regular basis were a red **Bell 206B Jet Ranger** and a blue **Hughes 500C** (reg. N9221F / msn 104-0656S). Light aircraft include a **Cessna A150M Aerobat** (reg. N9835J / msn A150-0644) and **Cessna 182P Skylane** (reg. N1394M / msn 182-64311). Notable "guest stars" were a **Consolidated PBY-6A Catalina** (reg. N6453C / BuNo. 64041 / msn 2112/170) air-tanker owned by Hemet Valley Flying Service; Joe Hughes's **Super Stearman** aerobatic conversion (reg. N121R / msn 75-5510); Tallmantz's vintage **Stinson L-1 Vigilant** (reg. N63230) and a **Beechcraft Model D18C** (reg. N648CF). Filming took place at Brackett Airport, California (N34 05.50 / W117 47.00), which depicted Spencer's base of operations. Aerial coordinator for the series was aerobatic pilot Art Scholl with Hollywood aviation company Tallmantz Aviation, Inc., providing some aerial logistics and aircraft.

Frank Tallman and Frank Pine were also employed on some episodes as pilots. The show was canceled mid-season due to poor ratings, but has always been fondly remembered by many aviation fans around the world.

Steve Canyon

USA / NBC Television / B&W / 1958-1959 / 1 season of 34 episodes

Regular Cast: Dean Fredericks, Jerry Paris, Ted de Corsia, Abel Fernandez, Robert Hoy, Ingrid Goude

Synopsis / Aviation Content: Larger-than-life USAF pilot Steve Canyon is always on hand to troubleshoot any problems encountered on the job. A purely comic-book style series that's actually based on the 1947 comic strip of the same name by Milton Caniff. Many U.S. military aircraft of the era are seen in various roles throughout the series, including the **Boeing KB-50J Stratofortress, B-47E Stratojet, B-52B Stratofortress** (s/n 52-0013), **JB-52B Stratofortress, Convair F-102A Delta Dagger** (s/n 56-1363, seen in opening titles), **Douglas A3D Skywarrior, B-66 Destroyer, C-47 Skytrain, Fairchild C-119G Flying Boxcar, Lockheed C-130A Hercules, F-104 Starfighter, T-33A Shooting Star, Martin B-57, McDonnell F-101 Voodoo, North American F-100D Super Sabre** (s/n 56-2904, 56-3281), and **Republic F-84F Thunderstreak**. Filming took place at various Californian locations, including Edwards and George AFB, Van Nuys Airport, and desert locations in the Mojave Desert. Large use of USAF stock footage throughout.

Tales of the Gold Monkey

USA / Universal Television / Color / 1982–1983 / 1 season of 21 episodes

Regular Cast: Stephen Collins, Jeff MacKay, Caitlin O'Heaney, Roddy McDowall, Marta DuBois, John Calvin, John Fujioka

Synopsis / Aviation Content: Adventure series about a former Flying Tigers pilot named Jake

Cutter and his commuter airline in Southeast Asia during 1938. The "gold monkey" reference is a statue in a local bar, which is one of the central settings in the show. Often mistaken for a *Raiders of the Lost Ark* (1981) rip-off, on which much of its action and style seems based, the show's concept was actually more influenced by the 1939 Howard Hawks film *Only Angels Have Wings*. Jake's aircraft is a 1938 **Grumman G-21A Goose** (reg. N327 / msn 1051). This airframe was originally delivered in December 1938 as the second of four in an order for the Peruvian Air Force. It had s/n 2TP-2H, subsequent s/ns were XX11-84 and FAP-323. It returned to the United States in 1953 as N327 with California-based Catalina Airlines. N327 was owned by Kodiak Western Airlines in 1982, when it was transformed into *Cutter's Goose*. Renowned aerial coordinator Davis Jones spent several weeks in Hawaii with N327 capturing various flying angles which would serve as library material for use throughout the series. A second Grumman Goose wreck was acquired and refurbished for the set on the Universal Studios backlot, where the Gold Monkey bar and a water inlet were constructed. It's believed this airframe might be ex–Catalina Airlines Inc.

Grumman G-21 Goose (reg. N13CS / msn 1007), which was derelict at San Pedro in the early 1980s. It was later acquired for display by the Cradle of Aviation museum in New York State. Other aircraft seen during the series include a Curtiss P-40E Warhawk (reg. N923), Douglas C-47 hulk, several *Tora!* Zero conversions, and much library footage use of a Boeing Clipper.

12 O'Clock High

USA / 20th Century–Fox Television / B&W & Color / 1964–1967 / 3 seasons totaling 78 episodes

Regular Cast: Robert Lansing, Paul Burke, Chris Robinson, Frank Overton, Barney Phillips, Paul Newlan, John Larkin, Lew Gallo, Andrew Duggan

Synopsis / Aviation Content: Developed from the classic 1949 film of the same name, the series follows the same story thread of a hard-nosed commander pulling a squadron of misfits into line. Actor Robert Lansing played base commander General Frank Savage, but was replaced in the second season by Paul Burke playing Colonel Joe Gallagher. The third sea-

The unmistakable *Cutter's Goose* as seen in the early '80s TV series *Tales of the Gold Monkey* (1982–1983). The aircraft was a Grumman G-21A Goose N327. Photograph: Ken Stoltzfus Collection, www.john2031.com.

Type	msn	Military s/n	Civil reg.
Boeing B-17G-75-DL Flying Fortress	31957	44-83316	—
Boeing B-17G-90-DL Flying Fortress	32325	44-83684	N3713G

son, starting in 1966, was broadcast in color. Very little flying took place throughout the series, which relied instead on stock footage from various other sources and motion pictures. The two B-17 bombers provided were mainly for set dressing.

B-17G (reg. N3713G) was hired from the Air Museum at Chino, California. It was flyable but didn't do any for the series; instead it provided shots of taxiing, departing, arriving and general background scenes. The aircraft was mostly marked *Piccadilly Lily* but was also marked as a number of other B-17 bombers depending on filming requirements. The aircraft was previously a DB-17P drone director and was retired from active duty by the USAF in 1959. B-17G (s/n 44-83316) was a fuselage section owned by the studio and served as background for crash scenes and any other requirements for the series. It had been a staff transport designated as a VB-17G in USAF service, then a display item at Norton AFB before Fox Studios purchased it for film work in 1964. A third B-17G (s/n 44-83387) cockpit section was used for studio-based flying scenes. There was much use of stock footage from the film *Twelve O'Clock High* (1949), including, of course, the famous Paul Mantz B-17 belly landing, and William Wyler's 1944 documentary *The Memphis Belle*. Filming took place at Chino Airport, California, where period airfield buildings were constructed.

We'll Meet Again

UK / LWT & ITV Television / Color / 1982 / 1 season of 13 episodes
Regular Cast: Susannah York, Michael Shannon, Patrick O'Connell, Lynne Pearson, James Saxon
Synopsis / Aviation Content: Romantic, soap opera–styled series, named after the famous 1939 Vera Lynn song, about U.S. bomber crews in England during World War II and the local ladies they meet. The production made use of

Boeing B-17G-105-VE Flying Fortress (s/n 44-85784 / msn 17-8693 / reg. G-BEDF) and was filmed in part at former RAF West Malling, Kent, England, during 1981.

Whirlybirds

Alternate Titles: *The Whirlybirds* / *Copter Patrol*
USA / CBS Television / B&W / 1957–1960 / 3 seasons totaling 111 episodes
Regular Cast: Kenneth Tobey, Graig Hill, Nancy Hale
Synopsis / Aviation Content: Adventure series about two helicopter pilots and the trouble they run into while hiring their machines out to clients. Very much a cult favorite today among helicopter and television fans alike, the show is fondly remembered for its wide use of the Bell Model 47 helicopter.

Type	msn	Civil reg.
Bell Model 47G-21	381	N975B
Bell Model 47J Ranger	1424	N2838B

The two Bell helicopters were leased from National Helicopter Service, Van Nuys, California, with a third Bell 47J (reg. N1538B) also used on occasion. Filming locations were at San Fernando Airport and National Helicopters base at Van Nuys. A mock-up chopper was built in a studio for flying close-ups with the actors.

Wings

UK / BBC Television / Color / 1977–1978 / 2 seasons totaling 25 episodes
Regular Cast: Tim Woodward, Nicholas Jones, Michael Cochrane, David Troughton, Sarah Porter, Anne Kristen, John Hallman
Synopsis / Aviation Content: Drama series about a group of Royal Flying Corps pilots during World War I headed by Tim Woodward playing fighter pilot Alan Farmer. Limited use of actual flyable aircraft included a **Fokker E.III Eindecker** (reg. G-AVJO / msn PPS/FOK/6), built by Personal Plane Services; a **Royal Aircraft Factory B.E.2c** (reg. G-AWYI / msn 001); two replicas from the Shuttleworth Collection, an **Avro 504K** (reg. G-ADEV / msn R3/LE/61400) and **Bristol Boxkite** (reg. G-

ASPP / msn BM.7279) and Cole Palen's **Avro 504K** (reg. N4929 / msn HAC1) in the USA. Full- and near-full-scale non-flying replicas were built of the Avro 504K (BAPC.122 and BAPC.177), Albatros C.III, B.E.2; Sopwith Pup, and Vickers F.B.5 Gunbus for ground and taxi scenes. Mostly used for the flying sequences were large-scale RC models of the above aircraft built and flown by expert British model-maker David Boddington. Aerial coordinator was British pilot Derek Piggott. Filmed at Old Warden Aerodrome, Bedfordshire, England, with the flyable B.E.2c being filmed in the United States, where it was based at the time.

Selected TV Miniseries / Movies

The Amazing Howard Hughes

USA / EMI Television & Roger Gimbel Productions / 1977 / Color / 215 minutes
Director: William A. Graham
Cast: Tommy Lee Jones, Ed Flanders, James Hampton, Tovah Feldshuh, Lee Purcell, Jim Antonio
Synopsis / Aviation Content: Fascinating account of the life and times of eccentric millionaire, aviation pioneer and filmmaker Howard Hughes from his childhood up to his death in 1976. Based on the 1971 book *Howard: The Amazing Mr. Hughes* by Noah Dietrich and Bob Thomas. Featured aircraft are two **Curtiss JN-4 Jenny** biplanes; a **Royal Aircraft Factory S.E.5**; and a **Grumman J2F-6 Duck** (BuNo. 33587 / reg. N67790), supplied by Tallmantz Aviation, Inc., who also oversaw aerial logistics. Also seen are a **Lockheed Model 12-A Junior Electra** (reg. NC1161V / msn 1203); an extensively converted **North American AT-6 Texan** as the "Hughes H-1 Racer"; a **Lockheed P-38 Lightning** as the "Hughes XF-11" (with a P-51D fuselage post-crash); and an early **Learjet** business aircraft. The *Hell's Angels* crash sequence was actually footage from the film *Ace Eli and Rodger of the Skies* (1973). The domestic DVD version is cut to 123 minutes.

By Dawn's Early Light

USA / Home Box Office (HBO) / 1990 / Color / 96 minutes
Director: Jack Sholder
Cast: Powers Boothe, Rebecca De Mornay, James Earl Jones, Martin Landau, Darren McGavin, Rip Torn, Jeffrey DeMunn, Peter MacNicol
Synopsis / Aviation Content: The crew of a B-52 bomber must proceed to target after a limited nuclear strike on the U.S. sees the president incapacitated. Excellent Cold War drama creates tension and fear as the situation worsens. Models and mock-ups built of the Boeing B-52 Stratofortress, EC-135, E-4, McDonnell Douglas F/A-18 Hornet and MiG-25 Foxbat. The only real aircraft used was a **Bell Model 204B** helicopter and a studio-based actual B-52 flight deck section, where much of the action takes place.

Deadly Encounter

USA / CBS Television & EMI Films Ltd. / 1982 / Color / 96 minutes
Director: William A. Graham
Cast: Larry Hagman, Susan Anspach, James Gammon, Michael C. Gwynne
Synopsis / Aviation Content: An ex–Vietnam War helicopter pilot is running a chopper business in Mexico when an old girlfriend shows up pursued by helicopter-equipped gangsters. Bad scripting and a weak narrative give way to spectacular helicopter flying and stunt work, which makes this one of the most highly rated helicopter movies ever made. An enjoyable production overall, with edge-of-your-seat helicopter visuals for the aviation fan, but general audiences may find it pretty lame.

Hagman's helicopter is a **Hughes 500C** (reg. N4EE / msn 113-0537S), owned by Glenn E. Miller, who appears in the film as a truck driver. This machine crashed on April 17, 1982, when it struck an aerial cableway along the Colorado River in Marble Canyon, Arizona. Miller was killed, as was the production's costumer Frank Novak and nurse Diane Doherty; a fourth passenger was seriously injured. The flight was not engaged in filming at the time, and a memoriam credit is given to the deceased in the final on-screen credits. Filming was completed with another Hughes 500C, this one having a "long skid" configuration, which is evident in the final canyon chase sequences.

The gangster helicopters are an unidentified red **Bell 206B Jet Ranger**; two **Aerospatiale SA.315B Lama** choppers—a gray (reg. N62345 / msn 2407) and red (reg. N62250 / msn 2334) model; and a blue **Aerospatiale SA.341G Gazelle** (reg. N341BB / msn 1421). Hagman's red biplane is a **Boeing-Stearman PT-13D Kaydet** (reg. N4766V / msn 75-5488), owned and flown in the movie by renowned aerobatic pilot Art Scholl. This same biplane famously appears in *Capricorn One* (1978) and here performs much the same stunt work, with a pursuing helicopter trying to knock it out of the sky using its skids. Two other unidentified Stearman aerobatic biplane conversions were also provided for filming.

The helicopter stunt coordinator and Hughes 500 pilot was Larry Kirsch; the Stearman biplane coordinator was Art Scholl. Other pilots were James Gavin, Lawrence Patrick Kirsch, Lee Meyers, Ross Reynolds, Bertrand Rhine III and Chuck Wentworth. Some of these pilots make a cameo appearance in the movie as members of Hagman's old squadron.

Filmed mainly in Guaymas, Mexico—the same location used for the aviation classic *Catch-22* (1970), with many of the background mountains recognizable from that film. The final chase was filmed in the Marble Canyon area in Arizona. The aircraft graveyard is the Pima Air & Space Museum in Tucson, Arizona, with much of their collection visible on screen, with the **Boeing B-29 Superfortress** *Sentimental Journey* (s/n 44-70016 / msn 10848) having a starring role. Other aircraft include their B-17, B-24, B-25, B-52, B-57, C-54, C-97, C-119, C-121, C-124, UH-19, CH-21, CH-37, H-43, CH-46, and UH-1F, among many others.

Enola Gay: The Men, the Mission, the Atomic Bomb

USA / NBC Television / 1980 / Color / 156 minutes

Director: David Lowell Rich

Cast: Patrick Duffy, Billy Crystal, Kim Darby, Gary Frank, Gregory Harrison, Stephen Macht, Walter Olkewicz, Robert Pine

Synopsis / Aviation Content: The fascinating story of the bomber crew's preparing for the mission to drop the atomic bomb on Hiroshima in 1945. Makes use of several B-29 aircraft, the two that were flyable being the only ones ever to appear on the U.S. civilian register.

Type	msn	Military s/n	Civil reg.
Boeing B-29-75-BW Superfortress	10848	44-70016	—
Boeing B-29-95-BW Superfortress	13681	45-21787	N91329
Boeing B-29A-60-BN Superfortress	11547	44-62070	N4249

B-29, s/n 44-70016, was a static airframe borrowed from the nearby Pima Air & Space Museum in Tucson, Arizona, and used for background scenes. There were two flyables: B-29 N91329, which came from the American Air Museum in California and is a former U.S. Navy P2B-1S, BuNo. 84029; and B-29A N4249, which came from the Confederate Air Force in Texas and was later re-registered as N529B, flying at airshows as *Fifi*. A B-29-35-MO fuselage (s/n 42-65401) was also used for studio filming of aircraft interiors. Two **Douglas C-47 Skytrain** transports and a **Lockheed P-38 Lightning** were also hired. The camera-plane was a Clay Lacy Learjet 23. Airfield apron scenes were filmed at Davis-Monthan AFB, Tucson, Arizona. Much use of World War II color film of B-29 bombers in action. Director David Lowell Rich is a former B-29 navigator.

Piece of Cake

UK / LWT Television / Color / 1988 / TV miniseries of 6 parts

Director: Ian Toynton

Cast: Tom Burlinson, Neil Dudgeon, George Anton, Nathaniel Parker, Boyd Gaines, David Horovitch, Richard Hope

Synopsis / Aviation Content: Drama series following a fictional RAF squadron deployed to France in the pre–Dunkirk period through to the height of the Battle of Britain. Based on the 1983 novel by English author Derek Robinson.

Notable miniseries as it was the first production since the classic film *Battle of Britain* (1969) to assemble together so many Spitfire and Buchon fighter aircraft. Because of this, the series has since developed a substantial cult following among Warbird enthusiasts.

Type	msn	Military s/n	Civil reg.
CASA 2.111B	167	B.2I-37	G-AWHB
CASA 352L	144	T.2B-262	G-BFHG
DeHavilland DH.98 Dragon Raptide	6862	Z7258	G-AHGD
Hispano HA-1112-M1L Buchon	170	C.4K-107	G-BOML
Hispano HA-1112-M1L Buchon	213	C.4K-40	D-FEHD
Hispano HA-1112-M1L Buchon	235	C.4K-172	G-HUNN
Supermarine Spitfire Mk. Ia	WASP.20/2	AR213	G-AIST
Supermarine Spitfire LF.Mk. IXb	CBAF.IX552	MH434	G-ASJV
Supermarine Spitfire LF.Mk. IXc	CBAF.IX2200	NH238	G-MKIX
Supermarine Spitfire LF.Mk. IXe	6S/730116	ML417	G-BJSG
Supermarine Spitfire PR.Mk. XI	6S/533723	PL983	G-PRXI

Five flyable Spitfires were supplied: one from a private owner—G-AIST; the Old Flying Machine Co. of Duxford—G-ASJV; Warbirds of GB Ltd. of Biggin Hill—G-MKIX, G-PRXI; and the Fighter Collection of Duxford—G-BJSG. Spitfire G-BJSG was rebuilt as a two-seater Spitfire Tr.Mk. 9 (new msn 6S/735188) in 1946, and then converted back again to "Mk. IXc" standard in civilian ownership around 1981. All hired aircraft flew without squadron codes or markings in order to avoid continuity problems in editing. Since the series is set in France during 1939–1940, the correct RAF fighter would have been the Hawker Hurricane; a lack of flyable ones meant the Spitfire was considered an acceptable substitute.

Six additional Spitfire mock-ups were also built for background set dressing; three had 50cc motors to turn their propellers, and one could even taxi under its own power. Three detailed replica cockpit sections were also built for actor close-ups.

The non-flyable CASA 2.111B (reg. G-AWHB) fuselage was used for Heinkel He 111 bomber interiors, and the CASA 352L stood in for the Junkers Ju 52. Both were hired from Aces High Ltd. The Dragon Raptide was a privately owned aircraft.

The miniseries' famous bridge fly-under was performed by the production's chief pilot Ray Hanna in Spitfire G-ASJV. Camera-planes were Aces High Ltd.'s B-25J, N1042B, a North Amer-ican T-6G Texan (for rear tail shots), an Agusta 109 and a Bell 206 Jet Ranger helicopter. There was some use of scale models for certain shots, and various outtakes were used from *Battle of Britain* (1969).

RAF locations were at South Cerney Airfield as "Kingsmere," and some scenes were at Duxford Aerodrome, the home base for several of the companies providing aerial logistics, etc. Some filming was also undertaken at former RAF Friston, East Sussex, on the English coast—revived as "Bodkin Hazel" after being farmland for some years. French scenes were filmed at Charlton Park as "St. Pierre," and Cambridge Airport stands in as a prewar "Le Touguet." Interiors and mock-ups were filmed at Elstree Studios, Hertfordshire, England.

GPS LOCATIONS

Cambridge Airport, Teversham, Cambridgeshire, England: N52 12.20 / E000 10.30

Duxford Aerodrome, Cambridgeshire, England (closed 1961): N52 05.50 / E000 07.80

RAF South Cerney, Gloucestershire, England (closed 1971): N51 41.25 / W001 55.25

Charlton Park, Malmesbury, Wiltshire, England: N51 36.05 / W002 04.10

Sole Survivor

USA / CBS Television & Cinema Center 100 / 1970 / Color / 95 minutes

Director: Paul Stanley

Cast: Vince Edwards, Richard Basehart, William Shatner, Lou Antonio, Lawrence P. Casey, Dennis Cooney, Brad David, Patrick Wayne, Alan Caillou

Synopsis / Aviation Content: The wreckage of a B-25 bomber discovered in the Libyan desert hides a supernatural secret for the aircraft's only survivor. A tense, well-crafted story based loosely on the fantastic real-life 1959 discovery of the crashed B-24 Liberator *Lady Be Good* by oil workers in Libya. The film's desert wreck was an ex–ANG **North American B-25J-30-NC Mitchell** (s/n 44-30979 / msn 108-34254),

A detailed close-up of the excellent job done by the art department to make this B-25 bomber look derelict for *Sole Survivor* (1970). Photograph: James H. Farmer Collection.

The Sikorsky S-55C N860 painted in USAF markings on the set of *Sole Survivor* (1970). Photograph: James H. Farmer Collection.

which had been in storage at the Air Museum in Ontario, California. The airframe was disassembled and trucked out to the filming location, where it was expertly dressed as a long-derelict crashed bomber. After filming it was reassembled, only to be scrapped by 1973. The helicopter was a civilian **Sikorsky Model S-55C** (reg. N860 / msn 55-1050), painted in USAF colors. It later went to Canada as CF-AGQ, then CF-AAQ before being written off in a crash in 1989. A B-25 studio mock-up was built from fiberglass based on molds taken off 44-30979. Filmed on El Mirage Dry Lake, Mojave Desert, California, in mid–1969.

The Tuskegee Airmen

USA / Home Box Office (HBO) / 1995 / Color / 106 minutes

Director: Robert Markowitz

Cast: Laurence Fishburne, Allen Payne, Malcolm-Jamal Warner, Courtney B. Vance, Andre Braugher, Christopher McDonald, Daniel Hugh Kelly, John Lithgow, Cuba Gooding Jr.

Synopsis / Aviation Content: An outstanding drama recounting the racial discrimination endured by African American pilots of the 332nd Fighter Group. The title refers to Tuskegee Airfield, Alabama, where the "colored" trainee pilots were trained as the 99th Fighter Squadron. A great lineup of World War II period aircraft throughout.

The B-17G was provided by the Lone Star Flight Museum in Galveston, Texas; Buchon reg. N109GU was provided by the Cavanaugh Flight Museum in Texas. All other Warbird aircraft were provided by private owners. Also provided were two **Boeing-Stearman PT-17-BW Kaydet** biplane trainers. Much use of wartime combat footage with B-17 sequences featuring stock footage from the documentary *The Memphis Belle* (1944) and the feature film *Memphis Belle* (1990). With several awards, nominations and television repeats, this telefilm gained a limited release into movie theaters in 1996—a rare feat for a television movie. The Tuskegee Airmen's story was later re-told in a major motion picture by Lucasfilm Ltd. titled *Red Tails* (2012).

Type	msn	Military s/n	Civil reg.
Boeing B-17G-105-VE Flying Fortress	17-8627	44-85718	N900RW
CCF Harvard Mk. 4	CCF4-124	(RCAF) 20333	N1466
Hispano HA-1112-M1L Buchon	235	C.4K-172	N109GU
North American AT-6D-NT Texan	88-17380	42-85599	N7421C
North American P-51D-20-NA Mustang	122-38942	44-72483	N151DM
North American P-51D-25-NA Mustang	122-39236	44-72777	N151D
North American P-51D-25-NT Mustang	124-44471	44-84615	N55JL
North American P-51D-30-NT Mustang	124-48311	45-11558	N6175C
North American SNJ-5 Texan	88-15194	BuNo.52006	N52006
Travel Air D4000	798	—	NC6478

Section Three—
Aircraft Manufacturers

Section Three serves as a cross-reference guide to Sections One and Two, enabling a reader to look up a single aircraft type to find a definitive list of films which have been made employing that airplane.

Aircraft are listed alphabetically by manufacturer, and the list includes a wide mixture of Warbirds, civilian airliners and in-service military types. While it is almost impossible to present a complete list of all film titles made with a particular aircraft type, the section below does competently list the most definitive films associated with any one selected aircraft. Also included in this section are film and television titles that aren't listed in earlier parts of the book. The term "flying" in the remarks column indicates, where it may not be immediately obvious, aircraft that had a flying role during a production.

Aero

A Czech Republic aviation manufacturer founded around 1919 and most notable for its successful military trainers, the L-29 Delfin, L-39 Albatros and L-59 Super Albatros. Also known as Aero Vodochody. Also builds components for other major manufacturers in the U.S. and Europe.

Aero Commander   *see*
Rockwell

Aerospatiale / Eurocopter

A French manufacturer founded in 1970 after the merger of Sud and Nord Aviation as Societe Nationale d'Industrie Aerospatiale (SNIAS), later renamed Aerospatiale. Well known for their military and civil aircraft, especially the Concorde (with BAC) and the wide range of helicopter types, including the hugely successful Ecureuil (Squirrel) series. The helicopter division was split in 1992 to become Eurocopter Group and in 2000 became a subsidiary of EADS, as did Aerospatiale itself in the same year. Became Airbus Helicopters in 2014.

ALOUETTE SERIES

First flight (SA.313B): March 12, 1955. Single-engined military and civil helicopter evolved through several upgrades and had very successful international sales, remaining in production up to 1985. Basic variants of the Alouette II design were the SA.313 and SA.315B Lama with the Artouste engine and SA.318 with the Astazou engine. The redesigned Alouette III were the SA.316 with the Artouste engine and SA.319 with the As-

Aero		SN or Reg. at Time of		
Type	msn	Filming	Title	Remarks / Film Markings
L-39ZA Albatros	5321	—	*Tomorrow Never Dies* (1997)	Marked as 28/08, flying scenes
L-39ZO Albatros	232337	G-OTAF	*Tomorrow Never Dies* (1997)	Marked as 28/02, flying scenes
L-39ZO Albatros	731002	G-BWTS	*Tomorrow Never Dies* (1997)	Marked as 28/02, ground scenes
L-39ZO Albatros	731013	G-BWTT	*Tomorrow Never Dies* (1997)	Marked as 28/08, ground scenes

Alouette Series Type	msn	SN or Reg. at Time of Filming	Title	Remarks / Film Markings
SA.313B Alouette II	1628	F-MJAO	*The Day of the Jackal* (1973)	—
SA.313B Alouette II	1679	JA9007	*You Only Live Twice* (1967)	Bond's arrival at the ninja school. Camera-chopper on this film was Alouette II reg. JA9012
SA.315B Lama	2225	HB-XDL	*The Cassandra Crossing* (1976)	—
SA.315B Lama	2261	N13583	*Birds of Prey* (TVM, 1973)	—
SA.315B Lama	2314	G-BCPA	*The Empire Strikes Back* (1980)	Camera-ship for Snowspeeder aerial backdrops
SA.315B Lama	2334	N62250	*Breakout* (1975)	Used in the jail bust sequence
		N62250	*Deadly Encounter* (TVM, 1982)	Gangster's helicopter
SA.315B Lama	2407	N62345	*Deadly Encounter* (TVM, 1982)	Gangster's helicopter
SA.316B Alouette III	1509	SX-HAC	*Sky Riders* (1976)	Greek-registered helicopter

tazou engine. This helicopter was very popular in the 1960s and 1970s with film studios as camera-platforms, and appearances on-screen were frequent, especially, of course, in French cinema.

Puma Series

First flight: April 15, 1965. Twin-engined utility helicopter has been a very popular transport helicopter with both military and civil operators. Followed by the SA.332 Super Puma in 1978. Doubles as the "Russian chopper" in many films, most notably the *Rambo* series.

Other Notable Titles: *Rambo: First Blood Part II* (1985) as Mi-24 Hind.

Gazelle Series

First flight: April 7, 1967. Sleek single-engined turbine helicopter featuring the unique Fenestron tail rotor, the Gazelle was originally designed as a lightweight army helicopter for France, but developed into a very successful type also built in England by Westland and in Yugoslavia by SOKO. The Gazelle is most famous in cinematic circles for its role as the sinister *Blue Thunder* in the film of the same name.

Other Notable Titles: *The Golden Lady* (1979); *Under Fire* (1983); *Batman* (1989); *The Fly II* (1989); *Die Hard: With a Vengeance* (1995); *28 Weeks Later* (2007).

Puma Series Type	msn	SN or Reg. at Time of Filming	Title	Remarks / Film Markings
SA.330J Puma	1227	ZS-RNK	*District 9* (2009)	Marked as MNU
SA.330J Puma	1501	N3263U	*Rambo III* (1988)	Doubles as Russian Mi-24 Hind

Gazelle Series Type	msn	SN or Reg. at Time of Filming	Title	Remarks / Film Markings
SA.341B Gazelle AH.1	1032	N341AH	*The Gauntlet* (1977)	—
		N341AH	*The Cat from Outer Space* (1978)	—
SA.341G Gazelle	1015	N58283	*Rambo III* (1988)	Doubles as Russian gunship
SA.341G Gazelle	1066	N37LR	*Blue Thunder* (1983)	Heavily modified, marked as N77GH / 02
		N51BT	*Blue Thunder* (TVS, 1984)	—
		N51BT	*Amerika* (TVMS, 1987)	—
SA.341G Gazelle	1075	N777GH	*Blue Thunder* (1983)	Heavily modified, marked as N77GH / 02
		N52BT	*Blue Thunder* (TVS, 1984)	—
		N52BT	*Amerika* (TVMS, 1987)	—
SA.341G Gazelle	1421	N341BB	*Deadly Encounter* (TVM, 1982)	Gangster's helicopter

CONCORDE

First flight: March 2, 1969. Four-engined, delta-wing supersonic airliner. A marvel of engineering, twenty were built over a ten-year period for Air France and British Airways. Not many film appearances, but Concorde F-BTSC did have a starring role in the last *Airport* film in 1979.

DOLPHIN SERIES

First flight: June 2, 1972. Single-engined utility helicopter as the SA.360 Dauphin and later developed into the twin-engined AS.365 Dauphin 2, which the USCG purchased as the HH-65A Dolphin.

Other Notable Titles: *The Guardian* (2006).

ECUREUIL (SQUIRREL) SERIES

First flight: June 26, 1974. Single-engined AS.350 helicopter became very popular in both the United States and Europe for film work, not only on screen but as platforms for aerial photography. Many action films use this helicopter extensively. Named the A-Star in the U.S. The AS.355 model is the twin-engined version. Dozens of on-screen appearances over the years.

Other Notable Titles: Many later *James Bond* films; *Cliffhanger* (1993); *The X-Files: Fight the Future* (1998); *The A-Team* (2010).

Concorde		SN or Reg. at Time of		
Type	msn	Filming	Title	Remarks / Film Markings
Concorde 100	101	G-AXDN	Never Say Never Again (1983)	Doubles as a B-1B Lancer bomber
Concorde 101	203	F-BTSC	The Concorde … Airport '79 (1979)	Crashed in 2000, triggering Concorde's retirement
Concorde 101	211	F-BVFD	Moonraker (1979)	Background

Dolphin Series		SN or Reg. at Time of		
Type	msn	Filming	Title	Remarks / Film Markings
AS.365C1 Dauphin	5023	G-BGNM	Octopussy (1983)	Marked as 06 and later as 51
HH-65A Dolphin	6270	(USCG)	Licence to Kill (1989)	—

Ecureuil Series		SN or Reg. at Time of		
Type	msn	Filming	Title	Remarks / Film Markings
AS.350B Ecureuil	1227	N300CE	Lethal Weapon 2 (1989)	—
		N300CE	Die Hard 2: Die Harder (1990)	—
AS.350B Ecureuil	1531	XA-MUA	Licence to Kill (1989)	Sanchez's helicopter
AS.350 B2 Ecureuil	1384	N5774J	True Lies (1994)	Unmarked terrorist chopper
AS.350 B2 Ecureuil	1408	N350SC	Die Hard 4.0 (2007)	—
		N350SC	Get Smart (2008)	—
AS.350 B2 Ecureuil	1682	N450CC	Mission: Impossible II (2000)	—
		N450CC	Batman Begins (2005)	—
		N450CC	Die Hard 4.0 (2007)	—
AS.350 B1 Ecureuil	2124	N547SA	Die Hard 4.0 (2007)	—
AS.350BA A-Star	2130	N410JC	Gone in 60 Seconds (2000)	—
		N410JC	The Fly Boys (2008)	—
AS.350BA A-Star	2298	N61HL	S.W.A.T. (2003)	Marked as: KCAL 9
AS.355 F1 Ecureuil 2	5063	F-GDMS	A View to a Kill (1985)	Zorin's helicopter
AS.355 F1 Ecureuil 2	5201	G-BPRJ	The World Is Not Enough (1999)	Marked as: King Industries
AS.355 F1 Ecureuil 2	5036	N811HS	Enemy of the State (1998)	—
AS.355 F1 Ecureuil 2	5139	N5793J	Bad Boys II (2003)	—
EC.130B4	3500	ZS-RWR	District 9 (2009)	Marked as: MNU
EC.135 T2	0496	JA135H	Inception (2010)	Flying

Tiger Series

First flight: April 1991. Twin-engined EC.665 army attack helicopter. One of the prototypes was seen in the 1995 Bond film *GoldenEye*.

Agusta / AgustaWestland

Founded in Italy in 1923 by Count Giovanni Agusta. Best known for its A109 helicopter, first flown in 1971. Merged with GKN-Westland helicopters in 2000 to form **AgustaWestland**.

Also known for license building many Bell products, such as the Model 47, 206 Jet Ranger and 204 / 205 "Huey" models.

Agusta-Bell   see   Bell

Airco   *see*   Dehavilland

Airship Industries

British manufacturer founded as Aerospace Developments in 1971; became the above entity in 1980 and built several non-rigid airship designs also known as "blimps." Best remembered for its prominent role in the Bond film *A View to a Kill*. Became Westinghouse Airships in 1990.

Airspeed

British manufacturer founded in 1931 most famous for their twin-engined Oxford aircraft built in large numbers for the RAF during World War II. Airspeed was merged with DeHavilland in 1951.

American Eagle

U.S. manufacturer founded in 1925 by Edward Porterfield. Merged with Lincoln Aircraft Co. in 1931 as Eagle-Lincoln. Well known for their two-seater parasol monoplane.

Tiger Series

Type	msn	SN or Reg. at Time of Filming	Title	Remarks / Film Markings
EC.665 Tiger	PT.1	F-ZWWW	*GoldenEye* (1995)	Helicopter stolen off navy ship

Agusta

Type	msn	SN or Reg. at Time of Filming	Title	Remarks / Film Markings
A109A	7349	N188S	*U.S. Marshals* (1998)	—
A109A	7133	N293G	*Jurassic Park* (1993)	Marked as N233G
A109A Hirundo	7220	N502RP	*Broken Arrow* (1997)	Flying
A109A II	7355	N7242N	*S.W.A.T.* (2003)	Flying
AW.101 Merlin	50012	G-17-510	*Skyfall* (2012)	UK Class B rego., flying
AW.159 Wildcat	478	ZZ408	*Skyfall* (2012)	Replicated as three choppers on screen

Airship Industries

Type	msn	SN or Reg. at Time of Filming	Title	Remarks / Film Markings
Skyship 500	1214/02	G-BIHN	*A View to a Kill* (1985)	Marked as Zorin Industries

Airspeed

Type	msn	SN or Reg. at Time of Filming	Title	Remarks / Film Markings
AS.6 Envoy	33	G-ADBA	*Q Planes* (1939)	Marked as E97 and E131
AS.40 Oxford II	3277	G-AHGU	*The Inn of the Sixth Happiness* (1958)	—

American Eagle

Type	msn	SN or Reg. at Time of Filming	Title	Remarks / Film Markings
A-1	277	NC6969	*Central Airport* (1933)	—

Antonov

Ukrainian manufacturer founded in 1946 by Oleg Antonov. One of the leading Soviet aircraft builders, well known for their large, high-wing transport designs. One of their best-known designs is the An-2 biplane built from 1946 to 2002, with over 18,000 airframes delivered.

Armstrong-Whitworth

Originally founded in 1912 as the Aerial Department of Sir W.G. Armstrong Whitworth & Co. and later named Sir W.G. Armstrong Whitworth Aircraft Co. in 1921. Acquired by Hawker Aircraft Ltd. in 1934 to help form Hawker Siddeley Aircraft Ltd. in 1935, but both companies traded under their original names. After a merger with Gloster Aircraft in 1961, Armstrong-Whitworth was merged into Hawker-Siddeley Aviation in 1963. Not to be confused with the 1927-formed Vickers-Armstrongs, which is a separate company—see: VICKERS.

Auster   *see*   Taylorcraft

Avro

Landmark British manufacturer was founded as A.V. Roe and Co. Ltd. (AVRO) in 1909 and became a subsidiary of Hawker Siddeley Aircraft Ltd. in 1935 but retained its original name. With such immortal designs as the Model 504, Lancaster and Vulcan V-bomber, the company continued in strong fashion through to its final merger with Hawker-Siddeley Aviation in 1963.

ANSON

First flight: March 24, 1935. Multi-role, twin-engined design for RAF and Commonwealth service during World War II. Remained in RAF service until 1968. Used in many aviation films over the years, *Journey Together* (1945) being one of the more prominent.

Other Notable Titles: *The Lion Has Wings* (1939); *Captains of the Clouds* (1942); *Journey To-*

Antonov		SN or Reg. at Time of		
Type	msn	Filming	Title	Remarks / Film Markings
(PZL-Mielec) An-2 Colt	1G22331	N87AN	Indiana Jones and the Kingdom of the Crystal Skull (2008)	Marked as NC48550 / Pan American
An-12BK Cub	7344801	3C-AAG	The Last King of Scotland (2006)	—
An-12BP Cub	43418039	Q-CIH	Lord of War (2005)	Crashed in Uganda soon after filming
An-26B Curl	13905	LZ-ABR	The Expendables 3 (2014)	Shark mouth painted on nose
An-124-100 Ruslan	19530501005	UR-82007	Die Another Day (2002)	Giant cargo plane in the final scene

Armstrong-Whitworth		SN or Reg. at Time of		
Type	msn	Filming	Title	Remarks / Film Markings
AW.660 Argosy E.Mk. 1	6792	XR137	Octopussy (1983)	Background

Avro		SN or Reg. at Time of		
Type	msn	Filming	Title	Remarks / Film Markings
504K	R3/LE/61400	G-ADEV	Reach for the Sky (1956)	Ex-RAF H5199, flying as E3404
		G-ADEV	Wings (TVS, 1977–1978)	Flying
		G-ADEV	Biggles: Adventures in Time (1986)	Marked as H5199, background only
504K (replica)	BAPC.177	G-AACA	Aces High (1976)	Non-flying replica marked as G1381
		G-AACA	Wings (TVS, 1977–1978)	Non-flying replica
504K (replica)	BAPC.178	—	Aces High (1976)	Non-flying replica marked as E373
504K (replica)	HAC1	N4929	Wings (TVS, 1977–1978)	Flying
621 Tutor I	—	G-AHSA	Reach for the Sky (1956)	Ex-RAF K3241, briefly seen as R2511

gether (1945); *Angels One Five* (1952); *The Purple Plain* (1954); *Mosquito Squadron* (1969).

LANCASTER

First flight: January 8, 1941. Four-engined heavy bomber, the legendary Type 683 saw 7,377 of the type built by war's end. Undoubtedly the 1955 film *The Dam Busters* cemented the Lancaster into cinematic film history. Due to dwindling numbers available, it's since starred in only a handful of productions, notably the British TV series *The Pathfinders.*

Other Notable Titles: *A Matter of Life and Death* (1946) models only.

YORK

First flight: July 5, 1942. The Avro Type 685 was a cargo transport development of the Lancaster. Easily recognizable from its square-slab fuselage and port hole–style windows. A total 259 were built and served up to 1964. *I Was Monty's Double* (1958) features some excellent views of the York in the air and on the ground.

VULCAN

First flight: August 30, 1952. Four-engined, delta-wing bomber. One of Britain's V-bombers, the Vulcan served from 1953 until 1984 with a total of 136 built.

Anson Type	msn	SN or Reg. at Time of Filming	Title	Remarks / Film Markings
Anson Mk. I	—	N9948	*The Sound Barrier* (1952)	—
Anson Mk. I	—	VH-FIA	*The Pacific* (TVMS, 2010)	Ex-RAF AW965, Japanese aircraft wreck
Anson C.Mk. XIX	—	TX181	*The Purple Plain* (1954)	Background

Lancaster Type	msn	SN or Reg. at Time of Filming	Title	Remarks / Film Markings
Lancaster B.Mk. I	—	R5868	*The Purple Twilight* (TVM, 1982)	UK production filmed at the RAF Hendon Museum
Lancaster B.Mk. I	—	PA474	*Operation Crossbow* (1965)	—
		PA474	*The Pathfinders* (TVS, 1972–1973)	Flying
		PA474	*Overlord* (1975)	—
		PA474	*Force 10 from Navarone* (1978)	Plus a takeoff file shot from *The Dam Busters* (1955) evident from the modified bomb bay
Lancaster B.Mk. I	—	TW862	*Appointment in London* (1953)	Marked as IH-S
Lancaster B.Mk. I	—	TW883	*Appointment in London* (1953)	Ground scenes only
Lancaster B.Mk. VII	—	NX636	*No Highway in the Sky* (1951)	Brief appearance
Lancaster B.Mk. VII	—	NX673	*Appointment in London* (1953)	Marked as IH-B
		NX673	*The Dam Busters* (1955)	Marked as AJ-P
Lancaster B.Mk. VII	—	NX679	*Appointment in London* (1953)	Marked as IH-C
		NX679	*The Dam Busters* (1955)	Marked as AJ-G / ED932
Lancaster B.Mk. VII	—	NX782	*Appointment in London* (1953)	Marked as IH-V
		NX782	*The Dam Busters* (1955)	Marked as ZN-G
Lancaster B.Mk. VII	—	RT686	*The Dam Busters* (1955)	Marked as AJ-M

York Type	msn	SN or Reg. at Time of Filming	Title	Remarks / Film Markings
York C.Mk. 1	—	MW101	*I Was Monty's Double* (1958)	—

Vulcan Type	msn	SN or Reg. at Time of Filming	Title	Remarks / Film Markings
Vulcan B.1A	—	XA913	*Thunderball* (1965)	Ground shots, along with three others
Vulcan B.1A	—	XH506	*Thunderball* (1965)	Flying shots

Prominently seen in the 1965 Bond film *Thunderball*, which included a full-scale mock-up built for underwater scenes.

Bede

Founded in 1955 by James A. and James R. Bede, building small single-seater aircraft, mainly with piston engines. Their 1973 micro-jet design is solely famous on the big screen for its brief but exciting appearance in the 1983 Bond film *Octopussy*. The aircraft only weighs 360 lbs. empty. The company went bankrupt in 1979, but kits are still available, and some minor companies have been established to help home-build pilots complete them.

Beechcraft

One of the best-known aircraft manufacturers in the United States was founded by Walter Beech and his wife Olive in 1932 in Wichita, Kansas. Became Beech Aircraft Corp. in 1936 and built many excellent types, including the Beech 18, Staggerwing, Bonanza and King Air among others. Purchased by Raytheon in 1980 and rebranded as such in 1994. Renamed Hawker Beechcraft Corp. in 2007.

BEECH 18 / C-45 EXPEDITOR

First flight: January 15, 1937. Hugely successful twin-engined aircraft, and like the DC-3, a time-

Bede

Type	msn	SN or Reg. at Time of Filming	Title	Remarks / Film Markings
BD-5J Acrostar	001	N70CF	*Octopussy* (1983)	"Micro-jet." Backup aircraft was a Bede BD-5J reg. N153BD / msn 5J-0004.

Beechcraft

Type	msn	SN or Reg. at Time of Filming	Title	Remarks / Film Markings
Baron 95-A55	TC431	N9750Y	*Airport 1975* (1974)	—
B200 Super King Air	BB-491	N622DC	*Jurassic Park III* (2001)	Some sources quote real-life reg. as being N622KM
B200 Super King Air	BB-534	N12CF	*The A-Team* (TVS, 1983–1987)	Appears in several episodes

Star of so many feature films and TV series is this Beechcraft Model 18 N476PA. It gained much screen time in *The Fly Boys* (2008) and is also known for making an appearance in *Con Air* (1997). Photograph: Steve Nation.

Beech 18		SN or Reg. at Time		
Type	msn	of Filming	Title	Remarks / Film Markings
UC-45F Expeditor	7881	N81GB	The A-Team (TVS, 1983–1987)	Ex-44-47473, appears in several episodes
AT-11 Kansan	4037	N63158	It's a Mad, Mad, Mad, Mad World (1963)	Ex-42-37444, used in famous billboard stunt
AT-11 Kansan	4616	CF-JNW	Don't Drink the Water (1969)	Ex-42-37620
SNB-1 Kansan	3824	N90264	Amelia Earhart: Final Flight (TVM, 1994)	Ex-BuNo. 51034, to SNB-5 standard, flying
SNB-1 Kansan	3894	BuNo. 51064	This Man's Navy (1945)	—
Model D18S	A-94	N250MC	The Day the Earth Moved (1974)	—
Model D18C	AA-20	N648CF	Spencer's Pilots (TVS, 1976)	Seen in occasional episodes
Model E18S	BA-281	N231H	Lost (TVS, 2004–2010)	Seen in occasional episodes
Model E18S	BA-428	ZS-IJO	Amelia (2009)	Electra stand-in, marked as NR16020
C-45G Expeditor	AF-222	N75WB	Octopussy (1983)	Ex-51-11665, marked as VN75WB
C-45G Expeditor	AF-420	N11863	Beautiful Dreamer (2006)	Ex-51-11863, background
TC-45G Expeditor	AF-82	N706FY	Spirit of the Wind (1979)	Ex-51-11525
C-45H Expeditor	AF-701	N403SE	1941 (1979)	Ex-51-10771, plus a wreck for studio use
Expeditor Mk. 3NM	CA-191	C-FGNR	Agent Cody Banks (2003)	Ex-RCAF 2318, floatplane conversion
Expeditor Mk. 3NM	CA-265	N476PA	The A-Team (TVS, 1983–1987)	Ex-RCAF 1579, "guest appearance"
		N476PA	Terminal Velocity (1994)	Flying
		N476PA	Amelia Earhart: Final Flight (TVM, 1994)	Flying
		N476PA	Con Air (1997)	Flying
		N476PA	All the Pretty Horses (2000)	Flying
		N476PA	Letters from Iwo Jima (2006)	Flying, as Japanese VIP transport
		N476PA	The Fly Boys (2008)	Flying
Expeditor Mk. 3NM	CA-267	N1042H	The Phantom (1996)	Ex-RCAF 1581, floatplane conversion
		N1042H	Godzilla (1998)	Floatplane conversion

less design that is still in commercial service today. Production continued up till 1969, when a total of 7,612 had been built for both the military and civilian markets. Known in civilian terms as the Beechcraft 18 or "Twin Beech" and in military service as the C-45 Expeditor, AT-7 Navigator and AT-11 Kansan. Famous on film for its use by Frank Tallman, who flew one through a billboard sign, the Beechcraft 18 is a very popular choice for filmmakers looking to hire an inexpensive classic design.

Other Notable Titles: *Bombardier* (1943); *Sands of the Kalahari* (1965), ZS-BVR; *Point Blank* (1967), N9943Z; *Fantasy Island* (TVS, 1977–1984), N772W; *The Last Emperor* (1987).

Bell

One of the iconic American helicopter manufacturers, Bell Aircraft Corp. was founded by Lawrence Bell in Buffalo, New York, in 1935. Initially building aircraft such as the P-39 Airacobra during World War II, Bell moved into helicopter production with the success of their Model 47 and later Model 204 / 205 types, which became the legendary "Huey" series for the army. Moved to Fort Worth, Texas, in 1951 to expand production and became a division of the Textron Corp. in 1960. Commercial helicopter production was started in Canada in 1985. Several products were license manufactured by Italian company Agusta under the Agusta-Bell (AB) brand name.

P-39 Airacobra

First flight: April 6, 1938. Single-engined fighter which sported the unique design feature of a rear-mounted engine with a connecting shaft to the front propeller. Production ran from 1938 to 1944 with a total of 9,590 built, plus another 3,303 of the upgraded P-63 Kingcobra.

Both types were largely obsolete by 1946.

Other Title: *Chain Lightning* (1950) as fictional Willis jet prototype.

X Planes

Bell's X-planes led the way for experimental developments after World War II with the X-1 itself being used to first break the sound barrier in 1947. This aircraft (s/n 46-062) was in fact used in Howard Hughes's 1957 film *Jet Pilot*.

Other Notable Titles: *The Right Stuff* (1983), models only.

Model 47

First flight: December 12, 1945. Recognized as the world's first mass-produced helicopter, the Bell Model 47 marked the beginning of a production period that lasted until 1973. Including overseas production, 6,471 were built, with the U.S. Army version named the Sioux. On the big and small screen, the Model 47 was the most recog-

P-39 Airacobra				
Type	*msn*	*SN or Reg. at Time of Filming*	*Title*	*Remarks / Film Markings*
P-39D Airacobra	unknown	41-28345	*Air Force* (1943)	Briefly seen
P-39D Airacobra	unknown	41-28347	*Air Force* (1943)	Briefly seen
P-39D Airacobra	unknown	41-28378	*Air Force* (1943)	Briefly seen

X Planes				
Type	*msn*	*SN or Reg. at Time of Filming*	*Title*	*Remarks / Film Markings*
X-1	unknown	46-062	*Jet Pilot* (1957)	—
X-2	unknown	46-674	*Toward the Unknown* (1956)	—

The Bell X-2 replica, complete with s/n 46–674, which was used in the TV series *Quantum Leap* (1989–1993). Photograph: James H. Farmer Collection.

Model 47		SN or Reg. at Time		
Type	msn	of Filming	Title	Remarks / Film Markings
Model 47B-3	37	NC177B	Red Skies of Montana (1952)	Flying
Model 47D	43	N189B	It Came from Outer Space (1953)	With open cockpit and 4-wheel undercarriage. Exported to New Zealand in 1959
Model 47G	6545	N480MW	Badlands (1973)	Flying.
Model 47G-2	1381	N975B	Whirlybirds (TVS, 1957–1960)	Flying
Model 47G-3	2604	N8417E	Air Patrol (1962)	—
Model 47G-3B-1	2921	N3079G	Batman—The Movie (1966)	Fitted with a fake "bat-wing," which reduced lifting by almost 50 percent, requiring careful flying. Owned by National Helicopter Service at Van Nuys, California
Model 47J Ranger	1424	N2838B	Whirlybirds (TVS, 1957–1960)	Flying
Model 47J Ranger	1581	N5151B	Air Patrol (1962)	—
Model 47J Ranger	1850	N73202	Paradise, Hawaiian Style (1966)	—
Model 47J Ranger	2839	N73960	A Perfect World (1993)	Flying
Model 47J Ranger	3130	N1134W	Air America (1990)	Marked as: Radio 1080 am
Model 47J Ranger	3302	N1190W	Thunderball (1965)	Floats fitted
Model 47J Ranger	unknown	N1538B	Whirlybirds (TVS, 1957–1960)	Flying

nized and utilized helicopter in the years before the Bell Jet Ranger and Hughes 500 came along. Widely referred to as the "M*A*S*H helicopter" after it was made famous in both the film and popular television series.

Other Notable Titles: Canyon Crossroads (1955); Air Patrol (1962); You Only Live Twice (1967), four Kawasaki Model 47G; Where Eagles Dare (1968); M*A*S*H (1970; TVS, 1972–1983), several OH-13 Siouxs provided by a local army base in California; Breakout (1975), Model 47G; The Wilby Conspiracy (1975), Model 47G and 47J Ranger.

Model 204 / 205 / UH-1 Iroquois / AH-1 Cobra

First flight (XH-40): October 22, 1956. The only aircraft, fixed or rotary winged, since the end of World War II to be mass produced directly for war. Approximately 7,000 saw service in the Vietnam War, with which this helicopter is synonymous. The UH-1 Huey is probably the most utilized military helicopter in the history of film aviation and has become the "DC-3" of the rotary world! With the advent of the "Vietnam film" in the late 1970s and throughout the 1980s, there was no shortage of work for the Huey in screen

roles. Many major action films up to the present day still use the faithful Huey in some shape or form, and a large number are still flying on the civilian market. Of all the films the Huey has starred in, the most famous is undoubtedly Apocalypse Now (1979), especially the scene accompanied by the classical music of "The Ride of the Valkyries."

Other Notable Titles: Many James Bond films; The Green Berets (1968); The Towering Inferno (1974), U.S. Navy UH-1N; King Kong (1976), Bell 204; The Deer Hunter (1978), Thai Police UH-1H; Apocalypse Now (1979), Philippine UH-1H; High Ice (TVM, 1980); Uncommon Valor (1983), two Bell 212; The A-Team (TVS, 1983–1987); Commando (1985); Rambo: First Blood Part II (1985), Bell 212; Heartbreak Ridge (1986); Platoon (1986); Good Morning, Vietnam (1987); Hamburger Hill (1987); Tour of Duty (TVS, 1987–1990); Die Hard (1988), Bell 204; Born on the Fourth of July (1989); Casualties of War (1989); Air America (1990); Die Hard 2 (1990), Bell 204; Fire Birds (1990); Alive (1993); Heaven and Earth (1993); Clear and Present Danger (1994), Bell 412; Operation Dumbo Drop (1995); Outbreak (1995); Broken Arrow (1996); Independence Day

Model 204...		SN or Reg. at Time		
Type	msn	of Filming	Title	Remarks / Film Markings
UH-1B Iroquois	343	N842M	Lost (TVS, 2004–2010)	Ex-61-0763, seen in Seasons 4 and 5
UH-1B Iroquois	745	63-8523	Terminator 2: Judgment Day (1991)	Reg. N3121A 1991–2013. Derelict in desert scenes
UH-1B Iroquois	1162	N87701	Twilight Zone—The Movie (1983)	Ex-64-14038, crashed during filming on July 23, 1982, killing three actors (Vic Morrow and two children) on the ground
UH-1D Iroquois	4695	N42331	Live Free or Die Hard (2007)	Ex-65-9651
		N42331	The Last Stand (2013)	As FBI chopper
UH-1D Iroquois	4738	N72376	The Right Stuff (1983)	Ex-65-9694
UH-1D Iroquois	5657	N313CF	Courage Under Fire (1996)	Ex-66-1174
		N313CF	Con Air (1997)	—
		N313CF	We Were Soldiers (2002)	Plus several others
UH-1D Iroquois	5787	N6131P	Hawaii Five-0 (TVS, 2010–)	Ex-66-16093, "guest appearance"
UH-1H Iroquois	13081	N431LH	The Expendables 3 (2014)	Ex-71-20257
UH-1H Iroquois	13560	G-HUEY	The Living Daylights (1987)	Ex-73-22077
TH-1L Iroquois	6426	N540GH	Dante's Peak (1997)	Ex-BuNo. 157831
Model 204B	2196	N1304X	Close Encounters of the Third Kind (1977)	Sprayer helicopter, ex–Air America Inc.
Model AB.204B	3002	HB-XCG	On Her Majesty's Secret Service (1969)	Hired from Heliswiss
Model AB.204B	3209	HB-XCQ	On Her Majesty's Secret Service (1969)	Hired from Heliswiss
Model AB.204B	3211	LN-ORZ	On Her Majesty's Secret Service (1969)	Hired from Heliswiss
Model 205A-1	30056	D-HAFL	Behind Enemy Lines (2001)	Flying
Model 205A-1	30101	D-HAFM	Cliffhanger (1993)	Flying
Model 205A-1	30206	N49641	The A-Team (TVS, 1983–1987)	Fire-bomber, "guest appearance"
		D-HOOK	Cliffhanger (1993)	Previously N49641, flying
		D-HOOK	Spy Game (2001)	Flying
		D-HOOK	Behind Enemy Lines (2001)	Flying
Model 205A-1	30289	N205SF	Live Free or Die Hard (2007)	Flying
		N205SF	Quantum of Solace (2008)	Flying
Model 212	30516	N212CR	The A-Team (TVS, 1983–1987)	"Guest appearance" in one episode
Model 212	30624	N370EH	The Puppet Masters (1994)	Flying
Model 212	30672	N72AL	Black Sunday (1977)	Flying
Model 212	30869	N16949	The A-Team (TVS, 1983–1987)	"Guest appearance" in one episode
Model 212	30973	N2768N	True Lies (1994)	Flying, bridge sequence
Model 214B-1 Big Lifter	28001	N214RM	Close Encounters of the Third Kind (1977)	Detainee helicopter
AH-1S Cobra	24039	N605DB	Courage Under Fire (1996)	Ex-76-22605
		N605DB	Con Air (1997)	—
AH-1S Cobra	24072	N2734D	Courage Under Fire (1996)	Ex-77-22734
		N2734D	Con Air (1997)	—

(1996); The Rock (1996); Six Days Seven Nights (1998); The Matrix (1999); Rescue Dawn (2006); Tropic Thunder (2008); Terminator Salvation (2009); The A-Team (2010); Battle: Los Angeles (2011), USMC UH-1H/N; Transformers: Dark of the Moon (2011), three NASA UH-1H.

MODEL 206 JET RANGER / OH-58 KIOWA

First flight: December 8, 1962. The Model 206 was originally designed as a light observation helicopter for the U.S. Army. In all, 2,377 were built

Model 206... Type	msn	SN or Reg. at Time of Filming	Title	Remarks / Film Markings
Model 206A Jet Ranger	004	N1351X	*King Kong* (1976)	Marked "Petrox Corp"
Model 206A Jet Ranger	067	VH-UHC	*Chopper Squad* (TVS, 1976–1979)	Yellow and white livery. Flew in TV movie only; VH-FHF was used in the subsequent TV series
Model 206A Jet Ranger	174	N209D	*Diamonds Are Forever* (1971)	Leads attack on oil rig
Model 206A Jet Ranger	236	N4709R	*Vanishing Point* (1971)	Highway Patrol helicopter
Model 206A Jet Ranger	335	N550JA	*King Kong* (1976)	NYPD police helicopter
Model 206A Jet Ranger	352	C-GJTV	*Iceman* (1984)	Flying
Model 206A Jet Ranger	563	N40MC	*Chopper One* (TVS, 1974)	As a police helicopter
Model 206A Jet Ranger	657	JDFH-03	*Live and Let Die* (1973)	Jamaica Defence Force
Model 206B Jet Ranger	854	G-BAKF	*Biggles: Adventures in Time* (1986)	Flying
Model 206B Jet Ranger	937	N20DB	*Dirty Mary Crazy Larry* (1974)	Seen in car chase sequence
		N20DB	*The Towering Inferno* (1974)	Seen in opening titles
		N20DB	*Mobile One* (TVS, 1975)	Marked as: KONE TV1
		N20DB	*Riding with Death* (1976)	Flying
		N20DB	*The Stunt Man* (1980)	Flying
Model 206B Jet Ranger	1192	N2995W	*Magnum P.I.* (TVS, 1980–1988)	"Guest appearance"
Model 206B Jet Ranger	1292	N59492	*Hooper* (1978)	—
		N59492	*Nice Dreams* (1981)	—
		N59492	*The A-Team* (TVS, 1983–1987)	"Guest appearance"
Model 206B Jet Ranger	1326	N3187D	*Airwolf* (TVS, 1984–1987)	"Guest appearance"
Model 206B Jet Ranger	1420	N59600	*The A-Team* (TVS, 1983–1987)	"Guest appearance"
Model 206B Jet Ranger	1474	N59577	*Speed* (1994)	Flying
Model 206B Jet Ranger	1531	C-GTPH	*First Blood* (1982)	Used in canyon shoot-out scene
Model 206B Jet Ranger	1557	N59642	*Close Encounters of the Third Kind* (1977)	Unmarked army helicopter
		N59642	*Moonraker* (1979)	Marked as N5364W, "Drax Airlines"
Model 206B Jet Ranger	1738	N90296	*Close Encounters of the Third Kind* (1977)	Unmarked army helicopter
Model 206B Jet Ranger	1792	N62FH	*Passenger 57* (1992)	Marked as AIA
Model 206B Jet Ranger	1801	N830RC	*Terminator 2: Judgment Day* (1991)	Flying
		N830RC	*Man Trouble* (1992)	Flying
		N830RC	*True Lies* (1994)	Flying
Model 206B Jet Ranger	1826	N49661	*Terminal Velocity* (1994)	Marked as KAZS 6
Model 206B Jet Ranger	1862	N49675	*Raise the Titanic* (1980)	Flying
Model 206B Jet Ranger	1923	N9902K	*Magnum P.I.* (TVS, 1980–1988)	"Guest appearance"
Model 206B Jet Ranger	1926	VH-FHF	*Chopper Squad* (TVS, 1976–1979)	Blue and white livery
Model 206B Jet Ranger	2615	N250CA	*Close Encounters of the Third Kind: The Special Edition* (1980)	Gobi Desert sequence
		N250CA	*Knight Rider* (TVS, 1982–1986)	"Guest appearances"
		N250CA	*Blue Thunder* (1983)	Flying
		N250CA	*Uncommon Valor* (1983)	Flying
		N250CA	*Dreamscape* (1984)	Flying
		N250CA	*Alien Nation* (1988)	Flying
		N250CA	*Forever Young* (1992)	Briefly seen in flyby
		N250CA	*Speed* (1994)	Flying
		N250CA	*Con Air* (1997)	Flying
Model 206B Jet Ranger	2642	N2757M	*Airwolf* (TVS, 1984–1987)	"Guest appearances"
Model 206B Jet Ranger	2761	N2766Y	*Airwolf* (TVS, 1984–1987)	"Guest appearance"
Model 206B Jet Ranger	2779	N2774L	*Close Encounters of the Third Kind: The Special Edition* (1980)	Gobi Desert sequence

Model 206... (Type)	(msn)	(SN or Reg. at Time of Filming)	(Title)	(Remarks / Film Markings)
		N230CA	Knight Rider (TVS, 1982–1986)	"Guest appearance"
		N230CA	Blue Thunder (1983)	Previous reg. N2774L
		N230CA	Uncommon Valor (1983)	Flying
		N230CA	Commando (1985)	Marked as 0-25886
		N230CA	Lethal Weapon (1987)	Flying
		N230CA	Darkman (1990)	Flying
Model 206B Jet Ranger	2811	N764CL	Knight Rider (TVS, 1982–1986)	"Guest appearances"
		N764CL	The A-Team (TVS, 1983–1987)	"Guest appearance"; also seen in opening titles
Model 206B Jet Ranger	2840	N1068A	The A-Team (TVS, 1983–1987)	"Guest appearance"
		N1068A	Blue Thunder (1983)	Flying
Model 206B Jet Ranger	2842	N25AJ	Independence Day (1996)	Flying
Model 206B Jet Ranger	3025	N5739V	Con Air (1997)	—
Model 206B Jet Ranger	3092	ZK-HSA	Race for the Yankee Zephyr (1981)	Flies in Bell factory livery
Model 206B Jet Ranger	3102	N5736L	Uncommon Valor (1983)	—
Model 206B Jet Ranger	3167	N57BL	Drop Zone (1994)	—
Model 206B Jet Ranger	3264	N200NP	Blue Thunder (1983)	Bell factory livery
Model 206B Jet Ranger	3363	N2044C	Knight Rider (TVS, 1982–1986)	"Guest appearances"
		N2044C	The A-Team (TVS, 1983–1987)	"Guest appearances"
		N2044C	Blue Thunder (1983)	—
		N2044C	Airwolf (TVS, 1984–1987)	Colorful "Santini Air" livery
Model 206B Jet Ranger	3429	N20802	Scarface (1983)	—
		N20802	The A-Team (TVS, 1983–1987)	Guest appearance"
		N20802	Airwolf (TVS, 1984–1987)	"Guest appearance"
Model 206B Jet Ranger	3470	N218SS	The X-Files (TVS, 1993–2002)	"Guest appearance" in final episode
Model 206B Jet Ranger	3634	N2282T	Airwolf (TVS, 1984–1987)	"Guest appearance"
Model 206B Jet Ranger	3957	N212LA	Volcano (1997)	Flying
Model AB.206B Jet Ranger	8013	HB-XCF	On Her Majesty's Secret Service (1969)	Hired from Heliswiss
Model AB.206B Jet Ranger	8339	G-BAKS	For Your Eyes Only (1981)	Marked "Universal Exports"
Model AB.206B Jet Ranger	8353	F-BUIA	The Concorde ... Airport '79 (1979)	Briefly seen
Model 206L Long Ranger	45116	C-FHJK	Iron Eagle IV (1995)	Doubles as a CH-136 Kiowa
Model 206L Long Ranger	45195	N3338H	The Osterman Weekend (1983)	—
Model 206L Long Ranger	45204	N73FA	Die Hard With a Vengeance (1995)	—
Model 206L Long Ranger	45448	C-GWCF	Iceman (1984)	Marked as C-GVVI
Model 206L Long Ranger	45510	N57497	The A-Team (TVS, 1983–1987)	"Guest appearance"
Model 206L Long Ranger	45561	N3886J	The A-Team (TVS, 1983–1987)	"Guest appearance"
Model 206L Long Ranger	45568	N3388H	Terminal Velocity (1994)	—
Model 206L Long Ranger	45653	N522RS	Jurassic Park (1993)	—
Model 206L Long Ranger	51062	N331WD	The A-Team (TVS, 1983–1987)	"Guest appearance"
		N331WD	Airwolf (TVS, 1984–1987)	"Guest appearance"
Model 206L Long Ranger	51067	N16EA	True Lies (1994)	—
Model 206L Long Ranger	52047	N911YY	Transformers: Dark of the Moon (2011)	Chicago Police
OH-58A Kiowa	40999	N38FA	Outbreak (1995)	Ex-70-15448, news chopper
OH-58D Kiowa Warrior	43151	88-0295	Fire Birds (1990)	—

as such from 1968 as the OH-58 Kiowa with other military types to follow. The design also sold into the civilian market and became one of the most popular helicopters of its day, with nearly 4,690 206A and B models built from 1966 to 2010. It has starred in literally dozens of productions over the years; the list below is only the briefest sampling of identified machines seen on the big and small screen.

Other Notable Titles: *Mobile One* (TVS, 1975); *Sky Riders* (1976); *Spencer's Pilots* (TVS, 1976); *Capricorn One* (1978); *Superman—The Movie* (1978); *The Survivor* (1981); *Deadly Encounter* (TVM, 1982); *The A-Team* (TVS, 1983–1987); *Rambo: First Blood Part II* (1985); *Air America* (1990); *The A-Team* (2010).

Model 222

First flight: August 13, 1976. Twin-engined civil helicopter; 237 were built by 1995, but for various reasons it never achieved the success of earlier Bell types. Best known for its extensive use in the *Airwolf* TV series.

Bell-Boeing

A joint program by Bell and Boeing to produce a tilt-rotor design known as the V-22 Osprey, which first flew in its present form in 1989. Development and service entry had been very slow due to technical issues, with the USMC MV-22B and USAF CV-22B not gaining active duty until 2006.

Other Notable Titles: *The A-Team* (2010), CGI model only.

Bleriot

Bleriot Aeronautique was a French aircraft manufacturer founded by Louis Bleriot in 1909 after his historic feat of flying the English Channel. Built both Bleriot and SPAD aircraft during World War I. One of the leading French manufacturers in its day.

Boeing

One of the most famous, enduring and bold of all aircraft manufacturers, Boeing has created military and civil aircraft designs that are known the world over. Also one of the very few U.S. aircraft manufacturers to still be doing business under its original namesake.

Founded in 1916 by William Boeing as Pacific Aero Products Co.; renamed the Boeing Airplane Co. in 1917; the Boeing Aircraft Co. in 1934, when it also acquired Stearman Aircraft Corp.; acquired the Vertol Aircraft Corp. in 1960; renamed the Boeing Co. in 1961; acquired Rockwell Intl. (aerospace holdings) in 1996; McDonnell Douglas in 1997; relocated its head office from Seattle to Chicago in 2001. Boeing aircraft have had a vast exposure on the silver screen, especially the B-17 Flying Fortress during the war years and the Model 747 in many disaster films.

Model 222				
Type	msn	SN or Reg. at Time of Filming	Title	Remarks / Film Markings
Model 222A	47085	N3176S	*Airwolf* (TVS, 1984–1987)	Crashed in 1992

Bell-Boeing		SN or Reg. at Time of Filming		
Type	msn		Title	Remarks / Film Markings
CV-22B Osprey	D1006	02-0025	*Transformers* (2007)	Flying
CV-22B Osprey	D1008	04-0027	*Transformers* (2007)	Flying
CV-22B Osprey	D1011	05-0030	*Transformers: Dark of the Moon* (2011)	Plus several others

Bleriot		SN or Reg. at Time of Filming		
Type	msn		Title	Remarks / Film Markings
Model XI Penguin (replica)	1	N6683C	*Lafayette Escadrille* (1958)	Flying
Model XI Penguin (replica)	1	N126HM	*Amelia* (2009)	Flying

MODEL 100 / F4B / P-12

First flight: June 25, 1928. Single-engined USAAC (P-12) / USN (F4B) pursuit biplane. The civilian version was known as the Model

100 and only four were built. Two of these were operated by Hollywood pilot Paul Mantz (N872H, N873H) in many of his films, especially N873H, which was a favorite for many years.

Other Notable Titles: *Hell Divers* (1931), *F4B-*

Model 100				
Type	msn	SN or Reg. at Time of Filming	Title	Remarks / Film Markings
Model 100	1143	NC / N872H	*Men With Wings* (1938)	Doubles as a Boeing P-12
		NC / N872H	*Task Force* (1949)	Doubles as a F8C-2 Helldiver
Model 100	1144	NC / N873H	*Test Pilot* (1938)	—
		NC / N873H	*Men With Wings* (1938)	Doubles as a Boeing P-12
		NC / N873H	*Keep 'Em Flying* (1941)	Doubles as a Stearman Kaydet
		NC / N873H	*International Squadron* (1941)	Doubles as a RAF Gladiator
		NC / N873H	*Thunder Birds* (1942)	Doubles as a Stearman Kaydet
		NC / N873H	*Blaze of Noon* (1947)	Also flies as camera-plane
		NC / N873H	*The Amazing Howard Hughes* (TVM, 1977)	Doubles as a Boeing F4B-1
F4B-3	1598	BuNo. A-8894	*Devil Dogs of the Air* (1935)	—

Model 247				
Type	msn	SN or Reg. at Time of Filming	Title	Remarks / Film Markings
Model 247	1712	NC13330	*Flight Angels* (1940)	Seen in opening titles.
Model 247	1724	NC13342	*Thirteen Hours by Air* (1936)	Provided by United Airlines, to 247D standard.
Model 247	1948	NC13362	*Men With Wings* (1938)	Doubles as the "Falconer bomber," to 247D standard.
Model 247	D1946	NC2666	*Without Orders* (1936)	—

One of Hollywood stunt pilot Paul Mantz's favorite aircraft, his Boeing Model 100 N873H that he flew for so many film productions including *Test Pilot* (1938), *Men with Wings* (1938) and *Keep 'Em Flying* (1941). Photograph: James H. Farmer Collection.

2; *Navy Born* (1936); *Wings of the Navy* (1939), F4B-4; *The Aviator* (2004).

MODEL 247

First flight: February 8, 1933. Twin-engined airliner; a total of 75 were built up to 1935.

Overshadowed and outsold by the legendary Douglas DC-3, the Model 247 featured in several early air disaster movies during the 1930s.

Other Notable Titles: *Stunt Pilot* (1939); *Flying Blind* (1941).

B-17 FLYING FORTRESS

First flight: July 28, 1935. Legendary four-engined heavy bomber of which a staggering 12,731 had been built for the war effort by 1945. Of all the bombers during World War II, the B-17 has won the most time in the limelight on the big screen. Not only was it made famous in the public eye during the war through newsreels and productions such as *Flying Fortress* (1942), *Air Force* (1943) and the William Wyler documentary *The Memphis Belle* (1944), but there was a large abundance of airframes available on the civilian market after the war. This meant there was easy, ready access to flyable B-17 aircraft for filmmakers, enough even to casually destroy them on camera, as happened for the famous Paul Mantz belly-landing scene in *Twelve O'Clock High* (1949).

Other Notable Titles: *I Wanted Wings* (1941); *Desperate Journey* (1942), mock-up; *Bombardier* (1943); *Aerial Gunner* (1943); *The Sky's the Limit* (1943); *Captain Eddie* (1945); *The Way to the Stars* (1945); *You Came Along* (1945); *The Best Years of Our Lives* (1946), B-17E; *Seven Came Back* (1947), SB-17H; *Above and Beyond* (1952); *Top of the World* (1955); *Ike* (TVMS, 1979); *Fortress* (2012), CGI only.

B-17 Flying Fortress		SN or Reg. at Time of		
Type	msn	Filming	Title	Remarks / Film Markings
Y1B-17 Flying Fortress	1973	36-149	*Test Pilot* (1938)	—
Y1B-17 Flying Fortress	1974	36-150	*Test Pilot* (1938)	No. 60
Y1B-17 Flying Fortress	1975	36-151	*Test Pilot* (1938)	No. 80
Y1B-17 Flying Fortress	1976	36-152	*Test Pilot* (1938)	No. 50
Y1B-17 Flying Fortress	1977	36-153	*Test Pilot* (1938)	—
Y1B-17 Flying Fortress	1978	36-154	*Test Pilot* (1938)	No. 81
Y1B-17 Flying Fortress	1979	36-155	*Test Pilot* (1938)	No. 10
Y1B-17 Flying Fortress	1980	36-156	*Test Pilot* (1938)	No. 51
Y1B-17 Flying Fortress	1981	36-157	*Test Pilot* (1938)	—
Y1B-17 Flying Fortress	1982	36-158	*Test Pilot* (1938)	No. 82
Y1B-17 Flying Fortress	1983	36-159	*Test Pilot* (1938)	No. 52
Y1B-17 Flying Fortress	1984	36-160	*Test Pilot* (1938)	—
Y1B-17 Flying Fortress	1985	36-161	*Test Pilot* (1938)	No. 89
B-17B Flying Fortress	2004	38-211	*Air Force* (1943)	No. 18
B-17B Flying Fortress	2020	38-261	*Air Force* (1943)	No. 07
B-17B Flying Fortress	2031	38-584	*Air Force* (1943)	No. 10, marked as 05564 / Mary Ann
B-17B Flying Fortress	2033	39-001	*Air Force* (1943)	No. 15
Fortress Mk. I	2044	(RAF) AN518	*Flying Fortress* (1942)	B-17C s/n 40-2043
Fortress Mk. I	2067	(RAF) AN530	*Flying Fortress* (1942)	B-17C s/n 40-2066
Fortress Mk. I	2077	(RAF) AN536	*Flying Fortress* (1942)	B-17C s/n 40-2076
B-17F Flying Fortress	4896	N17W	*The Thousand Plane Raid* (1969)	Ex-42-29782, flying
		N17W	*Tora! Tora! Tora!* (1970)	Flying
		N17W	*Memphis Belle* (1990)	Marked as DF-X / C-Cup
B-17F Flying Fortress	8296	N67974	*Command Decision* (1948)	Ex-42-3360, background
		N67974	*Chain Lightning* (1950)	Flying
B-17F Flying Fortress	17-6142	42-5846	*Hers to Hold* (1943)	Filmed at Vega's Burbank plant. Lost in combat late 1943
B-17G Flying Fortress	10334	43-39356	*The Lady Takes a Flyer* (1958)	USAF VB-17G, false civil reg. N39356

B-17 Flying Fortress		*(SN or Reg. at Time of*		
(Type)	*(msn)*	*Filming)*	*(Title)*	*(Remarks / Film Markings)*
B-17G Flying Fortress	31957	44-83316	*12 O'Clock High* (TVS, 1964–1967)	Non-flying, studio prop
B-17G Flying Fortress	32028	44-83387	*Twelve O'Clock High* (1949)	Studio cockpit filming
		44-83387	*12 O'Clock High* (TVS, 1964–1967)	Studio cockpit filming
		44-83387	*The Thousand Plane Raid* (1969)	Studio cockpit filming
		44-83387	*Tora! Tora! Tora!* (1970)	Studio cockpit filming
B-17G Flying Fortress	32155	N9323Z	*1941* (1979)	Ex-44-83514, doubled as a B-17E
B-17G Flying Fortress	32166	N83525	*The Thousand Plane Raid* (1969)	Ex-44-83525, flying
		N83525	*MacArthur* (1977)	Taxi scenes only
B-17G Flying Fortress	32187	N3703G	*Memphis Belle* (1990)	Ex-44-83546, marked as DF-A / *Memphis Belle*
B-17G Flying Fortress	32204	N9563Z	*The War Lover* (1962)	Ex-44-83563, flying
		N9563Z	*Tora! Tora! Tora!* (1970)	Flying
B-17G Flying Fortress	32233	44-83592	*Twelve O'Clock High* (1949)	Performed the famous belly-landing piloted by Paul Mantz
B-17G Flying Fortress	32325	N3713G	*12 O'Clock High* (TVS, 1964–1967)	Ex-44-83684
		N3713G	*The Thousand Plane Raid* (1969)	Flying
		N3713G	*Baa Baa Black Sheep* (TVS, 1976–1978)	Flying / background
B-17G Flying Fortress	32426	N809Z	*Thunderball* (1965)	Ex-44-83785 / Fulton retrieval system
B-17G Flying Fortress	32452	44-83811	*The War Lover* (1962)	Ex-NL5014N, ex–Israeli Air Force, derelict fuselage
B-17G Flying Fortress	32483	NL1212N	*Fighter Squadron* (1948)	Flying
		NL1212N	*Command Decision* (1948)	Ex-44-83842, marked as *Impatient Virgin III*
B-17G Flying Fortress	32513	N7227C	*Ike: The War Years* (TVMS, 1979)	Ex-44-83872
		N7227C	*Brady's Escape* (1983)	—
B-17G Flying Fortress	32518	N5232V	*The War Lover* (1962)	Ex-44-83877, flying
B-17G Flying Fortress	32524	N5229V	*The War Lover* (1962)	Ex-44-83883, flying
B-17G Flying Fortress	17-8246	F-AZDX	*Memphis Belle* (1990)	Ex-44-8846, marked as DF-S / *Mother & Country*
		F-AZDX	*Red Tails* (2012)	Flying
B-17G Flying Fortress	17-8552	F-BEEA	*Memphis Belle* (1990)	Ex-44-85643, marked as DF-U / *Baby Ruth*
B-17G Flying Fortress	17-8627	N900RW	*The Tuskegee Airmen* (TVM, 1995)	Ex-44-85718, Lone Star Flight Museum, Texas
B-17G Flying Fortress	17-8683	N621L	*Tora! Tora! Tora!* (1970)	Ex-44-85774, flying
B-17G Flying Fortress	17-8693	G-BEDF	*We'll Meet Again* (TVS, 1982)	Ex-44-85784, mostly seen in opening titles
		G-BEDF	*Memphis Belle* (1990)	Marked as DF-M / *Windy City*
B-17G Flying Fortress	17-8738	N3193G	*Tora! Tora! Tora!* (1970)	Ex-44-85829, flying
		N3193G	*Closing the Ring* (2007)	Briefly seen
B-17G Flying Fortress	17-8746	BuNo. 82855	*The High and the Mighty* (1954)	Ex-44-85837, USCG PB-1G conversion
B-17G Flying Fortress	17-8749	N620L	*Tora! Tora! Tora!* (1970)	Ex-44-85840, flying

B-29 / B-50 SUPERFORTRESS

First flight: September 21, 1942. Four-engined heavy bomber, the B-29 became the air force's first atomic bomber when it dropped the bomb on Hiroshima, and would go on to serve in the Korean War. Considering the fame and capabilities of B-29, it hasn't really achieved much exposure at the box office, probably because access to actual aircraft after the war was difficult, with most remaining in service and the decision by the USAF not to make them available to civil operators. Most 1940s and 1950s films made use of stock footage, studio mock-ups or derelict airframes. Two did make it to the U.S. civilian register in later years, N529B and N91329, and these made a small contribution in actual flying scenes for a handful of productions in the late 1970s and early 1980s. The later, tall-tail version with revised engines and nacelles was designated as the B-50.

Other Notable Titles: *The Beginning or the End* (1947); *Hell's Horizon* (1955); *Space Cowboys* (2000).

C-97 / KC-97 STRATOFREIGHTER

First flight: November 9, 1944. Four-engined cargo transport / aerial tanker. A total of 887 were built based on the original design of the B-29 Superfortress. The KC-97 version was the USAF's first capable aerial tanker. The civilian version was the Model 377 Stratocruiser, which first flew on July 8, 1947; 56 were built.

Other Notable Titles: *Strategic Air Command* (1955).

B-47 STRATOJET

First flight: December 17, 1947. Six-engined, swept-wing jet bomber had its maiden flight as the XB-47. In all, 2,042 airframes were delivered

B-29 / B-50 ... Type	msn	SN or Reg. at Time of Filming	Title	Remarks / Film Markings
B-29 Superfortress	10848	44-70016	*Enola Gay* (TVM, 1980)	Non-flying
		44-70016	*Deadly Encounter* (TVM, 1982)	Non-flying
B-29 Superfortress	10881	44-70049	*The Last Flight of Noah's Ark* (1980)	Shipped to Hawaii for filming
B-29 Superfortress	13681	N91329	*The Last Flight of Noah's Ark* (1980)	Ex-45-21787, flying
		N91329	*Enola Gay* (TVM, 1980)	Flying
B-29 Superfortress	13706	45-21812	*The Glenn Miller Story* (1954)	Background
B-29 Superfortress	unknown	42-65401	*The Wild Blue Yonder* (1951)	Studio filming
		42-65401	*Above and Beyond* (1952)	Studio filming
		42-65401	*Enola Gay* (TVM, 1980)	Studio filming
B-29 Superfortress	unknown	44-84084	*The Last Flight of Noah's Ark* (1980)	Shipped to Hawaii for filming
B-29A Superfortress	11547	N4249	*Enola Gay* (TVM, 1980)	Ex-44-62070, flying
		N529B	*The Right Stuff* 1983)	Flying
		N529B	*Roswell* (TVM, 1994)	Flying
B-29A Superfortress	11589	44-62112	*The Last Flight of Noah's Ark* (1980)	Studio filming
B-29A Superfortress	11699	44-62222	*The Last Flight of Noah's Ark* (1980)	Studio filming
B-50A Superfortress	15726	46-006	*Jet Pilot* (1957)	—

C-97 / KC-97 ... Type	msn	SN or Reg. at Time of Filming	Title	Remarks / Film Markings
KC-97G Stratofreighter	16669	52-2638	*Bombers B-52* (1957)	—

B-47 Stratojet Type	msn	SN or Reg. at Time of Filming	Title	Remarks / Film Markings
XB-47 Stratojet	15972	46-065	*Strategic Air Command* (1955)	—
B-47B Stratojet	450352	51-2299	*Strategic Air Command* (1955)	—
B-47B Stratojet	450371	51-2318	*Strategic Air Command* (1955)	—
B-47B Stratojet	450374	51-2321	*Strategic Air Command* (1955)	—
B-47B Stratojet	450389	51-2336	*Strategic Air Command* (1955)	—
B-47E Stratojet	43666	52-051	*Bombers B-52* (1957)	—
B-47E Stratojet	4501124	53-2311	*Bombers B-52* (1957)	—

by 1957, but shortcomings in the design and the advent of the much more successful B-52 meant the front-line service life of the B-47 ended the same year they finished building them. The aircraft is well represented in the 1955 James Stewart film *Strategic Air Command*.

Other Notable Titles: *Bailout at 43,000* (1957).

B-52 Stratofortress

First flight: April 15, 1952. Eight-engined strategic bomber is the most successful and longest-serving heavy bomber in the history of the USAF and one of the greatest symbols of American airpower. The B-52 was at the forefront of the Cold War as a nuclear bomber and conventional heavy bombing in Vietnam, the Gulf War and beyond. Given its stature in aviation history, the Stratofortress hasn't been that prolific on the silver screen, and is currently best remembered for its appearance in *Dr. Strangelove* (1964).

Other Notable Titles: *Dr. Strangelove* (1964); *Wild in the Sky* (1972); *Apocalypse Now* (1979), mocked-up tail section; *The Day After* (TVM, 1983), footage from 1979 docco. *First Strike*.

Model 707

First flight: July 15, 1954. Four-engined civilian airliner initially designated as the Model 367-80 or "Dash-80." It revolutionized the airline industry from 1958 and put Boeing on the map as a world leader in jet airliner technology. Total output of 1,011 had been built by 1991 when production stopped, with another 820 built for the military as the KC-135 Stratotanker. Perhaps best known on the silver screen for its appearance in the 1970 air disaster film *Airport*.

Other Notable Titles: *Superman—The Movie* (1978), VC-137C scale model only; *Iron Eagle II* (1988).

Model 727

First flight: February 9, 1963. Three-engined, T-tailed airliner was another huge success for Boeing, and 1,832 had been built by 1984 when production ceased. Not many big-screen appearances, but the airliner did gain much notoriety during the D.B Cooper hijack of 1971, which was made into a film in 1981.

B-52 Stratofortress		SN or Reg. at Time of		
Type	msn	Filming	Title	Remarks / Film Markings
B-52A Stratofortress	16493	52-003	*X-15* (1961)	Actual NASA NB-52A
RB-52B Stratofortress	16498	52-008	*X-15* (1961)	Actual NASA NB-52B
B-52B Stratofortress	16852	53-373	*Bombers B-52* (1957)	In SAC service
B-52E Stratofortress	17325	56-642	*A Gathering of Eagles* (1963)	In SAC service
B-25E Stratofortress	464071	56-700	*By Dawn's Early Light* (TVM, 1990)	Nose section for studio filming
B-52G Stratofortress	464221	57-6516	*A Gathering of Eagles* (1963)	In SAC service

Model 707		SN or Reg. at Time of		
Type	msn	Filming	Title	Remarks / Film Markings
Model 707-131	17661/22	N6232G	*Speed* (1994)	Destroyed at Mojave Airport for film
Model 707-131	B18987/486	N6721	*Airplane!* (1980)	TWA, brief ground scenes
Model 707-138	B18334/229	CN-ANS	*Black Hawk Down* (2001)	Ex-Qantas VH-EBK, derelict in background
Model 707-138	B18740/388	N707JT	*Pan Am* (TVS, 2011-2012)	Provided by owner John Travolta for ground scenes
Model 707-139	B17903/108	N778PA	*The Delta Force* (1986)	Marked as "American Travelways"
Model 707-330	B19315/545	D-ABUL	*Diamonds Are Forever* (1971)	Lufthansa Airlines
Model 707-349	C19354/503	N324F	*Airport* (1970)	Marked as "Trans Global Airlines"
Model 707-373	C18583/346	N374WA	*Skyjacked* (1972)	Marked as "Global Airlines"
		N374WA	*Magnum Force* (1973)	Marked as "Sovereign Airlines"

Model 727		SN or Reg. at Time of		
Type	msn	Filming	Title	Remarks / Film Markings
Model 727-30	18933/185	N7271P	U.S. Marshals (1998)	Doubles as a U.S. Marshals jet
Model 727-51	19122/319	N105RK	The Pursuit of D.B. Cooper (1981)	Marked as "Northern Pacific"
Model 727-63	19846/555	N32720	Accidental Hero (1992)	Used for wreck scene marked as N88892
Model 727-17	3C19504/527	N690WA	The Pursuit of D.B. Cooper (1981)	Marked as "Northern Pacific"
Model 727-173C	19507/449	N693WA	Mayday at 40,000 Feet! (TVM, 1976)	Marked as "Transcon Airways"
Model 727-29	119993/549	N408BN	Bad Boys (1995)	Destroyed for film

MODEL 737

First flight: April 9, 1967. Twin-engined airliner known as the "Boeing Baby" is the most successful of all the Boeing airliners to date, with production having gone past the 6,500 mark by 2010. Other Notable Titles: *Random Hearts* (1999).

MODEL 747

First flight: February 9, 1969. Four-engined "Jumbo Jet" airliner marked a new beginning in passenger airline transport and the dawn of the wide-body airliner. Over 1,400 had been delivered by 2010 and production continues on new versions. The most popular by far of any jet airliner to be utilized on the big screen with numerous titles made over the years exemplifying the Jumbo's size and presence. This was especially so during the 1990s, when the air-disaster genre made another flight into Hollywood.

Other Notable Titles: *The Survivor* (1981), mock-up; *Snakes on a Plane* (2006), CGI model; *Flight of the Living Dead* (2007), CGI model.

MODEL 757

First flight: February 19, 1982. Twin-engined narrow-body airliner saw a total of 1,049 built be-

Model 737		SN or Reg. at Time of		
Type	msn	Filming	Title	Remarks / Film Markings
Model 737-293	19308/40	N463GB	This Is a Hijack (1973)	Flying
Model 737-297Adv.	21739/561	N70723	Miracle Landing (TVM, 1990)	Flying

Model 747		SN or Reg. at Time of		
Type	msn	Filming	Title	Remarks / Film Markings
Model 747-121	19657/37	N473EV	Die Hard 2: Die Harder (1990)	Used in taxiing scenes only
Model 747-121	19658/47	F-GIMJ	Executive Decision (1996)	Marked as "Oceanic Airlines"; static wreck
Model 747-123	20106/79	N9667	Airport '77 (1977)	Marked as N13S / "Stevens Corporation"
Model 747-123	20390/136	N9675	Airport 1975 (1974)	Marked as "Columbia Airlines"
Model 747-146	19727/54	N703CK	Air Force One (1997)	Marked as "United States of America" / 28000
Model 747-146	20528/191	N704CK	Drop Zone (1994)	Marked as "PAC Atlantic Pacific"
Model 747-100SR	22293/477	N219BA	War of the Worlds (2005)	Used for wreckage scene on studio backlot
Model 747-236B	21831/440	G-BDXJ	Casino Royale (2006)	Non-flying, marked as N88892
Model 747-238B	20534/195	N614FF	Turbulence (1997)	Marked as N644FF
Model 747-269B	21541/332	N707CK	Executive Decision (1996)	Marked as "Oceanic Airlines"

Model 757		SN or Reg.		
Type	msn	at Time of Filming	Title	Remarks / Film Markings
Model 757-225	22200/20	G-MCEA	United 93 (2006)	Scrapped fuselage used for interior filming

fore deliveries stopped in 2004, airline service began in 1983.

Boeing-Stearman *see* Stearman

Boeing-Vertol *see* **Vertol**

Bombardier

Bombardier Aerospace is a division of the large Canadian conglomerate Bombardier Inc. It was formed in 1986 with the acquisition of Canadair Ltd., at which time it also acquired all their aircraft, such as the soon to be successful CRJ commuter jet series. Acquired Learjet in 1990, De-Havilland-Canada (DHC) in 1992 and continued production with their Dash-8 series.

Brantly

American manufacturer founded in 1945 as the Brantly Helicopter Corp. by Newby Brantly. Produced the unique looking B-2 helicopter from 1953. Acquired by Learjet in 1966; renamed Brantly-Hynes Helicopter, Inc., in 1975. Survived well for a small company that produced only one helicopter type.

Other Notable Titles: *Goldfinger* (1964); *Night of the Living Dead* (1968).

Brewster

Founded in 1924 as Brewster & Co., Aircraft Division on Long Island; became Brewster Aeronautical Corp. in 1932. Notable for its early war efforts and in building the F2A Buffalo fighter. U.S. Navy took over management of the plant in 1942 after allegations of war profiteering. License-built the Corsair as the F3A-1 until 1944. Shut down by 1946.

Notable Titles: *Dive Bomber* (1941), F2A Buffalo; *Flight for Freedom* (1943), F2A Buffalo stock footage.

Bristol

British manufacturer founded in 1910 as the British & Colonial Aeroplane Co. Ltd. by Sir George Whitehead. Became the Bristol Aeroplane Co. in 1920 and produced the Bulldog biplane fighter for the RAF in the 1930s. During World War II produced the Beaufighter multi-role fighter-bomber. After the war went on to make the successful Bristol Freighter.

Merged with other British aero manufacturers in 1960 to form the British Aircraft Corp. (BAC).

Bombardier		SN or Reg.		
Type	msn	at Time of Filming	Title	Remarks / Film Markings
Challenger 604	5505	G-OCSC	*Quantum of Solace* (2008)	Greene's jet to Austria

Brantly		SN or Reg. at Time of		
Type	msn	Filming	Title	Remarks / Film Markings
Model B-2B	445	G-ASXE	*You Only Live Twice* (1967)	Mr. Osato's helicopter as OS7241, landing inside volcano
Model B-2B	449	G-ATFH	*You Only Live Twice* (1967)	Mr. Osato's helicopter as OS7241, landing on office building rooftop

Bristol		SN or Reg. at Time of		
Type	msn	Filming	Title	Remarks / Film Markings
Bulldog IIA	7446	G-ABBB	*Reach for the Sky* (1956)	Ex-RAF K2227, static only, as K2496
F.2B Fighter	7575	G-AEPH	*Reach for the Sky* (1956)	Ex-RAF D8096, background
Beaufighter TT.Mk. 10	unknown	(RAF) RD788	*Ice Cold in Alex* (1958)	Brief flyby
Britannia Series 302	12918	XA-MEC	*Jet Over the Atlantic* (1959)	Flying; written off in 1965

Other Notable Titles: *Hell's Angels* (1930), F.2 Fighter; *The Lion Has Wings* (1939), Bulldog; *The Way to the Stars* (1945), Blenheim Mk. II.

TYPE 170 FREIGHTER

First flight: December 2, 1945. Twin-engined civil freight / passenger aircraft; 214 were built up to 1958. Fondly remembered aircraft amongst skystruck fans, the Freighter is best known on the big screen from 1957's *The Man in the Sky*.

British Aerospace (BAe)

Major British aerospace manufacturer was formed in 1977 through the merger of British Aircraft Corp. (BAC), Hawker-Siddeley Aviation, and Scottish Aviation. Also a partner in Airbus. Rebranded many existing aircraft with the "BAe" designation such as the HS.748 into the BAe.748, etc. Renamed BAE Systems in 1999.

Brown

American manufacturer founded by Lawrence Brown in 1926. Known for building several racing plane types.

Bucker

German manufacturer founded as Bucker Flugzeugbau GmbH in 1932 by Carl Bucker.

Built the pre–World War II German biplane trainers, the Bu. 131 and Bu. 133, in great numbers, which were also exported and license-built. Remains a favorite biplane aircraft to this day among sportsman pilots.

Canadair

Formed in 1944 from the original Canadian Vickers Ltd. (1911). Acquired by the Electric Boat

Type 170 Freighter		SN or Reg. at Time of Filming		
Type	msn	Filming	Title	Remarks / Film Markings
Wayfarer Mk. IIA	12781	G-AIFV	*The Man in the Sky* (1957)	Convt. to Mk. 21 Freighter
Freighter Mk. 21	12773	G-AIFM	*The Man in the Sky* (1957)	Background only
Freighter Mk. 31	M13134	ZK-EPF	*The Rescue* (1988)	Ex-RNZAF (s/n NZ5910), North Korean markings

British Aerospace		SN or Reg. at Time of Filming		
Type	msn	Filming	Title	Remarks / Film Markings
BAC.111-400	117	N97GA	*Transformers: Dark of the Moon* (2011)	Likely but not confirmed
BAe.125-600FA	256070	N322CC	*Raise the Titanic* (1980)	—
BAe.125-700A	NA0288	N198GT	*A Man Apart* (2003)	—
BAe.125-700B	257175	RA-02804	*The Da Vinci Code* (2006)	—
BAe.125-800A	258003	N803RK	*Quantum of Solace* (2008)	—
(HS.748) BAe.748	unknown	XW-PNA	*Air America* (1990)	Royal Air Lao

Brown		SN or Reg. at Time of Filming		
Type	msn	Filming	Title	Remarks / Film Markings
Model B-2	unknown	NX255Y	*Tail Spin* (1939)	Flying; destroyed in crash in 1939
Model B-2 (replica)	T-2	N255Y	*The Rocketeer* (1991)	Flying replica built by Bill Turner

Bucker		SN or Reg. at Time of Filming		
Type	msn	Filming	Title	Remarks / Film Markings
Bu. 133 Jungmeister	1015	N87P	*The Great Waldo Pepper* (1975)	Marked as *Ernst Kessler*
Bu. 133C Jungmeister	38	G-AYSJ	*Aces High* (1976)	Marked as: E622
Jungmann 1.131-E-2000	E3B 439	C-FLAE	*Amelia* (2009)	Flying

Co. in 1946, which became General Dynamics in 1954. License-built several notable U.S. types including the PBY Catalina, DC-4, F-86, T-33, F-104 plus original types like the CL-215 Scooper. Acquired by Bombardier Inc. in 1986.

Other Notable Titles: *Sky Riders* (1976).

Capelis

Formed as the Capelis Safety Airplane Corp. of California solely to design and build their Model XC-12 airliner. This unique prototype first flew in 1933 as a 12-seat passenger design with two 525 hp Wright Cyclones. Various design

faults and a lack of commercial interest meant the aircraft was soon grounded, and it was eventually sold to RKO Pictures in Hollywood as a non-flying movie prop. The full-scale aircraft, and a scale model used to create flying shots, made appearances on film into the 1950s.

CASA

CASA stands for Construcciones Aeronauticas SA, an aircraft manufacturer based in Spain and formed in 1923. After World War II they acquired the manufacturing rights to many German aircraft types. The 2.111 was based on the Heinkel He.

Canadair		SN or Reg. at Time of		
Type	msn	Filming	Title	Remarks / Film Markings
CL-44-D-4	21	G-ATZH	*O Lucky Man!* (1973)	Marked as XV196
CL-215-1A10	1076	TC-TKZ	*The Expendables 2* (2012)	Marked as XP 2112

Capelis		SN or Reg. at Time of		
Type	msn	Filming	Title	Remarks / Film Markings
Model XC-12	1	NX12762	*Five Came Back* (1939)	Non-flying, named *Silver Queen*
		NX12762	*Flying Tigers* (1942)	Non-flying, some taxiing scenes
		NX12762	*Invisible Agent* (1942)	Non-flying
		NX12762	*Night Plane from Chungking* (1943)	Non-flying
		NX12762	*Action in Arabia* (1944)	Non-flying
		NX12762	*Dick Tracey's Dilemma* (1947)	Non-flying, dismantled
		NX12762	*On the Isle of Samoa* (1950)	Non-flying

The one and only Capelis Model XC-12 was owned by RKO Pictures and was made famous through its appearance in *Five Came Back* **(1939) and** *Flying Tigers* **(1942). Photograph: James H. Farmer Collection.**

CASA		SN or Reg. at Time of		
Type	msn	Filming	Title	Remarks / Film Markings
CASA 2.111B	025	B.2I-77	Battle of Britain (1969)	To UK as G-AWHA for aerial filming
CASA 2.111B	150	B.2I-20	Battle of Britain (1969)	Studio filming
CASA 2.111B	167	B.2I-37	Battle of Britain (1969)	To UK as G-AWHB for aerial filming
		—	Piece of Cake (TVMS, 1988)	Studio filming
CASA 352L	155	G-BFHG	The Dirty Dozen: Next Mission (TVM, 1985)	Ex-Spain T.2B-262
		G-BFHG	Piece of Cake (TVMS, 1988)	Flying
CASA C.127	2094	EC-BSX	Cuba (1979)	Flying
CASA C-212-100 Aviocar	TC-9-92	F-GOGN	The World Is Not Enough (1999)	Flying

111, around 30 of which appeared in *Battle of Britain* (1969) and three in *Patton* (1970). The 352L was based on the Junkers Ju. 52, and several have doubled as such in a handful of films.

Acquired Hispano Aviacion in 1972.

Caudron

French manufacturer formed in 1909 by brothers Gaston and Rene Caudron. Produced many biplane types from World War I through to World War II. Acquired by French SNCAN in 1945.

Cessna

Iconic American light aircraft manufacturer was formed by Clyde Cessna in 1927 as Cessna-Roos Aircraft Co.; renamed Cessna Aircraft Co., Inc., in 1928. Built the Cessna Bobcat during World War II; postwar became a world leader in recreational and light aircraft design. Acquired by General Dynamics in 1985 with production ceasing in 1986; acquired by Textron Inc. in 1992 with production resuming in 1996, still in Wichita, Kansas, where the company was originally founded. Many, many hundreds of Cessna aircraft have been featured on screen; the titles below outline just a few of the more prominent.

Other Notable Titles: *Winged Victory* (1944), AT-8 / AT-17 Bobcat; *PT 109* (1963), Cessna Bobcats as Japanese bombers; *Spencer's Pilots* (TVS, 1976).

L-19 (O-1) Bird Dog

First flight: December 14, 1949. Single-engined spotter plane for the U.S. Army / USAF based on the Model 305. Output of 3,296 delivered as the L-19, redesignated as the O-1 in 1962. Several good views with Vietnam-era colors in *Air America* (1990).

T-37 Tweet

First flight: October 12, 1954. Twin-engined jet trainer for USAF served until 2009.

Caudron		SN or Reg. at Time of		
Type	msn	Filming	Title	Remarks / Film Markings
C.277 Luciole	7546/135	G-ATIP	The Blue Max (1966)	Spotter-plane marked as A8590
		EI-ARF	Darling Lili (1970)	Flying
		EI-ARF	Von Richthofen and Brown (1971)	Flying

Cessna		SN or Reg. at Time of		
Type	msn	Filming	Title	Remarks / Film Markings
UC-78B Bobcat	6117	N67832	Sky King (TVS, 1951–1959)	Ex-43-32179, flying
Model T-50 Bobcat	6695	N61115	The Trap (1959)	—

Cessna		(SN or Reg. at Time of		
(Type)	(msn)	Filming)	(Title)	(Remarks / Film Markings)
Model C-37 Airmaster	363	NC18037	The Tarnished Angels (1957)	—
Model 140	12361	N77029	Live and Let Die (1973)	Plus two others for stunt work
Model 150M Aerobat	A150-0637	N9828J	Iron Eagle (1986)	—
Model 152 Aerobat	152-83043	N46405	Con Air (1997)	—
Model 152 Aerobat	FA152-0345	G-BFRV	Some Mothers Do 'Ave 'Em (TVS, 1973–1978)	Featured in 1978 Christmas Special
Model 172	29697	N6497B	Drop Zone (1994)	—
Model 172	36873	N3973F	Terminator 3: Rise of the Machines (2003)	Well-known film flub: the ground shots had the aircraft marked with false reg. N3035C
Model 172C	172-49361	N1661Y	Flight (2012)	ground scenes only, as "N1661YG"
Model 172G	172-53829	N3660L	The Fly Boys (2008)	—
Model 172M	172-65417	ZK-DXO	Solo (1978)	—
Model 172N	172-68532	VH-IMW	The Survivor (1981)	—
Model 172P	172-75046	N54743	Licence to Kill (1989)	Stolen by Sanchez at airfield
		N54743	Drop Zone (1994)	—
Model 172P	172-76119	N96816	GoldenEye (1995)	CIA plane lent to Bond
Model 175	55151	N9351B	Drop Zone (1994)	—
Model 180D	180-50971	N6471X	Drop Zone (1994)	—
Model 182A	34007	N6007B	Drop Zone (1994)	—
Model 182A	34420	N3720D	Drop Zone (1994)	—
Model 182A	34937	N4837D	Terminal Velocity (1994)	—
Model 182Q	182-67013	N97200	Drop Zone (1994)	—
Model A185F	185-04318	N6964N	Licence to Kill (1989)	Drug-runners' floatplane
Model A185F	185-02279	N3357S	For Your Eyes Only (1981)	Marked as SX-JKR / Kerkyra Charter
Model U206G	U206-03525	ZK-EFI	Race for the Yankee Zephyr (1981)	Floatplane
Model 310B	35548	N5348A	Sky King (TVS, 1951–1959)	Flying
Model 310D	39117	N6817T	Sky King (TVS, 1951–1959)	Used for series publicity work only
Model 310	unknown	ZS-ATR	The Wilby Conspiracy (1975)	Flying
Model 310	unknown	3D-ABN	The Wild Geese (1978)	Doubles as a military attack aircraft
Model 340A	340A-0724	N340SB	2012 (2009)	Flying

L-19		SN or Reg. at Time of		
Type	msn	Filming	Title	Remarks / Film Markings
L-19A Bird Dog	unknown	51-4643	One Minute to Zero (1952)	—
L-19A Bird Dog	unknown	53-7994	Battle Hymn (1957)	—
O-1A Bird Dog	unknown	51-7353	Air America (1990)	—
O-1A Bird Dog	unknown	53-7978	Air America (1990)	—
O-1A Bird Dog	unknown	56-2563	Air America (1990)	—

T-37 Tweet		SN or Reg. at Time of		
Type	msn	Filming	Title	Remarks / Film Markings
T-37B Tweet	41026	67-14762	Airport 1975 (1974)	Was subsequently named the "Hollywood Tweet" among the USAF pilots who flew it

Of the 1,759 built, 577 were the armed attack version known as the A-37 Dragonfly.

Chance Vought   *see*   Vought

Chester

Founded in Chicago by Art Chester, the company was mainly concerned with air-racing.

Consolidated / Convair

Founded as The Consolidated Aircraft Corp. in 1923 by Reuben Fleet in Buffalo, New York.

Acquired Thomas-Morse Aircraft Co. in 1929; moved to San Diego in 1935. Merged with Vultee Aircraft, Inc., in 1941 to form the Consolidated-Vultee Aircraft Corp. by 1943 and was a major U.S. aircraft manufacturer during the war years. Renamed the Convair Aircraft Corp. soon after World War II. Acquired by the Electric Boat Co. in 1953 to form the Convair Division of General Dynamics Corp. by 1954. Convair branding was phased out by 1961. Further details see: GENERAL DYNAMICS.

Notable Titles: *Toward the Unknown* (1956), C-131B Samaritan; *Fail-Safe* (1964), B-58 Hustler; *Amazing Stories* (TVS, 1985–1987), Convair 880 N814AJ.

PBY Catalina

First flight: March 21, 1935. Legendary twin-engined amphibious flying boat was built in greater numbers than any other flying boat ever built. Served during World War II and became a

PBY Catalina Type	msn	SN or Reg. at Time of Filming	Title	Remarks / Film Markings
PBY-5A Catalina	1581	N9505C	*Always* (1989)	Ex-BuNo. 34027, marked as Tanker 53
PBY-5A Catalina	1643	N68623	*Steelyard Blues* (1973)	Ex-BuNo. 48281 / CF-IHJ, identification likely but not confirmed. Blown up during filming?
PBY-5A Catalina	1733	N5589V	*Tora! Tora! Tora!* (1970)	Ex-BuNo. 48371, destroyed during filming
PBY-5A Catalina	1759	N5593V	*SOS Pacific* (1959)	Ex-BuNo. 48397, flying. Thomas Kendall Catalina
PBY-5A Catalina	1764	N5592V	*Tora! Tora! Tora!* (1970)	Ex-BuNo. 48402, destroyed during filming
PBY-5A Catalina	1768	N5590V	*The Devil at 4 O'Clock* (1961)	Ex-BuNo. 48406, flying. Thomas Kendall Catalina
		N5590V	*Adventures in Paradise* (TVS, 1959–1962)	Likely used but not confirmed. Marked as *Tiare Tahiti*
PBY-5A Catalina	1817	FAC-619	*All the Way, Boys* (1973)	Ex-BuNo. 46453, Colombian Air Force
PBY-5A Catalina	1939	N5586V	*Tora! Tora! Tora!* (1970)	Ex-BuNo. 46575, destroyed during filming
PBY-5A Catalina	1955/13	N5587V	*Tora! Tora! Tora!* (1970)	Ex-BuNo. 46591, destroyed during filming
PBY-5A Catalina	1993/51	N5595V	*Tora! Tora! Tora!* (1970)	Ex-BuNo. 46629, destroyed during filming
PBY-6A Catalina	2069/127	N16KL	*Midway* (1976)	Ex-BuNo. 63998, flying
PBY-6A Catalina	2112/170	N6453C	*Spencer's Pilots* (TVS, 1976)	Ex-BuNo. 64041, "guest appearance" in first episode
PBY-6A Catalina	2145/203	N2886D	*Steelyard Blues* (1973)	Ex-BuNo. 64074, identification likely but not confirmed. Provided by Sis-Q Flying Service, Inc., who were apparently involved in filming
PBY-6A Catalina	2163/221	N6681C	*Kiss Them for Me* (1957)	Ex-BuNo. 64092
(Boeing) Canso	A22022	N6108	*Tora! Tora! Tora!* (1970)	Ex-RCAF 9793, flying marked as 24-P-4 / -9
(NAF) PBN-1 Nomad	unknown	BuNo. 02838	*High Barbaree* (1947)	Fuselage retained by MGM studios after filming

highly sought after civilian aircraft in post war years. Some very memorable moments in film history from *Wings of the Navy* (1939) through to *Always* (1989), the "Cat" has had a fair run at the box office.

Other Notable Titles: *Wings of the Navy* (1939); *Flight Command* (1940); *Flying Leathernecks* (1951), PBY-6A; *South Pacific* (1958); *Sink the Bismarck!* (1960); *The Guns of Navarone* (1961), Greek Navy Catalina.

B-24 Liberator / PB4Y Privateer

First flight: December 29, 1939. Four-engined heavy bomber saw action throughout World War II in many guises from bomber to cargo transport (C-87), tanker (C-109) and naval reconn. (PB4Y Privateer). A whopping 19,258 were built—more than any other U.S. aircraft built during the war. A relatively limited cinematic career reflects the real-life fact that the B-17 and B-29 were more popular in the eyes of the public.

Other Notable Titles: *Winged Victory* (1944); *Slattery's Hurricane* (1949), PB4Y-2M; *The Lady Takes a Flyer* (1958), PB4Y-2; *Unbroken* (2014), CGI models.

B-36 Peacemaker

First flight: August 8, 1946. Massive strategic bomber was America's "big stick" in the early days of the Cold War and formation of SAC. In all, 385 were built, but it was soon phased out by the much more refined B-52 Stratofortress. Excellent views and detail seen in the 1955 film *Strategic Air Command* for which the B-36 was a major advertisement!

F-102 Delta Dagger / F-106 Delta Dart

First flight: October 24, 1953. Single-engined, delta-wing jet fighter interceptor. The F-102 has a pointed tail whereas the developed F-106 has a flattened tail apex and a lengthened fuselage. Prominently used in the opening and closing titles of the 1950s TV show *Steve Canyon*.

Culver

Founded as the Culver Aircraft Co., Ohio in 1938. Naming and design rights went through many owners and companies well into the 1990s. Produced mainly air-racing and light aircraft types.

B-24 Liberator / PB4Y Privateer

Type	msn	SN or Reg. at Time of Filming	Title	Remarks / Film Markings
Liberator Mk. I	18	N24927	*Beautiful Dreamer* (2006)	Ex-RAF AM927, flying

B-36 Peacemaker

Type	msn	SN or Reg. at Time of Filming	Title	Remarks / Film Markings
B-36B Peacemaker	62	44-92065	*Jet Pilot* (1957)	—
B-36H Peacemaker	222	51-5702	*Strategic Air Command* (1955)	—
B-36H Peacemaker	234	51-5708	*Strategic Air Command* (1955)	—
B-36H Peacemaker	260	51-5721	*Strategic Air Command* (1955)	—
B-36H Peacemaker	286	51-5734	*Strategic Air Command* (1955)	—
B-36J Peacemaker	357	52-2216	*Strategic Air Command* (1955)	—

F-102 Delta …

Type	msn	SN or Reg. at Time of Filming	Title	Remarks / Film Markings
F-102A Delta Dagger	unknown	56-1226	*Beyond the Time Barrier* (1960)	—
F-102A Delta Dagger	unknown	56-1363	*Steve Canyon* (TVS, 1958–1959)	Seen in opening titles
F-106A Delta Dart	unknown	57-0236	*Beyond the Time Barrier* (1960)	—

Culver

Type	msn	SN or Reg. at Time of Filming	Title	Remarks / Film Markings
Dart G	G-11	NC20993	*The Tarnished Angels* (1957)	—
Dart GK	GK-48	NC20944	*The Tarnished Angels* (1957)	—

Curtiss / Curtiss-Wright

Founded by Glenn Curtiss in 1904 as the Curtiss Motor Co. After several changes finally became the Curtiss Aeroplane Co. in 1910. Merged with Wright Aeronautical Corp. in 1929 to become the Curtiss-Wright Aeroplane Co., specializing in both aircraft and aero engine manufacturing. Entered World War II as one of America's manufacturing giants with the SB2C Helldiver, P-40 series, C-46 Commando plus their engine and propeller divisions. Failed, however, to evolve with postwar aviation developments, and all aircraft assets were closed up by 1949. Engine division continued on under the Wright name into the 1950s.

Other Notable Titles: *King Kong* (1933), F8C-5 / O2C-1 Helldiver; *Flight Command* (1940), SBC-4 Helldiver; *Dive Bomber* (1941), SBC-4 Helldiver.

JN-4 Jenny

First flight: 1915. Single-engined biplane trainer for the U.S. Army is likely America's best-known World War I aircraft. Postwar it made up the backbone of civil aviation in the U.S. during the 1920s.

The "Jenny," as it was known, was used in numerous early Hollywood films, especially during the silent era, the abundant numbers meaning easy access to airframes for stunts and crashes. Some were restored in later years, a few of which still fly today.

Notable Titles: *The Great Air Robbery* (1919); *The Grim Game* (1919); *The Skywayman* (1920); *Now We're in the Air* (1927); *Hell's Angels* (1930); *The Dawn Patrol* (1930 / 1938); *Ace of Aces* (1933); *Men With Wings* (1938); *Blaze of Noon* (1947); *The Great Waldo Pepper* (1975), two Tallmantz Jennys; *Amelia Earhart* (TVM, 1976); *The Amazing Howard Hughes* (TVM, 1977); *The Red Baron* (2008), scaled replica, reg. OK-FUL-28.

C-46 Commando

First flight: March 26, 1940. Twin-engined cargo / troop transport; 3,181 were built by 1945, with the definitive variants being the C-46A and C-46D. Famous aircraft for its involvement flying the "hump" in the China-Burma-India Theater. Popular civil transport in the postwar years, especially in South America.

Other Notable Titles: *God is my Co-pilot* (1945), stock footage; *Dragonfly Squadron* (1954); *Roswell*

Curtiss / Curtiss-Wright		SN or Reg. at Time of		
Type	msn	Filming	Title	Remarks / Film Markings
Model D Pusher (replica)	101	N8Y	*West Point of the Air* (1935)	Replica built for the film by Billy Parker, owned for many years by Paul Mantz
		N8Y	*Men With Wings* (1938)	—
		N8Y	*Captain Eddie* (1945)	Stock footage from *Men With Wings*
		N8Y	*Blaze of Noon* (1947)	Likely used but not confirmed
AT-23A Condor	42	NC12390	*Bright Eyes* (1934)	—
F8C-4 Helldiver	unknown	BuNo. A-8425	*Hell Divers* (1931)	Flying, plus up to 16 others
F8C-4 Helldiver	unknown	BuNo. A-8438	*Hell Divers* (1931)	Flying, plus up to 16 others; was also camera-plane for takeoffs and landings
RC-1 Kingbird	unknown	BuNo. A-8846	*Devil Dogs of the Air* (1935)	—

JN-4 Jenny		SN or Reg. at		
Type	msn	Time of Filming	Title	Remarks / Film Markings
JN-4 Jenny	396	N5391	*The Spirit of St. Louis* (1957)	Likely used but not unconfirmed
JN-4C Canuck	1898	N10389	*The Spirit of St. Louis* (1957)	Likely used but not unconfirmed
JN-4D Jenny	400	N2821D	*The Spirit of St. Louis* (1957)	Likely used but not unconfirmed
JN-4D Jenny	47502	N6899	*The Spirit of St. Louis* (1957)	Likely used but not unconfirmed

(TVM, 1994); *Seven Years in Tibet* (1997); *Beautiful Dreamer* (2006), N53594.

P-40 WARHAWK

First flight (XP-40): October 14, 1938. Single-engined fighter bore the brunt of aerial combat in the early days of America's entry into World War II. Named Warhawk in USAAF service and Tomahawk and Kittyhawk in RAF service, it saw extensive use in the North African and Southwest Pacific Theatres. The P-40 was a follow-on from the prewar P-36 Hawk series, and although nearly 14,000 were built, it was largely obsolete by war's end. Perhaps the best-known P-40 film didn't actually feature any real P-40 fighters at all!—*Flying Tigers* (1942) made use of studio mock-ups with a few real Warhawks filmed on test flights. When the Warbird scene came along in the early 1970s, a reasonable number of restorations meant a good number of flyable aircraft have since found their way into motion pictures.

Other Notable Titles: *Flying Tigers* (1942), P-

P-40 Warhawk		SN or Reg. at Time of		
Type	*msn*	*Filming*	*Title*	*Remarks / Film Markings*
Kittyhawk Mk. I	15404	N94466	*Death Race* (TVM, 1973)	Ex-RAF AK933
		N94466	*Pearl Harbor* (2001)	—
Kittyhawk Mk. I	15376	N40PE	*1941* (1979)	Ex-RAF AK905, studio cockpit filming
Kittyhawk Mk. I	18723	N5672N	*Tora! Tora! Tora!* (1970)	Ex-RAF AK979, marked as: 20-15P
		N151U	*1941* (1979)	Gas station scene
Kittyhawk Mk. I	18796	N1207V	*Tobruk* (1967)	Ex-RAF AL152, crudely marked as NI-V with British roundel
		N1207V	*Tora! Tora! Tora!* (1970)	Marked as 27-15P
Kittyhawk Mk. I	18815	N62435	*1941* (1979)	Ex-RAF AL171, Grand Canyon scene
P-40M Warhawk	27490	G-KITT	*Red Tails* (2012)	Ex-43-5802, marked as 210855
P-40N Warhawk	28954	N85104	*Pearl Harbor* (2001)	Ex-42-105192
		N85104	*Valkyrie* (2008)	Brief flyby
P-40N Warhawk	29677	F-AZKU	*Red Tails* (2012)	Ex-42-105915
P-40N Warhawk	30158	N1195N	*Pearl Harbor* (2001)	Ex-42-106396
P-40N Warhawk	32824	N999CD	*Pearl Harbor* (2001)	Ex-44-7084
TP-40N Warhawk	33915	N923	*Death Race* (TVM, 1973)	Ex-44-47923, TP-40N conversion
		N923	*Baa Baa Black Sheep* (TVS, 1976–1978)	—
		N923	*Tales of the Gold Monkey* (TVS, 1982–1983)	As a Flying Tigers P-40

TP-40N N923 is a veteran of several films and TV series—the rear seat often covered over to make the plane appear to be a single-seater. This Warhawk stayed with Tallmantz until the company closed up shop in the mid–1980s. Photograph: Peter Nicholson.

This Curtiss Kittyhawk Mk. I (s/n AK933) was being used as a spares source on *Tora! Tora! Tora!* (1970) until reclaimed by its owner John Paul of California, who restored it to airworthy condition in 1970 as N94466. It later made brief appearances in the 2001 film *Pearl Harbor.* Photograph: James H. Farmer Collection. (That's Farmer in the back seat!)

40C mock-ups; *The Sky's the Limit* (1943); *China's Little Devils* (1945), P-40 mock-ups; *Winged Victory* (1944); *God Is My Co-Pilot* (1945), P-40E / F; *Jungle Patrol* (1948); *Hellfighters* (1968); *Sky Captain and the World of Tomorrow* (2004), P-40 mock-ups.

Dassault

French aircraft manufacturer founded in 1930 as Societe des Avions Marcel Bloch.

Renamed as Avions Marcel Dassault in 1947, then Avions Marcel Dassault-Breguet in 1971 and Dassault Aviation in 1990. Well known for its Mirage jet fighter series and Falcon range of private jets.

Davis

American manufacturer founded in 1929 as the Davis Aircraft Corp. by Walter Davis.

Built a series of high-wing monoplanes, some for air racing.

DeHavilland / Airco

Iconic British manufacturer is responsible for some of the finest aircraft ever to be built in the UK. Geoffrey DeHavilland joined the Aircraft Manufacturing Co. Ltd. (Airco) in 1914 designing aircraft during World War I. After the war, Airco closed and the DeHavilland Aircraft Co. Ltd. was founded in its place in 1920. The company then began developing aircraft in a constant winning formula with such classic designs as the Tiger Moth biplane, Mosquito fighter-bomber, Dove commuter, Comet jet airliner and Vampire jet fighter.

DeHavilland was merged into Hawker-Siddeley Aviation in 1963; one design at the time, the DH.125 private jet, became the HS.125, then BAe.125 in 1977.

Dassault		SN or Reg. at Time of		
Type	msn	Filming	Title	Remarks / Film Markings
Mystere-Falcon 20GF	145	F-BPJB	*The Concorde ... Airport '79* (1979)	Marked as "H Industries"

Davis		SN or Reg. at		
Type	msn	Time of Filming	Title	Remarks / Film Markings
Model D-1-K	510	NC151Y	*The Tarnished Angels* (1957)	—

AIRCO DH.4

First flight: August 1916. Single-engined biplane bomber of World War I, also built by Boeing in the U.S. Like the Curtiss "Jenny," the DH.4 was a popular postwar biplane for the U.S. Air Mail service, and many were also used in Hollywood films of the time.

Other Notable Titles: *The Big Parade* (1925); *The Air Mail* (1925); *Wings* (1927); *Hell's Angels* (1930); *Men With Wings* (1938); *Flight Angels* (1940).

DH.60 MOTH

First flight: February 22, 1925. Single-engined, two-seater biplane was also developed as the Cirrus Moth and Gipsy Moth.

DH.82 / DH.82A TIGER MOTH

First flight: October 26, 1931. Single-engined, two-seater biplane became a design classic and the "iconic representation" of the biplane era. Thousands built as basic trainers for pilots during World War II. In postwar years, many were ob-

DeHaviland / Airco Type	msn	SN or Reg. at Time of Filming	Title	Remarks / Film Markings
Airco DH.2 (replica)	WA4	G-BFVH	*Gunbus* (1986)	Doubles as a Vickers F.B.5 Gunbus

Airco DH.4 Type	msn	SN or Reg. at Time of Filming	Title	Remarks / Film Markings
DH.4M-1	ET-4	N3258	*Task Force* (1949)	Flying
			The Court-Martial of Billy Mitchell (1955)	Flying
			The Spirit of St. Louis (1957)	Marked as "110 / U.S. Air Mail"

DH.60 Moth Type	msn	SN or Reg. at Time of Filming	Title	Remarks / Film Markings
DH.60GM Gipsy Moth	86	G-AAMY	*Out of Africa* (1985)	Marked as G-AAMT
DH.60GM Gipsy Moth	117	NC916M	*The Tarnished Angels* (1957)	—
DH.60M Moth	757	CF-AAJ	*Amelia* (2009)	Briefly seen
DH.60M Moth	unknown	VP-AAM	*Safari* (1940)	—

DH.82 / DH.82A Tiger Moth Type	msn	SN or Reg. at Time of Filming	Title	Remarks / Film Markings
Tiger Moth	3101	G-ABTB	*Q Planes* (1939)	Flying
Tiger Moth	3544	G-AESA	*Q Planes* (1939)	Flying
Tiger Moth	3624	G-AEZC	*Q Planes* (1939)	Flying
Tiger Moth	3861	G-AHRM	*The Sound Barrier* (1952)	Flying
Tiger Moth	82186	VH-BIN	*Tail of a Tiger* (1984)	Ex-RAAF A17-684
Tiger Moth	82960	N523R	*Silver Streak* (1976)	Hired from actor and pilot Cliff Robertson
Tiger Moth	83028	G-ANNF	*Lawrence of Arabia* (1962)	Doubles as German biplane
Tiger Moth	83604	G-ANFM	*Thunderbird 6* (1968)	Performed a bridge fly-under stunt
		G-ANFM	*The King's Speech* (2010)	Flying
Tiger Moth	83653	(RAF) T7187	*Appointment in London* (1953)	To civilian market in 1955 as G-AOBX
		G-AOBX	*Aces High* (1976)	Background only as a German biplane
Tiger Moth	83900	G-AJHU	*The English Patient* (1996)	Ex-RAF T7471, marked as G-AFFC
Tiger Moth	85154	G-ANLC	*Lawrence of Arabia* (1962)	Doubles as German biplane
Tiger Moth	85829	VH-BVB	*Tail of a Tiger* (1984)	Ex-RAF s/n DE969
Tiger Moth	DHA428	VH-ASC	*Tail of a Tiger* (1984)	Ex-RAAF A17-387, as "Red Baron" fighter
Tiger Moth	DHA802	VH-SSI	*Tail of a Tiger* (1984)	Ex-RAAF A17-637
Tiger Moth	DHA861	VH-DFJ	*Tail of a Tiger* (1984)	Ex-RAAF A17-714
Tiger Moth	DHA1014	VH-GVA	*Tail of a Tiger* (1984)	Ex-RAAF A17-579
Tiger Moth	DHNZ155	ZK-BCZ	*Solo* (1978)	Ex-RNZAF NZ1475

tained for aero clubs and by recreational flyers. They have became a pilot's collector's item with many proudly preserved around the world. Many feature films have been made over the years with this aircraft; one notable title is the rare Australian film, *Tail of a Tiger* (1984). In many cases, the Tiger Moth has been a popular substitute for other World War I–era biplane types (German or British) not available for filming—the giveaway, of course, is always the upper-wing fuel tank!

Other Notable Titles: *The Blue Max* (1966), many for background only; *Ace Eli and Rodger of the Skies* (1973), one airframe crashed; *The Great Waldo Pepper* (1976), two airframes crashed; *King Solomon's Mines* (1985).

DH.89 DRAGON RAPIDE

First flight: April 17, 1934. Twin-engined short-haul biplane airliner of the 1930s.

DH.98 MOSQUITO

First flight: November 25, 1940. Twin-engined multi-role combat aircraft for the RAF is built of wood, which earned it the nickname of "Wooden Wonder." The design called for taking two of the most powerful engines available and bolting them to the lightest airframe that could be built. Incredibly photogenic, the Mosquito was immortalized on the big screen with its appearance in the 1964 film *633 Squadron*. Footage from this film has been used in several subsequent film and TV productions.

Other Notable Titles: *A Matter of Life and Death* (1946); *The Purple Plain* (1955), possibly RAF s/n RG177, RG238; *The Man Who Never Was* (1956); *Fate is the Hunter* (1964); *A Man Called Intrepid* (TVMS, 1979).

DH.100 / DH.115 VAMPIRE

First flight: September 20, 1943. Single-engined, twin-boom jet fighter served the RAF from 1945

DH.89 Dragon Rapide		SN or Reg. at Time of		
Type	msn	Filming	Title	Remarks / Film Markings
DH.89 Dragon Rapide	6862	G-AHGD	*Piece of Cake* (TVMS, 1988)	Ex-RAF Z7258
DH.89A Dragon Rapide	6340	G-AENN	*Q Planes* (1939)	—

DH.98 Mosquito		SN or Reg. at Time of		
Type	msn	Filming	Title	Remarks / Film Markings
Mosquito T.Mk. III	unknown	G-ASKH	*Mosquito Squadron* (1969)	Ex-RAF RR299, flying
		G-ASKH	*Another Time, Another Place* (1983)	—
Mosquito T.Mk. III	unknown	TV959	*633 Squadron* (1964)	Ground scenes, exterior cockpit shots
Mosquito T.Mk. III	unknown	TW117	*633 Squadron* (1964)	Flying
Mosquito B.Mk. 35	unknown	G-ASKA	*633 Squadron* (1964)	Ex-RAF RS709, flying
		G-ASKA	*Mosquito Squadron* (1969)	Flying
Mosquito B.Mk. 35	unknown	G-ASKB	*633 Squadron* (1964)	Ex-RAF RS712, flying
		G-ASKB	*Mosquito Squadron* (1969)	Flying
Mosquito B.Mk. 35	unknown	G-ASKC	*633 Squadron* (1964)	Ex-RAF TA719, flying
		G-ASKC	*Mosquito Squadron* (1969)	Derelict airframe
Mosquito B.Mk. 35	unknown	G-AWJV	*Mosquito Squadron* (1969)	Ex-RAF TA634, flying
Mosquito B.Mk. 35	unknown	RS715	*633 Squadron* (1964)	Studio filming
Mosquito B.Mk. 35	unknown	RS718	*633 Squadron* (1964)	Ground scenes, destroyed during filming
Mosquito B.Mk. 35	unknown	TA639	*633 Squadron* (1964)	Flying
Mosquito B.Mk. 35	unknown	TA642	*633 Squadron* (1964)	Ground scenes, destroyed during filming
Mosquito B.Mk. 35	unknown	TA724	*633 Squadron* (1964)	Ground scenes, destroyed during filming
Mosquito B.Mk. 35	unknown	TJ118	*633 Squadron* (1964)	Studio filming
		TJ118	*Mosquito Squadron* (1969)	Studio filming
Mosquito B.Mk. 35	unknown	VR803	*The Dam Busters* (1955)	Flying, briefly seen

to 1955. Also built as the DH.115 two-seater trainer and refined into the DH.112 Venom. Some excellent views seen in the 1952 film *The Sound Barrier*.

DH.104 Dove / Devon

First flight: September 25, 1945. Twin-engined short-haul airliner known as the Dove in civilian service and the Devon in RAF service. Production lasted until 1967.

DH.106 Comet

First flight: July 27, 1949. Four-engined aircraft was the world's first commercial jet airliner, entering service in 1952. The early Comet 1 variant suffered from structural design faults, resulting in several crashes, but the Comet 4 of 1958 clocked up an excellent record, with service lasting into the 1980s.

DeHavilland-Canada

Formed in 1928 as DeHavilland Aircraft of Canada Ltd. by parent company DeHavilland of the UK to produce their products for the Canadian market. In the postwar years the company evolved into an almost stand-alone entity with its original aircraft designs, beginning with the

DH.100 / DH.115 Vampire		SN or Reg. at		
Type	msn	Time of Filming	Title	Remarks / Film Markings
Vampire NF.Mk. 10	13005	WP232	*The Sound Barrier* (1952)	—
Vampire T.Mk. 11	unknown	XE937	*High Flight* (1957)	—
Vampire T.Mk. 11	unknown	XH318	*High Flight* (1957)	—

DH.104 Dove / Devon		SN or Reg. at Time of Filming		
Type	msn		Title	Remarks / Film Markings
Dove 1B	4196	G-ARBH	*The Wrong Arm of the Law* (1963)	—
Devon C.Mk. 2	unknown	WB531	*Octopussy* (1983)	Background

DH.106 Comet		SN or Reg. at Time of Filming		
Type	msn		Title	Remarks / Film Markings
Comet 1	06002	G-ALZK	*The Sound Barrier* (1952)	—
Comet 1	06004	G-ALYR	*The Sound Barrier* (1952)	—

DeHavilland-Canada		SN or Reg. at Time of Filming		
Type	msn		Title	Remarks / Film Markings
DHC-1 Chipmunk T.Mk. 10	DHB/F/0370	N7DW	*The Great Waldo Pepper* (1975)	Ex-RAF WG427, monoplane prototype
DHC-2 Beaver	274	C-GHCT	*Mother Lode* (1982)	Ex-L-20A, 51-16803, crashed during filming with it all caught on camera, can be seen in the finished film
DHC-2 Beaver	441	N9313Z	*At Play in the Fields of the Lord* (1991)	Ex-L-20A, 52-6078, marked as *Shoo Shoo Baby*
DHC-2 Beaver	724	C-GAEE	*Never Cry Wolf* (1983)	Ex-L-20A, 53-7915, marked as "Little Air"
DHC-2 Beaver	799	N1799F	*Six Days Seven Nights* (1998)	Original reg. CF-ICL
DHC-2 Beaver	1408	N9251Z	*Six Days Seven Nights* (1998)	Ex-L-20A, 58-2075, flying marked as F-0318
DHC-5A Buffalo	7	5Y-SRD	*The Constant Gardener* (2005)	Kenyan reg., ex–CC-115 (CAF) 115453
DHC-6-300 Twin Otter	647	N300WH	*Casino Royale* (2006)	Floatplane

DHC-1 Chipmunk, followed by the DHC-2 Beaver, DHC-3 Otter, DHC-4 Caribou, DHC-5 Buffalo, DHC-6 Twin Otter, DHC-7 and DHC-8 airliners. Acquired by Boeing in 1986, then Bombardier Inc. in 1992, who continued with production on the DHC-8 series.

Other Notable Titles: *The Green Berets* (1968), U-6A Beaver, C-7A Caribou; *The Edge* (1997), DHC-2 falsely marked as N9748C.

Douglas / McDonnell Douglas

The legendary U.S. aircraft manufacturer was founded as the Douglas Airplane Co. in 1920 by Donald Douglas. Renamed as the Douglas Aircraft Co. in 1925 and acquired Northrop Aircraft Corp. in 1932, only to separate again by 1939. Built the design classic DC-1, DC-2 and DC-3 airliners from 1933. Followed by an incredible array of aircraft types during and after World War II, including the A-20, A-26, SBD Dauntless, C-124, C-118, DC-4, DC-6, DC-7, DC-8 and DC-9. Merged with McDonnell Aircraft Corp. in 1967, who were already building the F-4 Phantom II, to form the McDonnell Douglas Corp. Went on to built the DC-10 and MD-11. Acquired Hughes Helicopters in 1984 and inherited the Model 500 and AH-64

helicopters. Acquired by Boeing in 1997, who then inherited the McDonnell Douglas C-17, F-15, F/A-18 and AH-64 programs.

DC-2 Series

First flight: May 11, 1934. Twin-engined passenger airliner introduced after the earlier DC-1 of 1933. The DC-2 appeared in many civil air disaster thrillers in the latter half of the 1930s and several movies in the early 1940s.

Other Notable Titles: *Lost Horizon* (1937); *The Man Who Found Himself* (1937); *Stunt Pilot* (1939); *The Bride Came C.O.D.* (1941); *Flying Blind* (1941).

B-18 Bolo

First flight: April 1935. Twin-engined medium bomber designed using the wings and other components of the DC-2 airliner. A total of 370 were built for the USAAC, but all were regarded as outdated before World War II even started.

Notable Titles: *I Wanted Wings* (1941); *Bombardier* (1943).

DC-3 / C-47 Skytrain Series

First flight: December 17, 1935. A legend—pure and simple! Twin-engined passenger airliner

DC-2 Series		SN or Reg. at Time of		
Type	*msn*	*Filming*	*Title*	*Remarks / Film Markings*
DC-2-120	1307	NC14274	*Bright Eyes* (1934)	Loaned by American Airlines. Used for "The Good Ship Lollipop," sung by Shirley Temple in the film
DC-2-120	1316	NC14283	*Death Flies East* (1935)	Loaned by American Airlines
R2D-1	1404	NC39165	*Back From Eternity* (1956)	Ex-BuNo. 9993, flying scenes

DC-3 / C-47 ...		SN or Reg. at Time of		
Type	*msn*	*Filming*	*Title*	*Remarks / Film Markings*
DST	1496	NC16002	*Flight Angels* (1940)	American Airlines aircraft
		NC16002	*Fly Away Baby* (1937)	Later to USAAF as C-49E s/n 42-56103
DST	1499	NC16005	*Flight Angels* (1940)	American Airlines aircraft
DC-3	1919	NC17333	*Flight Angels* (1940)	American Airlines aircraft
DC-3	1920	NC17334	*The Killer Inside Me* (2010)	Flying
DC-3	2169	N26MA	*The A-Team* (TVS, 1983–1987)	"Guest appearance" in first season
		N26MA	*Congo* (1995)	—
		N26MA	*Pearl Harbor* (2001)	Marked as 90385 / 17265
		N26MA	*Flags of Our Fathers* (2006)	USAAF markings
		N26MA	*Indiana Jones and the Kingdom of the Crystal Skull* (2008)	Marked as NC33673 / Pan American

DC-3 / C-47 ... (Type)	(msn)	(SN or Reg. at Time of Filming)	(Title)	(Remarks / Film Markings)
scenes		N26MA	Quantum of Solace (2008)	Marked as CP265; stunt-flying
DC-3	2236	N20TW	Act of Valor (2012)	Ex-NC25648
DC-3	2247	N408D	The A-Team (TVS, 1983–1987)	Flying
DC-3	4089	N79MA	Pathfinders: In the Company of Strangers (2011)	Ex-NC28381, marked as 414089 / 8C
DC-3A	1983	NC18111	Test Pilot (1938)	United Airlines aircraft
DC-3A	2005	N18939	Strategic Air Command (1955)	—
DC-3A	4126	N129H	Drop Zone (1994)	—
DC-3A	4812	N1047G	The Island (1980)	Ex-Western NC33671. Has the distinction of being the last civilian-built DC-3 delivered prior to massive military orders. Crashed landed and written off for film
DC-3B	1924	NC17314	Island in the Sky (1953)	Ex-C-84, s/n 42-57511, plus four other DC-3 aircraft
DC-3B	1931	NC17316	Hollywood Hotel (1937)	Later to USAAF as C-49F s/n 42-56620
C-47 Skytrain	6007	VH-EWE	Pacific Banana (1981)	Ex-41-18646, R-rated Australian film. Aircraft marked as "Banana Airlines." Fuselage became a McDonald's restaurant!
C-47 Skytrain	6051	VH-DAS	Sky Pirates (1986)	Ex-41-38668, non-flying, used in crash scene
C-47 Skytrain	6154	ZS-UAS	The Wild Geese (1978)	Ex-41-38695, Viewmaster conversion
C-47 Skytrain	6179	NC86551	You Gotta Stay Happy (1948)	Ex-41-38720
C-47 Skytrain	4564	N57626	Traffic (2000)	Ex-41-18472
C-47 Skytrain	9043	G-AKNB	The Eagle Has Landed (1977)	Ex-42-32814
C-47A Skytrain	9470	N484F	The Protectors (TVS, 1971)	Ex-42-23608
C-47A Skytrain	9581	ZS-GPL	Amelia (2009)	Ex-42-23719, briefly seen
C-47A Skytrain	9592	VH-TAN	A Town Like Alice (1956)	Ex-42-23730 and (RAAF) A65-12
C-47A Skytrain	9700	N47FK	Band of Brothers (TVMS, 2001)	Ex-42-23838, marked as 292912
C-47A Skytrain	9715	NC79077	This Island Earth (1955)	Ex-42-23853, interior refurbished by aliens with a remote-controlled flight-deck! Later to Mexico as XA-PUR
C-47A Skytrain	9798	G-DAKK	Band of Brothers (TVMS, 2001)	Ex-42-23936, marked as 293095 / N
C-47A Skytrain	9914	G-BHUA	Airline (TVS, 1982)	Ex-42-24052
C-47A Skytrain	10035	N12BA	Quantum of Solace (2008)	Ex-42-24173, marked as CP265, ground scenes
C-47A Skytrain	11970	VH-PWM	Sky Pirates (1986)	Ex-42-92196, ex–RAAF A65-21, flying
C-47A Skytrain	12050	DO-10	A Bridge Too Far (1977)	Ex-42-92268, marked as 721182 / I-C1
C-47A Skytrain	12060	N751A	Pathfinders: In the Company of Strangers (2011)	Ex-42-92277, marked as 292277 / Z4
C-47A Skytrain	12075	G-AGIZ	Calling Bulldog Drummond (1951)	Ex-42-92291 / RAF FL647, BEA colors
C-47A Skytrain	12107	ZS-BXF	Amelia (2009)	Ex-42-92320, briefly seen
C-47A Skytrain	12540	VH-MMF	Sky Pirates (1986)	Ex-42-92709, ex–RAAF A65-41, non-flying
C-47A Skytrain	12874	VH-EDC	The Pacific (TVMS, 2010)	Ex-42-93010, ex–RAAF A65-46, wreck as Japanese L2D Tabby
C-47A Skytrain	12970	DO-12	A Bridge Too Far (1977)	Ex-42-93096, marked as 314013 / I-C7

DC-3 / C-47 ...		(SN or Reg. at Time of Filming)		
(Type)	(msn)	Filming)	(Title)	(Remarks / Film Markings)
C-47A Skytrain	13073	N86U	The Great Wallendas (TVM, 1978)	Ex-42-93189, flying
C-47A Skytrain	13099	ZK-BEU	Race for the Yankee Zephyr (1981)	Ex-42-93212, marked as 69 / 1-7689
C-47A Skytrain	13504	42-93577	Thirty Seconds Over Tokyo (1944)	Tail falsely marked as 193577
C-47A Skytrain	13510	JA5025	Flight from Ashiya (1964)	Ex-42-93582
C-47A Skytrain	18949	N99131	Outbreak (1995)	Ex-42-100486, USAF livery
		N99131	Pearl Harbor (2001)	Marked as 90395
C-47A Skytrain	18983	42-100520	A Prize of Gold (1955)	—
C-47A Skytrain	19054	N3239T	Drop Zone (1994)	Ex-42-100591
C-47A Skytrain	19109	DO-7	A Bridge Too Far (1977)	Ex-42-100646, marked as 711212 / I-D3
C-47A Skytrain	19200	K-687	A Bridge Too Far (1977)	Ex-42-100737, marked as 823561 / I-C3
C-47A Skytrain	19291	K-685	A Bridge Too Far (1977)	Ex-42-100828, marked as 337185 / I-C6
C-47A Skytrain	19347	G-DAKS	Airline (TVS, 1982)	Ex-42-100884, marked as G-AGHY / Vera Lynn
		G-DAKS	The Dirty Dozen: Next Mission (TVM, 1985)	Marked as a German transport
		G-DAKS	Memphis Belle (1990)	Background
		G-DAKS	White Hunter Black Heart (1990)	Marked as BOAC / G-ADL
		N147DC	Band of Brothers (TVMS, 2001)	Flying
		N147DC	Red Tails (2012)	Marked as 2100884 / D
C-47A Skytrain	19975	G-BHUB	Airline (TVS, 1982)	Ex-43-15509, marked as G-AGIV / Alice
C-47A Skytrain	20118	K-688	A Bridge Too Far (1977)	Ex-43-15652, marked as 315317 / I-C8
C-47A Skytrain	20562	N3FY	MacGyver (TVS, 1985–1992)	Ex-43-16096, "guest appearance" in several episodes
C-47A Skytrain	14070/25515	DO-4	A Bridge Too Far (1977)	Ex-43-48254, marked as 700318 / I-D1
C-47B Skytrain	14365/25810	N9986Q	A Bridge Too Far (1977)	Ex-43-48549, marked as CS
C-47B Skytrain	14520/25965	43-48704	Flight Nurse (1954)	—
C-47B Skytrain	15014/26459	43-49198	Above and Beyond (1952)	—
C-47B Skytrain	15070/26515	254	Air America (1990)	Ex-43-49254, Thai Air Force
C-47B Skytrain	15290/26735	G-AMRA	Band of Brothers (TVMS, 2001)	Ex-43-49474
C-47B Skytrain	15770/27215	N9985Q	A Bridge Too Far (1977)	Ex-43-49954, marked as KG411 / CS
C-47B Skytrain	16124/32872	D-CXXX	The Airlift (TVM, 2005)	Ex-44-76540, background and taxi hots
C-47B Skytrain	16688/33436	G-ANAF	Indiana Jones and the Last Crusade (1989)	Marked as NC170GP
C-47B Skytrain	16784/33532	N9983Q	A Bridge Too Far (1977)	Ex-44-77200, marked as KK149 / YS
C-47B Skytrain	20604	43-16138	The Lady Takes a Flyer (1958)	Briefly seen
C-47B Skytrain	20735	43-16269	Above and Beyond (1952)	—
TC-47B Skytrain	16158/32906	44-76574	Air Cadet (1951)	—
C-50B Skytrain	4110	N340EL	Live and Let Die (1973)	Ex-41-7704, damaged for film

DC-3 / C-47 ... (Type)	(msn)	(SN or Reg. at Time of Filming)	(Title)	(Remarks / Film Markings)
C-53 Skytrooper	7313	N147M	Richie Rich (1994)	Ex-42-47371, marked as Billion Dollar One
C-53D Skytrooper	11675	N9984Q	A Bridge Too Far (1977)	Ex-42-68748, marked as KG637 / YS
R4D-4	6349	JA5040	Flight from Ashiya (1964)	Ex-BuNo. 07003, factory impressed DC-3A NC34956
R4D-6	14329/25774	BuNo. 17271	The Gallant Hours (1960)	Ex-C-47B, 43-48513

that evolved into the famous C-47 Skytrain / Dakota during World War II. An impressive 10,655 were built, and it still flies in commercial service over 75 years later. The *Dak* or *Gooney Bird*, as it's known, has probably featured in more Hollywood films over the years than any other aircraft built! A complete record of all its appearances is, of course, impossible, but the table list certainly covers the most notable of productions on the big and small screen. The definitive DC-3 / C-47 films to watch out for are *You Gotta Stay Happy* (1948), *Island in the Sky* (1953), *Race for the Yankee Zephyr* (1981) and the TV series *Airline* (1982). There are also exciting Dakota sequences in *The Wild Geese* (1978) and the Bond film *Quantum of Solace* (2008).

Other Notable Titles: *Test Pilot* (1938); *Flight into Nowhere* (1938); *Stunt Pilot* (1939); *Sky Murder* (1940); *Forced Landing* (1941); *A Guy Named Joe* (1943); *Operation Burma* (1945); *God Is My Co-Pilot* (1945); *The Beginning or the End* (1947); *Blaze of Noon* (1947); *The Secret Island* (1948), R4D; *The Big Lift* (1950); *The Thing* (1951), civil DC-3A in USAF livery; *Top of the World* (1955); *Battle of the V-1* (1958), G-AMSS or G-AMSU; *China Doll* (1958); *Steve Canyon* (TVS, 1958–1959); *McHale's Navy Joins the Air Force* (1965); *None But The Brave* (1965); *The Dirty Dozen* (1967); *The Green Berets* (1968), AC-47D; *The*

Hell with Heroes (1968), marked as "NC45347"; *Too Late the Hero* (1970), Philippine C-47; *Baa Baa Black Sheep* (TVS, 1976–1978); *Ike: The War Years* (TVMS, 1979); *Tales of the Gold Monkey* (TVS, 1982–1983), wreck on Universal Studios backlot; *The A-Team* (TVS, 1983–1987).

SBD Dauntless

First flight (XBT-2): April 22, 1938 / (SBD-1): May 1, 1940. Single-engined carrier-borne dive-bomber saw much action in the Pacific Theatre during World War II. Many surplus Dauntless dive-bombers were purchased by film studios postwar as wind machines, MGM Studios in particular had acquired quite a collection. Restored warbird examples are seen in some detail in the epic TV miniseries *War and Remembrance* (1988).

Other Notable Titles: *Flight for Freedom* (1943), stock footage; *Wing and a Prayer* (1944), as Japanese bombers; *Task Force* (1949).

DC-4 / C-54 Skymaster Series

First flight: June 7, 1938. Four-engined civil airliner that was drafted into military service as the C-54 Skymaster during World War II. Canadair built a Merlin-powered version as the North Star and British company AT(E)L converted 21 to vehicle-ferry configuration with a top-deck cockpit. The best DC-4 film is certainly *The High and*

SBD Dauntless Type	msn	SN or Reg. at Time of Filming	Title	Remarks / Film Markings
SBD-5 Dauntless	3883	—	Midway (1976)	Ex-BuNo. 28536 and ex–RNZAF NZ5062, studio filming
		N670AM	War and Remembrance (TVMS, 1988)	Flying
A-24A Banshee	2350	N15749	Tora! Tora! Tora! (1970)	Ex-42–60817, flying but scenes cut
		N15749	Midway (1976)	Stock footage from Tora! shot in 1969
A-24B Banshee	17371	N54532	War and Remembrance (TVMS, 1988)	Ex-42–54532, flying

A roughly kept Douglas Dauntless on a Hollywood backlot; several of these aircraft were obtained by film technicians for use as wind machines. Photograph: James H. Farmer Collection.

Originally built as an A-24A Banshee for the USAAF with s/n 42–60817, this aircraft has been restored as an SBD Dauntless warbird and was provided as a flying aircraft for *Midway* (1976) as N15749. Photograph: James H. Farmer Collection.

DC-4 / C-54 Skymaster Series

Type	msn	SN or Reg. at Time of Filming	Title	Remarks / Film Markings
C-54A Skymaster	10315	N4726V	*The High and the Mighty* (1954)	Ex-42-72210, marked as Topac
C-54A Skymaster	10408	G-APID	*Cuba* (1979)	Ex-42-72303, gimmick snack bar
C-54B Skymaster	10538	N4665V	*The High and the Mighty* (1954)	Ex-42-72433, marked as Topac
C-54E Skymaster	27320	44-9094	*Flight Nurse* (1954)	—
C-54G Skymaster	36010	45-557	*The Airlift* (TVM, 2005)	Background only marked as 5557
C-54G Skymaster	36032	45-579	*The Hunters* (1958)	Briefly seen
DC-4	42904	NC10201	*The Best Years of Our Lives* (1946)	—
AT(E)L.98 Carvair	10273/7	G-ASDC	*Goldfinger* (1964)	C-54A ex–USAF 42-72168

the Mighty (1954), with the Berlin Airlift flick *The Big Lift* (1950) also worthy of mention.

Other Notable Titles: *The Big Lift* (1950); *Above and Beyond* (1952); *The Glenn Miller Story* (1954); *Zero Hour!* (1957); *The Geisha Boy* (1958), DC-4 marked as a MATS C-54 with false s/n 42-3261.

A-26 INVADER

First flight: July 10, 1942. Twin-engined attack / light-bomber aircraft saw a very lengthy combat career from World War II, to Korea, to Vietnam plus many other wars around the world, particularly in Latin and South America. A popular type for civilian executive conversion and sprayer use. The definitive Invader film is without a doubt 1989's *Always*, which features some stunning aerial footage of several A-26 fire-bombers.

Other Notable Titles: *The Train* (1964), French AF Invaders.

A4D SKYRAIDER

First flight (XBT2D-1): March 18, 1945. Single-engined, carrier-borne tactical support aircraft.

It's been said the biggest trouble with the Skyraider was that they didn't build enough of them! Entered service as the AD Skyraider in 1946 with a total of 3,180 built by 1957. Redesignated as the A-1 in 1962.

Other Notable Titles: *We Were Soldiers* (2002); *Rescue Dawn* (2006), CGI only.

C-74 / C-124
GLOBEMASTER SERIES

First flight (C-74): September 5, 1945; (C-124): 1950. Four-engined heavy-lift cargo / troop transport with nose doors and a unique belly elevator.

DC-6 / DC-7

First flight (DC-6): February 15, 1946 / (DC-7): May 18, 1953. Four-engined civil airliners.

DC-6 was also built as the military C-118 Liftmaster. Both aircraft, along with the Constellation, represented the last of the piston-engined giants to enter airline service before the dawning of the jet age.

A-26 Invader		SN or Reg. at Time of Filming		
Type	msn	Filming	Title	Remarks / Film Markings
A-26B Invader	27400	N4805E	*Always* (1989)	Ex-44-34121, marked as Tanker 58
A-26B Invader	27817	N34538	*Roswell* (TVM, 1994)	Ex-44-34538, static shot only.
A-26B Invader	27992	N36B	*Cash McCall* (1960)	Ex-44-34713, *On Mark Marketeer* VIP conversion
A-26B Invader	28045	N9150	*Havana* (1990)	Ex-44-34766
A-26C Invader	18670	N4050A	*Badlands* (1973)	Ex-43-22523
A-26C Invader	28650	N4818E	*Always* (1989)	Ex-44-35371, marked as Tanker 59
A-26C Invader	29000	N9425Z	*Always* (1989)	Ex-44-35721, marked as Tanker 57 / 59

A4D Skyraider		SN or Reg. at Time of Filming		
Type	msn	Time of Filming	Title	Remarks / Film Markings
AD-4N Skyraider	7797	N409Z	*Flight of the Intruder* (1990)	Ex-BuNo. 126997
AD-6 Skyraider	10838	N39606	*Flight of the Intruder* (1990)	Ex-BuNo. 139606

C-74 / C-124 Globemaster Series		SN or Reg. at Time of Filming		
Type	msn	Filming	Title	Remarks / Film Markings
C-74 Globemaster I	13920	HP-379	*The Italian Job* (1969)	Ex-42-65409, derelict, fictional Chinese colors

DC-6 / DC-7		SN or Reg. at Time of Filming		
Type	msn	Time of Filming	Title	Remarks / Film Markings
DC-6B	43530	N6530C	*A Prize of Gold* (1955)	—
DC-6B	45077	EC-DCK	*Cuba* (1979)	—
DC-7C	45071	N5903	*American Graffiti* (1973)	Provided for final scene
DC-7C	44883	N741PA	*China Doll* (1958)	Provided for final scene

Other Notable Titles: *Crash Landing* (1958), DC-7C; *The Crowded Sky* (1960), DC-6B; *Fate is the Hunter* (1964), DC-6B; *King Kong* (1976), DC-7.

F-4 PHANTOM II

First flight: May 27, 1958. Twin-engined, 2-seater fighter / fighter-bomber began as a pre-merger McDonnell aircraft and saw extensive use in Vietnam. Last official U.S. armed forces retirement was in 1996. In all, 5,068 were built, with another 127 in Japan.

Notable Titles: *Ice Station Zebra* (1968); *The Concorde ... Airport '79* (1979), model only; *The Great Santini* (1979); *The Hanoi Hilton* (1987), file footage; *Flight of the Intruder* (1991).

DC-8

First flight: May 30, 1958. Four-engined jet airliner, entered service in 1959 competing with the Boeing 707. Also built as the DC-8 Super 60 and converted as the DC-8 Super 70.

DC-9 / C-9 SKYTRAIN II / MD-80 / MD-90

First flight: February 25, 1965. Twin-engined, T-tailed airliner began service in 1965 and was later rebranded as the MD-80, MD-90 and the Boeing Model 717 after 1997.

Other Notable Titles: *The Grey* (2011).

DC-10 / KC-10 EXTENDER / MD-11

First flight: August 29, 1970. Three-engined, wide-body airliner entered service in 1971, later rebranded as the MD-11 in 1990 after various upgrades. The KC-10 is a USAF aerial tanker of which 60 were built.

Other Notable Titles: *Air Force One* (1997), KC-10A; *Castaway* (2000), Fed-Ex MD-11.

AV-8 HARRIER

First flight (AV-8A): November 20, 1970. McDonnell Douglas version of the British Harrier VTOL jet fighter for service with the USMC. A

DC-8		SN or Reg. at Time of Filming		
Type	msn		Title	Remarks / Film Markings
DC-8-11	45282/10	N8005U	*Good Morning, Vietnam* (1987)	United Airlines freight conversion
DC-8-21	45594/35	N8021U	*The Pilot* (1980)	United Airlines aircraft
DC-8-33(F)	45272/118	N59AJ	*Hot Shots!* (1991)	—
DC-8-54AF	45675/200	N8041U	*The Pilot* (1980)	United Airlines aircraft

DC-9 / C-9 Skytrain II / MD-80 / MD-90		SN or Reg. at Time of Filming		
Type	msn		Title	Remarks / Film Markings
DC-9-32	47525/631	N1295L	*Cliffhanger* (1993)	Flying without tail cone
C-9B Skytrain II	47584/696	BuNo. 159114	*Top Gun* (1986)	Briefly seen
MD-82	49261/1153	N16807	*Flight* (2012)	Flight-deck / interior scenes
MD-82	49468/1409	N442AA	*Flight* (2012)	Post-crash wreck scenes
MD-88	49532/1338	N901DL	*Flight* (2012)	Post-crash wreck scenes
MD-88	49810/1588	N937DL	*Flight* (2012)	Exterior pre-crash scenes

DC-10 / KC-10 Extender / MD-11		SN or Reg. at Time of Filming		
Type	msn		Title	Remarks / Film Markings
DC-10 Series 10	46977/251	N908WA	*Commando* (1985)	World Airways aircraft

AV-8 Harrier		SN or Reg. at Time of Filming		
Type	msn		Title	Remarks / Film Markings
AV-8B Harrier II	68	BuNo. 162946	*True Lies* (1994)	Replica also created for studio filming
AV-8B Harrier II	202	BuNo. 164126	*True Lies* (1994)	—

total of 452 built, including prototypes and foreign orders.

Extensive views seen in the 1994 spy movie *True Lies*.

F-15 EAGLE

First flight: July 27, 1972. Twin-engined combat fighter first went into service in 1974.

Became a Boeing product in 1997 and has since been developed into the F-15E Strike Eagle and similar variants.

Notable Titles: *The Courage and the Passion* (TVM, 1978), YF-15A; *Air Force One* (1997); *Armageddon* (1998).

AH-64 APACHE

First flight: September 30, 1975. Twin-engined attack helicopter developed by Hughes Helicopters, but had become a McDonnell Douglas product by the time of service entry in 1984; a product of Boeing since 1997.

Definitive version is the AH-64D Apache Longbow.

Notable Titles: *Fire Birds* (1990); *Toy Soldiers* (1991); *Transformers: Dark of the Moon* (2011).

F/A-18 HORNET

First flight (YF-18A): November 18, 1978. Twin-engined carrier-borne naval fighter developed from the 1974 Northrop YF-17A Cobra. Well known on the big screen for its use in *Independence Day* (1996), plus several other "cameo" appearances in subsequent films. Became a product of Boeing in 1997.

Notable Titles: *Under Siege* (1992); *Independence Day* (1996); *The Rock* (1996); *Behind Enemy Lines* (2001); *Tears of the Sun* (2003); *Stealth* (2005); *Transformers* (2007); *Transformers: Revenge of the Fallen* (2009); *Battleship* (2012).

C-17 GLOBEMASTER III

First flight: September 15, 1989. Four-engined heavy-lift transport; over 260 built for the USAF and other nations, including Australia, Canada, the UK and Qatar. The C-17 has become a popular transport type on the big screen in recent years.

Built by Boeing from 1997.

Notable Titles: *Transformers* (2007); *Eagle Eye* (2008); *Iron Man* (2008); *Transformers: Revenge of the Fallen* (2009); *Iron Man 2* (2010).

Embraer

Brazilian aerospace manufacturer founded in 1969 as a government-owned corporation. The name is an abbreviation of Empresa Brasileira de Aeronautica. Their best known products are the EMB-110 Bandeirante and ERJ Regional Jet series.

Erco

Engineering and Research Corporation, founded in 1930, developed the unique Ercoupe light aircraft with twin tails and a control system that required no rudder pedals. It first flew in 1937 and production took place both before and after World War II.

Eurocopter *see* Aerospatiale

Fairchild / Fairchild-Hiller

Founded in 1924 by Sherman Fairchild as an aerial photographic business. Acquired the Kreider-Reisner Aircraft Co. in 1927 and entered aircraft manufacturing. Became the Fairchild Aviation Corp. in 1934 and went on to produce the

Embraer		SN or Reg. at Time of		
Type	msn	Filming	Title	Remarks / Film Markings
EMB-110 Bandeirante	110479	ZS-NVB	*The Dark Knight Rises* (2012)	Flying scenes in the UK

Erco		SN or Reg. at Time of		
Type	msn	Filming	Title	Remarks / Film Markings
Ercoupe 415-C	688	NC93365	*Operation Haylift* (1950)	Brief flyby only

World War II PT-19 trainer and C-82 Packet. After the war, produced the C-119 and C-123 for the USAF. Became Fairchild-Hiller in 1964 after acquiring Hiller Helicopters; acquired the Republic Aviation Corp. in 1967 and developed the A-10; acquired the Swearingen Aviation Corp. in 1972; license-built the F.27 Friendship and Pilatus Porter. Aircraft production stopped entirely in 1987. In some ways the Fairchild product has been given a rough treatment throughout aviation film history. Virtually every film featuring a Fairchild has had it crashing or coming to misfortune at some point in the story—whether it be the C-82 or C-119 for both *Flight of the Phoenix* (1965 / 2004) films, the C-123 Providers in *Air America* (1990) and *Con Air* (1997), or the FH-227 in *Alive* (1993), not to mention the A-10 Warthogs in the sci-fi movie *Terminator Salvation* (2009).

MODEL 71

First flight: 1928. Single-engined monoplane design, many with floats. Good views featured in *Captains of the Clouds* (1942).

MODEL 24

First flight: 1932. Single-engined monoplane was one of Fairchild's early successful designs with 1983 built from 1931 to 1947.

Notable Titles: *Men Against the Sky* (1940); *The Marines Fly High* (1940); *Fate is the Hunter* (1964).

C-82 PACKET

First flight: September 10, 1944. Twin-engined, twin-boom cargo / troop transport has the distinction of being the first practical, purpose-built cargo design to enter USAF service. Many sold on the civilian market, but most only saw limited use. Solely famous for its role in *The Flight of the Phoenix* (1965).

Other Notable Titles: *The Big Lift* (1950); *Invasion USA* (1952); *Earth vs. the Flying Saucers* (1956), library shot; *Beautiful Dreamer* (2006), cockpit doubles as a B-24!

C-119 FLYING BOXCAR / R4Q PACKET

First flight (XC-119A): December 17, 1947. Twin-engined, twin-boom upgrade of the C-82 Packet had a much more successful career, with 1,185 built; the last military retirement was in Taiwan in 1997. Best known on film for its leading role in the 2004 version of the *Flight of the Phoenix*.

Other Notable Title: *The Lady Takes A Flyer* (1958), R4Q-1 in background.

Fairchild / Fairchild-Hiller		SN or Reg. at Time of		
Type	msn	Filming	Title	Remarks / Film Markings
Model KR-21A	1053	N962V	*The Carpetbaggers* (1964)	—
Model 22C-7D	916	NC14339	*The Tarnished Angels* (1957)	—
PT-19A Cornell	unknown	N48672	*The Tarnished Angels* (1957)	Ex-USAAF trainer
FH-227D Friendship	573	N2784R	*Alive* (1993)	Brief flying shots

Model 71		SN or Reg. at Time of		
Type	msn	Filming	Title	Remarks / Film Markings
Model 71	675	NC2K	*Central Airport* (1933)	—
Model 71	unknown	CF-NBP	*Captains of the Clouds* (1942)	—
Model 71C	unknown	CF-BJE	*49th Parallel* (1941)	—

C-82 Packet		SN or Reg. at Time of		
Type	msn	Filming	Title	Remarks / Film Markings
C-82A Packet	10059	N6887C	*The Flight of the Phoenix* (1965)	Ex-44-23015, flying aircraft
C-82A Packet	10075	N4833V	*The Flight of the Phoenix* (1965)	Ex-44-23031, derelict fuselage
C-82A Packet	10080	N53228	*The Flight of the Phoenix* (1965)	Ex-44-23036, derelict fuselage
C-82A Packet	10094	44-23050	*Operation Haylift* (1950)	Provided by USAF, flying

C-119 ...		SN or Reg. at Time of Filming		
Type	msn	Filming	Title	Remarks / Film Markings
C-119B Flying Boxcar	10304	N13745	Black Thunder (1998)	Ex-48-322, Hemet Valley Flying Service
C-119F Flying Boxcar	10776	N8093	Always (1989)	Ex-RCAF 22111
C-119F Flying Boxcar	10955	N15501	Flight of the Phoenix (2004)	Ex-RCAF 22130, flying aircraft
C-119G Flying Boxcar	196	53-8093	Battle Hymn (1957)	Plus four others
R4Q-1 Packet	10549	BuNo. 126580	The Flight of the Phoenix (1965)	Wing and boom parts only
R4Q-2 Packet	10876	BuNo. 131691	Flight of the Phoenix (2004)	Derelict
R4Q-2 Packet	10885	N3267U	Flight of the Phoenix (2004)	Ex-BuNo. 131700, derelict
R4Q-2 Packet	10891	BuNo. 131706	Flight of the Phoenix (2004)	Derelict

C-123 PROVIDER

First flight: September 1, 1954. Twin-engined transport design based on the earlier Chase Avitruc glider. Fairchild acquired the production contract and built 309, most of which were upgraded to C-123K standard with auxiliary jet-pods. A popular aircraft with many action films in the 1990s, the best-known of these being *Con Air* (1997), but the best C-123 film is definitely *Air America* (1990).

Other Notable Titles: *Good Morning, Vietnam* (1987), Thai AF C-123K; *Air America* (1990), four flyable Thai AF C-123K.

PC-6 TURBO-PORTER / AU-23 PEACEMAKER

First flight: 1966. Singe-engined STOL turbo-prop utility aircraft license built from the Swiss Pilatus Porter / Turbo-Porter. 92 built by Fairchild

C-123 Provider		SN or Reg. at Time of Filming		
Type	msn	Filming	Title	Remarks / Film Markings
C-123B Provider	20014	N123K	Aces: Iron Eagle III (1992)	Ex-54-565, flying
		N123K	Operation Dumbo Drop (1995)	Florida-based flying scenes, marked as 702 and WH / 342
		N123K	Outbreak (1995)	Flying
C-123B Provider	20018	(RTAF) BL4k-22/16	Air America (1990)	Ex-54-569, "Tango 7" wreck marked as 671
C-123B Provider	20025	(RTAF) BL4k-1/16	Operation Dumbo Drop (1995)	Ex-54-576, some scenes in Thailand
C-123B Provider	20059	N3836A	The Living Daylights (1987)	Ex-54-610, C-130 stand-in for cargo-net fight
		N3836A	Tucker: The Man and His Dream (1988)	Brief appearance
C-123B Provider	20064	N546S	Terminal Velocity (1994)	Ex-54-615, white and blue livery
		N546S	A Man Apart (2003)	Flying
C-123B provider	20113	N22968	X-Men: Days of Future Past (2014)	Ex-54-664
C-123B Provider	20155	N94DT	Con Air (1997)	Ex-54-706, destroyed for film
C-123B Provider	20158	N709RR	Die Hard 2: Die Harder (1990)	Ex-54-709, fake 4-jet conversion
		N709RR	Con Air (1997)	Flying scenes. Fatally crashed in Alaska, 2010
C-123B Provider	20245	56-4361	Con Air (1997)	Derelict, ground scenes

PC-6 ...		SN or Reg. at Time of Filming		
Type	msn	Filming	Title	Remarks / Film Markings
PC-6B Turbo-Porter	2001	N346F	Drop Zone (1994)	Marked as Crazy Flamingo
AU-23A Peacemaker	2088	(Thai) JTh2-29/19	Air America (1990)	Marked as "238," plus 4 others

of which 36 went to the Thai Air Force as the AU-23A Peacemaker.

A-10 Thunderbolt II

First flight: May 10, 1972. Twin-engined close air support aircraft is notable as being Fairchild's last aircraft before the company closed its doors in the mid–1980s. Better known as the "Warthog"; 715 were built. Has starred in a "supporting role" in several action orientated films.

Notable Titles: *Courage Under Fire* (1996); *Jarhead* (2005); *Transformers* (2007); *Terminator Salvation* (2009); *Transformers: Revenge of the Fallen* (2009); *Battle: Los Angeles* (2011).

Fairey

British manufacturer founded in 1915 by Charles Fairey as Fairey Aviation Ltd. Built a steady string of designs including their best-known products, the Fairey Swordfish, Battle, Barracuda and Firefly during World War II, and the Fairey Gannet postwar. Began rotary-winged aircraft development, and along with the helicopter divisions of Bristol and Saunders-Roe, was merged into Westland Aircraft in 1960.

Other Notable Titles: *The Lion Has Wings* (1939), Battle; *Captains of the Clouds* (1942), Battle; *Ships with Wings* (1942), Swordfish.

Fleet

American manufacturer founded by Reuben Fleet in 1929 as a subsidiary to the Consolidated Aircraft Corp. Produced several light aircraft types such as the Finch and Canuck. The Fleet name was dropped from Consolidated by 1939, but the Canadian branch remained during World War II, license-building the Fairchild PT-19.

Further details see: CONSOLIDATED.

Fokker

A Dutch aircraft manufacturer founded by Anthony Fokker in 1912 as Fokker Aviatik GmbH; built several World War I types, including the fa-

Fairey Type	msn	SN or Reg. at Time of Filming	Title	Remarks / Film Markings
Swordfish Mk. II	unknown	G-AJVH	*Sink the Bismarck!* (1960)	Ex–RN LS326, marked as 5A
Swordfish Mk. III	unknown	(RN) NF389	*Sink the Bismarck!* (1960)	Marked as LS423/5B

Fleet Type	msn	SN or Reg. at Time of Filming	Title	Remarks / Film Markings
Model 2	333	NC748V	*The Tarnished Angels* (1957)	—
(Finch) Model 16R	92319	C-FDAF	*Amelia* (2009)	Briefly seen

Fokker Type	msn	SN or Reg. at Time of Filming	Title	Remarks / Film Markings
Fokker Dr.I (replica)	001	G-ATIY	*The Blue Max* (1966)	Replica built for the film, later to EI-APW
		EI-APW	*Darling Lili* (1970)	Flying
		—	*Aces High* (1976)	Stock footage from previous films
Fokker Dr.I (replica)	002	G-ATJM	*The Blue Max* (1966)	Replica built for the film, later to EI-APY
		EI-APY	*Darling Lili* (1970)	Flying
		—	*Aces High* (1976)	Stock footage from previous films
		G-ATJM	*Flyboys* (2006)	Flying
		N78001	*The Red Baron* (2008)	Flying, not widely used, rego. was temporary

Fokker		(SN or Reg. at Time of		
(Type)	*(msn)*	Filming)	*(Title)*	*(Remarks / Film Markings)*
Fokker Dr.I (replica)	DB1	N5523V	The Great Waldo Pepper (1975)	Tallmantz owned, flying. Some sources quote Dr.I replica, N864DR, as being the aircraft used
Fokker Dr.I (replica)	PFA/238-12654	G-BVGZ	Flyboys (2006)	Flying
Fokker D.VII	504/17	N6268	Men With Wings (1938)	Flying
		N6268	Stunt Pilot (1939)	Flying
Fokker D.VII (replica)	6880	N125QB	The Aviator (2004)	Flying, plus five others
Fokker D.VII-65 (replica)	01	F-BNDF	The Blue Max (1966)	Replica built for the film
		EI-APV	Darling Lili (1970)	Flying
		EI-APV	Von Richthofen and Brown (1971)	Flying
		—	Aces High (1976)	Stock footage from previous films
Fokker D.VII-65 (replica)	02	F-BNDG	The Blue Max (1966)	Replica built for the film
		EI-APT	Darling Lili (1970)	Flying
		EI-APT	Von Richthofen and Brown (1971)	Flying
		—	Aces High (1976)	Stock footage from previous films
Fokker D.VII-65 (replica)	03	F-BNDH	The Blue Max (1966)	Replica built for the film
		EI-APU	Darling Lili (1970)	Flying
		EI-APU	Von Richthofen and Brown (1971)	Flying
		—	Aces High (1976)	Stock footage from previous films
Fokker E.III (replica)	PPS/FOK/6	G-AVJO	Aces High (1976)	Built in 1965 by Douglas Bianchi
		G-AVJO	Wings (TVS, 1977–1978)	Flying
Fokker F.DVIIb/3m	4954	VH-USU	Smithy (1946)	Ex–NC1985, the actual Southern Cross aircraft

mous Dr. I Dreidecker. After World War I returned to the Netherlands in 1919, set up a new aircraft factory and began building many successful aircraft including the Fokker tri-motor series of aircraft. Fokker Aircraft Corp. was opened in the U.S. and, for a time, Fokker was the largest aircraft manufacturer in the world. Factories in the Netherlands were occupied by German forces during World War II and were almost totally destroyed by the end of the war. Fokker went on postwar to build the iconic turboprop airliner, the F.27 Friendship, and later the Fokker twin-jet series. The company was declared bankrupt in 1996. Fokker aircraft have been well represented on the big screen, especially in the World War I epic featuring the D.VII and Dr. I fighters. Most representations, as listed below, are replicas, original aircraft having long since perished.

Other Notable Titles: Fokker D.VII: *Wings* (1927); *Now We're in the Air* (1927); *Hell's Angels* (1930)—footage subsequently used in many other productions; *Lafayette Escadrille* (1958); *Von Richthofen and Brown* (1971), EI-APW or EI-APY.

Ford

Originally the Stout Metal Airplane Co., it was purchased by the Ford Motor Co. in 1924, who then utilized it to build the famous Tri-Motor series of aircraft so popular in the 1920s. With the onset of the Great Depression, Ford stopped production by 1936, but did return to aviation during World War II, building thousands of B-24 bombers. Many Tri-Motor aircraft have been seen on the silver screen and were especially popular during the 1930s with air-disaster movies.

Ford		SN or Reg. at Time of		
Type	msn	Filming	Title	Remarks / Film Markings
Model 4-AT-B Tri-Motor	4-AT-10	N1077	*Amelia* (2009)	Marked as N1077 / Ford
Model 4-AT-B Tri-Motor	4-AT-35	NC7121	*Only Angels Have Wings* (1939)	Marked as F-HLI
		NC7121	*Charter Pilot* (1940)	Flying
		NC7121	*Flying Wild* (1941)	—
Model 4-AT-D Tri-Motor	4-AT-24	NC5578	*Central Airport* (1933)	—
		NC5578	*Murder in the Clouds* (1934)	—
Model 4-AT-E Tri-Motor	4-AT-69	N8407	*The Family Jewels* (1965)	—
Model 5-AT-B Tri-Motor	5-AT-34	N9651	*Indiana Jones and the Temple of Doom* (1984)	Marked as "Lao Che Air Freight"
Model 5-AT-B Tri-Motor	5-AT-5	NC9607	*Air Hostess* (1933)	TWA Airlines
Model 5-AT-C Tri-Motor	5-AT-51	NC8413	*Air Hostess* (1933)	TWA Airlines
Model 5-AT-C Tri-Motor	5-AT-58	N8419	*Red Skies of Montana* (1952)	—
RR-4 Tri-Motor	5-AT-84	BuNo. A-8840	*Devil Dogs of the Air* (1935)	USMC staff transport

Other Notable Titles: *Hurricane Express* (film serial, 1932), possibly NC4814; *Central Airport* (1933); *Murder in the Clouds* (1934); *China Clipper* (1936); *Fugitive in the Sky* (1936); *The Man Who Found Himself* (1937); *Eternally Yours* (1939); *Flight for Freedom* (1943).

Gates Learjet *see* Learjet

General Dynamics

General Dynamics Corp. was formed in 1952 with Convair as an aircraft division. The Convair brand name was phased out by 1961 along with the San Diego plant by 1965.

Aircraft production continued with the introduction of the F-111 Aardvark from 1964 and F-16 Fighting Falcon from 1974, both built at Fort Worth, Texas. The F-16 program was sold to the Lockheed Corp. in 1992. General Dynamics acquired Gulfstream Aerospace in 1999.

Notable Titles: *The Jewel of the Nile* (1985), F-16 mock-up; *Iron Eagle* and *Iron Eagle II* (1986, 1988), Israeli F-16; *Independence Day* (1996), F-16 mock-up; *War of the Worlds* (2005), F-16 CGI model.

Gloster

British manufacturer founded in 1917 as the Gloucestershire Aircraft Co., which was shortened to the Gloster Aircraft Co. Ltd. in 1926. Acquired by Hawker Aircraft in 1934 and became a part of Hawker Siddeley Aircraft Ltd. in 1935. Famous for producing the Gladiator biplane and the Meteor and Javelin jet fighters in the postwar years. In 1961 it was merged with Armstrong-Whitworth as Whitworth Gloster Aircraft Ltd., then in 1963 disappeared altogether under Hawker Siddeley Aviation branding.

Government Aircraft Factory (GAF)

Australian manufacturer founded as the Dept. of Aircraft Production (DAP) prior to World War

Gloster		SN or Reg. at		
Type	msn	Time of Filming	Title	Remarks / Film Markings
GA.2A	unknown	TX145	*No Highway in the Sky* (1951)	Brief flyby appearance

GAF		SN or Reg. at Time of		
Type	msn	Filming	Title	Remarks / Film Markings
Prototype Nomad	N2-01	—	*The Flying Doctors* (TVS, 1985-1992)	Interior filming, ex-reg. VH-SUP
N22B Nomad	N22B-69	VH-MSF	*The Flying Doctors* (TVS, 1985-1992)	Flying aircraft

II, producing the Beaufighter and Beaufort. Post-war produced the Lincoln and Canberra bombers, then the Mirage III jet fighter. Famous original product is the Nomad utility aircraft as seen in *The Flying Doctors* TV series. Renamed Aerospace Technologies of Australia (ASTA) in 1987 and subsequently became a part of Boeing Australia.

Granville Bros.

Granville Bros. Aircraft, Inc., was founded in 1929 as Granville Bros. Aircraft Repair, which was a mobile repair station on the back of a truck. Soon became famous for their Gee Bee racer aircraft built from 1930 to 1934.

Great Lakes

American company founded in 1929 as Great Lakes Aircraft Corp., often remembered for their Model 2-T-1 biplane, which first flew in 1929.

Greenleaf (Player)

American company founded by William Player and Harry Thalman. Became the Plxweve Aircraft Co. division of Aero Industries with John Greenleaf as president.

Grumman / Northrop-Grumman

The famous Grumman "Iron Works," as it became known, was founded on Long Island by Leroy Grumman in 1929 as the Grumman Aircraft Engr. Corp. Shifted to its Bethpage location in 1937 and made a tremendous contribution to World War II with such classic naval aircraft as the Wildcat, Hellcat and Avenger. Opened the Calverton plant in 1954 for jet production; was renamed as the Grumman Aerospace Corp. in 1969; sold its Gulfstream division in 1978; became Northrop-Grumman Corp. in 1994 after merging with the Northrop Corp.; finished aircraft production in 1996 when the Calverton plant shut, which had built the A-6, E-2 and F-14. Grumman is best remembered for its hugely successful bulky and heavy naval aircraft types.

J2F Duck

First flight: April 24, 1933. Singe-engined amphibious biplane which saw service throughout the 1930s and World War II as a naval utility aircraft. Best known on film for its memorable role in the 1971 movie *Murphy's War*.

Other Notable Titles: *The Court-Martial of Billy Mitchell* (1955), N67790 or N1196N.

Granville Type	msn	SN or Reg. at Time of Filming	Title	Remarks / Film Markings
Gee Bee Z (replica)	T-4	NR77V	*The Rocketeer* (1991)	Flying replica built by Bill Turner

Greenleaf Type	msn	SN or Reg. at Time of Filming	Title	Remarks / Film Markings
Model CT-6A	1	NX19994	Power Dive (1941)	Doubles as a "plastic prototype"

Great Lakes Type	msn	SN or Reg. at Time of Filming	Title	Remarks / Film Markings
Model 2T-1A	199	N312Y	*The Rocketeer* (1991)	Flying

J2F Duck Type	msn	SN or Reg. at Time of Filming	Title	Remarks / Film Markings
J2F-6 Duck	unknown	N1214N	*Midway* (1976)	Background
		N1214N	*Baa Baa Black Sheep* (TVS, 1976-1978)	—
J2F-6 Duck	unknown	N67790	*Murphy's War* (1971)	Ex-BuNo. 33587
		N67790	*The Amazing Howard Hughes* (TVM, 1977)	Marked as 7790
J2F-6 Duck	unknown	N1196N	*Murphy's War* (1971)	Ex-BuNo. 36976

F3F

First flight: March 20, 1935. Single-engined biplane fighter for the U.S. Navy and the last biplane to enter naval service. All 147 built were retired by 1943.

G-21 & JRF Goose / G-44 & J4F Widgeon

First flight (G-21): May 29, 1937 / (G-44): June 28, 1940. Twin-engined amphibious utility flying boat is a classic Grumman design which saw both civilian and military service. The Goose is best known for its major role in the TV series *Tales of the Gold Monkey*. The G-44 Widgeon featured a more nimble hull and in-line engines, 42 were also built in France by aircraft manufacturer SCAN.

Other Notable Titles: *Crash Dive* (1943); *The Islanders* (TVS, 1960–1961).

F4F / FM Wildcat

First flight: September 2, 1937. Single-engined naval fighter, developed as a monoplane version of the biplane F3F. Early versions were largely export orders for the UK and France as the Martlet. Most later production was handled by General Motors when Grumman switched to full-time production on the Hellcat.

Other Notable Titles: *Wake Island* (1942); *Guadalcanal Diary* (1943); *We've Never Been Licked* (1943), as Japanese fighters; *Wing and a Prayer* (1944); *Fighting Seebees* (1944); *Task Force* (1949); *Windtalkers* (2002), CGI creations only.

TBF / TBM Avenger

First flight: August 7, 1941. Single-engined naval torpedo-bomber had its combat debut in the Battle of Midway in 1942. A total of 9,839

F3F Type	msn	SN or Reg. at Time of Filming	Title	Remarks / Film Markings
F3F-2	365	BuNo. 0967	*Dive Bomber* (1941)	—
F3F-2	376	BuNo. 0978	*Dive Bomber* (1941)	—
F3F-2	426	BuNo. 1028	*Flight Command* (1940)	—
F3F-2	427	BuNo. 1029	*Flight Command* (1940)	—
F3F-3	485	BuNo. 1451	*Dive Bomber* (1941)	—

G-21 ... Type	msn	SN or Reg. at Time of Filming	Title	Remarks / Film Markings
G-21 Goose	1007	N13CS	*Tales of the Gold Monkey* (TVS, 1982–1983)	Not confirmed, marked as *Cutter's Goose*
G-21A Goose	1051	N327	*Sea Hunt* (TVS, 1958–1961)	—
		N327	*Tales of the Gold Monkey* (TVS, 1982–1983)	Flying scenes, marked as *Cutter's Goose*
JRF-5 Goose	B-41	N1543V	*Sea Hunt* (TVS, 1958–1961)	Ex-BuNo. 37788
JRF-6B Goose	1153	N143DF	*Commando* (1985)	Ex-RAF FP503
JRF-6B Goose	1166	N11CS	*Tobruk* (1967)	Ex-RAF FP516. As German seaplane, Widgeon windscreen
G-44A Widgeon	1411	N444M	*Loulou Graffiti* (1991)	Ex-N41890
J4F-2 Widgeon	1317	N67867	*Crossroads* (1951)	Ex-BuNo. 32963
J4F-2 Widgeon	1323	N66432	*On an Island With You* (1948)	Ex-BuNo. 32969
(SCAN) Type 30	31	N4453	*Fantasy Island* (TVS, 1977–1984)	Used in opening titles; radial engine upgrade

F4F ... Type	msn	SN or Reg. at Time of Filming	Title	Remarks / Film Markings
FM-2 Wildcat	3268	N47201	*War and Remembrance* (TVMS, 1988)	Ex-BuNo. 55627
FM-2 Wildcat	5804	N6290C	*Midway* (1976)	Ex-BuNo. 86746
FM-2 Wildcat	5835	N90541	*Midway* (1976)	Ex-BuNo. 86777
		N5HP	*War and Remembrance* (TVMS, 1988)	Flying

were built, 7,546 of which by General Motors. A popular aircraft for civil applications such as spraying and fire-bombing. Excellent but brief views seen in 1977's *Close Encounters*, but the top Avenger film would be 1944's *Wing and a Prayer*.

Other Notable Titles: *Wing and a Prayer* (1944); *Sky High* (1951); *Battle Stations* (1956); *The Wings of Eagles* (1957); *S.O.S. Pacific* (1960).

F6F Hellcat

First flight: June 26, 1942. Single-engined naval fighter built in large numbers—12,274 from 1942 to 1945, the most for any type ever built by Grumman and within the shortest time period. Some good views seen in the 1951 film *Flying Leathernecks*.

TBF... Type	msn	SN or Reg. at Time of Filming	Title	Remarks / Film Markings
TBF-1C Avenger	4045	BuNo. 05997	unknown	Owned by MGM Studios, California
TBM-1C Avenger	unknown	N9394H	*On an Island With You* (1948)	Ex-BuNo. 46122
		N9394H	*Thunder in the East* (1953)	—
TBM-3 Avenger	3099	N86280	*Close Encounters of the Third Kind* (1977)	Ex-BuNo. 86280
TBM-3 Avenger	3181	N33BM	*Close Encounters of the Third Kind* (1977)	Ex-BuNo. 53119, marked as 33
TBM-3 Avenger	3565	N53503	*Close Encounters of the Third Kind* (1977)	Ex-BuNo. 53503, marked as 82
		N53503	*The Bermuda Triangle* (1979)	Documentary feature, Flight 19 sequence
TBM-3 Avenger	3847	N7075C	*Smokey and the Bandit II* (1980)	Ex-BuNo. 53785, plus one other
TBM-3 Avenger	3866	N9710Z	*Close Encounters of the Third Kind* (1977)	Ex-BuNo. 53804

F6F Hellcat Type	msn	SN or Reg. at Time of Filming	Title	Remarks / Film Markings
F6F-5 Hellcat	A-5634	N1078Z	*The Bermuda Triangle* (1979)	Ex-BuNo. 70222, documentary feature
F6F-5 Hellcat	A-11631	N4994V	*Route 66* (TVS, 1960-1964)	Ex-BuNo. 93879
		N4994V	*Close Encounters of the Third Kind* (1977)	Doubles as an "Avenger" stand-in

A Warner Bros.–owned Grumman Avenger derelict. Several studios purchased such airframes for back-lot filming. Photograph: James H. Farmer Collection.

Other Notable Titles: *Wing and a Prayer* (1944); *Task Force* (1949); *The Flying Missile* (1950), F6F-5K drones; *Flying Leathernecks* (1951); *Navy Log* (TVS, 1955–1958); *The Wings of Eagles* (1957); *South Pacific* (1958); *The Gallant Hours* (1960); *Baa Baa Black Sheep* (TVS, 1976–1978).

G-73 MALLARD

First flight: April 30, 1946. Twin-engined amphibian seaplane designed as a larger G-21 Goose replacement for commercial customers. Only 59 were built from 1946 to 1951.

Other Notable Titles: *Miami Vice* (TVS, 1984–1989).

HU-16 ALBATROSS

First flight: October 1, 1947. Twin-engined amphibious seaplane designed for SAR and utility duties. Numerous serial number, designation and inter-service exchanges meant a colorful history

for many airframes. In all, 466 were built from 1946 to 1961. The last HU-16E was retired from U.S. military service in 1983.

Other Notable Titles: *Battle Taxi* (1955), background only.

F9F PANTHER / COUGAR

First flight: November 21, 1947. Single-engined naval fighter originally built with a straight wing, then from 1951 with a swept wing, named the Cougar. Redesignated as the F-9 in 1962. Best known on film for its appearance in *The Bridges at Toko-Ri* (1954).

Other Notable Titles: *Flat Top* (1952); *Men of the Fighting Lady* (1954).

A-6 INTRUDER

First flight: April 19, 1960. Twin-engined naval attack aircraft. A total of 880 were built from 1959 to 1991, with 170 being the EA-6B Prowler, which

G-73		SN or Reg. at Time of		
Type	*msn*	*Filming*	*Title*	*Remarks / Film Markings*
G-73 Mallard	J-22	VH-LAW	*Sky Pirates* (1986)	Flying
G-73 Mallard	J-39	N2975	*Slattery's Hurricane* (1949)	Flying

HU-16 Albatross		SN or Reg. at Time of		
Type	*msn*	*Filming*	*Title*	*Remarks / Film Markings*
HU-16B Albatross	G-99	N44HQ	*Act of Valor* (2012)	Ex-51-025
HU-16D Albatross	G-425	N20861	*The Dark Knight* (2008)	Ex-BuNo. 141278, brief appearance
HU-16E Albatross	G-334	51-7245	*Flight from Ashiya* (1964)	Ex-USCG UF-2G s/n 7245
HU-16E Albatross	G-335	N29853	*The Expendables* (2010)	Built as a USAF SA-16A (s/n 51-7246), to USCG as a UF-1G (s/n 7246), upgraded to UF-2G, redesignated as an HU-16E in 1962

F9F Panther / Cougar		SN or Reg. at Time of		
Type	*msn*	*Filming*	*Title*	*Remarks / Film Markings*
F9F-5 Panther	unknown	BuNo. 125598	*The Bridges at Toko-Ri* (1954)	—
F9F-5 Panther	unknown	BuNo. 126000	*The Bridges at Toko-Ri* (1954)	—
F9F-5 Panther	unknown	BuNo. 126225	*The Bridges at Toko-Ri* (1954)	—

A-6 Intruder		SN or Reg. at Time of		
Type	*msn*	*Filming*	*Title*	*Remarks / Film Markings*
A-6A Intruder	I-87	BuNo. 151784	*Flight of the Intruder* (1990)	—
A-6A Intruder	I-167	BuNo. 152619	*Flight of the Intruder* (1990)	—
A-6A Intruder	I-310	BuNo. 155584	*Flight of the Intruder* (1990)	—
A-6E Intruder	I-528	BuNo. 158792	*Flight of the Intruder* (1990)	—
A-6E Intruder	I-619	BuNo. 161107	*Flight of the Intruder* (1990)	—

saw extensive use in Vietnam. Fantastic views of this aircraft in *Flight of the Intruder* (1990).

F-14 TOMCAT

First flight: December 21, 1970. Twin-engined naval defense fighter entered service in 1972 and was retired in 2006. In all, 712 were built, with 79 of these delivered to Iran pre–1979. Made famous worldwide for its big screen appearance in *Top Gun* (1986).

Other Notable Titles: *The Final Countdown* (1980), one was BuNo. 160382; *The Hunt for Red October* (1990); *JAG* (TVS, 1995–2005); *Executive Decision* (1996).

Gulfstream

American manufacturer of small private and commuter jet aircraft. Began in 1957 when the Grumman Aircraft Engr. Corp. built the Gulfstream civilian aircraft, which developed into a successful range of small civilian jets. Became the Grumman-American Division in 1962; in 1978 Grumman sold the division to American Jet Industries as Gulfstream-American Corp.; became Gulfstream Aerospace Corp. in 1983; acquired by General Dynamics in 1999; acquired Galaxy Aerospace in 2001, rebranding their line of jet aircraft. Like the Learjet, Gulfstream's range of jets

have been used by filmmakers in a variety of screen roles as symbols of power and wealth.

Hamilton

Founded in 1910 as the Hamilton Aero Mfg. Co. by Thomas Hamilton; became the Hamilton Metalplane Co. after merging with the Boeing Airplane Co. in 1926; was absorbed into the United Aircraft & Transport Corp. in 1929, and stopped aircraft production in 1932 to focus on propeller manufacturing.

Notable Title: *Only Angels Have Wings* (1939), H-47 Metalplane.

Handley Page

British manufacturer founded as Handley Page Ltd. in 1909 by Frederick Handley Page. Became well known during World War I for producing the O/400 and V/1500 heavy bombers and during World War II with the Hampden and Halifax bombers. Acquired Miles Aircraft Co. postwar as Handley Page (Reading) Ltd. Also produced the Victor V-bomber for the RAF plus the Hermes and Herald for civil airlines. Unable to compete, the company was liquidated in 1970; their last aircraft, the Jetstream, went on to success with Scottish Aviation, then BAe from 1977.

F-14 Tomcat Type	msn	SN or Reg. at Time of Filming	Title	Remarks / Film Markings
F-14A Tomcat	284	BuNo. 160665	*Top Gun* (1986)	—
F-14A Tomcat	300	BuNo. 160681	*Top Gun* (1986)	—
F-14A Tomcat	313	BuNo. 160694	*Top Gun* (1986)	—

Gulfstream Type	msn	SN or Reg. at Time of Filming	Title	Remarks / Film Markings
Gulfstream II	42	N8000J	*The A-Team* (TVS, 1983–1987)	"Guest appearance" in pilot episode
Gulfstream II	220	N315TS	*True Lies* (1994)	Juno's private jet
Gulfstream V	517	HB-IMJ	*Quantum of Solace* (2008)	Greene's jet to Bolivia
Gulfstream G450	4004	N4500X	*Transformers: Dark of the Moon* (2011)	Owned by director Michael Bay

Handley Page Type	msn	SN or Reg. at Time of Filming	Title	Remarks / Film Markings
HP.70 Halifax C.Mk. VIII	unknown	G-AJNW	*No Highway in the Sky* (1951)	Ex-RAF PP296, as "Rutland Reindeer" airliner
HP.137 Jetstream 1	209	N5VH	*Moonraker* (1979)	Marked as "Apollo Airways"

Hawker

British manufacturer founded in the bankruptcy of Sopwith Aviation in 1920 as H.G. Hawker Engineering. Renamed Hawker Aircraft Ltd. in 1933; purchased Gloster Aircraft in 1934. With Armstrong Whitworth Aircraft Co., formed Hawker Siddeley Aircraft Ltd. in 1935, with each company trading under its original name. Hawker produced some immortal fighter designs during and after World War II, including the Hurricane, Typhoon, Tempest and Hunter. The Hawker name was gone by 1963 but survives at U.S. company Raytheon in their small jet range.

Other Notable Title: *High Flight* (1957), Hawker Hunter F.Mk. 4.

HURRICANE

First flight: November 6, 1935. Single-engined fighter of World War II was instrumental in winning the Battle of Britain. While many Spitfire fighters were retained after the war for further service or preserved as gate guardians outside RAF Airfields, the same could not be said for the

Hawker Type	msn	SN or Reg. at Time of Filming	Title	Remarks / Film Markings
Hunter F.Mk. 51 seen	41H-680262	N72602	*The Right Stuff* (1983)	Ex–Denmark E-403, briefly
Hunter F.Mk. 6	8798	N-202	*The Man with the Golden Gun* (1974)	Nose section only
		N-202	*Octopussy* (1983)	Nose section only
Harrier T.Mk. 4A	212034	(RAF) ZB602	*The Living Daylights* (1987)	VTOL RAF fighter

Hurricane Type	msn	SN or Reg. at Time of Filming	Title	Remarks / Film Markings
Hurricane Mk. I	unknown	L1591	*Angels One Five* (1952)	RAF owned, static / studio scenes
Hurricane Mk. I	W/05422	L1592	*Angels One Five* (1952)	RAF owned, static
Hurricane Mk. I	unknown	P2617	*Angels One Five* (1952)	RAF owned, static as US-B / P2619
		P2617	*Reach for the Sky* (1956)	RAF owned, taxi scenes only as T4107
		P2617	*Battle of Britain* (1969)	RAF owned, taxi scenes only
Hurricane Mk. IIc	14533	G-AMAU	*Angels One Five* (1952)	Ex-RAF PZ865, flying
		G-AMAU	*Battle of Britain* (1969)	Flying
Hurricane Mk. IIc	41H/469290	LF363	*Angels One Five* (1952)	RAF owned, flying
		LF363	*Reach for the Sky* (1956)	RAF owned, flying as T4125
		LF363	*The One That Got Away* (1957)	RAF owned, ground scenes only
		LF363	*Battle of Britain* (1969)	RAF Memorial Flight, flying
Hurricane Mk. IIc	unknown	LF378	*Reach for the Sky* (1956)	Taxi scenes only as V5276
Hurricane Mk. IIc	unknown	LF751	*Battle of Britain* (1969)	Static only
Hurricane Mk. IIc	unknown	(Portugal) 544	*Angels One Five* (1952)	Flying
Hurricane Mk. IIc	unknown	(Portugal) 554	*Angels One Five* (1952)	Flying
Hurricane Mk. IIc	unknown	(Portugal) 600	*Angels One Five* (1952)	Flying
Hurricane Mk. IIc	unknown	(Portugal) 601	*Angels One Five* (1952)	Flying
Hurricane Mk. IIc	unknown	(Portugal) 624	*Angels One Five* (1952)	Flying
(CCF) Hurricane Mk. XII	42012	G-AWLW	*Battle of Britain* (1969)	Ex-RCAF 5377, flying
(CCF) Hurricane Mk. XIIa	72036	G-HURI	*Pearl Harbor* (2001)	Ex-RCAF 5711
(CCF) Sea Hurricane Mk. Ib	CCF/41H.4013	Z7015	*Battle of Britain* (1969)	Taxi scenes only
		G-BKTH	*Pearl Harbor* (2001)	—

Hawker Hurricane. Some survived, of course, and luckily for them the British film industry produced motion pictures such as *Angels One Five* (1952), *Reach for the Sky* (1956), and the *Battle of Britain* (1969), which saw a number of the type saved and restored.

Helio

American manufacturer founded in 1948 as the Koppen-Bollinger Aircraft Corp. for the purpose of building light STOL aircraft. Renamed as the Helio Aircraft Corp. in the early 1950s and became well known for their Courier and Super Courier range of STOL aircraft. Acquired by General Aircraft Corp. in 1969 and renamed the Helio Aircraft Co. with production continuing until 1974.

Hiller

American helicopter manufacturer founded in 1942 by Stanley Hiller as Hiller Industries; renamed United Helicopters, Inc., from 1944 to 1952, when it became Hiller Helicopters Corp. Best known for its Hiller Model 12 chopper, built for the U.S. Army as the H-23 Raven.

Acquired by Fairchild in 1964 as the Hiller Helicopter Division of the Fairchild-Hiller Corp.

Hispano

Spanish manufacturer founded in 1939 as La Hispano Aviacion S.A., which was merged with CASA in 1972. Their most famous product was the Hispano HA-1112 Buchon, a license-built version of the German Messerschmitt Bf. 109. Up

Helio		SN or Reg. at Time of		
Type	*msn*	*Filming*	*Title*	*Remarks / Film Markings*
U-10B Super Courier	636	N101BL	*Waterworld* (1995)	Ex–63-13183 and ex–Air America (s/n 183). Converted as a derelict but flyable floatplane

Hiller		SN or Reg. at Time of		
Type	*msn*	*Filming*	*Title*	*Remarks / Film Markings*
Model UH-12C	WH6003	N780ND	*From Russia with Love* (1963)	Seen at SPECTRE HQ and in finale
Model UH-12E4	2070	G-ASAZ	*Goldfinger* (1964)	Goldfinger's helicopter as NASAZ

Hispano		SN or Reg. at Time of		
Type	*msn*	*Filming*	*Title*	*Remarks / Film Markings*
HA-1112-M1L Buchon	067	G-AWHE	*Battle of Britain* (1969)	Ex–Spain C.4K-31, flying
		N109ME	*The Hindenburg* (1975)	Briefly seen
HA-1112-M1L Buchon	120	N700E	*Pearl Harbor* (2001)	Ex–Spain C.4K-77, flying
HA-1112-M1L Buchon	129	G-AWHF	*Battle of Britain* (1969)	Ex–Spain C.4K-61, flying, crashed during filming
HA-1112-M1L Buchon	139	G-AWHG	*Battle of Britain* (1969)	Ex–Spain C.4K-75, flying
HA-1112-M1L Buchon	145	G-AWHH	*Battle of Britain* (1969)	Ex–Spain C.4K-105, flying
HA-1112-M1L Buchon	156	D-FMBB	*Valkyrie* (2008)	Ex–C.4K-87
HA-1112-M1L Buchon	164	C.4K-114	*Battle of Britain* (1969)	Static only
HA-1112-M1L Buchon	166	G-AWHI	*Battle of Britain* (1969)	Ex–Spain C.4K-106, flying
HA-1112-M1L Buchon	170	C.4K-107	*Battle of Britain* (1969)	Taxi scenes only
		G-BOML	*Piece of Cake* (TVMS, 1988)	Flying
		G-BOML	*Memphis Belle* (1990)	Flying
HA-1112-M1L Buchon	171	G-AWHJ	*Battle of Britain* (1969)	Ex–Spain C.4K-100, flying
HA-1112-M1L Buchon	178	C.4K-121	*Battle of Britain* (1969)	Taxi scenes only
HA-1112-M1L Buchon	186	G-AWHL	*Battle of Britain* (1969)	Ex–Spain C.4K-122, flying
		G-AWHL	*Patton* (1970)	Doubles as P-51B, not used in finished film

Hispano (Type)	(msn)	(SN or Reg. at Time of Filming)	(Title)	(Remarks / Film Markings)
HA-1112-M1L Buchon	187	G-AWHM	Battle of Britain (1969)	Ex–Spain C.4K-99, flying
HA-1112-M1L Buchon	190	G-AWHD	Battle of Britain (1969)	Ex–Spain C.4K-126, flying
HA-1112-M1L Buchon	193	G-AWHN	Battle of Britain (1969)	Ex–Spain C.4K-130, flying
HA-1112-M1L Buchon	194	C.4K-134	Battle of Britain (1969)	Taxi scenes only
HA-1112-M1L Buchon	195	C.4K-135	Battle of Britain (1969)	Taxi scenes only
HA-1112-M1L Buchon	199	G-AWHO	Battle of Britain (1969)	Ex–Spain C.4K-127, flying
HA-1112-M1L Buchon	201	C.4K-131	Battle of Britain (1969)	Taxi scenes only
HA-1112-M1L Buchon	208	G-AWHP	Battle of Britain (1969)	Ex–Spain C.4K-144, flying
HA-1112-M1L Buchon	213	D-FEHD	Piece of Cake (TVMS, 1988)	Flying
		D-FEHD	Memphis Belle (1990)	Flying, marked as 15
HA-1112-M1L Buchon	220	G-AWHR	Battle of Britain (1969)	Ex–Spain C.4K-152, flying
HA-1112-M1L Buchon	223	G-AWHK	Battle of Britain (1969)	Ex–Spain C.4K-102, flying
		G-BWUE	Valkyrie (2008)	Flying
HA-1112-M1L Buchon	225	C.4K-159	Battle of Britain (1969)	Crashed before filming began
HA-1112-M1L Buchon	228	G-AWHS	Battle of Britain (1969)	Ex–Spain C.4K-170, flying
		G-AWHS	Patton (1970)	Doubles as P-51B, not used in finished film
HA-1112-M1L Buchon	234	G-AWHT	Battle of Britain (1969)	Ex–Spain C.4K-169, flying
HA-1112-M1L Buchon	235	C.4K-172	Battle of Britain (1969)	Taxi scenes only
		G-HUNN	Piece of Cake (TVMS, 1988)	Flying
		G-HUNN	Memphis Belle (1990)	Flying, marked as 14
		N109GU	The Tuskegee Airmen (TVM, 1995)	Flying
HA-1112-M1L Buchon	unknown	C.4K-30	Battle of Britain (1969)	Static only
HA-1112-M1L Buchon	unknown	C.4K-111	Battle of Britain (1969)	Static only
HA-1112-M1L Buchon	unknown	C.4K-154	Battle of Britain (1969)	Static only
HA-1112-M4L Buchon	40/2	G-AWHC	Battle of Britain (1969)	Ex–Spain C.4K-112, camera-plane

Hispano HA-1112M1L Buchon G-BOML (msn 170), painted as a Luftwaffe Bf 109 for the 1989 film *Memphis Belle*. Photograph: Derek Ferguson.

until the film *Battle of Britain* was made in 1969, the German Messerschmitt Bf. 109 was represented on Hollywood screens by various types of period aircraft that were simply refitted or repainted to look like the famous fighter. Commonly in the U.S., these were the P-51 Mustang in such films as *A Guy Named Joe* (1943), *Sahara* (1943) and *Fighter Squadron* (1948). In Europe a common type used was the Nord 1002 as seen in *633 Squadron* (1963) or the Messerschmitt Bf. 108 as in *Von Ryan's Express* (1965). With Group Captain Hamish MaHaddie's acquisition of the Spanish Air Force's retired Hispano fighters in 1966 for *Battle of Britain*, there was finally a fair representation of the German fighter on-screen. Since then, these carefully preserved Warbirds have appeared in a number of Hollywood films as the formidable German fighter.

Hughes

Founded by Howard Hughes in 1932 as the Hughes Aircraft Division of the Hughes Tool Co.; built the Hughes H-1 Racer, XF-11 prototype and H-4 Hercules flying boat. After World War II, founded the Aerospace Group, developing electronics and other aeronautical technologies. Also developed several successful helicopter types with the Hughes 300, 500 series and AH-64 Apache; the Helicopter Division was acquired by McDonnell Douglas in 1984. What remained of the Hughes Aerospace divisions was merged into the Raytheon Co. in 1997. Further details see: McDONNELL DOUGLAS.

SERIES 300

First flight: October 2, 1956. Single-engined three-seat light helicopter for civilian sales and military use as the TH-55A Osage. Manufacturing rights were acquired in 1986 by the Schweizer Aircraft Corp., who then continued production. Other Notable Titles: *Sky Heist* (TVM, 1975).

SERIES 500 / OH-6 CAYUSE / AH-6 LITTLE BIRD

First flight (YOH-6A): February 27, 1963. Single-engined utility helicopter first built as a

Hughes		SN or Reg. at Time of		
Type	msn	Filming	Title	Remarks / Film Markings
H-1B Racer	—	NR258Y	*The Aviator* (2004)	Models and CGI only
H-4 Hercules	—	NX37602	*Tucker: The Man and His Dream* (1988)	Brief scene inside Long Beach dome
		NX37602	*The Aviator* (2004)	Models and CGI only
XF-11	—	44-70155	*The Aviator* (2004)	Models and CGI only

Series 300		SN or Reg. at Time of		
Type	msn	Filming	Title	Remarks / Film Markings
Series 300	15-0025	ZK-HGD	*Race for the Yankee Zephyr* (1981)	Mock-up, marked as ZK-HHQ
Series 300	44-0059	N9341F	*Jaws 2* (1978)	Flying
Series 300	128-0399	N9542F	*Lone Wolf McQuade* (1983)	Flying
Series 300C	61-0120	N9666F	*The Gauntlet* (1977)	Flying
Series 300C	113-0258	ZK-HHQ	*Race for the Yankee Zephyr* (1981)	Flying
Series 300C	99-0829	N58384	*The A-Team* (TVS, 1983-1987)	"Guest appearance"

Series 500...		SN or Reg. at Time of		
Type	msn	Filming	Title	Remarks / Film Markings
Series 500C	52-0378S	N9103F	*Birds of Prey* (TVM, 1973)	Flying
Series 500C	72-0398S	N9128F	*The Sugarland Express* (1974)	Brief appearance
Series 500C	33-0459S	N9134F	*Capricorn One* (1978)	Gunship No. 2, most likely used but not confirmed
Series 500C	113-0537S	N4EE	*Deadly Encounter* (TVM, 1982)	Flying
Series 500C	14-0557S	N500WH	*Escape to Witch Mountain* (1975)	Flying

Series 500...		(SN or Reg. at Time of		
(Type)	(msn)	Filming)	(Title)	(Remarks / Film Markings)
Series 500C	24-0564S	N501WH	Capricorn One (1978)	Gunship No. 1
Series 500C	104-0656S	N9221F	Spencer's Pilots (TVS, 1976)	Flying in regular episodes
Series 500C	15-0699S	N506WW	240-Robert (TVS, 1979-1981)	Doubles as a county sheriff helicopter
Series 500C	115-0778S	N9267F	Magnum P.I. (TVS, 1980-1988)	"Guest appearance" in one episode
		N9267F	Airwolf (TVS, 1984-1987)	"Guest appearance" in several episodes
Series 500C	46-0811S	ZK-HKM	Race for the Yankee Zephyr (1981)	Briefly seen in opening credits
Series 500D	87-0184D	N8673F	The A-Team (TVS, 1983-1987)	"Guest appearance" in one episode
		N8673F	Airwolf (TVS, 1984-1987)	"Guest appearance" in several episodes
Series 500D	18-0254D	N9276F	Airwolf (TVS, 1984-1987)	"Guest appearance"
Series 500D	108-0349D	N58243	Magnum P.I. (TVS, 1980-1988)	TC's chopper, seen during opening titles, long skids with float bags. Crashed during filming on November 19, 1980
Series 500D	29-0460D	ZK-HMB	Race for the Yankee Zephyr (1981)	Seen in opening credits
Series 500D	119-0614D	N4943T	Magnum P.I. (TVS, 1980-1988)	TC's chopper, only seen in later seasons
Series 500D	129-0624D	N58428	Blue Thunder (1983)	Gunship conversion
		N58428	Deal of the Century (1983)	Gunship conversion
		N58428	The A-Team (TVS, 1983-1987)	"Guest appearance" in several episodes
		N58428	Airwolf (TVS, 1984-1987)	"Guest appearance" in several episodes
		N58428	Street Hawk (TVS, 1985)	"Guest appearance" in one episode
Series 500D	10-0654D	N58308	The A-Team (TVS, 1983-1987)	"Guest appearance" in a memorable chase scene shot in Malibu, California, with a UH-1H Huey
Series 500D	50-0701D	N1095A	Magnum P.I. (TVS, 1980-1988)	TC's chopper, most utilized helicopter, short skids
Series 500D	81-1075D	N5108E	The Osterman Weekend (1983)	Flying
Series MD 520N	LN024	N599DB	Speed (1994)	Flying
Series MD 530F	0600FF	N530MG	Komodo vs. Cobra (2005)	This is not the original N530MG Defender
Series MD 600N	RN023	N511VA	Die Another Day (2002)	Seen at the end of the final scene
Series MD 600N	RN042	N451DL	Casino Royale (2006)	MI6 helicopter
Series MD 900 Explorer	900-00010	N9208V	Die Another Day (2002)	Marked as CU-H13
AH-6J Little Bird	41-0937D	84-24319	Black Hawk Down (2001)	Flying
AH-6J Little Bird	unknown	89-25354	Black Hawk Down (2001)	Flying, most utilized for filming
AH-6J Little Bird	unknown	95-25371	Black Hawk Down (2001)	Flying
MH-6J Little Bird	unknown	81-23653	Black Hawk Down (2001)	Flying

military observation chopper but also developed for civil operators. Further evolved as the MD 500 by McDonnell Douglas from 1984. Like the Bell 206 series, the Hughes 500 has enjoyed a long and well-exposed career on the big and small screens. Of course, the list below only covers a very few of the aircraft employed over the years, but few can argue the fame this helicopter has gained from the *Magnum P.I.* TV series.

Other Notable Titles: *Diamonds Are Forever*

(1971); *Apocalypse Now* (1979), OH-6A; *Fire Birds* (1990); *Last Action Hero* (1993); *Outbreak* (1995); *Mission: Impossible* (1996); *The Italian Job* (2003), false reg. N723KP; *The A-Team* (2010).

Hunting *see* Percival

Israel Aircraft Industries (IAI)

Originally founded in 1953 as Bedek Aircraft Co., it became Israel Aircraft Industries Ltd. in 1967 and later Israel Aerospace Industries Ltd. Performs many upgrades for existing aircraft types both military and civilian. Some of its best known aircraft include the Westwind and Astra/Galaxy business jets plus the Nesher and Kfir jet fighters based on the French Mirage.

Other Notable Titles: *Iron Eagle* (1986) and *Iron Eagle II* (1988), Kfirs doubling as MiGs.

Junkers

German manufacturer founded in 1895 by Hugo Junkers became a pioneering aircraft company experimenting with metal construction while also producing aero engines. From 1933 the Nazi Party took control of the company, forcing Junkers to leave. He died two years later, but the company, under his name, went on to produce some of the finest German aircraft of World War

II such as the Ju 52 transport, Ju 87 Stuka and Ju 88 bomber / night fighter.

Kaman

Founded in 1945 as the Kaman Aircraft Corp. in Bloomfield, Connecticut, by Charles Kaman. Remains a contractor in the aerospace industry and is known as having manufactured two minor but notable helicopters, the H-43 Huskie and SH-2 Seasprite.

Notable Titles: *The Starfighters* (1964), HH-43B (59-1580); *Airport '77* (1977), SH-2 Seasprite.

Keith Rider

American manufacturer founded by Keith Rider around 1930, produced a series of air racing monoplanes. Company also known as simply "Rider."

Learjet / Gates Learjet

Iconic American private jet company was founded by Bill Lear in 1960 as the Swiss American Aviation Corp. In 1962 all tooling was shifted to the U.S. and the company became the Lear Jet Corp.; merged with Gates Rubber Co. in 1967 to be renamed Gates

Learjet Corp. by 1970; acquired by Bombardier Inc. in 1990, but aircraft are still produced under

Israel Aircraft...		SN or Reg. at Time of			
Type	msn	Filming	Title		Remarks / Film Markings
1124N Sea Scan	152	4X-CJC	*Live And Let Die* (1973)		Mr. Big's private jet

Junkers		SN or Reg. at Time of		
Type	msn	Filming	Title	Remarks / Film Markings
Ju 52/3mg4e	6595	HB-HOT	*Where Eagles Dare* (1968)	Ex-Swiss AF s/n A-107
		HB-HOT	*Valkyrie* (2008)	Hitler's transport marked as D-2600
Ju 52/3mg4e	6610	HB-HOP	*Valkyrie* (2008)	—

Keith Rider		SN or Reg. at Time of		
Type	msn	Filming	Title	Remarks / Film Markings
R3	A1	NR14215	*Test Pilot* (1938)	Flying, rebuilt as Marcoux-Bromberg Special
R4	unknown	NR261Y	*Test Pilot* (1938)	Flying, rebuilt as Schoenfeldt Firecracker
R5	unknown	NX264Y	*Tail Spin* (1939)	Flying, rebuilt as Marcoux-Bromberg Jackrabbit
R6	unknown	NX96Y	*Tail Spin* (1939)	Flying

the Learjet name. The Learjet is a well-recognized private jet on the big and small screens and is often used by filmmakers as a status symbol of power and wealth in fictional storytelling.

Lockheed / Lockheed-Martin

Founded by Allan and Malcolm Loughead in 1912 as the Alco-Hydro-Aeroplane Co.; became the Loughead Aircraft Mfg. Co. in 1916; the Lockheed Aircraft Co. in 1926; had settled in Burbank as the Lockheed Aircraft Corp. by 1935; formed a subsidiary as the Vega Airplane Co. in 1937. During World War II established itself as one of the giants in aircraft manufacture with the Lockheed Twin series, P-38 and C-69 / C-121 Constellation. Built the hugely successful Shooting Star series post–World War II; opened its Marietta, Georgia, plant in 1951 and went on to build the C-130, C-141 and C-5 transports for the USAF. Also built the F-104 and SR-71 through its secret "Skunk Works" plant. Built the civil L-1011 Tristar at Palmdale. Became the Lockheed Corp. in 1977;

acquired the F-16 program from General Dynamics in 1992; became Lockheed-Martin Corp. in 1995 after a merger with Martin-Marietta.

MODEL 10 / 12 / 14 / 18 / 37 TWIN SERIES

First flight (Model 14): July 29, 1937. Twin-engined series built by Lockheed as commuter airliners, first as the L-10 Electra, then L-12 Electra Junior, L-14 Super Electra and L-18 Lodestar. Developed into military bombers during World War II as the Lockheed Hudson for export, C-60 Lodestar, Lockheed Ventura and PV-2 Harpoon for a total of 7,223 built. Numerous appearances on the big screen over the years, a few memorable titles would be *A Yank in the RAF* (1941), *Casablanca* (1942), and *Captains of the Clouds* (1942).

Model 10 / 12 Notable Titles: *The Man Who Found Himself* (1937); *Sky Giant* (1938); *Happy Landing* (1938); *Secret Service of the Air* (1939); *Five Came Back* (1939), flying stand-in for non-flying XC-12; *Men Against the Sky* (1940); *Dive Bomber* (1941); *Eagle Squadron* (1942); *A Guy*

Learjet...		SN or Reg. at Time of		
Type	msn	Filming	Title	Remarks / Film Markings
Learjet 23	23-038	LN-NPE	*The Last Safari* (1967)	Striking zebra-style livery
Learjet 24	24-123	N25LJ	*S.W.A.T.* (2003)	—
Learjet 24	24-167	N664CL	*When Time Ran Out* (1980)	—
		N664CL	*Knight Rider* (TVS, 1982–1986)	"Guest appearances"
Learjet 24A	24A-096	N1972L	*Airport 1975* (1974)	Clay Lacy owned Learjet
		N464CL	*Capricorn One* (1978)	Re-registered from N1972L
		N464CL	*The Courage and the Passion* (TVM, 1978)	—
		N464CL	*The A-Team* (TVS, 1983–1987)	As USAF VIP jet
Learjet 25	25-064	N564CL	*The Concorde...Airport '79* (1979)	—
Learjet 35	35-034	N37TA	*Licence to Kill* (1989)	—

Lockheed...		SN or Reg. at Time of		
Type	msn	Filming	Title	Remarks / Film Markings
9C Orion	180	NC12222	*The Bride Came C.O.D.* (1941)	—
8A Sirius	151	NC117W	*Flying G-Men* (1939 / serial)	—
1 Vega	40	N199E	*Amelia Earhart* (TVM, 1976)	Marked as N965Y
5B Vega	100	NC48M	*West Point of the Air* (1935)	—
		NC48M	*Wings in the Dark* (1935)	—
		NC48M	*Men With Wings* (1938)	Marked as *Miss Patricia*
		NC48M	*Only Angels Have Wings* (1939)	Damaged during production
5C Vega	102	NC19958	*Flying Wild* (1941)	—
	108	NC19958	*The Face Behind the Mask* (1941)	—
		NC19958	*The Bride Came C.O.D.* (1941)	—
		NC19958	*Flying Wild* (1941)	—
	171	NC965Y	*Border Flight* (1936)	—

Named Joe (1943); *The Desert Fox* (1951), as a German VIP transport, likely Paul Mantz's N60775.

Model 14 / 18 Notable Titles: *A Yank in the RAF* (1941); *Captains of the Clouds* (1942); *Destination Tokyo* (1943), Hudsons doubling for Doolittle B-25s; *Bomber's Moon* (1943); *Tokyo Joe* (1949); *The Malta Story* (1953); *The Sea Shall Not Have Them* (1954); *Don't Drink the Water* (1969); *Above and Beyond* (TVMS, 2006).

Model 37 Notable Titles: *Aerial Gunner* (1943), B-34 Lexington.

P-38 Lightning

First flight: January 27, 1939. Twin-engined, twin-boom fighter design saw extensive service during World War II, definitive variants were the P-38J and P-38L, which made up well over half of the 10,039 built. Had a memorable appearance in the 1943 smash hit *A Guy Named Joe*.

Other Notable Titles: *A Guy Named Joe* (1943), P-38E / F; *Fury in the Sky* (1943); *Swing Shift Maisie* (1943); *A Walk in the Sun* (1946); *Von Ryan's Ex-*

Twin Series...		SN or Reg. at Time of		
Type	msn	Filming	Title	Remarks / Film Markings
Model 10-A Electra	1070	NR16056	*Flight for Freedom* (1943)	Later to USAAF as UC-36A (s/n 42-57215)
Model 10-B Electra	1036	NC14958	*Crack-Up* (1936)	Later to USAAF as UC-36C (s/n 42-57222)
Model 12-A Electra Junior	1203	NC1161V	*Amelia Earhart* (TVM, 1976)	Flying, owned by renowned aerobatic pilot Art Scholl
		NC1161V	*The Amazing Howard Hughes* (TVM, 1977)	Flying
		NC1161V	*The A-Team* (TVS, 1983-1987)	"Guest appearance"
Model 12-A Electra Junior	1208	N2072	*Amelia* (2009)	Flying, marked as NR16020
Model 12-A Electra Junior	1214	N16085	*Amelia* (2009)	Non-flying, marked as NR16020
Model 12-A Electra Junior	1216	NX17342	*Flight Angels* (1940)	Later to RCAF (s/n 7653)
Model 12-A Electra Junior	1220	NC17376	*Flying Blind* (1941)	—
		NC17376	*Casablanca* (1942)	Later to USAAF as UC-40D (s/n 42-57504)
Model 12-A Electra Junior	1245	NC18957	*Flying Wild* (1941)	—
Model 12-A Electra Junior	1258	NC19933	*Flight to Nowhere* (1946)	Ex-USAAF UC-40A (s/n 38-540)
Model 12-A Electra Junior	1287	F-AZLL	*Amelia* (2009)	Flying, marked as NR16020
C-40A Electra Junior	1262	VH-HID	*Unbroken* (2014)	Ex-USAAC 38-545
Hudson Mk. III	414-2421	(RAF) T9386	*Desperate Journey* (1942)	Was the first Mk. III built, retained by Lockheed
Hudson Mk. III	414-2518	(RAF) T9465	*Coastal Command* (1942)	—
L-18 Lodestar	18-2023	NC25633	*Emergency Landing* (1941)	To RAF (s/n AX763)
L-18 Lodestar	18-2068	NC34900	*Emergency Landing* (1941)	To USAAF as C-56C (s/n 42-53499)
C-60A Lodestar	18-2496	N30F	*North by Northwest* (1959)	Ex-42-56023. Cargo plane at the end of the film. This aircraft is often quoted with c/n 18-2492 but this is incorrect

P-38 Lightning		SN or Reg. at		
Type	msn	Time of Filming	Title	Remarks / Film Markings
P-38J Lightning	422-4318	N38BP	*Aces: Iron Eagle III* (1992)	Ex-44-23314

press (1965), model only; *The Amazing Howard Hughes* (TVM, 1977), doubles as Hughes XF-11.

C-69 / C-121
CONSTELLATION SERIES

First flight: January 9, 1943. Elegant four-engined commercial airliner design drafted into military service as the C-69 during World War II and C-121 post–World War II. Also had a great civilian career as the L-1049 Super Connie; last

civilian version was known as the Starliner. The last military NC-121K was retired in 1982.

Other Notable Titles: *Blaze of Noon* (1947); *You Gotta Stay Happy* (1948), L-749; *Skyliner* (1949); *Mame* (1974).

P-80 / F-80 / T-33 SHOOTING STAR / F-94 STARFIRE

First flight: January 8, 1944. Single-engined jet fighter and jet trainer. The pop culture iconic image

C-69...		SN or Reg. at Time of		
Type	msn	Filming	Title	Remarks / Film Markings
L-1049H Super Constellation	1049H-4830	N6937C	*The Aviator* (2004)	TWA markings

P-80...		SN or Reg. at Time of		
Type	msn	Filming	Title	Remarks / Film Markings
P-80A Shooting Star	080-1041	44-85018	*Air Cadet* (1951)	—
P-80A Shooting Star	080-1175	44-85152	*Air Cadet* (1951)	Studio filming
P-80A Shooting Star	080-1283	44-85260	*Air Cadet* (1951)	—
P-80B Shooting Star	080-1782	45-8568	*Air Cadet* (1951)	—
P-80B Shooting Star	080-1799	45-8585	*Air Cadet* (1951)	—
P-80B Shooting Star	080-1810	45-8596	*Air Cadet* (1951)	—
P-80B Shooting Star	080-1896	45-8682	*Air Cadet* (1951)	—
P-80B Shooting Star	080-1904	45-8690	*Air Cadet* (1951)	Crashed for film
P-80B Shooting Star	080-1906	45-8692	*Air Cadet* (1951)	—
F-80C Shooting Star	080-1942	47-181	*Sabre Jet* (1953)	—
F-80C Shooting Star	080-1943	47-182	*Sabre Jet* (1953)	—
F-80C Shooting Star	080-1945	47-184	*Sabre Jet* (1953)	—
F-80C Shooting Star	080-1949	47-188	*Sabre Jet* (1953)	—
F-80C Shooting Star	080-1964	47-203	*Sabre Jet* (1953)	—
F-80C Shooting Star	080-2017	47-556	*The McConnell Story* (1955)	—
F-80C Shooting Star	080-2131	48-874	*One Minute to Zero* (1956)	—
F-80C Shooting Star	080-2132	48-875	*One Minute to Zero* (1956)	—
F-80C Shooting Star	080-2180	49-432	*The McConnell Story* (1955)	—
F-80C Shooting Star	080-2248	49-500	*Chain Lightning* (1950)	Briefly seen
F-80C Shooting Star	080-2256	49-508	*Chain Lightning* (1950)	Briefly seen
		49-508	*One Minute to Zero* (1956)	—
F-80C Shooting Star	080-2258	49-510	*Chain Lightning* (1950)	Briefly seen
F-80C Shooting Star	080-2404	49-656	*The McConnell Story* (1955)	—
F-80C Shooting Star	080-2534	49-786	*The McConnell Story* (1955)	—
F-80C Shooting Star	080-2719	49-1892	*Air Cadet* (1951)	—
T-33A Shooting Star	580-5014	48-369	*Air Cadet* (1951)	—
T-33A Shooting Star	580-5051	49-901	*Air Cadet* (1951)	—
T-33A Shooting Star	580-5052	49-902	*Air Cadet* (1951)	—
T-33A Shooting Star	580-5230	50-377	*Air Cadet* (1951)	Studio filming
T-33A Shooting Star	580-7681	52-9546	*This Island Earth* (1955)	—
F-94A Starfire	780-7001	49-2479	*Jet Pilot* (1957)	—
(Canadair) Silver Star Mk. 3	T33-98	N99184	*Terminal Velocity* (1994)	Ex-RCAF 21098, *The Red Knight*
(Canadair) Silver Star Mk. 3	T33-273	N12413	*The Right Stuff* (1983)	Ex-RCAF 21273
(Canadair) Silver Star Mk. 3	T33-456	N333MJ	*The Right Stuff* (1983)	Ex-RCAF 21456

of the American Air Force in the 1950s, this aircraft was depicted on everything from kids' products, comics, cartoons, to the many Hollywood films made during this period.

Other Notable Titles: *Tarantula!* (1956); *Thundering Jets* (1958); *The Crowded Sky* (1960); *A Gathering of Eagles* (1963).

F-104 STARFIGHTER

First flight: March 4, 1954. Single-engined jet fighter is literally an engine with wings bolted on! Altogether, 2,580 built from 1953 to 1979, with 1,790 of these built outside the U.S. in Belgium, Canada, Italy, Japan, the Netherlands and West Germany. Excellent views of this aircraft can be seen in the 1983 film *The Right Stuff*.

Other Notable Titles: *The Starfighters* (1964), F-104A / C / D; *The Courage and the Passion* (TVM, 1978).

C-130 HERCULES

First flight: August 28, 1954. Four-engined turboprop transport. Classic, timeless design that re-

mains in production over sixty years after its first flight. It is employed in all kinds of roles in all branches of the U.S. military forces with large export orders to air forces around the world. Its had a few bright moments on the big screen, one of them being the Bond film *The Living Daylights* (1987).

Other Notable Titles: *The Green Berets* (1968); *Outbreak* (1995); *The Perfect Storm* (2000); *The A-Team* (2010), CGI created only; *Act of Valor* (2012).

L-1329 JETSTAR

First flight: September 4, 1957. Four-engined civilian business jet in service throughout the 1960s and 1970s; 18 delivered to the USAF as the C-140.

SR-71 BLACKBIRD

First flight (SR-71A): December 22, 1964. Twin-engined, high-altitude reconnaissance aircraft, the Blackbird first evolved as the A-12 and F-12 before 32 of the definitive SR-71 design were

F-104 Starfighter		SN or Reg. at Time of		
Type	*msn*	*Filming*	*Title*	*Remarks / Film Markings*
YF-104A Starfighter	183-1010	55-2964	*X-15* (1961)	Flying
F-104G Starfighter	683-2026	63-13243	*The Right Stuff* (1983)	Flying as NF-104A
(Fokker) F-104G Starfighter	683D-8002	63-13269	*The Right Stuff* (1983)	Flying as NF-104A

C-130 Hercules		SN or Reg. at Time of		
Type	*msn*	*Filming*	*Title*	*Remarks / Film Markings*
C-130A Hercules	182-3119	N121TG	*The Dark Knight Rises* (2012)	Ex-56-511, flying scenes in the UK
C-130E Karnaf	382-3940	(Israel) 311	*Iron Eagle II* (1988)	Ex-63-7870
C-130H Hercules	382-5223	89-9106	*The Delta Force* (1986)	Marked with false reg. 14X-FBB
C-130H Karnaf	382-4430	(Israel) 102	*Iron Eagle II* (1988)	Ex-71-1374
HC-130H Hercules	382-4993	83-0007	*The Guardian* (2006)	Background
HC-130H Hercules	382-4999	83-0506	*The Guardian* (2006)	Background
HC-130H Hercules	382-5002	83-0507	*The Guardian* (2006)	Background
C-130K Hercules	382-4274	(RAF) XV306	*The Living Daylights* (1987)	Paratroop jump
CC-130H Hercules	382-4994	(CAF) 130334	*Iron Eagle IV* (1995)	—
L-100-20	382-4385	ZS-GSK	*The Wild Geese* (1978)	Named *Boland*

L-1329 JetStar		SN or Reg. at Time of		
Type	*msn*	*Filming*	*Title*	*Remarks / Film Markings*
L-1329 JetStar 6	1329-5023	N711Z	*Goldfinger* (1964)	Auric Enterprises Inc. and USAF VC-140B
L-1329 JetStar	1329-5108	N680TT	*Cliffhanger* (1993)	Flying

built. Served with the USAF up to 1998 and NASA up to 1999. An excellent, if fictional, depiction seen in the second *Transformers* movie.

Notable Titles: *D.A.R.Y.L.* (1985); *Armageddon* (1998), background; *Space Cowboys* (2000), s/n 61-7975; *Transformers: Revenge of the Fallen* (2009).

L-1011 Tristar

First flight: November 16, 1970. Three-engined, wide-body airliner. Lockheed's only entry in the jet-powered airliner market eventually lost out to the better selling DC-10 and 747 jumbo airliners. Notable for its regular appearance, as a wreck, on the long-running TV series *Lost*. Also the subject of the TV movie *The Ghost of Flight 401* (1978), based on the true-life L-1011 crash in the Everglades during 1972.

Other Notable Titles: *The Ghost of Flight 401* (TVM, 1978).

F-117 Nighthawk

First flight (YF-117A): June 18, 1981. Twin-engined stealth fighter design served from 1982 to 2008 with a total of 64 built. A top secret aircraft, much of which remains a mystery today, often the subject of many minor action / aviation films.

Notable Titles: *Executive Decision* (1996); *Black Thunder* (1998); *Stealth Fighter* (1999); *Flight of Fury* (2007); *Transformers* (2007).

F-22 Raptor

First flight: September 29, 1990. Twin-engined stealth fighter with 195 production examples built

from 1996 to 2011 with USAF service entry in 2005. A popular choice of fighter aircraft for recent action-orientated films.

Notable Titles: *Transformers* (2007); *The Day the Earth Stood Still* (2008); *Iron Man* (2008); *Transformers: Revenge of the Fallen* (2009); *Iron Man 2* (2010); *Skyline* (2010); *Transformers: Dark of the Moon* (2011).

F-35 Lightning II

First flight: October 24, 2000. Single-engined, multi-role stealth fighter is being developed for the USAF, U.S. Navy and USMC. Its intended to replace many of the front-line fighters such as the F-15, F-16 and even the F-22.

Notable Titles: *Superman Returns* (2006); *Live Free or Die Hard* (2007), CGI creation.

LTV Aerospace   *see*   Vought

Luft-Verkehrs-Gesellschaft

German manufacturer founded in 1912, which produced several biplane types during World War I.

Martin

Founded in 1912 as the Martin Co. by Glenn Martin followed by a merger with the Wright Co. as the Wright-Martin Corp. in 1916. In 1918 became the Martin Aircraft Co. and produced the MB-1 World War I bomber. Shifted to Baltimore

L-1011 Tristar		SN or Reg. at Time of		
Type	msn	Filming	Title	Remarks / Film Markings
L-1011-1 Tristar	193A-1005	TF-ABG	*Last Flight Out* (TVM, 1990)	Ex–Eastern Airlines N304EA
L-1011-1 Tristar	193A-1009	N783DL	*Lost* (TVS, 2004–2010)	Fuselage barged to Hawaii for beach wreck scenes
L-1011-1 Tristar	193B-1065	N31018	*The Langoliers* (TVM, 1995)	Mostly used in ground scenes
L-1011-1 Tristar	193A-1087	N330EA	*Passenger 57* (1992)	Marked as Atlantic International / AIA
L-1011-500 Tristar	193Y-1184	N755DL	*Die Hard 2* (1990)	Marked as NEA

Luft-Verkehrs-Gesellschaft		SN or Reg. at Time of		
Type	msn	Filming	Title	Remarks / Film Markings
LVG C.VI	4503	G-AANJ	*Biggles: Adventures in Time* (1986)	Background only

in 1929 and began making larger aircraft such as B-10 and China Clipper flying boats. During World War II became noted for the B-26 Marauder, PBM Mariner and JRM Mars. Postwar built the B-57 Canberra and P5M Marlin. Aircraft production ended in 1960 with the focus moving to missile and space technology. Merged with American-Marietta Corp. in 1961 to become Martin-Marietta Aerospace Corp. before finally merging with the Lockheed Corp. in 1995 to form the Lockheed-Martin Corp.

B-26 MARAUDER

First flight: November 25, 1940. Twin-engined medium bomber; 5,266 built from 1940 to 1945. A few appearances in several wartime films as listed below.

Notable Titles: *A Guy Named Joe* (1943), as Betty bombers; *Air Force* (1943); *God Is My Copilot* (1945); *Target Unknown* (1951); *Sky Commando* (1953).

McDonnell / McDonnell Douglas *see* Douglas

Mil

Iconic Russian helicopter manufacturer founded by Mikhail Mil in 1947 as the Mil Moscow Heli-

copter Plant. Produced some notable designs such as the Mi-12 Homer, the world's largest helicopter, and the famous Mi-24 Hind gunship so often depicted in "western cinema." Several designs are also produced by PZL-Swidnik in Poland.

Other Notable Titles: *Behind Enemy Lines* (2001) Mi-17 Hip.

Miles

British manufacturer founded in 1943 as Miles Aircraft Ltd., which had originally been founded in the early 1930s as Philips and Powis Aircraft. Acquired by Handley Page Ltd. in 1947 as Handley Page (Reading) Ltd. Frederick Miles founded F.G. Miles Ltd. in 1948 and continued production under the Miles banner until 1961, when a merger with Auster created Beagle Aircraft Ltd. Produced in significant quantities were the Magister, Master and Martinet light aircraft. Miles Marine and Structural Plastics Ltd. later created the two S.E.5a replicas for *The Blue Max* (1966). See also: ROYAL AIRCRAFT FACTORY.

Mitsubishi

Iconic Japanese manufacturer was first established in 1870 and grew to be a major industrial giant in Japan, involved in shipping, heavy indus-

Martin		SN or Reg. at Time of		
Type	msn	Filming	Title	Remarks / Film Markings
M-130 Clipper	558	NC14716	*China Clipper* (1936)	Flying boat
JRM-1 Mars	9267	C-FLYL	*The A-Team* (2010)	Ex-BuNo. 76823
XB-51	unknown	46-685	*Toward the Unknown* (1956)	As fictional "Gilbert XF-120"
Model 404	14135	N636X	*View from the Top* (2003)	Flying

Mil		SN or Reg. at Time of		
Type	msn	Filming	Title	Remarks / Film Markings
Mi-8MTV-1 Hip	96078	ER-MHZ	*Stealth* (2005)	Provided by Heli-Harvest Ltd., NZ
Mi-8T Hip	105103	D-HOXQ	*Die Another Day* (2002)	Marked as P-71
Mi-24P Hind	340335	(Hungary) 335	*A Good Day to Die Hard* (2013)	Gunship helicopter
Mi-26T Halo	34001212465	EW-260TF	*A Good Day to Die Hard* (2013)	Transport helicopter
(PZL-Swidnik) Mi-2 Hoplite	525-523-038	SP-SAP	*For Your Eyes Only* (1981)	Marked as 8P-8AP. General Gogol's helicopter

Miles		SN or Reg. at		
Type	msn	Time of Filming	Title	Remarks / Film Markings
Messenger Mk. 2A	6378	G-AKBO	*633 Squadron* (1964)	Brief appearance

try and aviation. Built the legendary A6M Zeke "Zero" fighter during World War II, plus the G4M Betty bomber. Re-established itself postwar, again in heavy industry, and license-built the F-86 Sabre, F-104 Starfighter and F-4 Phantom II. Traditionally the "Hollywood Zero," as the term goes, has been played by the North American AT-6 Texan, either simply painted up or extensively modified, as for *Tora! Tora! Tora!* (1970). The three aircraft listed below are original, salvaged airframes painstakingly rebuilt from the ground up, all having their Hollywood debuts in the 2001 film *Pearl Harbor*.

Morane-Saulnier

French manufacturer founded in 1911 by brothers Robert and Leon Morane and Raymond Saulnier. Renowned for their parasol wing designs, the company produced a large number of various aircraft. It was placed under Nazi control during World War II, producing aircraft for the Reich. Continued light aircraft design postwar and was absorbed into Sud Aviation by 1965.

Naval Aircraft Factory (NAF)

American manufacturer founded in 1917 by the U.S. Navy for the building of naval aircraft in World War I. Built a handful of designs but is best known for its N3N Canary biplane trainer, of which 997 were produced. Also built 156 Catalina aircraft as the PBN-1 Nomad during World War II. The plant was closed in 1945.

Other Notable Titles: *Wings of the Navy* (1939) N3N Canary.

Nieuport

French manufacturer founded in 1902 as Nieuport-Duplex for the building of engine parts. Reformed in 1909 building aircraft and went on to produce the famous Nieuport Model 17 to Model

Mitsubishi		SN or Reg. at Time of Filming		
Type	*msn*	*Filming*	*Title*	*Remarks / Film Markings*
A6M2-21 Zero	3869	N712Z	*Pearl Harbor* (2001)	Ex-Japanese s/n X-133, marked as AI-157
A6M3-22 Zero	3858	N553TT	*Pearl Harbor* (2001)	Marked as AI-112
A6M5-52 Zero	5357	N46770	*Pearl Harbor* (2001)	Ex-Japanese s/n 61-120, marked as 61-120 / AI-120

Morane-Saulnier		SN or Reg. at Time of Filming		
Type	*msn*	*Filming*	*Title*	*Remarks / Film Markings*
L Parasol (replica)	001	N323SS	*Amelia* (2009)	Briefly seen
MS.230	1049	F-BGMR	*The Blue Max* (1966)	Doubles as a new German prototype
MS.230	1076	F-BGJT	*The Blue Max* (1966)	Back-up aircraft only
MS.500 Criquet	637	G-AZMH	*The Eagle has Landed* (1977)	Doubles as a German type
MS.502 Criquet	544	F-BBUI	*Broken Journey* (1948)	Flying
MS.760A Paris	69	HB-PAA	*On Her Majesty's Secret Service* (1969)	Marked as J-4117

Naval Aircraft Factory		SN or Reg. at Time of Filming		
Type	*msn*		*Title*	*Remarks / Film Markings*
N3N-1 Canary	unknown	BuNo. 0701	*Dive Bomber* (1941)	—
N3N-3 Canary	unknown	BuNo. 1978	*Dive Bomber* (1942)	—
N3N-3 Canary	unknown	BuNo. 2590	*Dive Bomber* (1942)	—
N3N-3 Canary	unknown	BuNo. 2717	*Dive Bomber* (1942)	—
N3N-3 Canary	unknown	N45091	*North by Northwest* (1959)	Ex-BuNo. 4420. Flew in the famous crop-duster scene; this aircraft is often mistaken for a Stearman biplane, as a derelict was used for the post-crash fire scene

Nieuport Type	msn	SN or Reg. at Time of Filming	Title	Remarks / Film Markings
Nieuport 17 (replica)	No. 001	N117TB	*Flyboys* (2006)	Baslee-built flying replica
Nieuport 17 (replica)	No. 002	N117DD	*Flyboys* (2006)	Baslee-built flying replica
Nieuport 17 (replica)	No. 003	N117KP	*Flyboys* (2006)	Baslee-built flying replica
Nieuport 17 (replica)	No. 004	N117MR	*Flyboys* (2006)	Baslee-built flying replica
Nieuport 17 (replica)	LCNC 1967	N1290	*Flyboys* (2006)	Flying replica
Nieuport 17 (replica)	PFA/121-12351	N1977	*Flyboys* (2006)	Flying replica
Nieuport 28 (replica)	512	N4728V	*Lafayette Escadrille* (1958)	Flying

Hollywood stunt pilot and businessman Garland Lincoln rebuilt in 1932 a number of Nieuport 28 airframes, some designated as the Garland-Lincoln LF-1 / LF-2. Three featured an I-strut between the wings for strengthening and a 200 hp Wright J-4. The first LF flew on August 10, 1932.

Nieuport 28	unknown	N4	see "Other Notable Titles" below	—
Nieuport 28	110Esub	N2539	see "Other Notable Titles" below	—
Nieuport 28	RFC-25	N11504	see "Other Notable Titles" below	—
Nieuport 28	348	N926	see "Other Notable Titles" below	—
Nieuport 28 (LF-1)	3	N12237	*Ace of Aces* (1933)	Built for the film
		N12237	*Lafayette Escadrille* (1958)	Flying
		N12237	*The Great Waldo Pepper* (1975)	Crashed before filming began
Nieuport 28 (LF-1)	512	N10415	*Ace of Aces* (1933)	Built for the film
		N10415	*Men With Wings* (1938)	
Nieuport 28 (LF-2)	1466	N75W	*Ace of Aces* (1933)	Built for the film
		N75W	*Men With Wings* (1938)	
Nieuport 28 (LF-2)	unknown	N5038	*Ace of Aces* (1933)	Built for the film

One of several Nieuport 28 fighters owned by Tallmantz Aviation for film work. This one apparently flew in *The Dawn Patrol* (1930 / 1938). Photograph: James H. Farmer Collection.

28 biplane fighters used during World War I, especially by U.S. pilots flying in French service. The Nieuport name and company slowly faded away in the 1930s, and like most vintage-era aircraft, could only appear on the big screen as replicas or rebuilds, such as the Garland-Lincoln Nieuports listed below.

Other Notable Titles: *The Dawn Patrol* (1930 / 1938); *Heartbreak* (1931); *The Lost Squadron* (1932); *Sky Devils* (1932); *Ace of Aces* (1933); *The Eagle and the Hawk* (1933); *Hell in the Heavens* (1934); *Stunt Pilot* (1939).

Noorduyn

Canadian company founded as Noorduyn Aircraft Ltd. in 1934 by Robert Noorduyn. Began producing the popular Norseman bush plane from 1935; during World War II, license-produced the North American Harvard and continued to do so after being acquired by Canadian Car & Foundry (CCF) in 1946.

Nord

French company formed in 1954 on the merger of French manufacturers SFECMAS and SNCAN. Merged with Sud Aviation in 1970 to form SNIAS, later renamed Aerospatiale. Best known aircraft include the Nord Pingouin liaison aircraft and the Nord Noratlas twin-boom transport.

North American

Founded as a holding company in 1928, it became North American Aviation, Inc., in 1935 and went on to become one of the giant U.S. manufacturers during World War II and beyond, building the famous AT-6 Texan, B-25 Mitchell, P-51 Mustang, F-86 Sabre, A-5 Vigilante and T-28 Trojan. Renamed North American Rockwell Corp. in 1967 after a merger with Rockwell Standard Corp., then Rockwell International Corp. in 1973. Further details see: ROCKWELL.

AT-6 (T-6) Texan / Harvard Series

First flight: April 1, 1935. Single-engined advanced trainer became one of the most respected trainers of all time with over 21,000 built in total, including production in Japan and Sweden. Widely known in film circles as the "Hollywood Zero" because of the aircraft's ability to be easily converted into the famous Japanese fighter. The list below identifies mostly these productions, along with the most notable ones as the classic American trainer.

Noorduyn		SN or Reg. at Time of		
Type	msn	Filming	Title	Remarks / Film Markings
Norseman Mk. I	1	CF-AYO	*Captains of the Clouds* (1942)	Flew as James Cagney's aircraft CF-HGO

Nord		SN or Reg. at Time of		
Type	msn	Filming	Title	Remarks / Film Markings
Model 1002 Pingouin II	188	F-BFYX	*633 Squadron* (1964)	Doubles as Messerschmitt Bf 109
Model 1002 Pingouin II	264	F-BGVU	*633 Squadron* (1964)	Doubles as Messerschmitt Bf 109
Model 3400	37	G-ZARA	*Empire of the Sun* (1987)	Background, marked as 2

AT-6…		SN or Reg. at Time of		
Type	msn	Filming	Title	Remarks / Film Markings
AT-6 Texan	59-1969	40-2143	*Air Force* (1943)	Briefly seen
AT-6A Texan	78-6227	41-15849	*Aerial Gunner* (1943)	—
AT-6A Texan	78-6648	41-16270	*Aerial Gunner* (1943)	—
AT-6C Texan	88-12044	G-BGOV	*Airline* (TVS, 1982)	Ex-41-33573, flying
AT-6D Texan	88-17380	42-85599	*The Tuskegee Airmen* (TVM, 1995)	Flying
AT-6D Texan	88-17890	42-86109	*Air Cadet* (1951)	Studio filming
AT-6F Texan	121-42541	N7446C	unknown	Ex-44-81819, Zero conversion

AT-6...		(SN or Reg. at Time of		
(Type)	(msn)	Filming)	(Title)	(Remarks / Film Markings)
SNJ-3 Texan	77-5963	BuNo. 6786	*Dive Bomber* (1941)	—
SNJ-4 Texan	88-13171	N7062C	*Tora! Tora! Tora!* (1970)	Ex-BuNo.27675, Kate conversion
		N7062C	*Baa Baa Black Sheep* (TVS, 1976–1978)	Flying
		N7062C	*War and Remembrance* (TVMS, 1988)	Doubles as a Douglas TBD-1
SNJ-5 Texan	88-14446	N7986C	*Tora! Tora! Tora!* (1970)	Ex-BuNo. 51698, Zero conversion
SNJ-5 Texan	88-15194	N52006	*The Tuskegee Airmen* (TVM, 1995)	Ex-BuNo. 52006, flying
SNJ-5 Texan	88-15757	N3242G	*Tora! Tora! Tora!* (1970)	Ex-BuNo. 43766, Kate conversion
		N3242G	*Pearl Harbor* (2001)	—
SNJ-5 Texan	88-16686	N3725G	*Tora! Tora! Tora!* (1970)	Ex-BuNo. 84875, Kate conversion
		N3725G	*Pearl Harbor* (2001)	—
SNJ-5 Texan	88-17652	N6438D	*Tora! Tora! Tora!* (1970)	Ex-BuNo. 90654, Kate conversion
		N6438D	*Baa Baa Black Sheep* (TVS, 1976–1978)	—
SNJ-5 Texan	88-17780	N7130C	*Tora! Tora! Tora!* (1970)	Ex-BuNo. 90712, Kate conversion
SNJ-5 Texan	121-41736	N3239G	*Tora! Tora! Tora!* (1970)	Ex-BuNo. 90950, Kate conversion
SNJ-5 Texan	SMA2-669	F-AZBL	*Empire of the Sun* (1987)	Ex-BuNo. 90669, Zero marked as: 3-189
Harvard Mk. II	66-2290	CF-MGZ	*For the Moment* (1993)	Ex-RCAF 2557
(CCF) Harvard Mk. 4	CCF4-16	N15796	*Tora! Tora! Tora!* (1970)	Ex-RCAF 20225, Zero conversion
		N15796	*Shack* (TVM, 1977)	—
		N15796	*Baa Baa Black Sheep* (TVS, 1976-1978)	—
		N15796	*Aces: Iron Eagle III* (1992)	Zero marked as 3-183
(CCF) Harvard Mk. 4	CCF4-20	N1264	*Tora! Tora! Tora!* (1970)	Ex-RCAF 20229, Kate conversion
(CCF) Harvard Mk. 4	CCF4-23	N2048	*Tora! Tora! Tora!* (1970)	Ex-RCAF 20232, Zero conversion
(CCF) Harvard Mk. 4	CCF4-27	C-FGUY	*Iron Eagle IV* (1995)	Ex-RCAF 20236
(CCF) Harvard Mk. 4	CCF4-83	N2047	*Tora! Tora! Tora!* (1970)	Ex-RCAF 20292, Kate conversion
		N2047	*Pearl Harbor* (2001)	—
(CCF) Harvard Mk. 4	CCF4-104	N15795	*Tora! Tora! Tora!* (1970)	Ex-RCAF 20313, Zero conversion
(CCF) Harvard Mk. 4	CCF4-117	N15799	*Tora! Tora! Tora!* (1970)	Ex-RCAF 20326, Zero conversion
		N15799	*The Final Countdown* (1980)	Flying
(CCF) Harvard Mk. 4	CCF4-124	N1466	*The Tuskegee Airmen* (TVM, 1995)	Ex-RCAF 20333, flying
(CCF) Harvard Mk. 4	CCF4-153	N15798	*Tora! Tora! Tora!* (1970)	Ex-RCAF 20362, Zero conversion
		N15798	*War and Remembrance* (TVMS, 1988)	Flying
(CCF) Harvard Mk. 4	CCF4-158	N9097	*Tora! Tora! Tora!* (1970)	Ex-RCAF 20367, Zero conversion

AT-6...		(SN or Reg. at Time of		
(Type)	(msn)	Filming)	(Title)	(Remarks / Film Markings)
(CCF) Harvard Mk. 4	CCF4-171	N7757	Tora! Tora! Tora! (1970)	Ex-RCAF 20380, Zero conversion
		N7757	Baa Baa Black Sheep (TVS, 1976-1978)	—
(CCF) Harvard Mk. 4	CCF4-199	N15797	Tora! Tora! Tora! (1970)	Ex-RCAF 20408, Zero conversion
		N15797	The Final Countdown (1980)	Flying
(CCF) Harvard Mk. 4	CCF4-215	N7754	Tora! Tora! Tora! (1970)	Ex-RCAF 20424, Zero conversion
(CCF) Harvard Mk. 4	CCF4-223	C-FHWU	Iron Eagle IV (1995)	Ex-RCAF 20432
(CCF) Harvard Mk. 4	CCF4-241	N4447	Tora! Tora! Tora! (1970)	Ex-RCAF 20450, Zero conversion
(CCF) Harvard Mk. 4	CCF4-242	CF-ROA	Iron Eagle IV (1995)	Ex-RCAF 20451
(CCF) Harvard Mk. 4	CCF4-264	N296W	Tora! Tora! Tora! (1970)	Ex-RCAF 20473, Zero conversion
		N296W	Baa Baa Black Sheep (TVS, 1976-1978)	—
(Noorduyn) AT-16 Harvard	14-641	B-64	A Bridge Too Far (1977)	Ex-42-12394, doubled as Allied fighter
(Noorduyn) AT-16 Harvard	14A-808	B-182	A Bridge Too Far (1977)	Ex-43-12509, doubled as Allied fighter
(Noorduyn) AT-16 Harvard	14A-1020	PH-BKT	A Bridge Too Far (1977)	Ex-43-12721, doubled as Allied fighter
(Noorduyn) AT-16 Harvard	14A-1184	PH-KLU	A Bridge Too Far (1977)	Ex-43-12885, doubled as Allied fighter
(Noorduyn) AT-16 Harvard	14A-1467	B-118	A Bridge Too Far (1977)	Ex-43-13168, doubled as Allied fighter
T-6G Texan	168-113	N2819G	Tora! Tora! Tora! (1970)	Ex-49-3009, Kate conversion, crashed during filming
T-6G Texan	182-72	51-14385	Empire of the Sun (1987)	Static only, Zero marked as 3-158
T-6G Texan	182-271	N6522	Tora! Tora! Tora! (1970)	Ex-JASDF 72-0151, Kate conversion
T-6G Texan	182-307	N6524	Tora! Tora! Tora! (1970)	Ex-JASDF 72-0159, Kate conversion
T-6G Texan	182-362	N6526	Tora! Tora! Tora! (1970)	Ex-51-14675, Kate conversion
T-6G Texan	182-366	N6529	Tora! Tora! Tora! (1970)	Ex-51-14679, Kate conversion
T-6G Texan	182-387	51-14700	Empire of the Sun (1987)	Derelict Zero in field
T-6G Texan	182-393	N6520	Tora! Tora! Tora! (1970)	Ex-51-14706, Kate conversion
T-6G Texan	SMA2-367	F-AZBK	Empire of the Sun (1987)	Ex-51-14367, Zero marked as 3-217
T-6G Texan	SMA2-049	F-AZAS	Empire of the Sun (1987)	Ex-51-15049, Zero marked as 3-281
T-6G Texan	unknown	(JASDF) 52-0030	Tora! Tora! Tora! (1970)	Zero conversion
T-6G Texan	unknown	(JASDF) 72-0158	Tora! Tora! Tora! (1970)	Zero conversion
T-6G Texan	unknown	(JASDF) 7 2-0175	Tora! Tora! Tora! (1970)	Zero conversion

Other Notable Titles: *Wings of the Navy* (1939), NJ-1; *I Wanted Wings* (1941); *A Yank in the RAF* (1941); *Captains of the Clouds* (1942); *Thunder Birds* (1942); *God Is My Co-Pilot* (1945), as "Zeros"; *Flying Leathernecks* (1951), as "Zero"; *Angels One Five* (1952), RAF Harvards; *From Here to Eternity* (1953), as "Zero"; *The Great Escape* (1963), as German aircraft; *PT 109* (1963), as "Zero"; *Patton* (1970), as U.S. fighters; *1941* (1979), six SNJ Texans.

One of the twelve U.S. Harvard trainers being converted into a Zero for the 1970 film *Tora! Tora! Tora!* Photograph: James H. Farmer Collection.

Veteran *Tora!* Kate conversion N3242G as seen at Santa Ana in 1973 under the care of Tallmantz Aviation, Inc., who used it in subsequent film work. Photograph: Peter Nicholson.

Frank Tallman converted this AT-6F Texan N7446C into a Zero replica for film work from the late 1950s. It was not used in *Tora! Tora! Tora!* filming in 1969. It has since been converted back to AT-6 standard for museum display. Photograph: Peter Nicholson.

O-47

First flight: July 1935. Single-engined observation aircraft with 239 built including the prototype. Quickly outdated and saw only minor stateside service during World War II.

B-25 MITCHELL

First flight: January 29, 1939. Twin-engined medium bomber built in great numbers for the USAAF during World War II. Like certain types after the war, the B-25 Mitchell was widely flown on the civilian market in various roles. By the time *Catch-22* came along in 1970, however, the Mitchell was becoming a bit worse for wear in many sectors until Tallmantz acquired 20 of them (17 eventually flew) for restoration and use in that film.

Since then, the B-25 has enjoyed, like other types, a return to stardom on the Warbird scene. Several have also been converted as cinema cameraplanes—Tallmantz's N1203 and N1042B are the best-known examples. Many of the *Catch-22* B-

O-47 Type	msn	SN or Reg. at Time of Filming	Title	Remarks / Film Markings
O-47A	25-554	N4725V	*The Flight of the Phoenix* (1965)	Ex-38-284, flyable mock-up

B-25 Mitchell Type	msn	SN or Reg. at Time of Filming	Title	Remarks / Film Markings
B-25B Mitchell	62-3016	40-2347	unknown	Recovered from a Hollywood studio in 1966, used for studio interior filming on several productions. May have been used in *Thirty Seconds Over Tokyo* (1944)
B-25C Mitchell	94-12762	42-32354	*The Twilight Zone* (TVS, 1959–1964), 1960 episode "King Nine Will Not Return"	Marked as 42-32359 / K9
B-25D Mitchell	87-7919	41-29754	*Thirty Seconds Over Tokyo* (1944)	Flying as *Ruptured Duck*
B-25D Mitchell	87-8076	41-29911	*Thirty Seconds Over Tokyo* (1944)	Flying, studio filming
B-25D Mitchell	87-8302	41-30137	*Thirty Seconds Over Tokyo* (1944)	Flying
B-25D Mitchell	87-8640	41-30475	*Thirty Seconds Over Tokyo* (1944)	Flying
B-25D Mitchell	87-8859	41-30694	*Thirty Seconds Over Tokyo* (1944)	Flying, studio filming as *Ruptured Duck*
B-25H Mitchell	98-21433	N10V	*Catch-22* (1970)	Ex-43-4432, marked as 6N
B-25H Mitchell	98-21644	N1203	*Them!* (1954)	Ex-43-4643
		N1203	*Catch-22* (1970)	Marked as 6A, camera-plane
B-25J Mitchell	108-24356	N3339G	*Baa Baa Black Sheep* (TVS, 1976–1978)	Ex-43-4030
		N3339G	*1941* (1979)	Background
B-25J Mitchell	108-35217	N9856C	*Catch-22* (1970)	Ex-43-28204, marked as 6G
		N9856C	*Pearl Harbor* (2001)	Marked as *Whirling Dervish*
B-25J Mitchell	108-32200	N7687C	*Catch-22* (1970)	Ex-44-28925, marked as 6F
B-25J Mitchell	108-32396	N86427	*Hanover Street* (1979)	Ex-44-29121
		N86427	*Cuba* (1979)	Damaged during filming
B-25J Mitchell	108-32474	N9117Z	*Pearl Harbor* (2001)	Ex-44-29199
B-25J Mitchell	108-32641	N9115Z	*Catch-22* (1970)	Ex-44-29366, marked as 6M
		N9115Z	*Hanover Street* (1979)	Flying
B-25J Mitchell	108-32782	N3698G	*1941* (1979)	Ex-44-29507, background
B-25J Mitchell	108-33162	N10564	*Catch-22* (1970)	Ex-44-29887, marked as 6Y
B-25J Mitchell	108-33214	N9456Z	*Catch-22* (1970)	Ex-44-29939, marked as 6C

B-25 Mitchell		(SN or Reg. at Time of		
(Type)	(msn)	Filming)	(Title)	(Remarks / Film Markings)
B-25J Mitchell	108-33352	N2849G	Catch-22 (1970)	Ex-44-30077, marked as 6Q
B-25J Mitchell	108-33485	N9455Z	Hanover Street (1979)	Ex-44-30210
B-25J Mitchell	108-33698	N3675G	1941 (1979)	Ex-44-30423, background
		N3675G	Forever Young (1992)	Flying
		N3675G	Pearl Harbor (2001)	Flying
B-25J Mitchell	108-33753	N9754Z	Tora! Tora! Tora! (1970)	Ex-44-30478, destroyed for film
B-25J Mitchell	108-33768	N9451Z	Catch-22 (1970)	Ex-44-30493, marked as 6V
B-25J Mitchell	108-33924	N9452Z	Catch-22 (1970)	Ex-44-30649, marked as 6V and 6W
B-25J Mitchell	108-34023	N8195H	Catch-22 (1970)	Ex-44-30748, marked as 6H
B-25J Mitchell	108-34076	N3699G	Catch-22 (1970)	Ex-44-30801, marked as 6K
		N3699G	Baa Baa Black Sheep (TVS, 1976-1978)	Flying
		N30801	Beautiful Dreamer (2006)	Doubles as a B-24 Liberator!
B-25J Mitchell	108-34136	N9089Z	633 Squadron (1964)	Ex-44-30861, also camera-ship
B-25J Mitchell	108-34200	N9494Z	Catch-22 (1970)	Ex-44-30925, marked as 6P
		N9494Z	Hanover Street (1979)	Flying
B-25J Mitchell	108-34254	44-30979	Sole Survivor (TVM, 1970)	Non-flying, scrapped in 1973
B-25J Mitchell	108-34307	N3174G	Catch-22 (1970)	Ex-44-31032, marked as 6D
B-25J Mitchell	108-47455	N7681C	Catch-22 (1970)	Ex-44-86701, marked as 6J
		N7681C	Hanover Street (1979)	Flying
B-25J Mitchell	108-47501	N8163H	Pearl Harbor (2001)	Ex-44-86747, marked as Ruptured Duck
B-25J Mitchell	108-47545	VH-XXV	Sky Pirates (1986)	Ex-44-86791
B-25J Mitchell	108-47597	N3507G	Catch-22 (1970)	Ex-44-86843, marked as 6B
B-25J Mitchell	108-47647	N6123C	Dark Blue World (2001)	Ex-44-86893
B-25J Mitchell	108-47694	XB-HEY	Catch-22 (1970)	Ex-45-8843, marked as 6S, derelict wreck

Tallmantz Aviation's B-25 N1042B, the legendary camera-plane used for over 25 years on so many film and television productions. Photograph: James H. Farmer Collection.

What's left of B-25C (s/n 42-32354) in an El Monte scrap yard in January 1970. It still bears the fictional markings of its starring role in a 1960 episode of *The Twilight Zone* titled "King Nine Will Not Return." Photograph: James H. Farmer Collection.

25 veterans have had further significant film appearances.

Other Notable Titles: *A Guy Named Joe* (1943), one was 40-2295; *God Is My Co-Pilot* (1945); *The Lady Takes a Flyer* (1958); *Gable and Lombard* (1976), N3699G; *Midway* (1976), footage from *Thirty Seconds over Tokyo*; *Smokey and the Bandit II* (1980), two from Planes of Fame, California.

P-51 MUSTANG

First flight (NA-73X): October 26, 1940. Single-engined fighter had a slow start with early variants like the A-36A but became a lethal and classic fighter design once the Merlin engine was fitted, the definitive variant being the P-51D. On film, many of the Mustang's early screen appearances were doubling as the German Messerschmitt Bf 109. This classic fighter, however, made its mark on movie aviation for the brief but striking appearance in the 1987 film *Empire of the Sun* doing fast flybys during an airfield strike. The best P-51 film would arguably be *Battle Hymn* (1957).

Other Notable Titles: *Sahara* (1943), as "Bf 109"; *A Guy Named Joe* (1943), as "Bf 109"; *Thirty Seconds Over Tokyo* (1944), as "Zero"; *Fighter Squadron* (1948), as "Bf 109"; *Mission Over Korea* (1953), as "Yak 9" fighters; *Dragonfly Squadron* (1954), ANG F-51D; *Battle Hymn* (1957), ANG F-51D; *The Lady Takes a Flyer* (1958); *12 O'Clock High* (TVS, 1964–1967); *Cannon* (TVS, 1971–1976); *Baa Baa Black Sheep* (TVS, 1976–1978).

P-51 Mustang		SN or Reg. at Time of		
Type	*msn*	*Filming*	*Title*	*Remarks / Film Markings*
P-51A Mustang	99-22354	N4235Y	*Aces: Iron Eagle III* (1992)	Ex-43-6251, doubled as a Messerschmitt Bf 109
P-51D Mustang	122-31514	G-PSID	*Empire of the Sun* (1987)	Ex-44-63788, flying
P-51D Mustang	122-38675	G-BIXL	*Memphis Belle* (1990)	Ex-44-72216, marked as AJ-L
P-51D Mustang	122-38942	N151DM	*The Tuskegee Airmen* (TVM, 1995)	Ex-44-72483, flying
P-51D Mustang	122-39198	44-72739	*Battle Hymn* (1957)	Studio-based scenes, restored as N44727
P-51D Mustang	122-39232	G-SUSY	*Memphis Belle* (1990)	Ex-44-72773, marked as AJ-C

P-51 Mustang		(SN or Reg. at Time of		
(Type)	(msn)	Filming)	(Title)	(Remarks / Film Markings)
P-51D Mustang	122-39236	N151D	The Tuskegee Airmen (TVM, 1995)	Ex-44-72777, flying
P-51D Mustang	122-39599	N314BG	Memphis Belle (1990)	Ex-44-73140
P-51D Mustang	122-39608	N51JJ	Empire of the Sun (1987)	Ex-44-73149, flying
		N51JJ	Memphis Belle (1990)	Flying, marked as AJ-S
P-51D Mustang	122-39977	N5483V	Star Wars (1977)	Ex-44-73518, provided the engine sound effect for the Millennium Falcon!
P-51D Mustang	122-40417	N167F	Saving Private Ryan (1998)	Ex-44-73877
		N167F	Memphis Belle (1990)	Flying, marked as AJ-N
		N167F	Red Tails (2012)	Flying, marked as A2-9
P-51D Mustang	122-40967	F-AZAB	Red Tails (2012)	Flying, marked as AI-7
P-51D Mustang	122-41500	44-74960	Battle Hymn (1957)	Flew as Hess's No. 18
P-51D Mustang	124-44471	N55JL	Cloud Dancer (1980)	Ex-44-84615
		N55JL	The Tuskegee Airmen (TVM, 1995)	Flying
P-51D Mustang	124-48124	N1051S	Memphis Belle (1990)	Ex-45-11371
P-51D Mustang	124-48311	N6175C	The Tuskegee Airmen (TVM, 1995)	Ex-45-11558, flying
(CAC) Mustang Mk. 21	1429	VH-BOB	Sky Pirates (1986)	Ex-RAAF A68-104, flying
(CAC) Mustang Mk. 21	1432	VH-AUB	Sky Pirates (1986)	Ex-RAAF A68-107, flying
(CAC) Mustang PR.Mk. 22	192-1517	G-HAEC	Empire of the Sun (1987)	Ex-RAAF A68-192, flying
		G-HAEC	Memphis Belle (1990)	Flying, marked as AJ-A
		G-HAEC	Saving Private Ryan (1998)	Flying
		G-HAEC	Red Tails (2012)	Flying, marked as AI-4

F-86 SABRE / F-100 SUPER SABRE

First flight: October 1, 1947. Single-engined, swept-wing fighter became famous for its part in the Korean War dogfighting against MiGs. Over 9,800 were built, including Sabres in Australia and Canada and as the naval FJ Fury. This famous Cold War–era fighter made several notable screen appearances in the films listed below. As often happened during this period (as with the Lockheed Shooting Star), film studios simply filmed operational aircraft at airbases taxiing and taking off, then cut them into the finished film, which is why this list (and the one for the P-80 / T-33) is so extensive. The F-100 Super Sabre first flew on May 25, 1953, and was a high-performance redesign of the original F-86 Sabre.

F-86...		SN or Reg. at Time of		
Type	msn	Filming	Title	Remarks / Film Markings
F-86A Sabre	151-513	48-144	Jet Pilot (1957)	—
F-86A Sabre	151-516	48-147	Jet Pilot (1957)	—
F-86A Sabre	151-529	48-160	Jet Pilot (1957)	—
F-86A Sabre	151-549	48-180	Jet Pilot (1957)	—
F-86A Sabre	151-559	48-190	Jet Pilot (1957)	—
F-86A Sabre	151-566	48-197	Jet Pilot (1957)	—
F-86A Sabre	151-577	48-208	Jet Pilot (1957)	—
F-86A Sabre	151-632	48-263	Bombers B-52 (1957)	Non-flying, marked as Lucky Lady
F-86A Sabre	161-229	49-1235	Jet Pilot (1957)	—
F-86A Sabre	161-279	49-1285	Jet Pilot (1957)	—
F-86E Sabre	172-269	51-12978	Sabre Jet (1953)	—
F-86E Sabre	172-280	51-12989	Sabre Jet (1953)	—
F-86E Sabre	172-282	51-12991	Sabre Jet (1953)	—
F-86E Sabre	172-308	51-13017	Sabre Jet (1953)	—

F-86...		(SN or Reg. at Time of Filming)	(Title)	(Remarks / Film Markings)
(Type)	(msn)			
F-86E Sabre	172-310	51-13019	Sabre Jet (1953)	—
F-86E Sabre	172-313	51-13022	Sabre Jet (1953)	—
F-86E Sabre	172-314	51-13023	Sabre Jet (1953)	—
F-86E Sabre	172-318	51-13027	Sabre Jet (1953)	—
F-86E Sabre	172-339	51-13048	Sabre Jet (1953)	—
F-86E Sabre	172-355	51-13064	Sabre Jet (1953)	—
F-86E Sabre	172-358	51-13067	Sabre Jet (1953)	—
F-86F Sabre	172-239	51-12948	Sabre Jet (1953)	—
F-86F Sabre	172-260	51-12969	Sabre Jet (1953)	—
F-86F Sabre	176-123	51-13192	The McConnell Story (1955)	—
		51-13192	Jet Attack (1958)	—
F-86F Sabre	176-145	51-13214	The McConnell Story (1955)	—
		51-13214	Jet Attack (1958)	—
F-86F Sabre	176-149	51-13218	Jet Attack (1958)	—
F-86F Sabre	176-164	51-13233	Jet Attack (1958)	—
F-86F Sabre	176-169	51-13238	The McConnell Story (1955)	—
		51-13238	Jet Attack (1958)	—
F-86F Sabre	176-228	51-13297	The McConnell Story (1955)	—
F-86F Sabre	176-229	51-13298	The McConnell Story (1955)	—
F-86F Sabre	176-266	51-13335	Jet Attack (1958)	—
F-86F Sabre	191-178	52-4482	The Hunters (1958)	Robert Mitchum's aircraft as 14482
F-86F Sabre	191-430	52-4734	The Hunters (1958)	Robert Wagner's aircraft as 14734
F-86F Sabre	191-723	52-5027	The Hunters (1958)	Marked as 15027
F-86F Sabre	191-803	52-5107	The Hunters (1958)	Marked as 15107
F-86F Sabre	191-835	N86F	The Right Stuff (1983)	Ex-52-5139, briefly seen
F-86F Sabre	191-836	52-5140	The Hunters (1958)	Marked as 15140
F-86F Sabre	191-940	52-5244	The Hunters (1958)	Marked as 15244
F-86F Sabre	191-966	52-5270	The Hunters (1958)	Marked as 15270
F-86F Sabre	193-114	52-5385	The Hunters (1958)	Marked as 15385
F-86F Sabre	193-142	52-5413	The Hunters (1958)	Marked as 15413
F-86F Sabre	193-154	52-5425	The Hunters (1958)	Marked as 15425
F-86F Sabre	193-211	52-5482	The Hunters (1958)	Marked as 15482, studio filming
F-86F Sabre	193-227	52-5498	The Hunters (1958)	Marked as 15498
F-86F Sabre	193-245	52-5516	The Hunters (1958)	Marked as 15516
F-86F Sabre	193-253	52-5524	The Hunters (1958)	Marked as 15524
F-86F Sabre	193-256	52-5527	The Hunters (1958)	Marked as 15527
F-100C Super Sabre	214-045	54-1753	Skyjacked (1972)	Doubles as Russian MiG
F-100C Super Sabre	217-064	54-1803	Skyjacked (1972)	Doubles as Russian MiG
F-100C Super Sabre	217-304	54-2043	Skyjacked (1972)	Doubles as Russian MiG
F-100C Super Sabre	217-317	54-2056	Skyjacked (1972)	Doubles as Russian MiG
F-100C Super Sabre	217-345	54-2084	Skyjacked (1972)	Doubles as Russian MiG
F-100F Super Sabre	243-239	56-3963	X-15 (1961)	—

SABRELINER

First flight: September 16, 1958. Twin-engined business jet with wings and tail section of a similar design to the F-86 Sabre which resulted in the name "Sabreliner." 212 were built for the USAF and U.S. Navy as the T-39 jet trainer. Many were later converted as personnel transports designated the CT-39. In 1982, Rockwell sold its Sabreliner Division as the Sabreliner Corp., which was a support company for owners and operators.

X-15

First flight: June 8, 1959. High-altitude, rocket-powered research aircraft.

Sabreliner		SN or Reg. at		
Type	msn	Time of Filming	Title	Remarks / Film Markings
CT-39A Sabreliner	265-45	61-0642	Stripes (1981)	In final scene

X-15		SN or Reg. at		
Type	msn	Time of Filming	Title	Remarks / Film Markings
X-15A-NA	240-2	56-6671	X-15 (1961)	Actual flying aircraft
X-15A-NA	240-3	56-6672	X-15 (1961)	Actual flying aircraft

Northrop / Northrop-Grumman

Founded in 1929 by Jack Northrop as the Avion Corp. Became Northrop Aviation Corp. under the United Aircraft & Transport Corp. in 1929. Became part of the Douglas Aircraft Corp. in 1932 and made several successful designs. Separated again by 1938 with Jack Northrop establishing the independent Northrop Aircraft Inc. in 1939, which built the twin-boom P-61 during World War II. Renamed Northrop Corp. in 1959 and built the F-89 and very successful F-5 / T-38 series. Merged with Grumman Aerospace in 1994 to form Northrop-Grumman Corp.

Other Notable Titles: *Apollo 13* (1995), NASA T-38 Talon (s/n 920); *Independence Day* (1996), B-2A Spirit; *Armageddon* (1998), NASA T-38 Talon, B-2A Spirit; *Iron Man 2* (2010), B-2A Spirit (s/n 82-1068).

Orenco

American company founded in 1916 as the Ordnance Engineering Corp. (ORENCO). Produced only a small number of biplane aircraft during World War I and a few postwar, but was taken over by the Baldwin Aircraft Corp. in 1922.

Pasped

American company founded in the mid–1930s by Fred Pastorious and Stanley Pederson; acquired by the Skylark Mfg. Co. in 1941.

Percival / Hunting Percival

British manufacturer founded by Edgar Percival in 1933 as the Percival Aircraft Co.; became Percival Aircraft Ltd. 1936. Joined the Hunting Group in 1944 and became Hunting Percival Air-

Northrop		SN or Reg. at Time of		
Type	msn	Filming	Title	Remarks / Film Markings
XF-89 Scorpion	unknown	46-678	Jet Pilot (1957)	—
F-89A Scorpion	unknown	49-2438	Jet Pilot (1957)	—
F-5E Tiger II	R-1118	M29-04	Bat*21 (1988)	Plus one other
M2-F2 Lifting Body	unknown	NASA 803	The Six Million Dollar Man (TVS, 1973-1978)	Opening titles is actual footage of this aircraft crashing at Edwards AFB, California, on May 10, 1967. Pilot Bruce Peterson survived with minor injuries

Orenco		SN or Reg. at		
Type	msn	Time of Filming	Title	Remarks / Film Markings
Model F Touriste	45	N2145	Task Force (1949)	Doubles as VE-7SF Bluebird

Pasped		SN or Reg. at		
Type	msn	Time of Filming	Title	Remarks / Film Markings
Skylark W-1	unknown	NC14919	Without Orders (1936)	Flying

Percival...		SN or Reg. at Time of		
Type	msn	Filming	Title	Remarks / Film Markings
P.28 Proctor 1	unknown	G-AIEY	Battle of Britain (1969)	Ju 87 Stuka mock-up, not used in final film
P.34 Proctor 3	unknown	G-ALOK	Battle of Britain (1969)	Ju 87 Stuka mock-up, not used in final film
P.44 Proctor 5	Ae.86	G-AIAE	Battle of Britain (1969)	Ju 87 Stuka mock-up, not used in final film

craft in 1954 and Hunting Aircraft in 1957. It merged with several other major aero manufacturers in 1960 to form British Aircraft Corp. (BAC). The Piston and Jet Provost are two of their successful aircraft.

Notable Titles: *High Flight* (1957) P.56 Provost; *The Wilby Conspiracy* (1975) SAAF Jet Provost (BAC Strikemaster).

Pfalz

German manufacturer founded in 1913 became famous for producing the D.III and D.XII series of biplane fighters for combat in World War I; the victorious French closed the factory after the war. Most on-screen appearances in films have been done with replicas.

Other Notable Titles: *The Dawn Patrol* (1930 / 1938), D.XII; *Von Richthofen and Brown* (1971), D.IIIa EI-ARC or EI-ARD.

Phillips

American company founded by James Phillips in 1936 as Phillips Aviation Co. for light aircraft development, acquired by Skylark Mfg. Co. in 1941.

Piasecki   *see*   Vertol / Boeing-Vertol

Pilatus

Swiss manufacturer founded in 1939 as Pilatus Flugzeugwerke AG. Became famous for produc-

Pfalz		SN or Reg. at		
Type	msn	Time of Filming	Title	Remarks / Film Markings
Pfalz D.IIIa (replica)	PPS/PFLZ/1	G-ATIF	*The Blue Max* (1966)	Replica built for the film
		EI-ARC	*Darling Lili* (1970)	Flying
Pfalz D.IIIa (replica)	PT.16	G-ATIJ	*The Blue Max* (1966)	Replica built for the film
		EI-ARD	*Darling Lili* (1970)	Flying

Phillips		SN or Reg. at		
Type	msn	Time of Filming	Title	Remarks / Film Markings
1-B Aeroneer	1	NX16075	*Power Dive* (1941)	—
CT-2 Skylark	101	NC19989	*The Tarnished Angels* (1957)	—

Pilatus		SN or Reg. at Time of		
Type	msn	Filming	Title	Remarks / Film Markings
P-2.05	36	F-AZCD	*Indiana Jones and the Last Crusade* (1989)	Doubles as German fighter
P-2.05	37	F-AZCC	*Indiana Jones and the Last Crusade* (1989)	Doubles as German fighter
PC-6B Turbo-Porter	735	HB-FFW	*GoldenEye* (1995)	Flying

An original Pfalz D.XII N43C rebuilt and owned by Frank Tallman from 1958 to 1968. Photograph: James H. Farmer Collection.

ing STOL type aircraft, especially the PC-6 Turbo-Porter, also built in the U.S. by Fairchild-Hiller. Now known as Pilatus Aircraft Ltd.

Piper

The iconic American light aircraft manufacturer was founded in 1937 as the Piper Aircraft Corp. by William Piper. Was one of four manufacturers during World War II to produce the Grasshopper series of spotter planes, Piper building the L-4, L-18 and L-21 based on their hugely successful Cub design. Acquired the Stinson Division of Convair in 1948. Went on to produce a winning range of single- and twin-engined light aircraft for business and recreational flying. There's a wide range of motion picture titles featuring Piper products; the most famous would no doubt be the five Cherokees seen in the Bond film *Goldfinger* (1964).

Pitcairn / Pitcairn-Cierva

American company founded in 1926 as the Pitcairn Aircraft Co. by Harold Pitcairn in order to build aircraft for his airmail service. In 1929 the company began building autogyro aircraft under the name Pitcairn-Cierva Autogyro Co., which was later renamed the Autogyro Company of America. The company went through several more name changes and ownerships before going out of business in 1948. Pitcairn is well remembered for its 1927 PA-5 Mailwing biplane and 1931 PCA-2 Gyroplane design.

Other Notable Titles: *Blaze of Noon* (1947) PA-7 Mailwing; *The Rocketeer* (1991) PCA-2 Gyroplane mock-up and model.

Pitts

An American company originated with Curtis Pitts in 1945 as Pitts Aero Service, becoming Pitts Aviation Enterprises in 1967, known for producing a small aerobatic biplane designated as the S-1 and S-2. Production was also undertaken by Aerotek, Inc., and later by Aviat Aircraft, both in Wyoming.

Potez

French manufacturer founded by Henry Potez in 1919 as Aeroplanes Henry Potez, which built a

Piper		SN or Reg. at Time of		
Type	msn	Filming	Title	Remarks / Film Markings
J-3C Cub	22015	N77524	Bird on a Wire (1990)	Marked as "Hauman's Speed Kill"
PA-18-150 Super Cub	unknown	XB-LOX	Licence to Kill (1989)	Crop-duster aircraft
PA-18-150 Super Cub	18-7409133	N8991Y	The Rum Diary (2011)	Opening credits only
PA-28-140 Cherokee	28-20068	N6056W	Goldfinger (1964)	Pussy Galore's Flying Circus
PA-28-150 Cherokee	28-1658	N5781W	Goldfinger (1964)	Pussy Galore's Flying Circus
PA-28-180 Cherokee	28-1400	N7489W	Goldfinger (1964)	Pussy Galore's Flying Circus
PA-28-180 Cherokee	28-1613	N7641W	Goldfinger (1964)	Pussy Galore's Flying Circus
PA-28-235 Cherokee	28-10264	N8729W	Goldfinger (1964)	Pussy Galore's Flying Circus
PA-28R-201T Arrow III	28R-7703118	N4013Q	Cloud Dancer (1980)	Flying, turbo config
PA-28R-201T Arrow III	28R-7803188	N3707M	Cloud Dancer (1980)	Flying, turbo config
PA-31 Navajo Chieftain	31-7405249	C-GROJ	Altitude (2010)	Falsely marked as "C-MYZX"

Pitcairn...		SN or Reg. at		
Type	msn	Time of Filming	Title	Remarks / Film Markings
PA-5	30	NC6708	Central Airport (1933)	—

Pitts		SN or Reg. at Time of		
Type	msn	Filming	Title	Remarks / Film Markings
Pitts S-2A Special	unknown	N9CC	The Pilot (1980)	Flying
(Aerotek) Pitts S-1S Special	1-0056	N31428	Cloud Dancer (1980)	Flying
(Aerotek) Pitts S-2A Special	2159	N31427	Cloud Dancer (1980)	Flying

series of small aircraft designs up to 1936, when it was absorbed into SNCAN and SNCASE. Revived after World War II but never achieved any further success, closing up in 1967.

Republic

Originally founded as the Seversky Aircraft Corp. in 1931, it was reorganized and became the Republic Aviation Corp. in 1939, going on to develop earlier Seversky designs into the legendary P-47 Thunderbolt during World War II. Postwar, Republic went into the jet age with the F-84 Thunderjet / Thunderstreak / Thunderflash series of jet fighters, followed by the F-105 Thunderchief. In 1965 Fairchild-Hiller Corp. acquired Republic to form the Republic Division, developing the A-10 Thunderbolt II.

Further details see: SEVERSKY.

Other Notable Titles: *God Is My Co-Pilot* (1945), P-43; *The Big Lift* (1950), P-47s as Russian fighters; *Dragonfly Squadron* (1954), as Russian Yaks; *Tarantula!* (1956), F-84 Thunderjet; *Ike: The War Years* (TVMS, 1979).

Rockwell

The aerospace division of Rockwell Standard Corp. was founded in 1967 when it acquired North American Aviation, Inc. It was renamed Rockwell International Corp. in 1973. Rockwell had previously acquired Aero Commander and its range of commuter aircraft in 1960, which it remarketed and built as a Rockwell product. The prime contractor for the space shuttle program; built the B-1 Lancer from the mid–1970s. Aerospace holdings merged with the Boeing Co. in 1996. Further details see: NORTH AMERICAN.

Other Notable Titles: *The Courage and the Passion* (TVM, 1978), B-1B Lancer; *Transformers: Revenge of the Fallen* (2009), B-1B Lancer.

Royal Aircraft Factory

British, government run manufacturer named as such between 1911 and 1918 for the research and production of combat types. Produced several well-known designs, including the B.E.2, F.E.2 and S.E.5 biplane fighter. Renamed the Royal Aircraft Establishment (RAE) in 1918.

| Potez | | SN or Reg. at | | |
Type	msn	Time of Filming	Title	Remarks / Film Markings
Model 43.1	3448	F-AMPI	*Broken Journey* (1948)	Flying

Republic		SN or Reg. at Time of Filming	Title	Remarks / Film Markings
Type	msn			
P-47D Thunderbolt	4272	44-33311	*Fighter Squadron* (1948)	—
P-47D Thunderbolt	5582	44-90437	*Fighter Squadron* (1948)	—
P-47D Thunderbolt	6398	44-20990	*Fighter Squadron* (1948)	—
P-47G Thunderbolt	21953	42-25068	*Fighter Attack* (1953)	Non-flying TP-47G conversion
F-84E Thunderjet	unknown	49-2031	*Jet Attack* (1958)	—
F-84E Thunderjet	unknown	49-2085	*Jet Attack* (1958)	—
F-84E Thunderjet	unknown	49-2306	*Jet Attack* (1958)	—
Model RC-3 Seabee	105	N87545	*The Man with the Golden Gun* (1974)	Amphibian. A mock-up was destroyed for the film
Model UC-1 Twin Bee	023	N65NE	*The Rum Diary* (2011)	Seabee conversion by United Consultants

Rockwell		SN or Reg. at Time of Filming	Title	Remarks / Film Markings
Type	msn			
Aero Commander 720	720-850-13	N825WD	*Clear and Present Danger* (1994)	Static only
Aero Commander 720	unknown	HP-668	*Quantum of Solace* (2008)	Background
Model 114 Commander	14399	N5854N	*Drop Zone* (1994)	Background

Royal... Type	msn	SN or Reg. at Time of Filming	Title	Remarks / Film Markings
B.E.2c (replica)	001	G-AWYI	*Biggles Sweeps the Skies* [canceled]	Built for a 1969 Universal Pictures film that was canceled; used Tiger Moth components. Exported to the U.S. in 1970
		G-AWYI	*Wings* (TVS, 1977-1978)	Flying

S.E.5

First flight: November 22, 1916. Single-engined biplane fighter with a top wing–mounted machine gun; over 5,200 were built. Some were featured in early Hollywood films but from the latter half of the 20th century, replicas were built, which are listed below. The first two are widely referred to as the Miles S.E.5a, since they were built at Miles Marine and Structural Plastics Ltd. by F.G. Miles.

Other Notable Titles: *Wings* (1927); *Hell's An-gels* (1930); *Flying Down to Rio* (1933); *Crimson Romance* (1934); *Stunt Pilot* (1939); *The Aviator* (2004), N1918P.

Ryan

American manufacturer that shot to stardom with their Ryan NYP monoplane built for Charles Lindbergh and named the *Spirit of St. Louis*. Founded as Ryan Air Lines Inc. in 1925 by Claude

S.E.5 Type	msn	SN or Reg. at Time of Filming	Title	Remarks / Film Markings
S.E.5a (replica)	SEM.7282	G-ATGV	*The Blue Max* (1966)	Replica built for the film
		EI-ARA	*Darling Lili* (1970)	Flying
		EI-ARA	*Von Richthofen and Brown* (1971)	Crashed during filming in September 1970
		EI-ARA	*Zeppelin* (1971)	Flying
S.E.5a (replica)	SEM.7283	G-ATGW	*The Blue Max* (1966)	Replica built for the film
		EI-ARB	*Darling Lili* (1970)	Flying
		EI-ARB	*Von Richthofen and Brown* (1971)	Flying
		EI-ARB	*Zeppelin* (1971)	Crashed during filming in August1970

The six biplanes below are Currie Wot airframes converted by Slingsby Sailplanes Ltd. as replica Royal Aircraft Factory S.E.5 fighters and designated by Slingsby as the Slingsby Type 56 S.E.5a.

S.E.5a (replica)	1590	EI-ARH	*Darling Lili* (1970)	Ex-G-AVOT, marked as A5435
		EI-ARH	*Von Richthofen and Brown* (1971)	Flying
		EI-ARH	*Zeppelin* (1971)	Flying
S.E.5a (replica)	1591	EI-ARI	*Darling Lili* (1970)	Ex-G-AVOU, marked as A4850
		EI-ARI	*You Can't Win 'Em All* (1970)	Flying
		EI-ARI	*Von Richthofen and Brown* (1971)	Flying
		EI-ARI	*Zeppelin* (1971)	Flying
S.E.5a (replica)	1592	EI-ARJ	*Darling Lili* (1970)	Ex-G-AVOV, marked as A7001
		EI-ARJ	*You Can't Win 'Em All* (1970)	Flying
		EI-ARJ	*Von Richthofen and Brown* (1971)	Flying
		EI-ARJ	*Zeppelin* (1971)	Flying
S.E.5a (replica)	1593	EI-ARK	*Darling Lili* (1970)	Ex-G-AVOW, marked as A5202
		EI-ARK	*Von Richthofen and Brown* (1971)	Flying
		EI-ARK	*Zeppelin* (1971)	Flying
S.E.5a (replica)	1594	EI-ARL	*Darling Lili* (1970)	Ex-G-AVOX, marked as A6262
		EI-ARL	*Von Richthofen and Brown* (1971)	Flying
		EI-ARL	*Zeppelin* (1971)	Flying
S.E.5a (replica)	1595	EI-ARM	*Darling Lili* (1970)	Ex-G-AVOY, marked as A1313
		EI-ARM	*Von Richthofen and Brown* (1971)	Flying
		EI-ARM	*Zeppelin* (1971)	Flying

Ryan and Ben Mahoney; became Mahoney-Ryan Aircraft Co. in 1927; built the M-1 and B-1 Brougham monoplane series on which Lindbergh's plane was based. Became the Ryan Aeronautical Co. in 1934 and went on to build the Ryan ST monoplane and PT-22 Recruit military trainer.

Other Notable Title: *Dive Bomber* (1941), ST-A as an RAF prototype.

Seversky

American manufacturer founded in 1931 as the Seversky Aircraft Corp. by Russian expatriate Alexander De Seversky. Developed several racing designs which evolved into the USAAC P-35 and P-43 fighters, which then led to the P-47 built after Seversky was reorganized into Republic in 1939. Further details see: REPUBLIC.

Other Notable Title: *Pilot #5* (1943), SEV-S2 mock-up as P-43 Lancer.

Scaled Composites

Small company located in the Mojave Desert, California, and a part of the Rutan Aircraft Fac-

tory since 1983, known for building many unique experimental aircraft designed by company founder Burt Rutan.

SCAN *see* Grumman / G-21 Goose

Scottish Aviation

Formed in 1935 as Scottish Aviation Ltd. in Prestwick, Scotland, performing aircraft maintenance. Post-World War II, built STOL types, the Pioneer and Twin Pioneer, plus the Bulldog after Beagle Aircraft Ltd. collapsed. Merged as part of British Aerospace (BAe) in 1977.

Short

Founded as Short Brothers in 1897 working in the field of balloons. In 1919 they became Short Brothers (Rochester & Bedford) Ltd., but the company was often just referred to as "Shorts." Eventually developed flying boats and became world-famous for their Empire Class designs, and

Ryan				
Type	msn	SN or Reg. at Time of Filming	Title	Remarks / Film Markings
B-1 Brougham	153	N7206	*The Spirit of St. Louis* (1957)	Flying, marked as N-X-211
B-1 Brougham	156	N7209	*The Spirit of St. Louis* (1957)	Flying, marked as N-X-211
B-1 Brougham	159	N7212	*The Spirit of St. Louis* (1957)	Flying, marked as N-X-211
Model ST-A	112	NC14956	*Without Orders* (1936)	Flying
Model ST-A	128	NC16039	*Test Pilot* (1938)	Flying
		NC16039	*Stunt Pilot* (1939)	Flying
		NC16039	*Tail Spin* (1939)	Flying
		NC16039	*High Barbaree* (1947)	Flying
		NC16039	*The Rocketeer* (1991)	Flying
Model ST-A	144	NC17344	*Flight Command* (1940)	Studio filming

Seversky				
Type	msn	SN or Reg. at Time of Filming	Title	Remarks / Film Markings
SEV-S2	43	NR70Y	*Test Pilot* (1938)	Flying

Scaled Composites				
Type	msn	SN or Reg. at Time of Filming	Title	Remarks / Film Markings
Model 151	001	N151SC	*Aces: Iron Eagle III* (1992)	As fictional "Messerschmitt 263"

Scottish Aviation				
Type	msn	SN or Reg. at Time of Filming	Title	Remarks / Film Markings
Prestwick Pioneer	115	G-AODZ	*The Roots of Heaven* (1958)	Hired from Film Aviation Services Ltd

in particular the S.25 Sunderland maritime flying boat of World War II; also recognized for the Stirling heavy bomber. Became Short Brothers and Harland Ltd. in 1947 and continued for a time with the Sandringham and Solent flying boat series.

Renamed Short Brothers Ltd. in 1977, then acquired by Bombardier, Inc., in 1989. Well known in later years for their Sherpa / Skyvan commuter series.

Siai-Marchetti

Italian manufacturer founded in 1915 as Societa Idrovolanti Alta Italia (SIAI); became Savoia-Marchetti in 1922. Built many successful aircraft designs in the 1920s and 1930s, including the SM.79 Sparviero bomber. Renamed SIAI-Marchetti in 1943 and survived via non-aviation activities postwar. Acquired by Agusta in 1983.

Sikorsky

Founded by Russian immigrant Igor Sikorsky in 1923 as the Sikorsky Aero Engr. Corp., which helped develop the concept of commercial flying boats. Became a part of United Aircraft & Transport Corp. in 1929 and was, for a period, merged with Chance Vought.

Later became a world leader in helicopter technology and from the late 1940s began exclusively developing large military rotary-winged aircraft with such types as the H-19 Chickasaw, H-34 Choctaw, H-3 Sea King and H-53 Sea Stallion. UK aircraft manufacturer Westland license-built many of Sikorsky's designs. The UH-60 Black Hawk is probably Sikorsky's most famous product, having had a starring role in the 2001 film *Black Hawk Down*. See also: WESTLAND.

MODEL S-51 / H-5 DRAGONFLY

First flight (XR-5): August 18, 1943. Single-engined general-purpose helicopter later used as a rescue chopper, also built by Westland in the UK. Best known for its use in 1954's *The Bridges at Toko-Ri*, in which actor Mickey Rooney flew one wearing a top hat.

Other Notable Titles: *Them!* (1954), H-5H.

Short		SN or Reg. at Time of		
Type	*msn*	*Filming*	*Title*	*Remarks / Film Markings*
Seaford Mk. I	S.1293	(RAF) NJ201	*The Sea Shall Not Have Them* (1954)	Background
Sea Otter Mk. I	—	(RN) JM909	*The Sea Shall Not Have Them* (1954)	Leading role
Solent Mk. 3	S.1295	N9946F	*Raiders of the Lost Ark* (1981)	Ex–G-AKNP, non-flying
Solent Mk. 3	S.1297	(RAF) WM759	*The Sea Shall Not Have Them* (1954)	Background
Sunderland Mk. I	S.1034	(RAF) P9606	*Coastal Command* (1942)	—

Siai-Marchetti		SN or Reg. at Time of		
Type	*msn*	*Filming*	*Title*	*Remarks / Film Markings*
SIAI-Marchetti SF.260TP	703/62-006	N260TP	*Quantum of Solace* (2008)	Black turboprop fighter

Sikorsky		SN or Reg. at Time of		
Type	*msn*	*Filming*	*Title*	*Remarks / Film Markings*
Model S-29-A	1	NC2756	*Hell's Angels* (1930)	Crashed during filming March 22, 1929. Pilot bailed out but mechanic killed in crash
Sikorsky S-38B	B414-20	N28V	*The Aviator* (2004)	Floatplane
XPBS-1	4400	BuNo. 9995	*Flight Command* (1940)	Crashed in 1942

Model S-51...		SN or Reg. at Time of		
Type	*msn*	*Filming*	*Title*	*Remarks / Film Markings*
HO3S-1 Dragonfly	unknown	BuNo. 123129	*The Bridges at Toko-Ri* (1954)	—

Model S-55 / H-19
Chickasaw Series

First flight: November 10, 1949. Single-engined utility helicopter named the Chicksaw in U.S. Army service and the Whirlwind by Westland in the UK, who built 431 including two for the Queen's Flight. Numerous appearances on film, with the definitive H-19 movie being *Battle Taxi* (1955).

Other Notable Titles: *A Gathering of Eagles* (1963); *The Poseidon Adventure* (1972).

Model S-58 / H-34
Choctaw Series

First flight: March 8, 1954. Single-engined ASW helicopter for the U.S. Navy as the Seabat,

later developed into a utility version for the U.S. Army as the Choctaw and for the USMC as the Seahorse—a total of 1,821 were built. Another 378 were built in the UK by Westland as the Wessex. Well known for its use on the TV series *Riptide*.

Other Notable Titles: *240-Robert* (TVS, 1979–1981); *Air America* (1990), Thai AF S-58T; *Men of Honor* (2000).

Model S-61 /
H-3 Sea King Series

First flight: March 11, 1959. Twin-engined ASW / SAR helicopter had a successful career with the U.S. Navy spanning from 1961 to 2006, and even longer with the USMC as a presidential

Model S-55... Type	msn	SN or Reg. at Time of Filming	Title	Remarks / Film Markings
SH-19A Chickasaw	55-153	51-3882	*The McConnell Story* (1955)	—
SH-19B Chickasaw	55-441	51-3947	*The McConnell Story* (1955)	—
SH-19B Chickasaw	55-535	52-7495	*Flight from Ashiya* (1964)	—
SH-19B Chickasaw	55-589	52-7513	*Bombers B-52* (1957)	—
SH-19B Chickasaw	55-611	52-7520	*Battle Taxi* (1955)	—
SH-19B Chickasaw	55-617	52-7526	*Battle Taxi* (1955)	—
SH-19B Chickasaw	55-693	52-7564	*Toward the Unknown* (1956)	—
SH-19B Chickasaw	55-812	53-4450	*On the Threshold of Space* (1956)	—
SH-19B Chickasaw	55-814	53-4452	*On the Threshold of Space* (1956)	—
H-19D Chickasaw	55-646	N91AS	*Airwolf* (TVS, 1984-1987)	Ex–52-7618, civil S-55B conversion
Model S-55	55-792	N22955	*Iceman* (1984)	Ex–RCAF 9621, marked as C-FJTB
Model S-55C	55-1050	N860	*Sole Survivor* (TVM, 1970)	Marked in false USAF markings

Model S-58... Type	msn	SN or Reg. at Time of Filming	Title	Remarks / Film Markings
H-34G.II	58-1097	N8292	*Charlie Chan and the Curse of the Dragon Queen* (1981)	Ex–W.Germany, flying
		N8292	*The Right Stuff* (1983)	Marked as Marines / 32
HSS-1N Seabat	58-1344	N95954	*Superman III* (1983)	Ex–BuNo. 148954
HUS-1 Seahorse	58-1519	N698	*Riptide* (TVS, 1984-1986)	Ex–BuNo. 150199, marked as *Screamin' Mimi* S-58DT turbine conversion

Model S-61... Type	msn	SN or Reg. at Time of Filming	Title	Remarks / Film Markings
SH-3A Sea King	61-069	BuNo. 148995	*The Final Countdown* (1980)	—
SH-3A Sea King	61-084	BuNo. 149010	*The Final Countdown* (1980)	—
SH-3A Sea King	61-134	BuNo. 149717	*The Final Countdown* (1980)	—
SH-3A Sea King	61-160	BuNo. 149894	*Top Gun* (1986)	—
SH-3D Sea King	61-367	BuNo. 152704	*Raise the Titanic!* (1980)	—
HH-3F Pelican	61-629	(USCG) 1467	*Top Gun* (1986)	Seen in ocean rescue scene
S-61A-4 Nuri	61-417	M23-09	*Bat*21* (1988)	Doubles as HH-3 Jolly Green Giant
S-61A-4 Nuri	61-796	M23-29	*Bat*21* (1988)	Doubles as HH-3 Jolly Green Giant
S-61N	61-762	C-GYCH	*Titanic* (1997)	Flying
S-61N	61-826	N15456	*Independence Day* (1996)	Doubles as presidential "Marine One"

helicopter. Popular model for export, and West-land built numerous variants for UK military forces. Minor roles in many films, but 1988's *Bat*21*, featuring the Malaysian version known as the "Nuri," has better detail than most.

Other Notable Titles: *The Right Stuff* (1983); *The Hunt for Red October* (1990); *Apollo 13* (1995).

Model S-62 / H-52 Seaguard Series

First flight: May 22, 1958. Single-engined SAR version for the USCG.

Other Notable Titles: *The Abyss* (1989).

Model S-64 Skycrane / CH-54 Tarhe Series

First flight: May 9, 1962. Twin-engined heavy-lift helicopter saw 89 built as the military CH-54 and 10 as the civil S-64. Remanufactured for the

fire-bombing role by Erickson Air-Crane, Inc., who also now own the design rights.

Other Notable Titles: *Swordfish* (2001).

Model S-65 / H-53 Sea Stallion Series

First flight: October 14, 1964. Twin / triple-engined heavy-lift transport helicopter.

Over 650 built since 1963, the USMC version is named Sea Stallion and the USAF SAR version the Super Jolly Green Giant. Later USMC CH-5E version was named the Super Stallion. The Stallion's most notable appearance on film is the 1974 air-disaster movie *Airport 1975*.

Other Notable Titles: *The Jackal* (1997); *The Sum of All Fears* (2002), USMC CH-53E.

Model S-70 / UH-60 Black Hawk Series

First flight: October 17, 1974. Twin-engined utility helicopter has a multi-role function, with

Model S-62...		SN or Reg. at		
Type	msn	Time of Filming	Title	Remarks / Film Markings
HH-52A Seaguard	62-051	(USCG) 1373	The Ghost of Flight 401 (TVM, 1978)	Brief appearance
HH-52A Seaguard	62-069	(USCG) 1388	Thunderball (1965)	Later to civil reg. N4341Q
HH-52A Seaguard	62-103	(USCG) 1419	Black Sunday (1977)	—

Model S-64...		SN or Reg. at		
Type	msn	Time of Filming	Title	Remarks / Film Markings
S-64E Aircrane	64-099	N4035S	Independence Day (1996)	As "Welcome Wagon" helicopter

Model S-65...		SN or Reg. at		
Type	msn	Time of Filming	Title	Remarks / Film Markings
HH-53B	65-086	66-14431	Airport 1975 (1974)	Later to MH-43J Pave Low III
HH-53C	65-274	69-5795	Firefox (1982)	Later to MH-43J Pave Low III
CH-53C	65-335	70-1625	Tomorrow Never Dies (1997)	MH-43J Pave Low III conversion

Model S-70...		SN or Reg. at		
Type	msn	Time of Filming	Title	Remarks / Film Markings
HH-60J Jay Hawk	70-1565	(USCG) 6008	The Guardian (2006)	—
HH-60J Jay Hawk	70-1585	(USCG) 6014	The Guardian (2006)	—
HH-60J Jay Hawk	70-1705	(USCG) 6023	The Guardian (2006)	—
HH-60J Jay Hawk	70-1789	(USCG) 6030	The Guardian (2006)	—
HH-60J Jay Hawk	70-1955	(USCG) 6034	The Guardian (2006)	—
HH-60J Jay Hawk	70-2283	(USCG) 6042	The Guardian (2006)	—
MH-60T Jay Hawk	—	(USCG) 6011	Man of Steel (2013)	—
S-70C-0	70-583	N70C	Salt (2010)	As unmarked army chopper
			Act of Valor (2012)	—
S-70C-5	70-1029	N2FH	The Manchurian Candidate (2004)	Marked as UAE
			Act of Valor (2012)	—

variants of the type in service with all branches of the U.S. armed forces. Many exported to foreign military and government agencies. The Black Hawk is most notable for its leading role in the 2001 film *Black Hawk Down* and the 2006 film *The Guardian*, featuring the USCG Jay Hawk variant in great detail—both movies are exceptional representations of this helicopter on the big screen.

Other Notable Titles: *Fire Birds* (1990); *Clear and Present Danger* (1994); *Armageddon* (1998); *The Perfect Storm* (2000); *Black Hawk Down* (2001); *Tears of the Sun* (2003); *Skyline* (2010); *Transformers: Dark of the Moon* (2011); *Act of Valor* (2012), SH-60B.

SIPA

French manufacturer known as Societe Industrielle Pour l'Aeronautique (SIPA) was founded in 1938, building parts for other manufacturers. Post-World War II it began building light trainer aircraft, especially the licensed Arado 396 as the S.121 two-seat advanced trainer. SIPA was absorbed into Aerospatiale in 1975.

Slingsby

British manufacturer founded in the early 1930s by Frederick Slingsby, building gliders and sailplanes as Slingsby, Russell & Brown Ltd; became Slingsby Sailplanes Ltd. in 1939 and built components for other aero manufacturers during World War II. Became Slingsby Aircraft Ltd. in 1967 and was then absorbed into the Vickers Group as Vickers-Slingsby Sailplanes Ltd. Ceased aircraft activities by 1982, but the company survived in other manufacturing areas. Built several replica aircraft for the film industry in the late 1960s as listed below.

Sopwith

Famous World War I–era British manufacturer was founded in 1912 by Thomas Sopwith.

Produced a number of early aircraft designs, but is best remembered for the Camel, Pup and 1½ Strutter biplane fighters; also produced a Triplane design in 1916. The company survived until 1920, when Sopwith and Harry Hawker

SIPA Type	msn	SN or Reg. at Time of Filming	Title	Remarks / Film Markings
S.121	57	F-BLKH	*The Eagle has Landed* (1977)	Doubles as departing German type

Slingsby Type	msn	SN or Reg. at Time of Filming	Title	Remarks / Film Markings
Type 56 S.E.5a—*See under:* ROYAL AIRCRAFT FACTORY				
Type 57 Camel F.1	1701	G-AWYY	*Biggles Sweeps the Skies* [canceled]	Sopwith Camel conversion for a 1969 Universal Pictures film which was canceled. Exported to the U.S. in 1970
Type 58 Rumpler C.IV	1704	G-AXAL	*Biggles Sweeps the Skies* [canceled]	Tiger Moth conversion for a 1969 Universal Pictures film which was canceled. Exported to the U.S. in 1970 as N1915E
Type 58 Rumpler C.IV	1705	G-AXAM	*Biggles Sweeps the Skies* [canceled]	Tiger Moth conversion for a 1969 Universal Pictures film which was canceled. Exported to the U.S. in 1970 as N1916E

Sopwith Type	msn	SN or Reg. at Time of Filming	Title	Remarks / Film Markings
Camel F.1 (replica)	3	N6254	*Lafayette Escadrille* (1958)	Flying
Camel F.1 (replica)	TM10	N8997	*The Great Waldo Pepper* (1975)	Features a red cowling
1½ Strutter	RA003	N4088H	*Flyboys* (2006)	Flying
Pup (replica)	BAPC.179	—	*Aces High* (1976)	Non-flying, marked as A7317

Sopwith Camel F.1 N6254 built by Tallmantz Aviation, Inc., starred in William Wellman's *Lafayette Escadrille* (1958) and several subsequent Tallmantz film projects. Photograph: James H. Farmer Collection.

started a new company, H.G. Hawker Engineering, which evolved into the famous Hawker Aircraft Co.

SPAD

French manufacturer named Societe de Production des Aeroplanes Deperdussin, founded in 1912 by Armand Deperdussin. Built a series of successful biplanes during World War I with the SPAD S.VII through SPAD S.XIV fighter range. Merged into Bleriot in the postwar years, with the SPAD name disappearing altogether.

Other Notable Titles: *Wings* (1927); *Now We're in the Air* (1927); *Hell's Angels* (1930).

Spartan

A British manufacturer founded in 1928 by Oliver Simmonds as Simmonds Aircraft Ltd.

Renamed Spartan Aircraft Ltd. in 1930, building 15 of their Spartan Arrow biplanes and a few other designs before closing in 1935. Not to be confused with the U.S.-founded Spartan Aircraft Co., which produced the well-known Spartan Executive 7W.

Stampe

Belgian manufacturer founded in 1922 as Stampe et Vertongen became well known for their

SPAD Type	msn	SN or Reg. at Time of Filming	Title	Remarks / Film Markings
SPAD S.VII	S-248	N4727V	*Men With Wings* (1938)	Flying
		N4727V	*Stunt Pilot* (1939)	Flying
		N4727V	*Captain Eddie* (1945)	Flying

Spartan Type	msn	SN or Reg. at Time of Filming	Title	Remarks / Film Markings
Arrow	78	G-ABWP	*Reach for the Sky* (1956)	Background

biplane trainer and recreational aircraft, the most famous being the Model SV.4 first flown in 1933; over 900 were eventually built. Colloquially known simply as the "Stampe," many have been preserved as private aircraft, so there have been a large number available to filmmakers for hire.

Other Notable Titles: *Von Richthofen and Brown* (1971).

Standard

The Standard Aircraft Corp. was founded in 1916 and was an American manufacturer which supplied a number of biplane types to the U.S. Army during World War I. The best known of these was the Standard J series that in postwar years went on to become a very popular type, along with the DH.4 and Curtiss JN-4, for civilian roles such as the mail service. In the 1950s, Hollywood pilot Paul Mantz rebuilt two airframes

that became a common sight in many motion pictures featuring vintage era aircraft.

Stearman / Boeing-Stearman

American manufacturer founded by Lloyd Stearman in 1927 as the Stearman Aircraft Corp., producing small biplane aircraft. Became a part of the United Aircraft & Transport Corp. in 1929; became the Stearman Aircraft Division of the Boeing Aircraft Co. in 1934; renamed the Wichita Division in 1939. Although the Stearman name ceased to exist at this point, the name has lived on through its most famous product, the Model 75 Kaydet, most often simply referred to as the "Stearman."

Model 75 / Kaydet Series

First flight (Model X70): January 1, 1934. Single-engined primary trainer; 8,584 were built during

Stampe		SN or Reg. at Time of		
Type	*msn*	*Filming*	*Title*	*Remarks / Film Markings*
Model SV.4B	64	G-AZSA	*Aces High* (1976)	Marked as: E954, doubles as S.E.5a
Model SV.4C	120	G-AZGC	*Aces High* (1976)	Doubles as S.E.5a
		G-AZGC	*High Road to China* (1983)	Marked as G-EOHE / *Dorothy*
Model SV.4C	141	G-BXNW	*Biggles: Adventures in Time* (1986)	Flying, marked as E6452
Model SV.4C	163	G-AXYW	*Aces High* (1976)	Doubles as S.E.5a
Model SV.4C	360	G-AWXZ	*Aces High* (1976)	Marked as E639 and E943, doubles as S.E.5a
		G-AWXZ	*Indiana Jones and the Last Crusade* (1989)	Marked as D-EKVY
		G-AWXZ	*The Mummy* (1999)	Marked as B5539
Model SV.4C	376	G-AZGE	*Aces High* (1976)	Marked as E940, doubles as S.E.5a
		G-AZGE	*High Road to China* (1983)	Marked as G-EQHF / *Lillian*
Model SV.4C	386	F-BBIT	*The Blue Max* (1966)	Doubles as an S.E.5 and Fokker D.VII
Model SV.4C	1060	F-BAUR	*The Blue Max* (1966)	Doubles as an S.E.5 and Fokker D.VII
		N901AC	*Pancho Barnes* (TVM, 1988)	Flying

Standard		SN or Reg. at Time of		
Type	*msn*	*Filming*	*Title*	*Remarks / Film Markings*
Model J-1	1582	N2825D	*The Spirit of St. Louis* (1957)	Tallmantz rebuilt and owned
		N2825D	*It's a Mad, Mad, Mad, Mad World* (1963)	Flying
		N2825D	*Thoroughly Modern Millie* (1967)	Marked as "721-K"
		N2825D	*Lucky Lady* (1975)	Flying
		N2825D	*The Great Waldo Pepper* (1975)	Flying
Model J-1	1598	N2826D	*The Spirit of St. Louis* (1957)	Tallmantz rebuilt and owned
		N2826D	*The Wings of Eagles* (1957)	Fitted with floats, marked as A-109
Model J-1	T4595	N62505	*The Court-Martial of Billy Mitchell* (1955)	Flying
		N62505	*Ace Eli and Rodger of the Skies* (1973)	Flying
		N62505	*The Rocketeer* (1991)	Flying

Stearman... Type	msn	SN or Reg. at Time of Filming	Title	Remarks / Film Markings
Stearman C2B	110	NC / R / X4099	Air Mail (1932)	Also flew as camera-plane
		NC / R / X4099	Central Airport (1933)	Also flew as camera-plane
		NC / R / X4099	Devil Dogs of the Air (1935)	Doubles as a Vought O2U Corsair
		NC / R / X4099	Ceiling Zero (1936)	Camera-plane
		NC / R / X4099	Flight from Glory (1937)	—
		NC / R / X4099	Men With Wings (1938)	Also flew as camera-plane
		NC / R / X4099	20,000 Men a Year (1939)	Also flew as camera-plane
		NC / R / X4099	Power Dive (1941)	Briefly seen
Stearman C3	190	NC6491	20,000 Men a Year (1939)	Flying
Stearman C3MN	172	NC6486	Keep 'Em Flying (1941)	Flying
Stearman C3R	5011	NC668K	Wings over Wyoming (1937)	Flying
Stearman C3R	5036	N794H	No Place to Land (1958)	Flying

Model 75... Type	msn	SN or Reg. at Time of Filming	Title	Remarks / Film Markings
PT-13D Kaydet	75-5247	N4826V	No Place to Land (1958)	Ex-42-17084, flying
PT-13D Kaydet	75-5488	N4766V	Capricorn One (1978)	Ex-42-17325, marked as A&A, flown by Frank Tallman
		N4766V	Deadly Encounter (TVM, 1982)	Flown by owner Art Scholl
		N4766V	The A-Team (TVS, 1983-1987)	Flown by owner Art Scholl for 1983 Pilot episode
PT-13D Kaydet	75-5497	N6692C	Tora! Tora! Tora! (1970)	Ex-42-17334, marked as "NC34307"
PT-13D Kaydet	75-5510	N121R	Spencer's Pilots (TVS, 1976)	Ex-42-17347, Super-Stearman conversion
		N121R	The Last Flight of Noah's Ark (1980)	Brief flyby
		N121R	Magnum P.I. (TVS, 1980-1988)	"Guest appearance" in one episode
PT-13D Kaydet	75-5629	I-KJNG	The English Patient (1996)	Ex-42-17466 and N88ZK, marked as "G-AFEA"
PT-13D Kaydet	75-5659	G-BAVN	The Aviator (1985)	Ex-42-17496, flying
PT-13D Kaydet	75-5660	N4866N	Amelia Earhart (TVM, 1976)	Ex-42-17497, flying
PT-17 Kaydet	75-1907	N53039	Charley Varrick (1973)	Ex-41-8348, flown by Frank Tallman
PT-17 Kaydet	75-2265	VH-JLA	Kangaroo Jack (2003)	Ex-41-8706, flying
PT-17 Kaydet	75-2793	N56949	The Pursuit of D.B. Cooper (1981)	Ex-41-25304, flying
PT-17 Kaydet	75-3047	YU-BAI	The Aviator (1985)	Ex-41-25540, flying
PT-17 Kaydet	75-3125	N59731	Skyward (TVM, 1980)	Ex-41-25618, flying
PT-17 Kaydet	75-4775	G-AROY	The Aviator (1985)	Ex-42-16612, flying
		G-AROY	Biggles: Adventures in Time (1986)	Flying
N2S-2 Kaydet	75-1335	N61445	Forever Young (1992)	Ex-BuNo. 3558, brief flyby
		N61445	The Kid (2000)	Flying
		N61445	Pearl Harbor (2001)	Flying
N2S-3 Kaydet	75-7016	N450SR	Space Cowboys (2000)	Ex-BuNo. 07412, aerobatic biplane
N2S-3 Kaydet	75-7394	G-ROAN	The Aviator (1985)	Ex-BuNo. 07790, damaged before filming started
N2S-3 Kaydet	75-7759	N68405	Airwolf (TVS, 1984-1987)	Ex-BuNo. 38138, "guest appearance" in one episode
		N68405	Sunset (1988)	Flying
		N68405	Independence Day (1996)	Flying, Russ Casse's crop-duster
N2S-4 Kaydet	75-3420	N450WT	Beautiful Dreamer (2006)	Ex-BuNo. 29989, background

World War II as the PT-13 / PT-17 Kaydet. Probably the most famous American biplane ever built, colloquially known as the "Stearman." Became a popular crop-dusting aircraft in the postwar years. On-screen the Stearman has had its fair share of fame with some very notable appearances, in particular *Thunder Birds* (1942), *Capricorn One* (1978) and *Independence Day* (1996).

Other Notable Titles: *Stunt Pilot* (1939); *Wings of the Navy* (1939); *Dive Bomber* (1941); *Keep 'Em Flying* (1941); *Thunder Birds* (1942); *God Is My Co-Pilot* (1945); *It Happened at the World's Fair* (1963), N6340; *The Cat from Outer Space* (1978), flown by Frank Tallman; *King Solomon's Mines* (1985); *Secondhand Lions* (2003).

Stinson

American manufacturer founded in 1920 as the Stinson Aircraft Co. by Edward Stinson; became the Stinson Aircraft Corp. in 1926, successfully selling small aircraft types. Later went through a series of changes, becoming a part of the Aviation Manufacturing Corp. before becoming the Stinson Division of the Vultee Aircraft Corp. in 1940. Made the well known L-5 Sentinel during World War II. Became a part of Consolidated-Vultee (Convair) before being sold off in 1948 to Piper Aircraft, with the Stinson name being absorbed into Piper branding.

Other Notable Titles: *Desperate Journey* (1942), Model A as a Junkers Ju 52.

Stinson		SN or Reg. at Time of		
Type	msn	Filming	Title	Remarks / Film Markings
SM-8A Junior	4098	NC930W	*The Tarnished Angels* (1957)	—
SR-5 Reliant	9210	NC13843	*Bright Eyes* (1934)	—
V-77 Reliant	77-166	CF-CAJ	*Amelia* (2009)	Briefly seen
L-1 Vigilant	unknown	N63230	*High Barbaree* (1947)	Ex-40-3102, marked as "NX63287"
		N63230	*Never So Few* (1959)	—
		N63230	*Spencer's Pilots* (TVS, 1976)	"Guest appearance" in one episode
L-5 Sentinel	unknown	42-98119	*Mission Over Korea* (1953)	—
L-5 Sentinel	76-121	42-98496	*Mission Over Korea* (1953)	To civilian reg. N9838F
L-5 Sentinel	76-560	N64669	*Catch-22* (1970)	Ex-42-98319
L-5G Sentinel	unknown	45-35025	*Mission Over Korea* (1953)	—
L-5G Sentinel	76-3597	45-35035	*Mission Over Korea* (1953)	To civilian reg. N3232S
Model R	8506	NC12152	*Flight at Midnight* (1939)	—
Model W	3054	NC12146	*Charter Pilot* (1940)	Flying
Model 108-1 Voyager	422	N97422	*This Island Earth* (1955)	Featured in the film's classic UFO kidnap scene

This Stinson L-1 Vigilant N63230 was often used as a camera-plane by its owner and operator, film pilot Paul Mantz. Photograph: James H. Farmer Collection.

Sud-Aviation   *see*
Aerospatiale

Supermarine

British manufacturer founded in 1912 as Pemberton-Billing Ltd., developing seaplanes.

Renamed Supermarine Aviation Works Ltd. in 1916, the company evolved their designs into the famous seaplane racers, which competed in the Schneider Trophy races of the late 1920s and early 1930s. In 1928 it was acquired by Vickers (Aircraft) Ltd. as Supermarine Aviation Works (Vick-

ers) Ltd. and in 1938 all aero interests were reorganized as Vickers-Armstrongs (Aircraft) Ltd., but the Supermarine and Vickers manufacturing names remained. Supermarine designs continued to fly until 1960, when Vickers-Armstrongs was merged into the newly formed British Aircraft Corp.

SPITFIRE

First flight: March 5, 1936. Legendary single-engined fighter of World War II, the Spitfire is one of the most famous fighter aircraft in history, its screen appearances—in such British classics as *The Malta Story* (1954) and *Reach for the Sky*

Supermarine		SN or Reg. at Time of		
Type	msn	Filming	Title	Remarks / Film Markings
Attacker F.1	unknown	WA485	*The Sound Barrier* (1952)	As fictional "901 prototype"
Type 517 Swift	unknown	VV119	*The Sound Barrier* (1952)	As fictional "902 prototype"

Spitfire		SN or Reg. at Time of		
Type	msn	Filming	Title	Remarks / Film Markings
Spitfire Mk. Ib	WASP.20/2	G-AIST	*Battle of Britain* (1969)	Ex-RAF AR213, flying
		G-AIST	*Piece of Cake* (TVMS, 1988)	Flying
Spitfire Mk. IIa	CBAF.14	G-AWIJ	*Battle of Britain* (1969)	Ex-RAF P7350, flying
Spitfire Mk. Vb	CBAF.1646	BL614	*Battle of Britain* (1969)	Taxi scenes only
Spitfire LF.Mk. Vb	CBAF.1061	G-AISU	*Battle of Britain* (1969)	RAF AB910, RAF owned, flying
Spitfire LF.Mk. Vb	CBAF.2403	EP120	*Battle of Britain* (1969)	Static only
		G-LFVB	*Dark Blue World* (2001)	Flying
		G-LFVB	*Pearl Harbor* (2001)	Flying
Spitfire LF.Mk. Vb	CBAF.2461	BM597	*Battle of Britain* (1969)	Static only
		G-MKVB	*Dark Blue World* (2001)	Flying
		G-MKVB	*Pearl Harbor* (2001)	Flying
Spitfire LF.Mk. Vc	WASP.20/223	G-AWII	*Battle of Britain* (1969)	Ex-RAF AR501, flying
		G-AWII	*Pearl Harbor* (2001)	Flying
Spitfire LF.Mk. VIIIc	6S/583793	G-BKMI	*Dark Blue World* (2001)	Ex-RAF MV154, flying
		G-BKMI	*Pearl Harbor* (2001)	Flying
Spitfire HF.Mk. IXe	CBAF.IX4494	G-AWGB	*Battle of Britain* (1969)	Ex-RAF TE308, flying, camera-plane
Spitfire LF.Mk. IX	CBAF.IX7263	G-AVAV	*Battle of Britain* (1969)	Ex-RAF MJ772, flying
Spitfire LF.Mk. IXb	CBAF.IX533	OO-ARD	*The Longest Day* (1962)	Ex-RAF MH415, flying
		G-AVDJ	*The Night of the Generals* (1967)	Flying
		G-AVDJ	*Battle of Britain* (1969)	Flying
Spitfire LF.Mk. IXb	CBAF.IX552	OO-ARA	*The Longest Day* (1962)	Ex-RAF MH434, flying
		G-ASJV	*Operation Crossbow* (1965)	Flying
		G-SAJV	*Battle of Britain* (1969)	Flying
		G-ASJV	*A Bridge Too Far* (1977)	Flying
		G-ASJV	*Hope and Glory* (1987)	Flying
		G-ASJV	*Piece of Cake* (TVMS, 1988)	Flying, performed a bridge fly-under
		G-ASJV	*Dark Blue World* (2001)	Flying

Spitfire (Type)	(msn)	(SN or Reg. at Time of Filming)	(Title)	(Remarks / Film Markings)
Spitfire LF.Mk. IXc	CBAF.IX1514	OO-ARB	The Longest Day (1962)	Ex-RAF MK297, flying
		G-ASSD	Battle of Britain (1969)	Flying
Spitfire LF.Mk. IXc	CBAF.IX1561	MK356	Battle of Britain (1969)	Static only
Spitfire LF.Mk. IXc	CBAF.IX1886	OO-ARF	The Longest Day (1962)	Ex-RAF MK923, flying
Spitfire LF.Mk. IXc	CBAF.IX2200	G-MKIX	Piece of Cake (TVMS, 1988)	Ex-RAF NH238, flying
Spitfire LF.Mk. IXe	6S/730116	G-BJSG	Piece of Cake (TVMS, 1988)	Ex-RAF ML417, flying
Spitfire PR.Mk. XI	6S/533723	G-PRXI	Piece of Cake (TVMS, 1988)	Ex-RAF PL983, flying
Spitfire F.Mk. XIVc	6S.432263	G-ALGT	Battle of Britain (1969)	Ex-RAF RM689, flying
Spitfire FR.Mk. XIV	6S/648206	N1148P	Aces: Iron Eagle III (1992)	Ex-RAF NH904
Spitfire LF.Mk. XVIe	CBAF.3495	SM411	Battle of Britain (1969)	Taxi scenes only
Spitfire LF.Mk. XVIe	CBAF.4497	TE311	Battle of Britain (1969)	Taxi scenes only
Spitfire LF.Mk. XVIe	CBAF.4610	TE476	Battle of Britain (1969)	Taxi scenes only
		G-XVIB	White Hunter Black Heart (1990)	Brief static scene
Spitfire LF.Mk. XVIe	CBAF.4640	RW382	Battle of Britain (1969)	Static only
Spitfire LF.Mk. XVIe	CBAF.4688	SL574	Battle of Britain (1969)	Static only
Spitfire LF.Mk. XVIe	CBAF.11414	TE288	Reach for the Sky (1956)	Static only, as AR251 / QV-X / ZD-S
Spitfire LF.Mk. XVIe	CBAF.11470	TE356	Battle of Britain (1969)	Taxi scenes only
Spitfire LF.Mk. XVIe	CBAF.11485	TE384	Battle of Britain (1969)	Taxi scenes only
Spitfire LF.Mk. XVIe	CBAF.IX4590	TE456	Reach for the Sky (1956)	Flying, as TE425 / PD-S
Spitfire LF.Mk. XVIe	unknown	RW345	Reach for the Sky (1956)	Static only, as TA614
Spitfire LF.Mk. XVIe	unknown	RW352	The Malta Story (1953)	Flying
		RW352	Reach for the Sky (1956)	Flying, as RA617 / QV-P / QV-S
Spitfire LF.Mk. XVIe	unknown	SL574	Reach for the Sky (1956)	Flying, as RV214 / QV-R
Spitfire LF.Mk. XVIe	unknown	SL745	Reach for the Sky (1956)	Static only, as TR627 / QV-T
Spitfire LF.Mk. XVIe	unknown	TB245	The Malta Story (1953)	Flying
Spitfire LF.Mk. XVIe	unknown	TB293	Reach for the Sky (1956)	Static only, as RV415 / QV-U
Spitfire LF.Mk. XVIe	unknown	TB382	Battle of Britain (1969)	Taxi scenes only
Spitfire LF.Mk. XVIe	unknown	TB863	Reach for the Sky (1956)	Studio filming
		TB863	Battle of Britain (1969)	Spares use
Spitfire LF.Mk. XVIe	unknown	TB885	Reach for the Sky (1956)	Static only, as R1247 / QV-V
Spitfire LF.Mk. XVIe	unknown	TE178	The Malta Story (1953)	Flying
Spitfire LF.Mk. XVIe	unknown	TE241	The Malta Story (1953)	Flying
Spitfire LF.Mk. XVIe	unknown	TE341	Reach for the Sky (1956)	Static only, as VT151 / ZD-S / QV-S
Spitfire LF.Mk. XVIe	unknown	TE358	Reach for the Sky (1956)	Flying, as AR251 / QV-X
Spitfire PR.Mk. XIX	6S.585121	PS915	Battle of Britain (1969)	Static only
Spitfire PR.Mk. XIX	6S.594677	PS853	Battle of Britain (1969)	RAF owned, flying
Spitfire PR.Mk. XIX	6S.683528	PM631	Battle of Britain (1969)	RAF owned, flying
Spitfire PR.Mk. XIX	6S.687107	PM651	Battle of Britain (1969)	Static only
Spitfire F.21	SMAF.4338	LA198	Battle of Britain (1969)	Static only

(1956)—being almost as famous as its real-life exploits. These films, unintentionally, also showed the slow demise of the Spitfire, depicted in junkyards or with late-model variants flying in place of early war variants. Not until *Battle of Britain* (1969) were early-model Spits once again depicted, albeit many retrofitted from Mk. IX and XVI versions. Since then this famous fighter has had a much-deserved revival on the Warbird scene with many being restored to flying condition.

Other Notable Titles: *The Lion Has Wings* (1939); *A Yank in the RAF* (1941); *Eagle Squadron* (1942); *The First of the Few* (1942); *Angels One Five* (1952), two in background; *The Sound Barrier* (1952); *Sink the Bismarck!* (1960); *The Thousand Plane Raid* (1968); *Goodbye Mr. Chips* (1969).

This Spitfire Mk. IXb G-ASJV (s/n MH434) flew in many film productions such as *Battle of Britain* (1969), *A Bridge Too Far* (1977) and *Dark Blue World* (2001), but is seen here while filming for *A Piece of Cake* (TVMS, 1988). Photograph: Derek Ferguson.

Tallmantz

Founded in 1961 as Tallmantz Aviation, Inc., by Hollywood pilots Paul Mantz and Frank Tallman. Not a manufacturer as such, but they did rebuild, replicate and restore many vintage-era aircraft for motion picture use, such as the Standard J-1, Sopwith Camel, Curtiss Jenny, Curtiss Pusher, *Spirit of St. Louis* replicas, and perhaps most famously, the ill-fated Phoenix P-1, based on a C-82 boom. The company closed in 1986.

Taylorcraft

American manufacturer founded in 1920 by Clarence and Robert Taylor as the Taylor Bros. Aircraft Manufacturing Co. Subsequently went through many business and organizational upheavals throughout the 1930s before becoming the Taylorcraft Aviation Corp. in 1938, at the same time opening Taylorcraft Aeroplanes (England) Ltd. in the UK. During World War II produced over 2,100 L-2 Grasshopper spotter planes.

Tallmantz Type	msn	SN or Reg. at Time of Filming	Title	Remarks / Film Markings
Phoenix P-1	1	N93082	*The Flight of the Phoenix* (1965)	Flyable scratch-build; crashed during filming, killing famed Hollywood stunt pilot Paul Mantz

Taylorcraft Type	msn	SN or Reg. at Time of Filming	Title	Remarks / Film Markings
Auster AOP.Mk. III	344	PH-NGK	*A Bridge Too Far* (1977)	Ex-RAF MZ231, marked as: RT607
Auster AOP.Mk. 5	1800	G-AOCP	*High Flight* (1957)	Ex-RAF TW462

Postwar, Taylorcraft went bankrupt, and in 1946 the UK plant was renamed Auster Aircraft Ltd., surviving up to 1960 with their "Auster" design. Taylorcraft, Inc., was reformed in 1947 and continued aircraft production, but at a much lower rate.

Thomas-Morse

American manufacturer originally founded in 1910 as the Thomas Brothers Co.; merged with the Morse Chain Co. in 1917 as the Thomas-Morse Aircraft Corp. Best known products are the S-4 Scout and MB series of fighter aircraft. Became the Thomas-Morse Division of the Consolidated Aircraft Corp. in 1929; the name had disappeared altogether by 1934.

Other Notable Titles: *Wings* (1927); *Hell's Angels* (1930); *The Dawn Patrol* (1930 / 1938); *The Lost Squadron* (1932); *Sky Devils* (1932); *Men With Wings* (1938); *Stunt Pilot* (1939); *The Amazing Howard Hughes* (TVM, 1977).

Transavia

Australian manufacturer founded in 1965 as the Transavia Corp. Pty. Ltd. to produce the PL-12 Airtruk agricultural aircraft originally designed in New Zealand by Bennett Aviation Ltd. A total of 118 aircraft were built from 1965 to 1985. The PL-12 is solely famous for its starring role in the futuristic 1985 film *Mad Max Beyond Thunderdome*.

Thomas-Morse Type	msn	SN or Reg. at Time of Filming	Title	Remarks / Film Markings
Model S-4B (replica)	1	N38923	*Lafayette Escadrille* (1958)	Marked as N1810
		N38923	*The Great Waldo Pepper* (1975)	Features a green cowling

Transavia Type	msn	SN or Reg. at Time of Filming	Title	Remarks / Film Markings
PL-12 Airtruk	1248	VH-EVY	*Mad Max Beyond Thunderdome* (1985)	Flying aircraft
PL-12 Airtruk	G353	VH-IVH	*Mad Max Beyond Thunderdome* (1985)	Likely used for static shots but not confirmed

A Thomas-Morse MB-3A biplane that was used in the pioneering aviation film *Wings* (1927). Photograph: James H. Farmer Collection.

Down and out before filming even started. Transavia PL-12 Airtruk VH-IVH was damaged in a landing accident in late 1984 while on its way to film for *Mad Max Beyond Thunderdome* (1985). It was replaced by Airtruk VH-EVY. Photograph: Terry Lee.

Travel Air

American manufacturer founded in 1925 as the Travel Air Manufacturing Co. by Walter Beech, Clyde Cessna and Lloyd Stearman. Produced a range of sporting designs but were forced out of business in 1929 by the Great Depression. The company assets were acquired by Curtiss-Wright, who continued producing Travel Air designs for a short period.

Model 2000 / 3000 / 4000

First flight: March 13, 1925. Single-engined sportsman biplane design produced as the Model 2000, 3000 and 4000. Many were modified for motion pictures to represent other World War I fighter types both British and German. When modified as the German Fokker D.VII, they were nicknamed the "Wichita Fokker"—Wichita coming from the Lloyd Stearman plant in Kansas, where the modifications were made.

Other Notable Titles: *The Air Circus* (1928); *Flying Fool* (1929), NC5282; *Hell's Angels* (1930); *The Dawn Patrol* (1930 / 1938); *Young Eagles* (1930); *The Lost Squadron* (1932); *Central Airport* (1933), NC477N; *Devil Dogs of the Air* (1935), NC406N; *Men With Wings* (1938); *Stunt Pilot* (1939); *Captain Eddie* (1945); *Blaze of Noon* (1947); *Lafayette Escadrille* (1958); *The Tuskegee Airmen* (TVM, 1995), NC6478.

Travel Air		SN or Reg. at Time of Filming		
Type	*msn*	*Filming*	*Title*	*Remarks / Film Markings*
Model 16-K	16K-2001	NC446W	*Air Mail* (1932)	Performed a hangar fly-through at Bishop Airport, California

Model 2000...		SN or Reg. at Time of Filming		
Type	*msn*	*Filming*	*Title*	*Remarks / Film Markings*
R Mystery Ship (replica)	RB0001	NR614K	*The Rocketeer* (1991)	Flying replica built by Jim Younkin

Valton-Lentokonetehdas

Finnish manufacturer founded in 1928; built several biplane designs during the 1930s. During World War II assembled German Junkers Ju 88 aircraft. Postwar, the company was absorbed into the large Finnish conglomerate Valmet.

Vertol / Boeing-Vertol

American manufacturer founded in 1940 by Frank Piasecki as the P-V Engineering Forum and renamed as the Piasecki Helicopter Corp. in 1946. Well known for its work on helicopter tandem-rotor designs, especially the H-21 "Flying Banana." Became the Vertol Aircraft Corp. in 1956; acquired by the Boeing Co. in 1960 as the Vertol Division; renamed Boeing-Vertol Co. in 1972 and Boeing Helicopter Co. in 1987. Built the hugely successful CH-46 Sea Knight / CH-47 Chinook range of heavy-lift helicopters, which were also built in Japan and Italy. Some excellent views of the USMC CH-46 Sea Knight in the sci-fi film *Battle: Los Angeles* (2011).

Other Notable Titles: *Lara Croft: Tomb Raider* (2001); *Green Zone* (2010); *Battle: Los Angeles* (2011), USMC CH-46E; *Transformers: Dark of the Moon* (2011), CH-47D; *Act of Valor* (2012), MH-47G.

Vickers

British engineering giant Vickers Ltd. formed an Aviation Department in 1911 and made several notable aircraft types during World War I. Merged with Sir W.G. Armstrong Whitworth & Co. in 1927 to form Vickers-Armstrongs Ltd.; aviation division became Vickers (Aircraft) Ltd. in 1928. Acquired Supermarine Aviation as a subsidiary in 1928; in 1938 all aero interests were reorganized as Vickers-Armstrongs (Aircraft) Ltd. but continued to build aircraft under the Supermarine and Vickers brand names. Vickers-Armstrongs merged with several other major British aero manufacturers in 1960 to form British Aircraft Corp. (BAC).

WELLINGTON

First flight: June 15, 1936. Twin-engined medium bomber which fought in the early years of World War II. Although largely outdated bombers, they were, however, built up to 1945 and are well known for their geodesic construction designed by Barnes Wallis of Dambusters fame. Several notable early World War II feature film titles used the "Whimpy" in leading roles.

Other Notable Titles: *The Lion Has Wings* (1939); *One of Our Aircraft is Missing* (1942);

Valton-Lentokonetehdas		SN or Reg. at Time of		
Type	msn	Filming	Title	Remarks / Film Markings
VL Viima II	unknown	G-BAAY	Aces High (1976)	Ex-Finnish AF VI-3, marked as C-1501

Vertol...		SN or Reg. at Time of		
Type	msn	Filming	Title	Remarks / Film Markings
Kawasaki KV-107/II-2	4003	N185CH	Starman (1984)	Flying
Kawasaki KV-107/II-2	4004	JA9503	You Only Live Twice (1967)	Picks up car via magnet
Kawasaki KV-107/II-2	4011	N192CH	Under Siege (1992)	Ex-JA9505, marked as 2406
		N192CH	X2: X-Men United (2003)	Flying
CH-46A Sea Knight	2003	N191CH	King Kong Lives (1986)	Ex-BuNo. 150267, carries Kong's cage
Model 234ER	MJ-016	N241CH	Demolition Man (1993)	As a police assault chopper
		N241CH	The Lost World: Jurassic Park (1997)	Marked as "ingen"

Vickers		SN or Reg. at Time of		
Type	msn	Filming	Title	Remarks / Film Markings
Valetta T.Mk. 3	unknown	WG266	High Flight (1957)	—

Eagle Squadron (1942), as German bomber; The Malta Story (1953).

Vought

Founded as Lewis & Vought Corp. in 1917 by Birdseye Lewis and Chance Vought. Became the Chance Vought Corp. in 1922. Became a part of the United Aircraft & Transport Corp. in 1929 and was, for a period, merged with Sikorsky. Although named as Chance Vought, it was often simply referred to as Vought. Best known during World War II for building the Corsair naval fighter, which remained in production until 1952. Purchased by Ling-Temco in 1961 and renamed LTV (Ling-Temco-Vought) Aerospace Corp. by 1965, building the F-8 Crusader and A-7 Corsair II. Went through several name and organizational changes until sold by LTV in 1991. Still exists in the aerospace industry, but as a mere shadow of its former self.

Notable Titles: Wings of the Navy (1939), O3U-6 / SBU-1; Dive Bomber (1941), OS2U Kingfisher; Captain Eddie (1945), OS2U Kingfisher; Tora! Tora! Tora! (1970), OS2U Kingfisher replica.

O2U Corsair

First flight: 1926. Single-engined scout biplane for the U.S. Navy.

SB2U Vindicator

First flight: January 4, 1936. Single-engined carrier-borne dive-bomber soon outmoded by later types but remained in service with training units until the end of World War II. Many excellent views featured in the 1941 film Dive Bomber.

F4U Corsair

First flight: May 29, 1940. Single-engined naval fighter became a legend during World War II, it

Wellington		SN or Reg. at Time of		
Type	msn	Filming	Title	Remarks / Film Markings
Wellington T.10	unknown	MF628	The Dam Busters (1955)	Flying

O2U Corsair		SN or Reg. at Time of		
Type	msn	Filming	Title	Remarks / Film Markings
O2U-1 Corsair	unknown	BuNo. A-7817	The Flying Fleet (1929)	—
O2U-1 Corsair	unknown	BuNo. A-7938	Devil Dogs of the Air (1935)	—
O2U-1 Corsair	unknown	BuNo. A-7939	Devil Dogs of the Air (1935)	—

SB2U Vindicator		SN or Reg. at Time of		
Type	msn	Filming	Title	Remarks / Film Markings
SB2U-2 Vindicator	unknown	BuNo. 1333	Dive Bomber (1941)	—
SB2U-2 Vindicator	unknown	BuNo. 1381	Dive Bomber (1941)	—

F4U Corsair		SN or Reg. at Time of		
Type	msn	Filming	Title	Remarks / Film Markings
F4U-1A Corsair	3884	N83782	Baa Baa Black Sheep (TVS, 1976-1978)	Ex-BuNo. 17799
F4U-4 Corsair	unknown	N97359	Baa Baa Black Sheep (TVS, 1976-1978)	Ex-BuNo. 97359
F4U-7 Corsair	unknown	N33693	Baa Baa Black Sheep (TVS, 1976-1978)	Ex-BuNo. 133693, brief use only in series
F4U-7 Corsair	unknown	N33714	Baa Baa Black Sheep (TVS, 1976-1978)	Ex-BuNo. 133714
FG-1D Corsair	3367	N6897	Baa Baa Black Sheep (TVS, 1976-1978)	Ex-BuNo. 92106
FG-1D Corsair	3393	N3466G	Baa Baa Black Sheep (TVS, 1976-1978)	Ex-BuNo. 92132
FG-1D Corsair	3694	N3440G	Baa Baa Black Sheep (TVS, 1976-1978)	Ex-BuNo. 92433, 2-seater conversion
FG-1D Corsair	3890	N62290	Baa Baa Black Sheep (TVS, 1976-1978)	Ex-BuNo. 92629

A Vought Corsair as used for the TV series *Baa Baa Black Sheep* **(1976–1978). Photograph: James H. Farmer Collection.**

remained in production postwar and saw service in Korea five years later. Demand for the Corsair was so great, Goodyear and Brewster opened production lines, with the total number built reaching 12,586. The Corsair is best remembered in film aviation for its starring role on the TV series *Baa Baa Black Sheep*.

Other Notable Titles: *Sands of Iwo Jima* (1949); *Flying Leathernecks* (1951); *Flat Top* (1953); *Battle Stations* (1956); *The Wings of Eagles* (1957); *China Doll* (1958).

Vultee

Founded in 1932 as the Airplane Development Corp. by Gerard Vultee. After several owners and name changes in the 1930s, became Vultee Aircraft Inc. in 1939 and produced the BT-13 Valiant and A-31 Vengeance. Merged with Consolidated Aircraft Corp. in 1941 and renamed Consolidated-

Vultee Aircraft Corp. in 1943, which was later renamed Convair. Further details see: CONSOLIDATED.

BT-13 / BT-15 Valiant

First flight: March 24, 1939. Single-engined monoplane basic trainer with a fixed undercarriage. Vultee's venerable BT-13 / BT-15 trainers have had limited exposure on the silver screen; their most famous exploit has been doubling as the "Val" Japanese dive-bombers in the 1970 film *Tora! Tora! Tora!*, which gained them subsequent film and television work. Over 10,300 were originally built.

Other Notable Titles: *Thunder Birds* (1942); *A Guy Named Joe* (1943), at least three; *Winged Victory* (1944), one was 42-89464; *The Story of Will Rogers* (1951); *Fighter Attack* (1953); *Dragonfly Squadron* (1954); *Midway* (1976) as "Vals"; *MacArthur* (1977) as "Vals."

Vultee		SN or Reg. at Time of		
Type	msn	Filming	Title	Remarks / Film Markings
Model V-1AD Special	25	NC16099	*The Tarnished Angels* (1957)	Marked with false reg. NC158

BT-13...	msn	SN or Reg. at Time of Filming	Title	Remarks / Film Markings
Type				
BT-13 Valiant	54A-308	N63163	*Tora! Tora! Tora!* (1970)	Ex-40-917, Val conversion
BT-13A Valiant	74-1414	N54865	*Tora! Tora! Tora!* (1970)	Ex-41-1306, Val conversion
BT-13A Valiant	74-2307	N67208	*Pearl Harbor* (2001)	Ex-41-11297, Val conversion
BT-13A Valiant	74-2819	N65837	*Tora! Tora! Tora!* (1970)	Ex-41-10502, Val conversion
BT-13A Valiant	74-6656	N56336	*Tora! Tora! Tora!* (1970)	Ex-41-22578, Val conversion
		N56336	*Pearl Harbor* (2001)	Crashed during filming
BT-13A Valiant	74-6991	N2200S	*Tora! Tora! Tora!* (1970)	Ex-41-22771, Val conversion
BT-13A Valiant	74-7356	N56478	*Tora! Tora! Tora!* (1970)	Ex-41-22926, Val conversion
		N56478	*Baa Baa Black Sheep* (TVS, 1976–1978)	Flying
		N56478	*Pearl Harbor* (2001)	Flying
		N56478	*Letters from Iwo Jima* (2006)	Background
BT-13B Valiant	79-1220	N56867	*Tora! Tora! Tora!* (1970)	Ex-42-90263, Val conversion
		N56867	*Baa Baa Black Sheep* (TVS, 1976–1978)	Flying
BT-13B Valiant	79-1703	N63227	*Tora! Tora! Tora!* (1970)	Ex-42-90626, Val conversion, crashed during filming
BT-15 Valiant	74A-11513	N67629	*Tora! Tora! Tora!* (1970)	Ex-42-42171, Val conversion
		N67629	*Pearl Harbor* (2001)	Flying. unknown variant
	unknown	N18102	*Tora! Tora! Tora!* (1970)	Val conversion

Two of the Val replicas used for the TV series *Baa Baa Black Sheep* (1976–1978). **Photograph: James H. Farmer Collection.**

WACO

American manufacturer founded in 1919 as the Weaver Aircraft Co. of Ohio (WACO) by George Weaver and others. Weaver departed in 1923 and it became the Advance Aircraft Co., then renamed the Waco Aircraft Co. in 1928. Produced a long line of light aircraft designs, each distinguished by a unique Waco three-letter code that describes the aircraft configuration. During World War II designed the CG-4 glider widely used in the 1944 D-Day invasion. The company failed to achieve any postwar success and disappeared in 1947. The Waco name is pronounced as "wah-co" not "way-co."

Excellent views seen of a Waco floatplane in *Raiders of the Lost Ark* (1981) and an aerobatic version in *Terminal Velocity* (1994).

Other Notable Titles: *Lilac Time* (1928), Waco 10; *Young Eagles* (1930); *Ace of Aces* (1933), Waco 7.

Wallis

Small British manufacturer founded around 1960 as Wallis Autogyros Ltd. by RAF Wg. Cdr. Ken Wallis for research into the non-civilian use of autogyros. The Wallis design has become legendary for its appearance in the 1967 Bond film *You Only Live Twice*, in which Wallis himself performed the flying.

Wedell-Williams

American manufacturer founded in 1929 by James Wedell and Harry Williams, building air racing aircraft. Assets sold to Eastern Airlines in 1936.

Westland

British manufacturer founded in 1935 as Westland Aircraft Ltd., who built the well-known

Westland Wessex Mk. 60 G-AZBY was one of two background helicopters in the Stanley Kubrick film *Full Metal Jacket* (1987). It's seen here as a local liquor store gimmick in Christchurch, New Zealand, in 2003. Photograph: Simon D. Beck.

WACO		SN or Reg. at Time of		
Type	msn	Filming	Title	Remarks / Film Markings
Cabin biplane	unknown	CF-GHV	*Captains of the Clouds* (1942)	—
Cabin biplane	unknown	CF-GHY	*Captains of the Clouds* (1942)	—
ATO	A-65	CF-BPM	*Amelia* (2009)	Briefly seen
GXE	1149	NC4008	*The Tarnished Angels* (1957)	—
UBF-2	3692	N13075	*Raiders of the Lost Ark* (1981)	Floatplane, marked as OB-CPO
UPF-7	5533	N30136	*Terminal Velocity* (1994)	Wing stunt performed on a C-123K
YMF-5	F5030	C-GKLH	*Iron Eagle IV* (1995)	—
YMF-5	F5C-102	C-GZPR	*Amelia* (2009)	Briefly seen

Wallis		SN or Reg. at Time of		
Type	msn	Filming	Title	Remarks / Film Markings
WA.116 Agile	B.203	G-ARZB	*You Only Live Twice* (1967)	Autogyro named *Little Nellie*

Wedell-Williams		SN or Reg. at Time of		
Type	msn	Filming	Title	Remarks / Film Markings
Model 44 Racer	104	NR536V	*Tail Spin* (1939)	Flying

Westland		SN or Reg. at Time of		
Type	msn	Filming	Title	Remarks / Film Markings
Whirlwind HCC.Mk. 8	WA266	(RAF) XN126	films unknown	Sighted at Pinewood Studios
Whirlwind HAR.Mk. 10	WA355	(RAF) XP339	*Octopussy* (1983)	Background
Wessex Mk. 60	WA686	G-AWOX	*Full Metal Jacket* (1987)	Derelict, marked as EM17
Wessex Mk. 60	WA739	G-AYNC	*Full Metal Jacket* (1987)	Flying, marked as EM18
Wessex Mk. 60	WA740	G-AZBY	*Full Metal Jacket* (1987)	Derelict, marked as EM16

Lysander during World War II. Postwar, moved into helicopter development with licenses from U.S. manufacturer Sikorsky, building the Dragonfly (H-5), Whirlwind (H-19), Wessex (H-34) and Sea King (H-3). Merged with the helicopter divisions of Bristol, Fairey and Saunders-Roe to form Westland Helicopters Ltd. in 1961. Slowly went into decline in the early 1980s, became a subsidiary of GKN in 1994, and merged with Agusta in 2000 to form AgustaWestland.

Appendix I: Aviation Film Pilots and Technicians

James Appleby (–August 23, 2010). Motion picture pilot and stunt pilot. Served in the Army Air Corps and USAF; flew 157 missions into Germany during World War II. Worked for Tallmantz Aviation, Inc., throughout its existence as a pilot and builder of replica vintage aircraft. Best-known aviation films are *Catch-22* (1970) and *The Great Waldo Pepper* (1975).

Florence Lowe "Pancho" Barnes (July 22, 1901–March 30, 1975). Pioneer aviator and Hollywood's first female stunt pilot. Helped create the Associated Motion Picture Pilots (AMPP) in 1931, a union-based organization safeguarding industry standards for movie pilots. Proprietor of the Happy Bottom Riding Club from the mid–1930s, a renowned bar, café, restaurant and hotel. It became a favorite hangout for test pilots from nearby Edwards AFB but was destroyed by fire in 1953. It was prominently depicted in the 1983 film *The Right Stuff*.

Tony Bianchi (June 7, 1946–). Aviation film pilot and aerial and technical supervisor. Has managed Personal Plane Services (PPS) Ltd. at Booker Aerodrome since 1977, a company founded by his father Doug Bianchi in 1947 for the restoration, servicing and operation of vintage aircraft. Doug Bianchi then founded Bianchi Aviation Film Services (BAFS) in the 1960s for servicing the film industry with aircraft, pilots and technical expertise. Tony Bianchi has flown for the film and television industry since 1963 and has been involved in over ninety productions. A few of his more notable credits include *Aces High* (1976), *Wings* (TVS, 1977–1978), *High Road to China* (1983), *Indiana Jones and the Last Crusade* (1989) and *The Mummy* (1999).

Jack Canary (1916–August 19, 1968). North American Aviation employee who worked on the AT-6, B-25, P-51 and F-86. The chief pilot for gathering the *Tora! Tora! Tora!* (1970) Japanese replicas until he was killed in a crash while flying one of the BT-15 trainers to Long Beach for conversion. Had previously helped build the Fokker triplanes for *The Blue Max* (1966).

Frank Clarke (December 29, 1898–June 12, 1948). Prominent early Hollywood stunt pilot well known for his involvement with many of the classic, silent-era aviation films. Clarke died in a non-work-related plane crash in 1948. His films included *Stranger than Fiction* (1921), *The Cloud Rider* (1925), *Wings* (1927), *The Air Patrol* (1928), *The Legion of the Condemned* (1928), *Flying Fool* (1929), *Hell's Angels* (1930, chief pilot), *The Lost Squadron* (1932), *Sky Bride* (1932), *Ace of Aces* (1933), *The Great Air Mystery* (1935), *Border Flight* (1936), *Men with Wings* (1938), *The Flying Deuces* (1939), *Flight Command* (1940), *Flying Devils* (1940), *Dive Bomber* (1941, standby pilot) and *Captains of the Clouds* (1942, chief pilot).

John Crewdson (May 15, 1926–June 26, 1983). Often credited as "Captain John Crewdson," a British pilot who managed the UK-based Film Aviation Services Ltd., providing aeronautical expertise to film production companies. His credits include converting three Tiger Moth biplanes for *Lawrence of Arabia* (1962); obtaining, servicing and flying three B-17 bombers and one derelict for *The War Lover* (1962) and providing the Mosquito pilots for *633 Squadron* (1964). Other credits include *I Was Monty's Double* (1958), *Operation Bullshine* (1959), *Jet Storm* (1959), *From Russia with Love* (1963), *Dr. Strangelove* (1964), *On Her Majesty's Secret Service* (1969), *The Spy Who*

Loved Me (1977) and *For Your Eyes Only* (1981). Crewdson was killed in a non-work-related helicopter crash off the Norfolk coast in 1983 while flying his SA.318 Alouette II (G-AWAP).

B.H. DeLay (August 12, 1891–July 4, 1923). Beverly Homer DeLay. Early Hollywood stunt pilot during the silent era. Killed in 1923 when his aircraft broke up in flight while performing at an air show.

J.W. "Corkey" Fornof (December 5, 1945–). Aerial coordinator, pilot and stunt pilot on many action and aviation-themed films including several of the Bond films, *The Rescue* (1988), *Jurassic Park* (1993), *Roswell* (TVM, 1995), *Face/Off* (1997), *Six Days Seven Nights* (1998) and *Mission: Impossible II* (2000). Fornof's Bede Miro-Jet (N70CF) was used for the Bond film *Octopussy* (1983).

Lyn Garrison (April 1, 1937–). Canadian fighter pilot, aviation film advisor and Warbird collector. Joined the RCAF in 1950 and served until 1964 flying the T-33 Silver Star, F-86, Hawker Sea Fury, P-51 and Lancaster. Served with the United Nations on the DHC Otter and Caribou. From 1963 began salvaging, collecting and restoring aircraft, and helped establish the Air Museum of Canada. Personally acquired as many as forty-five classic aircraft, especially Canadian serving types. Began Blue Max Aviation Ltd. with the Irish Air Corps. in 1966, preserving a number of replica biplane types from the 1966 film *The Blue Max*. A mercenary combat pilot in the Nigerian Civil War and the Football War between El Salvador and Honduras, flying the P-51 and Corsair. Garrison is also noted for his humanitarian work toward the impoverished nation of Haiti.

James W. Gavin (March 13, 1935–August 13, 2005). Renowned Hollywood pilot and aerial coordinator who mostly flew helicopters for aerial camera-work and coordinated aerial sequences. Co-founded Cinema Air, Inc., in the late 1970s with fellow pilot Tom Friedkin, providing the film industry with aircraft and aviation expertise. Two of their Bell Jet Rangers (N230CA, N250CA) featured in numerous productions throughout the 1980s. Co-founded the Motion Picture Pilots Association (MPPA) in 1997 to help safeguard industry standards. Also often credited as a second unit director for aerial sequences. Some of his aviation-themed credits include *The Flight*

of the Phoenix (1965), *Skyjacked* (1972), *Birds of Prey* (TVM, 1973), *Sky Heist* (TVM, 1975), *Baa Baa Black Sheep* (TVS, 1976–1978), *Airport 1975* (1974), *Airport '77* (1977), *The Concorde ... Airport '79* (1979), *The Last Flight of Noah's Ark* (1980), *Blue Thunder* (1983), *Iron Eagle* (1986), *War and Remembrance* (TVMS, 1988), *Always* (1989), *Die Hard 2* (1990), *Forever Young* (1992), *Terminal Velocity* (1994) and *Pearl Harbor* (2001).

Dick Grace (January 10, 1898–June 25, 1965). Early Hollywood stunt pilot who specialized in crashing aircraft on film. Most famous for his work on *Wings* (1927), for which he crashed up to four biplanes before the cameras. Served in both world wars and was a B-17 copilot in the second. One of the few early stunt pilots who lived to an old age! Films include *Wings* (1927), *Lilac Time* (1928), *The Lost Squadron* (1932), *Sky Bride* (1932) and *Devil's Squadron* (1936).

Mark Hanna (August 5, 1959–September 26, 1999). Co-founder of the Old Flying Machine Co. (OFMC) with father Ray Hanna. Learned to fly at sixteen years old in a T-34, served in the RAF as a fighter pilot, and saw a tour of duty in the Falklands. Killed in Spain when his Hispano Buchon fighter (G-BOML), crashed during an air show. Notable film and TV credits include *Empire of the Sun* (1987), *Piece of Cake* (TVMS, 1988), *Air America* (1990), *Memphis Belle* (1990) and *Saving Private Ryan* (1998).

Ray Hanna (August 28, 1928–December 1, 2005). New Zealand–born pilot who served in the RAF from 1949 to 1971. Was a squadron leader and a founding member of the RAF Red Arrows display team; also flew civilian 707 and L-1011 airliners. Established in 1981, with son Mark, the Old Flying Machine Co. (OFMC) at Duxford, England, flying and preserving fighter aircraft such as the Spitfire and Mustang. Film and TV credits include piloting and aerial coordination duties for *Empire of the Sun* (1987), *Piece of Cake* (TVMS, 1988), *Memphis Belle* (1990), *Saving Private Ryan* (1998), *Dark Blue World* (2001) and *Flyboys* (2006).

John "Jeff" Hawke. RAF flight lieutenant, film aerial coordinator and pilot. Credits include piloting for *The War Lover* (1962) and *633 Squadron* (1964); flying the B-25 camera-plane for *Battle of Britain* (1969); assembling, flying and coordinating the five B-25 bombers for *Hanover Street*

(1978); plus aerial coordination duties on *Gunbus* (1986) and *Empire of the Sun* (1987). Killed in a non-work-related plane crash.

Steve Hinton (April 1, 1952–). Well-known Hollywood film pilot and aerial coordinator. Has been involved with the Planes of Fame Air Museum since the age of seven (it was then known as the Air Museum), becoming the museum's president in 1994. First began doing film and television work in 1977 as a pilot, stunt pilot and aerial coordinator. Also an accomplished air show performer and air racer, having won several air racing championships with some at Reno. Type rated on 150 aircraft from vintage biplanes to Warbirds to modern jets. A short selection of his aviation-themed titles include *Baa Baa Black Sheep* (TVS, 1976–1978), *1941* (1979), *Airwolf* (TVS, 1984–1987), *Iron Eagle* (1986), *War and Remembrance* (TVMS, 1988), *Always* (1989), *Flight of the Intruder* (1991), *The Rocketeer* (1991), *Aces: Iron Eagle III* (1992), *Forever Young* (1992), *Drop Zone* (1994), *Air Force One* (1997), *Con Air* (1997), *Turbulence* (1997), *Six Days Seven Nights* (1998) and *Pearl Harbor* (2001).

J. David Jones (May 13, 1936–July 14, 1997). Well-known Hollywood film pilot, camera-pilot and aerial coordinator. Film and television credits include *Catch-22* (1970), *Tora! Tora! Tora!* (1970), *King Kong* (1976), *Capricorn One* (1978), *Apocalypse Now* (1979), *The Final Countdown* (1980), *Magnum P.I.* (TVS, 1980–1988), *Tales of the Gold Monkey* (TVS, 1982–1983), *Airwolf* (TVS, 1984–1987), *Fire Birds* (1990), *Speed* (1994), *Waterworld* (1995), *Courage Under Fire* (1996), and *Con Air* (1997).

John "Johnny" Jordan (April 12, 1925–May 16, 1969). Aerial unit cameraman and second unit director well known for his innovative filming techniques. Lost part of his leg while filming the Bond movie *You Only Live Twice* (1967) when another helicopter rotor blade came too close while shooting from an Alouette II helicopter (reg. JA9012). Developed a special aerial harness for filming on mountain slopes for the next Bond film *On Her Majesty's Secret Service* (1969). Killed when he fell from the tail turret of a B-25 camera-plane during the filming of *Catch-22* (1970) in 1969. Other aerial-related titles include *Chitty Chitty Bang Bang* (1968) and *Battle of Britain* (1969).

Skeets Kelly (1913–August 18, 1970). Highly respected cameraman and aerial cameraman whose career stretched back to 1936. Aviation-related work includes *The War Lover* (1962), *Those Magnificent Men in their Flying Machines* (1965), *The Blue Max* (1966), *Chitty Chitty Bang Bang* (1968) and *Battle of Britain* (1969). He was also a second unit cameraman on *Lawrence of Arabia* (1962). Killed during the production of *Zeppelin* (1971), when the Alouette camera-helicopter he was on collided with an S.E.5a biplane replica.

Clay Lacy (August 14, 1932–). American aviation businessman and pilot. Founded his company Clay Lacy Aviation, Inc., in 1968, flying Learjet aircraft, and has since become a leader in charter and corporate jet services. Several of his aircraft are fitted out as camera-planes for aerial photography, having completed many, many projects for film, television and commercials. A selection of Lacy's aviation-themed film credits include *Airport 1975* (1974), *Capricorn One* (1978) *The Concorde … Airport '79* (1979), *The Great Santini* (1979), *Firefox* (1982), *The Right Stuff* (1983), *Top Gun* (1986), *Iron Eagle II* (1988), *Flight of the Intruder* (1991), *Turbulence* (1997) and *Behind Enemy Lines* (2001).

Jimmy Leeward (October 21, 1936–September 16, 2011). American pilot, stunt pilot and aerial coordinator also well known for his air racing abilities. Killed when his P-51D Mustang (N79111) plummeted into the ground at the Reno Air Races in Nevada. Aviation-themed films included *Cloud Dancer* (1980), *The Tuskegee Airmen* (TVM, 1995) and *Amelia* (2009).

Garland Lincoln. Early Hollywood businessman and stunt pilot; was a pilot on *Hell's Angels* (1930). Rebuilt several Nieuport biplanes which were designated as the Garland-Lincoln LF-1 and LF-2 for lease work to film productions.

Ormer Locklear (October 28, 1891–August 2, 1920). Credited as being one of Hollywood's first major stunt pilots. Known as the "king of the wingwalkers," Locklear perfected the aerial stunt known as the "transfer," whereby a stunt man jumped from one aircraft to another in midair. Only made two films, *The Great Air Robbery* (1919) and *The Skywayman* (1920), before being killed performing a spin stunt for the latter title.

T.G. "Hamish" Mahaddie (March 1911–January 16, 1997). Full name Thomas Gilbert Mahaddie. Joined the RAF in 1928, gained his wings in 1935 along with the nickname "Hamish," which he had for the rest of his life. Was a bomber pilot during WW2 from 1939 to 1943, then was assigned recruitment duties of Pathfinder crews. While still in the RAF, he acquired the Lancaster bombers for *The Dam Busters* (1955). Retired from the RAF in 1958 with the rank of group captain. Became a consultant in the film industry and acquired the eleven Mosquitos for *633 Squadron* (1964). Mahaddie actually bought one of them afterward (s/n RS712), which he kept until 1972; it also appeared in *Mosquito Squadron* (1969). He also worked on *Operation Crossbow* (1965) and assisted with the famous Autogyro, *Little Nellie*, in the Bond film *You Only Live Twice* (1967). Mahaddie is most revered among Warbird and film fans for his unparalleled work in obtaining the multitude of aircraft for the *Battle of Britain* (1969). Over 115 aircraft were acquired by Mahaddie during a two-year period; he also secured assistance from the Spanish Air Force, RAF and various companies within the aviation industry to provide assistance for this classic film. His on-screen credits vary from "T.G. Mahaddie" and "Hamish Mahaddie" to "Group Captain T.G. Mahaddie." Appears as himself in the classic *World at War* (TVS, 1973–1974) documentary series.

Paul Mantz (August 2, 1903–July 8, 1965). Hollywood pilot, stunt pilot, aerial photographer / coordinator / supervisor, and technical advisor. With a career spanning thirty-five years in the film industry and dozens of titles, Mantz was, and is, the industry's leading, undisputed aviation film pilot and will probably always remain so. Began flying in 1919 and served as a cadet in the Army Air Service. Started his business United Air Services, Inc., in 1931 at Burbank and began flying for motion pictures, *Air Mail* (1932) being one of his first. Film work continued into the 1930s with a sizeable collection of modern, vintage and camera aircraft being accumulated for hire to film studios. Became the first pilot to provide private air travel to movie stars and celebrities alike and was an advisor to aviatrix Amelia Earhart, helping to convert her ill-fated Lockheed 10-E. During World War II, he was commissioned into the USAAF as a major with the First Motion Picture Unit (FMPU), producing training and propaganda films for the military; the group became known as the "Culver City Commandos." Started Paul Mantz Air Services after the war and purchased over 470 ex–World War II aircraft at Searcy Field, Oklahoma; he kept several types for film work, but scrapped the rest, making a healthy profit. Converted two B-25 Mitchell (N1203 and N1042B) bombers as film camera platforms. Won the 1946, 1947 and 1948 Bendix Trophy Air Race in two modified P-51C Mustang (NX1202 and NX1204) fighters. Highly regarded for his motion picture aerial stunt work, which included hangar fly-throughs and the B-17 belly landing for *Twelve O'Clock High* (1949). Helped develop the Cinerama Camera process with *This is Cinerama* (1952), *Cinerama Holiday* (1955), *Seven Wonders of the World* (1956), and *How The West Was Won* (1962), and the CircleVision process with *America The Beautiful* (1958). Combined talents with pilot Frank Tallman to form Tallmantz Aviation, Inc., in 1961, which expanded further their aviation business with Hollywood. Killed when his scratch-built Tallmantz Phoenix P-1 aircraft crashed near Yuma in 1965 while filming for *The Flight of the Phoenix* (1965); the film is dedicated to his memory. An impressive, but not complete, list of Mantz's film work includes *The Galloping Ghost* (1931), *Air Mail* (1932), *Central Airport* (1933), *Devil Dogs of the Air* (1935), *West Point of the Air* (1935), *Ceiling Zero* (1936), *China Clipper* (1936), *Men With Wings* (1938), *Test Pilot* (1938), *Tail Spin* (1939), *Only Angels Have Wings* (1939), *20,000 Men a Year* (1939), *Men Against the Sky* (1940), *Charter Pilot* (1940), *I Wanted Wings* (1941), *The Bride Came C.O.D.* (1941), *International Squadron* (1941), *A Yank in the RAF* (1941), *Flying Cadets* (1941), *Keep 'Em Flying* (1941), *Flying Blind* (1941), *Dive Bomber* (1941), *Captains of the Clouds* (1942), *Thunder Birds* (1942), *A Guy Named Joe* (1943), *Air Force* (1943), *High Barbaree* (1945), *Gallant Journey* (1946), *The Best Years of Our Lives* (1946), *Jungle Flight* (1947), *The Beginning or the End* (1947), *Blaze of Noon* (1947), *Fighter Squadron* (1948), *Command Decision* (1948), *Twelve O'Clock High* (1949), *Task Force* (1949), *Chain Lightning* (1950), *Sky King* (TVS, 1951–1959), *Flying Leathernecks* (1951), *Above and Beyond* (1952), *The Bridges at Toko-Ri* (1954), *Strategic Air Command* (1955), *Top of the World* (1955), *The Court-Martial of Billy Mitchell* (1955), *Toward the Unknown* (1956), *Jet Pilot* (1957), *The Spirit of St. Louis* (1957), *The Wings* *of Eagles* (1957), *A Gathering of Eagles* (1964) and *The Flight of the Phoenix* (1965).

Leo Nomis (May 5, 1892–February 5, 1932). Early Hollywood stunt pilot who flew in *Hell's Angels* (1930), *The Dawn Patrol* (1930) and *The Lost Squadron* (1932). Killed while performing a spin stunt on *Sky Bride* (1932).

Frank Pine (November 5, 1917–September 19, 1984). Motion picture pilot and aerial coordinator. Owned a crop-duster business at Chino Airport before joining Tallmantz Aviation, Inc. After Paul Mantz was killed in 1965, Pine became the chief pilot on the Tallmantz B-25 camera-planes. Became manager of Tallmantz after Tallman's death in 1978 and ran the company until his own death in 1984. Numerous film, television and commercial filming projects; his most prominent feature films include *The Flight of the Phoenix* (1965), *The 1000 Plane Raid* (1969), *Catch-22* (1970), *Airport 1975* (1974), *Breakout* (1975), *The Great Waldo Pepper* (1975), *Amelia Earhart* (TVM, 1976), *Airport '77* (1977), *The Winds of Kitty Hawk* (TVM, 1978) and *The Concorde ... Airport '79* (1979).

Art Scholl (December 24, 1931–September 16, 1985). Noted aerobatic pilot and aerial cameraman. Completed aerial work for numerous film and television productions. Some aviation-themed titles include *The Great Waldo Pepper* (1975), *The Pursuit of D.B. Cooper* (1981), *Blue Thunder* (1983) and *The Right Stuff* (1983). Killed while performing a spin sequence for *Top Gun* (1986); the film is dedicated to his memory.

Frank Tallman (April 17, 1919–April 15, 1978). Hollywood Pilot and Aerial Coordinator. Began flying as a teenager. Initially served as a civilian instructor for the USAAF during World War II before being accepted for combat training with the U.S. Navy. Was preparing for combat as an SBD Dauntless pilot when the war ended. Attained the rank of lieutenant commander with the USN Reserve in the post-war years while collecting and restoring vintage aircraft in his spare time. Had amassed a large collection of flyable, early aircraft by the end of the 1950s which were being hired out to film studios. Began Tallmantz Aviation Inc. with famed Hollywood pilot Paul Mantz in 1961, which set up his future film and TV ca-

reer. Lost a leg in 1965 due to a non-work related accident and had to requalify on all his aircraft. He also lost his business partner Paul Mantz when his aircraft crashed during a film shoot in Imperial Valley. Gained significant fame in the film industry during the 1970s for his aviation expertise on *Catch-22* (1970), *Murphy's War* (1971) and *The Great Waldo Pepper* (1975). Killed in 1978 when his Piper Aztec (N5641Y), hit a peak in the Santa Ana Mountains while flying in poor weather. Tallman has an extensive film list, some of his best aviation credits are *Lafayette Escadrille* (1958), *It's a Mad, Mad, Mad, Mad, Mad World* (1963), *The Carpetbaggers* (1964), *The Thousand Plane Raid* (1969), *Catch-22* (1970), *Murphy's War* (1971), *Ace Eli and Rodger of the Skies* (1973), *Airport 1975* (1974), *The Hindenburg* (1975), *The Great Waldo Pepper* (1975), *Lucky Lady* (1975), *Spencer's Pilots* (TVS, 1976), *Baa Baa Black Sheep* (TVS, 1976–1978), *Amelia Earhart* (TVM, 1976), *MacArthur* (1977), *The Amazing Howard Hughes* (TVM, 1977) and *Capricorn One* (1978).

Allen H. Wheeler (September 27, 1903–January 1, 1984). RAF Air Commodore and collector of vintage aircraft, having restored a Bleriot monoplane. Served as technical advisor for *Those Magnificent Men in Their Flying Machines* (1965), also overseeing the construction, filming and servicing of the vintage replica flying machines; *The Blue Max* (1966), *Mosquito Squadron* (1969) and *Aces High* (1976).

Al Wilson (December 1, 1895–September 5, 1932). Early Hollywood stunt pilot, actor and producer. Killed while performing aerobatics at an air show in Ohio. Film credits include *The Eagle's Talons* (1923), *Air Hawk* (1924), *The Cloud Rider* (1925), *The Flying Mail* (1926), *The Air Patrol* (1928) and *Hell's Angels* (1930).

Marc Wolff (August 25, 1947–). Sometimes credited as Marc Wolfe. One of the most prolific helicopter pilots, helicopter stunt pilots and aerial coordinators in the film industry since the 1970s. A few of his most prominent aviation-themed films include *Air America* (1990), *Memphis Belle* (1990) and *Black Hawk Down* (2001). Wolff has also specialized in aerial cinematography piloting for numerous action-themed films, including many of the later James Bond titles.

Appendix II: Tallmantz Aviation, Inc.

Probably the most famous film aviation company ever, Tallmantz Aviation, Inc., dominated the field. They had the largest aircraft collection, which combines the aircraft of Hollywood pilots Paul Mantz and Frank Tallman who, in 1961, merged talents to form Tallmantz Aviation in Santa Ana, California. The aircraft listed span from the 1930s till Tallmantz's closure in 1986. This collection was utilized in feature films, TV movies, TV series, commercials and promotional films. Their unique B-25 cameraplanes (N1203 and N1042B) were, for several decades, the best platforms for aerial photography.

In 1963, Tallmantz opened the Movieland of the Air Museum at Orange County Airport to display the vast collection of aircraft to the public; it closed in 1985. In the 1960s Tallmantz also opened the International Flight and Space Museum, housing several military types (such as the F-101, YF-107, XF-85 Goblin, and others). As well as aircraft hire and aerial photography, Tallmantz offered the film industry pilot hire, aerial logistics, technical advice, aerial coordination and stunt flying. The list below is not absolute, but is representative of their array of aircraft.

Type	msn	Civil reg.	Ownership dates / remarks
Dedicated Camera-Planes			
Douglas A-26C Invader	28784	N4815E	1963–1976
North American B-25H Mitchell	98-21644	N1203	1946–1975, named *The Smasher*
North American B-25J Mitchell	108-33768	N9451Z	1971–1986, ex–*Catch-22* (1970)
North American B-25J Mitchell	108-34098	N1042B	1962–1986
Scratch-Builds / Replicas (in order of build date)			
Curtiss D Pusher	101	N8Y	Built 1934
Bleriot XI	1	N6683C	Built 1953
Curtiss JP-1 Pusher	1	N8234E	Built 1960, ¾ scale
Phoenix P-1	1	N93082	Built 1965; crashed, killing Paul Mantz
Bleriot XI	1	N1197	Built 1967
Spirit of St. Louis	TM-3	N1967T	Built 1967, for Paris Airshow
Curtiss JN-4D Jenny	TM-4	N2062	Built 1969
Curtiss JN-4D Jenny	TM-7	N33627	Built 1973
Sopwith Camel F.1	TM-10	N8997	Built 1974
Aviation Golden Era			
Beechcraft C-17L Staggerwing	100	NC16441	—
Boeing Model 100	1144	N973H	—
Curtiss-Wright CW-1 JR	1145	N10967	—
Curtiss-Wright F6C-4	1	N982V	—
Curtiss JN-4 Jenny	396	N5391	—
Curtiss JN-4C Canuck	1898	N10389	—
Curtiss JN-4D Jenny	400	N2821D	—
Curtiss JN-4D Jenny	47502	N6899	—
Curtiss JN-4D Jenny	unknown	N6898	—
DeHavilland DH.4M-1	ET-4	N3258	—
DeHavilland DH.90A Dragonfly	7508	N2304	—

(Type)	*(msn)*	*(Civil reg.)*	*(Ownership dates / remarks)*
DeHavilland DH.82A Tiger Moth	82960	N523R	—
DeHavilland DH.82A Tiger Moth	DE-298	N524R	—
DeHavilland DH.82A Tiger Moth	DHC-16	N6970	—
Fairchild Model KR-21A	1053	N962V	Painted as a Fokker D.VII
Fairchild Model M-62A	T423056	N1332N	Painted as a PT-19
Fleet Model 2	291	N725V	—
Fleet Model 2	223	N648M	—
Lockheed L-12A Electra Junior	1243	N60775	1951–1961, re-reg. NC16020
Lockheed Orion 9C	180	N12222	—
Lockheed Sirius 8A	151	NC117W	Paul Mantz camera-plane
Lockheed Vega 1	40	NC199E	Later marked as NC965Y
Lockheed Vega 2D	unknown	N968Y	—
Maurice Farman S.11	25A	N96452	—
Morane-Saulnier A-1	20308	N5130K	—
Orenco F-4 Tourister	45	N2145	—
Pitcairn PA-7 Mailwing	144	N54W	—
Pitcairn PA-7S Mailwing	147	N95W	—
Ryan B-1 Brougham	153	N7206	Purchased for *The Spirit of St. Louis* (1957)
Ryan B-1 Brougham	156	N7209	Purchased for *The Spirit of St. Louis* (1957)
Ryan B-1 Brougham	159	N7212	Purchased for *The Spirit of St. Louis* (1957)
Sikorsky S-39A	905	NC804W	—
Sikorsky S-51	5139	N92813	—
Stampe SV.4C	190	N1606	—
Standard J-1	1582	N2825D	Rebuilt for *The Spirit of St. Louis* (1957)
Standard J-1	1598	N2826D	Rebuilt for *The Spirit of St. Louis* (1957)
Standard J-1	T4595	N62505	—
Stearman-Hammond YS-1	307	N15522	—
Travel Air Mystery Ship	RD-200	NX613K	To Pancho Barnes in 1968
Waco UPF-7	5538	N30141	—
Waco UPF-7	5680	N32049	—

World War I

Fokker E.III Eindecker	401	N3363G	Replica built by Jim Appleby
Fokker D.VII	504/17	N4729V	—
Fokker Dr.I Triplane	DB1	N5523V	Replica
Garland Lincoln LF-1	3	N12237	—
Nieuport 28	002	N2SR	Replica, crashed in 1974
Nieuport 28	512	N4728V	—
Nieuport 28	7171.2	N8539	—
Pfalz D.XII	1	N43C	1958–1968. Tallman rebuild
Royal Aircraft Factory S.E.5e	unknown	N4488	Replica built in 1922
Sopwith Camel F.1	3	N6254	Replica
Sopwith Pup	OE1	N4308	Replica built in 1972
Sopwith Triplane	ET-1	N5492	Replica built in 1967
SPAD S.VII	S-248	N4727V	—
Thomas-Morse S4C	1	N38923	Replica built in 1970
Thomas-Morse S4C	38898	NR502	—
Travel Air 2000	707	N6268	"Wichita Fokker"
Travel Air 2000	871	N8100	—

World War II

Beechcraft AT-11 Kansan	4037	N63158	—
Boeing B-17F Flying Fortress	8296	N67974	Ex-Stillwater surplus
Boeing B-17G Flying Fortress	32166	N83525	1968–1972
Boeing-Stearman PT-17 Kaydet	75-1652	N53422	—
Boeing-Stearman N2S-3 Kaydet	75-7613	N9090H	—
Boeing-Stearman N2S-3 Kaydet	75-7732	N5001V	—
Boeing-Stearman N2S-3 Kaydet	75-8024	N63588	—
Cessna UC-78B Bobcat	6117	NC67832	Flew in *Sky King* TV series

(Type)	(msn)	(Civil reg.)	(Ownership dates / remarks)
Consolidated PBY-5A Catalina	CV-548	N5609V	BuNo. 21232, 1947–1949
Curtiss Kittyhawk Mk. I	18796	N1207V	1958–1966
Curtiss TP-40N Warhawk	33915	N923	1959–1984, 2-seater version
Douglas A-20G Havoc	21305	N67932	s/n 43-21658, ex–Stillwater surplus
Douglas A-24B Shrike	17371	N54532	1964–1970 (s/n 42-54532)
Douglas A-24B Shrike	17521	N74133	1964-1966 (s/n 42-54682)
Douglas B-23 Dragon	2722	N52327	s/n: 39-036
Grumman FM-2 Wildcat	4752	N90523	Owned by Tallman 1960
Grumman FM-2 Wildcat	5618	N4629V	Owned by Tallman 1958–1968
Grumman J2F-6 Duck	unknown	N67790	Flew in *Murphy's War* (1971)
Grumman J2F-6 Duck	unknown	N1196N	Flew in *Murphy's War* (1971)
Grumman TBF-1C Avenger	unknown	NX9394H	—
Lockheed P-38L Lightning	422-8270	N9957F	1962-1966 (s/n 44-53015)
Lockheed PV-2 Harpoon	15-1385	N7486C	—
North American AT-6F Texan	121-42541	N7446C	Zero replica
North American SNJ-5 Texan	88-15757	N3242G	*Tora!* Kate replica
North American Harvard Mk. 4	CCF4-16	N15796	*Tora!* Zero replica
North American B-25D Mitchell	100-23702	N7493C	1957–1969 (s/n 43-3376)
North American B-25H Mitchell	98-21433	N10V	Purchased for *Catch-22* (1970)
North American B-25J Mitchell	108-32200	N7687C	Purchased for *Catch-22* (1970)
North American B-25J Mitchell	108-32310	N3516G	1959–1960 (s/n 44-29035)
North American B-25J Mitchell	108-32641	N9115Z	Purchased for *Catch-22* (1970)
North American B-25J Mitchell	108-33162	N10564	Purchased for *Catch-22* (1970)
North American B-25J Mitchell	108-33214	N9456Z	Purchased for *Catch-22* (1970)
North American B-25J Mitchell	108-33352	N2849G	Purchased for *Catch-22* (1970)
North American B-25J Mitchell	108-33485	N9455Z	1960 (s/n 44-30210)
North American B-25J Mitchell	108-33924	N9452Z	Purchased for *Catch-22* (1970)
North American B-25J Mitchell	108-34023	N8195H	Purchased for *Catch-22* (1970)
North American B-25J Mitchell	108-34076	N3699G	Purchased for *Catch-22* (1970)
North American B-25J Mitchell	108-34200	N9494Z	Purchased for *Catch-22* (1970)
North American B-25J Mitchell	108-34307	N3174G	Purchased for *Catch-22* (1970)
North American B-25J Mitchell	108-34317	N3515G	1959–1960 (s/n 44-31042)
North American B-25J Mitchell	108-35217	N9856C	Purchased for *Catch-22* (1970)
North American B-25J Mitchell	108-35235	N5256V	1960 (s/n 43-28222)
North American B-25J Mitchell	108-47455	N7681C	Purchased for *Catch-22* (1970)
North American B-25J Mitchell	108-47597	N3507G	Purchased for *Catch-22* (1970)
North American B-25J Mitchell	108-47694	XB-HEY	Purchased for *Catch-22* (1970)
North American P-51C Mustang	103-26385	NX1204	1946–1984 (s/n 42-103831)
North American P-51C Mustang	111-29080	NX1202	1946–1950 (s/n 44-10947)
North American P-51D Mustang	124-48389	N5467V	1960–1966 (s/n 45-11636)
Stinson L-1 Vigilant	unknown	N63229	s/n 40-291
Stinson L-1 Vigilant	unknown	N63230	s/n 40-3102
Stinson L-5 Sentinel	76-560	N64669	Purchased for *Catch-22* (1970)
Vought FG-1D Corsair	2900	N63382	—
Vought FG-1D Corsair	3694	N3440G	—
Vought FG-1D Corsair	3111	N9154Z	—
Vought FG-1D Corsair	unknown	N9153Z	—
Vultee BT-13B Valiant	79-1220	N56867	*Tora!* Val replica

Post–World War II / Modern Era

Douglas DC-7B	45193	N8210H	—
DeHavilland DH.100 Vampire	EEP42390	N6878D	—
DeHavilland DH.100 Vampire	EEP423	N6883D	—
Piper PA-23 Apache	23-1055	N3131P	Paul Mantz's personal aircraft
Piper PA-23 Aztec	23-2755	N5641Y	Crashed 1978, killing Frank Tallman

List developed from an original source by Scott Thompson / www.aerovintage.com

Appendix III: Blue Max Aviation Ltd.

This museum collection began with nine World War I replica fighters originally commissioned by 20th Century–Fox for the 1965 film *The Blue Max*. In addition, they also acquired several Tiger Moth and Stampe biplanes to fill out the backgrounds. Upon completion of filming, the nine replicas and several other aircraft were sold to ex–RCAF pilot and Warbird collector Lyn Garrison, who began Blue Max Aviation Ltd. at Western Aerodrome, Ireland, in early 1967. Later added to this unique collection were six Currie Wot S.E.5a biplanes acquired from Shillelagh Productions, Inc., for *Darling Lili* (1970), filmed in 1967. The local Irish Air Corps provided aircrews and expertise for the aircraft. This collection would go on to star in several other productions, namely *You Can't Win 'Em All* (1970), *Von Richthofen and Brown* (1971), *Zeppelin* (1971), *Aces High* (1976) and the unfinished *I Shot Down Richthofen, I Think*. The list below ranks all acquired aircraft in order of their Irish registrations. In 1986, much of the collection was sold to Frank Ryder's Fighting Air Command in Texas; the U.S. registrations are also listed below. From there, the collection was eventually broken up.

Ireland	msn	Type	Previous reg.	Subsequent reg. / remarks
EI-APT	02	Fokker D.VII-65	F-BNDG	N903AC
EI-APU	03	Fokker D.VII-65	F-BNDH	N904AC
EI-APV	01	Fokker D.VII-65	F-BNDF	N902AC; ZK-FOD
EI-APW	001	Fokker Dr.I	G-ATIY	—
EI-APY	002	Fokker Dr.I	G-ATJM	—
EI-ARA	SEM.7282	Miles S.E.5a	G-ATGV	Crashed Sep. 15, 1970
EI-ARB	SEM.7283	Miles S.E.5a	G-ATGW	Crashed Aug. 18, 1970
EI-ARC	PPS/PFLZ/1	Pfalz D.IIIa	G-ATIF	N906AC; ZK-FLZ
EI-ARD	PT.16	Pfalz D.IIIa	G-ATIJ	N905AC; ZK-JPI
EI-ARE	386	Stampe SV-4C	F-BBIT	—
EI-ARF	7546/135	Caudron C.277 Luciole	G-ATIP; F-AQFB	N907AC
EI-ARG	1049	Morane-Saulnier MS.230	F-BGMR	N230MS
EI-ARH	1590	Currie Wot S.E.5a	G-AVOT	—
EI-ARI	1591	Currie Wot S.E.5a	G-AVOU	N908AC
EI-ARJ	1592	Currie Wot S.E.5a	G-AVOV	N909AC
EI-ARK	1593	Currie Wot S.E.5a	G-AVOW	N910AC
EI-ARL	1594	Currie Wot S.E.5a	G-AVOX	N912AC
EI-ARM	1595	Currie Wot S.E.5a	G-AVOY	—
EI-AVU	1060	Stampe SV.4C	F-BAUR	N901AC

Appendix IV: U.S. Aircraft Carriers on Film

USS *Abraham Lincoln*
CVN-72
Commissioned: 1989 / Still in service
Stealth (2005)

USS *Antietam*
CV-36 / CVA-36 / CVS-36
Commissioned: 1945 / Decommissioned: 1963
Task Force (1949)

USS *Bairoko*
CVE-115
Commissioned: 1945 / Decommissioned: 1955
Task Force (1949)

USS *Carl Vinson*
CVN-70
Commissioned: 1982 / Still in service
Behind Enemy Lines (2001), *Stealth* (2005)

USS *Constellation*
CV-64
Commissioned: 1961 / Decommissioned: 2003
Behind Enemy Lines (2001), *Pearl Harbor* (2001)

USS *Coral Sea*
CV-43 / CVB-43 / CVA-43
Commissioned: 1947 / Decommissioned: 1990
The Right Stuff (1983)

USS *Enterprise*
CV-6
Commissioned: 1938 / Decommissioned: 1947
Flight Command (1940), *Dive Bomber* (1941)

USS *Enterprise*
CVA-65 / CVN-65
Commissioned: 1961 / Decommissioned: 2016
Top Gun (1986)

USS *Franklin*
CV-13 / CVA-13 / CVS-13 / AVT-8
Commissioned: 1944 / Decommissioned: 1964
Battle Stations (1956)

USS *Harry S. Truman*
CVN-75
Commissioned: 1998 / Still in service
Tears of the Sun (2003)

USS *Independence*
CV-62 / CVA-62
Commissioned: 1959 / Decommissioned: 1998
Flight of the Intruder (1991)

USS *John C. Stennis*
CVN-74
Commissioned: 1995 / Still in service
Stealth (2005)

USS *Kearsarge*
CV-33 / CVA-33 / CVS-33
Commissioned: 1946 / Decommissioned: 1970
The Bridges at Toko-Ri (1954), *The Eternal Sea* (1955)

USS *Kitty Hawk*
CVA-63 / CV-63
Commissioned: 1961 / Decommissioned: 2009
Clear and Present Danger (1994)

USS *Langley*
CV-1 / AV-3
Commissioned: 1920 / Struck off: 1942
The Flying Fleet (1929)

USS *Lexington*
CV-16 / CVA-16 / CVS-16 / CVT-16 / AVT-16
Commissioned: 1943 / Decommissioned: 1991
Midway (1976), *War and Remembrance* (TVMS, 1988), *Pearl Harbor* (2001)

USS *Nimitz*
CVAN-68 / CVN-68
Commissioned: 1975 / Still in service
The Final Countdown (1980)

USS *Oriskany*
CV-34 / CVA-34
Commissioned: 1950 / Decommissioned: 1976
The Bridges at Toko-Ri (1954), *Men of the Fighting Lady* (1954)

USS *Princeton*
CV-37 / CVA-37 / CVS-37 / LPH-5
Commissioned: 1945 / Decommissioned: 1970
Flat Top (1952), *Men of the Fighting Lady* (1954), *Battle Stations* (1956)

USS *Saratoga*
CV-3
Commissioned: 1927 / Decommissioned: 1946
Hell Divers (1931), *Devil Dogs of the Air* (1935)

USS *Yorktown*
CV-10 / CVA-10 / CVS-10
Commissioned: 1943 / Decommissioned: 1970
Wing and a Prayer (1944), *Tora! Tora! Tora!* (1970)

References and Bibliography

First Hand Email Correspondence and Interviews

Graham Adlam—UK aircraft provider, *Pearl Harbor* (2001).

Bruce Benson—South Coast Helicopters Inc., numerous film productions.

Ed Bertschy—Background, *The Hunters* (1958).

Igor Best-Devereux—History of Eardley-Billing Biplane.

Tony Bianchi—Pilot, numerous productions.

Matthew Boddington—Historian, *The Blue Max* (1966).

Steve Darke—Thai aviation historian.

Rex Dovey—Pilot, *Race for the Yankee Zephyr* (1981).

Mike Durant—Aircraft background, *Black Hawk Down* (2001).

James H. Farmer—Hollywood aviation historian.

Corky Fornof—Pilot, numerous film productions.

Tom Friedkin—Helicopter film pilot, *Blue Thunder* (1983).

Pete Gillies—Western Helicopters Inc., *Capricorn One* (1978).

Antony I. Ginnane—Producer, *Race for the Yankee Zephyr* (1981).

Benno Goethals—Aircraft data, *A Bridge Too Far* (1977).

Gerry Goodwin—Autogyro pilot, *Mad Max 2* (1981).

Jim Greaves (Shuttleworth Trust)—History of various film replica aircraft.

Richard Hart—National Helicopter Service Inc.

Steve Hinton—President, *Planes of Fame* Museum and veteran film pilot.

Orin "Spike" Kinghorn—Helicopter pilot.

Peter Kynsey—Pilot, *The Aviator* (1985).

Terry Lee—Helicopter pilot, *Mad Max Beyond Thunderdome* (1985).

David Legg—Catalina historian / author.

Chuck Lunsford—C119 historian, *Flight of the Phoenix* (2004).

Michael Mason—Stearman owner, *Independence Day* (1996).

Wally McDonnell—Pilot, *The Flight of the Phoenix* (1965).

Peter McKernan / Peter McKernan Jr.—Helicopter pilots, numerous film productions.

Tim Moore—Aircraft data, *Biggles* (1986).

Guy Nockels—Production Manager, *Flight of the Phoenix* (2004).

Mary Olson—Siller Helicopters Inc., *Independence Day* (1996).

Bruce Orriss—Hollywood aviation historian.

Robert Parmerter—Beech 18 historian.

Bill Pike—Pilot, *Sky Pirates* (1986).

Rick Shuster—Helicopter film pilot, *Con Air* (1997).

Don Spary—Helicopter pilot, *Race for the Yankee Zephyr* (1981).

Bob Thayer—Steward-Davis Inc., *The Flight of the Phoenix* (1965).

Scott Thompson—B-25 & B-17 histories.

Ray Vuillermin—Pilot, *Tail of a Tiger* (1984).

Bill Walker—RCAF historian.

Harry Wadley—Helicopter pilot, *Close Encounters of the Third Kind* (1977).

Herb Watkins—Helicopter mechanic, *Close Encounters of the Third Kind* (1977).

Bob West—C-119 pilot, *Flight of the Phoenix* (2004).

Jonathon Whaley—Pilot, *Indiana Jones and the Last Crusade* (1989).

Karl Wickman—Helicopter pilot, *Capricorn One* (1978).

Dorcey Wingo—Helicopter pilot.

Scott "Scooter" Yoak—Helicopter conversions, *Blue Thunder* (1983), *Rambo III* (1988).

Books

Andrade, John M. *US Military Aircraft Designations and Serials*. 1979, Midland Counties Publications Ltd.

Ashley, Mark. *Flying Film Stars*. 2014, Red Kite Books.

Falconer, Jonathan. *RAF Bomber Command In Fact, Film And Fiction*. 1996, Sutton Publishing Ltd.

Falconer, Jonathan. *Filming The Dam Busters*. 2005, Sutton Publishing Ltd.

Farmer, James H. *Broken Wings: Hollywood's Air Crashes*. 1984, Pictorial Histories Publishing Co.

Farmer, James H. *Celluloid Wings: The Impact of Movies on Aviation*. 1984, TAB Books Inc.

Greenwood, Jim, and Maxine. *Stunt Flying in the Movies*. 1982, TAB Books Inc.

Howe, Stuart *Mosquito Survivors*. 1986, Aston Publications.

Jackson, A.J. *British Civil Aircraft 1919–1972 Vol. II / Vol. III.* Putnam Books.

Marson, Peter J. *The Lockheed Twins.* 2001, Air-Britain (Historians) Ltd.

Miller, Jay *The X-Planes: X-1 to X-45.* 2001, Midland Publishing.

Mosley, Leonard. *Battle of Britain.* 1969, Ballantine Books Inc.

Robertson, Bruce *British Military Aircraft Serials 1878–1987.* 1987, Midland Counties Publications Ltd.

Smith, Carl. *Pearl Harbor.* 2001, Osprey Publishing Ltd.

Tallman, Frank. *Flying the Old Planes.* 1973, Doubleday.

Veronico, Nicholas A.; A. Kevin Grantham; Scott Thompson *Military Aircraft Boneyards.* 2000, MBI Publishing Co.

Wheeler, Allen H. *Building Aeroplanes for "Those Magnificent Men."* 1965, G.T. Foulis & Co. Ltd. London.

Periodicals

AAHS Journal: "The Making of Battle Hymn" by James H. Farmer, Vol. 23, No. 1.

Aeroplane Monthly: "Filming The Dam Busters" by Jonathan Falconer, April 2005.

Aeroplane Monthly: "Turkish Delight!" by Lewis Benjamin, October 2008.

Aeroplane Monthly: "Angels One Five" by Gary R. Brown, May 2012.

Aeroplane Monthly: "On Set with the Red Tails" by Simon O'Connell, December 2012.

After The Battle: "The War Lover" by Jerry Scutts, Issue 150, 2010.

Air & Space Magazine: "The Making of Air Force One" by George C. Larson, August 1997.

Air Classics: "Big Screen Banzai!" by Bob O'Hara, February 1969.

Air Classics: "Tora! Tora! Tora!" by Bob O'Hara, October 1969.

Air Classics: "Catch-22 Air Force" by James H. Farmer, December 1972.

Air Classics: "The Mitchells of Hanover Street" by Denis Calvert, June 1979.

Air Classics: "The Last Flight of Noah's Ark," April 1980.

Air Classics: "The Right Stuff Part 1" by James H. Farmer, December 1983.

Air Classics: "The Right Stuff Part 2" by James H. Farmer, January 1984.

Air Classics: "The Making of The Iron Eagle" by James H. Farmer, February 1986.

Air Classics: "The Making of Top Gun" by James H. Farmer, July 1986.

Air Classics: "Empire of the Sun," January 1988.

Air Classics: "The Hunters" by Jim H. Farmer, June 1988.

Air Classics: "War and Remembrance" by James H. Farmer, November 1988.

Air Classics: "The Making of Always" by James H. Farmer, February 1990.

Air Classics: "Making Flight of the Intruder" by James H. Farmer, August 1990.

Air Classics: "The Making of Air America" by James H. Farmer, October 1990.

Air Classics: "The Making of Memphis Belle" by James H. Farmer, November 1990.

Air Classics: "The Making of Flyboys" by James H. Farmer, November 2006.

Air Classics: "Steve Canyon Returns" by James H. Farmer, April 2008.

Air Classics: "Battle Hymn Revisited (Parts 1 & 2)" by James H. Farmer, February & March 2009.

Air Classics: "The Missing Bridge of Toko-Ri" by James H. Farmer, August 2013.

Air Pictorial: "633 Squadron" by Graeme Weir, September 1963.

Air Power: "Fighter Squadron" by James H. Farmer, May 1978.

Air Progress, 1956–57 Edition: "Stand-in for a Star" by Ruth & Don Downie.

Air Progress, Spring 1958 Edition: "How Hollywood Filmed" Pylon by Tom Henebry.

Air Progress Aviation: "Stearman Versus Helicopter" by Wayne Thomas, Fall, 1978.

FlyPast: "Film Star Stearmans" by Peter Kynsey, June 1984.

FlyPast: "Reach for the Sky—The Film" by Francois Prin, July 1986.

FlyPast: "Reach for the Sky 2—The Film" by Francois Prin, August 1986.

Flypast: "Taking the Cake—Slice One" by Francois Prins, October 1988.

Flypast: "Taking the Cake—Slice Two" by Francois Prins, November 1988.

Flypast: "Memphis Belle Action" by Duncan Cubitt, August 1989.

Flypast: "The Battle of Britain" by Francois Prins & Finding the Stars by Robert Rudhall, Sept. 1989.

Flypast: "The Battle of Britain" by Francois Prins, October 1989.

Flypast: "Catch 22" by Scott Thompson, August 1990.

Flypast: "Tora! Tora! Tora!" by Scott Thompson, December 1990.

Pilot: "Filming Piece of Cake" by Robert Eagle, October 1988.

Scale Models: "Hell's Angels Meet The Dawn Patrol" by Harry Z. Woodman, July 1973.

Sport Aviation: "Cloud Dancer" by Jack Cox, July 1978.

Sport Flying: "Darling Lili" by Gerald T. von Aspe, July 1968.

Sport Flying: "Tora! Tora! Tora!" August 1969.

Warbirds: "Hollywood Airnotes" by James H. Farmer, April 1987.

Warbirds: "Hollywood Airnotes" by James H. Farmer, August 1987.

Warbirds: "Hollywood Airnotes" by James H. Farmer, Sept./Oct. 1987.

Warbirds: "Hollywood Airnotes" by James H. Farmer, Jan./Feb. 1988.

Warbirds: "Hollywood Airnotes" by James H. Farmer, April/May 1989.

Warbirds International: "Black Sheep Bent Wings" by Michael O'Leary. March/April 2008.

Warbirds Worldwide No. 10: "Filming Memphis Belle" by Andy Height and Paul Coggan.

Warbirds Worldwide No. 11: "Filming Memphis Belle" by Andy Height and Paul Coggan.

Wings: "Hollywood's Flying Tiger" by James H. Farmer, August 1979.

Principal Internet Resources

www.uswarplanes.net

www.joebaugher.com

www.ukserials.com

www.rwrwalker.ca (RCAF aircraft)

www.aerofiles.com

www.scramble.nl

www.warbirdregistry.org

www.preservedaxisaircraft.com

www.faa.gov

www.airport-data.com

www.airfleets.net

www.imdb.com

www.impdb.org

www.aerovintage.com